Utah's History

UTAH'S HISTORY

Richard D. Poll
General Editor

Thomas G. Alexander,
Eugene E. Campbell,
David E. Miller
Associate Editors

Utah State University Press
Logan, Utah 84322-7800

00   99   98   5   6   7   8

Library of Congress Cataloging-in-Publication Data
Utah's history.
         Includes bibliographies and index.
         1. Utah–History. I. Poll, Richard Douglas, 1918-
F826.U9 1989   979.2   89-16477
ISBN 0-87421-142-5

Editors of This Volume

Richard D. Poll, general editor, professor of history, Western Illinois University

Thomas G. Alexander, associate editor, professor of history, associate director of the Charles Redd Center for Western Studies, Brigham Young University

Eugene E. Campbell, associate editor, professor of history, Brigham Young University

David E. Miller, associate editor, professor emeritus of history, University of Utah

Contributors to This Volume

Thomas G. Alexander
Department of History
Brigham Young University

James B. Allen
Department of History
Brigham Young University

Maureen Ursenbach Beecher
Historical Department
The Church of Jesus Christ of
  Latter-day Saints

John F. Bluth
Harold B. Lee Library
Brigham Young University

Bruce L. Campbell
Department of Sociology
Arizona State University

Eugene E. Campbell
Department of History
Brigham Young University

John E. Christensen
Austin, Texas

James L. Clayton
Department of History
University of Utah

J. Michael Cleverley
American Consulate General
New York, New York

Jill Mulvay Derr
Historical Department
The Church of Jesus Christ of
  Latter-day Saints

Marvin S. Hill
Department of History
Brigham Young University

Thomas K. Hinckley
Department of Geography
Brigham Young University

Wayne K. Hinton
Department of History
College of Southern Utah

Gustive O. Larson
Provo, Utah

Robert L. Layton
Department of Geography
Brigham Young University

Glen M. Leonard
Historical Department
The Church of Jesus Christ of
   Latter-day Saints

Ann Vest Lobb
Los Angeles Unified School
   District

T. Edgar Lyon
Institute of Religion
University of Utah

Kathryn L. MacKay
American West Center
University of Utah

Dean L. May
Historical Department
The Church of Jesus Christ of
   Latter-day Saints

David E. Miller
Department of History
University of Utah

Helen Z. Papanikolas
Utah State Historical Society

Charles S. Peterson
Department of History and
   Geography
Utah State University

F. Ross Peterson
Department of History and
   Geography
Utah State University

Richard D. Poll
Department of History
Western Illinois University

S. Lyman Tyler
American West Center
University of Utah

Richard O. Ulibarri
Department of History
Weber State College

Ted J. Warner
Department of History
Brigham Young University

Table of Contents

Maps

Tables

Illustrations

Preface

Utah's History began with a discussion early in the 1970s concerning the need for a substantial single-volume survey of the development of territory and state, based on recent research and written for adult readers. The discussants were David E. Miller of the University of Utah and Eugene E. Campbell and Thomas G. Alexander of Brigham Young University. Since none of the three wished to tackle the task alone, they decided to recruit associates—fellow historians and in a few cases graduate students—to produce the components for a cooperative work. Miller accepted responsibility for the pre-1847 period, Campbell for the territorial years, and Alexander for the twentieth century.

As the chapters were written it seemed advisable that one person be given general editorial oversight so that the final product would not be an anthology of articles about Utah history but a volume sufficiently comprehensive and integrated to serve as a college-level text as well as a general-purpose narrative and reference work. Richard D. Poll of Western Illinois University was enlisted for this assignment. He is responsible for revising the individual chapters to varying degrees, recruiting several additional contributors, selecting the pictures and supervising the preparation of the maps and statistical tables, and working with the Brigham Young University Press on the design and production of the volume. The interpretive viewpoints of the chapter authors were in all cases preserved and the associate editors counseled with the authors and reviewed the sections for which they wrote introductory statements.

A challenge that confronted both authors and editors was to keep *Utah's History* from being just another volume of Mormon history.

Given the circumstance that since 1847 the Latter-day Saints have almost certainly never comprised less than two-thirds of the Utah population—a situation without parallel among the territories and states of the American Union—this task was not easy, especially since most of the published research focuses on Mormon themes. An effort has been made to achieve a perspective as broad as the state and as long as its record in artifacts and documents. But no work of synthesis can go very far beyond the spade work already done by the specialists. Hopefully, one of the services that *Utah's History* will perform is to suggest—by its gaps and disproportions—where the current generation of scholars and researchers may most profitably place their attention.

While the individual authors were producing their chapters, S. George Ellsworth's text for the public schools, *Utah's Heritage* (1972), appeared. The editor gratefully acknowledges his frequent recourse to this text to identify areas that otherwise might have been overlooked in the cooperative book and to check many matters of fact. Other sources that were particularly helpful are included in the General Bibliographical Essay at the end of chapter 36.

Thomas Hinckley, Brigham Young University, designed the maps and was assisted in their execution by B. Kelly Nielsen and George W. Southard, photo mechanical, and B. Kelly Nielsen, Susanne Farrell, Robert Cook, Carolyn Cook, Gary L. Clifford, Paul E. Hoban, Jr., and Scott Scherbel, cartographic drafting. David E. Miller's *Utah History Atlas* (1977 ed.) was a very helpful reference, and Miller also reviewed the maps. Howard Allen Christy, Brigham Young University, prepared many of the statistical tables.

In the selection of pictures Margaret Lester of the Utah State Historical Society, William W. Slaughter of the LDS Church Historical Department, David Washburn of the University of Utah's Marriott Library, Neil Burt and Richard Bennett of Brigham Young University's Harold B. Lee Library, Wes Soulier of the Union Pacific Railroad, and Rell Francis of Springville, Utah, were very helpful. The Charles Redd Center for Western Studies, Brigham Young University, funded part of the cost of preparing pictures for the volume.

Kathryn J. Frandsen and Gail W. Bell read the manuscript for Brigham Young University Press and made valuable suggestions. McRay Magleby was production designer, and was assisted by Kerry Lynn Herrin; Frandsen, Bell, and John Drayton saw the book through the production process. Their encouragement and advice were very helpful.

Direct quotations have been identified in the context of the chapters, and source footnotes have not been used. Chapter bibliographies are selective; works most heavily relied upon by the chapter authors are normally included. Citations to *Utah Historical Quarterly* are so frequent that the abbreviation *UHQ* is used throughout.

The editor acknowledges the cooperation of the authors and associate editors, who almost always humored him in his suggestions, even when they did not regard them as improvements. Gene Poll showed wifely patience and understanding, read many of the chapters, and made valuable suggestions.

RICHARD D. POLL

August 1, 1977

Preface
to the 1989 Reprint

In the eleven years since *Utah's History* appeared, the original editorial team has dispersed. David Miller died in 1978, without ever having the opportunity to make classroom use of the volume to which he contributed so much. Eugene Campbell died in 1986 after only a short retirement. My retirement from Western Illinois University in 1983 left only Thomas Alexander active in the halls of ivy; he is now Director of the Charles Redd Center for Western Studies at Brigham Young University and Chairman of the Board of State History for Utah. Two of the chapter authors have also died, Gustive O. Larson and T. Edgar Lyon.

Thanks to the cooperation of Utah State University Press, it has been possible to correct a number of typographical and minor factual errors that escaped detection in the original printing. Substantive textual changes have been made on pages 156–57 and 620–21. Except for Tables K and L, pages 701–704, charts and tables have not been updated. A Supplementary Bibliography, pp. 681–682, lists the most important books on Utah history that have appeared since 1978.

I am grateful to Nikki Naiser and Linda Speth, of Utah State University Press, for their close attention to details and their expeditious handling of this project. Thanks also to the teachers and students whose acceptance of *Utah's History* has made this new printing necessary and feasible.

RICHARD D. POLL
May 1989

Part I
Introduction
Utah Before the Mormons

David E. Miller

Upon hearing the word *Utah* the average American usually thinks of the Mormons who first migrated to the Salt Lake Valley in 1847, conducted a remarkable colonization program during the next several decades, and went on to make Salt Lake City the headquarters and center of the worldwide Church of Jesus Christ of Latter-day Saints. But Utah's varied history goes back a hundred centuries before the Mormons or any other person of European extraction set foot inside the state's present boundaries.

We are indebted to anthropologists and archaeologists for bringing to light substantial information regarding the earlist known inhabitants of this region. The first was evidence of those nomads belonging to the Desert Culture (ca. 10,000 B.C. to A.D. 300), who migrated from place to place in search of game and edible seeds and plants. Peoples of the Desert Culture built no permanent dwellings, but season after season and century after century some of them returned to the shelter of several natural caves—such as Danger and Hogup caves—where they left substantial evidence of their occupancy and life-style.

More advanced cultures developed in the southern and eastern portions of our state. One of these is known as the Anasazi Culture (ca. A.D. 300 to A.D. 1300). These "ancient ones" left ample evidence of a relatively advanced civilization in and around their numerous stone-masonry buildings, still standing in the villages which they evacuated around the year 1276. The Fremont and Sevier Fremont cultures were contemporaries of the Anasazi, occupying much of the territory to the north and west.

1

By the time Europeans invaded Utah's territory three major nations of Indians (Ute, Shoshone, and Navajo) occupied the area. Some were probably descendants of earlier cultures; some, such as the Navajo, were recent newcomers to America's Southwest. White-Indian relations in Utah followed a pattern similar to that of other areas of the United States as people of European antecedents pushed westward into lands already occupied by the various Indian tribes.

The earliest white incursions into present Utah were two groups of Spaniards operating out of New Mexico during the last half of the eighteenth century. The first of these was led by Juan María Antonio Rivera who, in 1765, led a small group northwestward from Santa Fe through southwestern Colorado and as far as the Colorado River near present Moab, Utah. A second and more important expedition was conducted eleven years later under the leadership of two Franciscan fathers—Francisco Atanasio Domínguez and Silvestre Vélez de Escalante. The excellent daily journal kept by the two men supplies the earliest eye-witness descriptions of the natural environment, terrain, and peoples encountered as they traveled through eastern, central, and southern Utah. The expedition's cartographer, Miera y Pacheco, prepared a remarkable map showing some 377 geophysical features, and boundaries of various Indian nations encountered. The Spaniards founded no permanent settlements and established no missions inside of present Utah.

After the Domínguez-Escalante expedition there was relatively little white contact with Utah until the 1820s, when fur-hunting mountain men swarmed into the region to explore and trap every stream and lake. Recent research has disclosed that the major clash between British and American trappers vying for control of the whole Oregon country occurred at Mountain Green on Utah's Weber River in May 1825. Although the mountain men explored most of Utah and some left excellent journals describing their activities, they left no permanent settlements. By the time of the Mormon migration most of them had abandoned the region.

Brigham Young and other leaders of the Mormon migration relied heavily on information supplied by the fur men, the reports of John C. Fremont who had explored extensively in the Far West, and information gleaned from the experiences of several members of California-bound wagon trains that had crossed Utah in 1846. The Mormons followed the tracks of those wagons all the way into the Great Basin.

Utah's aboriginal inhabitants, the fur hunters, and the Mormon settlers were all influenced and considerably controlled by the ge-

2

ography, natural resources, and physical features encountered in our state. Water has always been the most important natural resource. It is the most important factor that determines where cities and towns can be established, industry developed, and agriculture practiced. The earliest wagon roads followed streams where water and grass supplied the energy for horse power, crossed mountain passes, and traversed desert wastes on trails leading from one water source to another. Permanent Mormon settlements were located where a few acres of relatively flat land could be brought under irrigation. Thus it is quite proper that we begin this volume with a chapter describing Utah's natural features, some of which are famous throughout the world, and then that we go on to examine various facets of our history prior to the Mormon migration.

Chapter 1
Utah: The Physical Setting

Robert L. Layton

Every event that may be viewed in the context of time may also be seen in the context of space. Place and time are in a real sense the warp and the woof of the canvas that conveys the picture of the past. Without both warp and woof there is no picture, and without appreciation of their interweaving the meaning of the picture cannot be fully understood. Jamestown's Captain John Smith said it in a different way in his *Historie of Virginia:* "Historie without Geographie is like a Vagrant that wandereth without a Certaine Habitation." It is appropriate then to begin a book about Utah that emphasizes time with a chapter that emphasizes space.

Just as time extends infinitely into the past and future, place may be anything from a point with no dimensions to the infinity of space in all directions. As the content of a segment of time is called the history of Utah, a small area—84,990 square miles—of the earth's surface is arbitrarily named Utah. Viewed from space there is no change from red to blue at its border as on the map in the atlas. Yet place may be defined, and Utah may be distinguished from all other places. Place may be an office occupied by Brigham Young and defined in terms of furniture, size of room and other such details, or the entire building, or the political unit—a city—where it is found, or a range of mountains next to which it stands. The physical characteristics of each place differentiate it and have some impact upon the events that occur through time in its location.

People commonly define places other than human artifacts in terms of such characteristics as landforms, climate, vegetation, soils, minerals, and other elements that may be present in concentrations useful to man. These interrelated features occur in similar combinations in various locations over the face of the earth. Some of the physical landscape of Utah, for example, may appear quite familiar to visitors from parts of central Asia or northwestern Argentina. Yet what people do with similar environments differs greatly, and the resulting cultural landscapes may not be familiar at all. As the well-known geographer, Preston E. James, has stated: "The use of the physical landscape by a given people is determined by their attitudes, their objectives, and their technical abilities." The cultural features of the landscape, arbitrarily delimited as Utah, differ greatly from 1776 to 1876 to 1976, yet Fathers Domínguez and Escalante would easily recognize the landforms in 1976 and the Mormon farmer of 1876 would find the weather "changeable" as usual and quite familiar. These physical aspects of place, which affect but do not control what is done, warrant description as background for the historical events—this book's primary concern.

Landforms

From a vantage point in space the western region of North America appears as a slightly wrinkled tan and green expanse. From a commercial jet plane the wrinkles are more impressive, and at ground level they may be simply awesome. They are, however, simply wrinkles where the section of the earth's crust known as the North American Plate is slowly sliding along and over another section known as the Pacific Plate, and a smaller section called the Gorda Plate.

If time lapse photography were available for the past several millions of years, we could watch as the area now known as Utah folded, heaved, buckled, cracked, and bent, while rain, snow, flowing water, and, in some areas, ice constantly wore away at every elevation. We could observe in succession areas lowered and invaded by shallow seas and occupied by vast swamps, periods of dry climate with vast areas of sand dunes, and layer after layer of sand, gravel, clay, and other sediments being laid down and buried only to be uplifted. Here and there during the eons of time we might also observe volcanic activity spread cinder cones, lava, and other materials over the surface, while under the surface masses of molten materials pushed up, bulging overlying rock strata and cooling slowly into crystalline rock, later to be exposed as the overlying strata eroded away. Compressed in time such movements would seem a jumble of frantic activity, and the hills by no means "everlasting." Yet these activities are still in process, and their sum in the past accounts for both the resources we now extract from the earth and the very form of the land itself.

Whether viewed from space or analyzed by tedious travel on the ground, the wrinkles exhibit a pattern. It may be defined in different terms, but the differences in various classification schemes are small since in the area of Utah, or even the expanded original territory of Deseret, the landforms are rather definite. (See pp. 717–19 for two maps incorporating commonly used systems.) The divisions developed by Nevin M. Fenneman are recognized even by those who may disagree in specific instances with his boundaries, and they are convenient for more particular comment on the landforms.

Basin and Range Province

Fenneman classes most of western Utah as part of the Basin and Range Province. This region, stretching from the Sierra Nevada on the border of Nevada and California to the western slope of the Wasatch Range in Utah, is a succession of undrained depressions divided by dozens of small ranges of mountains. John C. Fremont, who recognized the region as one of interior drainage, defined the basin as extending throughout the drainage of all its streams. Many today use the term *Great Basin* to include all of the interior drainage, including the watersheds of the Truckee in the west and such rivers as the Bear, Weber, Provo, and Sevier in the east. Fenneman draws the line at the base of the Wasatch and High Plateaus, and includes as the *Great Basin* only a section of the Basin and Range Province.

Whatever the definition used, the region appears from the air as a series of small mountain ranges being slowly drowned in a sea of alluvial materials washed down from their slopes. Many of these basins, or bolsons, have distinct lake beds, or playas, in their lowest section where waters flowing in during periods of high precipitation form shallow lakes that soon evaporate, leaving behind their salts. Where the playa is well developed, it will be almost exactly flat, filled with fine clays, and so impregnated with salts that no vegetation grows—ideal for emergency landing strips or race tracks, but of no value for farming. That section of the province referred to as the *Great Basin* is a collection of smaller basins with many playas, the most spectacular being the Bonneville Salt Flats next to the Nevada border.

Extending from the playa to the foot of the mountains is usually a long gentle slope underlain by a variety of alluvial material. Streams emerging from the canyons, bearing a heavy load of sediments as they cascade down the steep canyon, drop much of their

7

load as the flatter gradient of the valley is reached and the velocity of flow decreases. The quantity of sediment may be such, particularly during floods, that the stream literally dams itself and shifts channels, moving back and forth over the area beyond the mouth of the canyon until a fan-shaped deposit, or alluvial fan, is built up. Such fans vary greatly in size and in the slope of their surface; they may coalesce and constitute the entire slope to the lowest part of a valley, or they may be superimposed on a more gentle slope of finer alluvium stretching beyond their limits. They have been the preferred locations for settlement in much of Utah. In any case, the material of the valley floor beyond the mountains is usually a mixture of everything from boulders to fine clay.

Along the upper parts of the valleys and the base of the mountains, the landforms in most of the Basin and Range area of Utah also show evidences of having been shorelines of ancient Lake Bonneville, which at its highest level covered approximately 19,750 square miles. The two most prominent shorelines are the Bonneville level at about 5,100 to 5,200 feet above sea level and the Provo level some 300 feet lower, the difference in the present elevation of the shorelines being due to warping of the earth's crust and faulting since the disappearance of the lake. At each of these levels the notch cut into the slope of the mountains and deposition by wave action is clearly evident. The most prominent features, however, are the large deltas formed in the lake by the streams coming out of the Wasatch and the many fossil bars of sand and gravel deposited along the shores. These deposits are discussed in geomorphology and geology texts throughout the world; in a more immediate sense they have served as sources of sand and gravel for much of the construction in Utah.

With the drop in the level of Lake Bonneville, the streams eroded canyons into those deltas to reach the new base level or to flow on out into the valley. The remnant delta areas are now locally called *benches*. Their surfaces are almost level, having been deposited into water rather than sloping, as is characteristic of alluvial fans. As water has again been brought to them over the years since pioneer settlement, these bench lands along the Wasatch Front have become preferred locations for fruit growing and residential development. Hill Field takes advantage of the flat surface of the fossil delta of the Weber River for its 14,000-foot runway.

As the streams continued to bring materials down from the mountains, they deposited alluvial fans just beyond the mouths of the canyons cut into these deltas. These low fans provided the

The Green River (from the right) joins the Colorado River (from the bottom of the picture) in southeastern Utah's Canyonlands National Park.

original sites for Salt Lake City, Provo, American Fork, and many other communities. While urban development has obscured a clear view of the fans, it will still be obvious to anyone standing in the central business district of Salt Lake City or Provo that the land slopes not only to the south but also to the east and to the west. Such a site ideally met the requirements of the Mormon pioneers. A grid-pattern street system could be laid out with slopes such that water could run by gravity along every street. Soils were well drained and free from frost early in the spring. Wells can be sunk to tap underground water that flows through the loose materials of the fan even when the main stream on the surface ceases to flow in late summer. In some cases groundwater is trapped so that artesian conditions exist; self-flowing wells are still common in many places.

Where sufficient inflow of water exists along the east side of the Great Basin, the remnant lakes—Great Salt Lake, Utah Lake, and Sevier Lake—remain prominent features of the landscape. Sevier Lake is presently bereft of inflow most years because of water withdrawal from the Sevier River for irrigation. Utah Lake, while only averaging about eight feet in depth, was a source of fish for both Indians and pioneers; it still provides some fishing and boating in addition to serving as a reservoir. Great Salt Lake, with depths not much over thirty feet, provides recreational use and, interestingly enough, some fishing in fresh water bays at the mouth of the Bear River. Brine shrimp and shrimp eggs from the salty main area of the lake are sold to hatcheries and as food for tropical fish in home aquariums. Covering an average area of some 1,500 square miles, depending upon its fluctuating elevation, the Great Salt Lake is the largest natural lake in the western part of the United States and is one of the saltiest lakes in the world. It is a source of table salt, potash, and, more recently, magnesium; the value of the minerals in the lake is estimated at over $4 billion.

Rising above the valleys and basins with their playas are the mountains of the Basin and Range Province, and to the east the wall of the Wasatch and the High Plateaus. The basin ranges vary from low hills a few miles in length to impressive peaks over 12,000 feet in the Deep Creek Mountains (Haystack Peak) and over 13,000 feet (Wheeler Peak) in the Snake Range just west of the Utah border in Nevada. There is a wide variety of rock types, and a complexity of faulting, folding, and igneous activity may be observed. A high degree of mineralization has occurred and old and new mining districts are scattered through the region. Most of the minerals are metallic—precious metals (gold, silver, and platinum), lead, zinc, and copper—but some clays and nonmetals are also produced. Neither coal nor petroleum has been found in commercial amounts, though some hope exists for future discoveries of oil or gas.

The largest mining operation is located at Bingham in the Oquirrh Range west of the Salt Lake Valley. In the center of the range a body of molten material was forced up under the overlying formations, carrying with it copper and other minerals. Because this intrusive mass has an area less than forty square miles, it is called a *stock*. The huge open-pit copper mine, said to be the largest in the world, is excavating ore from the exposed upper section of this intrusive mass. Other mines in the region producing lead, zinc, and silver have worked ores surrounding the intruded rock.

Rocky Mountains Province

The Rocky Mountains Province is represented in Utah by two very dissimilar ranges, the Wasatch and the Uintas. The Wasatch extends some 200 miles north and south from the Soda Springs region of Idaho to Nephi, Utah, where it ends with Mount Nebo, 11,877 feet and the highest peak in the range. The Wasatch is complex in geology with a wide variation of rock types. Southeast of Salt Lake City sandstones and quartzites stand nearly vertical in Mount Olympus while to the north a downfold or syncline underlies Emigration Canyon and softer beds have eroded to give a low spot, favored both by the incoming pioneers in their wagons and later pioneer aviators. To the south another intrusive mass, this time a form of granite, occupies the area on the border of Salt Lake and Utah counties and again provides mineralization both within and surrounding the area at such places as Alta, Park City, and Brighton. Granite from this intrusion was used to build the Mormon temple in Salt Lake City.

The Uintas, on the other hand, run some 150 miles east from the Wasatch to the border of Colorado. This east-west orientation is rare for mountain ranges in North America, but not unique as often stated. The range is higher than the Wasatch, with many peaks over 12,000 feet and some over 13,000, including Kings Peak, the highest point in Utah at 13,498 feet. In contrast to the complexity of the Wasatch, the Uintas consist of a core of quartzites flanked on either side by upturned sedimentary beds. The range is heavily glaciated and from the air appears as though a flat mass of dough had been cut for biscuits. Only where the glaciation eroded far enough to eliminate the former flat surface do some sharp-pointed peaks or knifelike ridges appear.

Glaciation also occurred in the section of the Wasatch southeast of Salt Lake City. In both the Uintas and the Wasatch the glaciated areas have many lakes, some of which have been dammed and some of which play an important part in the water supply of the region. Glaciation also gives rise to a landscape valued for its scenery, and in recent years for its ski slopes.

For most of the population of Utah since the time of the Mormon pioneers, the abrupt and spectacular western front of the Wasatch is a daily fact of life. The range has been created by faulting along its western side and geologically is still in the process of being lifted. Recent fault scarps are evident in many locations. Interrupted ridge lines and attendant triangular facets on west-facing spurs are classic and are shown in textbooks throughout the world. Canyons which in other circumstances would widen as they approach the valley floor exit from the Wasatch in a sharp V, a pertinent fact to pioneers trying to descend one of these canyons with wagons. Minor earthquakes are frequent, though not of sufficient intensity to be felt by those living in the area, and the danger of more severe earth movement is very real.

One of the more interesting features of both the Wasatch and Uinta ranges is that they are cut by streams originating elsewhere and passing directly through the range. The Green River, entering Utah from Wyoming, cuts directly through the Uintas in a spectacularly scenic canyon. This peculiar river course is said to occur because at one point in the geologic past the entire area was buried in softer deposits and the river that flowed across this ancient surface has been able to cut downward as these deposits eroded away and the present hard core of the Uintas became exposed.

The Wasatch, Bear, Weber, and Provo rivers begin in the western end of the Uinta Range within a short distance of each other, and each cuts directly through the Wasatch into the Great Basin. In this case the explanation is that the rivers were there prior to the uplifting and have been able to cut downward and maintain their course rather than be diverted as has been the case with smaller streams. In practical terms, the result is absolutely critical since these streams support much of the agriculture and most of the urban population in Utah. Their canyons also provide "water level" routes through the Wasatch and are important in both rail and highway transportation.

Colorado Plateaus Province

To the south and east of the Rocky Mountain Province lies the area of Colorado Plateaus. The portion of this physiographic province found in Utah is divided into three sections—the High Plateaus, the Uinta Basin, and the Canyonlands. Each falls into the general classification because the layers of underlying sedimentary rock are essentially horizontal, or at best gently tilted, yet each differs from the others.

The High Plateaus section extends southward from Mount Nebo through Utah and into Arizona. Viewed from the valley floor, the edge of the plateaus seems a continuation of the Wasatch Range. But from the air, or from a road across the summit areas, the plateaus show areas of rolling surface quite in contrast to the sharp ridges of the Wasatch, and even where canyons have cut into the plateaus so that only ridge remains, the horizontal character of the rocks is evident. In total, the high plateaus are about 200 miles in length and roughly 40 miles across. The summit areas reach elevations of over 11,000 feet, with Delano Peak at 12,173 feet the highest point, and large areas of gently rolling land exist above 10,000 feet.

Cutting through the center of the High Plateaus is the valley of the Sevier River and its tributaries. These streams occupy a graben, a structural valley caused by faulting rather than stream erosion. This valley system divides the region into a series of eastern and western plateau blocks, with those on the east being the larger in summit area. The valley also concentrates the drainage from much of the region into the Sevier River system, providing a source of water for irrigation, and a flat valley floor suitable for agriculture that is low enough to provide a reasonable growing season.

The Uinta Basin is just that: a basin that, except for the canyon of the Green River as it cuts through the upturned beds of the Roan Plateau, would be a vast shallow lake. Streams a few miles from the Green River flow northward into the basin, join the Duchesne River on the west or the White River on the east, and go thence to the south-flowing Green. The sedimentary beds upturned against the south slope of the Uinta Range dip under the basin and outcrop again on the south of the Roan Plateau.

The remaining area of the plateaus, the Canyonlands section, is also well named. Here the beds of sandstones and limestones dip gently to the north and form steep cliffs at the upturned outcroppings to the south. The entire region has been uplifted with few disturbances of the almost-horizontal beds and the streams crossing the surface have subsequently eroded deep, steep-sided canyons, which follow the meandering pattern established when the stream flowed near sea level and cut sideways rather than downward. Such patterns now provide spectacular scenery for sightseers but extreme difficulty for road builders.

Within the Canyonlands section, the horizontal beds and somewhat even surface are broken by uplifted areas such as the San Rafael Swell and by volcanic ranges such as the LaSal, the Abajo, and the Henry mountains, adding to the variety of scenery and having considerable impact on the climate and the possibilities for land use. Mountain grassland, for example, allows summer grazing of sheep and cattle, and heavier precipitation at the high elevations provides irrigation water for hay crops, increasing the number of livestock that may be supported.

The various sections of the Colorado Plateaus contain coal, petroleum, natural gas, and other hydrocarbons including oil shales, natural waxes, solid asphalts, nonmetallic minerals such as potash; and metallic minerals such as uranium and vanadium. The coal is extensive and of excellent quality for fuel, although not the best for making coke for steel production. It has a low sulphur content and a high heat value. These minerals have been of some importance in the past but bear the possibility of sufficient exploitation in the future to alter the entire economy of the region.

Climate

The climate of Utah is often referred to as *semiarid*. The description may also point out that while most of the state is semiarid—having a balance between precipitation and evaporation such that shrubs and grasses predominate—some areas are truly arid and the higher elevations are sufficiently humid to produce large trees. Such generalities are indeed true, but they mask a myriad of detail and offer no understanding of why these conditions exist. Nor do such generalities explain local conditions which have critical impact upon what the people of Utah have done in the past and presently do with their land. (See map, p. 720, which shows some of the significant patterns in distribution of precipitation and temperatures.)

The key to weather and climate is the balance between incoming solar energy and energy being radiated away from the earth's surface. The amount of incoming energy is dependent upon latitude, or the angle of the sun's rays, and upon elevation. There is a difference in average temperature of about 2°F for each degree of latitude away from the equator, or a difference of about 6°F to 8°F between a station in southern Utah and one in the north at the same elevation. Elevation in turn makes a difference of about 3°F per thousand feet due in great part to the thinner layer of atmosphere, allowing more intensive radiation. Both of these factors are influenced strongly in short range by cloudiness that may reflect incoming radiation and that also may reflect outgoing radiation back to earth. In a region such as Utah, with many clear days and nights, both incoming and outgoing radiation are strong and the weather is marked by large differences between daytime and nighttime temperatures.

Precipitation in Utah, as elsewhere on earth, occurs when air is cooled to the point where the water vapor, always present, condenses. Such cooling may occur when the air is in contact with a cold surface of earth or water and it results in fog or frost, but for the most part it occurs when warmer, lighter air is lifted by an inflow of heavier cold air. The warmer air expands as it rises and is cooled in the process to the point where a cloud is formed. Differences in surface temperatures giving rise to areas of warmer or colder air may be at scales from hundreds of miles to a few feet. Air over the Gulf of Alaska may be warmer than air over the

Great Basin and western United States, or air over a parking lot may be warmer than air over the lawn in a nearby park. In either case movement may occur.

Where heating is local and an inflow of colder, heavier air lifts a column of warmer air, the column may be cooled sufficiently in rising and expanding to result in a cloud of small area but great vertical development. This is a convectional system, more commonly called a thunderstorm, because such convectional storms frequently result in lightning and thunder. Such storms are typical of Utah in the summer, when warm, moist air drifts northward from the Gulf of Mexico. They are particularly frequent over the mountains, where air temperature contrasts between adjacent mountains and valleys are often pronounced. Convectional storms are characterized by heavy precipitation of short duration and are local in area. High runoff as compared to infiltration into the soil is normal, and on occasion flash flooding results. Southern Utah receives about half its precipitation from such storms; in northern Utah they are of lesser importance. Throughout the state the frequency and number of such storms varies greatly from year to year.

Storm systems called *mid-latitude cyclones,* associated with low pressures, occur when differences in air pressure over large areas cause a flow of air from the higher pressure into the lower across hundreds or thousands of miles. The cooler, heavier air flows from the north, hugging the ground and pushing in under the warmer southern air along an often well-defined line called a *cold front.* The warmer, lighter air flows into the low pressure area from the south and tends to ride up over the cold air in the eastern sector of the system, along an often well-defined line called a *warm front.* In both the cold-front and the warm-front areas of such a storm system the warmer air is lifted, cooled through expansion, and may provide precipitation. Viewed from space these mid-latitude cyclones appear as giant whirlpools which move from west to east along the boundary between warmer southern and colder northern air as this boundary shifts and twists, sometimes far to the north and sometimes to the south of Utah.

If a cold front moves over Utah, the weather is characterized by a relatively warm period with winds from the south; then wind comes from the north and a sharp drop in temperature occurs as the front, or boundary between the two air masses, passes over. Precipitation tends to be brief and occasionally heavy, followed by clear, crisp weather. Weather characteristic of passage of a warm front, in contrast, brings little wind and prolonged periods of gentle precipitation. Such warm-front weather is relatively rare in Utah. Northern Utah receives more precipitation from such cyclonic storms than does the southern part of the state.

The third system for cooling large amounts of air sufficiently to yield precipitation is simply forcing the air to rise over a physical barrier such as a mountain. This lifting mechanism, termed *orographic*, is critical to Utah in many ways. First it may be said that orographic lifting is a negative factor in that much of the moisture passing inland from the Pacific Ocean is condensed out of the air as it is forced to rise over the Sierra Nevada or Cascade Range. If these ranges did not exist and the land sloped gently from the ocean to the western edge of the Great Basin, precipitation in Utah would be much greater and, in fact, Lake Bonneville would again fill its basin.

As it is, the air moving across the area of Nevada and Utah still retains some moisture which may be squeezed out by cooling as it is lifted over the higher mountains. Such orographic effect is easily seen in precipitation figures showing about thirteen inches per year near Great Salt Lake, around twenty inches on the east side of Salt Lake Valley, and around forty in the upper parts of Big Cottonwood Canyon. The vegetation also reflects this variation and is easily observed. In a sense the pushing of air up and over the mountains is like running a partially saturated sponge through a wringer. The sponge moves along but the water comes out of the wringer. Heavy snow may occur along the Wasatch and no snow in the Uinta Basin; Brian Head, east of Cedar City, may have plenty of snow for the skiers, but Cannonville or Escalante remains dry.

In actuality the process of wringing water from the air passing through the state is often a combination of cyclonic and orographic and even convectional factors all at the same time, and it is seldom simple. Landform features disturb the flow of air and local moisture may be added by evaporation from Great Salt Lake (although this lake is not a major factor) such that precipitation may be quite erratic. Ogden and Provo may receive rain while Salt Lake remains dry; a cold front passing during March may dump eighteen inches of snow in Bountiful north of Salt Lake City and one inch in southern Salt Lake Valley. Storms that usually pass through the state from the northwest or west *may* come from the south, causing unusual precipitation patterns.

High pressure systems are also important in the weather and climate of the state. Areas of higher pressure normally pass through, alternating with the lows. High pressure, however, may become established for a long period, shunting the jet stream of the upper atmosphere, and its attendant storm systems on the surface, to the north or south. Such a Great Basin High, as it is sometimes termed, is marked by stagnation of air and consequent high levels of pollution. Air near the surface becomes colder than air at higher levels and flows into the lowest parts of the valleys. Smoke, dust, automobile exhaust, particles from tires, and other pollutants pushed into this cold layer tend to remain. Heavy fogs may occur. The temperature at the ski resorts in the high Wasatch may be warmer than downtown Salt Lake City. Chances for precipitation under such conditions of high pressure are nil. Such periods with their attendant pollution are recorded in the first pioneer diaries; they were particularly serious in the 1920s and 1930s when thousands of coal-burning stoves and furnaces spewed soot into the air of the communities along the Wasatch Front. The fall and early winter of 1976–1977 was an extreme example of prolonged dominance of high pressure and lack of precipitation, affecting even the high mountain areas.

Day-to-day weather in Utah is always a combination of regional and local factors. In addition to the succession of lows and highs and the movement of large masses of air from the Gulf of Mexico in summer there is the local phenomenon of mountain valley winds and air drainage. With the setting sun and consequent cessation of incoming energy, cooled, heavier air flows down the canyons and into the lowest areas of the valleys below. Such air movement provides protection from frost for orchards and natural air conditioning for fortunate residents near the canyon mouth. The up-canyon breezes generated during the day are not so strong or so evident as the down-canyon winds.

Data for the growing season—the all-important period between killing frosts—must always be interpreted in the light of the specific location of the recording station. A station in a lower area of the valley may record frost weeks prior to a station on the slope near the mouth of one of the canyons. A station near Great Salt Lake may be influenced somewhat by the tempering influence of the warm lake water in early fall. Locations within Salt Lake Valley, where a number of recording stations have existed for decades, show a range of average days growing season from 144 at Midvale to 202 at the Salt Lake Airport. In Utah Valley, Spanish Fork records an average of 168 days between 32°F temperatures, while a few miles away the Elberta station at about the same elevation records a season of only 128 days. Heber City, in a higher valley east of Salt Lake City, clearly shows the effect of both elevation

17

and air drainage with an average period between frosts of only 77 days. Manti in the valley of the San Pitch River in the High Plateaus shows 129 days, again severely restricting possible crops. St. George, interestingly enough, shows an average frost-free period of 210 days, only 8 days longer than Salt Lake City, but it shows an average January temperature of 39°F compared to 27°F in Salt Lake, a very appreciable difference, which led the pioneers to call the lower Virgin and Santa Clara valleys "Dixie." (See map, p. 720.)

There is no evidence that the climate or "average weather" is changing in Utah, or that it has changed in the period covered by this history. There have indeed been cycles of wetter, colder or drier weather, and extremes of each are often seen as omens. The current generation will not likely forget the record-breaking dry months of 1976–1977; certainly the ski resort operators will not. These cycles and radical variations have come and gone for at least the last few thousand years and seem likely to continue. This is not to discount their serious short-range economic impact, but they remain just irregularly patterned variations.

Hydrology

From the discussion of landforms and climate it will be obvious that most of the streams in Utah are small in volume, short in length, and variable in seasonal flow. The Green and the Colorado, the two largest rivers, actually import water from Wyoming and Colorado, respectively. Even these larger rivers show enormous changes in volume from season to season and year to year, reflecting variations in the weather. Since major areas of the American Southwest depend upon the water of the Colorado and its tributaries, programs for regulating, conserving, and utilizing these resources have generated steadily increasing political concern and economic investment in Utah and her neighboring states in the twentieth century.

In many cases Utah's smaller streams are completely dry in late summer. In this respect the river lines on a map convey little information. The same width of blue ink shown in Utah, coastal Oregon, or Georgia may indicate streams which actually vary in flow by a factor of fifty or a hundred times. A network of blue lines in Ohio may be the result of the cartographer's leaving out nine of ten smaller streams due to lack of space, while the same density of blue lines in Utah may indicate every stream which has water for even a few months during favorable wet years.

Vegetation

If Escalante were to return, he would find the vegetation of the physical landscape altered—the consequence of grazing, crop cultivation, and the deliberate and accidental introduction of many new varieties of plants. Areas where native bunch grasses flourished when the Mormon pioneers arrived are now covered with an introduced European species variously called June Grass or Cheat Grass, which is useless for grazing and a real fire hazard in summer and fall. Other former grasslands have been invaded by sagebrush and juniper as the grasses were overgrazed. Valley floors have been put into cultivation and now bear no trace of native vegetation. A map of vegetation as it exists today in Utah is not a map of original native vegetation except in broad terms.

In these broad terms vegetation is most closely related to elevation and landform. Valley floors at lower elevations are usually abundant in grasses and small herbaceous plants, often with some shrubs. Higher areas of the valleys and lower sections of the mountains show more brush and small trees, while large trees are confined to the higher elevations in the mountains, the canyon bottoms, and along the streams through the valley floors. This distribution reflects the orographic precipitation pattern, coupled with the decreasing evaporation at higher elevations due to cooler temperatures. There is in a real sense in Utah a double tree line, the upper limit being one of constant cold temperatures and the lower a deficiency of moisture. The restriction of forest to the higher elevations is visible not only on the vegetation map but also in a general way on a map showing national forests, even though areas designated as national forests correspond in boundary only roughly with forest vegetation and include large areas of grass and brush land. (See map, p. 738.)

Varieties of grasses, brush, and trees number in the hundreds and are complex in distribution. Much of the state below about 7,500 feet falls into the Upper Sonoran Zone, with grasses such as grama grass, salt grass, rice grass, and galleta, along with brush such as sagebrush, creosote brush, black brush, salt brush, greasewood, and others. Along streams phreatophytes such as cottonwood and willow trees are evident. In favored locations pinyon and juniper, or even scrub oak or mountain ash, may occur in this zone. Above about 7,500 feet is a transition zone of piñon and juniper, merging into yellow pine and Douglas fir, above which quaking aspen and several varieties of spruce and fir are common; and, in the Uintas, extensive stands of lodgepole pine are found. Above

19

the tree line there is a wide variety of small herbs and grasses.

Specific distribution of vegetation depends upon many factors, including latitude, elevation, groundwater and soil composition, depth, and salinity. Landform is an influence in terms of exposure as well as elevation. A glance at the spurs running eastward from the crest of the Wasatch shows clearly that north-facing slopes where evaporation is lower are clothed in forest while south-facing slopes have grass or brush. Where vegetation is heavy, soils are strongly influenced over time by the input of organic material.

Soils

As with other physical features, soils in Utah are varied and complex in pattern. The "General Soil Map of Utah," published by the Soil Conservation Service of the United States Department of Agriculture and the Utah Agricultural Experiment Station at Utah State University, shows seventy-one classes of soil, and then notes that each area outlined contains more than one kind of soil and explains that the map is to be used for general planning only. Over much of the agricultural land of the state a farmer may be dealing with several significant variations in soil in a single field. In the alluvial area at the mouth of a canyon, for example, he may have heavy clay in one area, sand in another, and gravel or cobbles in another corner, or he may be blessed with an area of silt loam.

It is possible to group soils into certain general patterns. It may be said, for example, that most of the soils in Utah are thin and poorly developed. Such soils are generally termed lithosols, occurring on steep slopes or in areas where weathering has not been deep. On lower slopes and in valleys and basins where deposition has occurred, soils of better quality may be found. In some favored areas, as in the valleys west of the Wasatch Range, some soils compare with the flat lands of the Central States and are highly productive. In the area to the east of Monticello and the Abajo Range, there is even an area of wind-deposited silt, called *loess*, which provides excellent soil for dry farming.

Conclusion

As mentioned earlier, geographer Preston James says that what man does with his physical environment depends upon his attitudes, his objectives, and his technical abilities. Yet he is influenced and in some instances even controlled by that environment. Gold ore or silver ore, for example, must be present to be mined, whatever the characteristics of the inhabitants. Yet the choice may be, as it was in the pioneer generation, not to mine the ore. A given valley floor may be left idle except for a few trails and temporary camps. Or it may be used for grazing sheep or cattle, or intensive farming under irrigation, or for siting a steel mill. Or it may be buried under roads, parking lots, and high-rise office buildings.

The history of Utah is in a fundamental sense the story of the choices made in the use of an arbitrarily defined place on the surface of the earth by various groups of people with different and changing attitudes, objectives, and technical abilities—but working within the same physical parameters.

Chapter 1
Bibliographical Essay

Very few publications are available that deal solely with Utah in terms of physical background. The choice is usually between a regional or national study, or a specialized paper on some small part of the state.

Geology and Landforms are covered in books such as Nevin M. Fenneman, *Physiography of Western United States* (1931); Wallace W. Atwood, *The Physiographic Provinces of North America* (1940); Charles B. Hunt, *Natural Regions of the United States and Canada* (1974); and Lehi F. Hintze, *Geologic History of Utah* (1973). The Fenneman work is old, but still a classic study, with considerable detail. Atwood is a more popular treatment with less detail and some comment regarding man's use of each area. Information in Hunt's book is not restricted to landforms, but includes comments about vegetation, soils, and climate as well as the impact of geographic factors on man's use of the land in historical times and at present; the illustrations are excellent. Hintze's fine book is more technical and specialized, with maps and diagrams giving an overview of the geologic history of the state.

Climate is covered in general terms by books such as U.S. Department of Agriculture, *Climate and Man* (1941); Water Information Center, Port Washington, N.Y., *Climates of the States,* Vol. 2, (1974); and Robert C. Burnham, "The Climates of Utah" (master's thesis, University of Utah, 1950). Both *Climate and Man* and *Climates of the States,* Vol. 2, have tables of data for temperatures, precipitation, growing seasons, and other aspects of Utah climate; the latter is somewhat more up to date and the description of climates and weather, though brief, is very good. Burnham's thesis is an attempt to map climates according to the Koeppen system, complete with map, and it has some detail not available in the shorter discussions.

21

Vegetation and Soils are covered in hundreds of specialized reports for small areas. On a statewide basis, Robert Foster, "Distribution of Major Plant Communities in Utah" (Ph.D. dissertation, Brigham Young University, 1968), gives a description of major plant communities and a map of their distribution. The map mentioned in the chapter text, Soil Conservation Service of the U.S. Department of Agriculture and Utah Agricultural Experiment Station at Utah State University, "General Soil Map of Utah" (1973), offers a good generalized view of distribution of soils. Local detailed studies of recent data are available from the Soil Conservation Service for a number of agricultural areas of the state.

Goverment documents and maps are a major primary source of information. The U.S. Geological Survey publishes maps at a scale of 1:500,000 in both shaded relief and contour editions. The state is covered in the 1:250,000 scale series offering greater detail, and much of the state is covered by large-scale topographic sheets at a scale of 1:24,000 or 1:62,500. Information on maps and other Geological Survey publications may be obtained free from the Federal Distribution Center, Denver, Colorado, or the U.S. Geological Survey Public Inquiries Office, Salt Lake City, Utah. A recent and excellent map covering energy resources is *Map 36: Energy Resources Map of Utah* (1975), published by the Department of Natural Resources, Utah Geological and Mineral Survey. This and many other maps and documents are available from the Utah Geological and Mineral Survey, 606 Black Hawk Way, Salt Lake City, Utah 84108.

Government reports and statistical materials are available on items such as climate throughout most of the time since the Mormon pioneers entered Salt Lake Valley. Daily weather data is available in some cases for about eighty years. An example of an extremely perceptive and valuable report is John Wesley Powell, *Report on the Lands of the Arid Region of the United States* (1879). Significant reports by other early geological surveyors are listed with chapter 5.

An important source of contemporary information is the Geological Survey's *National Atlas of the United States* (1970). Available in most libraries, the atlas contains a wealth of information on both physical and cultural features of all the states, including many historical maps that will supplement this history.

Chapter 2
The Earliest Peoples

S. Lyman Tyler

To adjust the framework of the Utah story from geological time, it may be helpful to recall how brief is the written history of the area which became the state. Although Spain claimed the region for three centuries after Columbus and Cortez, the vast expanses north of New Spain emerged from Indian lore only late in that period. The first record which precisely documents events in Utah—the journal of the Domínguez-Vélez de Escalante expedition—was written while signatures were still fresh on the American Declaration of Independence. Thus the history of Utah encompasses only the last half-century of Spanish possession, 27 years as a part of Mexico, and a little more than 125 years in the United States. Before 1850 Utah had no political limits or status, and Utah Territory did not shrink to the present state boundaries until 1868.

The story of man in Utah, however, goes back much farther than the written records. Indian cultures, identified through the work of anthropologists, archeologists, and historians as Desert, Basket Maker, Pueblo, Fremont, Ute, Paiute, Gosiute, Shoshoni, Navajo, and others, have been present in the Great Basin-Colorado Plateau region for about 10,000 years. Indian peoples had their own boundaries that separated the territory of one group from another, but these had no relationship to the present boundaries of Utah. (See map, p. 721.)

The Desert Culture

During the 1920s and 1930s archeologists began to report discoveries in the American Southwest that carried the story of man back more than a hundred centuries. In the 1950s excavations in caves near Wendover, Utah, produced evidence of continuing seasonal occupancy going back to about 9000 B.C. and tending to confirm the earlier findings. As the hunting and gathering patterns that typified desert regions like the Great Basin were analyzed, it seemed apparent that the lifeways were similar enough to identify them as the Desert Culture. The people were primitive, but it should be remembered that agricultural civilizations capable of furnishing a livelihood based on the regular planting and harvesting of crops and the domestication of animals did not exist anywhere on earth 10,000 years before the beginning of the Christian era.

Within the Great Basin and Colorado Plateau there are different elevations and climatic conditions. Plants and animals can be found on a mountainside, on tablelands, or by streams flowing from higher ground that are not normally seen in the lower desert areas. Different seasons also bring variety to the foodstuffs available on mountain and desert. The peoples of the Desert Culture learned where to find and how to make use of the plants and animals around them for food, clothing, shelter, and medicinal purposes. Living and moving about in extended family units of fifteen to thirty men, women, and children, these people had few tools and a relatively simple life-style, but they survived.

The Western Shoshone still depended on hunting and gathering to furnish a livelihood when the white man arrived in their area. They say their land was "rich enough to provide for all their needs until the white man destroyed its resources."

The Anasazi

Anasazi is a Navajo word which means "the ancient ones." Archeologists have labeled the early Anasazi period *Basket Maker* and the later Anasazi period *Pueblo*. Each of these major divisions is further subdivided to assist in giving a time sequence to pre-Pueblo and Puebloan development.

A preagricultural, ancestral stage, probably prior to or about the time of Christ, has been assumed for the Basket Maker. This was followed by an early agricultural stage, then a period of further development and dependence upon agriculture in a semi-agricultural, semihunting stage in which pottery appeared. Basket Maker remains have been found in the Four Corners Region of Utah, Arizona, New Mexico, and Colorado. These people probably reached their highest development in the San Juan drainage basin.

It is interesting to trace the developments in building through the Basket Maker and on into the Pueblo period. Although it is

24

believed that house structures were built and used earlier, excavations near Durango, Colorado, indicate that house construction was well developed early in the fourth century A.D. During the Modified Basket Maker Period (A.D. 500–700), houses were entered through a passageway leading from the ground outside. Later, in the Developmental Pueblo Period (A.D. 700–1100), this ground entrance became smaller and was used to provide ventilation; the entrance for residents became the conventional pueblo hole in the roof, from which one descended by ladder to the floor inside.

From about A.D. 1100 to 1300 the Pueblo Culture was most widely extended and also reached a climax in the development of the house structure. Masonry walls, often plastered and decorated, ceremonial *kivas,* storage space, and living quarters characterized these Anasazi communities. Built in cliff caves, on mesa tops, and in sheltered box canyons, the pueblos housed from a few families to several hundred people. Fine pottery, cotton cloth, feather robes, and jewelry reflect the craftsmanship of these "ancient ones." Their archeological remains dot southeastern Utah, with some of these impressive sites now federally administered in Hovenweep National Monument.

During the last part of the thirteenth century the Anasazi withdrew from their settlements in Utah and Colorado, and only the pueblo villages of New Mexico and northern Arizona remained. Several reasons have been suggested for this retreat. A period of successive dry years and crop failures may have been a cause. The lowering of stream beds and the elevation of crop lands through many years of flood-water irrigation may have produced a condition where the water could no longer flow over the land as necessary to produce crops. The incursion of nomads whose new weapons, like the bow and arrow, were more effective than the *atlatl* (spear thrower) may have forced the pueblo dwellers to relocate and redesign their dwellings to make them less accessible from the outside, and ultimately to abandon the region. When Columbus came to America, the great age of Utah's "ancient ones" was already blending into Indian mythology.

The Fremont Culture

North and northwest of the area occupied by the Anasazi the somewhat parallel Fremont Culture developed after about A.D. 400, retaining some traits of the Desert people but adding Basket Maker-Pueblo characteristics. The Fremont was different from the Desert Culture in that corn, beans, and squash were raised, and by

A.D. 800 or 900 the people were living in simple but more or less permanent dwellings. Products of the small settlements included baskets, pottery, and clay figurines which seem to have had a special religious significance. From contacts with the Plains Indians the Fremont people adopted the buffalo hide and other leather products; on the other hand, they did not adopt the more sophisticated elements of the nearby Pueblo Culture.

At the end of the thirteenth century a cultural regression occurred among the Fremont peoples which paralleled the retreat of the Anasazi from Utah and may have had similar causes. They were replaced, displaced, or absorbed by peoples of a different cultural and linguistic background, who probably began to move into the region sometime after A.D. 1000.

The Shoshoni Peoples

There is a tradition among the Southern Paiutes that helps to bridge the gap between the peoples known only from archeological remains and the Indians who were living in the same area when the white man arrived. It describes a people who anciently made an arduous trek eastward from a land of high mountains and endless waters to the red mountains. There, under the benign influence of their gods, Tobats and Shinob, they developed a happy way of life in which irrigated gardens, abundant game, and wild seeds amply met their needs. Then came many years without moisture, and the streams dried up and the game fled. As famine threatened, they appealed to Tobats and Shinob, and after three days Shinob appeared, heard their problem, and instructed them to take counsel from the animals. Since that time the Southern Paiutes have been nomads. "Leaving their homes in the caves, they have followed the game from high land to low and gathered in gratitude the foods which the gods distribute every year over the face of *tu-weep,* the earth."

Anthropologists have developed various methods to identify different groups of Native Americans. Reference has been made to culture traits and culture areas. Another method relates to the use of language. Even as the peoples of western Europe are described as speaking Germanic and Romance languages, so the native peoples of the Americas have been grouped into large, inclusive language families. Thus, the Ute, Paiute, and Shoshoni spoke languages identified as Shoshonean (just as English is a Germanic language), and Shoshonean is a branch of the Uto-Aztecan language family (as the Germanic tongues are Indo-European). Uto-Aztecan also includes the languages spoken by the Hopi, Pima,

26

Papago, Yaqui, Comanche, Aztec, and some other tribes of Mexico and the American Southwest.

The Northern Shoshoni, the Gosiutes and other Western Shoshoni, the Southern Paiutes, and the Utes are all Shoshonean speakers. The Northern Shoshoni were located in what is now northern Utah, southern Idaho, and Wyoming. The Gosiute were found in northwestern Utah and northeastern Nevada along with other Western Shoshoni. The southern Paiute were in southwestern Utah, southern Nevada, and northern Arizona. (See map, p. 722.)

Chiefly situated to the north and east of present Utah, the Northern Shoshoni developed many of the characteristics of the nomadic Plains Indians. Hunting and trading were the basis of their economy when they appeared in history in the early nineteenth century.

The Gosiutes occupied what seems today some of the dreariest territory in the American West, and the life-style which they developed led early white observers to label them *Digger Indians.* They roamed the desert in family bands, gathering seeds and insects, trapping small game, hunting antelope and deer, wearing skin blankets in winter and little of anything in summer, and improvising wickiups of brush for shelter. They were few in number, peaceable in disposition, and reliant on medicine men to placate the invisible forces with which their world was filled.

The Southern Paiute lived on lands almost as formidable, except for a limited irrigation potential. Some of these bands, therefore, augmented nature's harvest with small gardens; but even among these clothing and housing were meager. Basketmaking was a functional art form. Like the Gosiutes, these Paiutes used the bow and arrow for hunting but rarely for warfare. In the eighteenth and early nineteenth centuries their women and children were sometimes taken by Ute raiding parties to be sold to the Spanish and Mexicans in New Mexico.

During the period before Anglo-Americans began to push them around, the Utes were described in terms of eastern and western bands. The eastern bands occupied the mountainous areas of Colorado and part of northern New Mexico. From their homeland they went on to the plains to hunt and farther south into New Mexico to trade with the Pueblo Indians. Spaniards and mountain men spoke of the Yamparka or White River band, the Tabeguache (later known as the Uncompahgre), the Moache, the Capote, and the Weeminuche. The Weeminuche were found both in southwestern Colorado and southeastern Utah, adjacent to a group the Spanish identified as Payuchis, or Ute people.

27

The Western Utes occupied approximately the eastern two-thirds of the present state of Utah, south of the Shoshoni and north of the San Juan River and the Southern Paiute. They were divided into bands known as the Uintahs in northeastern Utah, the Timpanogos around Utah Lake, the Pahvants around Fillmore and Sevier Lake, the Sanpete (or Sanpitch) in the same general north-south area but ranging farther east, and the Weeminuche. Utah Valley was a favorite gathering place of the western Utes, which may be the reason why it was the first point of major conflict between the Indians and the Mormon settlers.

Unlike the Gosiutes and Southern Paiutes, the Utes adopted the horse into their culture soon after Spaniards brought it into the Southwest in the late sixteenth century. Like the Plains Indians, they exploited the buffalo when available; their food, clothing, and *tepee* shelters reflected their primary reliance on hunting. Tribal groupings larger than extended family units were useful in hunting and warfare, but ties of obligation were loose and whites who later sought to negotiate with the Utes found that the jurisdiction of individual "chiefs" was often uncertain.

The area occupied by all the Ute bands in what is now Utah, Colorado, and New Mexico was very large—some 200,000 square miles—and they moved beyond that heartland to hunt and trade. Their far-ranging and predatory manner of living virtually guaranteed friction if outsiders moved into their country. After a half-century of conflict, the Uintah, Timpanogos, Pahvant, Yamparka (White River), and Uncompahgre were eventually settled on reservations in northeastern Utah and came to be known as the Northern Utes. The Moache, Capote, and Weeminuche were moved onto a reservation in southwestern Colorado and were called the Southern Utes. A small group of the latter remained in Utah and became identified as the Allen Canyon Utes.

The Navajo

Although the Navajo probably comprise half of the Indian population of Utah today, "old Navajoland" was centered in northern New Mexico. The Athapascan-speaking Navajo were relatively recent arrivals in the Southwest, having probably migrated from western Canada not long before the arrival of the Spanish. Under pressure from Utes and Comanches, and to find grazing for the livestock they acquired from the Spaniards, the Navajo gradually moved westward in the eighteenth and early nineteenth centuries, scattering their flocks and hogans over northeastern Arizona and southeastern Utah. They crossed the San Juan River regularly to

The architects and builders of the Anasazi culture constructed many remarkable homes and fortifications before evacuating southeastern Utah near the close of the thirteenth century. This one, built on a solid rock foundation, displays the "keyhole" doorway that is quite common in other ruins located in Hovenweep National Monument.

trade with the Weeminuche and other bands of the Utes, and there is evidence that a few were living north of the river as early as the 1700s. The rapid growth of the Navajo populace in San Juan County, however, is largely a twentieth-century phenomenon.

First Contacts with Spaniards

Beginning in 1540 and continuing during the sixteenth century, Spanish explorers moved north from New Spain to discover the territory occupied by the Pueblo Indians in New Mexico and Arizona. They heard of a Lake of Copala in the mysterious land north of the Colorado and San Juan rivers, and eventually the territory west of the Rocky Mountains came to be known as the Land of Teguayo. East of the Rockies was Quivira, the land of the Plains Indians and the buffalo.

A form of the word *Yuta* was probably first recorded in the 1620s by the Franciscan missionary, Father Geronimo de Zarate Salmeron. He likely wrote it down as it sounded coming from the lips of the Indians of Jemez Pueblo, his assigned station on the northwestern Pueblo frontier. Later Spanish chroniclers followed his example. By Yuta they meant Ute people; the Spanish did not identify different Ute bands until the eighteenth century.

Early in the seventeenth century Spaniards began to raid the Utes to acquire slaves for trade elsewhere in New Spain. Before midcentury the Utes had acquired the horse, which greatly aided them in hunting and transporting larger game like the buffalo and eventually becoming slave traders themselves. As the Spanish learned that Utes had been trading with Pecos and Taos pueblos for many years, they sought to regulate this trade to their own advantage. Records refer to a treaty made with the Utes as early as the 1670s. Father Alonso de Posada, in New Mexico from 1640 to 1654, reported to the King of Spain in the 1680s that the Utes were all along the northern frontier and shared the buffalo plains northeast of Santa Fe with the Apaches. Fray Alonso stated further: "These Indians are fond of the Spaniard, are well built, brave and energetic, for only these carry on campaigns against the valiant Apachas with a courage equal to theirs ... they do not retreat; they win or die." He explained that the San Juan and Colorado "divides Yuta and Apacha." Here the term *Apacha* includes the Navajo as well as those now designated Apaches.

Ute pressure against the Navajo in northern New Mexico began in the 1720s. As earlier noted, fear of such attacks caused the Navajo to move westward, sometimes leaving their farms and losing part of their flocks. The Navajo sought peace with the Spaniards, and the Franciscan missionaries assigned to work with them in the 1740s encouraged them to move nearer to the pueblos of Encinal and Caboletta, where they would receive protection from their enemies.

While assigned to the Navajo mission, Fray Carlos Delgado learned of the Land of Teguayo that lay northward through Ute country. He resolved to go there, being told that the remote land included people from various nations, both "civilized" and "heathen." One "division" or "city" was reported by the Navajo to be so large that "one cannot walk around it within eight days." In that country "lives a king of much dignity and ostentation, who, as they say, neither looks or speaks to anyone, except very briefly, such is his severity."

Fray Carlos never made his exploration, and the myth persisted. The desire of the Spanish for new discoveries, for precious metals, and for souls to convert to Christianity seems to have led the Indians to conjure up stories to satisfy them. Still, concepts of "civilization" are relative. The pueblo villages may have been to the nomadic tribes surrounding them what Rome was to the German tribes in ancient times, and the deserted structures that lay northward in the Four Corners area may have seemed fabulous indeed to the Navajo, who thought of them as the homes of the Anasazi— the ancient ones.

During the 1760s and 1770s a new surge of interest in the land north of New Mexico and Arizona developed in connection with the extension of the Spanish frontier into Alta California and the desire to establish a land route between Santa Fe and Monterey. The story of the epic exploration of Fathers Domínguez and Escalante is for another chapter, but some of their observations about the native inhabitants of Utah are appropriate here. Escalante divided the Ute people they encountered into two major groups: the "Yutas we knew before," or the Eastern Utes including the Payuchis of southeastern Utah; and those they had not known before, including the Lagunas in the vicinity of Utah Lake and the Yutas Cobardes, or timid Utes. Groups encountered were listed as the Huascaris (Cedar Indians), the Parusis (Shivwits), the Yubuincariris (Uinkarits), the Ytimpabichis (Timpeabits), and Pagampabichis (Kaibab Indians).

The Indians identified as timid Utes were the Southern Paiutes. They lived in houses made of willow or cane framework covered with brush in the summer and with earth or animal skins in cold weather. From Utah Lake southward to the Colorado River, west of the Payuchis, the bands encountered were reported to be increasingly gentle and more sedentary. They possessed skill in basket handicrafts, some agriculture, the ability to spear fish and conduct communal rabbit drives, and they made extensive use of plant food and small animals. Their clothing was of poorer quality than that of the Eastern Utes. In a letter written later, Father Escalante stated:

From the poorly understood relations of the heathen Indians, many were persuaded that on the other side of the Colorado . . . lived a nation similar to the Spanish, wearing long beards, armor like our old sort, with breast-plate, steel helmet, and shoulder-piece; and these, no doubt, are the bearded Utes of whom the Reverend Father Custodio and I speak in the diary of the journey which we made through those lands in 1776; who live in ran-cherias *and not in* pueblos. *They are very poor; they use no arms other than their arrows and some lances of flint, nor have they any other breast-plate, helmet, or shoulder-piece than what they brought out from the belly of their mothers.*

Although another set of myths about exotic Indian civilization thus died, and although promises of missionary settlement among the Great Basin natives were not fulfilled, there seem to have been continuing contacts between Spaniards and Utes as far north as Utah Lake from 1776 until after the arrival of the Mormons sixty years later. Spanish references usually mention Yuta Indians and do not always name particular bands. An example is the record of Manuel Mestas, a *Genizaro* or Indian of mixed blood, being among the Timpanogos Yutas about 1800. He was said to be seventy years old, a Yuta interpreter "for approximately fifty years," and "the one who reduced them to peace." Several charges of horse stealing against the Utes were referred to Mestas for action during 1805 and 1806; he recovered at least seventeen horses and mules, several of which had passed through more than one Indian band.

Another example of Spanish contact is from the records of the trial of Mauricio Arze and Lagos Garcia, charged with trading with the Yutas without a license. Since it was illegal to trade except at authorized times and places, the traders known to history are those who were caught in illicit business and tried in cases for which the court records have survived. Arze and Garcia left Abiquiu on March 16, 1813, en route to Lake Timpanogas. The party traded with the Indians there for three days and then left for the Sevier River. West of the river they encountered an armed and hostile band of Sanpete Utes, although the Sanpetes were reported to have been friendly when contacted by the Dominguez-Escalante company. Several statements in this trial suggest that members of the trading party knew the country well, that they could converse in the Ute language, and that the only group of Indians they had not previously contacted was the Sanpetes.

The First Anglo-Americans

The Spanish received word about 1800 of activities on the part of Anglo-Americans to the north of their holdings in Texas and the Southwest. The Spanish reacted by organizing a group of Ute and Genizaro spies that were sent among the Kiowas, Pawnees, and other Great Plains tribes south of the Missouri River. They were to keep Santa Fe constantly informed concerning British and American activity in that area. Utes were with Spanish officers observing Zebulon Montgomery Pike while he was operating in Colorado in 1807. James Workman and Samuel Spencer were probably in Ute territory two years later, accompanying a Spanish caravan. It is fair to speculate that there were other Anglo-American as well as Spanish incursions into the "land of the Yutas" in the years that followed.

As the 1820s saw the fur trade invade the Great Basin and the Colorado Plateau, and the Mexican revolution broke Spanish power over the Indian trade in the Southwest, a new era dawned for the Native Americans. Their lives increasingly intertwined with mountain men, explorers, cross-country emigrants, and Mormon pioneers; by midcentury their history was becoming a very different, sadder tale.

Chapter 2
Bibliographical Essay

The story of man in the mountain-plateau-basin region of the American West has lengthened in time span considerably during the past several decades. The work of Alfred V. Kidder, first published in 1924 and now available in paperback as *An Introduction to the Study of Southwestern Archaeology* (1969), synthesized the conclusions reached by the early 1920s. The discoveries of Mark R. Harrington reported in two articles, "Paiute Cave," *Southwest Museum Papers* (No. 4, 1930), and "Gypsum Cave, Nevada," *Southwest Museum Papers* (No. 8, 1933), extended knowledge of early man further to the north and west.

H. M. Wormington's *Prehistoric Indians of the Southwest* (1947), published by the Colorado Museum of Natural History, included chapters on "The Most Ancient Cultures" and "The Anasazi Culture" written in language that is relatively easy for the layman to understand. The seminal work by Jesse D. Jennings, *Danger Cave*,

University of Utah Anthropological Papers, No. 27 (1957), considerably enlarged concepts concerning the Desert and Fremont cultures. Professor Jennings' "Early Man in Utah," *UHQ,* January 1960, places these cultures in perspective with those that followed in an article written for the layman. The work edited by Jennings and Edward Norbeck, *Prehistoric Man in the New World* (1964), with chapters on "The Desert West" by Jennings and "The Greater Southwest" by Erik K. Reed, synthesizes the knowledge available to that date and places those culture areas in perspective in western North America and in the Americas generally.

The Spanish period can be studied in S. Lyman Tyler, "The Spaniard and the Ute," *UHQ,* October 1954, and "The Myth of the Lake of Copala and Land of Teguayo," *UHQ,* October 1952; in Julian H. Steward, *Basin-Plateau Aboriginal Socio-Political Groups,* Bureau of American Ethnology Bulletin 120 (1938); and in the works on the Domínguez-Escalante expedition listed in chapter 3.

Joseph G. Jorgensen, "The Ethnohistory and Acculturation of the Northern Ute," Ph.D. dissertation, University of Indiana (1964), surveys Northern Ute history from precontact through the Spanish period and down to the early 1960s. The same author's *The Sun Dance Religion* (1974) gives less historical detail than the above work and more attention to religious concepts.

A special issue of the *UHQ,* Spring 1971, with C. Gregory Crampton as guest editor, is entirely devoted to Indian tribes or groups that have had some relationship to Utah, past or present, and should be examined by students of the Indian. Helen Z. Papanikolas (ed.), *The Peoples of Utah* (1976), includes important material on the Gosiute, Navajo, Southern Paiute, and Ute by both Indian and Anglo-American authors.

Chapter 3
The Spanish Epoch

Ted J. Warner

L ong before the first white men set foot in what is now the state of Utah, the Spaniards had learned of this region through vague Indian legends. Spanish explorers came within a few days' journey of Utah's southern boundary less than a half-century after Columbus, but two more centuries elapsed before—to our present knowledge—a European crossed that line. Then a remarkable expedition brought two Spanish Franciscans and a handful of companions across the Colorado Plateau and through the Great Basin while signatures were drying on the Declaration of Independence and Washington was crossing the Delaware. The Domínguez-Escalante discoveries were not substantively exploited, however, and today Utah carries only a few place names as reminders of the years under the dominion of Spain.

Kingdoms of the North

Native accounts in the days of Cortes and Coronado mentioned the fabulous lands of Lake Copala and El Gran Teguayo located to the northwest of the pueblo villages of present New Mexico and Arizona—probably in the vicinity of Utah Lake and Great Salt Lake. Soldiers, private adventurers, and missionaries formulated plans and numerous expeditions actually set forth during the sixteenth and seventeenth centuries in search of these "mysterious kingdoms of the north." Francisco de Ibarra, Antonio de Espejo, Juan de Oñate, Diego de Peñalosa Briceño, Fray Alonso de Posada, and Fray Carlos Delgado eagerly received reports, and several of them led expeditions in the general direction of Utah. All failed to reach their objective and they remained frustrated in their search for the fabulous kingdoms on the northern frontiers of New Spain.

At one time it was widely believed that the European discovery of Utah occurred over four hundred years ago. Based upon the writings of Pedro de Castañeda, the chronicler of the Coronado expedition, early writers contended that Don García López de Cárdenas penetrated southeastern Utah in 1540. Searching for a large river reportedly lying northwest of Tusayan (the Hopi villages in northeastern Arizona), Cárdenas marched for twenty days northwestward through a desert country until he was stopped by the huge gorge of the Colorado River. Some early students of Utah history believed this was located in Utah just north of the present Arizona-Utah state line, probably in the region of Glen Canyon. Recent scholarship, however, has clearly demonstrated that López de Cárdenas, guided by Hopi Indians, followed a well-known trail in a more westerly direction from waterhole to waterhole, until he reached the south rim of the Grand Canyon of the Colorado River in Arizona at a place now identified as Grand View.

There are numerous suggestions in documents preserved in the Spanish Archives of New Mexico, the Archivo General de Nación, Mexico City, and the Archivo General de Indias in Seville, Spain, that Spaniards on authorized as well as unauthorized expeditions penetrated southeastern Utah before 1776. A recently rediscovered journal in the archives in Seville reveals that one Juan María Antonio Rivera, whose diary is referred to in the Domínguez-Escalante journal, was on the Colorado River in the Moab area as early as 1765.

The Domínguez-Escalante Expedition

The most thoroughly documented evidence of early Spanish exploration in Utah is the 1776 expedition of Fray Francisco Atanasio Domínguez and Fray Silvestre Vélez de Escalante, who entered Utah as they sought an overland route from Santa Fe, New Mexico, to the newly founded missions in Alta, California. Their journal and letters afford the earliest descriptions of the people, geography, and plant and animal life of the state.

This expedition has generally been referred to as the *Escalante Expedition,* although he was only the junior partner in the enterprise. The role of Father Domínguez, Escalante's religious superior and the one who in fact ordered Escalante to accompany him on the expedition, has been misunderstood and neglected by most historians. Domínguez was the actual leader, the one who had the major responsibility for undertaking it, its chief planner, organizer, the one who made the difficult and hard decisions en route, and the one to be held accountable for its success or failure. The journal is usually called "Escalante's Journal," but it was signed by *both* men prior to being submitted to the authorities in Santa Fe, with Father Domínguez signing *first*. A careful reading of the journal and other letters about the expedition indicates that it was a joint effort on the part of the two Franciscans and not that of Escalante alone.

Utah has recognized only the contributions of Father Escalante. There are numerous Escalante placenames in the state: Escalante Desert, Escalante River, Escalante Mountains, Escalante Valley, Escalante Canyon, Escalante Forest, and a town of Escalante. Vélez de Escalante would be the first to protest this injustice to his superior. Recently through the efforts of the Domínguez-Escalante State-Federal Bicentennial Committee a number of sites associated with the expedition have been named after Domínguez: Domínguez Hill, where the expedition first viewed Utah Valley from the mouth of Spanish Fork Canyon; Domínguez Dome, where they cast lots and determined to return to Santa Fe; and Domínguez Butte on the south shore of Lake Powell.

None of the Escalante placenames were affixed by the expeditioners themselves. As a matter of fact, most of them are not even along the route of march. Had the expedition named things they would have no doubt used the correct name of the padre. His family name was "Vélez" and his contemporaries referred to him as such. Apparently early scholars not familiar with the nomenclature of Spanish names assumed that the last written name was his family name and he became thereby simply Father Escalante. "Escalante," however, refers only to the birthplace of his father, Senor Vélez, who was from the town of Escalante in Spain. It is proper to refer to him as Vélez de Escalante and the journey as the Domínguez-Vélez de Escalante Expedition, but, since it seems virtually impossible to change common usages, the expedition will likely always be called the Domínguez-Escalante Expedition and the keeper of the diary will continue to be known as Father Escalante.

Plans for the Expedition

In 1775 Father Domínguez, who was born in 1740 in Mexico City, was sent to New Mexico as canonical visitor, a responsibility given only to clergymen of the highest caliber. He had a threefold mission to accomplish. First, he was to inspect all the New Mexico missions and make a complete report of both their spiritual and economic status. Second, he was to determine the historical value of the archives in Santa Fe, inasmuch as they had been ravaged by the Pueblo Indians in the revolt of 1680. Finally, he was to search for an overland route from Santa Fe to Monterey, California, for economic, political, defensive, and missionary reasons. Father Domínguez arrived in Santa Fe in March 1776.

The year before another young Franciscan had arrived in New Mexico and been assigned as resident missionary friar in the Indian village of Zuni. Here "in this out of the way place" and at "the end of Christendom in this New World," Fray Silvestre Vélez de Escalante administered to the spiritual needs of the Christian Zuni Indians at his mission of Nuestra Señora de Guadalupe de Zuni. A native of the Villa de Treceño, in the Valle de Vandaliga, in Santander, Spain, he was only twenty-four years old. While serving at Zuni he developed considerable interest in the Moqui, or Hopi Indians, to the northwest of Zuni and in the reports of other tribes farther west. He also entered into a lengthy and important correspondence with another Franciscan missionary, Fray Francisco Garcés, who was then laboring and exploring in Southern Arizona along the Gila and Salt rivers.

In the summer of 1775, Vélez de Escalante spent a week in Hopiland. He called the Hopi "wretched infidels, obstinate in their foolish libertinism." He was keenly disappointed in finding them no more disposed to listen to him preach the gospel than they had been receptive to missionaries before him. One of his reasons for traveling to Hopi was to find out everything possible with regard to the communications Spaniards at Monterey sought with those of New Mexico. He wanted to visit the Cosnina (Havasupai) Indians who lived six days west of Oraibi, the westernmost Hopi village, but did not do so. He did learn that nine days west of the Cosninas were the Jomascabas and that fourteen days west of these were the Chirumas, described by Vélez de Escalante as "warriors, thieves, and savages, because they eat the human flesh of those they kill in their campaigns." This information convinced him that the way to Monterey was not in that direction, but must be sought through lands of the Yutas (Ute Indians) to the west and the northwest of Hopi.

On April 15, 1776, Father Domínguez ordered Escalante to come to Santa Fe to discuss the Monterey project. Together on June 7, they quickly recognized the need for an exploring expedition and decided to undertake it within a month's time. They so informed Governor Don Pedro Fermín de Mendinueta, who agreed to support them. Men were recruited and July 4, 1776, was set as the date for their departure.

Several unforeseen developments delayed them. First, the Comanche Indians attacked the town of La Cienaga and Domínguez assigned Escalante as chaplain to accompany the presidial soldiers on a ten-day scouting campaign against the invaders. Later Escalante was sent to Taos on urgent business; while there he was stricken with an acute pain in his side. Domínguez hastened to Taos, found his friend out of danger, but instructed him to remain there for a week to recuperate fully.[1]

Meanwhile, Fray Francisco Garcés, "The Trails Priest," had journeyed from the mouth of the Colorado River to the Hopi village of Oraibi. He was not welcomed by the Hopi either, but from there he wrote to Father Escalante, who received the letter in Santa Fe. Inasmuch as Garcés had, in effect, opened a trail from the coast to Santa Fe via Hopi, the two Franciscans were forced to review their plans. After consulting with the governor, the group decided that their own expedition would still be useful even if they failed to reach Monterey. Both fathers felt that the knowledge acquired of the lands through which they intended to travel would be of great use in future missionary and political plans.

Eight men were selected to participate with the two Franciscans on the expedition. Most important was don Bernardo Miera y Pacheco, a retired military engineer and at that time a resident of Santa Fe. Upon the expedition's return he prepared some very interesting and useful maps of the regions traversed by the party. The maps show most of the major campsites and name many of them—using names supplied by the padres and recorded in the daily journal. Miera also filed an important summary of the expedition which recommended the establishment of a number of military garrisons or forts in the lands they had visited. His recommendations were never acted upon.

In addition to Miera y Pacheco the expedition included: don Juan Pedro Cisneros, the alcalde mayor of Zuni; his servant Simon Lucero; don Joaquin Laín of Santa Fe; Lorenzo Olivares of El Paso del Norte; Juan de Aguilar of Bernalillo; and two brothers, Andrés Muñiz and Antonio Lucrecio Muñiz. Of these it would

---

[1]The pain which afflicted Vélez de Escalante was probably a severe kidney ailment which plagued him most of the time he served in New Mexico and which, no doubt, caused him considerable pain and discomfort while on the expedition. This kidney trouble eventually was the cause of his death. He died in Parral, Mexico, in 1780, while returning to Mexico City. He was scarcely thirty years old.

appear that the two priests trusted Cisneros most and relied considerably on his judgment. On August 14 in present southwestern Colorado two additional men, Juan Domingo and Felipe, joined the expedition.

From Santa Fe to Utah Lake

On July 29, 1776, the expedition finally set forth on its "Splendid Wayfaring." (See map, p. 723.) It covered fairly well-known territory for the first three weeks, through northwestern New Mexico and the extreme southwestern corner of Colorado. The explorers reached the Gunnison River and proceeded up its North Fork to the villages of the Sabuaganas Yutas. Here they met two Laguna or Timpanogotzis (Ute) Indians from the Utah Lake region. Realizing that they would be traversing their homeland the priests employed the Lagunas, Silvestre and Joaquin, as guides. This increased the expedition number to fourteen. Eleven-year-old Joaquin stayed with the padres all the way back to Santa Fe.

The expedition entered the present state of Utah on September 11, 1776, at a point almost due east of present Jensen on present Cliff Creek—just west of the Utah-Colorado boundary. They called their first encampment in Utah *Arroyo del Cibola,* because at this place they killed a buffalo (cibola). They remained there the next day and proceeded westward until they arrived at the banks of a stream they called the *Río de San Buenaventura*—the Green River of today. Camp was established in a cottonwood grove opposite the mouth of present Brush Creek—some six miles north of Jensen and about a mile south of the Dinosaur National Monument. The fathers recognized the Buenaventura as the boundary between the Yutas on the south and the Comanches on the north; Miera noted this fact on his map. On September 16 the expedition waded across this river at a ford known to the Indian guide, Silvestre.

The fathers directed their course to the southwest until they arrived at the junction of the Río de San Damián (Uinta) and the Ribera de San Cosme (Duchesne River). Going westward up the Duchesne and Strawberry rivers and crossing the summit (rim of the Great Basin) they descended along the Río de San Lino (Diamond Creek) to the Río de Aguas Calientes (Spanish Fork River). This they followed downstream to the settlements of the Laguna (Ute) Indians on the eastern shores of Utah Lake, where they arrived on September 23-24, 1776.

This "great valley and lake of the Tympanocuitzis" they named *La Valle de Nuestra Señora de la Merced.* Here they found the most docile and affable nation of all that they had encountered. The fathers proclaimed the gospel with very positive results, according to the journal. The Indians urged them to remain and then pleaded with them to return as soon as possible in order that they might become Christians. Domínguez and Escalante promised the Utah Indians that upon completion of their present assignment they would return within a year; that missionaries would come to instruct them, and Spaniards would come to live with them, teaching them to plant crops, raise cattle, and have food and clothing like Europeans. Father Domínguez preached to the Indians and promised them that if they submitted "themselves to live in the manner ordered by God and as the padres would teach them, our Great Chief whom we call King would send them everything that was needed, because, on seeing how they wished to be Christianized, He would already be regarding them as His children and would be caring about them as though they were already His people."

The fathers were enthusiastic in their descriptions of Utah Valley. They reported that it was "so spacious, with such good land in beautiful proportions, that in it alone a province like New Mexico can be established and can be maintained here well supplied with every kind of grain and cattle." Throughout this valley, as well as those to the south, southwest, north, east, and southeast, they reported much good pasture and abundant water. The climate was good. The surrounding mountains contained ample timber and firewood. Streams and rivers—four of them they reported discharging into the lake from the east side—provided abundant water for irrigation.[2] Utah Lake they described as teeming with several kinds of edible fish. Geese, beaver, and other land and water animals also were in abundance.

So impressed were the travelers that they remained in the valley for three days, enjoying a much-needed rest. The Indians informed them that their lake connected with another one to the north, which stretched for many leagues. The waters of the second lake were reportedly noxious and extremely salty. The Indians assured the padres that anyone getting a part of his body wet in that water instantly felt a severe itching. The Lagunas reported that around this salt lake (Great Salt Lake) there lived a populous and peaceful tribe named the Puaguampe, which in Spanish means

---

[2]That the Spaniards suggested irrigation in Utah is interesting inasmuch as it was once claimed that the Mormon pioneers were the first people to practice irrigation in the trans-Mississippi West. The Spaniards had been irrigating in New Mexico for 178 years by this time and certain Indian tribes in the Southwest had been irrigators for centuries.

The Dominguez-Escalante expedition forded the Colorado river at this point on November 7, 1776.

"Hechiceros," or witch doctors or wizards. This tribe reportedly spoke the Comanche language, ate grasses, and drank from several springs of good water found around the lake. Their huts were built of dry grass with roofs of earth. They were not enemies of the Lagunas. This is the earliest vague written description of the Salt Lake Valley and its inhabitants.

Miera's map contains interesting notes concerning this region. He depicts "Laguna de las Timpanogos" (present Utah Lake and Great Salt Lake) as one body of water with only a narrows connecting the two parts (not the forty-mile long Jordan River). To the east of the northern and larger part of the lake, the mapmaker noted that "The Comanche region reaches as far as here. Preventing their expansion are the very abundant rivers and lakes on the east, north and northeast of their habitations." Directly on the west side of Great Salt Lake he shows a very large river flowing westward. He notes that this "must be the Río de Tizon [Colorado River], previously discovered by the Adelantado Don Juan de

The Crossing of the Fathers Dominguez and Escalante now lies far beneath the waters of Lake Powell's Padre Bay.

Oñate, which he could not cross on account of its great width and depth. It can be navigated." He was obviously confused, but the conceptions of a river flowing westward out of Great Salt Lake was not dispelled until 1826 when four trappers circumnavigated it in bullboats looking for possible beaver streams. They found that there was no outlet. In 1833 Joseph R. Walker of the Bonneville expedition explored part of the Great Basin and, of course, found no such river.

Another Miera note states: "They say there are many large tribes of Indians on the other side [of the lake], who lived in organized communities. The Timpanogos Indians say that the tribes living on the west side of their lake, and on the high ridge of mountains which is seen in that direction from their huts ... were formerly their friends, and that they make the tips of their arrows, lances, and macanas [war clubs] of a yellow metal, in accordance with ancient traditions." It is curious that the mention of a "yellow metal" (*metal amarillo*) did not seem to excite greater interest

43

on the part of the Spaniards. "Yellow metal" usually suggested gold and such a report would have supported their petition for missions in Utah. Escalante, however, put his finger on a practice which had misled Spanish explorers and missionaries since the days of Coronado when he wrote that "long experience has shown that not only the infidel Indians, but even the Christians, in order to raise themselves in our esteem, tell us what they know we want to hear, without being embarrassed by the falsity of their tales." Apparently he discounted this report, or at any rate concluded that the Indian informants were talking about copper rather than gold. The natives in this area were probably using copper from the Bingham Copper region and had developed a method for hardening it.

Back to Santa Fe

From Utah Valley the expedition once again proceeded toward its destination, traveling south and southwest. Along the way the Spaniards encountered many other peaceful and friendly Indians, all speaking the Yuta language. The padres preached to them as well as the language barrier permitted and reported that "they all received the gospel with pleasure." These Indians had as "thick and dense a beard as the Spaniards." Miera evidently regarded the heavily bearded Indians on the lower Sevier River as such interesting curiosities that he sketched them on one version of his map. These people also pierced the cartilage of their noses with a piece of bone. This was a widespread and numerous nation. Their special name was Tyrangapui in their language, but the Spaniards called them the Yutas Barbones or "Bearded Utes."

Miera's "Bearded Indian Map" accurately shows present Sevier Lake without a western shore—since the expedition had not circumnavigated that body of water. He placed his own name on the lake and then went on to make his most serious geographic mistake. Evidently believing that the Sevier River was the same stream the company had crossed in mid-September (the Buenaventura-Green River) the cartographer lifted it out of its channel, brought it across the Wasatch Range, and discharged it into Lake Miera—Sevier Lake. Thus was born the mythical Buenaventura River, that later was shown as draining Sevier Lake and finally reaching the Pacific at San Francisco Bay. This erroneous information was carried on most maps of the West for more than a half-century until dispelled in 1845 when John C. Fremont's report of his 1843–44 exploration was published. Failing to find the mythical river, Fremont significantly announced that the whole region

44

through which it supposedly flowed was without exterior drainage. He called it the *Great Basin*!

After another six days journey the Spanish party found itself with very little food. The governor of New Mexico had supplied them with what was expected to be sufficient provisions for the entire journey, but they had distributed much of it among the Yutas. Although they had killed two buffalos and had obtained some dried fish from the Lagunas, by this time their supplies were almost exhausted. On October 5 the Laguna guide, José María, whom they had employed before leaving Utah Lake, deserted after a quarrel involving members of the party. Three days later a heavy snowstorm struck; the group suffered greatly from the almost intolerable cold.

On October 8, being snowbound and virtually out of provisions at a point just north of present Milford, the fathers made the momentous decision to abandon the quest for Monterey and return instead to Sante Fe. Miera, Laín, and Andrés Muñiz vigorously protested this decision and demanded that they press on, accusing the padres of robbing them of profits which they expected to reap by reaching California. The fathers replied that many times since leaving Santa Fe they had informed their companions that they had no other destination than the one which God might give to them and that they were not motivated by any temporal aim. In order that the cause of God might be better served, and to make their companions see more clearly that not through fear nor by their own will had they decided to abandon the trail to Monterey, they decided to implore Divine intercession. The will of God was to be determined by the drawing of lots. Into a hat were placed two slips of paper; one with the word *Monterey* on it, and on the other, *Cosnina.*

Lots were drawn on October 11 at a spot about midway between present Milford and Cedar City. Before the drawing, Father Domínguez set forth the reasons why he felt they should abandon the attempt to reach Monterey. The ground was soft and muddy and progress was very slow; they were suffering terribly from the cold and from a sharp north wind; they had received no information from any Indians about Spaniards in California, indicating that their destination was still a long way off; the mountains in all directions were now covered with snow; the weather was changeable; they could expect to find the mountain passes blocked with snow and would then have to remain snowbound on some uninhabited mountain without food; they risked starvation; even if they got to Monterey that winter they would not be able to return to

45

Santa Fe until June of the next year; and finally delays in returning to the Utah Indians might prove harmful to their conversion. He felt that the Indians in waiting for baptism would become frustrated and consequently make their ultimate conversion more difficult.

The slip with the word *Cosnina* was then drawn. According to the padres, God had willed it! All thereupon agreeably and gladly accepted the result. The expedition would return to Santa Fe.

The explorers now directed their course to the south through Cedar Valley, down Ash Creek, and across the Virgin River where they soon reached the high tablelands of the canyon of the Colorado River. For a month they wandered over extremely difficult trails seeking a place where that great river could be forded. October 26 found them at the mouth of present Paria River, where Lee's Ferry would be established nearly a century later. At that point the padres attempted to cross the Colorado, but without success. Also at that spot a horse was slaughtered for food—the second one to find its way into the pot. After a frustrating week the company set out again on November 1 in search of the ford which, Indians had assured them, lay nearby.

The small party explored the lower reaches of Glen Canyon, camping on Wahweap Creek (at the present site of the Wahweap Marina slightly north of the Utah-Arizona boundary) and on the Colorado opposite the mouth of Navajo Creek (where another horse was killed) before reaching a spot where the mighty Colorado could be forded. The crossing was accomplished on November 7, 1776, at a point about thirty miles below the mouth of the San Juan River, three miles north of the present Utah-Arizona boundary. The journal entry about the crossing that day states:

We went very early to inspect the canyon and the ford. . . . In order to lead the animals down the side of the canyon mentioned it was necessary to cut steps in a rock with axes for the distance of three varas or a little less [eight feet]. The rest of the way the animals were able to get down, although without pack or rider. We went down to the canyon and having traveled a mile we descended to the river and went along it downstream about two musket shots sometimes in the water, sometimes on the bank, until we reached the widest part of its current where the ford appeared to be. One of the men waded in and found it good, not having to swim at any place. We followed him on horseback a little lower down, and when half way across, two horses which went ahead lost their footing and swam a short distance. We waited, although in some peril, until the first wader returned from the other side to guide us and then we crossed with ease, the horses on which we crossed not having to swim at all. We notified the rest of our companions . . . that with lassoes and ropes they should let the pack saddles and other effects down a not very high cliff to the bend of the ford, and they should bring the animals by the route over which we had come. They did so and about five o'clock in the afternoon they finished crossing the river, praising God our Lord and firing off a few muskets as sign of the great joy which we all felt at having overcome so great a difficulty and which had cost us so much labor and delay.

The steps they carved out of Padre Creek Canyon's west wall were once one of the choice historic sites in Utah. The fording place was affectionately known as "The Crossing of the Fathers." It is now covered by the waters of Lake Powell; boaters, fishermen, and water skiers now know the area as "Padre Bay."

Once across the Colorado the weary travelers directed their course southward, searching in vain for the villages of the Cosninas. They then turned southeastward to the Hopi town of Oraibi, arriving on November 17. The Hopi were civil enough and willing to provide much-needed supplies, but when the Franciscans attempted to preach to them they remained obstinate. The natives wished to be friends with the Spaniards, but not Christians.

From Hopi the expedition proceeded to Zuni, Escalante's home mission, where they remained from November 24 until December 13. They were detained for four days at Acoma, "The Sky City," because of a snowstorm. From Acoma they journeyed through Laguna, Alamo, Isleta, Albuquerque, and Santo Domingo. On January 2, 1777, they arrived in Santa Fe—the trek of almost 2,000 miles completed. The next day the padres reported to the governor and delivered the diary and itinerary (*diario y derrotero*) of their 158-day odyssey.

The Aftermath

Demand for overland communication between New Mexico and California had been the major stimulus for the expedition. An overland route was thought to be necessary as a means of protecting California from a threatening Russian advance down the Pacific Coast and as an economic saving in transportation. Insofar as the original intention of the expedition was concerned, it was a complete failure; it did not open a trail to Monterey from Santa Fe. However, by means of this expedition a large portion of the interior of North America was explored for the first time by white men, the Great Basin was visited, and the Indian tribes around

47

Utah Lake and the Sevier River were made friends of the Spaniards.

Spain failed to follow up on the Domínguez-Escalante Expedition of 1776 because by that time the missionary spirit was almost spent. Conditions in New Spain made impossible the further extension of the frontier at that time. Nine years earlier the king of Spain had ordered the expulsion of the Jesuits from the New World, fearful of their growing political and economic power and that the special Jesuit allegiance to the Pope was creating a state within a state. Since there were hardly enough Franciscans and Dominicans to man their own mission stations, it was impossible to take over those of the Jesuits and at the same time establish additional outposts in new and distant lands. Thus the two padres were not able to keep the solemn promises they had made to the Yuta Indians that they would return within a year. Had they been able to do so, that part of the Great Basin might have become an important and valuable part of the Spanish realm.

Other results of the 1776 expedition included: the first expedition of white men known to have entered and explored major portions of Utah; the daily journal provides the earliest eye-witness descriptions of the physical features, plant and animal life, and especially the various native peoples encountered; the expedition "discovered" Green and Duchesne rivers, Utah Lake, Sevier River and Lake, Virgin River, the lower end of Glen Canyon, Crossing of the Fathers, and many other places. The Miera y Pacheco map also afforded the world its first visual representation of Utah as seen by one who had actually traveled through it.

Perhaps the first scholar to make use of the Domínguez-Escalante journal was the German geographer, Baron Alexander von Humboldt, who studied a manuscript copy in Mexico City and included a brief discussion of it along with a map of the Lake Timpanogos (Utah Lake) area in his *Political Essay on the Kingdom of New Spain,* published in 1811. The journal was first published in Spanish in 1854 in Mexico City in *Documentos para las historia de Mexico.* While the journal and map appeared too late to be of any use to Brigham Young and the Mormon pioneers, the Humboldt work was available and may have been studied prior to their trek west.

After this initial exploration there seems to have been almost continuous contact with the Utah Indians by Spanish traders from New Mexico until some years after the coming of the Mormons to the Great Basin. Documents in the Spanish Archives of New Mexico reveal that fur traders penetrated as far north as Utah Lake for the purpose of trade. Inasmuch as Indian traders could often create difficulties with the Indians, the Spanish authorities attempted to curb such contact and numerous *bandos,* or decrees, were issued to prohibit trade with the Utes. The repetition of these bandos and the increasingly severe penalties prescribed indicate that mere decrees could not keep the traders out of Utah. Furs were the most important item sought by the Spaniards, but the Indians insisted on selling them captive natives as slaves. Thus an additional important market was opened in the Great Basin. As late as the 1850s companies of Mexican traders continued to frequent the Sevier Valley. Such slave trading operations resulted in friction between the Mormons and the Mexicans and the passage of laws by the Utah territorial legislature forbidding such traffic.

The route envisioned by the padres of 1776 was pushed from the Sevier Valley to southern California in 1830 by a party of Santa Fe traders headed by William Wolfskill. It was still called the Old Spanish Trail when the Mormon pioneers two decades later made the western half of it a part of their corridor to the Pacific.

Chapter 3
Bibliographical Essay

S. Lyman Tyler has published important articles on Spanish and Indian legends concerning the Utah region. See particularly his "The Myth of the Lake of Copala and Land of Teguayo," *UHQ,* October 1952; "The Report of Fray Alonso de Posada in Relation to Quivira and Teguayo," with H. Darrell Taylor, *New Mexico Historical Review,* October 1958; and Tyler's "The Spaniard and the Ute," *UHQ,* October 1954.

Concerning the 1540 expedition of Cárdenas, see Hubert Howe Bancroft, *History of Utah* (1889); Katharine Bartlett, "How Don Pedro de Tovar Discovered the Hopi and Don García López de Cárdenas Saw the Grand Canyon. . . ," *Plateau,* January 1940; and Herbert E. Bolton, *Coronado, Knight of Pueblos and Plains* (1949). Donald Cutter, of the University of New Mexico, located the journal telling of Juan María de Rivera's 1765 visit to southeastern Utah; see his "Prelude to a Pageant in the Wilderness," *Western Historical Quarterly,* January 1977.

The original journal of the Domínguez-Escalante Expedition has not yet come to light. It was submitted to the governor of New Mexico on January 3, 1777, but is now apparently lost. Several days after it was submitted it was borrowed back by Father Domínguez and a copy was made by Fray José Palacio, secretary to Domínguez. This copy is now located in the Newberry Library,

Chicago. Another manuscript copy, dated January 26, 1777, is in the Archivo General de Indias, Seville, Spain. The Archivo General de Nación, Mexico City, also has two manuscript copies, one made in 1792 and the other in 1797 (in Chihuahua, Mexico). Other handwritten copies are located in Madrid (three), London, Paris, and the Library of Congress, Washington, D.C. The number of copies suggests the interest which the expedition produced in the late eighteenth and early nineteenth centuries, long before the journal appeared in print.

The journal (*Diario y Derrotero*) was first published in Spanish in *Documentos para la historia de Mexico*, Segunda serie, Tomo I (Mexico City, 1854). This is not a particularly accurate rendition. The first English translation was published in 1909 by the Rev. W. R. Harris in *The Catholic Church in Utah*. It contains so many errors as to be of almost no value. The second English translation was by Herbert S. Auerbach: "Father Escalante's Journal with Related Documents and Maps," *UHQ*, January 1943. Especially useful are the notes and maps. *Pageant in the Wilderness: The Story of the Escalante Expedition to the Interior Basin, 1776* (1951) was Herbert E. Bolton's last major publication prior to his death and it does not measure up to his usual work. The latest translation is by Fray Angelico Chavez (trans.) and Ted J. Warner (ed.), *The Dominguez-Escalante Journal: Their Expedition through Colorado, Utah, Arizona, and New Mexico in 1776* (1976). This contains both the English and Spanish texts and has extensive notes which resulted from field work by research teams who retraced the trail in 1975.

Other articles and books which should be consulted in relation to the expedition are: Eleanor B. Adams, "Fray Silvestre and the Obstinate Hopi," *New Mexico Historical Review*, April 1963; her prize-winning account of the two Franciscans, "Fray Francisco Atanasio Domínguez and Fray Silvestre Vélez de Escalante," *UHQ*, Winter 1976; Adams and Fray Angelico Chavez, *The Missions of New Mexico: A Description by Fray Francisco Atanasio Dominguez, with other Contemporary Documents* (1956 and 1976), also includes a number of previously unpublished letters of both padres. Auerbach's articles in *UHQ* are useful: "Father Escalante's Itinerary," July, October 1941, and "Father Escalante's Route (as depicted by the Map of Bernardo de Miera y Pacheco)," January, April 1941. A beautiful Bicentennial volume is Walter Briggs, *Without Noise of Arms: The 1776 Dominguez-Escalante Search for a Route from Santa Fe to Monterey* (1976). Joseph Cerquone has also contributed a small volume, *In Behalf of Light....* (1976).

Bolton, "Escalante in Dixie and the Arizona Strip," *New Mexico Historical Review,* January 1928, and his "Escalante Strikes for California," in John Francis Bannon (ed.), *Bolton and the Spanish Borderlands* (1964), are excellent studies. C. Gregory Crampton, "The Discovery of the Green River," *UHQ,* October 1952, discusses the route in this area. David E. Miller, "Discovery of Glen Canyon, 1776," *UHQ,* July 1958, traces the trail in the area of the Crossing of the Fathers. Ted J. Warner, "The Significance of the Domínguez-Vélez de Escalante Expedition," in *Charles Redd Monographs in Western History: Essays on the American West, 1973–1974* (1975), Thomas G. Alexander (ed.), attempts to set the expedition in perspective. In 1975 under grants from the Four Corners Commission and the Bicentennial Commission, a complete reexamination of the Dominquez-Escalante Route was completed. Results of that field work, edited by David E. Miller, were published in 1976.

Leland H. Creer, *The Founding of an Empire* (1947) contains a discussion of the Spanish-American slave trade in the Great Basin. LeRoy R. and Ann W. Hafen, *Old Spanish Trail: Santa Fe to Los Angeles* (1954), is an excellent documentary study. Joseph J. Hill, "Spanish and Mexican Exploration and Trade Northwest from New Mexico into the Great Basin, 1765–1853," *UHQ,* January 1930, is an informative summary based on documents then available.

Chapter 4
The Fur Trade and
The Mountain Men

David E. Miller

During the half-century prior to the migration of the Mormons to the Salt Lake Valley, many fur companies and individual trappers played important roles in opening up the area that eventually became the state of Utah. Reports of a possibly rich booty in furs first attracted significant numbers of white men to this region. Fur hunters discovered the trails and mountain passes that became the major highways to the West. All the wagons that eventually brought settlers to the Great Basin traveled routes known decades earlier by mountain men. The pony express, stage coach, and telegraph followed the same paths. Trading posts along the way became resting, repairing, and recruiting stations: Fort Laramie, Fort Bridger, Fort Hall. The mountain men, who knew more about the West than anyone else, often served as guides for migrating, exploring, and military groups. They were the first experts on Utah geography.

International Rivalry and the Cold Fur War

The story of fur trade begins late in the eighteenth century, when events occurred on the distant northwest coast of North America that would have a tremendous impact on the history of Utah and the United States.

Long before Domínguez and Escalante shepherded their small party into the Great Basin in 1776, Russian explorers had discovered Alaska, found the adjacent waters teeming with sea otter, and developed a thriving maritime fur trade with China. Gradually news of this lucrative business filtered back from Canton to western Europe, where merchants and statesmen from several nations were fired up with a keen urge to claim a share. In 1774 Spain sent Juan Perez northward from Mexico to investigate the reports. Four years later Captain James Cook of the British Royal Navy sailed along the northwest coast on an official investigation. The reports, he found, were true; vast numbers of the sleek "sea beavers" were there for the taking, and the natives were eager to trade.

The year Cook's official report was published (1784) found John Ledyard in Paris meeting with Thomas Jefferson, U.S. minister to France. Ledyard had gone ashore with Cook in Alaska and had witnessed with his own eyes the potential wealth in furs. His account fired Jefferson's imagination; the future president's vision of national expansion was born!

Soon American merchants in the rapidly expanding China trade were in hot competition with the British and Russians for control of the sea otter traffic. One of these Yankee skippers, Captain Robert Gray, in 1792 crossed the bar into the mouth of Columbia River, named the stream after his ship, and claimed its whole drainage system for his nation. Thus the United States "by right of discovery" gained its first claim to the whole Oregon Country, not yet named and certainly not defined in its boundaries. Within two decades American seamen gained the upper hand in the competition for control of the maritime fur trade. The United States claim to the whole region was bolstered when Jefferson's Lewis and Clark Expedition (1804–1806) pushed all the way across the continent to establish Fort Clatsop at the Columbia's mouth.

Meanwhile the rich supply of sea otter was being rapidly depleted through overhunting, and the fur trade was shifting from maritime to overland expeditions—from sea otter to beaver. The competition for control of this new trade developed into a major factor in the diplomatic relations of the United States. In 1803 the nation purchased Louisiana from France without a clear definition of its western or northern boundaries. The Anglo-American Convention of 1818 established the 49th parallel from the Lake of the Woods west to the Continental Divide to define the boundary between Canada and the United States, but beyond that point neither government was willing to relinquish claims. As a result the whole vast area lying west of the divide and south of Russian-owned Alaska was left open to be jointly occupied by both nations for a period of ten years. Hopefully a division could be agreed upon within that time. In the interim, nationals of both countries were to have free and unrestricted access to the entire Oregon Country. As the decade drew to a close the fur competition was at its height; no division was possible. Joint occupation actually continued until 1846, at which time the 49th parallel was made the boundary to Puget Sound.

Having been virtually eliminated as a competitor for Oregon, Spain by the Adams-Onis Treaty of 1819 ceded to the United States all her claims to the area lying north of the 42nd parallel, while the United States ceded to Spain any American claims south of that line in the disputed area. Thus the line that eventually became Utah's northern boundary and the southern boundary of Oregon was established. Great Britain, however, was not a party to the treaty; the English recognized no southern boundary for the Oregon Country.

Coming of the Mountain Men

The apparently insatiable American and European markets for pelts from which to make beaver felt hats was by this time the magnet which drew trappers and traders deeper and deeper into the Intermountain West. Early in the 1820s pelts brought $10 and more in the St. Louis market and comparable prices in other centers of the trade. As the beaver streams of the Columbia and Missouri were trapped out, adventurous representatives of companies and of individual free enterprise pushed into the "land of the Yutas." Beginning in 1824 they came from three directions: independent French-Canadian-American trappers from New Mexico—primarily Taos and Santa Fe; Hudson's Bay Company expeditions from the north and northwest led by Peter Skene Ogden; and Americans from the east, northeast, and north—based primarily in St. Louis.

On March 20, 1822, William Henry Ashley placed the following notice in the *Missouri Republican* of St. Louis:

To Enterprising Young Men

The subscriber wishes to engage one hundred young men to ascend the Missouri River to its source, there to be employed for one, two, or three years. For particulars enquire Major [Andrew] Henry, near the lead mines of the county of Washington, who will ascend with and command the party; or of the subscriber, near St. Louis.

[Signed] William H. Ashley

Ashley and Henry were most gratified by the response to their advertisement. Soon the ranks were filled with eager men, a score of whom were destined to become the most famous "mountain men": Jedediah S. Smith, James Bridger, David E. Jackson,

Thomas Fitzpatrick, James Clyman, William L. Sublette, Daniel T. Potts, Hugh Glass, John H. Weber, Milton G. Sublette, Moses (Black) Harris, Jim Beckwourth, and others.

After some severe setbacks, two detachments of Ashley-Henry trappers reached the upper Sweetwater River early in 1824 and turned westward to cross the Continental Divide by way of South Pass. (This famous gateway to the Far West is not a narrow, rugged gorge as the name might suggest, but a half-mile-wide saddle with such gentle approaches that the traveler is never certain just when he reaches the summit.) Jedediah Smith was evidently the leader of this advance party. The pass had been traversed from west to east in 1812 by men from John Jacob Astor's trading post on the Columbia, but the 1824 "rediscovery" is of far greater importance because the pass soon became the major highway to Oregon, California, and then Utah. It was a welcome landmark for fur men, missionaries, farmers, goldrushers, sightseers, Mormons, and the builders and operators of the pony express, stage lines, and overland telegraph during the decades prior to the completion of the transcontinental railroad. Only the railroad and modern automobile—not dependent on grass and readily available water—could strike a more direct course a half-hundred miles to the south. (See map, p. 724.)

During the fall of 1824, while John H. Weber and a sizeable crew pushed northward along the Bear River in present Wyoming (unknowingly headed for Utah's Cache Valley), Jedediah Smith and six companions left the upper waters of Green River to spy out British activities in the Oregon Country. By November 26 they reached the Hudson's Bay Company's Flathead Post at present Eddy, Montana, where they found Peter Skene Ogden making arrangements for his first "Snake country expedition." Ogden had recently been assigned to direct the company's campaign against the Americans.

Hudson's Bay Company and the North West Company (both British) had until recently been competing with each other for the fur business of Canada and the Pacific Northwest. However, the two had merged in 1821 under the name of the older Hudson's Bay Company. Thus by the time the international fur competition extended into the area which is now Utah, there was one consolidated British firm to oppose various American groups. The whole Pacific Northwest was the potential prize.

Governor George Simpson, the Hudson's Bay Company's ranking officer in Oregon, mistakenly believed that the only inducement that would draw Americans into the area was the lure of the rich beaver supply. So he instructed Ogden to strike deeply into the jointly claimed region and to ruin the beaver supply as rapidly as possible—a kind of "scorched stream" policy which was not altered during the whole fur era. The policy was unavailing, for the horde of permanent American settlers who swarmed eventually into the Pacific Northwest tipped the scales in favor of the United States and led to the extension of the 49th parallel in 1846. But neither Simpson nor Ogden could see that far into the future; Ogden had been given a job to do and he intended to give it his undivided attention.

Ogden's huge brigade of 131 persons, with 268 horses and 352 traps, set out from Flathead Post on December 20, 1824, and trapped its way to Bear River at the present site of Alexander, Idaho, April 26, 1825. That "sly cunning Yankee" (as Ogden's chief clerk, William Kittson, described Jedediah Smith) and his companions were never far away from the British camp during those four months. Upon their arrival at the Bear, Smith's group headed upstream in search of their fellow Americans, while the British outfit followed the same river southward into Cache Valley. Ogden knew that Michel Bourdon of the Northwest Company had "discovered" and named Bear River and followed it into the heart of Cache Valley in 1819. He hoped that the whole region had not been trapped since, but he soon discovered that the Americans had beaten his men to the Bear and reaped the best of the crop. Near the present site of Franklin, Idaho, Ogden learned from the Indians that a large group of Americans had wintered there and then headed southward—Weber's company. It was doubtless from this site that Jim Bridger made his now famous exploration down Bear River to learn that it discharges into the Great Salt Lake.

Both Ogden and Kittson kept careful journals of this expedition's progress. In addition to detailed descriptions of the daily workings of a large fur brigade, the journals supply the earliest contemporary eyewitness descriptions of northern Utah. The brigade marched southward across the 42nd parallel into present Utah on May 5, 1825, and found the terrain swarming with huge black crickets and the air filled with seagulls—the earliest mention of these two species destined to become important in later Utah history. (See map, p. 726.)

From the south end of Cache Valley the brigade crossed the divide into present-day Ogden Valley. The journals describe the valley as a "hole" since it is completely surrounded by mountains. Both the "hole" and the river now bear Ogden's name. Neither Ogden nor Kittson followed the river down to its confluence with the Weber, but some of their companions probably did so. Ogden next followed his trappers southward over the "hole's" rim into the valley of Weber River and established camp at the present site of Mountain Green. The clash that occurred here might have had international repercussions.

The Affair at "Deserter Point"

While Ogden's brigade was making its way through Cache Valley, American trappers followed Bear River to its mouth and explored southward along the west face of the Wasatch Range, gleaning skins along the way. Some of Ogden's men doubtless encountered them on Ogden and Weber rivers. From the Americans the British trappers learned that they could expect a much better price for their catch from the American company than Hudson's Bay was paying. Why not desert the British and join the Americans? Almost at once a plot was hatched for an attack on Ogden's camp with the intent to plunder and drive the English out of the region.

Ogden was unaware of these developments until a rowdy crowd of flag-waving Americans rode up Weber Canyon and camped within a hundred yards of his camp. The date was May 23, 1825. Leader of the Americans was a trapper named Johnson Gardner. He informed Ogden that the ground they were on was United States soil and that the British must either leave or be driven out. Ogden replied that the country was jointly occupied and that he had no intention of leaving, but he carefully avoided action that would lead to the hostilities which he thought the Americans were trying to precipitate. He soon learned of the conspiracy among his own men, some of whom defiantly deserted, taking horses and furs with them to the American camp. The tension mounted for two days before Ogden, faced with a virtual mutiny, decided to retreat to Snake River. He had lost 23 men and 700 beaver pelts. (Those who deserted were "freemen" or free trappers who regularly signed on with the company from which they obtained traps, horses, and other supplies at a fixed rate. At the end of the season's hunt freemen turned in the furs they had collected, also at a fixed price, hoping that they would come out ahead. After settling accounts preparations would begin at once for the next season's hunt.)

This infamous incident occurred at Mountain Green on Weber River, at a point significantly labeled *Deserter Point* on Kittson's map. Since the more detailed of Ogden's two reports to company headquarters was dated July 10, 1825, from the "headwaters" of Missouri River, officials in London assumed that the affair had oc-

Antoine Robidoux carved this message on November 13, 1837, in Uinta Basin's Westwater region while enroute to establish his trading post on the Uinta River.

curred east of the Continental Divide in United States territory and refused to intercede diplomatically. Actually the incident happened south of the 42nd parallel in an area claimed only by Great Britain and Mexico, and any attempt to collect damages might have resulted in a complicated international tangle. Details and location of the incident were not known until the Ogden and Kittson journals were published in 1950.

Johnson Gardner, who led the American attack, was evidently a free-lance trapper who had joined the Ashley men for convenience. He acted without the knowledge of, or authority from, company leaders. This is definitely indicated by the fact that both Samuel Tullock and Robert Campbell, who spent some time in Ogden's Snake River camp during the 1827–1828 winter, apologized for the American action and stated that it would not have happened had any company officials been present.

The fracas at Deserter Point was the only incident of its kind during the Anglo-American competition—the only time the cold fur war threatened to erupt into a shooting war. But it had its impact on Hudson's Bay Company policies. Within three years reforms favorable to the trappers were instituted and by 1830 many of Ogden's deserters had returned to the British fold. In addition, British fur men seemed willing to consider what is now northern Utah to be pretty much an American sphere of influence as far as the beaver trade was concerned. Ogden's 1828–1829 brigade, after discovering the Humboldt River, traversed the west side of Cache Valley and the unproductive area north of Great Salt Lake. But he never again attempted to trap the major streams of Cache Valley; he never returned to the valley that now bears his name; he never visited the site of Ogden City.

Ashley, Henry, and the Rendezvous

American trappers continued to ply their trade south of the 42nd parallel even though the area legally belonged to Mexico. William H. Ashley, Andrew Henry, and their successors in the St. Louis-based trade tapped the richest fur areas in the West and in the annual rendezvous they developed an efficient and colorful mechanism for handling this exotic business. Ashley himself came to the mountains in 1825 and made the first boat trip of record down the Uinta Basin section of Green River while waiting for his men to gather for the first intermountain trade fair.

Most of the American fur trappers of the 1820s and 1830s stayed year-round in the beaver country for two or three years or more. In the Missouri River drainage area they took their pelts periodically to trading posts which were established at strategic locations. So great were the distances from St. Louis to the lands beyond the Continental Divide, however, that Ashley developed a new approach. He arranged for supplies to be brought to a designated spot in the West in 1825, and at the appointed summer date his company trappers, as well as independent mountain men and Indians who had pelts and hides to trade, gathered for what became a hectic social as well as business activity. In addition to obtaining supplies for the coming winter season and disposing of their furs, trappers enjoyed all kinds of sports—athletic contests, horse races, drinking parties, shooting matches, and fights. As the rendezvous became an annual institution, hundreds of natives usually assembled for the festivities.

The first four rendezvous were held on Henry's Fork of Green River (Wyoming) in Cache Valley and then twice at Bear Lake. Thereafter they convened at various locations in what are now southwestern Wyoming and eastern Idaho until the dwindling of the trade led to their discontinuance after 1840. Ownership of the business which sponsored the rendezvous passed in 1824 from Ashley and Andrew Henry to Ashley alone; then to Ashley and Jedediah Smith in 1825; to Smith, David E. Jackson, and William L. Sublette in 1826; and four years later to the Rocky Mountain Fur Company, of which Jim Bridger is the best remembered partner. This group sold out to the aggressively competitive American Fur Company late in 1834. Before the fur era came to an end, Americans quite thoroughly explored and trapped all of Utah's major streams and lakes and carried much information about the Colorado Plateau and the Great Basin to Missouri and the East.

Jedediah Smith

Jedediah Strong Smith was the outstanding leader among the American trappers. His activities around Great Salt Lake Valley were so extensive that he could ultimately refer to the area as his "second home" in the wilderness. In seeking new fur country for his partnership, he blazed trails between that valley and both southern and northern California, and he did some pathfinding into Oregon as well. (See map, p. 725.)

Finding the area immediately north and west of Great Salt Lake unprofitable, Smith decided to examine the unknown land to the south and southwest. Accompanied by some sixteen men, he left the Cache Valley rendezvous August 16, 1826. As far as Utah Valley he covered familiar terrain; beyond, the party moved through arid country scarcely traversed by white men since the

Domínguez-Escalante expedition fifty years earlier. After replenishing food supplies from the friendly Paiutes of Utah's Dixie, the trappers continued down the course of Virgin River to the Colorado. They visited the Mojave villages opposite the formations now known as the Needles. Via the Mojave River (which was nothing more than a dry wash much of the way) the expedition left the Great Basin over Cajon Pass and was soon at the gates of the Mexican missions and ranches in the San Bernardino-Los Angeles region.

Details of Smith's experiences at San Gabriel and San Diego belong to California history. Suffice it to say that he and his party were considered to be spies and trespassers; he was eventually ordered to leave by the same route he had come. But in spite of his promise, the "sly cunning Yankee" went from Cajon Pass to the north end of San Joaquin Valley. Here he decided to leave the bulk of the expedition while he and two companions, Robert Evans and Silas Gobel, returned to the rendezvous to report on his explorations. By now it was May 1827. The trio crossed the Sierra on a second attempt, after being turned back once by deep snow, and made their way across present Nevada and the Gosiute region of western Utah. Passing Great Salt Lake and crossing the high flooding Jordan River, the emaciated party finally reached the rendezvous at Bear Lake on July 3. A major celebration was held since most of the trappers had given up hope of ever seeing Jedediah and his companions again. A small cannon, recently wheeled halfway across the continent, was fired in their honor.

During his ten days at the rendezvous Smith was busy organizing a second brigade for the return to California. Having had his fill of the desert country which he had just crossed, he decided to take his eighteen companions and their supplies via southern California again. Most of the route to the Colorado was virtually the same as the previous year. After three days of rest at the Mojave villages Smith began another crossing of the river, not suspecting Indian treachery. When he and eight companions had rafted to the middle of the stream, Mojave warriors fell on the remaining men, slaughtering all of them. Only after a few well-placed long shots brought down three of the attackers and after a fearful night on the west bank did Smith and the other survivors escape into the desert. After several forced marches the bedraggled men reached a ranch at San Bernardino. Fortunately, enough trade goods had been salvaged from the attack to purchase horses for all, and the little brigade made it to Stanislaus River and united with those who had remained in California the previous season.

Misfortune continued to accompany Smith and his companions. They moved northward through the Sacramento Valley into Oregon where an Indian party killed all but Jedediah and three others in a surprise attack. That battered remnant remained at Fort Vancouver from August 1828 to March 1829; then Smith made his way to the rendezvous at Wind River, Wyoming.

In 1830 Jedediah Smith sold his partnership interest in the fur trade and left the mountains forever. His tragic death at the hands of a Comanche hunting party occurred May 27, 1831, while he was serving as guide for a Santa Fe-bound wagon train and scouting for water in the Cimmaron Desert. He was 32 years old.

Etienne Provost

Canadian born in 1794, Etienne Provost (also spelled Provot, Provatt, and Proveau in various documents, but pronounced "Pro-vo") was the most notable mountain man operating from the Taos, New Mexico, base. For many years he was believed to have been a member of the Ashley-Henry brigade that crossed South Pass in 1824, but it is now definitely established that he was at that time working as a partner with one LeClerc from headquarters in New Mexico. If Provost wrote a journal, it has never been found, but he left his mark and name on Utah.

Provost's brigade evidently entered Utah by the same general route that had brought Catholic missionary-explorers to the area almost a half-century earlier. He is known to have been on the Green River south of the Uinta Mountains during the summer of 1824. By way of the headwaters of the Duchesne River he came to the river that now bears his name (anglicized) and followed it to Utah Lake during that same season. Late that fall, somewhere on Provo, Jordan, or Weber River, his brigade was attacked by the Snake Indian chief, Bad Gocha; seven men were killed and only Provost and three or four others escaped.

The next year he returned to the Great Basin with a trapping party of about thirty men. He met Peter Skene Ogden on Weber River in May and witnessed but did not take part in the Ogden-Gardner fracas at Deserter Point. Two weeks later he met William Ashley at Duchesne River and accepted an invitation to guide the American's party via the upper Provo and Weber rivers to the rendezvous on Henry's Fork of Green River. By September 1826 Provost was in St. Louis "doing business with B. Pratte & Company." His future activities evidently did not bring him again inside the present boundaries of Utah unless he entered present Daggett County on visits to the Green River tributaries.

Osborne Russell

One of the last of the trappers active in northern Utah was Osborne Russell. At least he was one of the last to write an account of his activities. Russell had joined Nathaniel Wyeth's westbound migration in 1834 and by the end of 1842 he had made five trips into Utah, one of which extended as far south as Utah Lake. Russell's most interesting account of his expeditions and descriptions of the physical features, flora, and fauna of the region are outstanding. He also provides some valuable information concerning the location and habits of the Indians just a few years before the permanent settlement of the area by white men.

Discovery of Great Salt Lake

One important contribution of the fur men was the discovery and partial exploration of Great Salt Lake. Of the numerous men listed by historians as probable or possible discoverers of the lake, only two are now known to have been in the area early enough to have first set eyes on its waters—James Bridger and Etienne Provost. It is possible that others arrived at the lake long before either of these, but as yet there is no proof of such an accomplishment.

The twenty-year-old Bridger was a member of John Weber's Ashley brigade during the fall of 1824. As the group advanced into Cache Valley, speculation concerning the probable mouth of Bear River led Bridger to agree personally to conduct an exploration to determine the issue. Doubtless from the American winter camp near present Franklin, Idaho, Bridger set out, with possibly one or more companions, to learn the facts. It is likely that he traveled on horseback rather than by bullboat, which would have required a long walk back to the camp.

Sometime during the fall or winter of 1824–1825 Jim Bridger saw Great Salt Lake from the high ground near where Bear River breaks out of Cache Valley, followed the stream to its mouth, tasted the water, and returned to report that the river empties into a salty body of water. He evidently believed it to be an arm of the Pacific. Before many months, as the trappers continued their trade, the salty body was found to be a lake. William Kittson's 1825 map labeled it *Large Bear Lake.*

The earliest written record in support of the Bridger claim of discovery is the testimony of Robert Campbell, who, as a member of the Ashley-Smith Company, was in Cache Valley in 1826. In response to a request from G. K. Warren for "the facts" concerning the discovery, Campbell wrote this letter from St. Louis on April 4, 1857:

64

Your letter of the 25th ultimo reached me at a very fortunate period to enable me to give you a satisfactory reply to your inquiry as to who was the first discoverer of the Great Salt Lake. It happened that James Bridger and Samuel Tullock both met at my counting room after a separation of eighteen years, and were bringing up reminiscences of the past when your letter reached me. I read it to them, and elicited the following facts:

A party of beaver trappers who had ascended the Missouri with Henry Ashley found themselves in pursuit of their occupation on the Bear river, in Cache [or Willow] Valley, where they wintered in the winter of 1824–25; and in descending the course which the Bear river ran, a bet was made between two of the party, and James Bridger was selected to follow the course of the river to determine the bet. This took him to where the river passes through the mountains, and there he discovered the Great Salt Lake. He went to its margin and tasted the water, and on his return reported his discovery. The fact of the water being salt induced the belief that it was an arm of the Pacific ocean; but, in the spring of 1826 four men went in skin boats around it to discover if any streams containing beaver were to be found emptying into it but returned with indifferent success.

I went to Willow or Cache valley in the spring of 1826 and found the party just returned from their exploration of the lake, and recollect their report that it was without any outlet.

Mr. Tullock corroborates in every respect the statement of James Bridger, and both are men of strictest integrity and truthfulness. I have known both since 1826. James Bridger was the first discoverer of Great Salt Lake.

P.S. A party of Hudson Bay Company trappers came to the same place in the summer of 1825, and met the party that had discovered the Salt Lake that season.

In the meantime, Provost may have seen the lake before Bridger conducted his exploration. He is known to have been in the region during the fall of 1824 and to have suffered an attack by Indians. If the attack occurred on Jordan River, was it at or near the stream's source on Utah Lake or on the lower Jordan—toward Great Salt Lake? Or did the treachery take place on Provo River, or even on the Weber? Regardless of what the correct answer may be, Provost was likely in a position from which he *may* have discovered the lake during the fall of 1824, before Bridger did. On the other hand, there is no definite *proof* that he *ever* saw it!

The earliest eyewitness account of a white man's having seen the lake is Kittson's journal entry of May 12, 1825: ". . . [Charles] McKay went on a high mountain where he had a view of the country around us. A large lake into which Bear River falls in, is not above 12 miles from this and bearing about S.W. from this spot. . . ." By that date Bridger and others had already seen the lake; thus any member of Ogden's party is eliminated as a possible discoverer.

As American trappers worked along the west face of the Wasatch, their knowledge and curiosity about Great Salt Lake increased. During the spring of 1826 four of them—James Clyman, Moses Harris, and possibly Louis Vasquez and Henry G. Fraeb—spent three weeks paddling bullboats around the lake searching for an outlet or beaver streams flowing in from the west. They found neither. The lake lies in a basin with interior drainage only. It was a barrier to the mountain men and it continued to be a barrier to the Westward Movement until it was finally bridged by steel rails early in the twentieth century.

Soon after its discovery the lake gained the descriptive title *Salt Lake* to distinguish it from *Sweet Lake*—present Bear Lake. Before 1830 the name *Great Salt Lake* had already been adopted. In 1833 Captain B. L. E. Bonneville sent Joseph Reddeford Walker on a trapping expedition to California via the north end of the lake and the Humboldt River. Information brought back from that trek was reflected in Bonneville's 1837 map, the first sketch to show islands in Great Salt Lake. The fact that Bonneville—who never saw it—attached his own name to the lake doubtless influenced geologist Grove Karl Gilbert to christen the lake's ancient predecessor *Lake Bonneville.*

Trading Posts in the Uinta Basin

Relatively little information is available concerning fur trade activities in the Uinta Basin or along the Colorado and its numerous tributaries. Although William Ashley was here early, most of the trappers who worked the region in the 1820s were apparently based in New Mexico. One of these, Antoine Robidoux, evidently in 1837 built a trading post on the west fork of Uinta River slightly below present White Rocks. Marcus Whitman visited there in 1842 and John C. Fremont in 1844. Miles Goodyear and others occasionally stopped, but none of their descriptions supply details on fur trade operations in the vicinity. At the confluence of Green and White rivers, near where Provost and LeClerc had wintered in 1824–1825, Christopher "Kit" Carson established an unpretentious trading post in 1833. A third fur outpost was Fort Davy Crockett, founded in 1837 on the north bank of Green River in Brown's Hole, near the present Utah-Colorado line. The founders, Philip Thompson, William Craig, and one Sinclair, named their post for the late hero of the Alamo. Forts Robidoux, Kit Carson, and Davy Crockett served as general supply and trading posts for the major part of a decade before being abandoned or destroyed by Indians.

By the early 1840s the fashion in men's hats had shifted from felt to silk; the beaver of Utah was on the verge of extinction; and the era of the mountain men was at an end. Fort Bridger, the trading post which James Bridger founded on Black's Fork of Green River (Wyoming) in 1843, and Fort Buenaventura, the stockaded home which Miles Goodyear built on Weber River at the site of present Ogden City in the mid-1840s, were the only tangible monuments to the fur era which the Mormon pioneers encountered when they moved into the land of the trappers' rendezvous.

Chapter 4
Bibliographical Essay

The best single volume dealing with the fur trade as it related to Utah is Dale L. Morgan's *Jedediah Smith and the Opening of the West* (1953). This book was subsequently reprinted in 1964 and is available in paperback. Although Smith is the central figure in this volume, Morgan very effectively broadens the scope to include major aspects of the whole fur trade activity. Maurice S. Sullivan's two Jedediah Smith volumes are also very good: *The Travels of Jedediah Smith* (1934) and *Jedediah Smith, Trader and Trail Breaker* (1936). Smith's journals are reportedly located in the Missouri Historical Society archives awaiting publication. Hopefully, this record will soon be forthcoming, for Smith's own account of his activities will doubtless shed much additional light on the whole fur trade era.

Peter Skene Ogden's journals may be found in *Publications of Hudson's Bay Record Society*. Volume XIII (1950) includes Ogden's 1824–1826 journals and the 1824–1825 journal of William Kittson. Volume XXVIII (1971) carries Ogden's 1827–1829 journals; David E. and David H. Miller did the fieldwork and supplied the introduction, annotation, and maps for this volume. Ogden's June 27 and July 10, 1825, letters concerning the fracas at Deserter Point appear in Volume IV (1941) of the same series.

Gloria Griffin Cline, *Peter Skene Ogden and the Hudson's Bay Company* (1974) is the only book-length biography of that outstanding trapper-explorer worthy of consideration. Although somewhat weak in geographically tracing Ogden's various expeditions, the volume supplies a wealth of information concerning company operations.

David E. Miller's "Peter Skene Ogden's Journal of His Expedition to Utah, 1825," *UHQ*, April 1952, and "William Kittson's Journal Covering Peter Skene Ogden's 1824-25 Snake River Expedition," *UHQ*, April 1954, treat in detail Ogden's first entry into Utah and his clash with American trappers on the Weber River during the last week of May 1825.

LeRoy R. Hafen, "Mountain Men," *UHQ*, October 1958, and "Etienne Provost," *UHQ*, Spring 1968, are very good. The latter article deals with the variant spellings of Provost. Hafen's biography, with W. J. Ghent, of Thomas Fitzpatrick, *Broken Hand* (rev. ed. 1973), is the definitive work on that famous mountain man. Hafen also edited the ten-volume collection, *The Mountain Men and the Fur Trade of the Far West* (1965-1972), which contains short biographies of several hundred trappers.

Osborne Russell's *Journal of a Trapper* (1955), edited by Aubrey Haines, carries the informative accounts of his various trips into Utah.

J. Cecil Alter, *James Bridger* (rev. ed. 1962), deals with one of the most celebrated of the mountain men. Robert Campbell's letter to G. K. Warren regarding Bridger's discovery of Great Salt Lake appeared in *Reports of Explorations and Surveys, to Ascertain the Most Practical and Economical Route for a Railroad from the Mississippi River to the Pacific Ocean* (1861), Volume XI.

Other important documentary collections are Dale L. Morgan, ed., *The West of William H. Ashley* (1964), and Harrison C. Dale, ed., *The Ashley-Smith Explorations and the Discovery of a Central Route to the Pacific, 1822-1829* (rev. ed. 1941). The latter is somewhat outdated as a result of more recent work.

In 1971 appeared the first volume to throw much light on the activities of numerous expeditions that came into the Uinta Basin and on into the Great Basin from New Mexico. David J. Weber, *The Taos Trappers,* is well worth reading.

Hiram M. Chittenden's three-volume *American Fur Trade of the Far West,* first published in 1902 and reissued in 1935 with some updating, has been considerably superseded by more recent research and the publication of additional journals. Long considered a historical masterpiece, Chittenden's work is still valuable for a great deal of general information. Paul C. Phillips and J. W.

Smurr, *The Fur Trade* (1961), is a useful two-volume survey which deals only sparingly with the Far West. Fred R. Gowans' *Rocky Mountain Rendezvous* (1976) locates and describes the various rendezvous sites, 1825–1840.

Chapter 5
Explorers and Trail Blazers

David E. Miller

During the half-dozen years prior to the westward trek of the Mormon pioneers John C. Fremont completed two major explorations inside present-day Utah, and several companies of California-bound emigrants transformed pack trails into wagon roads. These expeditions supplied reliable and important information regarding the Great Basin and opened roads that would become the major highways into Salt Lake Valley.

The Bartleson-Bidwell Party, 1841

In 1841 the Bartleson-Bidwell Party drove the first overland wagons through Utah. With the west coast as its destination, they left Independence, Missouri, in May 1841. This company was an offshoot of a larger expedition captained by John Bartleson, guided by mountain man Thomas Fitzpatrick, and accompanied by Father Pierre Jean De Smet and other Oregon-bound missionaries; fifteen women and children were in the original company, which numbered over sixty persons. Because John Bidwell had been an active organizer of the company and because he kept a daily journal of its progress the expedition is identified as the Bartleson-Bidwell Company, or sometimes as simply the Bidwell Company.

As this group arrived at Soda Springs (Idaho) following the Oregon Trail, Bartleson, Bidwell, and several others determined to leave the regular trail and follow Bear River southward through Cache Valley. They planned to skirt the north end of the Great Salt Lake and strike for Mary's River (Humboldt), which they would follow across Nevada and into California. Several members

71

of the company had been led to believe that one or more rivers flowed out of the Great Salt Lake to the west coast and that, if the going got too rough for wagons, boats could be built and the party could float downstream to San Francisco. This fact alone shows how little was known about the Great Basin a half-dozen years before the Mormon migration; the Buenaventura River myth still endured.

Fitzpatrick and De Smet refused to leave a well-traveled trail in favor of the supposed shortcut; they continued toward Fort Hall (Idaho) and Oregon, taking half the single men and all the families but one. However, thirty-two men and one woman took the new route. Benjamin Kelsey's young wife, Nancy, and their infant daughter, Ann, became the first white females known to have crossed Utah and Nevada. There were probably ten wagons in this small train; the Kelsey family had two of them.

The Bartleson-Bidwell Company left the big bend of Bear River at the present location of Alexander, Idaho, on August 11 and traveled southward into Cache Valley before crossing Long Divide into lower Bear River Valley. With considerable difficulty and delay the group passed the north end of the Great Salt Lake and the west edge of Great Salt Lake Desert. They reached the east base of Pilot Peak on September 13—the first white people known to have drunk from the freshwater springs located there.

After a brief rest the company skirted the south end of Pilot Range to arrive at Johnson Springs by way of Silver Zone Pass. The month's travel had proved too difficult for wagons; two had been left northeast of Pilot Peak and the rest were abandoned at Johnson Springs. After transferring the baggage to pack animals and giving surplus items to a delighted Indian, the party headed south and then west across Nevada. Mounted on horses, oxen, and mules, they finally straggled into Dr. John Marsh's ranch in the San Joaquin Valley on November 4. It had taken them six months to complete the tedious journey from Missouri.

The Bartleson-Bidwell Company took a most difficult route from Soda Springs to Pilot Springs. No other emigrant group followed their tracks to that point. However, beyond Pilot Peak—as far as Johnson Springs—their wagons left the first imprints on a segment of trail eventually to become part of Hastings Cutoff. (See map, p. 727.)

John C. Fremont in Utah

Much of Captain John C. Fremont's time in the West was spent mapping trails already comparatively well known to trappers and mountain men; hence some historians have given him the title "Pathmarker" rather than "Pathfinder." However, his numerous explorations did lead him into unknown regions; he was *first* in many instances. His own native ability and training, coupled with enthusiasm for his exploring tasks, made him an outstanding leader whose men followed him faithfully. His marriage to Jessie Benton, daughter of expansionist Missouri Senator Thomas Hart Benton, not only gave Fremont the active encouragement of an ambitious wife but also assured him valuable government support. With this backing he went on his early expeditions into the West well equipped with scientific instruments, weapons, and supplies. Likewise, the nature of his Washington contacts insured early publication of his findings. His *Report of the Exploring Expedition to the Rocky Mountains in the Year 1842, and to Oregon and North California in the Years 1843–44,* published in 1845, was one of the first authoritative publications concerning the American West. It supplied valuable information to the reading public and especially to the thousands of emigrants then on the way or planning to go to the Great Basin or the Pacific coast.

An excellent case study of Fremont's activities in the West and his contributions to its ultimate occupation is his exploration of Utah. Here he was not only pathmarker but scientific investigator and trailblazer as well. The Great Salt Lake had been a barrier to trappers, explorers, and emigrants. Since it was relatively unknown, many rumors and myths had developed concerning it: whirlpools, subterranean outlets to the Pacific, lake monsters, and abundant wildlife and vegetation on the islands were all supposed to exist. Fremont helped dispel some of these myths and supplant them with accurate information. He also produced the first authentic description of the Great Basin. (See map, p. 728.)

The first of Fremont's five explorations, traveled in the summer of 1842, took him only over South Pass and into the Wind River Mountains, but it fired his enthusiasm for a larger effort. Thus, thirty-nine men, well equipped and armed, left St. Louis in May 1843. Oregon was their goal, but Fremont's assignment and disposition led him to depart from the beaten paths. So it was that he and thirteen companions left the overland trail at Soda Springs and headed toward Cache Valley and the phenomenal body of salt water of which he had heard so much and knew so little. He would explore this lake personally.

On September 3, 1843, the Fremont Party made its first approach to the Great Salt Lake through the swampy land at the mouth of Bear River. Here the willows and rushes were so high that even a view of the lake proper could not be obtained and the captain had to seek a different approach. The group did, however, spend the night on low ground, where Fremont calculated the elevation of the lake to be 4,200 feet above the Gulf of Mexico. This was the first scientific measurement of the surface altitude of the Great Salt Lake, and subsequent observations and calculations proved it correct. While in the marshes the party feasted on wild waterfowl so numerous in the vicinity, "rising for the space of a mile round about at the sound of a gun, with a noise like distant thunder." (In 1928 approximately 64,000 acres of this region was created into the Bear River Migratory Bird Refuge, one of the largest in the United States.)

Having been thwarted in their attempt to reach the lake via Bear River, Fremont and his party turned southward to try a Weber River approach. Following the west base of the Wasatch past present Brigham City, Willard, and "ten or twelve" hot water springs, the company arrived at the Weber River some six miles west of present Ogden on September 5. Early the next morning the expedition headed for Little Mountain to the west. Wrote Fremont:

We reached the butte without any difficulty, and ascending to the summit, immediately at our feet beheld the object of our anxious search—the waters of the Inland Sea, stretching in still and solitary grandeur far beyond the limit of our vision. . . . It was one of the great points of the exploration. . . . I am doubtful if the followers of Balboa felt more enthusiasm when . . . they saw for the first time the great Western ocean.

As they gazed on the spectacle before them, their enthusiasm for the proposed boat trip mounted rapidly. Charles Preuss, Kit Carson, Baptiste Bernier, and Basil Lajeunesse were selected to accompany Fremont on the expedition that he called "the first ever attempted on this interior sea." It seems almost incredible that such an explorer was uninformed concerning the bullboat trip around the lake made by James Clyman, Moses Harris, and two others in 1826. Even Bonneville had heard of that voyage ten years earlier.

The vessel was an "India-Rubber" boat that Fremont describes as being eighteen feet long and "sufficiently large to contain five or six persons and considerable baggage." The sides, bow, and stern were "air-tight cylinders eighteen inches in diameter." Made of waterproof linen with seams "pasted in a very insecure manner," the boat was very frail. A bellows was used to inflate the bags.

"We carved a large cross which is there to this day," reported Kit Carson concerning the now-famous crucifix which was carved September 9, 1843, and which is located at the crest of Fremont Island in the Great Salt Lake. This "large" cross is only seven inches tall.

On the morning of September 9 the five explorers towed their boat and its cargo of supplies and scientific gear through a mile of shallow water before they could float the craft and climb aboard. When they reached sufficient water depth that the lake bottom could not be touched with the oars, all the old myths concerning whirlpools and currents began to cause uneasiness. About halfway across "two of the divisions between cylinders gave way, and it required the constant use of the bellows to keep in a sufficient quantity of air."

After several hours of hard rowing, the party reached the island about noon and ascended to the highest point. Here, 800 feet above the water, Fremont and Preuss conducted a telescopic survey of the lake and its islands and drew a map that is as accurate as could be expected of one drawn from a single position at the crest of the rocky island. Fremont searched the shores for a possible connection with other bodies of water, but found none. The island had "neither water nor trees of any kind." It is no wonder that he entered in his report: "In the first disappointment we felt from the dissipation of our dreams of the fertile islands, I called this Disappointment Island." In 1850 Captain Howard Stansbury renamed the island in honor of Fremont, "who first set foot upon its shores."

Two objects left on the island have occasioned much searching and speculating in the years since Fremont's report was printed in 1845. The brass cover of the object end of the captain's "spy glass" was accidentally left, and almost everyone who hàs visited the island has attempted to locate it. The cap was actually found by Jacob Miller during the 1860s when the Miller brothers of Farmington, Utah, were using the island as a stock range. The cap was subsequently misplaced, however, and has not been seen for several decades. On the other hand, a cross carved on a peculiar rock formation near the summit has intrigued visitors to Fremont Island since Stansbury's day. Despite speculations to the contrary, it was definitely cut by members of Fremont's party. According to Kit Carson: "We ascended the mountain and under a shelving rock, cut a large cross which is there to this day." It is not known whether the crucifix was cut for religious purposes or just to pass the time.

Before leaving the island after one night "in perfect security for the first time in a long journey," Fremont filled one of his water bags with lake water, which he boiled down after his return to shore. "Roughly evaporated over the fire," he reported, "the five gallons of water yielded fourteen pints of very fine-grained and very white salt, of which the whole lake may be regarded as a saturated solution." Thus was added another "first" to Fremont's career, for Great Salt Lake water had never before been scientifically analyzed.

Having completed his initial survey of the lake, Fremont directed his course northward to Fort Hall and thence down the Snake and Columbia rivers to Fort Vancouver, arriving November 19. Six days later the company left to return via "Tlamath" Lake and the east slopes of the Sierra Nevadas. A major objective of the expedition was to discover and explore "the reputed Buenaventura river," a river often depicted on maps of that day as draining either the Great Salt Lake, Sevier Lake, or Utah Lake into the Pacific. Joseph R. Walker, on his famous trip to California in 1833, had established that no river flows westward out of the Great Basin. Yet Fremont, with Carson as guide, continued to search into the winter of 1843–1844. Finally convinced that no such river existed and that it was impractical to continue his southerly course, Fremont and his weary band crossed the mountains in midwinter and arrived at Sutter's Fort in Sacramento Valley on March 8, 1844.

The following May found the captain entering the present limits of Utah on his way east over the Old Spanish Trail. In southern Utah he was overtaken by Joseph Walker, who joined the party as an additional guide. Of Utah Lake, which was reached on May 24, Fremont wrote:

Its greatest breadth is about 15 miles, stretching far to the north, narrowing as it goes, and connecting with the Great Salt Lake. This is the report, and which I believe to be correct; but it is fresh water, while the other is not only salt, but a saturated solution of salt; and here is a problem which requires to be solved.

It is astonishing that Fremont did not calculate the elevation of Utah Lake as he had done that of the Great Salt Lake. This would have shown the freshwater body to be approximately 300 feet higher and hence certainly not an arm of the lake to the north. The Fremont Party left the region on May 27 and returned to the states by way of Spanish Fork Canyon, Fort Robidoux, and Fort Davy Crockett. The captain had virtually circled the vast region that he appropriately named the Great Basin.

The year 1845 found Jessie Benton's husband again in Utah. This time he came by way of the White River and Uinta Basin to reach the upper waters of the Provo River, which he followed to Utah Lake. From that point he turned to the north, and along the Jordan River he learned the true relationship between the lakes at each end of that stream. He camped where Salt Lake City now stands on October 13 and spent the better part of two weeks exploring the vicinity. With Carson and several others he made the first known visit by white men to Antelope Island, where they killed several antelope. Upon their return to the mainland the horsemen encountered an Indian who claimed ownership of the island and the animals on it. Fremont paid for the game taken, which had prompted him to give the island its name.

The exploring party then went west, intending to reach California via a route along the south shores of the Great Salt Lake and across Great Salt Lake Desert. Although Jedediah S. Smith and two companions had crossed the south edge of this wasteland on their return from California in 1827 and Joseph R. Walker had traveled along the north edge in 1833, no one had traversed the center. In making his desert crossing Fremont really blazed the trail that was soon to become a segment of the famous Hastings Cutoff. (See map, p. 728.) Although Indians in the vicinity warned that no man had ever made it across the barren waste, the well-prepared company, guided by the signal fires of Carson's advance party, reached Pilot Peak (which Fremont named) with comparative ease; only a few animals were lost. California-bound pioneers—especially the Donner Party—were to spend many painful hours plodding through this desert with wagons just one year later.

After a brief rest at Pilot Springs, Fremont's party continued westward. Before reaching what had been known as Ogden or Mary's River (which Fremont renamed Humboldt), the company was divided; Lieutenant T. H. Talbot led one segment that picked up the well-established California Trail and followed it west. Captain Fremont led the other segment across present central Nevada. Members of the expedition reached Sutter's Fort during the following winter in time to provide Lansford W. Hastings with exciting information regarding a possible new shortcut to California.

On his brief visits to northern Utah, John C. Fremont made several original contributions: he was the first white man known to have visited any of the Great Salt Lake islands; he was the first to compute the altitude and geographic location of the lake and other points; he was the first to map the lake more or less accurately; he was first to analyze its waters; he was first to name any of its islands; he was first to make official soundings of its depth; and he was first to cross the middle of Great Salt Lake Desert, blazing a portion of what became Hastings Cutoff. His survey stimulated interest and further exploration of the Great Basin, which he named, along with two of its most important landmarks—Pilot Peak and Humboldt River. He was the first to give accurate, reliable information concerning the whole region.

The Fremont report, which appeared in 1845, contained descriptions of numerous fertile valleys west of the Wasatch Range—Cache Valley in the north and Utah and other valleys to the south—and suggested the possibility of establishing military forts and settlements. The report came to the Mormon leaders at Nauvoo as they were planning to migrate westward in search of a secure home. The account was studied very carefully by Brigham Young and his associates; it was their most valuable source of information concerning the Great Basin. There is hardly a doubt that this publication was a factor, as Fremont later claimed, in the

Mormon decision to settle in Salt Lake Valley. It should be noted, however, that the report did not include an account of Fremont's 1845 visit to the site of present Salt Lake City.

Fremont's 1853 expedition through Utah is of less importance in the state's history than the earlier expeditions. In an attempt to find a feasible route for a transcontinental railroad, Fremont's party entered present Utah from the east by way of the Colorado River. He explored the stream that now bears his name, and after a very difficult winter trek he reached the Mormon settlement of Parowan by way of Fremont Pass. After a few days of rest, he and his companions continued to California over the old Spanish Trail. He never returned to Utah, although his 1856 presidential candidacy involved him in the Republican Party effort to make a national political issue out of the Mormon practice of plural marriage in the territory.

Hastings Cutoff

Closely related to Fremont's 1845 expedition was the great overland migration of 1846. By then the western wagon traffic had gained significant momentum. Thousands of people had caught "Oregon fever"; many sold good farms and gave up thriving businesses as the lure of the West captivated their imaginations. A notable shift in the ultimate destination of the land-hungry migrants was also taking place; more and more people were thinking of California as the land of opportunity. Eagerness to shorten the established routes by miles and days led to the opening of Hastings Cutoff and the building of a wagon road across Utah.

Memorable in the history of the 1846 migration are the promotional activities of Lansford W. Hastings, who unwisely encouraged several groups of emigrants to depart from the well-worn Oregon Trail at Fort Bridger and break a new wagon road south of the Great Salt Lake. As anyone could see by looking at the maps available in the mid-1840s, the direct course west from Fort Bridger avoided the lengthy journey northwestward to Fort Hall and then southwestward to the Humboldt River, saving between 200 and 450 miles—the equivalent of fifteen to thirty days in travel time. What Hastings failed to point out clearly, and what those who took his advice could not know, were the difficulties to be encountered along the proposed route.

Hastings had reached Oregon in the 1842 migration, and the following year he traveled south to California. There he fell in love with the Sacramento Valley and the San Francisco Bay Area. Convinced that California rather than Oregon should be the major goal of the westward migration, he returned to the states by way of Mexico in 1845. That same year he published his now famous *Emigrants' Guide to Oregon and California,* which vaguely described the Oregon Trail and other routes to the Pacific, but which vigorously extolled the virtues of California. Hastings may have envisioned there a populous new state, filled with Americans who might choose him as their governor or senator. Most historians agree that such ambitions helped motivate this eager and capable promoter.

Hastings had traveled only once to Oregon, and that was before the California Trail (Fort Hall-Raft River-City of the Rocks-Humboldt River) was opened to wagon traffic in 1843. He described the Fort Hall route as very feasible for wagons, but continued:

The most direct route, for the California emigrants, would be to leave the Oregon route, about two hundred miles east of Fort Hall; thence bearing west southwest, to the Salt Lake; and thence continuing down to the bay of St. Francisco. . . .

This last vague reference meant that the suggested route would connect with the regular California road somewhere along the Humboldt, although no mention is made of that stream. At the time of his writing Hastings seems to have been unaware of the strategic location of Fort Bridger, which had not been established when he made his journey to Oregon in 1842. The *Emigrants' Guide* recommends Soda Springs as "the point at which the routes will most advantageously diverge. . . ." However, in 1846 Hastings became the active promoter of the "west from Fort Bridger" route.

After seeing his *Guide* safely into print, Hastings returned to California. At Sutter's Fort he learned early in 1846 from Captain Fremont and Lieutenant Talbot what they had experienced in crossing the Great Basin the year before. As a result, what had before been no more than a vague hope rapidly evolved into a real prospect, and Hastings began his promotional campaign in earnest.

With his book already enjoying wide circulation, Hastings determined to traverse the new route himself before actually attempting to direct wagon traffic over it. Late in April he headed east in a party that included his friend James M. Hudspeth and two mountain men, Caleb Greenwood and James Clyman. According to Clyman's journal, fifteen other men and boys, three women, two children, and "about 150 mules and horses" completed the party. Having followed the regular road east to the vicinity of present Elko (Nevada), Hastings, Hudspeth, Clyman, and a few others split off from the company to backtrack along the Talbot Route to

Pilot Springs. By June 2 Hastings' group had followed the Fremont tracks eastward to Salt Lake Valley.

Clyman, who had known this region for twenty years, guided the small party up Parley's Canyon, over Big Mountain, and on to the Weber River by the route that would be recommended to the Donner Party. From the present site of Henefer they went upstream to Echo Creek, followed it to its headwaters, crossed Bear River near the present site of Evanston, and eventually intersected the Oregon Trail at Bridger Gap. June 7 found them at Fort Bridger.

Hastings had finally traversed a route he had so casually advocated in the *Guide*. The only part that he thought might pose serious problems was Great Salt Lake Desert, but having crossed it on horseback, he failed to appreciate exactly how difficult the soggy portions of that wasteland would be for wagons. Eager to influence as many groups as possible, he and Hudspeth headed eastward along the Oregon Trail. Clyman also continued eastward but not for the same purpose; he realized that the new route was not practical for wagons and urged California-bound emigrants not to take the cutoff.

Hastings' actions were irresponsible on two counts. First, even on horseback he should have realized that heavy wagons might bog down in the desert mud and he should have clearly explained this risk to the wagonmasters he met. Second, he seems to have deliberately failed to indicate the distance between the springs on the east and west edges of the desert. Most migrants expected the distance to be a negotiable forty miles, but eighty miles through treacherous terrain without grass or water for the animals could be disastrous. Had the truth been known, it is likely that no wagon would have taken Hastings Cutoff.

By July 2 Hastings was well into his promotional program. A few miles east of South Pass he recruited Wales B. Bonney, returning to the states from Oregon, to intercept oncoming trains with the "good news." The Hastings letter that Bonney carried eastward urged "those bound for California to concentrate their numbers and strength, and to take a new route which had been explored by Mr. H., from Fort Bridger via the south end of the Salt Lake, by which the distance would be materially shortened." Many, if not most, of the 1846 migrants were already acquainted with Hastings' *Guide,* and most of them had heard reports that John C. Fremont had pioneered a new route fit for wagon traffic. Combining the magic name of Fremont with assurances that the author of the *Guide* would personally escort them over the path he had just traversed, numerous California-bound migrants were naturally tempted. How many expeditions Bonney contacted is not known; the Donner Party was one.

Hastings himself returned to Fort Bridger, arriving July 16 in company with some who had agreed to try his proposal. Others arrived within a few days. Most of those who took Hastings Cutoff in 1846 had left Independence, Missouri, in mid-May, evidently intending to travel as one large train of some 150 wagons. William H. Russell was elected captain. However, as often happened during the great overland migration, dissatisfaction soon led various outfits to split off from the main company. Among these smaller groups were the four companies known to have traveled over Hastings Cutoff with some direction from the promoter: the Bryant-Russell, Harlan-Young, Lienhard, and Donner parties. There is some contemporary evidence of other small groups, but most of them apparently overtook and joined or closely followed the Harlan-Young Company. T. H. Jefferson, who in 1846 took the Hastings route and in 1848 published a first-rate map of the whole trail west from Independence, seems to belong in this category, as do James Mathers and George McKinstry.

The Bryant-Russell Party

The first group to follow Hastings' recommended course did so without wagons. At Fort Laramie William Russell evidently resigned his leadership position with the large emigrant company for various reasons, sold his wagons, and decided to set out for California with several others on mule and horseback. Edwin Bryant was among that group; he was an editor of the Louisville (Kentucky) *Courier-Journal,* and had intended to write a book about his adventures. The result, *What I Saw in California,* published in 1848, gives the most graphic descriptions of the Utah country crossed by any group that season. As a result of this fine account, the expedition is commonly known as the Bryant-Russell Party.

After conferring with Hastings, Bryant and Russell agreed to try the new route with Hudspeth as guide. The company of nine well-mounted and well-supplied men left Fort Bridger on July 20. Instead of backtracking the trail he had followed with Hastings and Clyman, Hudspeth headed southwestward to Bear River over a route that was later followed by most of the 1846 wagons and the Mormon migration of 1847. (Joseph R. Walker had led the Joseph C. Chiles Party over the same route in 1843 on the way to Fort Hall and California.) The 1846 horsemen then followed the Bear River northwest to the present site of Evanston, Wyoming, rode westward to Lost Creek, and followed it to its confluence with the Weber River near Devils Slide. After some exploration of the area, the group left Lost Creek via the low divide between present Croydon and Henefer, a route that appealed to Hudspeth as a likely wagon road around the worst stretch of the rugged upper canyon of the Weber. (He would soon be guiding the Harlan-Young wagons that way.)

From near the present site of Henefer, Bryant and his associates turned southward up Main Canyon, over the divide to Dixie Creek, and on to East Canyon. This was the approximate route the Donner Party would test with wagons—the route Hastings had evidently always intended. Once on East Canyon Creek Hudspeth guided his small party northward, downstream to the Weber, and westward through lower Weber Canyon. Even on good mules the men found that part of the narrows now known as Devil's Gate almost impassable, but they made it through without loss. Hudspeth then explored back upstream to determine the feasibility of bringing wagons through the two canyons of the Weber. He was evidently convinced, for he met the Harlan-Young Party at the mouth of Echo Canyon on July 27, started them along that almost impossible route, and returned to his fellow riders. The Bryant-Russell Party then made its way easily across the site of downtown Salt Lake City, over the Jordan River, and on to Twenty Wells (Grantsville) and the excellent springs near present Iosepa in Skull Valley.

By August 3 the party stood at the crest of Cedar Mountain looking northwest toward Pilot Peak, some seventy miles away. "Now, boys, put spurs to your mules and ride like H---!" exclaimed Hudspeth as he turned back to do some additional exploring. The mounted group arrived at Pilot Springs without serious trouble and noted the wagon tracks left there in 1841 by the Bidwell Party. They eventually reached California in good condition.

The Harlan-Young Party

The first wagons to transform major portions of Hastings Cutoff into a wagon road were those of the party named for George W. Harlan and Samuel C. Young. Harlan had been personally influenced by Lansford W. Hastings and by his *Guide* to sell a fine Michigan farm and migrate to California. After parting early from the large Russell train, Harlan, Young, and several other families traveled west together, eventually reaching Fort Bridger on July 16 in company with Hastings. Four days later the party of at least forty wagons left the fort with Hastings personally guiding them.

For the few miles to Sulphur Creek they followed the course pioneered in 1843 by Walker and the eight Chiles wagons. Then the 1846 company took a new trail southward to reach Bear River nearly twenty miles south of present Evanston. After fording the Bear River they made their way to Yellow Creek, followed it into present Utah, and crossed over a low divide into Echo Canyon, two miles upstream from Castle Rock. Here, evidently convinced that he had followed an unnecessarily circuitous course from Fort Bridger, Hastings instructed his party to continue down the canyon that he had ascended a few weeks earlier while he turned back to seek a more direct route. He intended to rejoin his company at the confluence of Echo Creek and Weber River.

Hurrying eastward, Hastings easily located a more satisfactory route, and on July 27 intercepted the Lienhard Company on Sulphur Creek southwest of the fort. It took a full day for him to put their wagons safely on the new cutoff, which followed the creek westward to the Bear River, crossed that stream some nine miles south of Evanston, and then turned west to Yellow Creek and Echo Canyon. He then hurried ahead to catch the Harlan-Young Party, intending to guide them over the mountains to Salt Lake Valley. However, the advance wagons had made very good time and had already met James Hudspeth at the mouth of Echo Canyon.

In order to avoid the worst part of upper Weber Canyon, Hudspeth directed the wagons northwestward over the divide into Lost Creek Valley, thence down the Weber River into Morgan Valley. They had reached that point and Hudspeth had returned to the Bryant-Russell Party when Hastings overtook them. Since Hudspeth had just been through Devil's Gate and had evidently assured the company's leaders that wagons could make it, Hastings was not able to dissuade them. However, lower Weber Canyon proved to be almost impossible for wagons to travel, and the Harlan-Young Party made it only at the cost of backbreaking labor and at least one wagon and team that crashed into the chasm.

Having examined Devil's Gate firsthand, Hastings turned back to warn those behind against taking that route. He soon met the Lienhard Company near present-day Peterson, explained the hardships to be encountered in the lower canyon, and again hurried eastward to leave a similar warning for the Donner Party—a note prominently placed on August 4 at the Weber crossing near the present site of Henefer. Having completed this mission Hastings overtook the Harlan-Young train at the mouth of Weber Canyon and escorted them to the south end of the Great Salt Lake.

Slowed by the illness of John Hargrave, the company was over-taken by the Lienhard wagons on August 8. James F. Reed, who had picked up Hastings' letter at Henefer, rode into camp that same day and induced Hastings to return with him to mark the course for the Donner wagons to take.

While Hastings was gone, the Harlan-Young and Lienhard out-fits moved slowly across the north end of Tooele Valley to Twenty Wells, where Hargrave died. On August 12, immediately after the funeral, Hastings, who had just returned, and those who were de-pending upon him moved on, and four days later the advance wagons began the long, waterless drive over the desert from the Iosepa Springs. More than thirty years later both Samuel Young and Jacob Harlan wrote accounts of the difficult, near-tragic cross-ing. Large numbers of livestock were lost; several wagons had to be temporarily left bogged in the desert mud. But after a few days of rest the Harlan-Young Party pushed on to their destination.

The Lienhard Party

Because he kept a journal, Heinrich Lienhard's name is associ-ated with a small group of predominantly Swiss and German im-migrants who left Independence with the Russell Company. Split-ting off from the main group, they arrived at Fort Bridger on July 23—three days after the Harlan-Young Party had set out for Salt Lake Valley. Persuaded by what they had heard and read, the Lienhard Company decided to follow. At Sulphur Creek they met Hastings, who pointed out the shorter route to Echo Canyon. After the Lienhard wagons had cut tracks along this new trail, it be-came an important segment of the Hastings Cutoff. The Mormons and others followed it during the years before the building of the transcontinental railroad.

After Hastings had departed for the lower Weber, Lienhard fol-lowed the well-marked wagon tracks westward through Echo and upper Weber canyons and into the present Morgan Valley. As has already been noted, Hastings again intercepted them there and at-tempted to persuade them to return upstream to present Henefer and then strike to the south. The Swiss-German company decided to disregard this advice; if the Harlan-Young Company had suc-ceeded in getting wagons through Devil's Gate, so could they. Lienhard's description of passing the narrows is graphic:

On August 6 we ventured upon this furious passage, up to this point decid-edly the wildest we had encountered, if not the most dangerous. We devoted the entire forenoon and until fully one o'clock in the afternoon to the task of

In the 1930s Charles Kelly photographed these remains of oxen and wagons that were abandoned by the Donner Party in the mud of the Great Salt Lake Desert. The dark peak at the left is Floating Island; Silver Island can be seen in the background.

getting our four wagons through. In places we unhitched from the wagon all the oxen except the wheel-yoke, then we strained at both hind wheels, one drove, and the rest steadied the wagon; we then slid rapidly down into the foaming water, hitched the loose oxen again to the wagon and took it directly down the foaming riverbed, full of great boulders, on account of which the wagon quickly lurched from one side to the other; now we had to turn the wheels by the spokes, then again hold back with all the strength we had, lest it slip upon a low lying rock and smash itself to pieces. . . .

After emerging from Weber Canyon the company moved quickly through present Davis County, where Lienhard was so favorably impressed that he would gladly have remained had there been just one white family living in the area. After crossing the Jordan River the party was with or near the Harlan-Young Company during the balance of its transit of Utah. Lienhard's excellent journal gives the fullest details of the desert crossing. His seems to have been the only wagon train of the 1846 migration that lost neither livestock nor wagons in the saline wasteland. Finally reaching the Humboldt on September 8, he significantly noted that Hastings Cutoff should more appropriately be called *Hastings Longtripp.* Wagons that had left Fort Bridger a couple of weeks after him, but had taken the regular road by way of Fort Hall, had already arrived at the junction.

The Donner Party

After leaving Independence the families of George and Jacob Donner, James Reed, and several others overtook and joined the Russell Company. West of South Pass they separated again, elected George Donner as captain, and moved on to Fort Bridger, arriving on July 27. The leaders had already decided to take Hastings' shortcut, even though James Clyman, an old friend of Reed, strongly advised against it when he met the group at Fort Laramie. Some of the emigrants had Hastings' *Guide* with them and had evidently also been influenced by reports of Fremont's crossing of Great Salt Lake Desert. Their meeting with Wales Bonney has already been noted. When the Donners reached Fort Bridger there was no question about the route they would take from that point. On July 31 they headed westward along a road that at least sixty wagons had traveled before them. After F. W. Graves and his family overtook and joined them on August 16 the Donner Party numbered twenty-three wagons and eighty-seven persons. Only forty-seven of them would eventually reach their destination.

Reed's journal details the company's progress from Fort Bridger. He wrote almost daily until his banishment from the group on October 5, near present Valmy, Nevada. The last very brief entry is dated October 4, the day a quarrel between Reed and John Snyder erupted into a fight in which Snyder was killed. Reed was tried and banished from the company the next day.

The Donner Party followed the Harlan-Young-Lienhard route from Fort Bridger to the present site of Henefer, where they arrived on August 6. There they found the letter that Hastings had pressed into a split stick and securely wedged into the top of a large sagebrush. The message was simple: The Weber Canyon route was absolutely unfit for wagon traffic. However, if the expedition would send a messenger after him, Hastings would return and point out the better, shorter route wagons could follow into Salt Lake Valley. As noted, James Reed hurried after Hastings and found him with the earlier wagon parties, probably at the Adobe Rock camp west of the Oquirrh Mountains. True to his promise, Hastings rode eastward with Reed as far as the summit of Big Mountain where Hastings and Clyman had stood on June 3. Hastings pointed out the directions the wagons should take. (See map, p. 727; current names have been applied to the route he described.) Reed was to follow down Little Emigration Canyon to East Canyon Creek, thence northward down that stream to just above the narrows where East Canyon Dam now stands. There he would find Dixie Creek flowing in from the east; he should ascend Dixie Creek to the summit from which he would have an easy downhill grade via Main Canyon to the Donner camp. Reed marked the trail as he went and arrived at the Henefer campsite on August 10. His trip had taken four days.

No time was lost as the company now moved up Main Canyon and over into East Canyon. By August 14 they were cutting brush and trees from Little Emigration Canyon, a job that required two more days. On August 18 the wagons rolled across Reed's Gap (Big Mountain Pass) into the upper reaches of Parley's Creek's north fork. By the evening of August 21 they had climbed over Little Mountain and were camped a couple of miles upstream from the mouth of Emigration Canyon. It required another whole day to drag all the wagons up Donner Hill—a spur of mountain that seemed to them to block the mouth of the canyon—and into Salt Lake Valley. Allowing for the four days of relative inactivity at camp while Reed was seeking out Hastings, the Donners had hacked out a wagon road between Henefer and the valley in eleven days. In 1847 the Mormon vanguard covered the same ground in three days, following the Donner tracks every mile of the way except for a short by-pass around Donner Hill.

After searching all day for a ford, the Donner Party crossed the Jordan River somewhere between present-day 2100 and 2700 South Streets and struck a direct course for the north tip of the Oquirrh Range, where they intercepted the two-week-old Harlan-Young and Lienhard tracks. As the wagons moved westward from Adobe Rock toward Twenty Wells, Luke Halloran died of consumption on August 25. The Donners had taken the sick man into their company at Fort Bridger, hoping to nurse him back to health. He was buried the next day at Twenty Wells beside the grave of John Hargrave. The track ahead was easily followed, and by August 28 the company had pulled into the Skull Valley campsite at present Iosepa. There the Donners found a board with a few bits of paper stuck to it; on the ground were additional scraps. Here Hastings had obviously left a second message that the birds had pecked to pieces. Former schoolteacher Tamsen Donner pieced the fragments together with the help of several children. The message read: "2 days—2 nights—hard driving—cross desert—reach water."

This was the beginning of the long, dry drive—dry, that is, as far as drinking water was concerned, but often very wet underfoot. They expected the drive to be not more than forty or fifty miles, but ahead lay over eighty miles of some of the most difficult terrain in the West, half of it sticky mud that would suck the wagons down to the hubs and sap the strength of tired and thirsty oxen and horses. Cutting and bundling huge piles of grass and filling every available container with water, the party set out on August 30. A relatively easy thirteen-mile pull northwestward across Skull Valley brought the expedition to Redlum Springs where the brackish water and coarse grass was of little use to men or animals.

From there a natural route led over the Cedar Mountains via Hastings Canyon. The last half-mile below the summit has an incline of more than 30 degrees—a tough challenge for horses and oxen drawing heavy wagons.

Once over Hastings Pass the Donners got their first glimpse of the country ahead. Immediately before them was a small rocky ridge now known as Grayback, and beyond that was the first distant view of Pilot Peak, approximately seventy miles straight ahead. (Present U.S. Highway I-80 crosses the old trail in this region, a half-dozen miles west of Low Pass.) After crossing the Grayback, where the old Dugway road can still be seen, the trail wound in and out among the sand dunes and smooth mud flats. (The trail is still clearly visible because of the discoloration that resulted from the wagon wheels churning up the subsurface materials.) After approximately four miles of this terrain, the emigrants entered the completely flat, barren portion of Great Salt Lake Desert and headed for the northeast end of Silver Island and Pilot Peak beyond.

After the first day's travel into the desert the Donner leaders began to realize that the distance was much greater than they had been led to believe. By the end of the second day the situation was becoming desperate. Some families began lightening loads by discarding heavy items from the ever slower-moving wagons. At first glance the surface seemed dry and solid, but horses and wagons mired deeper with every mile of progress. By the third day the whole episode had become a struggle for survival. Many animals dropped and died in their tracks; five wagons had to be abandoned. Before night every drop of water had been consumed, and the Pilot Springs were still more than twenty-five miles away.

The only hope was to make a desperate attempt to reach water. Oxen loosened from their yokes and all the loose livestock made a beeline for the water that they either smelled or sensed; many of them were never seen again. Some men rode ahead to return with meager quantities of water for those who could not make it to the springs without help. Ultimately all of the Donner Party managed to make their way to the water. Most of the wagons and livestock were also brought in, but some were not. Abandoned wagons and the bleaching bones of animals were for many years grim witnesses to the fact that the shortest line is not always the best road between two points.

The terrible tragedy suffered by the Donner Party at and near Donner Lake during the 1846–1847 winter is too well known to require retelling. However, it should be pointed out that the company's experiences in Utah contributed materially to that disaster. Time lost and energy expended in building the road from Henefer to Salt Lake Valley was the first factor. If James Hudspeth had not made the mistake of sending the Harlan-Young wagons through the canyons of Weber River, that company would have opened Hastings' road through the mountains and the Donners would have saved several days. However, crossing Great Salt Lake Desert was the greater contributor. Losses of energy, supplies, livestock, and equipment in that wasteland did more to weaken and demoralize the group than any other experience prior to the final tragedy.

Obviously the Donners could not know that the road they cut through the Wasatch Range would, in just eleven months, become a highway for the Mormon vanguard of 1847.

Chapter 5
Bibliographical Essay

These accounts of the pre-Mormon migrations across Utah are based on the available journals and reminiscences of the emigrants plus careful field reconnaissance to identify and map the routes. John Bidwell's journal has been published at various times; one of the most recent and best is *A Journey to California, 1841, The First Emigrant Party to California by Wagon Train: The Journal of John Bidwell* (1964), with an introduction by Francis P. Farquhar. For a detailed account and map of the Bartleson-Bidwell trek through Utah see David E. Miller, "First Wagon Train to Cross Utah," *UHQ,* Winter 1962.

Much of the Fremont portion of this chapter is quoted by permission from David E. Miller, "John C. Fremont in the Great Salt

Lake Region," *The Historian,* Autumn 1948. For broader biograph-ical material *Fremont, Pathmarker of the West* (1939) by Allan Nevins is available. Best sources, however, are Fremont's published jour-nals: (a) *Report of the Exploring Expedition to the Rocky Mountains in the Year 1842, and to Oregon and North California in the Years 1843–44* (1845) and (b) *Memoirs of My Life* (1887). The latter volume con-tains a reprint of the 1845 report as well as accounts of the 1845 and 1853 expeditions. Mary Lee Spence and Donald Jackson have recently edited two volumes of Fremont's collected works and cor-respondence, *The Expeditions of John Charles Fremont* (1970–73). *Kit Carson's Own Story of His Life* (1926) was reissued in 1966 as *Kit Carson's Autobiography,* edited by Milo M. Quaife.

Two separate works contain basic documents dealing with the 1846 migrations: J. Roderic Korns, ed., *West From Fort Bridger* (*UHQ,* 1951), and Dale L. Morgan, ed., *Overland in 1846: Diaries and Letters of the California-Oregon Trail* (1963). Included in one or both are major portions of the records of Edwin Bryant, James Clyman, George McKinstry, James Mathers, Heinrich Lienhard, James F. Reed, Samuel C. Young, and George Harlan. *West from Fort Bridger* also reproduces T. H. Jefferson's map of the route from the fort to the Humboldt.

Thomas F. Andrews, "Lansford W. Hastings and the Promotion of the Salt Lake Desert Cutoff: A Reappraisal," *Western Historical Quarterly,* April 1973, sympathetically examines motives and activi-ties of Hastings and migrating Americans in 1846. Fred R. Go-wans and Eugene E. Campbell's *Fort Bridger* (1975) describes the outpost that was the point of departure for Hastings Cutoff.

Special works deal with the Donner Party. Geoge R. Stewart's *Ordeal by Hunger* (rev. ed., 1960) is the best. A second important work is C. F. McGlashan, *History of the Donner Party* (1968); this is a reprint from an 1880 edition of the first formal history of that ill-fated company. *Fatal Decision* (1950), by Walter M. Stookey, is of lesser value. By special permission portions of this chapter dealing with the Donners are quoted from David E. Miller, "The Donner Road Through the Great Salt Lake Desert," *Pacific Historical Re-view,* February 1958.

Maps showing the routes of these various explorations, together with a brief commentary for each, are found in *Utah History Atlas* (1977 ed.), compiled by David E. Miller. Hastings' *The Emigrants' Guide to Oregon and California* was reprinted in 1969 with an in-troduction by Mary Lee Spence. Most readers will be surprised at the vagueness of the author's description and reference to the shortcut (pp. 135–138).

Part II
From Colonization
to Statehood
Introduction

Eugene E. Campbell

The Mormons who colonized Utah were religious refugees seeking an isolated location where they could practice their faith in comparative freedom. Convinced that their founder, Joseph Smith, was a prophet appointed by God to establish the Kingdom of God as a basis for Christ's millennial reign on earth, these Latter-day Saints had been forced to leave communities in New York, Ohio, Missouri, and most recently in Illinois. The Church of Jesus Christ of Latter-day Saints, persecuted because of its belief in the Book of Mormon and because of its religious zeal, millennial beliefs, economic solidarity, political unity, and practice of plural marriage, had survived and grown due to strong leadership and a vigorous missionary system in the years since its organization in 1830.

Composed of converts from throughout the United States and Canada plus thousands of proselytes from the British Isles, the Scandinavian countries, France, Germany, Switzerland, and the Pacific islands, the Mormon pioneers not only accepted a new religion but heeded the call to gather to Zion in order to build the nucleus of the Kingdom. The millenarianism that had driven them from their homes seemed to give them the strength and dedication necessary to survive in the arid Great Basin, which they chose as their home in 1847.

Brigham Young, their leader in the westward migration, was a remarkable man. With only a few weeks of formal education he developed leadership skills within the Mormon organizational structure that enabled him to accept the leadership role after Joseph Smith's murder in 1844. Before his death in 1877, Young planned and supervised the movements of approximately 80,000 Mormons from various parts of the world in a movement to colonize over 300 settlements in and near the Great Basin. He also served as the president of his church, the first governor of the State of Deseret and of the Territory of Utah, and the regional superintendent of Indian affairs.

The period of Utah's history from settlement to statehood was dominated by three basic themes—colonization, confrontation, and conformity. Successful colonization was made possible by developing irrigation skills and by cooperatively using natural resources. Church members accepted calls to go on colonizing missions with the same dedication that characterized their proselyting assignments. The Mormon pattern was to establish base colonies in the arable valleys and then to expand colonizing efforts into the surrounding regions. Salt Lake City, Ogden, Provo, Tooele, Manti, Nephi, Fillmore, Parowan, Brigham City, and Logan were such centers during the early years. Some specialized colonies were established to mine iron, coal, and lead and to raise cotton, grapes, and other fruit. Still others were founded primarily to control and civilize the Indians.

Tragically for the Indians of the region, there was a limited amount of arable land with irrigating water available, and the Mormon pioneers colonized areas that the Indians had occupied for centuries. Church leaders tried to compensate the Indians by teaching them the art of farming and even by baptizing them, but wherever the Indians failed to adapt to the white men's ways they were defeated and ultimately forced to leave their lands.

The necessity and desire of the Mormon leaders for a self-sustaining society led them to foster numerous economic experiments, including beet sugar, iron, and silk industries and cotton production. Efforts were also made to reinstitute the United Order, a communal system taught by Joseph Smith. While many of these undertakings failed, the Mormons were successful in building a strong agricultural base for their expanding population. Believing that precious metal mining would bring an undesirable element into the population and create materialistic attitudes among the Mormons, church leaders opposed mining and let Utah's metallic wealth pass into the hands of the non-Mormons.

Mormon women played an important role in the development of territorial Utah. Because of the plural marriage system and the calling of men to do missionary work and serve as lay leaders of ecclesiastical units, Mormon women carried more than a normal share of the pioneering burdens. Many of those who survived became remarkable managers and leaders in addition to rearing large families. Some became women's rights advocates, medical doctors, nurses, editors, poets, and political leaders.

Utah pioneering did not end with the conquest of lands along the Wasatch Front. From the farming lands at the base of the Uintas to the mining regions of Carbon and Emery counties and the livestock lands of Kane, Wayne, and San Juan counties, the settlement of the Colorado Plateau required courage and ingenuity. The promise of the region was barely sensed during the territorial years.

Polygamy and theocratic domination of the civil government led to serious confrontations with federally appointed territorial officials and were the primary reasons that Utah's statehood applications were denied for over forty years. Friction began when the first territorial appointees arrived in Utah in 1851, and they reached a climax in 1857 when United States President James Buchanan felt obliged to send an army of 2,500 men to install a non-Mormon governor and to quell a reported Mormon rebellion against the government. Twenty-five years of intermittent troubles followed, involving federal officials as well as army personnel, miners, railroad officials, non-Mormon merchants, and a handful of ministers of other Christian faiths. A new crisis developed in the 1880s when federal laws put hundreds of Mormon leaders into prison and threatened to destroy the Mormon Church as a legal institution. The threat was ended by the Manifesto of 1890 that called for the end of the contracting of plural marriages and by a political manifesto that announced the withdrawal of the church from partisan politics.

Conformity to American attitudes and practices, including monogamy, separation of church and state, and *laissez faire* economics, came slowly. Declining isolation brought about first by the gold rush and then by the transcontinental telegraph and railroad, both of which were completed in Utah, increased non-Mormon influences in the territory. The discoveries of precious metals brought many non-Mormons to new boom towns, and some amassed fortunes. A second generation of Mormon leaders, no doubt influenced by their contact with these successful and influential gentiles, began to advocate conformity with American patterns of living. No longer preoccupied with the imminence of Christ's second coming and undifferentiated by the practice of polygamy, these young men helped to prepare the way for statehood, which was finally achieved in January 1896.

Chapter 6
The Rise of the Mormon Kingdom of God

Marvin S. Hill

While the fur men explored the Great Basin, a religious movement began in western New York that would largely determine the history of Utah. In 1830 at Fayette a millennialist group was organized that in less than two decades became one of the ten largest religious denominations in the United States. By choosing to make the Great Basin its central gathering place, The Church of Jesus Christ of Latter-day Saints (Mormons) brought the first permanent white settlers into the vast region. Insight into the nature and early history of the Mormons is basic to understanding what transpired later in Utah.

Origins of Mormon Theocracy

Within the last quarter century historians, anthropologists, and sociologists of religion have made students aware that millennial religions arise during periods of sharp social change and anxiety and that they seek to reorganize and revitalize the social order, bringing into being a new culture as well as a new religion. The Mormons seem to be such a group. Through a series of revelations received by their prophet, many of the individualistic aspects of American capitalism, politics and government, marriage, and other social relationships were restructured to effect a society where religious values transfused every institution and helped promote more effective social control.

Joseph Smith, the founder and central figure of early Mormonism, was the son of an itinerant laborer and farmer by the same name who migrated from Vermont to Palmyra, New York, in 1816 after a succession of economic misfortunes had made it difficult for him to provide for his family. The Smiths were among thousands of New Englanders who moved during this period into western New York, a region alive with social ferment.

The Smith family attended periodic religious revivals, and several members of the family joined the Presbyterian Church. Young Joseph, however, would join neither the Presbyterians nor the Methodists, to whom he was somewhat attracted. According to his account he came away from the revivals disturbed by their contradictory views; it was impossible for him to come to "any conclusion who was right and who was wrong." After some soul searching in 1819 or 1820 he inquired in prayer as to which church in Palmyra he should join; he was informed in a vision not to join any—their professors were "all corrupt," teaching "the commandments of men . . . ."

In thus explaining the origin of the movement, Joseph Smith stressed what was central to his own thinking—a dislike for the religious diversity that characterized nineteenth-century America. Pluralism promoted controversy, and controversy encouraged social conflict, doubt, and disorientation. Many Americans in upstate New York and in Ohio felt similarly; many also feared the emergence of an openly competitive economic order where social rank and individual worth were based on wealth and where acquisitiveness seemed to threaten spiritual values and the sense of community. To offset these tendencies Smith and his followers planned the organization of a social refuge where priesthood leaders under divine inspiration would direct the political, social, and economic, as well as religious, life of the community. Under the direction of their prophet leader, the Mormons sought to eliminate the economic and political reasons for social division by establishing a cooperative economic system, termed the Law of Consecration and Stewardship, and by voting as a group. The collective aspects of Mormon society accounted largely for its success in colonizing the western frontier, but this collectivism also seemed to run counter to the more individualistic orientation of other nineteenth-century Americans. In New York, Ohio, Missouri, and Illinois the Latter-day Saints (as the Mormons were called) found their way of life opposed by "gentiles" whose ultimate recourse to violence necessitated recurring Mormon migrations and their final exodus to Utah.

New York Experiences

Mormonism first gained attention around Palmyra when Joseph Smith announced that he had, under divine guidance, found buried in a hill near his home a history recorded on gold plates, telling of early inhabitants of America who, once Christian, had fallen into apostasy. As a result, their theocratic civilization was destroyed by their enemies, the ancestors of the American Indian. But the record, published in 1830 as the Book of Mormon, was more than a history. It was a "voice from the dust" that warned the living generation that a similar fate awaited them unless they repented and turned to Christ. To the adherents of the new faith a sense of impending judgment seemed to hang over the American people, and this foreboding was the starting point for their peculiar social and political organization. Their early writings were filled with apocalyptic pessimism, deepened by the brutal maltreatment they received at the hands of their neighbors in a succession of locations from New York to Illinois.

The Book of Mormon initially attracted converts to Mormonism, and their increasing numbers made church organization necessary. In 1829, according to Smith, the Aaronic and Melchizedek priesthoods were "restored," soon to be given to male members of what was initially called the Church of Jesus Christ. The officers in the church were given biblical titles such as elder, seventy, deacon, teacher, and bishop. Hostility toward the idea of a "hireling" clergy and working on a voluntary basis quickly became the nucleus of an energetic missionary system.

As head of the church, Joseph Smith was called a "seer, a translator, a prophet, and an apostle of Jesus Christ." While the Saints were committed to the United States Constitution as a divinely inspired document and to the idea of government by the people, they placed greater emphasis on government under God, whose spokesman, the prophet, was their leader. In their church government a sustaining vote of all priesthood leaders was a prerequisite for establishing doctrine and policy, but the underlying ideals were theocratic. The prophet, acting in God's name, made decisions touching every aspect of life. Only rarely did a member disagree or oppose the decisions of the prophet or of other church authorities without experiencing general group disapproval. The principle of theocratic authority was maintained as a hierarchical structure developed over the next several years, headed by a First Presidency of three members, a Quorum of Twelve Apostles, and various High Councils.

The new church, with its jeremiads, its proclamations of apostasy, restoration, *one* true church, and one authoritative priesthood, was deeply resented, and the Mormons—as they soon were called—

had to hold their meetings secretly to avoid persecution. This increasing opposition left them still more alienated from their neighbors and their culture. They were warned in a revelation that "the enemy is combined" and that they should gather and flee; they were also promised by revelation that "in time ye shall have no king nor ruler, for I will be your king and watch over you—wherefore, hear my voice and follow me, and ye shall be a free people, and ye shall have no laws but my laws when I come."

Ohio and Missouri: Social Reorganization and Conflict

After most of the Saints had gone from New York to the vicinity of Kirtland, in northeastern Ohio, and had joined new converts there, "the laws of the kingdom" were given. A number of moral imperatives similar to the Ten Commandments were included in the law, and those unwilling to obey were cast out. Included in the new imperatives was the Law of Consecration and Stewardship. The definitive study by Leonard J. Arrington, Feramorz Y. Fox, and Dean L. May describes the law as a "prescription for transforming the highly individualistic economic order of Jacksonian America into a system characterized by economic equality, socialization of surplus incomes, freedom of enterprise, and group economic self-sufficiency."

The new economic system required that each church member consecrate his property and annual surplus to the bishop of the church (later called the Presiding Bishop), and that the member receive back a portion of that surplus according to his needs. Property thus accumulated by the church was to be used to care for the poor, to buy additional church property, and to assist generally in building up the Kingdom of God. While some of the institutions of capitalism were thus retained, including the allocation of resources according to supply and demand, its purpose was to curb acquisitiveness and competition among the Saints, to pool resources, and to promote social unity. A revelation stated that they were to "be alike . . . and receive alike, that ye may be one."

But not all the Saints were content to part with their property, despite divine injunctions. A prominent member withdrew his consecration of farm land and told the members residing there to move off. Those members who were committed to the law were then commanded to go to western Missouri where missionaries had found converts at Independence. Joseph Smith visited these members in 1831 and designated the area as the site of the New Jerusalem, or Zion, the central gathering place for the church. Here they were instructed to build a temple to which Christ would return in the coming millennium. The charge proved impossible to carry out, but the dream of returning to Jackson County to fulfill this obligation was cherished by many who later helped to build stakes of Zion and other temples in the Intermountain West.

For a year after the prophet's visit, the Mormons in Missouri grew steadily in numbers without any overt hostility displayed by the old settlers. However, some feared that the Saints might monopolize the available grazing land. As more and more immigrants collected, many slave owners became afraid that the Mormons would gain the balance of political power. Some church members offered to sell out and emigrate, but most of the Mormons in the area lacked capital. A few church members unwisely intimated that the Lord had given them Zion (Jackson County) as an everlasting inheritance. Squatters who had occupied and improved land to which they had no legal claim were angry when Mormons gained legal title and demanded the squatters' removal. In addition, the Saints' economic exclusiveness under the Law of Consecration was resented by non-Mormon merchants.

When a Mormon newspaper editor informed free Negroes of the laws that might prevent their immigration into the state, Missourians took this as an open invitation for free blacks to immigrate, and their distrust turned to rage. Planters (who feared the influence of free blacks on their slaves), businessmen, other leaders of the community, and aroused citizens took immediate action to expel the Mormons. The Mormon press was destroyed, and some of the Mormon leaders were beaten. Finding no sympathy when they appealed to the Missouri courts, the Saints were forced in November 1833 to flee to adjoining Clay County.

Mormon leaders sought the intervention of the Missouri governor to recover their lands, but the small contingent of the state militia that the governor sent could not persuade the county judges to allow legal redress. An expeditionary force of Mormons from Kirtland in the spring of 1834, designated "Zion's Camp," was too small to be effective, and the Saints were forced to bide their time. After two years in Clay County, they were requested to leave peacefully and settle in north-central Missouri in a county designated by the state legislature. They established the city of Far West in Caldwell County as their headquarters.

In the process of these relocations the faltering effort to live the Law of Consecration was abandoned. But the memories of the first "United Orders" went west with the Saints and helped motivate several approaches to collectivist economics in the era of Brigham Young.

101

Meanwhile the principal gathering place became Kirtland, and dreams of establishing a large city in Ohio flourished. By the summer of 1835 from 1,500 to 2,000 converts came to Kirtland, providing the Mormons with sufficient numbers to become a political force. The theocratic tendencies that brought politics within the realm of church control also encompassed marriage relationships; in 1835 the Mormon prophet attracted criticism by marrying a couple under the authority of the priesthood rather than by civil power, and reports that Smith himself had begun to practice plural marriage precipitated controversy within the church. Monopolization of land and control over other aspects of the economy also brought opposition. As a means of increasing the money supply and promoting business, Smith organized the Kirtland Anti-Banking Society, but its collapse within a few months caused anti-Mormon activity to increase. Threatened with lawsuits and violence in Kirtland, the prophet fled to Far West early in 1838.

Far West became a center of Mormon gathering, and converts were urged to seek refuge there from the wrath of God soon to be poured out upon the earth. Mormon communities were also established at DeWitt in Carroll County and at Adam-ondi-Ahman in Daviess County. As opposition again manifested itself among land speculators, politicians, and other non-Mormons alarmed by the influx of Latter-day Saints, a wave of apocalyptic fervor spread through Far West. A secret band called *Danites* soon recruited as many as 300 men who were prepared to use violence against external foes and internal dissenters. In a millennialist and militant spirit the first counselor in the First Presidency, Sidney Rigdon, delivered a Fourth of July oration that Joseph Smith endorsed. He told the Saints that calamitous days were imminent, and he informed the Missourians that persecution would be tolerated no longer; should any mob descend upon the Saints "it shall be between us and them a war of extermination."

Political differences added to the tension, and on election day in August in Gallatin a bloody free-for-all erupted that brought in its aftermath a civil war in Daviess County. After a series of forays by armed bands on both sides, Missouri Governor Lilburn W. Boggs declared the Mormons in rebellion and urged their extermination. A band of anti-Mormon militia attacked a settlement at Haun's Mill, killing seventeen and wounding twelve. After this the Saints at Far West were besieged; the prophet sought peace. While he and other church leaders were incarcerated to await trial for treason and murder, the people from Far West and other church settlements fled the state. The extermination order, the massacre at

Haun's Mill, and their general treatment in Missouri remained vivid in Mormon minds and contributed to a growing sense of solidarity and alienation.

Nauvoo: Kingdom on the Mississippi

The fleeing Latter-day Saints were welcomed in Illinois by the citizens of the western part of the state for humanitarian and political reasons. Both Whigs and Democrats went out of their way to befriend the homeless refugees, who thus found themselves again the object of political conflict even before Joseph Smith escaped from Liberty Jail in Missouri in April 1839 and returned to his people. He had encouraged the Saints by letter not to abandon their gathering, arguing against Rigdon and others who urged dispersion. But equally important in sustaining the collectivist impulse were the Twelve Apostles, headed by Brigham Young, who in Smith's absence organized a migration of the poor so that they would not be left in Missouri. The Twelve Apostles thus assumed a role in church leadership second only to the prophet.

Following his arrival in Illinois, Smith, armed with hundreds of petitions, went to Washington to try to persuade the Van Buren administration to compensate the Mormons for their Missouri losses. Smith was told that the matter was a state responsibility and that redress must be sought through Missouri courts. This rejection reinforced Smith's conviction that if the American people were to have a just government, the Saints must take the initiative in providing it. Orson Pratt recorded a Smith prophecy at this time that the United States government could not "stand as it now is but will come so near desolation as to hang as it were by a single hair."

With a sense of urgency the prophet began to establish another refuge for his people. He negotiated with several land owners to secure Illinois and Iowa land north of Quincy on credit. Naming his new headquarters *Nauvoo,* he began publishing a newspaper, the *Times and Seasons,* which advertised the advantages of the new gathering place and recorded progress in erecting private and public houses, mills, and shops. When some of the Saints began experimenting once more with the consecration of private property, Smith quickly objected, denouncing what he called "the folly of common stock." At Nauvoo the system of tithe paying was implemented, while the church depended increasingly on private capital investment as well as tithes of cash, goods, and labor to provide resources for necessary projects.

Pictured is the Joseph Smith homestead in Nauvoo, Illinois, as it looks today.

The transformation of swampland along the Mississippi River into what may have become the largest city in Illinois by 1845 was a remarkable accomplishment.[1] Without any heavy industry or substantial export enterprises, Nauvoo grew to perhaps 12,000 inhabitants on the basis of credit and the exchange of services among the Saints. Construction was the largest industrial activity; housing, commercial buildings, and church-managed public works absorbed labor and the money that was gradually accumulated. The early 1840s were hard times in Illinois and the Middle West, and few of the Saints approached affluence.

The first immigrants resulting from missionary efforts launched in Great Britain arrived in Nauvoo in 1840. Nearly 5,000 British

---

[1]Contemporary estimates of Nauvoo's population went as high as 22,000, but recent historians reduce that figure by as much as 10,000. The tendency to include all the Mormons in Iowa and western Illinois in reckoning the Nauvoo populace accounts for part of the inflation and also underlies the frequently made claim that the Mormon capital was the largest city in the state. Chicago grew spectacularly between 1840 and 1850, and in the absence of reliable census data for the years between, any assertion about which was first must be tentative.

Mormons migrated to America during the next five years, boosting the population of Nauvoo and its outlying settlements by almost a third. To administer to the spiritual and temporal needs of the expanding church, administrative modifications in the roles of stakes (geographic units), high councils, and the Council of the Twelve were made. The creation of geographic subdivisions called *wards,* which were initially both municipal and ecclesiastical units, and the designation of bishops to preside over each set a pattern that would be followed in the Utah settlements.

Developing Opposition in Illinois

With the encouragement and help of John C. Bennett, the quartermaster general of the state militia and an opportunistic new convert, Joseph Smith secured for the city an act of incorporation that gave the Saints considerable legal and military autonomy. Although the charter was similar to others granted in Illinois during this period, requiring that the Mormons obey the constitutions of the United States and of Illinois, it was ambiguous with respect to obedience to the *laws* of the state. Smith took an expansive view of the powers the charter bestowed, maintaining "there is nothing but what we have power over, except where restricted by the Constitution of the United States." A comparably expansive view of home rule was later displayed in the formative years of the Mormon commonwealth in the Great Basin.

As the prophet gradually implemented his concept of Nauvoo sovereignty, protests developed in Hancock County and elsewhere in Illinois. Party politics were also a source of conflict: when the Mormons first arrived in Illinois they voted for the Whig Party candidates, but after the Democrats helped secure the Nauvoo Charter, Smith openly praised their candidate for governor and urged the Saints to sustain Democrat Stephen A. Douglas, for "his friends are our friends." Whig newspapers denounced this "corrupt bargain" and became bitter critics, charging that the Mormons cared only for the well-being of their own group.

In the meantime, a military force was organized under the city charter and Joseph Smith was commissioned by Governor Thomas Carlin as "Lieutenant General" of this Nauvoo Legion. Within six months the Mormons had an army of 1,500 men. While the Legion was ridiculed in some local newspapers, others viewed it with fear. Thomas Sharp, editor of the *Warsaw Signal,* was one of the first to call Smith "a dangerous man."

Important in alienating many Gentiles, as well as some Mormons, in Illinois were some of the new doctrines and rituals that were introduced in Nauvoo. Reflecting the prophet's increasing emphasis on the importance of kinship and family life in the Kingdom of God, the doctrine of baptism for the dead was introduced, tying the Saints to their immediate ancestors. Also initiated was the practice of "sealing" church members to individual church leaders as a means of building loyalty to that leader and as a means of increasing his status in the kingdom. So they could perform these and other sacred rites, the Saints were instructed to build another temple, and to this project impressive contributions of capital and labor were made from 1841 until the city and its crowning structure were abandoned in 1846.

The endowment, a secret ceremony restricted to church members in good standing, was instituted in 1842 in anticipation of the completion of the temple. It became another allegiance-strengthening element in the Latter-day Saint community; most adult members received their endowment before leaving Nauvoo. The endowment also became a factor in alienating apostates and non-Mormons because of similarities between it and some of the rituals of Freemasonry, which had a considerable vogue among the Saints until recognition of the Nauvoo Lodge was withdrawn shortly after Smith's death.

In April 1843 Smith dictated a revelation authorizing plural marriage, which he himself had begun to practice. The revelation held that all contracts made under priesthood authority in accord with the "new and everlasting covenant" endure for eternity. This revelation—the basis for the present-day Mormon doctrine and practice of eternal marriage—also explained that Abraham and other ancient Hebrews received many wives from the Lord and that such a system was justified for Latter-day Saints. Evidence is plentiful that the prophet took care to prevent plural relationships from becoming promiscuous. The institution was family-oriented and was intended to strengthen social and kinship ties in the kingdom. There began to emerge at Nauvoo a small, closely knit, elitist leadership joined together by blood and plural marriage, absolutely committed to the prophet and his program.

Yet the John C. Bennett scandal threatened to rend the kingdom in two in the summer of 1842. Bennett, then mayor of the city and a general in the Legion, was charged by the prophet with attempting to seduce several Nauvoo women, all in the name of the new doctrine. Bennett shortly left the church and fled the city, hastening to publish *The History of the Saints* (1842), which purported to expose Smith's polygamous relationships. The book was widely discussed in Illinois and was generally believed; within the church it was generally discredited, but some who were implicated in its accusations were temporarily or permanently alienated.

The Bennett scandal became public on the eve of statewide elections, and both candidates for governor called for repeal of the Nauvoo Charter. Democrat Thomas Ford was the victor. Whatever his initial intentions may have been with regard to the charter, an incident in Nauvoo forced him to take action. The governor of Missouri sought the extradition of Joseph Smith as an accessory in the attempted murder of ex-governor Boggs. Porter Rockwell, the alleged killer, and the prophet were arrested in Nauvoo by Adams County officials and were then released by the city council on the ground that they were being held for reasons of "religious prejudice." Both men then went into hiding to avoid confrontation with state officials.

Hancock County anti-Mormons like Thomas Sharp were infuriated. Outgoing governor Carlin termed Smith's release a "gross usurpation of power" and said "it cannot be tolerated." In the midst of rising protest, Ford informed the legislature in his inaugural address that the people of the state "anxiously desire that these charters . . . be modified so as to give the inhabitants of Nauvoo no greater privileges than those enjoyed by others of our fellow citizens." The governor thus gave voice to what many Illinois citizens feared: that Mormons stood above ordinary political and legal processes and would be governed only by their own ecclesiastical authorities. The charter, however, was not repealed until January 1845.

Political Conflict, Violence, and Exodus

Relations between Mormons and state citizens continued to deteriorate through 1843 as Missouri efforts to prosecute Smith were frustrated and as Smith encouraged followers to vote in a way that antagonized both Democrats and Whigs. The citizens of Adams and McDonough counties resolved in July that no Mormons were to settle among them and those that had done so must leave. In September a gathering of anti-Mormons at Carthage, the Hancock County seat, called for support not only from Hancock but also from adjoining counties, and they urged Missouri officials to make another extradition request. They also promised military support to apprehend the prophet—countering Mormon theocratic tendencies with threats to go beyond law to violence.

Believing that failure to compensate Mormons for their losses in Missouri constituted a grievous moral lapse that endangered the nation, Joseph Smith announced in January 1844 that he would be a candidate for the American presidency, promising that if elected he would "protect the people in their rights and liberties." He organized a vigorous campaign, instructing all church spokesmen to support his candidacy while proselyting. The *Times and Seasons* warned that the nation was "approaching an awful crisis." "The Lord, the Mighty God," it declared, "has ordained him [Joseph] a deliverer and savior to this generation, if they hear his counsel."

The prophet also sought social control and security in other ways. On March 11, 1844, he organized a Council of Fifty to be the executive, legislative, and judicial arm of the Kingdom of God. This "shadow government" played a leading role in decision-making in Nauvoo, on the trek west, and in Utah. (See chapter 9.) Composed mostly of Mormons, the council made elaborate plans for colonization in Texas or Oregon, where the Saints could have a society imperial in size and ruled by their own government. George Miller, who was a member of the Fifty, said if the prophet won the election the "dominion of the kingdom would be forever established in the United States," but if not they could fall back on Texas or Oregon "and have a kingdom anyway." But the organization of the Fifty was soon whispered in Nauvoo and became a source of open rebellion. The leader of the rebels was William Law, formerly a member of the church's First Presidency.

When some of the dissenters were excommunicated from the church in April they responded by organizing a new church with Law as their prophet. They found friends not only at Warsaw and Carthage, but also at Quincy where a growing number were opposed to Mormonism. The crisis reached a climax in June when the dissenters began the publication of the *Nauvoo Expositor,* the only issue of which denounced the marriage practices and politics of Mormon leadership. Joseph Smith feared the paper would encourage a general apostasy among the Saints and a mob uprising in the county, so as mayor he urged the city council to declare the *Expositor* a public nuisance to be suppressed. Despite some limited opposition Smith had his way, and the newspaper and its press were destroyed.

Up and down the Mississippi River the reaction was immediate and was overwhelmingly against the Mormons. Hundreds flocked to Carthage to determine, as one observer put it, whether the "law should have its corse [sic] on Smith or not." Sharp emotionally editorialized in the *Warsaw Signal:* "War and Extermination is Inevitable, Citizens ARISE ONE AND ALL."

The prophet and his city council were quickly charged at Carthage with promoting a riot. Again unable to act in Nauvoo, the county authorities appealed to Governor Ford who ruled that the Mormons must submit to the processes of the Carthage court. He wrote to Smith that there must be no obstacles to the arrest, neither by *habeas corpus* nor otherwise.

Despairing of a fair trial, Smith fled to Iowa, intending to seek refuge in Far West. But when convinced by his wife and some of the elders that his flight might bring an attack on Nauvoo, he returned and submitted to arrest. There was talk at Carthage on June 26 that Smith's life would be taken, but, disregarding this as rumor, the governor went to Nauvoo on the morning of June 27 to address the Saints and to search for bogus money rumored to be printed there. While Ford was in Nauvoo, members of the Warsaw and Carthage militia broke into the Carthage jail and shot the prophet and his brother Hyrum to death.

Sharp and others implicated in the killing—five of whom were found innocent in a trial at Carthage in May 1845—anticipated that without Joseph Smith the Mormons would disperse. Instead, the controversial living prophet became a martyr for his people, and the commitment to the gathering and the building of the kingdom continued. Despite some controversy over the issue of succession, within a short time a majority of the members of the church rallied around Brigham Young and the Twelve Apostles as they made plans for the future. Temple building was pursued with redoubled vigor even as the prospects for Nauvoo became more bleak. As anti-Mormon activity increased following the Carthage acquittals, Governor Ford informed Young that statewide public sentiment made it impossible for him to properly defend the Mormons. After several episodes of vigilantism and violence, a small force of state militia was sent to Nauvoo to keep peace, but only with the expectation of an early Mormon departure. Young pledged in September 1845 that if the Saints could sell their land and houses at an acceptable price, they would leave Illinois when "grass grows and water runs." The fulfillment of that pledge is the subject of another chapter.

The Kingdom of God in Retreat

Although the Latter-day Saints still retained deep loyalties toward the United States and its republican form of government, they believed that they were leaving a nation on the brink of ruin. Brigham Young wrote in the *Times and Seasons* in November 1845: "The direful eruption must take place. It required not the spirit of

109

prophecy to see it." Orson Pratt wrote to the Saints in the eastern states to "be determined to get out from this evil nation . . . be determined to flee out of Babylon. . . . Judgment is at the door."

Fused into one mind and one spirit by their common ideals and common adversities, the Mormons had become a "peculiar people," a people whose sense of identity had become so intense that one astute student, Thomas F. O'Dea, called it "incipient nationalism." George Whitaker spoke the mind of the Saints on the eve of the exodus from Nauvoo when he said, "We are going to a better country where we can live in peace, free from mobs and strife, where we could worship God according to our own conscience, none to molest or make us afraid." He might have added that they departed a singularly united and committed people, ideally suited to conquer and govern a vast frontier.

Thus it was that the Mormon experience in the Middle West shaped what was to come in Utah. Millennialist in orientation, certain that man-made institutions would shortly fail, the Latter-day Saints sought virtual independence through mutual cooperation under uniquely theocratic leadership. Their peculiar beliefs, their new revelations, and their social order that brought civil, political, and social matters under direct church control, had already proved appealing to many Americans as well as European converts and had stood the test of severe challenge from non-Mormons. Now there would be an opportunity to apply the social order in an environment where the Saints would be the majority of the population. Church domination of local government, including legislatures and courts, would follow the theocratic pattern. Economically, the practice of cooperative enterprise and centrally planned activities would be expanded. Socially, plural marriage would play an increasing role in the Mormon life-style; and religiously, the temple ceremonies formulated at Nauvoo would influence much of Mormon thinking. Ecclesiastical organizations developed in Ohio, Missouri, and Illinois would expand and adapt to serve and direct the tens of thousands of converts who would flock to the intermountain Zion.

The establishment of the Mormon Kingdom of God in the Great Basin and its ultimate accommodation to secular political, economic, and social pressures and influences would prove to be the central theme in the history of Utah.

Chapter 6
Bibliographical Essay

The sources on early Mormonism are legion, but not all are of equal worth. A convenient point of departure into almost any phase is James B. Allen and Glen M. Leonard, *The Story of the Latter-day Saints* (1976); this volume provides a sound historical survey and a selective but extensive, classified, and up-to-date critical bibliography of books, articles, and unpublished studies. General works such as Joseph Smith's *History of The Church of Jesus Christ of Latter-day Saints,* ed. by Brigham H. Roberts, 7 vols., and his other published writings are basic; they are available in many editions. Brigham H. Roberts, *A Comprehensive History of The Church of Jesus Christ of Latter-day Saints: Century I* (1930), 6 vols., devotes most of its first three volumes to the Joseph Smith era.

A biography of Joseph Smith that has considerable limitations is Fawn M. Brodie's *No Man Knows My History* (1946, rev. ed. 1971). A necessary corrective is Marvin S. Hill's "Secular or Sectarian History: A Critique of *No Man Knows My History,*" *Church History,* March 1974. A biography by Donna Hill, *Joseph Smith The First Mormon* (1977), is based on extensive research and is less critical of Smith. Also helpful in reassessing Smith are many articles appearing in *BYU Studies,* beginning with the Spring 1969 issue; *Dialogue: A Journal of Mormon Thought,* beginning with the first issue in 1966; and the publication of the Mormon History Association, *Journal of Mormon History,* since 1974.

On the origins and nature of early Mormonism, Mario DePillis' "Quest for Religious Authority and the Rise of Mormonism," *Dialogue,* Fall 1966, is important for the theme developed in this chapter. Stress is placed on Mormon apocalyptics and antipluralism in Marvin S. Hill's "The Role of Christian Primitivism in the Origin and Development of the Mormon Kingdom, 1830-1844" (Ph.D. dissertation, University of Chicago, 1968). On Mormonism in New York see the Spring 1969 issue of *BYU Studies* for the introductory essay by Leonard J. Arrington and James B. Allen and for Marvin S. Hill, "The Shaping of the Mormon Mind in New England and New York."

Kirtland has been studied with insight by Robert Kent Fielding in "The Growth of the Mormon Church in Kirtland, Ohio" (Ph.D. dissertation, Indiana University, 1957). This can be supplemented by such other works as Max H. Parkin, *Conflict at Kirtland* (1967), which illuminates the causes of strife, and Willis Thornton, "Gentile and Saint at Kirtland," *Ohio Archeological and Historical Quarterly,* January 1954, which adds to understanding of the political issues. See also Marvin S. Hill, Larry T. Wimmer, and Keith Rooker, "The Kirtland Economy Revisited: A Market Critique of Sectarian Economics," published by the Charles Redd Center for Western Studies at Brigham Young University.

The Law of Consecration and Stewardship has been quite thoroughly studied by Leonard J. Arrington, Feramorz Y. Fox, and Dean L. May in *Building the City of God* (1976). No satisfactory study of the origins of the temple ordinances or plural marriage exists; works on polygamy as it developed in Utah are cited in the bibliographies for chapters 15 and 17.

The best study of early Missouri is Warren A. Jennings, "Zion Is Fled: The Expulsion of the Mormons from Jackson County, Missouri" (Ph.D. dissertation, University of Florida, 1962), which covers more ground than the title would suggest. No comparable work exists for the later years in Missouri, but Leland Gentry's "History of the Latter-day Saints in Northern Missouri from 1838 to 1839" (Ph.D. dissertation, Brigham Young University, 1965) is crammed with useful sources.

Robert B. Flanders' *Nauvoo: Kingdom on the Mississippi* (1965) is excellent. Also informative is David E. and Della S. Miller's *Nauvoo: The City of Joseph* (1974). For an interpretive essay on the general relationship between Mormon social aims and religious values and their quest for refuge, see Marvin S. Hill, "Mormon Religion in Nauvoo: Some Reflections," *UHQ*, Summer 1975. Klaus J. Hansen, *Quest for Empire: The Political Kingdom of God and the Council of Fifty in Mormon History* (1967), is an important interpretive study that spans the Illinois and early Utah phases of kingdom building. Dennis Michael Quinn's "Mormon Heirarchy, 1832-1932: An American Elite" (Ph.D. dissertation, Yale University, 1976) challenges many accepted views of this subject.

There is no fully adequate study of anti-Mormonism, either in Illinois or in any other state. Important for politics is Thomas Ford's *History of Illinois* (1854). Dallin H. Oaks and Marvin S. Hill, *Carthage Conspiracy: The Trial of the Accused Assassins of Joseph Smith* (1975), throws much light on anti-Mormon attitudes as they related to Smith's killing and the expulsion of the Saints from Illinois.

Chapter 7
The Mormon Migrations
To Utah

Eugene E. Campbell

As the preceding chapters have detailed, until 1847 Utah was a wilderness, inhabited by small bands of Indians and traversed periodically by Spanish missionaries and traders, American and British fur trappers, government explorers, and California-bound pioneers. But the Mormons quickly changed that pattern. Although their church had been organized for only seventeen years, it had several thousand members and a proselyting and emigrating system geared to bring many thousands more to its "Zion" in the mountains. The Mormons also had a history of persecution and a body of beliefs and practices—including polygamy and theocratic government—that would make the Utah story unique in the annals of the American West.

Why Utah?

Some years after colonizing Utah, one of the Mormon leaders said humorously, "We came here willingly because we had to." Yet there were other places they might have gone. Texas, California, Oregon, Vancouver Island, and Canada were all suggested as possible locations for the unpopular Saints. While Joseph Smith was still alive, he predicted that his people would go to the Rocky Mountains; he made some preparations to seek out an acceptable location there, but failed to send out an exploring party. He sent representatives to investigate Texas while it was an independent nation, and he offered to provide the United States government with a force to occupy and settle Oregon, so apparently he was not exclusively committed to the mountains. His untimely death at the hands of an Illinois mob left it for other men to determine the new home for his followers.

Brigham Young and his associates made the definite commitment to move west in 1845 when it became apparent that the Mormons could not survive peaceably in Nauvoo. Late in the summer they resolved to send a pioneering company to Great Salt Lake Valley, a clear indication of one direction of their thinking. The plan was not carried out, but during the winter of 1845–46 active preparations were made for a mass migration. The church leaders spent winter evenings listening to one of their number read from Fremont's 1843–44 journal and from Hastings' *Emigrants' Guide to Oregon and California*, while the *Nauvoo Neighbor* supplied the church members with information concerning the Far West.

The following circular from the Nauvoo High Council, published in the January 20, 1846, *Times and Seasons*, alerted the Saints to where, when, and why they were going:

TO THE MEMBERS OF THE CHURCH OF JESUS CHRIST OF LATTER-DAY SAINTS, AND TO ALL WHOM IT MAY CONCERN: GREETINGS.

Beloved Brethren and Friends:—We the members of the High Council of the Church, . . . embrace this opportunity to inform you, that we intend to send out into the Western country from this place, some time in the early part of the month of March, a Company of Pioneers, consisting mostly of young, hardy men, with some families. These are destined to be furnished with an ample outfit; taking with them a printing press, farming utensils of all kinds, with mill irons and bolting cloths, seeds of all kinds, grain, etc.

The object of this early move is to put in a spring crop, to build houses, and to prepare for the reception of families who will start as soon as grass shall be sufficiently grown to sustain teams and stock.

Our Pioneers are instructed to proceed West until they find a good place to make a crop, in some good valley in the neighborhood of the Rocky Mountains, where they will infringe upon no one, and be not likely to be infringed upon. Here we will make a resting place, until we can determine a place for a permanent location. In the event of the [U.S.] president's recommendation to build block houses and stockade forts on the route to Oregon, becoming a law, we have encouragements of having that work to do; and under our peculiar circumstances we can do it with less expense to the government than any other people. . . .

Should hostilities arise between the government of the United States and any other power, in relation to the right of possessing the territory of Oregon, we are on hand to sustain the claim of the United States government to that country. It is geographically ours; and of right, no foreign power should hold dominion there, and if our services are required to prevent it, those services will be cheerfully rendered according to our ability.

The patriotic tone of the letter suggests that the ultimate choice of a home for the Mormons was perhaps contingent upon the outcome of the Polk administration expansionist projects and the government's response to Mormon overtures. The location of the proposed "resting place" was somewhat indefinite and possibly temporary, giving encouragement to Samuel Brannan and others who were interested in settling in California.

The "Brooklyn" Saints

The Mormons in the eastern states had meanwhile been making preparations to go to California by sea. On November 8, 1845, the *New York Messenger*, a church newspaper, carried an announcement made by Apostle Orson Pratt that led 238 Mormons to sail on the ship *Brooklyn* from New York City to San Francisco by way of Cape Horn. It read in part:

The time is at hand for me to take a long and last farewell to these eastern countries, being included with my family, among tens of thousands of American citizens who have a choice of death or banishment beyond the Rocky Mountains. I have preferred the latter. It is with the greatest joy that I forsake this Republic; and all of the Saints have abundant reason that they are counted worthy to be cast out as exiles from this wicked nation. . . .

Brethren, awake!! Be determined to get out of this evil nation by next spring. We do not want one saint to be left in the United States by that time. Let every branch in the north, south, east, and west be determined to flee Babylon, either by land or by sea. . . .[1]

Samuel Brannan, the last editor of the short-lived *Messenger,* was placed in charge of the sea migration. Although he had no previous experience as a Mormon official, he was able to stock the *Brooklyn* with agricultural and mechanical equipment as well as dry goods, books, and a printing press. Evidence indicates that he acquired these supplies through a deal made with A. G. Benson and Company, in which he promised these land speculators every alternate section and city lot that the Saints might acquire in the West. This proposed contract was rejected by the church leadership.

---

[1] It should be noted that the letter from the Nauvoo High Council was much more patriotic in tone than Pratt's announcement. Rhetorical outbursts such as Pratt's were not uncommon during early periods of Mormon persecution, but there seems to have been a basic Mormon commitment to the United States as long as it did not conflict with their concept of obligation to the Kingdom of God.

A storm delayed the ship's departure, and it is only a coincidence that the *Brooklyn* cleared New York harbor on February 4, 1846—the same day that the first company left Nauvoo. The voyage was a reasonably pleasant one, punctuated by two severe storms, the deaths of ten voyagers, the births of two children christened Atlantic and Pacific, and some discipline problems that led to the excommunication of four prominent members. While in Honolulu they discovered that the United States was on the verge of war with Mexico and that their destination might well be a war zone. They made active military preparations, but found northern California under the control of American forces when they landed in Yerba Buena (San Francisco) on July 31, 1846.

After a few weeks in the Bay Area, Brannan detailed a company to begin an agricultural colony near the junction of the Stanislaus and San Joaquin rivers, near present-day Modesto, in preparation for the coming of the main body of the Saints. In April 1847 this ambitious young leader and two companions rode through the Sierras en route to Fort Hall and the Oregon Trail. At the Green River they met the advance company of Mormon pioneers on June 30. Brannan followed them into Salt Lake Valley and participated in the early exploration of the region. On August 9 he left for California, convinced that the church leaders had made a mistake in stopping in the Great Basin. Meeting some eastbound members of the Mormon Battalion near Donner Lake, he told them, as Daniel Tyler remembered:

The saints could not possibly subsist in the Great Salt Lake Valley, as according to the testimony of the mountaineers, it froze there every month in the year, and the ground was too dry to sprout seeds without irrigation, and irrigated with the cold mountain streams the seeds planted would be chilled and prevented from growing; . . . He considered it no place for an agricultural people, and expressed his confidence that the saints would emigrate to California the next spring. On being asked if he had given his views to President Brigham Young he answered that he had. On further inquiry as to how his views were received he said in substance that the president laughed and made some rather insignificant remark, "but," said Brannan, "when he has fairly tried it, he will find that I was right and he was wrong, and will come to California."

As he stopped at Sutter's Fort, Brannan rented a place for a store, hardly anticipating that gold would be discovered nearby a few months later, and that he would become California's first millionaire. Brannan never returned to Utah. Only a few of his group left California to help build the Mormon kingdom in the Great

116

Basin, although many of them later helped establish a church colony at San Bernardino.

Nauvoo to Winter Quarters

Although the high council circular indicated that the first departures from Nauvoo would be early in March, the first contingent of Mormon emigrés crossed the Mississippi on February 4, 1846. Continuing vigilante pressure by the citizens of neighboring communities, who found it difficult to believe that the Saints were really planning to leave the temple that they were still constructing, had built up during the winter. The premature departure was apparently precipitated by efforts of federal officials to arrest church leaders on ill-founded charges of counterfeiting money and by rumors that federal troops might interfere with the planned move west. In consequence, some Mormons left before their preparations were complete.

Tradition notwithstanding, mobs did not chase the Saints down to the river's edge at the first exodus, nor was Nauvoo under siege at the time. Neither is it true that the Mississippi River froze over "for the first time in history" to allow the refugees easy passage. Eliza R. Snow's account that "nine babes were born that first night at Sugar Creek" may have been based on the experience of the "poor camp" refugees in September; there was no pressing reason for expectant mothers to leave the relative comforts of Nauvoo to bear their children under such difficult circumstances. Brigham Young remained in Nauvoo until February 15 and returned later in the month for several days, while many other members of the church stayed in Nauvoo through the spring and early summer. The last six or seven hundred destitute Saints who became the "poor camp" were driven out of Nauvoo by a guerrilla force in September.

The early departure caused considerable suffering and made the trek across Iowa unduly difficult. What was intended to be a well-planned and orderly exodus became a near disaster. Unprepared families, fearful of being left behind, delayed the advance company and necessitated the sharing of equipment and supplies. Cold weather and spring thaws added to the problems occasioned by insufficient organization and inadequate provisions, more than offsetting the advantages of traveling through a partially settled prairie-country.

Pursuant to plans, the leaders with the advance company established resting and supply stations at Garden Grove, halfway across Iowa, and at Mount Pisgah, twenty-five miles farther west. They planted and fenced crops and built shelters for the benefit of those who were following. On April 15, learning that his frail wife, Diantha, had safely borne a son back in Nauvoo, William Clayton wrote the words to his now-famous hymn, "Come, Come, Ye Saints."

The slow and difficult progress across Iowa forced the Mormon leaders to reconsider their plan to continue on to the Great Basin in 1846. They had voted to send an advance party to the Bear River Valley, but the call of the Mormon Battalion plus the general exhaustion of the migrants made an advance party infeasible. Since they now had government permission to camp on Indian lands, they decided to establish settlements on the Missouri River that could serve as outfitting points for those journeying to the Great Basin in 1847 and the years following. Kanesville (Council Bluffs) on the Iowa side ultimately became an important Mormon colony, while Winter Quarters, a few miles north of the present site of Omaha on the west bank, became the temporary headquarters of the Mormon Church. By the end of 1846 more than 3,500 people were housed in dugouts and log cabins at Winter Quarters.

The Mormon Battalion

Since his inauguration in March 1845, President James K. Polk had received several requests from Mormon representatives for aid in their proposed westward migration, but he had not responded. When war with Mexico broke out in May 1846, Polk saw an opportunity to give Mormons help while securing their services for the country. Responding to suggestions from Jesse C. Little, a church agent, and Thomas L. Kane, the prominent, idealistic, and somewhat eccentric young Pennsylvanian who was just beginning his self-appointed career as "friend of the Mormons," Polk authorized Colonel (later General) Stephen W. Kearny to "receive into the service as volunteers a few hundred of the Mormons who are now on their way to California, with a view to conciliate them, attach them to our country, and prevent them from taking part against us." This action was meant to be a favor, for there were more volunteers than the Army of the West could accept, and Kearny had no real need for the Mormon troops. Although Brigham Young said he "would rather have undertaken to raise two thousand men a year ago in twenty-four hours than one hundred in one week now," he realized that there would be many advantages from such a voluntary enlistment. Reassuring the skeptical and fearful Saints, he actively aided in recruiting the 549 men who became the Mormon Battalion.

Captain James Allen, who represented the army as recruiter and who also served as the first commander of the battalion, was able to make some unusual and important concessions to the Mormons. He promised the Mormon leaders that their people could remain on government lands, and this agreement was ratified by Indian leaders. Allen also promised the volunteers that they would not be divided among other military units, that they could choose their own company officers, that they would be sent to California, that they could be accompanied by their wives and children if they desired, and that some of the wives would be hired as laundresses. The battalion was also permitted to accept forty-two dollars in cash apiece in lieu of a uniform allowance, thus providing a sizable fund to aid the Saints in their westward migration.[2]

The battalion left Council Bluffs on July 20, 1846, and marched over two thousand miles in a little over five months. (See map, p. 729.) Sickness and then death claimed Captain Allen at Fort Leavenworth, and the march to Santa Fe was complicated by command problems and poor morale. Most of the women and children and approximately 150 of the men who were slowed by sickness separated from the main body before or shortly after it reached the newly captured New Mexican capital. There Lieutenant Colonel Philip St. George Cooke took command of the troop.

The three "sick detachments" went to the site of present-day Pueblo, Colorado, where they spent the winter with a contingent of forty-three Mormons from Mississippi. These Saints had made their way to Fort Laramie during the summer of 1846, expecting to join the migration to the Great Basin. Discovering that the movement had been postponed a year, they sought a wintering place and learned of some fur trappers' cabins near the headwaters of the Arkansas River. Communication of this information to the Mormon Battalion led to the sending of the ill soldiers and noncombatants to wait there also. The Pueblo community thus numbered 287 Mormons during the 1846-47 winter. Seventeen of them met Young's advance party of pioneers at Fort Laramie and accompanied them into Salt Lake Valley in 1847. The rest arrived in Salt Lake Valley on July 29.

---

[2]It is unfortunate that the belief became prevalent among the Mormons that the call of the Mormon Battalion was an act of persecution by the federal government and that only the loyal response by the battalion members saved the church from destruction. This belief was emphasized at the first reunion of the battalion veterans in 1855, when they chose as their theme, "A Ram in the Thicket," comparing themselves to the sacrificial ram in the Old Testament story of Abraham and Isaac.

This view of Nauvoo as seen from the opposite bank of the Mississippi River is the work of Henry Lewis; it is of special interest because it shows the completed temple on the hill, numerous buildings and mills on the lower land and river front, and a Mississippi River island now covered by the waters backed up behind the Keokuk Dam.

The remaining 350 battalion men and the five women who stayed with them reached San Diego on January 29, 1847, just two weeks after the last battle of the Mexican War was fought in California. Their trek had been arduous, but they had not fired a shot at a hostile soldier. After serving as occupation troops in Los Angeles, San Diego, and other parts of southern California, the soldiers were discharged. Eighty-five men reenlisted for another eight-month term and the others, numbering about 260, made plans to join their families and friends in the Great Basin. After meeting

Brannan and Brown at Donner Lake, about half of the veterans chose to seek winter employment in California, and six of these participated in the discovery of gold at Coloma on January 24, 1848. Several others were among the first to prospect for gold in that region. Most of the battalion veterans came into Salt Lake Valley in small groups during October and November 1847. The knowledge that they had gained and the income that they had generated were significant in the success of the colonizing enterprise in Salt Lake Valley.

Winter Quarters to Salt Lake Valley

The winter of 1846–47 at Kanesville and Winter Quarters was spent in active preparation for the movement of the main body of Saints to the Rocky Mountains. On Christmas Day the Council of Fifty decided to send a pioneer company to choose a definite site for the initial settlement; the company would shortly be followed by as many families as were prepared to go. This readiness was to include eighteen months' provisions.

In an official announcement on January 14, 1847, called "The Word and Will of the Lord," Brigham Young indicated the type of organization that would be followed to avoid the difficulties experienced in the evacuation of Nauvoo. The members continued to be formed into semimilitary divisions with captains over hundreds, fifties, and tens, with a president and two counselors at the head, under the general direction of the Twelve Apostles. They were required to covenant to keep the "commandments of the Lord our God," and to share in caring for the widows, the fatherless, the poor, and the families of those who had gone into the army. It was to be a cooperative venture in the spirit of Christian brotherhood.

The pioneer company, originally composed of 144 men, was changed at the last moment when one of the men returned to Winter Quarters because of sickness. Three women, Clarissa Decker Young, Ellen Sanders Kimball, and Harriet Page Wheeler Young, wives of Brigham Young, Heber C. Kimball, and Lorenzo Dow Young respectively, were permitted to travel with their husbands. Two sons of Harriet Young, one by a former husband and one by Lorenzo Young, accompanied their mother. (Clarissa Young was also a daughter of Harriet.) Stephen Markham and A. P. Rockwood were appointed captains of hundreds; Addison Everett, Tarlton Lewis, James Case, John Pack, and Shadrach Roundy were named captains of fifty, which appears a bit superfluous in a group of less than 150. A military organization, derived from the

Nauvoo Legion, was superimposed on the "revealed order of march," with Brigham Young as lieutenant general, Markham as colonel, and Pack and Roundy as majors. Another interesting aspect of the company was the presence of three Negro slaves, Hark Lay, Green Flake, and Oscar Crosby.

The first elements of the advance company moved out from Winter Quarters on April 5, 1847; the remainder soon followed. They chose to stay on the north side of the Platte River in order to avoid competition for forage and wood with the emigrants on the Oregon Trail across the river. (See map, p. 729.) The trip to Fort Laramie was pleasant, although the pioneers had to be on guard against Indian depredations, and the pioneers experienced some difficulties with huge herds of buffalo. Orson Pratt, who had brought scientific instruments from Europe, made careful calculations of the elevations as well as observations of the flora and fauna along the route. William Clayton, after attempting to measure distances by counting the revolutions of a wagon wheel, collaborated with Pratt and Appleton Harmon in constructing an odometer to keep track of the distances covered each day.

After crossing the North Platte River near Fort Laramie, the pioneer group met seventeen of the Mississippi Saints, who gave them detailed news of the battalion sick detachments at Pueblo. They also learned of the large number of people moving west on the Oregon Trail. In anticipation of the numerous Mormon companies to follow, the leaders decided to build a ferryboat capable of carrying loaded wagons across the North Platte east of the mouth of Sweetwater River, near present Casper, Wyoming. This venture proved to be profitable since hundreds of Oregon and California emigrants were willing to pay for ferrying service over the next several years.

On June 26 the company met Moses "Black" Harris, a fur trapper and trader, who gave them a great deal of information about the Great Basin; most of it was discouraging as far as prospects for a permanent colony were concerned. He did recommend Cache Valley as the most likely place for a successful settlement, and also informed them that the Great Salt Lake had no outlet. Harris left his company and traveled with the Saints through South Pass the following day. At their evening camp on June 26 they met Thomas "Peg-leg" Smith, another mountain man, who also encouraged them to go to Cache Valley. James Bridger and two companions met the Mormons on June 28 at the Little Sandy River. His view of the Great Basin was much more favorable than that of Harris or Smith, but he thought it would be unwise to take large numbers of people to the Great Basin until it had been proved that crops could be raised in the area. Bridger's report of the area around Utah Lake was enthusiastic.[3]

Two days later Samuel Brannan met the advance party at the Green River crossing; he had copies of his newspaper and information about California. He followed Young's group to Salt Lake Valley, but, as earlier noted, he was unable to induce them to continue on to the coast. After reaching Fort Bridger on July 7, the pioneers left the Oregon Trail and followed Hastings Cutoff. While encamped near Bear River on July 10, they met Miles Goodyear. He acknowledged that garden vegetables were doing well at an out-of-the-way trading post on the Weber River at present Ogden, but he was pessimistic about the Mormon proposal to colonize Salt Lake Valley.

Near this point Young became severely ill with "mountain fever" and was unable to advance with the company. Orson Pratt, with twenty-three wagons and forty-two men, was sent ahead to locate the Donner-Reed Trail. (See map, p. 728.) After traversing Echo Canyon to present-day Henefer, Pratt and John Brown rode down Weber Canyon for several miles before deciding against that route. Later that day they found the Donner-Reed tracks, and by July 19 the advance party reached the summit of Big Mountain, where they could see over a great extent of country. Pratt and Brown climbed farther than their companions and were able to see portions of Salt Lake Valley. Two days later Pratt and Erastus Snow were the first of the pioneer company to enter the valley, having followed the Donner Trail over Little Mountain, down Emigration Canyon, and over Donner Hill. With only one horse, the two men took turns walking and riding over major portions of the valley before returning to the vanguard camp in the canyon.

On July 22 the first wagons moved downstream toward the mouth of Emigration Canyon. Finding the route over Donner Hill quite unsatisfactory for a permanent road, the Mormons spent four hours cutting a new road around the north end of Donner Hill to rejoin the Donner tracks on the high ground north of present Hogle Zoo. This stretch of less than a half-mile was the only piece of original road the Mormon pioneers were required to build.

---

[3]The story that Bridger offered $1,000 for the first bushel of corn grown in the Salt Lake Valley has been altered in the *Journal History* to read that "Bridger would give $1,000 if he only knew if we could raise an ear of corn."

Shortly after noon on July 22 the wagons of the vanguard rolled into Salt Lake Valley, following the Donner tracks southwestward to a campsite in the vicinity of present 500 East between 1700 and 2100 South streets. During that same day Orson Pratt and eight others conducted an extensive examination of the area to locate the best site for plowing and planting. The nine horsemen reported to the camp that evening that the spot lay a couple of miles to the north. So on the following morning, July 23, Pratt guided the wagons to a point on the east bank of City Creek near present 400 South and Main streets. Plowing was begun at once. In a solemn prayer that evening, Pratt dedicated the land as a place for the future home of the Saints.

The remaining wagons, including Brigham Young's, entered the valley on July 24, 1847. When Young, the president of the Quorum of the Twelve, rose from his sick bed in Wilford Woodruff's carriage (at a point not far from the "This is the Place" monument) and uttered some version of the now-famous words, "This is the right place," the location had already been identified and dedicated; irrigation, plowing, and planting were well under way.

Selection of the Western "Resting Place"

When, then, was the decision made to establish the initial colony in Salt Lake Valley? As early as August 23, 1845, the Council of the Twelve approved a 3,000-man expedition to the valley and the Council of Fifty later worked on plans for a smaller pioneer company of 1,000. Other announcements that fall indicated a plan to go somewhere west of the Rocky Mountains, but the announcements were not specific on the location. The high council circular of January 20, 1846, suggested "some valley in the neighborhood" of the mountains.

Father Pierre Jean De Smet, the pioneer Oregon missionary, wrote many years later concerning his meeting the Mormons near Council Bluffs in 1846, where he answered questions concerning the basin of the Great Salt Lake. He wondered if his information might have been a determining factor in the choice of that valley, a speculation that has intrigued historians because there is no firm evidence that De Smet ever entered Utah. However, as late as June 6, 1847, Brigham Young sent a letter to Samuel Brannan via Fort Hall that indicated that his mind was not made up at that time. He wrote that "the leaders planned to settle . . . west of the mountains, perhaps in the Great Basin. . . . The camp will not go to the West Coast or to your place at present; they have not the means."

It seems likely that Young decided on Salt Lake Valley after talking to Harris, Smith, and Bridger. Goodyear also gave helpful information. By the time the pioneer company reached Fort Bridger, the valley had definitely become the goal. However, it should be remembered that Young had visions of a great empire, and the choice of Salt Lake Valley did not eliminate other valleys, or even California and Oregon, as additional gathering places for the Latter-day Saints.

Later Arrivals and Departures

The detachments of the Mormon Battalion and the rest of the Mississippi Saints from Pueblo arrived in the valley five days after the pioneer group. Brigham Young and the other apostles remained only long enough to establish the colony before beginning their return trip to Winter Quarters. Twenty-four pioneers and forty-six battalion men left the valley on August 16 and were followed in ten days by Young's company of 107 persons.

Discharged members of the battalion began arriving from California in the fall, and additional large companies began arriving from Winter Quarters. Apostles Parley P. Pratt and John Taylor were the leaders of four companies, totaling approximately 1,500 people, who followed the pioneer party westward in 1847. They met Brigham Young and his returning group on Sweetwater River and received welcome news concerning the Salt Lake settlement. Their arrival at the new site in October increased the total to more than 1,650 people who wintered in the valley. (Approximately 230 of those who had arrived during the summer returned to Missouri or California before winter set in.)

Young, who after December 1847 was the head of a newly organized Mormon First Presidency, led the migration that came in three large divisions from Winter Quarters to Salt Lake City in 1848. Battalion veterans returning from San Diego and the gold fields helped to bring the valley population to approximately 4,000 by the year's end. Before the organized Mormon migration ended forty years later, some 80,000 Saints completed the trek west—and an estimated 6,000 died along the way.

Life in the Valley

The first days in the valley were spent in farming, in home building, and in exploring the neighboring valleys. "As if by force of habit," according to Leonard Arrington's *Great Basin Kingdom,* "the advance company was divided into cadres or committees for work." One group staked out, plowed, harrowed, and irrigated thirty-five acres, planting potatoes, corn, buckwheat, beans, turnips, and other garden produce. Another group laid out a city in 135 ten-acre blocks, with a site for the temple in the center. Others were assigned to build cabins and a fort, "sixty to hoke, twelve to mould and twenty to put up walls." A public adobe yard was established, an adobe wall was constructed around the three open sides of the fort, and within a month twenty-nine log houses were built within.

Another committee of the advance party located timber in a nearby canyon, constructed a road, extracted logs for the cabins, and dug a pit for a whipsaw. A boat was made for use on the streams, a blacksmith shop was set up, corrals were built, and a community storehouse was erected. Others were assigned to hunt, to try their luck at fishing in the mountain streams, and to extract salt from the Great Salt Lake. In eight days their combined efforts netted "one hare, one badger, one white wolf, and three sage hens," four fish, 125 bushels of coarse salt, and a barrel of "fine white table salt." Within eight days of the initial planting, Stephen Markham reported that "about three acres of corn was up two inches above ground and beans and potatoes were up and looking well." Such phenomenal growth seemed to justify the plan to establish the Saints permanently in the area.

Luckily for the colonists, the first winter proved to be a mild one. John Taylor, writing on December 7, 1847, reported that his group had been plowing "almost incessantly," and had been successful in planting 2,000 acres of fall wheat. The next summer Parley P. Pratt reported to his brother—Orson was by then back in England—that:

... the winter was mild and pleasant, several light snows soon melted off. The cattle did well all winter in the pasture without being fed. Horses, sheep and cattle, were in better order in the spring than they were when we arrived, I mean those which were not kept up and worked or milked, but suffered to live where there was grass.

The spring planting of grain and garden crops also showed promise. Unfortunately, late frosts destroyed a considerable portion of the spring wheat and vegetables, and at the same time millions of crickets began to invade the fields. Harriet Young wrote:

[May] 29th: Last night we had a severe frost. Today the crickets have commenced on our corn and small grain. They have eaten off 12 acres for Brother Rosacrants, 7 for Charles and are now taking Edmunds.

Today 29th: They have destroyed 3/4 of an acre of squashes, our flax,

*two acres of millet and our rye, and are now to work in our wheat. What
will be the result we know not.*

In the circumstances, some Saints despaired of surviving in the
valley. After two weeks of fighting the voracious insects, the pioneers were somewhat relieved to gain an ally in their battle when
thousands of white-winged gulls landed in the fields and began to
devour the pests. The gulls helped stem the tide of cricket devastation, and their coming has since been regarded as a miracle by
many, although little was said about it at the time. Perhaps the
fact that the frost had destroyed so much and that the gulls left
before the crickets were eliminated muted the Saints' enthusiasm.
Similar aid by the seagulls in subsequent years has all but been ignored in Utah folklore.

Despite these setbacks a partial crop was harvested in July and
August. The Salt Lake High Council issued an epistle on August 9
in which they enthused over the fertility of the soil and claimed
that the wheat harvest had exceeded expectations. Parley Pratt reported that they would raise ten or twenty thousand bushels of
grain above what would be consumed by the present inhabitants
of the valley.

Pratt's estimate may have been valid for the "present inhabitants," but the needs of the additional thousands who came to
the Salt Lake Valley in 1848 and the long, cold winter of 1848–49
put a severe strain on the resources of the colony. It was this second winter that gave the settlers their hardest test. Many of them
were reduced to eating rawhide, sego lily roots, and thistles,
although vigorous efforts were made by the church leaders to encourage sharing of foodstuff. Bishops of the nineteen ecclesiastical
wards requested that those with surplus food turn it in for distribution among the needy. In February 1849 a survey was made
and rations were set at three-fourths of a pound of breadstuff per
person per day.

No one starved during this period, but it is not likely that anyone gained weight. Some decided to quit the valley and seek a
new life in California. The news of the discovery of gold probably
added to the dissatisfaction of some, but remarkably few left to be
among the first of the Fortyniners. Doubtless President Young's
blunt counsel against such a move had considerable influence.

Early Explorations

Although the major effort of the first two years was, of necessity,
to establish a base of operations in Salt Lake Valley, the Mormon

leaders did not neglect the task of seeking other places for settlement. Young indicated on the day he arrived in the valley that "he intended to make every hole and corner from the bay of San Francisco" known to the Mormons. Every explorer was expected to determine the natural resources of places visited, including water supply, soil fertility, availability of timber and other building materials, altitude of surrounding mountains, and presence of minerals.

As one would expect, Salt Lake Valley and those valleys nearby were explored first. On July 26 nine men were chosen to accompany Young to such places as the warm springs and Ensign Peak. The following day a group that included eight apostles and Samuel Brannan traveled to the southern tip of the Great Salt Lake and enjoyed the exhilarating experience of bathing in the salt water at Black Rock. "No person could sink in it," wrote Wilford Woodruff, "but would roll and float on the surface like a dry log." He concluded that the lake was one of the "Wonders of the World." The party continued westward into Tooele Valley before returning.

Jesse C. Little and three companions spent a week exploring north of Salt Lake Valley to the Bear River and eastward into Cache Valley. About the same time Albert Carrington and two companions traveled to the south end of Salt Lake Valley and climbed the low divide that separates it from Utah Valley. The task of exploring beyond that point was accomplished by Parley Pratt and a small company in December. They launched a boat on Utah Lake and spent parts of two days exploring the region. When the rest of the company returned to the settlement, Pratt and a companion went on horseback west to Cedar Valley and over a low pass into Rush Valley. Traveling north past present-day Stockton, they emerged into Tooele Valley and then returned home after a week's journey.

Both the northern and southern routes to California were traversed by Mormon companies during the fall of 1847. In August Captain James Brown, a member of the battalion sick detachment, and others accompanied Samuel Brannan back to his colony at San Francisco. Three months later Jefferson Hunt, senior captain of the battalion, who had just arrived from San Francisco, volunteered to lead a group to southern California to secure cattle and other needed supplies. Accompanied by eighteen men, Hunt was successful in reaching the Chino Rancho by way of the Old Spanish Trail, although members of his party were forced to eat some of their horses to survive. The men returned over the same route in the spring of 1848 with much-needed animals and seeds. Other members of the battalion who had completed eight-month reenlistments came to Utah over the southern route in the same season. Led by Henry G. Boyle, they brought the first wagons over the trail from California.

A fifty-man company, headed by Parley P. Pratt, was formed on November 23, 1849, for the purpose of choosing locations for additional colonies south of Salt Lake Valley. This group made detailed observations in present-day Utah, Juab, Sanpete, Sevier, and Iron counties, as well as reconnoitering Little Salt Lake Valley and the Virgin and Santa Clara valleys. Returning by way of Mountain Meadows and Pahvant Valley, they were forced to stop at Chalk Creek (Fillmore) because of heavy snow. Half of the company pushed on to Provo, while the remainder stayed in the wintery camp until the following March. A year later this campsite was chosen to be the territorial capital. This company, equipped with an odometer and a thermometer, brought back a report that was the basis for establishing a line of colonies from Utah Valley to the Sevier and Virgin rivers.

The Mormon colonists benefited in several ways from the presence of United States government explorers in Utah from August 1849 to August 1850. Captain Howard Stansbury, the Corps of Topographical Engineers, and a surveying party explored and mapped around the Great Salt Lake and Utah Lake and east to Fort Laramie. His findings influenced later stagecoach and railroad routes, and his published report includes accurate descriptions of the region and observations about the early settlement. One of the party, Lieutenant John W. Gunnison, published *The Mormons, or Latter-day Saints, in the Valley of the Great Salt Lake* (1852), one of the best early accounts of the Mormon colony.

Thus in a brief three-year period the Latter-day Saints evacuated Nauvoo, established temporary communities in present-day Iowa, Nebraska, and Colorado, aided in the conquest and Americanization of California, and made a permanent settlement in Great Salt Lake Valley. They also explored much of the Great Basin and were ready to reclaim the area with an expanded colonization program.

Chapter 7
Bibliographical Essay

General histories of Utah that concentrate on the Mormon migrations and other aspects of the nineteenth century include Hubert Howe Bancroft, *History of Utah* (1889, repr. 1964); Orson F.

Whitney, *History of Utah,* 4 vols. (1892–1904), which includes a volume of biographies; Levi Edgar Young, *The Founding of Utah* (1923); Gustive O. Larson, *Outline History of Utah and the Mormons* (1958 and revisions); and S. George Ellsworth's comprehensive junior high school textbook, *Utah's Heritage* (1972). Concentrating on the early period are Leland H. Creer, *Founding of an Empire: The Exploration and Colonization of Utah, 1776–1856* (1947); and Andrew Love Neff, *History of Utah, 1847–1869* (1940). See also Nels Anderson, *Desert Saints: The Mormon Frontier in Utah* (1942), and Ray B. West, Jr., *Kingdom of the Saints: The Story of Brigham Young and the Mormons* (1957).

The Mormon exodus receives chapter-length treatment in James B. Allen and Glen M. Leonard, *The Story of the Latter-day Saints* (1976), which also contains an extensive and up-to-date bibliography on this and virtually all other aspects of Mormon history. B. H. Roberts, *Comprehensive History of the Church...,* Vols. II and III (1930), details the migration of 1847, and Russell R. Rich's church history, *Ensign to the Nations* (1972), contains several chapters on the pioneer trek and early years in Salt Lake Valley. Wallace Stegner, *The Gathering of Zion* (1964), is a very readable and objective account by a friendly non-Mormon.

Details of the move from Nauvoo are recounted in Robert B. Flanders, *Nauvoo: Kingdom on the Mississippi* (1965), and David E. and Della Miller, *Nauvoo: The City of Joseph* (1974). An important recent monograph is Lewis Clark Christian, "A Study of the Mormon Westward Migration Between February 1846 and July 1847 with Emphasis On and Evaluation of the Factors That Led to the Mormons' Choice of Salt Lake Valley as the Site of Their Initial Colony" (Ph.D. dissertation, Brigham Young University, 1976). A detailed account of the journey of the pioneer company of 1847 is contained in the publication of the Clayton Family Association, *William Clayton's Journal: A Daily Record of the Journey of the Original Company* (1921).

A Concise History of the March of the Mormon Battalion (1881, repr. 1964), by Daniel Tyler, and Frank Golder's *March of the Mormon Battalion* (1928), based on the journal of Henry Standage, are still the standard works on that interesting episode. Charles S. Peterson, John F. Yurtinus, David E. Atkinson, and A. Kent Powell, *Mormon Battalion Trail Guide* (1972), contains valuable information and maps.

Paul Bailey, *Sam Brannan and the California Mormons* (1943), is still the best book on the voyage of the *Brooklyn.* Annaleone D. Patton's *California Mormons* (1961) contains useful information on individuals but lacks objectivity. See also Eugene E. Campbell, "A History of The Church of Jesus Christ of Latter-day Saints in California, 1846–1946" (Ph.D. dissertation, University of Southern California, 1952), and John F. Yurtinus, "A Ram in the Thicket: A History of the Mormon Battalion in the Mexican War" (Ph.D. dissertation, Brigham Young University, 1975). The story of the Mississippi Saints has been told in Lamar C. Berrett, "The History of the Southern States Mission" (master's thesis, Brigham Young University, 1960).

Leonard J. Arrington, *Great Basin Kingdom* (1958), contains a detailed account of the economic activities involved in the colonizing process. Milton R. Hunter's *Brigham Young the Colonizer* (1940) and Joel E. Ricks' *Forms and Methods of Early Mormon Settlement in Utah* (1964) are excellent sources on specific colonies. Richard H. Jackson, "Righteousness and Environmental Change: The Mormons and the Environment," in Thomas G. Alexander, ed., *Essays on the American West, 1973–1974* (Charles Redd Monographs in Western History, Brigham Young University, 1975), presents a revisionist view on the appearance of Salt Lake Valley in 1847, as well as of the Mormon role in developing irrigation. William G. Hartley, "Mormons, Crickets and Gulls: A New Look at an Old Story," *UHQ*, Summer 1970, places the dramatic incident in historic perspective.

Most biographies of the pioneer generation tend toward hagiography. The definitive story of Brigham Young remains to be written; available works range from the laudatory Preston Nibley, *Brigham Young, the Man and His Work* (1936) to the adversely biased Stanley P. Hirshson, *The Lion of the Lord* (1969). Morris R. Werner, *Brigham Young* (1925) is a well-written but skeptical treatment. Studies that incorporate recent research are Leonard J. Arrington, *Charles C. Rich: Mormon General and Western Frontiersman* (1974); Juanita Brooks, *John D. Lee: Zealot, Pioneer Builder, Scapegoat* (rev. ed., 1972); Andrew Karl Larson, *Erastus Snow: The Life of a Missionary and Pioneer for the Early Mormon Church* (1971); and Harold Schindler, *Orrin Porter Rockwell: Man of God, Son of Thunder* (1966).

Personal records that throw light on the Nauvoo-to-Utah pioneering include Parley P. Pratt, ed., *Autobiography of Parley Parker Pratt* (1874, repr. 1961); Juanita Brooks, ed., *On the Mormon Frontier: The Diary of Hosea Stout, 1844–1861,* 2 vols. (1964); and Robert G. Cleland and Juanita Brooks, eds., *A Mormon Chronicle: The Diaries of John D. Lee,* 2 vols. (1955).

Chapter 8
Early Colonization Patterns

Eugene E. Campbell

The Mormon settlement of Utah was a remarkable accomplishment by a group of strong leaders and thousands of dedicated, obedient followers who were intent on establishing the Kingdom of God on earth. Their combined efforts produced the most impressive colonizing program in the history of the American West. By the time of Brigham Young's death in 1877, more than 300 settlements had been established in the present states of Utah, Idaho, Wyoming, Arizona, Nevada, California, and Hawaii. The colonizing momentum was maintained for another decade, after which it declined along with the flow of convert immigrants that had sustained the temporal kingdom-building for half a century.

The Sequence of Settlement

The most spectacular colonizing period, from 1847 to 1857, saw approximately 100 towns founded. These included not only a cluster of settlements in and near Salt Lake Valley, but a line of settlements from Salt Lake City to San Bernardino in southern California, and several outposts on the fringes of the territory coveted by the Mormons. Unfortunately, most of the outlying settlements were experiencing difficulties by 1857, and the approach of the United States Army served as the occasion to call the colonists home. (See map, p. 730.)

A new program began after the so-called Utah War. Between 1858 and 1868 another hundred communities were founded within the present limits of Utah, and colonization extended into southern Idaho, southeastern Nevada, and Arizona north of the Grand Canyon. Indian troubles led to temporary withdrawal from some locations in southern Utah, and water and other problems caused a few of the more remote settlements to be abandoned. The last ten years of President Young's life saw another 125 settlements established, according to the reckoning in Milton R. Hunter's *Brigham Young the Colonizer* (1940). East-central Utah, eastern and southern Arizona, and more of southern Idaho saw Mormon villages established, and the valleys of northern and central Utah were filled in.

In the 1880s and 1890s special emphasis was given to colonies of refuge, as Mormon polygamists escaped the "judicial crusade" in Utah by settling in northern Mexico, southern Alberta, and unoccupied locations in Idaho, Wyoming, and other adjoining states. The discontinuance of organized church-sponsored emigrations from Europe and the East came at about the same time and was doubtless related to the fact that Utah was running out of capacity to sustain more agricultural settlements of the type that had absorbed the earlier fruits of the "gathering."

Most of the Utah towns that today have more than 500 people, and almost all of the villages that today have fewer than that, were founded under Mormon Church auspices in the territorial years. The table on "Utah's Urban Beginnings" (p. 684) shows the extent of Mormon settlement and also shows that the exceptions are mining, railroad, livestock, and Indian reservation-related towns and bedroom suburbs along the Wasatch Front. The style of their founding is a far cry from that which prevailed in the pioneer generation.

The Mormon System

One unique aspect of the colonization of Utah was the establishment of organized towns under the direction of leaders called by the Mormon Church authorities. In some cases the leaders would "call" others to aid in the project; in other cases several men received calls from the hierarchy, with one member of the group designated as their leader. These calls were received as revelations from God, and in some cases they were even designated as missions. Sites were usually preselected, and personnel were assigned to give a seasoning of men and women familiar with pioneering to the colonies of newly arrived immigrants. Some settlements were assigned special missions—fishing, Indian trading and proselyting, iron mining, or wine making—and some took on definite ethnic characteristics as Scandinavians and Germans joined the convert influx from the British Isles and the Eastern states.

134

Attempts were made to secure a variety of talents and skills in each community. Not every settlement possessed such a range of training and experience as the company called to the Cotton Mission in 1861, but the following list, compiled by Juanita Brooks, illustrates this concern:

31 farmers; also 1 horticulturist, 2 gardeners, 2 vine dressers, and 1 vintner
2 with molasses mills
2 dam builders
14 blacksmiths
2 wheelwrights and 1 machinist
1 mill builder, 2 millwrights, and 3 millers
10 coopers to make barrel containers for either liquids or solids
1 adobe maker with 5 masons to lay the walls
1 plasterer and 1 painter
3 carpenters, 1 turner, 1 joiner, 1 shinglemaker
3 cabinetmakers and 1 chair maker
1 mineralogist and 2 miners
2 wool carders, 1 weaver, 1 tailor, 1 hatter, 1 brush maker, and 1 manufacturer who did not designate his product
1 tanner and 5 shoemakers
4 musicians and 1 fiddler
3 schoolteachers, 4 clerks, 1 lawyer, and 1 printer
2 surveyors to divide the land
2 daguerreans to preserve their portraits for posterity
1 butcher, 1 baker, 1 castor oil maker
1 tobacco maker
1 drum major and 1 sailor

Another factor that made for successful colonization was that towns were formed, forts were built, and large fields were worked on an organized, cooperative basis in the early years. The plan for the towns followed the basic principles, although not the details, of the City of Zion concept developed by Joseph Smith and others in 1833. This plan called for each community to be laid out in a square grid pattern, with ample land for each family to have its own home, orchard, and garden. Zoning regulations required that factories and farms be beyond the town boundaries. Wide streets with homes sitting back from them gave a feeling of spaciousness and planning, while the public squares provided room for churches, schools, and other community buildings. In actual practice, most early Utahns found it more convenient to have their barns and domestic animals near their homes than outside the city limits.

The plan had been experimented with in Ohio, Missouri, and Illinois, and it proved to be particularly well adapted to the arid Great Basin. Limited water resources mandated settling in small communities near mountain streams flowing from the canyons. These villages were more easily protected against Indian attack than were individual farmsteads, and they also provided an enriched social, cultural, and religious atmosphere.

The necessity to provide experienced people for each new colonizing venture meant that some of Utah's early settlers went through the pioneering experience two, three, or more times. Not all such calls were joyfully received. It took a great deal of faith and devotion to leave a new farm, home, and orchard and start over again in some remote part of the wilderness; some of the Saints were understandably reluctant. John D. Lee, called to leave Salt Lake Valley with the Iron Mission, told Brigham Young: "The whole idea is repugnant to me! If I could pay as much as two thousand dollars in money or goods, if I could furnish and fit out a family to take my place, I would rather do it than go." But he went, and he moved many times thereafter. Elijah Averett told how his father came home after a hard day in the fields to learn that he had been called to Utah's "Dixie." He dropped in his chair and said: "I'll be damned if I'll go!" After sitting a few minutes with head in hands, he stood up, stretched, and said, "Well, if we are going to Dixie, we had better start to get ready."

This principle of the "call" was the main key to Mormon colonizing success, but it was taken so seriously as a test of religious faith that it led some people to suffer a miserable existence in an inhospitable spot long after prudence would have led them to abandon the effort. The settlements on the Muddy River, now partially submerged under Lake Mead, are good examples. The heroism of the "Hole-in-the-Rock" pioneers of San Juan County was possible only with a people too devoted and obedient to ask, "Is this trip necessary?"

Early Utah Settlements

As soon as Great Salt Lake City was a going concern, the outreach of colonization began. Illustrative of the pattern are the first settlements on the Weber River and in Utah, Tooele, and Sanpete valleys. Each became a nucleus around which new villages, largely populated by newly arrived Saints, were established. (See map, p. 730.)

Within a year after the arrival of the Mormons in Salt Lake Valley, small towns were settled in the southern part of the valley

East of the temple block in Great Salt Lake City in 1855 stood the Deseret Store, General Tithing Office, and the Bishop's Storehouse (center); the territorial mint and Deseret News buildings (right center); the Lion House, Beehive House, and other properties of Brigham Young (right); and part of the never-completed city wall (upper left).

and in what became Davis and Weber counties to the north. Of particular interest was the possible acquisition of Fort Buenaventura, Miles Goodyear's post that stood on the east bank of the Weber River at the west end of present 2800 Street in Ogden. Captain James Brown, leader of the sick detachment of the Mormon Battalion, returned from California in January 1848 not only with the back pay of the incapacitated soldiers, but with some gold of his own to invest in Goodyear's place. Other colonists joined the Brown family to establish Brownsville, which soon became Ogden, Utah's second largest city.

After occupying Goodyear's buildings, the settlers moved to higher ground because the river overflowed its banks. The Browns were successful in raising wheat, corn, cabbage, turnips, potatoes, and watermelons, the latter from seeds brought from California.

They also milked about twenty-five cows, purchased from Goodyear, and were the first Mormons to produce cheese in the area. According to Milton R. Hunter, Brown's produce was instrumental in helping the Saints in Salt Lake Valley survive the starvation period during the winter and spring of 1848–49. Brown sold his grain at reasonable prices and killed a number of fat cattle and shared the meat with destitute colonists.

Apparently the Brownsville leader was not always so generous, for when Brigham Young gave him permission to build toll bridges over the Weber and Ogden rivers, he insisted on collecting tolls even when the streams were low enough to ford. Young sent him a written reprimand.

Within two years approximately thirty families joined the settlement at Brownsville, and a few settled two or three miles to the northeast on the north bank of the Ogden River. In the fall of 1849, Brigham Young, Heber C. Kimball, and Jedediah M. Grant visited the colonists and advised them to build their city on the south side of the Ogden River, where they could utilize the waters of both streams for irrigation. (A number of the early Utah settlements were relocated after experience disclosed what could and could not be accomplished with the available water.)

Lorin Farr was sent to take charge of affairs in Weber County in 1850. He became Ogden's first mayor and served in that position for twenty years. He was also chosen as the first president of the church's Weber Stake in 1851. Not only was he the political and religious leader, but he promoted irrigation, milling, and ultimately the railroad that made Ogden an important transportation center.

Utah Valley, which had delighted Domínguez and Escalante, Jim Bridger, and John C. Fremont, was a logical place for an early settlement. The attractive and fertile region, with its large freshwater lake, was well known to Mormon explorers and travelers by 1849. The church leaders first proposed to use it as a stock range and a source of fish for the Salt Lake Valley populace, but, when they were advised against such projects because of potential Indian problems, they decided to establish a permanent settlement.

Thirty-three families, numbering about 150 people, were called in March 1849 to go to Utah Valley for the purpose of "fishing, farming and instructing the Indians in cultivating the earth and teaching them civilization." John S. Higbee was named as president of the company that arrived at Provo River on April 1. The colonists built Fort Utah on the south bank of the stream about a mile and a half east of the lake, and began farming the rich riverbottom lands to the south and west. In September Young and a small party visited the fort and recommended that the city be built on higher ground farther to the east. This new location became the nucleus of Provo, which was incorporated by the State of Deseret legislature on February 6, 1851.

Other settlements established in 1850 and 1851 included Lehi, Alpine, American Fork, Pleasant Grove, Springville, Spanish Fork, Salem, and Payson. This line of settlements utilized every mountain stream and was so spaced that the outlying farms and pasture lands of each community could touch the next and all the settlers could rally to meet external dangers or unusual internal challenges. With Provo as stake center as well as county seat, Utah Valley presented a particularly striking illustration of the City of Zion concept of colonization. At first there were difficulties with the Indians, including fights at Fort Utah and Battle Creek (as Pleasant Grove was first called) and the 1853 Walker War. But the colonists soon became so numerous that the Indians no longer constituted a serious threat.

Located south of Great Salt Lake and separated from Salt Lake Valley by the Oquirrh Mountains, Tooele Valley was partially explored by Brigham Young and others of the advance company in late July 1847. Two years later the Mormon leader and about a dozen companions made a more thorough exploration and recommended that a settlement be established. A few colonists built cabins on Settlement Creek, near the mouth of the canyon, but as with many other Utah colonies the initial location was criticized and a new site was chosen a mile or two to the north. At the same time Apostle Ezra T. Benson and his family settled and built a grist mill at Twin Springs (present Stansbury Park), some nine miles nearer to the lake.

Tooele County was established by the State of Deseret in January 1850. A few months later John Rowberry was called to preside over the Saints in Tooele Valley, a position that he held with only one brief interruption for twenty-seven years. The valley was fertile but lacked sufficient water to sustain a large population. However, careful use of the water resources from Middle Canyon and Settlement Canyon permitted cultivation of several hundred acres, and the settlement continued to grow. Within a year the nucleus of another settlement was established on the west side of the valley at Willow Creek, and in 1852 a townsite was surveyed and the town of Grantsville was established.

In the fall of 1849 the first deviation from the pattern of contiguous colonization near the mother settlement, Great Salt Lake

City, occurred. A group of Saints under the leadership of Isaac Morley was called to settle near the encampment of Ute Chief Wakara's band to teach them the arts of agriculture. Morley led 225 colonists through Utah Valley and past the site of Nephi, then eastward through Salt Creek Canyon to reach Sanpitch (later named Sanpete) Valley on November 22. Morley's choice of location at present Manti did not receive enthusiastic approval, but when he announced that God had chosen the site and that he intended to stay there even if only ten agreed to follow his leadership, the matter was settled.

The founders of Manti spent a cold and difficult winter in "dugouts on Temple Hill," but they survived and were able to establish friendly relations with Wakara and his people. The Utes did not take comfortably to farming, but other Mormons followed the pioneers into Sanpete Valley; in time Manti became the site of the second temple built by the Saints in the West.

The Mormon Corridor

When the theodemocratic State of Deseret was organized in March 1849, the proposed boundaries embraced practically all of present Utah, Nevada, and Arizona and portions of Oregon, Wyoming, Colorado, New Mexico, Idaho, and California, including the ports of San Pedro and San Diego. The Mormon leaders envisioned controlling this vast region by means of colonization, with their headquarters in Utah. (Fillmore was founded for this purpose, but by the time the "state capital" was ready for occupancy, Deseret had been trimmed and renamed by Congress and Salt Lake City was clearly the logical capital of the territory that remained.)

An important aspect of the plan for Deseret was the so-called Mormon Corridor to the Pacific, which would provide a more convenient way for immigrants to come to the Great Basin than by the overland trail, and which would also provide an all-weather route to southern California for purposes of trade. By the end of 1850 the settlements in Utah Valley were in place. Manti was intended to fit into this scheme, but it proved to be out of the way. In the fall of 1850 a company was called to settle Little Salt Lake Valley, approximately 250 miles south of Salt Lake City on the route to the sea; Parowan was founded early in 1851 as an agricultural center, and the iron mining community of Cedar City was established a few months later. At the same time another group of Mormon settlers was establishing San Bernardino at the California end of the corridor.

Other communities established along the route to the sea included Nephi and Fillmore in 1851, Santa Clara in 1854, Las Vegas in 1855, and Beaver in 1856. It should be noted that practically all of these colonies were meant to serve a double purpose. Santa Clara and Las Vegas were also Indian missions; Cedar City was committed to mining, and in 1856 a church group was sent to Las Vegas to mine lead. Parowan was a farming base for the iron mining mission, and San Bernardino was a gathering place for California Mormons.

Despite this promising beginning, the Mormon Corridor did not materialize. European Mormons were unsuccessful in chartering ships to bring them around South America to the California ports, and so the only immigrants to use the route were the few converts who came from Australia, New Zealand, and the Pacific islands. The settlements did make it possible to communicate more easily with California and the Pacific missions, and they also served as bases for exploration and further colonization along the Virgin, Santa Clara, and Muddy rivers.

The "Outer Cordon"

In addition to this corridor to the sea, the Mormon leaders established other settlements far from the central colonies in the 1850s. Historians, including Hunter and Andrew Love Neff, have suggested that the primary purpose of these settlements was to possess and appropriate all the best agricultural lands of the area and to occupy strategic points commanding the entrances to the intermountain country. According to this concept, the Carson Valley Mission was to command the trail from northern California, the Elk Mountain Mission (Moab) was to control the crossing of the Colorado on the Old Spanish Trail, the Las Vegas Mission was to hold the great oasis in the desert on the trail to southern California, and San Bernardino was to control access to that trail from Los Angeles and to serve as a base of supplies and receiving station near a Pacific port. Fort Supply and Fort Bridger, in the Green River region, would control the Oregon-California Trail entrance to the Great Basin, and Fort Lemhi on the Salmon River would be the northern outpost.

However, detailed studies of the "outer cordon" colonies have brought the whole concept into question. Did Mormon authorities really try to encircle the region with colonies to control the strategic routes? If so, the plan was unsuccessful, for every colony had failed or was in trouble before the coming of the United States Army in 1857. In fact, the coming of the army served more as an excuse to recall the colonies than as a reason for their termination. A brief analysis of the reasons for founding and then abandoning these outposts follows.

Interest in civilizing and converting the Indians, who were believed by Mormons to be children of Israel, was manifest by the founders of the earliest Utah settlements. Harmony, on the rim of the Great Basin in southwestern Utah, was founded by John D. Lee and others in 1852 primarily to teach religion and farming to the Indians, and two years later the most successful and enduring Indian mission was established by Rufus C. Allen, Jacob Hamblin, and others among the Paiutes on the Santa Clara River.

The most extensive proselyting effort among the Indians was launched at the April 1855 church conference, when about 100 men were called on colonizing missions. Forty-one of those who answered the call gathered at Manti in mid-May to prepare for the trip to the Elk Mountain region (present La Sal Mountains). After a difficult journey, the colonists arrived in Grand Valley and chose a spot for a fort on Grand (Colorado) River, where the city of Moab now stands. They experienced immediate success with the Utes, many of whom accepted Mormon baptism and were ordained to the priesthood. However, after three and a half months of contact with the teaching, farming, and fort-building activities of the colonists, the erstwhile friendly Indians began stealing crops and finally shot and killed three missionaries. This was not a general uprising, but was probably a product of rivalry between Utes and Navajos; it understandably disheartened the settlers, and they decided to abandon the mission. The Mormons made no attempts to occupy the Colorado crossing or the region to the east of it for more than twenty years.

The same 1855 conference heard thirty men called to establish a mission at Las Vegas Springs for the purpose of teaching the gospel to the "wild Piede Indians." This group of Mormons, headed by William Bringhurst, also wanted to establish a post on the route to San Bernardino, but their records indicate that the work with the Indians was paramount. They were successful in converting many of the Paiutes and in establishing an Indian farm in addition to their own agricultural projects. The colony was reinforced in 1856 by a group of men who, according to Heber C. Kimball, were not sufficiently employed in Salt Lake City. "These are all good men but they need to learn a lesson," he confided in a letter to one of his sons; some of the same coterie was sent to the outposts on the Salmon and Green rivers.

142

When a lead-mining mission was also sent to Las Vegas in 1856 under the leadership of Nathaniel V. Jones, Bringhurst refused to cooperate. This conflict led to division among the colonizers and the Indians and to the temporary disfellowshiping of President Bringhurst by Brigham Young. The mining missionaries abandoned their project in January 1857, and the Indian missionaries were informed by Young on February 23 that they were at liberty to close down the mission and return home. Most returned at once, although some remained until 1860.

The most obvious flaw in the "outer cordon" concept was the establishment of the Salmon River Mission at Fort Lemhi, almost 400 miles north of Salt Lake City and far from any normal transportation routes or natural boundaries of the Great Basin. The twenty-seven men who responded to the April 1855 call were evidently influenced in their site selection by an ex-Hudson Bay Company employee who knew that Lemhi Valley was the summer home of several Indian tribes. Results were favorable for about two years; native converts were made, and wagonloads of dried fish were sent to Utah.

President Young and an entourage of almost 150 people visited Fort Lemhi in May 1857. The Mormon leader was pleased with the work in progress, but was surprised that the settlement was so far north, rather than near Fort Hall. Young decided to make the best of the situation, and he sent additional settlers to strengthen the fort and to establish a midway post at the mouth of the Blackfoot River. Unfortunately for the colonists, the Utah War led to deteriorating relations with both the Indians and other white residents of the area. On February 25, 1858, a raid on the Lemhi village by supposedly friendly Indians resulted in the death of two Mormons, the wounding of others, and the loss of most of their livestock. Soon after this, on advice from Salt Lake City, the Salmon River Mission was permanently abandoned.

Although a great deal of Mormon traffic went through Carson Valley en route to San Francisco, there was no attempt to found a colony there until eight years after the pioneer entry into the Great Basin. A trading post called *Mormon Station* had been established in 1850, but there is a question as to whether any of the seven partners were active Mormons; certainly they had not been officially called by the church—nor was John Reese, a Salt Lake merchant who bought out the original owners and who opposed any extension of the Mormon-dominated Utah territorial government to the region.

In 1855 the Mormon leadership took the first official action toward Carson Valley. Since it was a part of Utah Territory, Governor Brigham Young sent Apostle Orson Hyde to act as probate judge and to organize a county government. As a result of Hyde's recommendations, some 250 colonizing missionaries were called to western Nevada in 1856. They were also instructed to proselyte and civilize the Indians. This resulted in difficulties with the non-Mormon and inactive Mormon settlers, who resented being brought under the political control and cultural influence of the church. Discovery of gold in the area added to the problems. Rumors that the colony was to be recalled kept the Saints in a state of tension, and several leading members soon returned to their former homes. Within a year word was received concerning the approach of the United States Army, and the remaining colonists were instructed to return to Salt Lake City.

The friction caused by colonizing areas that were already populated by non-Mormons contributed to the outcome of the Carson Valley effort, as it had similarly resulted in antagonism and expulsion in Ohio, Missouri, and Illinois.

Of all the outpost colonies, Fort Bridger and Fort Supply seem best to fit the concept of controlling trails and holding territory. Fort Bridger occupied a strategic spot on the Oregon, California, and Mormon trails. The owners, James Bridger and Louis Vasquez, seemed friendly to the Mormons at first, but they resented attempts by the territorial legislature to control their commercial relations with the Indians. Other mountain men living in or near the fort were operating ferries across the many branches of the Green River, and they resented Mormon attempts to move in. However, Mormon leaders wanted to use Fort Bridger as a supply station for the thousands of converts coming into the Great Basin because it was an ideal spot to prepare for the difficult hundred-mile journey through the Wasatch Mountains. It was also a strategic location for missionary work among the Indians.

The 1853 outbreak of the Walker War led Governor Young to rescind all licenses to trade with the Indians and to send a large posse to arrest Bridger, who was accused of violating the law in this regard. Bridger fled, and the Mormons attempted to purchase the fort, finally succeeding in 1855. But the Mormon colonists who went to occupy the post found armed mountain men defending it; so they built Fort Supply some twelve miles to the southwest. Fort Bridger was ultimately occupied by the Mormons, but in 1857 both posts were abandoned and destroyed in the face of the approaching federal troops.

The largest Mormon colonizing venture within the state of California was attempted at San Bernardino in the summer of 1851 by approximately 500 church members who made the long trek from Utah under the leadership of apostles Amasa M. Lyman and Charles C. Rich. The colony was conceived as a port of entry for converts coming from the Pacific missions, as a gathering place for members of the *Brooklyn* colony and other Saints who were living in the northern part of the state, as a way-station for missionaries going to and from their fields of labor, and as a vital link in the chain of colonies that formed the Mormon Corridor. It was also a reluctant response by the church leadership to the "California fever" that affected some of the Great Basin populace as the gold rush produced a new state and new fortunes.

Although the colony grew to more than 3,000 people in five years and although its story is an interesting chapter in California history, in terms of Mormon plans for the Great Basin it must be regarded as a costly failure. Many of the participants lost their gold field earnings and the fruits of years of labor when the colony was recalled. Institutionally, the church suffered considerably, for nearly half of the settlers either refused to leave San Bernardino at the call of the church, or returned reluctantly a year or two later. In either case, they were lost to the church.

The traditional explanation for the abandonment of San Bernardino is the policy of retrenchment followed by Brigham Young on the eve of the Utah War. Other outlying colonies were recalled, and even the handful of missionaries in the Hawaiian Islands were ordered home, leaving some 4,000 newly converted members without adequate leadership. But the evidence shows that San Bernardino was already in serious difficulty. It was in April 1857, three months before the first news of the army, that Young recalled Rich and Lyman and publicly stated that "this was about the last year any Saint could stay in California."

Part of the blame for the failure must be placed on Young, who was unenthusiastic about the colony from the start. But even if church leadership had given whole-hearted support, San Bernardino would have had a difficult time surviving. Undemocratic political policies patterned after the theocratic customs of the mother colony, the practice of plural marriage, misunderstandings concerning Mormon attitudes toward the Indians, and unfortunate disputes over land all brought hostile reactions from non-Mormon elements and caused serious differences in the ranks of the Saints. It is doubtful that a Mormon community with such attitudes and practices could have survived unless it was either isolated or in complete control of the region. Perhaps the possibility of gaining such control in San Bernardino Valley would have justified such a colonizing effort, but not a half-hearted one.

In summary, it appears that the "outer cordon" concept must be reconsidered in the light of the facts about each of the colonies. Most of the settlements in question were organized for particular reasons rather than pursuant to a carefully worked-out strategic plan. In any case, all were abandoned, and a less ambitious but more realistic program of colonization emerged after 1858.

Other Specialized Colonies

As has already been noted, several of the Mormon colonies were established for reasons other than just to occupy agricultural land and develop homes and communities. These were specialized missions to produce or procure specific articles needed by other communities, or to control and instruct the Indians. Thus groups were called to produce iron, lead, copper, grapes, and other semitropical products. The following cases are illustrative.

Early explorers recognized a large deposit of iron ore near present-day Cedar City, and it was here that the Iron Mission was established in the fall of 1851 with its support base, Parowan, nearby. Apostle George A. Smith, who headed the mission, reported that it initially consisted of a hundred and twenty men, thirty-one women, and eighteen children under fourteen years of age. During the year, additional colonists moved in and brought the total to 360.

Both iron ore and coal were found in abundance near Cedar City, and the settlers there organized a company for mining and smelting. Hoping to increase the productivity of the colony, Brigham Young early in 1852 called upon Franklin D. Richards and Erastus Snow in England to raise capital and recruit converts who were skilled in iron mining and manufacturing. They responded by organizing the Deseret Iron Company, optimistically capitalized at nearly five million dollars, and by recruiting some funds and workers. Arriving in Cedar City in November, the two apostles purchased the existing iron works and began expanding the project. The production of 2,500 pounds of an excellent grade of iron in March 1853 seemed to be a sure sign of success.

Unfortunately, a series of difficulties developed. The high cost of charcoal made necessary the locating and developing of new veins of coal and the spending of time and energy in building a road to the higher grade deposits. The Walker War caused the leaders to suspend operations during the summer in order to build fortifications, and in September a flash flood destroyed the bridges and dams and deposited huge boulders in the area. The iron works were flooded and large amounts of charcoal, wood, and lumber were washed away.

The colonists recovered from these disasters and by 1855 prospects were again bright; in April alone nearly eleven tons of iron were manufactured. But their new furnace had to be blown out twice after a short period of successful operation because of malfunctions. The extremely cold winter of 1855–56 hampered operations because of the difficulty of obtaining coal, and grasshopper devastation of crops struck the community the following summer. By 1857 the ironworks were almost completely shut down. Many colonists were moving away and the involvement of the Cedar City militia in the tragic Mountain Meadows Massacre caused other families to leave the Iron Mission. The coming of Johnston's Army into Utah in 1858 with ample supplies of iron led to the termination of the local endeavor, and the completion of the transcontinental railroad in 1869 made imported iron available at a fraction of what it had cost for local manufacture. Sporadic efforts were made to produce iron near Cedar City in the 1880s, but the mineral that gave Iron County its name did not figure prominently in the Utah economy until the twentieth century.

The lead mining mission has been mentioned in connection with the Las Vegas Indian Mission. Despite the jurisdictional dispute between leaders, the mining missionaries made almost superhuman efforts to fulfill their calling. The lead ore was located high in the mountains twenty-seven miles southwest of Las Vegas and twelve miles from water. The lack of proper smelting equipment was an added problem. The yield, too, was low, in part because of what the Mormon miners described as a "hard bluish material" in the ore; an experienced smelter suspected that it was silver. The project was abandoned after only sixty tons of ore had been mined. Five years later the famous Potosi silver mines were discovered by non-Mormons near the spot.

Although the Cotton Mission did not develop on a large scale until 1861, it should be included in a survey of specialized pioneer colonies. Small groups were sent to the Virgin and Santa Clara valleys as early as 1857 to test the agricultural potential of the warm climate, and they demonstrated the feasibility of growing cotton by producing 155 bales in 1860. The following year 309 families were called to go to Utah's "Dixie" to raise not only cotton but figs, olives, grapes, sugar, almonds, and tobacco. The variety of their skills has already been noted. At about the same time some thirty families of Swiss immigrants were assigned to Santa Clara to produce grapes and other fruit for the cotton missionaries. These hardy German-speaking settlers came to be known as "Utah Dutchmen."

St. George, founded by the cotton missionaries, became the center of Dixie, and the colonists were successful in producing sizable amounts of cotton, wine, and molasses. During the American Civil War the market demand for Utah cotton remained strong, but plans for a factory at Washington, near St. George, had barely been carried to completion in 1866 when the falling price of imported cotton from the East destroyed most of the demand for the local product. The wine industry became an important source of trade and revenue, especially when mining camps opened at Silver Reef, Utah, and Pioche, Nevada. Eventual closure of the mines and competition with California wines led to a decline in this industry, and local addiction to the potent Dixie vintages caused church leaders to discourage production. The colony remained on a precarious economic footing for many years. It had to be subsidized by the church, which supplied food, clothing, and machinery and which used tithing money to finance such job-creating projects as the building of a tabernacle and the first Mormon temple to be finished in the West.

Despite the failure of the outlying settlements and some of the specialized colonies, the overall colonizing program was very successful. The interior colonies continued to expand from one valley to the next as new immigrants came to the region each year. This was especially true after the outpost colonies were discontinued and the leaders were content to expand in a more natural way. Furthermore, President Young, who at first had a negative impression of the feasibility of colonizing to the north of Ogden, changed his policy after 1857 and encouraged the settlement of the rich lands in northern Utah and southeastern Idaho.

Character of the Colonizers

One reason for the success of the Great Basin colonization was the number of capable men in the hierarchy of the Mormon Church. Instead of concentrating the leadership in Salt Lake City, Young sent the apostles out to head important colonies. George A. Smith, and later Erastus Snow, directed the settlements in southern Utah. Lorenzo Snow organized an important colony in Brigham City. Orson Hyde presided over settlements in the Green River country, Carson Valley, and finally Sanpete Valley. Ezra T. Benson served as an early leader in Cache Valley. Amasa M. Lyman and Charles C. Rich founded San Bernardino, and Rich later led in colonizing the Bear Lake region.

In addition to these general authorities, hundreds of Mormon bishops and presiding elders directed the building of individual settlements. These men not only served as spiritual leaders, but they acted as probate judges, watermasters, directors of construction projects, and supervisors of tithing houses. Many served for ten, twenty, even thirty years, as did some of the stake presidents who supervised them.

Finally, note should be taken of the thousands of Mormon men and women who faced the often traumatic experiences that were part of adapting British, Scandinavian, New England, Southern, and other cultures to the rigorous demands of survival in the arid West. In *The Gathering of Zion* (1964) Wallace Stegner expressed it this way: "That I do not accept the faith that possessed them does not mean that I doubt their frequent devotion and heroism in its service. Especially their women. Their women were incredible."

Utah's Urban Beginnings

Listed in the approximate order of their founding are the cities and towns of Utah that the 1970 United States Census showed to have at least 500 inhabitants. Unless identified with mining, smelting, or railroad origins, the communities with settlement dates were founded primarily for agricultural purposes and primarily by Mormons. A case can be made for a different "founding" date in some instances. The "expansion communities" are so listed because they owe their existence to largely unplanned overflow from adjacent cities. Population figures are from 1970:

1847		1850	
Salt Lake City	175,885	Harrisville	603
Bountiful	27,853	Pleasant Grove	5,327
Farmington	2,526	Lehi	4,659
1848		Alpine	1,047
Ogden	69,478	American Fork	7,713
Centerville	3,268	Lindon	1,644
Holladay	25,000	Payson	4,501
West Jordan	4,221	Spanish Fork	7,284
1849		Springville	8,790
Kaysville	6,192	Layton	13,603
Provo	53,131	North Ogden	5,257
Granger	13,800	**1851**	
Tooele	12,539	Parowan	1,423
Manti	1,803	Brigham City	14,007

Salem	1,081	**1863**	
Willard	1,045	Monroe	918
Santaquin	1,236	Salina	1,494
Nephi	2,699	**1864**	
Fillmore	1,411	Richfield	4,471
Cedar City	8,946	Kanab	1,381
Grantsville	2,931	Panguitch	1,318
Midvale	7,840	Clinton	1,768
Pleasant View	2,028	**1866**	
1852		Honeyville	640
Mount Pleasant	1,516	**1867**	
Ephraim	2,127	West Point	1,020
1853		**1869**	
Perry	909	Eureka (mining)	753
1856		**1870**	
Beaver	1,453	Randolph	500
Washington	750	Lewiston	1,244
Wellsville	1,267	**1871**	
Mapleton	1,980	Sandy (railroad)	6,438
1859		**1872**	
Plain City	1,543	Murray (smelting)	21,206
South Jordan	2,942	Park City (mining)	1,193
Logan	22,333	Riverdale	3,704
Providence	1,608	**1875**	
Heber City	3,254	Escalante	638
Midway	804	**1876**	
Coalville	864	Sunset	6,268
Fairview	696	**1877**	
Richmond	1,000	Castle Dale	541
Smithfield	3,342	Ferron	663
Gunnison	1,073	Huntington	857
Moroni	894	Orangeville	511
1860		Price	6,218
Kamas	806	Syracuse	1,843
Hyde Park	1,025	**1878**	
Hyrum	2,340	Vernal	3,908
Morgan	1,586	**1879**	
Huntsville	553	Riverton	2,820
1861		Wellington	922
Saint George	7,097	**1880**	
1862		Moab	4,793
Hebron (Enterprise)	844	Milford (railroad)	1,304

		1907	
1884		Delta	1,610
Green River (railroad)	1,033	**1909**	
Helper (railroad)	1,964	Wendover (railroad)	781
1887			
Monticello	1,431	**Expansion Communities**	
1890			
Garland	1,187		
Tremonton	2,794	Clearfield	13,316
1896		East Carbon City	2,900
Hurricane	1,408	Kearns	18,200
		North Logan	1,405
1904		Orem	25,729
Blanding	2,250	River Heights	1,008
1905		Roy	14,356
Duchesne	1,094	South Ogden	9,991
Roosevelt	2,055	South Salt Lake	7,810
1906		Washington Terrace	7,241
Magna (smelting)	8,000	Woods Cross	3,124

Information derived from Milton R. Hunter, *Brigham Young the Colonizer* (1940), pp. 361-367; Andrew Jenson, *Encyclopedic History of The Church of Jesus Christ of Latter-day Saints* (1941), *passim;* and "Cities and Towns: 1970 Census (Incorporated places and unincorporated places of 1,000 or more)," *Utah Highway Map 74/75* (1974).

Chapter 8
Bibliographical Essay

Of the general histories listed in Chapter 7, Leland H. Creer, *Founding of an Empire*... (1947) and B. H. Roberts, *Comprehensive History of The Church*.... Vols. III and IV (1930), deal most extensively with the early colonization of Utah. Milton R. Hunter, *Brigham Young the Colonizer* (1940; rev. ed. 1973), is still the fundamental monograph on the subject. Leonard J. Arrington, *Great Basin Kingdom* (1958), emphasizes the economic aspects and gives valuable information on the Iron, Lead, and Cotton missions. Joel E. Ricks, *Forms and Methods of Early Settlement in Utah*... (1964), stresses the formation of centers of settlement—mother colonies throughout the region—from which the immediate vicinity was colonized. See also Lowry Nelson, *The Mormon Village: A Pattern and Technique of Land Settlement* (1952).

Andrew Love Neff, *History of Utah* (1940), contains much information but is also responsible for the "outer cordon" concept that was questioned by Eugene E. Campbell in "Brigham Young's Outer Cordon: A Reappraisal," *UHQ,* Summer 1973. Campbell asserts that several of the so-called "outer cordon" colonies were established after Brigham Young had retreated from his expansive dreams of empire and were merely bases for missionary work among the Indians.

Important studies of individual Mormon settlements include Fred R. Gowans and Eugene E. Campbell, *Fort Bridger: Island in the Wilderness* (1975) and *Fort Supply: Brigham Young's Green River Experiment* (1976); Joseph S. Wood, "History of San Bernardino" (Ph.D. dissertation, University of Utah, 1968); and Albert R. Page, "Orson Hyde and the Carson Valley Mission" (Master's thesis, Brigham Young University, 1970). *The History of a Valley: Cache Valley, Utah-Idaho* (1956), ed. by Joel E. Ricks and Everett L. Cooley, contains chapters on specific aspects of colonization by several Utah historians.

Dale Beecher's study of the role of Mormon bishops in the colonizing process, *The Office of Bishop* (1975), is an important contribution. The lives of individual colonizers illustrate important aspects of the total story. In addition to the biographies and journals of Brigham Young, Charles C. Rich, John D. Lee, Hosea Stout, Erastus Snow, and Porter Rockwell listed in Chapter 7, the following are helpful: Leonard J. Arrington, *From Quaker to Latter-day Saint: Bishop Edwin D. Wooley* (1976); Charles S. Peterson, "Jacob Hamblin, Apostle to the Lamanites, and the Indian Mission," *Journal of Mormon History* (1975); and two publications by Peterson on Lot Smith, "A Mighty Man Was Brother Lot. . . ," *Western Historical Quarterly*, October 1970, and *Take Up Your Mission* (1973).

Many of the works listed in Chapter 17 include information and insights on the pioneering work of Mormon women. Mary Ann Hafen, *Recollections of a Handcart Pioneer of 1860 with Some Account of Frontier Life in Utah and Nevada* (1938) and Juanita Brooks, ed., *Not by Bread Alone: The Journal of Martha Spence Heywood, 1850–56* (1977) describes women's experiences in crossing the plains and colonizing outlying communities.

Chapter 9
Governmental Beginnings

Eugene E. Campbell

Had the pioneers of 1847 been permitted to express their convictions and capabilities in isolation, they might have produced a unique and autonomous theocratic society in their new home. But this was not to be. Even as Brigham Young led the Mormon vanguard to the Salt Lake Valley, General Winfield Scott was advancing on Mexico City. Whatever may have been the hopes or expectations of the Mormon leaders when they picked the Great Basin for a haven, the American victory in the Mexican War subjected them to the vicissitudes of national and sectional politics. Under territorial government they were tied to the United States in a subordinate status for almost half a century. What happened in the first decade was, in important respects, a foreshadowing of what kept Utah from becoming a state until 1896.

Ecclesiastical Government

The organization of The Church of Jesus Christ of Latter-day Saints, which had been functioning as the Mormons' instrument of government since the repeal of the Nauvoo Charter in January 1845, continued to serve the Mormon people as they migrated westward and established their first settlements in Utah. Often called a *theodemocracy*, this ecclesiastical organization was based upon the concept that God had conferred his priesthood on the church leaders and that they had the right and duty to govern as his representatives on earth. However, this rather absolute power was tempered by the principle of common consent. As Brigham Young said on one occasion, "It is the right of the Twelve to nominate officers, and the people to receive them." In the great majority of cases the membership approval was unanimous and rather perfunctory; there were cases, however, where the people rejected officers and proposals offered by their theocratic leaders.

Upon the death of Joseph Smith, no one was immediately designated to take his place as church president and prophet. Brigham Young, as head of the Quorum of the Twelve Apostles, succeeded in establishing that council as the authoritative body of the priesthood, and he functioned as president by reason of his position as the senior apostle. He and his counselors, Heber C. Kimball and Willard Richards, were sustained as the First Presidency of the church on December 27, 1847, after returning to Winter Quarters and Council Bluffs from the pioneer trip to Utah.

Since the presiding apostles remained in Salt Lake Valley only a month before returning to the encampments on the Missouri, it was necessary for them to appoint leaders to govern in their absence. At a mass meeting held on August 22, 1847, it was agreed that a president, a high council, and other needed officials should be appointed. Young indicated that he wanted "Uncle" John Smith, uncle of the murdered prophet, to preside if he were in the next company en route to the Great Basin. This appointment was made official on September 9 when Young and his companions, having met the expected company, wrote a letter from "twenty miles east of South Pass" that designated Smith, "with liberty for him to select his two councilors," and that nominated twelve men for the high council. It continued:

... we also nominate John Van Cott to be marshall of your city, and Albert Carrington to be your clerk, historian, and deputy postmaster, and that he keep barometrical and thermometrical observations daily—we recommend that General Charles C. Rich be the Chief Military Commander of the City, and that a perfect organization be instituted and sustained in companies of ten, fifty and hundred.

The principle of common consent was followed on October 3 at a general conference in Salt Lake Valley, in which all of the officers nominated by the leaders were sustained. A month later the community of approximately 1,500 people was divided into ecclesiastical wards, and bishops were appointed to be in charge of temporal affairs and to adjudicate disputes. Cases could be appealed to the high council, the resident apostles, and finally to the First Presidency.

The high council passed a variety of laws concerning vagrants, disturbing the peace, adultery and fornication, drunkenness, robbery, and malicious destruction of property by fire. Control of fuel and building materials and of domestic animals was also included. Since there was no jail, the punishments designated were fines and whipping, although the actual administration of "39 lashes on the bare back" was rarely carried out. In one case the marshal offered to pay the fine of the guilty person rather than administer ten lashes with the whip, but the offer was refused and the punishment was inflicted.

The accomplishments of the church government in the first two years are impressive; it provided the people of the Great Basin with executive, legislative, and judicial branches of government. It furnished laws for the protection of the people and provided for the enforcement of them. It made provision for the construction of forts, roads, bridges, a temple, a council house, and many other civic improvements. It inaugurated a system of currency for the convenience of the people. It provided judicial procedures by which the people might obtain redress for wrongs and be given a fair trial by their peers. Finally, it provided the initiative for the creation of a territorial or state government under the Constitution of the United States.

The Council of Fifty

Superimposed on this relatively simple picture of early theocratic government was the enigmatic Council of Fifty, the organizational arm of the "Political Kingdom of God." Although historians make differing assessments of the overall importance of this agency, its prominence during the first years of Mormon settlement in Utah seems to justify an examination of its origins and purposes.

On March 11, 1844, three and a half months before his death, Joseph Smith organized a special council that he charged with the task of establishing the political kingdom of God on earth. According to one of the first members, this action was based on a revelation the Mormon prophet received on April 7, 1842, and the formal designation for the group was "The Kingdom of God and His Laws with the keys and powers thereof and the judgment in the hands of his servants." It is generally referred to in the extant documents as the Council of Fifty. Its purpose seems to have been to establish a political organization that would be ready to rule the world when "Christ shall come to usher in the Millennial Reign." It was to work in close cooperation with God's church on earth, but it was not identical to it. Most members of the Council of Fifty held high church positions, but nonmembers could be on the council as well. (The millennial expectations on which the council was based were discussed in an earlier chapter.)

The most difficult aspect of the Council of Fifty for the historian to cope with is its secrecy. The evidence seems clear enough to assert that the council played a leading role in the early colonizing of Utah and that in 1849, having assumed the Salt Lake high council's municipal functions, the Fifty tried to set up a state government as the best method of maintaining the political independence of the Saints within the confines of the United States. The extent to which the council actually initiated projects in this transitional period is unclear. With the passage of time, authority over both secular and religious concerns of the Latter-day Saints became concentrated in the First Presidency and the Quorum of the Twelve Apostles; the Council of Fifty became a ratifying body whose deliberations were often perfunctory. Its periodic revivals were at times when the millennial expectations of the Mormons were running high, and its role—if any—after the 1880s is obscure.

The State of Deseret

Although the stake presidency and high council functioned as the highest governmental units in Utah until late 1848, two members of the Council of the Twelve Apostles and the Council of Fifty, Parley P. Pratt and John Taylor, came into the valley in October 1847 and were regarded as the highest authorities there. Shortly after his arrival, Pratt reminded the stake high council that its laws were only temporary—that permanent arrangements would be in the hands of the Council of Fifty as soon as its members were present. This prediction became a reality on December 9, 1848, when the Fifty met at Heber C. Kimball's house to determine what type of secular government should be established. The Guadalupe-Hidalgo Treaty had transferred the Utah region to the United States from Mexico, creating the option of statehood or territorial government. The council decided to apply for a "territorial government of our own," implying that officers be chosen from Mormon leadership. A petition stating the proposal was drawn up, and Dr. John M. Bernhisel carried it to Washington, D.C., leaving Utah on May 3, 1849. The document bore 2,270 signatures, including Brigham Young's.

After the plan for territorial government was devised and dispatched, a *de facto* government was selected in an uncontested election on March 12. It was headed by Young and manned entirely by prominent Mormons. Almost immediately, however, the leadership group began to have second thoughts about the desirability of territorial status. News from the East, including recommendations from Thomas L. Kane,[1] led to the conclusion that statehood should have been sought instead. If California and New Mexico were going for it, why not Deseret? Statehood would give the Mormons the self-government that they really wanted.

However, the decision makers in Great Salt Lake City, probably the Council of Fifty, concluded that there wasn't time to go through the steps of electing delegates, drafting a constitution, ratifying it, and then petitioning Congress. They also knew that if they asked for statehood without going through this procedure, they couldn't succeed. So they created a record. During two weeks in July, a committee wrote a constitution, borrowing mostly from a copy of Iowa's. Then they invented convention minutes and election documents, named members to a legislature, and sent the papers back to Kanesville, Iowa, where Apostle Orson Hyde printed them at the *Frontier Guardian* office because the Salt Lake valley did not yet have an operating press.[2] Almon W. Babbitt then took copies of the pamphlet back to Washington and went to work with Kane and Bernhisel in an effort to secure statehood.

Unfortunately, the application for statehood was doomed to defeat without any real consideration of its merits. It became part of the Compromise of 1850 (a result of the slavery issue), which admitted California into the Union as a free state, and which designated Utah and New Mexico as territories with the right to decide by popular sovereignty whether they would eventually become slave or free states. That they would reject slavery seemed a foregone conclusion, but the fact that they had a choice was a gesture to the South. But even if there had been no slavery controversy raging in Congress at the time, it does not seem likely that Deseret would have been admitted to the Union. The liberal boundaries of

---

[1]Colonel Thomas L. Kane (1822-1883), whose family had good connections in Pennsylvania and national politics, had formed close ties with the Mormons when Kane had been cared for when he had become seriously ill during a visit to the church settlements on the Missouri River in 1846. He had earlier played a role in the calling of the Mormon Battalion, and he would continue to be an unofficial political adviser to Brigham Young until the latter's death. Despite contemporary rumors, there is no evidence that Kane secretly joined the Mormon Church.

[2]This 16-page pamphlet, *Constitution of the State of Deseret, with the journal of the convention which formed it, and the proceedings of the legislature consequent thereon* (Kanesville, 1849) confused generations of historians until Peter Crawley did the detective work that established its deceptive character. Crawley, *The Constitution of the State of Deseret* (Provo: Friends of the Harold B. Lee Library, 1982), pp. 1-27.

the proposed state embraced almost one-sixth of the nation's territory, including most of southern California, which conflicted with the claims of that new state. Then, too, the population of Deseret was far below the number usually required for statehood. There was some expression of anti-Mormon sentiment in Congress and in the press, but it apparently had very little influence on the final vote to create the territory.

Deseret in Action

Although Utah Territory was formed on September 9, 1850, the State of Deseret had been functioning since March 1849 and it continued to do so until early 1851, when the territorial administration gradually took over. Brigham Young served as Deseret's governor, and prominent churchmen held most of the elective and appointive posts. A significant record of accomplishments was compiled by officials of the State of Deseret during these two years of quasiofficial government.

To provide local government for the rapidly expanding colonies, seven counties were organized and their boundaries were prescribed by the General Assembly; they were Salt Lake, Weber, Davis, Tooele, Utah, Sanpete, and Iron. Great Salt Lake City, Ogden, Provo, Manti, and Parowan were incorporated as cities and were chartered early in 1851. At this time the counties had no governing officials, but merely served as legislative and later as judicial districts. In the colonizing ventures the church leaders appointed men to preside until cities were chartered and elections were held. In Great Salt Lake City, for example, the charter was granted and the first officers were appointed by the governor and the legislature. The first regular election was held in April 1851, and all of the appointed officers retained their positions with the exception of two councilmen. The city was divided into municipal wards according to the number of aldermen; the tax rate for the city was fixed; and other necessary officers such as treasurer, marshal, and assessor were appointed. A similar procedure was followed in the other incorporated cities of Deseret.

Among the more important services rendered by the State of Deseret were those related to the judiciary. Just as the state government superseded that of the church, so did the civil courts replace the stake high council and the bishop's courts of the theodemocracy. The latter courts had been adequate for the first years of the small isolated settlements, but with the coming of California's gold rush, many legal disputes developed that the church

158

courts were incapable of resolving. These courts could render fair decisions, but in cases involving Mormons and non-Mormons they were almost certain to be accused of partiality, especially if the non-Mormon was the loser in the case. This problem was not entirely solved by the establishment of civil courts, because the chief justice and associate justices of Deseret were all church leaders and most of the magistrates of the lower courts were still ward bishops. Despite some claims of prejudice and unfairness, however, the courts rendered an important service to both settlers and transients in the region. Captain Howard Stansbury, who was surveying in the Salt Lake Valley in 1849, reported favorably on Mormon justice:

Their courts were constantly appealed to by companies of passing emigrants, who, having fallen out by the way, could not agree on the division of their property. The decisions were remarkable for their fairness and impartiality, and if not submitted to, were sternly enforced by the whole power of the community.

John W. Gunnison, one of Stansbury's associates and a military surveyor in Utah in 1853, expressed similar sentiments. With reference to another problem involving transients, Gunnison noted that the value of crops was "so enormously greater than in the states" that the remuneration demanded for damage done by trespassing emigrant livestock "looked to the stranger as an imposition and an injustice," even though it reflected market conditions.

One of the most significant enactments of the State of Deseret was the February 28, 1850, chartering of the University of Deseret, which eventually became the University of Utah. Another law provided for an organized militia based on the Nauvoo Legion, which had maintained its existence during the years of migration and early settlement. The General Assembly also authorized Governor Young to contribute a block of Utah's best marble to the Washington Monument, then being erected. The stone sent by the people of Deseret became part of the monolith in the nation's capital, along with blocks from the various states and territories and from Sunday Schools, fire companies, and temperance societies.

Other important enactments included the incorporation of The Church of Jesus Christ of Latter-day Saints; the incorporation of The Perpetual Emigrating Fund Company; the regulation of the manufacture and sale of spiritous liquors; and several enactments for the control and conservation of the region's natural resources.

Utah Territory

Word that President Millard Fillmore had signed the organic act creating Utah Territory and had appointed the first group of territorial officers reached Great Salt Lake City on January 27, 1851, in a copy of the New York *Tribune*, which came to Utah via Los Angeles. Brigham Young was on a preaching tour at the time, so Daniel H. Wells, the chief justice of Deseret, went to Davis County at the head of a body of cavalry and a brass band to inform Young of his appointment as governor. Although the news was not official, Young felt that it was reliable enough to justify his taking office, and so on February 5, 1851, he took the oath of office as chief executive of Utah Territory.

In addition to his appointment as governor, Young was also designated superintendent of Indian affairs. Other officials appointed by Fillmore were:

Sec. of the Territory	B. D. Harris	Non-Mormon
Chief Justice	Lemuel Brandebury	Non-Mormon
Associate Justice	Perry E. Brocchus	Non-Mormon
Associate Justice	Zerubabbel Snow	Mormon
U.S. Marshal	Joseph L. Heywood	Mormon
U.S. Attorney	Seth M. Blair	Mormon

The organic act also provided for a territorial legislature and a delegate to Congress. Since they were elected by the people, they were chosen by the same theodemocratic process that had operated in the State of Deseret. According to D. Michael Quinn, "up to 1890 the [Mormon] General Authorities were the source of first approval for every political nomination in Utah that they regarded as important." This included not only candidates for territorial elective offices but appointees recommended to the governor by the legislative assembly.

Members of the thirteen-member Council and twenty-six-member House of Representatives were for many years selected by this process and were unanimously elected. The presiding officers of the two bodies were usually members of the First Presidency or Council of the Twelve Apostles (See Table, pp. 694–96), and most of the members also belonged to the Council of Fifty. The organic act called for annual forty-day sessions of the legislature beginning in December. Illustrative of the accord among the lawmakers during the first two decades of the Utah Territory is the report that one session was completed "without the occurrence of a negative vote on any question or action."

The territorial delegates to the United States House of Representatives were also quasi-ecclesiastical figures. John M. Bernhisel and his successors for more than forty years were selected and set apart by the First Presidency, and there were no contested elections for the office until the non-Mormons fielded a candidate in 1867. (See Table, pp. 694-96.) There is evidence that the delegates were chosen to match the political majority in Washington, and that they sometimes changed their party identification when that majority changed. At the local level there was occasional interpersonal competition for city or county offices, but partisan elections did not characterize Utah politics until the Liberal and People's parties were organized in 1870. The church leadership regularly selected candidates for mayor and city councilmen in Salt Lake City, Ogden, and Provo, and no candidate without this approval was elected to any of these offices until 1889.

The territory over which Brigham Young was to preside was extensive, although much smaller than the original State of Deseret. (See map, p. 731.) It was bounded north and south by the 42nd and 37th parallels; the summits of the Rocky Mountains and the Sierra Nevada completed the boundaries. Estimates placed the Indian population in the wide range from 12,000 to 35,000; if the most conservative figure is taken, then whites and Indians were almost equal in number when the territory was born. But the whites increased rapidly in numbers and the displaced natives decreased until the middle of the twentieth century. Fed largely by the gathering of the Latter-day Saints, the population of Utah Territory was reported by the decennial censuses to be:

> 1850— 11,380
> 1860— 40,273
> 1870— 86,786
> 1880—143,963
> 1890—210,779

Territorial Government in Action

Because of the solidarity and sensitivity of Utah's inhabitants and the ambitions and attitudes of the typical territorial appointees of the nineteenth century, Fillmore's well-meant attempt to combine Mormons and non-Mormons in executive and judicial offices was hardly likely to succeed. Brigham Young's relationship with the incoming officials was damaged when he proceeded to take a census and call for an election of legislators even before they arrived in Utah. Since the secretary of the territory was supposed to supervise the census-taking, according to the organic act,

161

Utah's nineteenth-century governors began with Brigham Young (upper left), first head of the territory, and ended with Heber M. Wells (lower right), first chief executive of the state.

162

and was supposed to certify the validity of the election, it appears that the governor acted precipitately. When Secretary B. D. Harris arrived, he refused to deliver the $24,000 that Congress had appropriated for territorial expenses. Associate Justice Perry E. Brocchus, who came to Utah expecting to be elected a Congressional delegate, quickly antagonized the people by criticizing plural marriage in a public meeting. Harris and Brocchus then encouraged Chief Justice Lemuel H. Brandebury and Indian Agent Henry R. Day to return to the east with them and report the impossibility of carrying out their assigned responsibilities in Utah because of the domination of the Mormon Church over the lives and minds of the people.

Fortunately for the people, their elected representative, Bernhisel, was able to counteract many of the accusations and ultimately the "runaway officials" were discredited. Their reports of the practice of polygamy could not be denied, however, and Bernhisel later reported unhappily that the public announcement of the unconventional marriage practice in August 1852 left the Saints in a weaker political position than before.

Meanwhile the territorial legislature went about what it perceived to be its business, which consisted largely of enacting into law Governor Young's recommendations. Its 1851 session reenacted the legislation adopted earlier under the State of Deseret and also created Millard County, christened its county seat in Fillmore in honor of the Whig president, and designated the still-to-be-founded city as the territorial capital. (After the first territorial capital building was finished in 1855, the legislature met there for one session, but economic and demographic realities had by then established that Great Salt Lake City would be the center of both Utah Territory and the Mormons' "Great Basin kingdom." The lawmakers soon legislated to fit the facts, and for many years the legislature met in the Social Hall and the Council House, both church-built structures.)

In the 1850s the legislature increased the number of counties from seven to twenty-two (see map, p. 732), including eight that disappeared in the following decade when the territorial boundaries were cut back to the present limits of the state and when the population proved insufficient to sustain several of the units established west of Utah and Great Salt lakes. The number of chartered cities grew from five to seventeen, but no provision was made for government for the other villages and towns that soon dotted the territory. Consequently the scope of county government was broad. The elected county court, which consisted of a probate judge and three selectmen, had jurisdiction over the conservation and disposition of timber and water resources; the districting for road, school, voting, and other purposes; the levying of taxes; the construction of public buildings; the care for orphans, the insane, and stray animals; and the election or appointment of lesser officials. Since the probate judge was not only the chairman of the county court but usually a Mormon bishop, it is not surprising that priesthood quorums and other instrumentalities of the Mormon Church were often involved in activities that would elsewhere be performed by public agencies.

One very important legislative act was passed on February 4, 1852, because the federally appointed justices, Brandebury and Brocchus, had abandoned their positions. This act gave the local probate courts authority to exercise original jurisdiction in both civil and criminal cases. This, in effect, made it possible for the local courts to practically displace the federal courts, a situation that prevailed in Utah until Congress repealed the territorial statute in 1874.

The Steptoe Incident

The public announcement of plural marriage, followed by the election of Democrat Franklin Pierce to the United States presidency, made a change in the territorial governorship politically expedient. Bernhisel advised Brigham Young to be cautious in his public utterances and to be more friendly to the federally appointed officials. Young's statement in a public meeting a few months later was hardly what the delegate had in mind: "I am and will be Governor, and no power can hinder it until the Lord Almighty says, 'Brigham, you need not be Governor any longer'."

Not wishing to violate the principles of popular sovereignty but determined to make a change in Utah, President Pierce took advantage of Lieutenant Colonel Edward J. Steptoe's presence in the territory and offered the governorship to him. Steptoe had come into Salt Lake Valley in August 1854 at the head of a military and civilian party. His instructions were to study the feasibility of a military road through the territory and to assist in capturing the murderers of Captain John W. Gunnison and seven others who had been killed in an 1853 Indian massacre that some publicists had erroneously charged against the Mormons. Instead of accepting the governorship, Steptoe apparently became convinced that Young should be reappointed and signed a mammoth petition to that effect. He and his party left for California in the spring of 1855. Pierce offered the position to others and when they declined he simply let things stand. Brigham Young remained Utah's governor by default.

The Utah War

In spite of this respite, events and attitudes were developing that would not only lead to the replacement of Young as governor but would cause Utah to be "invaded" by the United States Army in 1857-58.

An important contributor to this unfortunate episode was the involvement of Mormon polygamy in national politics. The passage of the Kansas-Nebraska Act in 1854, granting popular sovereignty on the question of slavery to those territories, unleashed a flood of opposition that led to the organization of the Republican Party. Some Republican orators used the marriage customs of Utah, which would certainly be supported by popular vote in the territory, as an argument against the principle of "squatter sovereignty." By 1856 Republicans were insisting on the right and duty of Congress to "prohibit in the Territories those twin relics of barbarism—Polygamy and Slavery." The Democrats, not wishing to imply support of polygamy by their support of slavery, became as vehement as were their political opponents in denouncing the Mormon institution of polygamy.

James Buchanan, the Democratic victor in 1856, decided even before entering the White House to appoint a new governor for Utah. By May 1, 1857, he was further convinced that the Mormons were in a state of rebellion and would not accept a new chief executive unless they were forced to do so. So he decided to have force available.

Several developments in addition to partisan politics led to these decisions. The fervor of the "Reformation" movement among the Saints in the winter of 1856-1857 produced rhetoric about the pending fate of the wicked, apostate and Gentile alike, that generated concern when it appeared in the national press. At the same time new troubles involved some of the territorial officials. Letters and verbal reports from three Indian agents, Utah surveyor general David H. Burr, former U. S. mail contractor W. F. M. McGraw, and territorial supreme court justices George P. Stiles and William W. Drummond alleged that the Mormons in Utah were unwilling to accept and cooperate with non-Mormon officials; that they were alienating the Indians from the federal government; that they had destroyed the supreme court records and had so dominated the lower courts that there was no justice for non-Mormons; that Brigham Young and other leaders were disrespectful of federal officials, both living and dead; that the priesthood government was violent and despotic; and that a state of rebellion existed. They also asserted that many Utahns were unwillingly subject to the church leaders and that they longed to escape the "cruelties" of Mormon society.

These circumstances not only insured that the second of what would ultimately become seven formal applications for statehood from Utah—this one launched in 1856—would die in Congress. They also produced a state of national opinion of which this editorial comment in *Harper's Weekly*, April 25, 1857, is typical:

> *The matter has, in fact, passed beyond the line of argument, and it is time at once for the Government of the United States to interpose. We do not call for fire or slaughter. No Highland clan sort of operation—no Glencoe massacre. But, at whatever cost, the United States must declare and vindicate its supremacy . . . .*

Without investigating the situation in Utah or communicating his intentions to the people there, President Buchanan appointed Alfred Cumming of Georgia to be governor and ordered General William S. Harney to organize and command a military force to accompany the new appointee to Great Salt Lake City. Unfortunately, Harney's orders came from Secretary of War John B. Floyd, who was bitterly anti-Mormon and who advocated the need for military force, while Cumming's instructions were from Secretary of State Lewis Cass, who urged him to uphold the law but not to interfere with any of the Mormons' "peculiar opinions." Thus a conflict of attitudes was created at the outset between the army leadership and the governor.

On May 26, 1857, Army Chief of Staff Winfield Scott confidentially advised Floyd against the expedition on the basis of logistics and the late start. But two days later Floyd ordered the gathering of 2,500 troops at Fort Leavenworth "to march thence to Utah as soon as assembled." The expedition was further delayed when Harney was reassigned to Kansas; he was not replaced by Colonel Albert Sidney Johnston until September, after advance units of the military were on their way west under the temporary command of Colonel Edmund B. Alexander. Quartermaster Corps Captain Stewart Van Vliet was sent ahead to Utah to make arrangements for food and forage, but he carried no official information concerning the intentions of the troops and unguarded supply trains that were then strung out along the overland trail.

Utah's inhabitants became aware of the approaching army July 24, 1857, when Porter Rockwell, A. O. Smoot, and Judson Stoddard, returning from business in the East, rode into a Pioneer Day celebration in Big Cottonwood Canyon with the alarming news. Fearful of what an army might do to their whole program, Brigham Young and the other Mormon leaders decided to resist if the troops tried to force their way into the territory. Millennial enthusiasm rose as fiery speeches predicted the nearness of God's kingdom and the fall of the United States government. Colorful Heber C. Kimball expressed his intense feelings in these words:

Send 2500 troops here, our brethren, to make a desolation of this people! God Almighty helping me, I will fight until there is not a drop of blood in my veins. Good God! I have enough wives to whip the United States, for they will whip themselves . . . .

The Nauvoo Legion was mustered and practical measures were instituted to make resistance possible. Grain and other staples were stored, fortifications were built, raiding parties were selected to harass the army and supply trains, and exploring groups were sent out to locate oases where the Saints could survive if forced to abandon their homes.

Captain Van Vliet entered this scene on September 7, 1857. After interviewing the church leaders and inspecting their resistance measures, he was invited to attend a conference session in which the people listened to a recounting of their persecutions in Missouri and Illinois and then pledged unanimous support to Young's resistance policy. Van Vliet was convinced that the Mormons were not in rebellion against the authority of the United States, but that they felt justified in preparing to defend themselves against an unwarranted military invasion. He was unsuccessful in making his quartermaster arrangements. As he returned to the expeditionary force and then to Washington, Van Vliet became a strong advocate of peaceful reconciliation.

In view of the facts that in mid-August Brigham Young sent dispatches east to his old friend, Colonel Thomas L. Kane, and that on September 14 Congressional delegate Bernhisel left with Van Vliet for the capital, it seems likely that the Mormon leadership also hoped for a peaceful outcome. The bellicose speeches and actions that followed may have been intended primarily as a demonstration of Mormon solidarity that might, as a *Millennial Star* editorial put it, capture the public fancy and "make the General Government show their true colors in reference to their designs with Utah."

Whatever the ultimate hopes or intentions, Young at this point seized upon a technicality to justify the proposed military preparations. Since he had not been replaced by a duly certified and legally installed governor, he issued a proclamation as territorial governor on September 15, 1857, declaring that a state of martial law existed and that the militia would resist any invasion of Utah. Under this authority, guerrilla forces under Lot Smith, Robert Burton, Porter Rockwell, and others and several hundred Nauvoo Legion soldiers in Echo Canyon under the command of Daniel H. Wells prepared to face the United States Army.

Elements of pathos and comedy combined in the events that followed. Nauvoo Legion horsemen, under strict orders to avoid bloodshed, burned three supply trains, interrupted military communications, and employed all manner of delaying tactics. There were no combat casualties, unless account be taken of the infantryman who was reported to have "died of fright" during a nocturnal raid designed to drive off the army's livestock. The Saints had heard of Harney's boast that he would "winter in the valley or in hell," and, unaware that he had been replaced, they did their best to make the choice for him.

Meanwhile Van Vliet had met Colonel Alexander's forces west of South Pass with the news of probable Mormon resistance. The temporary commander tried to organize his troops at Hams Fork on the Green River while awaiting Johnston's arrival, but he finally decided to try to enter the Salt Lake Valley by Bear River Valley rather than by the fortified Echo Canyon route. Early winter weather forced him to give up the plan, and when Colonel Johnston took command he had little choice but to establish winter quarters near Fort Bridger. Both Fort Bridger and Fort Supply had by then been abandoned and burned by the Mormons. Johnston called his city of tents and improvised shelters *Camp Scott.*

Thus a combination of bungling on the part of the Buchanan administration, vacillating military leadership, hit-and-run raids, and inclement weather stopped the Utah Expedition a hundred miles short of its destination. Approximately 2,500 American soldiers and several hundred civilian officials, freighters, and camp followers spent a miserable winter at Camp Scott, while the eastern press began to have second thoughts about the whole enterprise and both Buchanan and Brigham Young weighed their options for 1858.

Despite their initial successes, in their winter speeches the Mormon leaders reflected awareness that it would be impossible to stop an invasion by a reinforced army in the spring. Sermons now began to speak about retreating into the desert if necessary, and contingency plans were made. However, hopes for a negotiated peace rose when Colonel Kane arrived in Great Salt Lake City late in February, having come by way of Panama and California with a quasiofficial letter from President Buchanan. Despite the failure of the efforts that Kane, Bernhisel, and Van Vliet had made to persuade the president to send an investigating commission to Utah, Buchanan was willing to let Kane go to the Mormon capital with his unofficial blessing. The subsequent policy of the administration clearly suggests that some hope was placed on the successful outcome of this private diplomacy.

After apprising himself of the attitudes of Young and his associates and assuring them that the government had no interest in warring against them, Kane rode on to Camp Scott, arriving on March 12, 1858. He found Colonel Johnston suspicious of his proposals, but he was finally able to induce Cumming to go with him to the Salt Lake Valley, accompanied only by a detachment of Mormon troops. Cumming arrived on April 12, and three days later he sent word to Johnston and Buchanan that he had been received as governor and treated with kindness and respect.

Smooth relations between the Saints and the government were not, however, immediately established. Still fearful of the bellicose-sounding army, which the administration was known to have asked Congress to reinforce with new regiments, the Mormons abandoned all of the settlements in the northern part of the territory, including the capital. They gathered in wagon boxes and makeshift shelters or moved in with friends in Utah Valley and the settlements to the south, ready to retreat farther if the army failed to carry out Cumming's promise that it would enter the Great Basin peacefully and establish its camps away from the population centers. Army personnel, anxious for revenge and spoiling for a fight, were distrustful of Cumming's negotiations and insisted on marching into the Salt Lake Valley in fulfillment of their assignment.

While Cumming was pursuing his attempts at reconciliation, a two-man peace commission arrived in Great Salt Lake City on June 7. Appointed by Buchanan to pacify the Mormons with a proclamation of amnesty, dated April 6, Lazarus W. Powell and Ben McCulloch had excellent qualifications and proved to be reasonably good diplomats. The timing of their appointment, before any word had been received in Washington about Kane's reception, Cumming's activities, or the change in Mormon strategy, strongly supports the conclusion that the president, anxious to extricate the government from a costly and hazardous venture, decided to stake more on the advice of Kane, Van Vliet, and Bernhisel than he had been willing to do, at least publicly, a few months earlier.

The commissioners announced on June 12, 1858, that all differences between the people of Utah and the United States had been happily settled. A premature movement of Johnston's forces threatened momentarily to upset the peace, but the misunderstandings were cleared up and the Mormons accepted the government offer of amnesty and the establishment of a federal military post in their midst. The army moved quietly through abandoned and silent Great Salt Lake City on June 26 and soon established itself forty miles to the southwest in Cedar Valley; the post was named *Camp Floyd*. After a few days the Saints traveled back to their deserted homes and the Utah War was over.

The Mountain Meadows Massacre

One indirect but tragic result of the military invasion was the massacre of 120 emigrants September 7-11, 1857, at Mountain Meadows, a campsite thirty-five miles southwest of Cedar City on the California trail.

At about the same time that word was received in the small southern Utah settlements of the approach of the United States Army, the Fancher Train, a party composed of several families from Arkansas and a group of horsemen who called themselves the *Missouri Wildcats*, made its way through central Utah; it was following the southern route to California because of the lateness of the season. Unwise actions by members of the party, including failure to keep their animals under control while going through Mormon communities and the expression of anti-Mormon sentiments, antagonized the Saints who had already been stirred to a war fever by the fiery preaching of Apostle George A. Smith and others. The climax of this bad feeling was reached at Cedar City when the local citizens followed their instructions to husband their supplies because of the threatening war situation and refused to sell food to the Fancher Train. The angry emigrants expressed hope that the invading army would punish the Mormons, and they threatened to raise another military force when they arrived in California. Leaving Cedar City, the emigrants traveled to Mountain Meadows, where they stopped to rest their livestock before the long hard journey across the Nevada-California desert.

A meeting was held in Cedar City under the leadership of Mormon Stake President Isaac C. Haight, and proposals were made to wipe out the emigrants before they could get to the coast to carry out their threats. Calmer heads prevailed, and a rider was sent

170

north to obtain Brigham Young's advice. (His instructions to let the emigrants pass were received on September 12, one day too late.)

Meanwhile a band of Indians, attracted by the herds of fat cattle and apparently encouraged by some Mormons, had been following the train, and decided to attack the Mountain Meadows encampment. The attack failed, and the Indians turned to their erstwhile friends and allies, the Mormons, demanding help in overcoming the beleaguered camp. John D. Lee, the Mormon in charge of Indian affairs in southern Utah, became involved and ultimately played a major role in carrying out the massacre plan, although he later insisted that he had opposed the whole scheme and had acted only under duress.

When three men who had escaped from the besieged camp to seek aid were killed by Mormons and Indians, the local Mormon leaders decided that they could not wait for Brigham Young's advice; it would be too dangerous to let the Fancher party spread the word in California that Mormons were helping Indians attack emigrant trains. Under a flag of truce, Lee was able to convince the emigrants to lay down their arms with a promise of safe conduct back to Cedar City. Then Mormon militia men, acting under military orders, killed the disarmed men, while the Indians were permitted to kill the women and older children. Seventeen small children were spared and ultimately, with government help, were returned to relatives in Arkansas.

Federal government attempts to apprehend and punish the participants in this bloody deed failed as the tight-knit Mormon society closed ranks and protected its members. John D. Lee was apprehended almost twenty years after the incident and, following two trials, was executed by a firing squad at the scene of the crime. The tragic massacre increased the Mormon reputation for fanaticism and made relationships with federal officials more difficult.

Conclusion

The political developments in Utah during the first decade of white settlement are interesting for a number of reasons. During the first four years, three separate forms of government were utilized, each with a different source of authority. In each form—church, State of Deseret, and Utah territorial—Brigham Young was the leader, and it is doubtful that the citizens of Utah could detect any day-to-day difference in the way they were governed. When non-Mormon territorial officials arrived in 1851, there was a difference. These men found it uncomfortable to try to function within the prevailing theocratic atmosphere and finally called on the federal government to correct what they felt was an un-American system. After the Utah War almost forty more years of difficulty and antagonism would elapse before the problem could be resolved and Utah could become the nation's forty-fifth state.

Chapter 9
Bibliographical Essay

The general histories by Bancroft, Whitney, Neff, Creer, and Anderson, listed in chapter 7, all contain information on early governmental developments. The volumes of B. H. Roberts, *Comprehensive History of the Church* (1930), which cover the Utah period, heavily emphasize politics; Vols. III and IV deal with this period.

Leland H. Creer's *Utah and the Nation* (1929) treats Utah's rather tempestuous relationship with the federal government in a way that suggests the Mormons were basically loyal. Klaus Hansen's *Quest for Empire* (1968) challenges this concept and maintains that the early founders of Utah were so committed to the establishment of the political Kingdom of God that their attitudes and actions were often antagonistic to federal authority. Hansen feels that the mysterious Council of Fifty holds the key to a proper understanding of governmental development in Utah. D. Michael Quinn, "The Mormon Hierarchy, 1832-1932: An American Elite" (Ph.D. dissertation, Yale University, 1976), assigns less emphasis to the Council of Fifty but emphasizes the leading role of the Mormon hierarchy in early Utah politics.

J. Keith Melville, *Highlights in Mormon Political History* (Charles E. Merrill Monograph Series in the Humanities and Social Sciences, Brigham Young University, 1967), discusses political activities in the Iowa colonies as well as Mormon involvement in the Compromise of 1850.

Dale L. Morgan, "The State of Deseret," *UHQ,* January 1940, is probably the best study of that episode in Utah's history. Unpublished monographs that throw light on aspects of early politics and government include Eugene E. Campbell, "The Government of Utah, 1847-51" (master's thesis, University of Utah, 1940); Charles Koritz, "The Government of Early Utah Communities" (master's thesis, Brigham Young University, 1972); Richard Draper, "Babylon in Zion: The Mormon Concept of Zion as a Cause for Mormon-Gentile Conflict, 1846-1857" (master's thesis, Arizona State University, 1974); Louis G. Reinwand, "Interpretive Study of Mormon Millennialism ..." (master's thesis, Brigham Young University, 1971).

Norman F. Furniss, *The Mormon Conflict, 1850–59* (1960), covers the causes and course of the Utah War. *The Utah Expedition, 1857–58: A Documentary Account ... (1958)*, collected and edited by LeRoy and Ann Hafen, provides valuable sources on the political and military aspects of the expedition. Albert L. Zobell's "Thomas L. Kane, Ambassador to the Mormons," *Utah Humanities Review*, October 1947, analyzes Kane's important contribution to the peaceable settlement of the unfortunate affair.* Richard D. Poll, "The Mormon Question, 1850-65" (Ph.D. dissertation, University of California, Berkeley, 1948), gives a careful analysis of political developments with special emphasis on public opinion and congressional action.

Juanita Brooks, *Mountain Meadows Massacre* (1950; rev. ed. 1962), is certainly the best source of information concerning that tragic event. Her biography of *John D. Lee* (1962) throws a great deal of light on the whole Mormon colonization program as well as the massacre.

---

*Two works by Gustive O. Larson bear on 1850s politics: *The "Americanization" of Utah for Statehood* (1971) and "The Mormon Reformation," *UHQ,* January 1958.

Chapter 10
The Mormon Gathering

Gustive O. Larson

The founding of Utah, as noted in earlier chapters, resulted from the Mormon concept of building an earthly Kingdom of God in the Great Basin. The mission of the Mormons, as outlined by their early leaders, was to gather "scattered Israel" preparatory to Christ's personal rule on earth. In the performance of this mission, more than 100,000 men, women, and children were recruited, organized, and brought to Utah from the Eastern States, Europe, and the islands of the Pacific during the territorial period. Most of them were Britons, Scandinavians, and Germans, whose emigration was assisted by a unique Mormon enterprise—the Perpetual Emigrating Fund Company.

The "Gathering"

The gathering began when The Church of Jesus Christ of Latter-day Saints was born in 1830. The message of "the Restoration" was carried by dedicated missionaries out of western New York and Ohio into every state of the Union, to Canada, and finally in 1837 to Great Britain. Within eight months of their arrival in England, Heber C. Kimball and his associates baptized 2,000 converts. The Mormon apostles enjoyed continued success, and 5,000 converts sailed from Liverpool to join the Nauvoo congregation before its exodus to the West.

The Chartist Petition of 1838 sheds light on the enthusiastic response of the poor in Great Britain to the message of the missionaries from America. In demanding that the working class be given a voice in the government, the petitioners complained of oppressive taxes and overwhelming suffering:

Our trades are trembling on the verge of bankruptcy; our workmen are starving. Capital brings no profit, and labor no remuneration. The home of the artificer is desolate, and the warehouse of the pawnbroker is full. The workhouse is crowded and the manufactory is deserted. We have looked on every side; we have searched diligently in order to find out the causes of distress so sore and so long continued. We can discover none in nature or in providence.

Such conditions favored a proselyting program in which temporal welfare was inseparably connected with spiritual; Mormonism, with its promise of economic relief, could not fail to attract wide attention. Thousands responded to announcements such as the one that appeared in the *Millennial Star* in February 1842:

In the midst of the general distress which prevails in this country on account of want of employment, the high price of provisions, the oppression, priestcraft and iniquity of the land, it is pleasing to the household of faith to contemplate a country reserved by the Almighty as a sure asylum for the poor and the oppressed—a country every way adapted to their wants and conditions—and still more pleasing to think that thousands of the Saints have already made their escape from this country, and all its abuses and distress, and that they have found a home, where, by persevering industry they may enjoy all the blessings of liberty, peace and plenty.

In 1847, while the Mormons were preparing to leave Winter Quarters for their trek overland to Salt Lake Valley, the Saints in England prepared their own petition to Queen Victoria, asking for aid in emigrating to Vancouver Island (Canada). The petition was 168 feet long and contained nearly 13,000 signatures. Noting that most government schemes for emigration had experienced difficulty in finding willing participants, it pledged "to send twenty thousand people of all trades and from most districts in Scotland, England and Wales at once, or as soon as vessels can be found. . . ." The British government did not respond to this petition, but it did not obstruct the Mormon emigration during the following decades.

After Brigham Young had been sustained as church president at Council Bluffs on December 27, 1847, the First Presidency and Quorum of the Twelve Apostles issued a General Epistle urging all of the scattered Saints to gather to the temporary church settlements on the Missouri. The epistle also urged church members to be prepared to push on to the Great Basin as soon as feasible:

To all Saints in England, Scotland, Ireland, Wales and adjacent islands and countries, we say emigrate as speedily as possible to this vicinity, look-

ing to, and following the counsel of the Presidency at Liverpool: shipping to New Orleans and from thence direct to Council Bluffs . . . . for here is land on which, by their labor they can speedily better their condition for their future journey. And to all Saints in any country bordering upon the Atlantic we would say, pursue the same course, come immediately and prepare to go west—bringing with you all kinds of choice seeds, of grain, vegetables, fruit, shrubbery, trees and vines, everything that will please the eye, gladden the heart, or cheer the soul of man, that grows upon the face of the whole earth . . . .

Plans for solid community buildings were reflected later in the epistle. The emigrating converts were to bring:

. . . the best stock of beast, bird and fowl of every kind. Also the best tools of every description, and machinery for spinning or weaving and dressing cotton, wool, flax and silk, etc., or models and descriptions of the same by which they can construct them; the same in relation to all kinds of farming utensils and husbandry, such as corn-shellers, grain threshers and cleaners, smut machines, mills and every implement and article within their knowledge that shall tend to promote the comfort, health, happiness and prosperity of any people. So far as it can be consistently done, bring models and drafts, and let the machinery be built where it is used, which will save great expense in transportation. . . .

Before the 1848 companies started west from Winter Quarters, Young undertook to strengthen the proselyting and gathering program of the church. Wilford Woodruff was sent to take charge in Canada and Jesse C. Little, John Brown, Ezra T. Benson, Amasa Lyman, and others were assigned to supervise the work in the states and urge the Mormons to come west. Orson Pratt left to preside in Britain, and Orson Hyde took charge of the remaining exiles in Iowa until they could go to the Salt Lake Valley.

The Great Basin presented a real challenge to the gathering program, but those called on missions almost always accepted with enthusiasm. In 1849 proselyters were sent to Scandinavia, Germany, France, Switzerland, Italy, Spain, the South Seas, and even to far-off Australia. By 1852 they had invaded South America, South Africa, Japan, China, and India. The Asiatic, African, and Latin American ventures proved short-lived, but Mormonism had come to stay in Europe and the islands of the Pacific.

The Perpetual Emigrating Fund Company

Eight thousand refugees from Nauvoo remaining on the Pottawattamie lands in Iowa in 1849 were a reminder to the Saints in Salt Lake City of an unfulfilled pledge. Brigham Young proposed that a revolving fund be created "agreeable to our covenant in the Nauvoo Temple that we would never cease our exertions ... till all the Saints who were obliged to leave Nauvoo shall be located at some gathering place of the Saints." A committee of the Council of Fifty was appointed to raise a fund during October conference; the committee quickly collected $5,000 cash and thirteen yoke of oxen. Bishop Edward Hunter was appointed to carry the funds back to the states to buy cattle, to take the oversight of the property, and to bring the poor to the new Zion. A letter of instruction to him explained that money from the cash fund was to be advanced as a *loan* to be paid back by the beneficiaries for repeated use by others who waited their turn to come to Zion. Hence it was to become a perpetual emigrating fund.

To legalize the various activities involved in management of the fund, officials incorporated it under the laws of the State of Deseret on September 14, 1850, as the Perpetual Emigrating Fund Company.

The first census of Utah Territory showed the 1850 population to be 11,380. That year, when proselyting activities were extended from England to the European continent, there were 27,000 Mormons in Great Britain; 10,319 had already sailed to America. With the addition of many of these who had not yet reached the Salt Lake Valley and considerable numbers who were joining the movement in Scandinavia, the church membership abroad was 33,000 in 1850—three times the number already in the West. The situation gave urgency to the services of the emigrating company.

Additional contributions swelled the Emigrating Fund over the next three years, and the hesitating flock in Iowa was urged to come west. "We wish you to evacuate Pottawattamie and the states and next fall be with us ..." wrote Brigham Young in the fall of 1851. The following year the mission was accomplished by special effort as the Mormons poured into the migrating stream along the Oregon-California Trail. Twenty-one companies of sixty wagons each—including about 10,000 settlers—made the trek. A major part of the Nauvoo membership of the church was now reunited in the Salt Lake Valley.

Meanwhile the swelling Latter-day Saint membership in Britain eagerly awaited its turn to embark on chartered ships bound for the American Zion. When the General Epistle from Winter Quarters reached England early in 1848, Mission President Orson Spencer lost no time in expressing its message in the *Millennial Star:*

The channel of Saints emigration to the land of Zion is now opened. The long wished for time of gathering has come. Good tidings from Mt. Zion!

The resting place of Israel for the last days has been discovered. . . . Now rejoice and lift up your heads, O ye pure in heart, and let the laboring and the heavily laden, that have been bowed down under the weight of accumulated oppressions in every nation prepare themselves to come to their inheritance in the land of promise. . . . Let all who can gather up their effects, and set their faces as a flint to go Zionward in due time and order . . . .

Local leaders were asked to indicate how many members were prepared to emigrate in February. They were advised that the expense per person would probably be £10, covering passage from Liverpool (via New Orleans and St. Louis) to Council Bluffs.

Passengers for the scheduled sailings were readily available, and early in March two ships were launched. In July Orson Pratt arrived in England to succeed Spencer as president of the mission, and two more companies of emigrants were dispatched under his direction in September. Nine companies followed in 1849, six companies in 1850, and four in early 1851. Further shipping was then suspended during investigation of an approach to the Great Basin from the West Coast (the "Mormon Corridor") so emigrants might possibly avoid the unhealthy river trip inland from New Orleans. When no satisfactory shipping arrangements materialized around Cape Horn or across the Isthmus of Panama, emigration was resumed by way of the Mississippi River. However, an important change in the program excluded any stopover on the Pottawatamie lands in Iowa, partly because the evacuation of the Saints from Iowa was completed in 1852 and partly because the customary halt had too often resulted in apostasy and failure to complete the journey. Now, only those who could make the through trip to the Salt Lake Valley either on their own or with Perpetual Emigrating Fund (PEF) help were permitted to undertake the journey.

In the meantime, Franklin D. Richards had arrived in Great Britain in March 1850, and, in cooperation with President Pratt, promptly introduced the Emigrating Fund to the Saints. A ready response brought contributions ranging from a few shillings to £400, which reached a total of £1,410 by 1852. Two vessels departing in January of that year carried 750 Mormon emigrants, of whom 251 were beneficiaries of the fund. The total expense of the operation, however, exceeded the funds on hand by £1,000.

Having determined that it could send a passenger from Great Britain to Utah for an outlay of £10 sterling, the fund company accepted that amount from 957 emigrants in 1853. In addition it assisted 400 others with PEF loans, and another 955 paid their own way. This total of 3,212 Britons was increased by 314 emigrants from the European mainland, and 297 Scandinavians and seventeen Germans. An expenditure of some £30,000 was required to transport these companies to their new homes in America.

Friends and relatives played an important part in the gathering of the Saints from Europe. Many in Utah, who were eager to bring members of their families or close friends, were not only permitted but were encouraged to pay their way by depositing either cash or articles that were readily convertible to cash with the PEF office in Salt Lake City. This office, in turn, directed the agents abroad to send the persons named under the care of the company. The popularity of this system soon necessitated an admonition from Brigham Young that the Saints "not waste their time or ours by continually running to the President's office to know whether this, that, or the other person can be sent for until they have deposited or have in hand the full amount necessary . . . and that too in money or its equivalent."

Variations in procedures were made to fit circumstances, but basically the emigrating process now served four classes of people: (1) PEF emigrants who signed notes under transportation contracts with the company; (2) Saints sent for by friends or relatives in Utah; (3) the £10 passengers who were encouraged to deposit any personal surplus funds with the company; and (4) those who paid their own way while enjoying the advantage of company organization and protection.

The total number of emigrants leaving Europe for Utah in 1854 dropped to 2,034, but those assisted by PEF money rose to 1,073. The rising cost of transportation and teams made it necessary to increase the £10 plan to £13 that year. By that time 21,911 Mormons had emigrated from Liverpool to America (including 5,000 to Nauvoo before the exodus). Of these, 2,885 had come as PEF emigrants (after 1852), 957 had come under the £10 plan, and eighty-six had emigrated under the £13 plan. The balance had been sent for by Utahns or had paid their own way while enjoying the services of the fund company, which had spent a total of about £125,000. Indicative of a developing international pattern in the European emigration to Utah are the following statistics from the continent in 1855: 972 from Scandinavia; forty-five from the Swiss-Italian Mission; seventy-five from France; thirteen from Germany; and one from Prussia. Also in 1855 the New Orleans-Mississippi River route was abandoned for health reasons in favor of entry into the United States at Philadelphia, New York, or Boston, and in favor of travel by rail westward to the Mississippi and the railhead beyond.

The infiltration of converts into the Mormon emigration movement for purely economic reasons became a problem as soon as the church began to organize and reduce the costs of transAtlantic travel. A sifting process by the church leadership resulted in 15,197 excommunications in the European missions between 1850 and 1854. In 1855 President Young sent a firm warning to the president of the British Mission to "be wary of assisting any ... whose chief aim and intention may be to get to America."

Handcarts to Zion

The financial strain on the emigrating company made it impossible for the company to continue to finance overland wagon trains. Young discussed the possibilities of handcart transportation in 1851, but no decision was made until 1855 when he wrote to Franklin D. Richards in England:

We have not much of interest to communicate more than you are aware of—such as meeting heavy liabilities constantly falling due here and in St. Louis for this year's emigration. ... We cannot afford to purchase wagons and teams as in time past, I am consequently thrown back upon my old plan—to make handcarts and let the emigration foot it, and draw upon them the necessary supplies, having a cow or two for every ten. ... I want to see it fairly tried and tested, at all events ... indeed, we will be obliged to pursue this course or suspend operations, for ought that I can see at the present.

On October 29 he instructed that the plan be implemented in 1856, and that the immigrants were to be equipped with handcarts at the railhead in Iowa City. Associated with this plan was the proposed establishment of an overland express and freight company, whose way stations would become resting places for future immigrants. Although the Brigham Young Express and Carrying Company was launched early in 1857 and numerous stations were established as contemplated, the Utah War led to the abandonment of the project. Meanwhile, the handcart experiment went forward without this support.

According to plan, five handcart companies of emigrants, numbering 1,891 in all, crossed the plains and mountains from Iowa City to Salt Lake Valley in 1856. The carts built in Iowa were designed either for pushing or pulling and were constructed to carry from 100 to 500 pounds of food and clothing. Some of the carts were painted and carried inscriptions such as "Merry Mormons," "Zion's Express," or "Truth Will Prevail." The first three companies left Iowa City in June and arrived safely in Salt Lake Valley between September 26 and October 2.

The last two companies, whose members did not leave Liverpool until May 3 and May 25, were delayed in Iowa City while waiting for their carts. They nevertheless set out in late July. When they reached Florence (Winter Quarters) in August, they earnestly debated waiting there until the next spring, but impatience, enthusiasm, and faith prevailed over prudence, and both companies pushed out onto the plains. October found them toiling up Sweetwater River in the high Rockies, where each member's scant allotment of clothing gave little comfort on the frosty mornings. Then unseasonably early snows trapped the Martin Company just west of Devil's Gate and the Willie Company a few miles east of South Pass. Here relief parties from Utah found them freezing and near starvation. Before total rescue was accomplished, more than 200 of them had been buried in frozen graves.

While the tragedy of the Martin and Willie companies must not be minimized, the handcart enterprise as a whole should not be measured in terms of what happened to those two companies. Out of a total of 3,756 emigrants leaving Europe for Utah in 1856, approximately half were PEF passengers listed to travel by handcart; 385 were booked to go through on their own means, and the balance were to remain in the states for a season. With a threatened invasion of Utah by the United States Army pending in 1857, Mormon immigration from abroad dropped to 1,994; 567 of those crossed the plains with handcarts. The fund was inactive in 1858 and 1859, with the result that foreign immigration dropped to 179 and 809 respectively in those years. Nevertheless, approximately 2,000 Mormons arrived in Salt Lake Valley in 1859, including American-born Saints and immigrants who had previously arrived in the states. In 1860 a total of 1,588 immigrants arrived, including two companies of handcarters totalling 268. Thus in the five-year period from 1856 to 1860, about 8,000 immigrants came to the United States bound for Utah. Of these, over 3,000 walked the full distance from the railroad terminal in Iowa to Salt Lake City, pushing or pulling a handcart.

The Church Teams

The local accumulation of cattle and horses purchased to supply the annual immigration companies required some adjustment in procedure. "We are rich in cattle," wrote Brigham Young in February 1861, "but do not abound in money either at home or abroad, and we desire to operate so as to use our small amount of money and large numbers of cattle in the best possible manner for accomplishing the most good." Previously Joseph W. Young had

An emigrant wagon train makes its way down Echo Canyon in the 1860s, the poles of the overland telegraph helping to mark the way.

accompanied an eastbound twenty-wagon ox team train to bring machinery and merchandise to Utah and had returned to Salt Lake City the same season. In a sermon on "oxteamology" preached in the Tabernacle on his return, Young outlined how, with proper care of the oxen, such church trains could serve both the church's commercial and immigration needs, no longer necessitating the purchase of additional animals in the East. This was the beginning of the procedure where church team trains left Salt Lake Valley each spring to meet the Utah-bound immigrants at the Iowa railway terminal.

The Mormon outfitting post moved from Iowa City west to Florence, Nebraska Territory, in 1857. Here it remained on the Missouri River until 1864. Then the railroad, creeping westward, crowded it to Wyoming, a little village located seven miles north of Nebraska City. In 1868 Benton, and later Laramie, became railway terminals and frontier outfitting posts.

Under the new plan, the church teams picked up the freight and passengers where the railroad dropped them. The call to supply teams, men, and provisions for the church trains went out annually to the ward bishops throughout Utah. In addition to a teamster for each outfit, one extra man for approximately every four wagons went along on horseback as herder and scout. These men were selected by the bishops and called on missions that usually took about six months. In Salt Lake City the teams assembled in a "train" that usually started east the last week in April; captains were appointed over every company of fifty teams. The teams were well provisioned and those required for transportation were augmented by extra cattle. These extra cattle, in addition to serving as a supply of meat, were intended for the eastern market—primarily for Mormon immigrants with sufficient means to purchase their own.

The church team plan made possible the importation of vital machinery and merchandise, and it facilitated the eastern marketing of surplus cattle and other commodities. (Among the products sent east, perhaps the most unusual cargo was 4,300 pounds of cotton in 1863, grown by the Cotton Mission in Utah's Dixie.) As the surplus cattle found a ready market among the independent Zion-bound immigrants, Brigham Young estimated that the people of the territory saved from ten to thirty thousand dollars from funds that had previously been paid to non-Mormons in the East for cattle and wagons.

Excepting the years of 1865 and 1867, the church team trains continued throughout the 1860s to meet the arriving immigrants and the shifting railroad terminal points. In 1868, the last year before the railroad was completed, 500 teams and $27,000 were provided in a special effort to assist foreign immigration; a total of $70,000 was raised by the Saints in Utah and by the missions for the purpose of "gathering the Lord's poor." Summarizing the accomplishments of the period, it appears that 1,956 wagons conducted by 2,483 men employing 17,443 oxen were sent east to receive the immigrants. A total of 20,426 Europeans were assisted to Utah; not more than 726 of those came by their own teams. These figures do not include immigrants from the states. The dollar value of this largely contributed service from 1861 to 1868 has been estimated at $2,400,000.

Mormon Immigration by Railroad

The immigrants of 1869 rode into Utah on the railroad, enjoying its relative comforts the entire distance to Ogden. (The comforts were limited, however, for those who journeyed in cattle cars.) Their June arrival marked the close of the church team operations, and the frontier outfitting post passed into history. The church faced a new problem in maintaining the annual influx of immigrants: the wagon trains of the preceding decade had operated with comparatively little cash outlay, whereas railroad transportation required cash for fares. These fares from Liverpool to Salt Lake City varied during the next few years, ranging from £15/10/0 in 1871 to £12/16/0 in the depression year 1875.

In Europe, savings were encouraged through the Emigration Deposit Fund and the Individual Emigration Account toward the day when such savings would cover transportation to Zion. With these measures supplementing the annual call for PEF contributions, the fund continued to operate on a decreasing scale, bringing another 34,593 immigrants to Utah between 1869 and 1887, when the company was disincorporated by the Congressionally enacted Edmunds-Tucker Law. Before its dissolution, the company had aided, either directly or indirectly, a grand total of over 100,000 emigrants to move to Utah Territory. Katherine Coman, in her *Economic Beginnings of the Far West* (1912), judged it "the most successful example of regulated immigration in United States history."

Financing the Immigration

Financing the annual flow of converts to Utah presented a continual challenge that could not have been met without the willing contributions of time, service, and products by church members. Cash contributions were limited but produce, readily convertible into cash, purchased overseas passage and equipment for overland travel. While many beneficiaries of loans were able to repay substantial amounts on their contracts through labor and products, indebtedness to the Emigrating Fund continued to grow until, when Brigham Young died in 1877, it amounted to $1,000,000. By 1880, it had reached $1,640,000 including interest. Half of this amount was stricken from the books as a Jubilee Year gesture, but most of it had already become uncollectible by the statute of limitations.

The complicated financing of the Perpetual Emigrating Fund Company allows for only educated estimates of the amount spent, but these do provide an impressive picture of overall operations. Leonard J. Arrington, on the basis of Mormon sources, placed the figure at some $8,000,000 expended on emigration operations by 1900. He also calculated that "the cost of all this immigration, as measured by the cost to the immigrants if they had used commercial channels instead of PEF, was approximately $25,000,000," and he estimated in *Great Basin Kingdom* (1957) "that the church through the PEF expended (or would have expended if commercial channels had been used) approximately $12,500,000."

The dissolution of the company in 1887 merely strengthened the social and economic forces that were already slowing down its operations. The immigration program was closely related to economic opportunities in Utah and was particularly related to available land and water. As the cultivatable lands were appropriated, a reactivated colonization program in the late 1870s expanded the Mormon commonwealth and provided new locations for settlement, first inside Utah borders, then beyond into neighboring territories and across international boundaries into Mexico and Canada. With decreasing promise of further agricultural areas to sustain new settlements, the call for "gathering" declined toward the end of the nineteenth century, and missionaries were instructed not to urge emigration. Concurrently, improved conditions in their homelands lessened the pressure on foreign Saints to emigrate.

Zion's Melting Pot

Of the more than 100,000 Latter-day Saints who were either directly or indirectly helped to emigrate to Utah, at least 85,000 came from Great Britain and the northern European countries. Within the United Kingdom, England contributed the bulk of the emigrants, followed by Wales and Scotland; Ireland contributed only a few. In numbers of emigrants Great Britain was followed by Denmark, Sweden, and Norway. The Swiss-German Mission, while adding considerably fewer converts, ranked next in its yield of migrants to Utah. Later the Netherlands added considerable numbers. Southern Europe was generally unresponsive to Mormon proselyting in the nineteenth century.

Reports up to 1855, when 21,911 emigrants had sailed from Liverpool, show the nationalities as follows: British—19,535; Scandinavian—2,000; French—125; Italian—125; German—100; and one other. In the eight-year period from 1861 to 1868, sixty percent of the total European emigration to Utah came from Great Britain, thirty-five percent came from Scandinavia, and two percent came from the Swiss-German Mission. Later, from 1878 to 1880, the United Kingdom dropped to forty-eight percent, the Scandinavian countries rose to thirty-nine percent, and the Swiss-German Mission contributed eight percent of the total.

Upon arriving in Utah, foreign converts often rejoined relatives and old friends or were sent in groups to strengthen outlying settlements. This resulted in the development of isolated nationality clusters where immigrants clung to their mother tongue and retained many characteristics of their homelands. Among such social groups were the Scandinavians who migrated to Sanpete County and the Swiss who were sent to grow grapes in the lower Virgin River Valley.

The Wine Mission, like the Iron, Cotton, and other special-purpose colonies discussed in another chapter, is a reminder that the Mormon kingdom was an economic as well as a social melting pot. That the gathering was concerned with temporal as well as spiritual gifts is illustrated in Brigham Young's 1849 letter to Orson Pratt, who was presiding in England:

We want a company of woolen manufacturers to come with machinery and take our wool from the sheep, and convert it into the best clothes, and the wool is ready. We want a company of cotton manufacturers who will convert cotton into cloth and calico, etc., and we will raise the cotton before the machinery can be ready. We want a company of potters; we need them. The clay is ready and the dishes wanted. . . . Silk manufacturers and all others will follow in rapid succession. We want some men to start a furnace forthwith; the coal, iron, and moulders are waiting. We have a printing press, and any who can take good printing and writing paper to the valley will be blessing themselves and the Church.

A sample of immigrant occupations appears in a list of 1,146 heads of families entered in the British Mission shipping books from 1849 to 1852. They appear in the following order of frequency (110 miscellaneous vocations are not included in this list):

laborers	207	mariners	16
miners	96	bricklayers	14
farmers	68	cloth workers	13
shoemakers	54	brickmakers	12
tailors	39	cordwainers	6
ministers	38	butchers	10
weavers	38	boilermakers	10
blacksmiths	36	painters	9
iron workers	36	sawyers	9
carpenters	33	mechanics	9
wheelwrights	28	spinners	9
colliers	26	servants	9
shipwrights	22	millers	9
engineers	22	stone masons	9
masons	21	plasterers	8
bakers	19	shopmen	5
gardeners	16		

The Gentiles

The dream that motivated the Mormon gathering to Utah—the establishment of a "land of Zion" in an isolated wilderness—began to be dispelled when the argonauts of 1849 passed through the Great Basin. Thousands trekked along what became a national highway to the Pacific, and a sprinkling of gold seekers found Salt Lake Valley attractive enough to stay. Next came non-Mormon merchants, freighters, and federal territorial appointees. The Utah War of 1857-58 brought Johnston's Army of 2,500 officers and enlisted men, plus enough civilian employees and camp followers to build almost overnight a city of 7,000 at Fairfield. Many of these became permanent citizens of Utah. The federal appointees who came with this military escort grew into a steady stream of carpetbaggers destined to play a significant role in Mormondom. The Civil War, which cancelled out Camp Floyd, brought 700 California volunteers to establish Fort Douglas as a new gentile center. Mining discoveries in the mid-1860s produced a small influx of outsiders, and the completed transcontinental railroad really opened up Utah to the outside world in 1869.

In the last three decades of the territorial period mining, transportation, commercial, governmental, educational, and religious activities increased the gentile movement into Utah as the Mormon immigration declined. The varied roles and contributions of the non-Mormons are discussed in other chapters. Here it need only be noted that their political impact contributed to the abandonment of the Mormon effort to build the theodemocratic Kingdom of God, even as their economic and social impact helped to move the gathered Saints—for better or worse—into the mainstream of American development.

Evaluation of the "Gathering"

Commentators on the class of people attracted to pioneer Utah differed widely in their judgments. Three American presidents were persuaded to address Congress on the need for legislation to curb the Saints' immigration, which was assumed to be an effort to sustain the Mormon polygamy system. In a novel approach in 1879 Secretary of State William M. Evarts asked the aid of foreign governments in stopping the emigration of potential lawbreakers—polygamists—from their shores. Many in Congress accepted at face value such allegations as one made in 1887 that "the menace of bringing in so large a number of immigrants by the Mormons was to be found in their continued illiteracy after arriving in Utah and their practical slavery to the Church." Evarts' appeal was regarded by the American and foreign press with some amazement, and it produced no action overseas. As for illiteracy, the 1880 census showed that only five percent of the Utah population over ten years of age were unable to read, as compared with 6.6 percent for the nine surrounding territories. Utah delegate John T. Caine, in a reply to the slavery charge, reported in the House of Representatives in 1889 that "as yet, ninety percent of all Mormon families in Utah own their own homes."

In contrast to repeated references to the Mormon immigrants as ignorant and superstitious are the personal observations of men such as Richard Burton, William Chandless, *Utah Gazeteer* Editor Robert W. Sloan, and James Linforth, who acted as an agent both in proselyting and in directing the annual immigrations from abroad. The first three are representative of many non-Mormons who had firsthand contact with the immigrants; in describing the immigrants they used such terms as "good, plain, honest sort, simple-minded, but not uneducated," and "sober, industrious, thrifty, moral, educated." Territorial Governor Arthur L. Thomas, who referred to them as coming from the lower classes of England and Scandinavia, admitted that "they are not without intelligence sufficient to utilize their general experience in practical affairs; they are industrious in a slow plodding way, frugal and easily governed." Burton, whose extensive travels gave him a basis for comparison, observed in *The City of the Saints* (1862):

Morally and spiritually, as well as physically, the proteges of the Perpetual Emigrating Fund gained by being transferred to the Far West. . . . Physically speaking, there is no comparison between the condition of the Saints and the class from which they are mostly taken. In point of morality the Mormon community is perhaps purer than any other of equal numbers.

While the beneficiaries of the fund company's activities were, as Burton pointed out, often drawn from the poor, the harvest of the "gathering" encompassed all economic and social classes. Among the converts were many leaders of superior caliber whose contributions to the budding state of Utah, and indeed to the nation, amply justify the emigrating enterprise. The Mormon success in utilizing sparse agricultural resources to build a thriving commonwealth in the vast wilderness of the Great Basin speaks well for the character of the men and women who accomplished it.

Chapter 10
Bibliographical Essay

The unique immigration program of the Mormon Church naturally required consideration in the early general histories of Utah and the Latter-day Saints, including T. B. H. Stenhouse, *Rocky Mountain Saints* (1873); Edward W. Tullidge, *History of Salt Lake City* (1886); and the earlier cited works of Bancroft, Roberts, and Neff.

The first volume devoted specifically to this subject is *Route from Liverpool to Great Salt Lake City* (1855), edited by James Linforth, with comments and illustrations by Frederick Piercy; a 1962 edition, edited by Fawn M. Brodie, is available. James A. Little covered emigration from the East to Utah from 1848 to 1852 in *From Kirtland to Salt Lake City* (1890). Under the title "The Gathering," Andrew Jenson published summaries of organized companies arriving from Liverpool in Vols. XII of *The Contributor*, 1891-1892. The files of the British Mission publication, *Millennial Star,* are replete with information about all aspects of the nineteenth-century emigration from Europe.

More recently the subject has occupied the attention of a number of scholars and students, beginning with a master's thesis by Gustive O. Larson at the University of Utah, 1926, which was summarized as "Story of the Perpetual Emigrating Fund Company," *Mississippi Valley Historical Review,* September 1931, and then published with some amplifications as *Prelude to the Kingdom* (1947). Three doctoral dissertations devoted to phases of the subject followed, two of which were published: William Mulder, *Homeward to Zion* (1957), which treats the Scandinavian emigration, and P. A. M. Taylor, *Expectations Westward* (1965), which centers on the British Saints. M. Hamblin Cannon summarized his dissertation in "Migration of English Mormons to America," *American Historical Review,* April 1947, and "The English Mormons in America," *Ibid.,* October 1952. Richard L. Evans, *A Century of Mormonism in Great Britain* (1937), summarizes emigration by years in the appendix. Leonard J. Arrington, *Great Basin Kingdom* (1958), deals with many economic aspects of the "gathering" movement.

The centennial of the handcart tragedy produced several articles: Gustive O. Larson, "Mormon Handcart Story," *Improvement Era,* June-July, 1956; LeRoy R. Hafen, "Handcarts to Utah, 1856-1860," *UHQ,* October 1956; and a popularized version by Wallace Stegner, "Ordeal by Handcart," *Colliers,* July 6, 1956. Hafen, together with his wife Ann Hafen, published a definitive study, *Handcarts to Utah* (1960).

William Mulder pointed out some unique features of the emigrating program in "Mormonism's 'Gathering': An American Doctrine with a Difference," *Church History*, September 1954. Other analytical studies are Wilbur S. Shepperson, "The Place of the Mormons in the Religious Emigration of Britain, 1840-1860," *UHQ*, July 1952; and three articles in the same journal by P. A. M. Taylor, "Why Did British Mormons Emigrate?" July 1954; "Mormons and Gentiles on the Atlantic," July 1956; and "The Mormon Crossing of the United States, 1840-1870," October 1957.

Some specialized studies of national origins in the Mormon gathering include these master's theses: Keith C. Warner, "History of the Netherlands Mission ... , 1861-1966," Brigham Young University, 1967, with an appendix listing emigrants by years; Douglas Alder, "German-Speaking Immigration to Utah, 1850-1956," University of Utah, 1959, with similar statistics; Sheryl Richard Benson, "Emigration of Swedish Mormons to Utah, 1905-1955," University of Utah, 1965; Brent A. Barlow, "History of the Church ... in Ireland since 1840," Brigham Young University, 1967, also with emigration statistics; Frederick S. Buchanan, "Emigration of Scottish Mormons to Utah, 1849-1900," Brigham Young University, 1961; and Marius A. Christensen, "History of the Danish Mission of the Church....," Brigham Young University, 1966, with statistics on emigration by years. The Scandinavian studies were greatly aided by Andrew Jenson's *History of the Scandinavian Mission* (1927), one of many fact- and data-laden volumes by the indefatigable assistant church historian of The Church of Jesus Christ of Latter-day Saints.

Helen Z. Papanikolas, ed., *The Peoples of Utah* (1976), is a good reference work on both Mormon and non-Mormon builders of the state. Several chapters deal with Gentile arrivals during the territorial period.

Chapter 11
Economic Beginnings

Dean L. May

In 1860 Brigham Young summarized the biases that had influenced his efforts to shape early Utah economy. "There is no happiness in gold," he told the Saints, "Not the least .... We have the real wealth here .... We have the good, fine flour, good wheat, horses, cattle, beef, vegetables, fruit, sheep, and wool,... This is real wealth. This people is a rich people." Young's preaching seems to have evoked the response he wished, as there were, in fact, marked differences between Utah's pattern of economic development and that of neighboring states. In the first decades of settlement the work forces of Colorado, Idaho, Nevada, and Montana were dominated by miners. During the same period fifty percent of Utah's workers were farmers, with only an insignificant handful engaged in mining. Typically, the other mountain states continued for two to four decades to put most of their manpower into extracting and processing minerals, not reaching, even in Idaho, the high ratios of agriculture to mining found in Utah. (See Tables, p. 714.)

Utah's economy developed differently from the economies of her neighbors for several reasons. Most importantly, initial white settlement was by an organized group of refugees seeking secure homes rather than quick wealth. Moreover, these Mormon settlers were motivated by a common ideology and set of loyalties that urged them to a relatively planned and balanced economic development and that stressed agriculture over mining and other pursuits as the basis for a sound economy. Brigham Young and other leaders wished to minimize outside trade, discouraging their followers from commercial and banking enterprises. They also opposed the mining of precious metals. The success of the Mormon leadership in placing an agrarian stamp upon the developing economy had the unintended consequence of encouraging a handful of non-Mormons and Mormon nonconformists to monopolize trade in imported goods and financial services. The group quickly achieved an economic and political importance far out of proportion to their numbers. Reinforced by military personnel stationed in the area, they fostered development of Utah's mineral resources, a course made practical by the advent of rail transportation in 1869. Thus, not until two decades after the initial Mormon settlement did others begin to superimpose mining and commercial activities upon the agrarian economy of the territory.

Perhaps the most fascinating aspect of Utah's early economic development, then, is the interplay of ideology, planning, and circumstance. As we examine specific ways in which nineteenth-century Utahns dealt with problems of initiating viable systems of transportation, resource development, trade, and manufacturing in their new-found land, the underlying theme of plans shaped by ideology and modified in turn by the necessities of circumstances will appear again and again.

Transportation and Communication

The migration of 1847 took the Mormons far beyond the frontier into an economic and social isolation similar to that experienced by the very earliest European settlers on the American continent. The voyage of John Winthrop and the first Puritan companies to New England took seventy-five days; that of the pioneer company from Council Bluffs to the Salt Lake Valley took ninety-seven days. The extreme isolation of the earliest settlements in the Great Basin was initially seen by the Saints and their leaders alike as an advantage. But though they had gained an opportunity to control their own destiny, there were economic costs that could not be avoided. During the next two decades a large proportion of the time and energies of church leaders would be spent in coping with the problems of transporting new settlers to western Zion and in building transportation and communication links between the scattered communities separated by the mountains and deserts of the Mormon refuge.

A tacit allocation of responsibility for economic activities between Mormons and non-Mormons in Utah commenced very early after settlement. High transportation costs added greatly to the expense of all imported goods, while diminishing the return from exported goods. Church leaders felt escape lay in fostering local production of all essential commodities. Self-sufficiency thus became the avowed objective of Mormon economic planners, and it became a necessary condition of life for thousands of common people, who rarely could afford the luxury of sugar, tea, or ready-made clothing. Transporting of persons, however, was a different matter. Church leaders felt a particular obligation to assist in the gathering of faithful Saints. Thus agricultural and industrial development and personal transportation enjoyed the advantage of considerable church subsidy, central planning, and direction under the early years of Utah's economic development.

Transportation of goods, on the other hand, was left largely to private entrepreneurs. These entrepreneurs, moreover, tended to be non-Mormons, as the strong official stand against importing and retailing of products from the East kept most faithful Mormons out of trade. As early as 1849 large overland freight trains brought stateside goods to Utah, the promoters finding a ready market at profitable prices. Much to the annoyance of church leaders, these gentile merchants prospered, quickly gaining political as well as economic influence through their more placid relationships with Washington officials.

During the first decades in Utah Brigham Young and his advisers developed a series of programs to assist in what they saw as the most crucial problem of transportation facing them—bringing immigrants to Zion. Some of these plans were as simple as the establishment of church-maintained savings banks to help British members save the few pounds needed for ship passage. Others involved sweeping geopolitical considerations, such as the establishment of strategically spaced outposts along routes from California and from the Missouri River to the Great Basin, so immigrants might have friendly stopping places and sources of supply en route. Expectations concerning the "Mormon Corridor" to San Bernardino and San Diego were not realized, but the overland route from the eastern states was the focus of several church-sponsored enterprises in the prerailroad era.

Mormon leaders made plans in 1849 for the Great Salt Lake Valley Carrying Company, or "Swiftsure Line," to carry both freight and passengers from the Missouri River to California. For reasons never publicly explained the project was shelved, but it possibly provided the germ for the 1857 Brigham Young Express and Carrying Company, or the YX Company, as it was commonly called. This time a government mail contract would provide a financial base for passenger and freight lines. The entire system would be supported by a chain of colonies and way stations, built with contributed resources and labor, which would stretch at fifty-mile intervals from the Missouri River to Salt Lake Valley. Mail carrying had already begun under a contract granted to Hiram Kimball, a church agent, and some of the settlements along the route were being established when the whole enterprise was brought to an end by the revocation of the mail contract and the onset of the Utah War. Brigham Young placed the loss at "probably nigh $200,000."

The overall program of transporting immigrants was successful despite these disappointments primarily because of the Perpetual Emigrating Fund Company, another product of far-reaching plans laid in 1849. Assisting the program was a network of church-appointed travel agents who chartered transatlantic vessels and arranged riverboat and rail connections in the United States and the outfitting and piloting of immigrant trains overland. Converts were greeted in Salt Lake City by church officials who made every effort to find temporary shelter and employment for the converts until permanent arrangements could be made. The imaginative but ill-starred handcart venture, 1856-60, and the successful church team trains of the 1860s have been discussed in other chapters. In spite of a growing sum of uncollected debts, the Perpetual Emigrating Fund Company continued operations until it was dissolved in 1887 under the Edmunds-Tucker Act.

Transportation by non-Mormons to Utah primarily involved freighting goods for retail sale or transshipment to other western localities or carrying mail. The first importers could perhaps be most aptly described as large-scale peddlers. Buying an inventory of goods and hiring a wagon train, often with borrowed capital, they would rent temporary quarters when they arrived in Salt Lake City, and they would sell their wares at scarcity prices to Utah residents and California-bound transients. The first firm to use the Mormon capital as a more or less permanent retailing center began operations when the gold rush traffic was at its peak in 1849. Livingston and Kinkead opened that year and Holladay and Warner opened the next; both firms stayed in business, eventually producing considerable fortunes. Something of the nature of such enterprises can be seen in the account of William Chandless, who hired out as a teamster on a Livingston and Kinkead train coming from Kansas in 1855. Each of the thirty-eight wagons carried 3,500 to 4,500 pounds of goods. They were loaded, according to Chandless, with "Tea, coffee, rice, sugar, tobacco, soap, candles, mustard, spices &c., of all kinds, also casks of whiskey, . . . boxes of hats, shoes, and ready-made clothes, . . . dressed leather, bags of nails and shot, sheet iron, bar iron, block tin, and stoves of all shapes and sizes."

It should be noted that though large firms carried significant proportions of the overland freight, very probably most goods were carried by smaller itinerant entrepreneurs. Possessing a few wagons and teams, these men made a living very much like commercial ship owners of the seventeenth century or truckers of the twentieth century, hauling cargo from one place to another and making their own business arrangements. Sometimes they turned a profit by outright purchase of goods shipped; sometimes they were paid only freighting charges. William Jennings and William H. Hooper were two men who went from such modest beginnings in freighting to become economically and politically prominent in the Mormon community.

The United States mail service was extended to Great Salt Lake City when the post office was established in 1850, but the first contractors had great difficulty maintaining regular monthly service. The eastern route to Missouri was often impassable because of inclement weather, and after the California terminus was shifted from Sacramento to San Diego in 1854 most contract mail went by this route during the winter months. After the failure of the YX Company, the mail contracts were held for several years by the firm of Russell, Majors, and Waddell, which profited handsomely from freighting supplies for the Utah Expedition and to Camp Floyd. The firm later suffered heavy losses as a result of the imaginative Pony Express scheme, which from April 1860 to October 1861 brought Salt Lake City within seven days of Washington, D.C., and within four days of Sacramento. Before two years were completed, the pony express was rendered obsolete by the overland telegraph. (See map, p. 734.) In 1861 the Butterfield Overland Mail, a stagecoach line previously operating over only southern routes, was given the contract for central overland mail. Express, mail, and commercial passenger traffic to and from the Great Basin became dominated shortly thereafter by Ben Holladay, a member of the old firm of Holladay and Warner. He sold his interests to the New York-based Wells, Fargo, and Company a judicious three years before the transcontinental railroad tie was made. Throughout the prerailroad period, church and business travelers carried much of the mail in and out of Utah, supplementing to a considerable extent the formal United States mail system.

Development of internal roads and of transportation and communications networks was left almost entirely to the Mormons until the late 1860s, when the mining potential of Utah gave non-

Mormons an interest in gaining access to outlying areas. The long stretches of mountain and desert lands between settlements made road building especially burdensome to towns that had few inhabitants in proportion to the miles separating them from neighboring towns. Roads to newly colonized areas were often cleared by the new colonists themselves, with their labor being credited to individual church tithing accounts. On occasion townsmen from the community on the leading edge of a settlement were asked to build part of the roadway connecting them to new settlements beyond. County governments were formally responsible for road building and maintenance, but church-sponsored projects supplemented and in some areas replaced the county effort. In any case, road building consisted of little more than choosing wagon routes along well-drained surfaces with reasonable inclines, removing boulders, trees, and underbrush where necessary, scraping out approaches to fordable areas in streams and rivers, and building occasional bridges.

There was some initial experimentation with canal transportation. A canal was built to haul granite from Little Cottonwood Canyon to the temple site in Salt Lake City, but the structure did not prove to be practical. An ambitious design for a multipurpose canal to connect the Utah Valley and Salt Lake Valley settlements was conceived in 1854 and passed by the territorial legislature. For reasons that remain obscure, the project was never begun. Generally, the terrain of the Great Basin and the settlement patterns of the Mormons did not make canal transportation viable. For Utah, as for most of the rest of nineteenth-century America, the railroad proved the most practical solution to inland transportation problems.

Regional communication was facilitated by informal use of travelers as mail carriers, by attendance of local church leaders at semiannual Mormon conferences (normally held in Salt Lake City), and by near-annual visits of Brigham Young to all the settlements. Probably the most important channel of communication for Mormons was the *Deseret News,* founded in 1850. It published newsletters from all areas of settlement, practical hints on improving farming and stockraising, sermons by high church officials, brief news items from beyond the mountains, and miscellaneous commercial and social notes. *The Valley Tan,* 1858-60, and the *Union Vedette,* 1863-67, served the non-Mormon community; the latter promoted mining exploration in the area.

Brigham Young and other Utahns were subcontractors for the transcontinental telegraph, the completion of which in October

Dies used for stamping Deseret coinage, like tithing and co-op scrip and Deseret currency, illustrate the chronic shortage of money in pioneer Utah. Pictured are the coin dies, a three-dollar bill, Brigham City scrip, and the five-cent bishop's general storehouse bill.

1861 opened a new era in Great Basin communications. The day Salt Lake City was tied to the system Young called church officials to his office to consider the building of a north-south line connecting Utah settlements to the church center. Construction was delayed until the Civil War ended, permitting purchase of the necessary wire and supplies. In 1866, 500 miles of line were completed and put into operation. Built almost entirely by volunteer laborers under supervision of local church officials, the system was extended eventually to almost every Mormon settlement from Idaho to Arizona. The Deseret Telegraph Company served the region until 1900, when it was sold to Eastern interests. Its wires carried news of mining discoveries in the mid-1860s and news of the approaching railroad in 1869—developments that would greatly transform the economic structure of the commonwealth Brigham Young and the Mormon leaders were attempting to build.

Resource Development

Early visitors to the Great Basin, among them Escalante and Fremont, commented on the potential of the region for the raising of livestock. Later non-Mormon visitors were convinced that mining showed the most promise as a base for the local economy. The first need of Brigham Young's settlers in 1847, however, was for food, and the incoming tide of immigrants each fall made the production of sufficient foodstuffs a constant high priority. From 1850 to 1860 the population of the territory increased 254 percent, and the increase for each subsequent decade to 1890 was 115 percent, 66 percent, and 44 percent respectively. Had new settlers been arriving at a constant rate during the first decade there would have been an average of nearly 3,000 new mouths to feed each year— and the new immigrants always arrived too late in the season to be able to contribute substantially to that year's crops. A general famine struck in the winter of 1855-56 and there were sporadic famines, particularly in outlying areas, through the 1870s that reminded the Saints that self-sufficiency in the production of food was a vital condition of survival. Crop farming was thus developed in a region not especially congenial to it, and crop farming would remain for decades the main economic activity of most Utahns. The persistence with which every irrigable scrap of land was sought out and cultivated is one of the more remarkable aspects of early Utah history.

The resource most critical to the development of an economy based on agriculture in Utah was, as the Mormons were quick to recognize, water. Wherever a dependable stream of water could be diverted for irrigation purposes settlements were made. Where such conditions did not prevail, settlement was not possible. Most Mormon farmlands thus predictably lay in narrow strips flanking streams flowing from nearby mountain canyons. The settlement itself was usually a compact cluster of houses surrounding a church and public square, frequently situated on the alluvial fan built up by the stream as it issued from the canyon. Each settlement was limited in size by the amount of land that could be enclosed within the irrigation net. (See Typical Mormon Townsite, p. 733.) Probably the peak population for most rural towns in Utah was reached before the turn of the century and remained stable or declined thereafter, unless federal capital was applied to the building of larger-scale irrigation systems or such other industries when tourism or mining provided a basis for further growth.

The question of how land should be distributed arose immediately upon settlement, and Brigham Young offered a characteristically forthright and idealistic response: "No man should buy or sell land. Every man should have his land measured off to him for city and farming purposes, what he could till. He might till it as he pleased, but he should be industrious and take care of it." Joseph Smith's doctrines that all the earth's resources belong to God and that men are granted what they can use as a "stewardship" that they are to improve and leave undiminished for future generations are clearly evident in Young's statement. Young's terms were translated into actual policy as new settlements were founded throughout the region. In many such settlements holdings were kept deliberately small to assure that there would be enough land for future settlers. It was a policy that with few exceptions, however, was applied only during the pioneering period. Once the initial allotments of farmlands and town lots were made, settlers generally sold or traded lands and improvements as they wished. Though there were occasional interventions by church leaders in particular cases, attempting to assure compliance to the original ideals, the volume of transactions quickly became too great for regular control to be exercised. The Consecration Movement of the 1850s and the United Orders of the 1870s (discussed in the next chapter) seem in some measure to have been deliberate attempts to counter the inequalities of wealth that had arisen through disregard of the original principles of land distribution enunciated by Brigham Young in 1847.

The long-delayed opening of a Federal Land Office in Salt Lake City in 1869 largely confirmed the property holdings as they existed at the time, despite the hopes of a few gentiles who squatted on public and private lands just prior to the opening of the office, apparently expecting that the federal administrators would favor their claims over those of the Mormons. Settlements founded after that date continued to follow the church guidelines except in areas where purchase from prior settlers was necessary.

The necessary development of irrigation imposed a set of challenges hitherto not faced by North Americans—adding considerably to the capital investment needed before successful farming could take place and necessitating the evolution of new laws and institutions for apportioning and managing irrigation water. The problem, of capital investment was not so great as it might have been for the 1847 pioneers, who had the good fortune to make their first western settlement in a locality where seven small streams—the pioneers called them creeks—traversed a valley from east to west at distances no greater than two or three miles from one another. The streams, though small, flowed throughout the summer. They could easily be dammed with brush and logs, and it was possible to bring large tracts of land under cultivation with relatively short canals.

Canal building, like fence construction, was a community enterprise, with individual farmers obligated to build a section in proportion to the number of their acres to be served by the new facility. Management of such construction projects and supervision of water use was under the direction of the bishops of the various wards. Eventually, however, a new institution—the Cooperative Ditch Company—was created to fill these responsibilities, with day-to-day water management under the direction of a watermaster chosen by company members. Though the ditch companies were ostensibly secular institutions, disputes continued to be settled in church courts as well as in county courts, as indicated in the 1873 dictum issued in Sanpete County that where water disputes were concerned "Let the priesthood rule." In fact, the church courts—governed not by legal precedent, but rather by church leaders' sense of justice—evolved a body of law more appropriate to irrigated agriculture than older common law principles governing such matters. The common law doctrine of riparian rights, which dominated the regions from which the Mormons had come, gave property owners the right to use waters of lakes and streams adjoining their lands, provided the flow and quality of the water remained undiminished. Irrigation, of course, reduces the flow of water, and required, therefore, that a new body of law be evolved. The Mormons quickly recognized the inappropriateness of riparian rights to their circumstances, and they acted on the assumption that the stream and lake waters belonged to the public and thus were subject to appropriation by individuals or by public agencies as designated by the legislature. The Mormon approach was no doubt influential in shaping the formal law now governing water disputes in civil courts in the West.

The Mormon doctrine that man enjoys natural resources only in *usufruct,* the legal right of using another's profits, was applied by Brigham Young to mill sites and timber as well as to water and land. In the same statement with which he enunciated the policy on land distribution, Brigham Young is reported to have said that "there shall be no private ownership of the streams that come out of the canyons, nor the timber that grows on the hills. These belong to the people: all the people." Mill sites and control of canyon resources were accordingly assigned to important church leaders as a public trust; they enjoyed the right to charge an access fee to pay the cost of building and maintaining roads and other improvements. After 1850 the county courts were empowered to make such assignments and to see that these resources were used in the public interest, a responsibility they continued to exercise.

Mineral resource development, as earlier noted, was left largely to non-Mormons and to a later period in Utah history. There were some notable exceptions, though the earliest of these proved to be of little consequence. Iron ore was discovered in the Cedar Valley of southern Utah as early as 1849, and in the winter of 1850-51 a colony was founded at Parowan that was to provide the agricultural base for a subsequent iron-producing mission. Technical difficulties, floods, and other problems plagued the enterprise, however, and by 1860 it had been largely given up until greater capital and expertise could be applied to the effort.

Coal mining was taken up at Coalville in the 1850s and at Wales, Sanpete County, in the late 1860s. There were, in addition, attempts, under church sponsorship, to develop lead mines at Minersville in 1859 and at Las Vegas and in Meadow Valley, Nevada. Mormon interest in developing mineral resources, however, was clearly directed towards practical, industrial minerals, such as coal, lead, and iron—all in short supply in Utah and available only through costly overland transportation. Even in these cases the commitment was usually not sufficient to launch the enterprises, and the settlements usually lapsed into rural farm communities undistinguishable from other Mormon towns. Precious minerals were sought only through special church projects to raise money for official use, and church members were strongly discouraged from such pursuits unless they were specifically called to do so. The semisecret mission to the California gold fields, 1849-50, produced more grief than gold.

The year 1862 saw approximately 750 United States Army troops from California establish Camp Douglas overlooking Salt Lake City. Their commander, Patrick E. Connor, whose biases were revealed when he officially reported that the Mormons were "a community of traitors, murderers, fanatics, and whores," allied with non-Mormon businessmen in promoting prospecting and mining as a possible means of diluting Mormon influence in Utah. Encouraging his troops to spend their time prospecting and using government funds to publish the promining *Union Vedette,* he organized Utah's first mining districts in 1863. The initial claims were to silver veins in the Bingham area, but gold and silver were both discovered shortly thereafter in several localities. Because of their high value per weight, it was possible, starting in 1865 before rail transportation, to mine both gold and silver. Production by 1869 had reached $187,000 in gold and $2,000 in silver. The next year, with rail lines completed to Salt Lake City from Ogden, mineral production increased sevenfold, with one-third of the total value in lead and copper. From that time the shape of Utah's economy was irrevocably altered, and the placid orderly Mormon farm communities were henceforth punctuated by raw mining towns, different in social and economic character from the earlier settlements.

Commerce and Banking

Without question the overwhelming majority of commercial and banking transactions taking place in Utah before 1869 consisted of either informal, two-party barter arrangements or tithing house exchanges. A banking function was performed by the church when its leaders, acutely aware of the chronic deficiency in specie, attempted to alleviate the problem by issuing notes in 1847 and again in 1858, and by minting gold coins—the famous Deseret coinage—from 1847 to 1851 and again in the activities of the tithing houses located at every Mormon settlement in the West.

The tithing houses were general stores, receiving goods of all kinds as tithing payments and redistributing the goods received either locally or through the General Tithing Office in Salt Lake City. Tithing scrip, redeemable in merchandise from tithing stores, was often paid for labor on church projects and for other purposes, performing many of the functions of currency in a money-short economy. "Loans" were made through extension of credit and "savings" were permitted through building favorable balances in tithing record books. The local bishops were thus merchants and bankers (as well as spiritual leaders and often probate judges); in nineteenth-century Utah they were sometimes compensated with a share of the tithes for their management services. Traveling bishops and other church agents supervised the gathering of surpluses to the General Tithing Office, from whence they were diverted to other areas of need, used in church-sponsored projects, or converted to cash for investment in various Kingdom-building enterprises. During the territorial period the tithing system was the most substantial mechanism for capital formation in Utah.

The system was homely—handling such local commodities as butter, eggs, grain, and livestock and sometimes performing postal services and even collecting and disbursing local taxes. But it undoubtedly met the needs of the great bulk of Utah's early citizenry. Living at a near subsistence level, the pioneer population had little opportunity to patronize mercantile establishments and even less opportunity to utilize commercial banks. Many Utah towns did not have a store at all, other than the tithing house, until the late 1860s; the occasional need for manufactured goods was supplied by itinerant peddlers and by annual or semiannual trips to Salt Lake City.

The earliest stores in the Mormon capital, as noted, were established during the peak of the California gold rush, and the timing was probably no coincidence. Some merchants doubtless foresaw that Salt Lake City would become an important stopping place for the California immigration and intended all along to trade there. Others, discouraged by the long journey and by reports of large cargoes being brought to the gold fields by sea, chose to unload their goods in the Great Basin and, finding the profits sufficient, stayed. By 1854 no less than twenty-two merchants were listed as doing regular business in Salt Lake City. John and Enoch Reese, Mormon brothers, had been in business since 1850; J. M. Horner and Company was capitalized at $200,000; the firm of Holladay and Warner was prospering on a large scale; and Fanny Brooks was finding a market for her bonnets and bagels.

The fortunes of pioneer merchants were greatly affected by a series of chance circumstances, occurring at close intervals. The gold rush, which brought both customers and a supply of money into Utah, was the first. As the flush of this windfall was fading, Johnston's Army was sent to the territory. Upon receipt of this news a number of merchants packed up and quit the region, expecting that a protracted seige, with possible armed resistance, would destroy their businesses. Those who stayed, however, found

205

that Camp Floyd created a new market for retail goods and for freighting and wholesale supplying under profitable government contract. A probably apocryphal story credits Brigham Young with having counseled the Mormon businessmen of nearby Provo to "raise your prices," and there is documentation for his claiming to have made $100,000 out of the auctioning of Camp Floyd assets in 1861. The Walker Brothers and William Nixon, among others, also benefited from this windfall.

Still another occupation force, the California and Nevada volunteers at Fort Douglas, provided a supplementary market for cash goods and offered government contracts for supplies and services. During the next few years several Jewish merchants, including Frederick and Samuel Auerbach, located in Salt Lake City. By 1886 the mining activities of the Fort Douglas soldiers had begun to show clear economic consequences, and the non-Mormon firms alone were as numerous as had been all mercantile businesses a decade earlier.

At this point President Young, long irritated by the handsome profits being siphoned away from the local economy through extensive merchandising activities, began to seize the initiative. Organized fixing of prices for agricultural commodities had been initiated under church auspices in 1864 to prevent the Saints from undercutting one another in supplying mining and military camps. In 1866 Young encouraged a boycott of those firms that were unsympathetic to Mormonism. The boycott boosted the volume of trade enjoyed by Mormon merchants, but did little to reduce the adverse balance of payments problem, Mormons now importing what previously had been imported by non-Mormons. After much deliberation the church president, no doubt influenced by the success of cooperative stores in Brigham City and elsewhere, decided that if the demand for imported goods could not be eliminated, at least the profits could be reduced and the stores could be managed in the public interest.

In October 1868 Young proposed establishment of a church-wide cooperative system, Zion's Cooperative Mercantile Institution, which would be based in a wholesale and retail establishment in Salt Lake City and would supply retail stores in every Mormon town. "We can get what we wish by sending to New York for it ourselves," he told the Saints. "We have skill and ability to trade for all we need." Salt Lake merchants at first hesitated, but were persuaded when Young hinted at a plan to make Provo the wholesale center for the trade net. Large Mormon firms such as William Jennings' Eagle Emporium and William H. Hooper's store were absorbed into the chain—providing an immediate inventory of goods that could be retailed in Salt Lake City and the dozens of local cooperatives being organized the length and breadth of the territory.

Z.C.M.I. was not a full consumers' cooperative in the sense that dividends were returned according to number of shares held rather than to amount of purchases. But every effort was made to keep shares sufficiently low in price to be within the reach of most families, and home commodities were accepted as payment on shares to encourage those without cash to enter the system. Moreover, the board of directors was dominated by men who felt their primary obligation was the consuming public, a fact of considerable significance. The stores identified themselves with a sign showing an "all-seeing eye" under the inscription "Holiness to the Lord." Though most Z.C.M.I.s later became dominated by men of wealth, who through purchase of shares gained policy control, the immediate benefits seemed obvious to most Mormons. Prices were lowered on many items, dividends were considerable, the dozens of communities were served by retail stores that previously had had no mercantile establishment other than the tithing house. Several non-Mormon firms sold their goods to Z.C.M.I. and left the territory or moved to Corinne, the railroad boom town in Box Elder County. Enjoying the benefits of lowered transportation costs and sustained by the church through the financial panics of 1873 and 1893, Z.C.M.I. remains a major retail institution in Mormon areas of the mountain west. It was surely one of Brigham Young's more successful temporal accomplishments.

It should be noted that the farmers and wage workers of Utah, as well as the businessmen, benefited from the series of events that built the mercantile firms. The forty-niners provided a ready market for locally produced foodstuffs and livestock, and they often sold cumbersome wagonloads of stateside goods at bargain prices. The military encampments also provided jobs and a market for Utah products, as did the mining camps. Indeed, one of the significant Mormon economic roles in the West between 1864 and 1890 was to provide the truck gardening and freighting services so much in demand in adjacent mining areas.

Banking, like overland freighting and merchandising, was also an enterprise pioneered in Utah by non-Mormons. There was a natural evolution from one enterprise to the other, as freighters seeking to enjoy retail profits for themselves became established merchants and then began to offer credit to and accept notes from retail customers. Finally, as the economy became more complex, some of them offered specialized banking services, either as a separate business or as an adjunct to an established firm. The Walker brothers followed roughly this evolution in Utah, as did the firm initiated by Ben Holladay and continued by Wells, Fargo, and Company.

In banking, as in merchandising, specific historical circumstances were important agents of change. There were no *bona fide* banks in Utah until gold and silver mining began in 1864. Four firms, also involved in freighting and trade, then opened banks in Salt Lake City to serve the mining enterprises north and west of the capital. Utah's first bank under federal charter, the Miners' National Bank of Salt Lake City, was founded in 1866 with the same primary objective.

Several other gentile banks were established before the Deseret National Bank was set up by Mormon merchants William H. Hooper and Horace S. Eldredge, recently dispossessed of their mercantile businesses by Z.C.M.I. The new business operated under the Z.C.M.I. symbols and honored Brigham Young by naming him president of the board of directors. Legally the bank was not a church enterprise, but being the only Mormon-owned commercial bank in Utah for many years, it cooperated in meeting the economic needs and social goals of the church. A child of the institution—Zion's Savings Bank and Trust Company—also endured into the twentieth century and maintained a close cooperative relationship with the church in its financial operations.

Gentile firms continued to dominate banking in Utah, with only two of the banks established between 1864 and 1880 being Mormon-owned. And in this area as in merchandising, the Mormon involvement was primarily a defensive action, representing in part a capitulation to economic changes that were long resisted. To preserve the autonomy needed to make decisions in the interest of God's Kingdom, Mormon leaders were quite willing, when pushed, to fight fire with fire.

Manufacturing

Though Mormon leaders were loathe to see the growth of mercantile and banking firms, they pushed vigorously and at every opportunity the development of local manufacturers. The key to development of the economy, they felt, lay in persuading the people of Utah to invest in local enterprise, providing jobs for local artisans and providing markets for the products of Utah agriculture, thereby "cutting the threads," as Brigham Young put it, that bound the Saints to the outside world. The problem was not unlike that faced by leaders of developing nations today—whether to curtail consumption in order to develop local industry and thereby insure autonomy, or whether to integrate into a larger exchange system by specializing in the production of raw materials for manufacture. Convinced that the inevitable tendency of the world's economic, social, and religious systems was toward self-destruction, Mormon leaders tenaciously pursued the first alternative—developing local industry—almost to the end of the territorial period.

The list of goods William Chandless observed being shipped to Utah in 1855 could almost serve to identify the industries church leaders supported in their efforts to foster economic development of the region. Iron was a vital necessity to a pioneer economy, and the overland cost of shipping such items as nails, sheet iron, bar iron, or cast iron stoves and utensils was enormous. A common rate for such freighting was one dollar per 100 pounds per 100 miles, which would raise the cost of a pound of nails from ten cents in Atchison to $1.30 in Salt Lake City. So great was the need for iron that tire irons and wagon fittings were systematically salvaged to be melted down and manufactured into nails and other needed items. Wagons abandoned by California-bound gold-seekers were collected and burned, the salvaged iron regarded as a providential boost to the Utah economy. The heroic but ultimately unsuccessful effort of the "Iron Mission" in the 1850s has already been described.

Another vital need, which had been solved before Chandless made his 1855 journey, was for paper, especially to print the *Deseret News*. The heavy, bulky nature of newsprint made it, like iron, very costly to freight overland. An English convert with experience in papermaking was enlisted to design and set up a paper factory. Using rags collected through church efforts, he produced a crude but useable product, which in 1853 was improved through importation of new machinery. The mill operated successfully under the church department of public works until 1868, and it then was transferred to the *Deseret News,* which continued its operation until 1883.

Early efforts to produce sugar had a less happy conclusion. In 1851 Apostle John Taylor, then in Europe, organized a company to manufacture beet sugar. He brought machinery and seeds as well as experienced workers with him to Utah in 1852; forty Santa Fe prairie schooners were needed to haul the equipment overland to the Great Basin. The plant was set up initially in Provo, where farmers were already growing sugar beets from seed sent before arrival of the machinery. Initial efforts to produce sugar failed, however, and Brigham Young took over the obligations of the company, setting the factory up first at Temple Square and then on a church farm four miles south of the city, known since as Sugar House. There, a three-story adobe factory was completed in 1855 and more than 22,000 bushels of sugar beets were processed into molasses during a seven-week period of operation. The product proved unpalatable, however, and failure of the sugar beet crop in 1855 and 1856 due to grasshopper infestations spelled the doom of the enterprise.

Church leaders searched for an alternative by experimenting with several varieties of sugar cane, which they hoped could be raised in southern Utah. Housewives resorted to boiling carrots and willow shoots in their search for a palatable sweetener. Finally the molasses of sorghum cane became the staple sweetener of Mormon cuisine. The sugar beet industry was finally made viable in the last decade of the century when a factory was established at Lehi under church subsidy; it eventually became profitable.

The textile industry also began with bold plans and ended with modest results. Taylor recruited both workers and capital for this enterprise at the same time he was arranging for the sugar beet factory. The machinery was purchased and apparently shipped as far as St. Louis in 1853, but it was 1862 before a mule train was organized to bring it, along with more recently purchased machines, to Salt Lake City. A factory on Big Cottonwood Creek, near Salt Lake City, became operative in 1863. The 240-spindle mill proved, however, to be too large for the local sheep industry to supply it adequately with raw wool. (Apparently Mormon households took a large portion of the crop for hand spinning and weaving until the 1870s.) The mill was dismantled and sent to southern Utah, where steps were being taken to produce cotton in sufficient quantity to make effective use of the machinery.

Cotton growing had been successful in southern Utah, partly owing to the high prices of cotton in the States during the Civil War. But with the cessation of hostilities the price dropped, and the establishment of a local mill seemed the only possible way of rescuing the "Cotton Mission." Machinery from the ill-fated woolen factory was accordingly shipped to Washington, a small town a few miles upstream from St. George on the Virgin River. There a new mill was built, which expanded through the 1870s and 1880s and continued operations until 1910.

Support and sometimes management of church enterprises such as the sugar factory and the textile mill was provided by the Department of Public Works, formally established under Daniel H.

Wells in 1850. The department provided work for hundreds of new converts, erecting nearly all public structures, including city walls, general church meetinghouses, and recreational facilities. The first light industry in the region was established by the department on Salt Lake City's Temple Square—a machine shop (1852-64), a foundry (1854-64), and a nail factory (1859-65). Employees were paid largely in drafts useable at the General Tithing Office. Though normally employing 200 to 500 men, the department is known to have provided jobs for as many as 2,000 workmen at a time, who worked on projects costing as much as a quarter of a million dollars a year in cash, labor, and commodities. The program thus provided Brigham Young with a flexible instrument for giving employment to those in need, disposing of surplus commodities, and achieving the erection of needed public buildings and other facilities.

Young's continuing insistence that local industries be established to provide basic needs took the form of specific cooperative programs in many communities as an adjunct to the cooperative retail merchandising system organized in 1868. Since 1847 small establishments—gristmills, sawmills, tanneries, and carpentry shops—had been set up, some as public and some as private ventures. The impending arrival of the railroad threatened to bring down the barrier of high transportation costs that had favored local industries, and though Brigham Young welcomed rail travel for immigrants, he wished to counter, insofar as possible, the increased dependency upon outside manufactures that the cheaper transportation might bring.

He accordingly recommended that each community found producers' cooperatives to manufacture essential goods for the local population. Some communities, including Paris, Idaho, and Hyrum and Brigham City, Utah, responded by developing extensive holdings of dairy and livestock farms, sawmills, and such light industries as tanneries, hat factories, broom factories, textile mills, and tin shops—all community-owned and managed. Brigham City, where Apostle Lorenzo Snow had begun organizing cooperatives in 1864, became eighty-five percent self-sufficient; its fame as a model cooperative economy reached the ears of Edward Bellamy, who visited the town while writing his critique of late nineteenth-century American society, *Looking Backward* (1888).

A common pattern for Mormon cooperatives was to begin as a retail store and then to invest part of the profits in a sawmill or dairy. These latter enterprises tended to be profitable for a time, though lumber operations were limited by supplies of accessible

Tithes from the orchards and farms of southern Utah arrive at the General Tithing Store, which stood where the Hotel Utah now stands.

timber and fluctuating demand for the product. Next profits were invested in enterprises appropriate to local resources and expertise; carpenter shops accompanied sawmills, for example, and tanneries were coupled with livestock industries. These cooperative aggregates disappeared before the end of the century, abandoning or divesting themselves of one enterprise after another until only the retail store was left. This, too, was eventually sold to private interests. Competition from more efficiently produced goods hauled by railroad was a major cause of the demise of the Mormon cooperatives, with the panic of 1893 administering the final blow. A few dairy and livestock cooperatives and retail stores survived until the middle of the twentieth century, but these were exceptional.

Conclusion

In 1847 Brigham Young had expressed his determination "to cut every thread" of trade and commerce tying his people to the outside world. Two decades later the steel rails being built towards the Great Basin were reinforcing ties Young and his people had never successfully severed. No steel mills were functioning in Utah, textile output was small, sugar production was nil, and heavy industry was nonexistent. A growing community of non-Mormons was encroaching upon the isolation the Mormons had sought in their escape from Illinois mobs, and a mining boom promised further to strengthen the gentile forces.

But if ambitious plans had gone awry, there were nonetheless notable successes. The cooperative retail system was prospering. Home industries of all kinds were being launched in many Utah towns. Substantial public buildings decorated a thriving young city—entrepot of trade and transportation serving several states in all directions. Farming communities housing a polyglot population of nearly 80,000 dotted a landscape that twenty years earlier had been nearly empty. Much of this impressive achievement was due to farsighted planning and central direction. Yet for every directed economic decision thousands were made independently—for every church-sponsored business hundreds were launched by private entrepreneurs. Though social pressures were put upon all who objected to the impositions on personal freedom Brigham Young's structured approach to economic planning involved, the system remained, in its broad lines, voluntaristic, retaining strong elements of individualism. Indeed, perhaps the most distinctive aspect of the economic achievement of the Mormons in the period from 1847 to 1869 was the unique blend of central planning, local cooperative endeavor, and private enterprise—a demonstration that in some circumstances, at least, these can flourish together with reasonable harmony and substantial achievement.

Even the few non-Mormons in the area, though resented and sometimes preached against, were nonetheless free to manage their enterprises. As the decade of the 1860s came to a close, they were beginning to build an alternative society within Utah characterized by an economic system strikingly different from what Leonard J. Arrington has called the "well-organized, relatively self-sufficient ecclesiastical commonwealth" that was Brigham Young's ideal. The gentile world was quite as apart from that of the Mormons in its individualistic hell-for-leather scramble to extract the mineral riches from Utah's hills as was the Jacksonian entrepreneur from the idealized Jeffersonian yeoman farmer. These two economies coexisted in the Great Basin until the 1890s, when Mormons began to gradually adapt their communitarian system to the one prevailing in greater America.

Chapter 11
Bibliographical Essay

The starting point for any study of economic development in early Utah remains Leonard J. Arrington's classic, *Great Basin*

Kingdom (1958). This volume summarized previous work in the field and placed it into an interpretive framework that has set the tone for a whole new generation of younger scholars. In fact, through this volume and numerous supporting studies published before and since *Great Basin Kingdom,* Arrington has almost single-handedly defined the field of Mormon economic history.

Helpful information on trade and transportation activities of non-Mormons in Utah can be found in Ray Allen Billington, *Westward Expansion: A History of the American Frontier* (1960), and in Oscar Osburn Winther, *The Transportation Frontier: Trans Mississippi West, 1865-1900* (1964). A basic work on Mormon migration that treats the Perpetual Emigrating Fund Company is Gustive O. Larson, *Prelude to the Kingdom* (1947). Arrington has studied the Deseret Telegraph in "The Deseret Telegraph—A Church-Owned Public Utility," *Journal of Economic History,* Spring 1951. The history of early newspapers in Utah is outlined in J. Cecil Alter, *Early Utah Journalism* (1938). Lawrence L. Linford's "Establishing and Maintaining Land Ownership in Utah Prior to 1869," *UHQ,* Spring 1974, clarifies the complicated procedures required of Mormons in claiming and establishing title to their lands in the Great Basin. A recent study on the development of irrigated agriculture in Utah is by Arrington and Dean L. May, "A Different Mode of Life: Irrigation and Society in 19th Century Utah," *Agricultural History,* January 1975. The whole *Utah Historical Quarterly,* Summer 1963, is devoted to the mining industry, with articles that discuss all aspects of mining in early Utah.

An excellent study of banking in early Utah is by Arrington, "Banking Enterprises in Utah, 1847-1880," *Business History Review,* December 1955. See also his "The Mormon Tithing House: A Frontier Business Institution," *Ibid.,* March 1954, and "Coin and Currency in Early Utah," *UHQ,* January 1952. The Mormon cooperative movement is treated in Arden B. Olsen, "Mormon Mercantile Cooperation in Utah," *Journal of Marketing,* October 1941. The cooperative movement is also treated in Leonard J. Arrington, Feramorz Y. Fox, and Dean L. May, *Building the City of God: Community and Cooperation Among the Mormons* (1976). There is little written on non-Mormon mercantile activities in Utah prior to 1869, but interesting anecdotal material can be found in a Daughters of the Utah Pioneers Historical Pamphlet, *Merchandising in Deseret* (1941).

Several travel accounts from the period contain observations on economic activities in Utah. One by an observer particularly interested in Mormon economic affairs is William Chandless, *A Visit to*

Salt Lake; . . . and a Residence in the Mormon Settlements at Utah (1857). S. N. Carvalho's *Incidents of Travel and Adventure in the Far West* (1854, repr. 1971) is also of interest, though Carvalho was not as keen an observer of economic activities as was Chandless. Also helpful are William Kelly, *Across the Rocky Mountains . . . With a Visit to the Celebrated Mormon Colony, at the Great Salt Lake* (1852); J. W. Gunnison, *The Mormons, or Latter-day Saints, in the Valley of the Great Salt Lake . . . .* (1856); and Richard F. Burton, *The City of the Saints and Across the Rocky Mountains to California* (1862). Many published diaries by Mormons contain scattered observations that offer insights into economic events of the period. These are indexed and made accessible through Davis Bitton, *Guide to Mormon Diaries and Autobiographies* (1977). Almost every issue of the *Utah Historical Quarterly* has contained articles of interest and relevance, and articles pertaining to Mormon economic history frequently appear in *Western Historical Quarterly, BYU Studies,* and *Journal of Mormon History.*

Chapter 12
Towards a Dependent Commonwealth

Dean L. May

Several important events surrounding the year 1869 underscore the tremendous consequences of the completion of the transcontinental railroad for Utahns.

In 1865 John Pierce, surveyor general for Utah-Colorado, suddenly reversed his earlier opposition to the granting of land titles in Utah Territory, explaining that "the true policy of the government in regard to Utah is to encourage the emigration to that territory of a population less hostile to the United States," and that to encourage this, the "gentile emigration must have the chance of acquiring title to the land, and must be protected in that title." Acting on Pierce's suggestion, Congress finally voted in 1868 to appoint a surveyor general for the territory and to apply there the preemption and homestead laws. A federal land office was opened the next year in Salt Lake City.

Production of nonferrous metals in Utah, begun shortly before Pierce's report, increased from $190,000 in 1869 to $1.5 million in 1870, the year rails were extended from Ogden to Salt Lake City. Corinne—the first Utah town settled by non-Mormons—began its colorful but short career as a trading and railroad center in 1869. Episcopal Bishop Daniel S. Tuttle settled in Salt Lake City the same year, a prominent representative of the burgeoning non-Mormon religious effort that had begun only a few years earlier.

In October 1869 William S. Godbe, E. L. T. Harrison, and Eli B. Kelsey were excommunicated from the Mormon Church, partly because they opposed the economic programs of church leaders and partly because they advocated rapprochement with federal officials and gentiles living in Utah. A group with similar views began to coalesce around these "Godbeites" and the next year they, together with prominent non-Mormons, formally organized the Liberal Party, a political party opposed to church policies.

The Mormon cooperative movement began in 1869 with the founding of Z.C.M.I. Five years later Brigham Young launched a strenuous effort to establish the United Order among his people—an economic reorganization inspired by his vision of a commonwealth of small, nearly self-sufficient town communes. The model United Order, as Young saw it, would be the antithesis of Corinne, differing dramatically from patterns of trade and commerce prevailing elsewhere in the United States.

The timing of these events was not coincidental; though they are interrelated in several ways, their nexus was the railroad, which tied Utah to the outside world and ended the isolation of the Great Basin Kingdom.

Railroad Building

Though the railroad was almost certain to diminish church influence in the territory, Brigham Young was one of its outspoken advocates, supporting petitions to Congress as early as 1852 and 1854. When the Pacific Railroad Act was passed on July 1, 1862, he subscribed to $5,000 worth of stock in the newly organized Union Pacific Railroad Company, becoming a director three years later. In 1866 he told the General Assembly of the Mormon quasi-state of Deseret that he was "happy" to note that during the next year "the Iron Horse will approach several hundred miles nearer our isolated position in the tops of the mountains." He urged the legislators and their constituents to "lend your material aid and energies to the more speedy accomplishment of that great national work."

Despite his enthusiasm, Young was aware that the railroad posed a danger to Mormon Church hegemony in the Great Basin. He accordingly took several "defensive measures." His investment in the railroad was to gain at least some voice and influence in determining policy and to assure that the church would receive a share of benefit from the new transportation facility.

Brigham Young's influence with the railroad management was insufficient to persuade them to build the line through Salt Lake City. He was successful, however, in contracting for local Mormon labor to construct the road within Utah. This minimized the flow of non-Mormons into the area and provided needed jobs and income for resident Saints. Though the railroads defaulted on some of their contract obligations, they liquidated part of their in-

Utah workers excavate the railroad right-of-way down Weber Canyon in 1868 under a contract between Brigham Young and the Union Pacific Railroad.

debtedness by transferring railroad construction materials and rolling stock (locomotives and cars). This gave the church president part of the capital he needed to pursue a final solution to transportation problems in the Mormon domain through rail transportation.

One week after the driving of the golden spike at Promontory, Utah, on May 10, 1869—a ceremony that Young did not attend—construction began in Ogden on the Utah Central Railroad that was to connect Salt Lake City with the transcontinental line. Ward organizations provided volunteer labor along the line, and on January 10, 1870, just 113 days after construction began, the church head drove the last spike in Salt Lake City before a cheering crowd of 15,000 persons. During the period of Mormon ownership the railroad was managed in the interest of overall church objectives and programs, and profits from ore shipments were used to subsidize transportation of immigrants, church officials, and freighting of goods purchased by the church. (See map, p. 735.)

Before the Utah Central Line was completed, work had begun on the Coalville and Echo Railway, which would facilitate development of coal deposits in Summit County. This venture proved less successful because of the obstructionist tactics of some Union Pacific officials who saw a threat to their own lucrative coal-carrying trade from Wyoming mines to Salt Lake City. In May 1871 the Utah Central Railroad began extension southward from Salt Lake City as the Utah Southern Railroad. The need for construction materials diluted Mormon influence on the project almost from the beginning, with the Union Pacific providing rails and rolling stock in exchange for bonds and stock in the railroad. The line remained under Mormon influence until 1879, at which time it had been built as far south as Juab Valley. Rail magnate Jay Gould and other non-Mormon businessmen finally completed the route as far as Frisco, providing access to mining claims in the San Francisco Mountains near Beaver. In 1880 the entire line, including the Utah Central, was combined into a Union Pacific-controlled company called the *Utah Central Railway System.* Mormon influence on the southern routes thereafter was minimal.

Part of the church leaders' motivation in supporting the Utah Northern Railroad, which began construction in August 1871, was to divert the Montana trade from Corinne towards Ogden and through Logan and other Mormon settlements to the north. Ward-organized laboring crews carried on the work until 1874 when the road reached the northernmost Mormon settlements near Franklin, Idaho; they were paid in shares of stock, making ownership of the venture unusually broad, and giving the various localities a strong identification with the railroad. Financial difficulties plagued the enterprise, however, and after several reorganizations that led again to outside control, the line was built to Blackfoot, Idaho; Dillon, Montana; and finally over Butte, Montana, to a connection with the Northern Pacific at Garrison, Montana, in 1884. It became part of the Oregon Short Line system in 1889 and eventually was taken into the Union Pacific. Though suffering from chronic financial problems, the Utah Northern Railroad was successful in diverting freight bound for Montana mines through Mormon-dominated areas. By the end of the 1870s Corinne had lost much of its population and was becoming a Mormon agricultural town, little different from hundreds founded under Brigham Young's direction. The completion of the Denver and Rio Grande Western Railroad to Salt Lake City in 1882 opened up eastern Utah to settlement and coal mining, but its general impact on the Utah economy was limited during the territorial period.

With completion of a serviceable railroad net, putting most Mormon towns within a few hours or at most within two or three days of rail transportation, a major economic problem of the first decades of settlement was solved. Transportation was no longer a preoccupation of church leadership, since immigration was facilitated and freighting costs were drastically reduced. Traffic between towns not served by the railroad continued over rough, unpaved wagon roads, most of them unchanged since early settlement. Life in these remote towns was altered, but not fundamentally, by the coming of the rails. The citizens of a number of Mormon towns, however, were startled to find new settlements growing up nearby, peopled by gentiles and apostates, liberally supplied with saloons, and, for a time, flush with the wealth of mining profits.

Mining

Unquestionably, the most powerful event of economic importance in the decades after the railroad tie was completed was the development of the mining industry, made possible by the dramatically less expensive transportation of ores the railroad afforded. The earliest extensive mining activity took place in Bingham Canyon, south and west of Salt Lake City, and in Little Cottonwood Canyon, southeast of the city. Producing silver, lead, and, in the Bingham area, copper, work in these mining districts began in the mid-1860s and continued to be significant through the turn of the century. Indeed the Bingham mines, concentrating after 1900 on copper rather than on silver, gold, and lead, remain of major economic importance to Utah.

By the time the railroad arrived most mining areas in and near the Salt Lake Valley had been thoroughly prospected and claims had been filed. From that time various districts experienced booms as the discovery of particularly rich lodes and the building of railroads and other access roads made shipping of ores profitable. East of Salt Lake City mines were opened at Alta, in Little Cottonwood Canyon in 1869, and in Parley's Canyon and Big Cottonwood Canyon shortly thereafter. (See map, p. 736.)

West of Salt Lake City, attention turned quickly from Bingham on the eastern slopes of the Oquirrh Mountains to the western slope of that range. The mining town of Stockton was developed by General Connor in 1864, and in 1870 the Ophir mines were discovered immediately to the south. Still further south on the west slope of the Oquirrhs, the Tintic area was opened in 1870–71. The quicksilver deposits that led to settlement of Mercur, between the Ophir and Tintic mines, were not discovered until 1882. Separating silver from mercury was extremely difficult with the technology available, however, and it was not until 1893, with the discovery of the cyanide separation process, that the Mercur mines flourished, producing millions of dollars worth of gold, silver, and lead.

Demands for cheap freighting to and from mining areas stimulated railroad construction. The Utah Central Railroad reached Sandy in September 1871; narrow-gauge roads were built from the railroad west to the Bingham area and east to the Little Cottonwood mines. The Bingham Canyon and Camp Floyd Railroad was completed in 1873, and the Jordan Valley Railroad up Little Cottonwood Canyon was completed to Alta in 1875. When the Utah Southern Railroad reached Juab Valley in 1874, it was in a position to receive wagon traffic from the Tintic mines, but a spur reaching the mines directly was not completed until 1883.

There was little mining in southern Utah until 1875, when two prospectors at Squaw Springs west of Milford in the San Francisco Mountains discovered a ledge of galena ore so rich that, according to the tale, it could be whittled, the slivers curling off the ore in shapes like the horns of a mountain sheep. The Horn Silver Mine, as it came to be known, proved the richest silver producer in Utah. The mine was sold in 1879 to Jay Cooke, a New York financier, whose connections assured completion of the railroad to Frisco by 1880. Production declined greatly in the 1880s, though efforts were made to work lower-grade ores until 1905.

The Silver Reef District in the eastern part of Washington County had a short but active career as a producer of silver-lead ores. Silver was discovered in the mid-1860s by John Kemple, but he did not return to begin mining until 1874. He soon became discouraged and left the claim to others, who in 1875 began to extract rich ores from sandstone. A rush followed, and within a few months a camp of some 1,500 people sprang up, many from nearby mining areas in Nevada. Production was drastically curtailed in 1879, to be resumed intermittently in this century. Output for the entire period from 1875 to 1909 was estimated at nearly eight million dollars in value.

Silver-lead ore was located in the Parley's Park area east of Salt Lake City in 1869, and in 1872 the fabulous Ontario Ledge was found. Acquired by George Hearst, the father of publisher William Randolph Hearst (and great-grandfather of Patty Hearst), the Ontario mine soon became the largest in the territory. From 1877 to 1904 it yielded almost 38,000,000 ounces of silver and paid almost fourteen million dollars in dividends. Other rich mines in the vicinity gave Park City a national fame in the late nineteenth century that it would not regain until its ski slopes brought new life to an almost ghost town sixty years later.

The 1870s and 1880s were an erratic period of individualistic entrepreneurial activity in Utah mining—a time of fabulous strikes, overnight boom towns, and precipitous busts. Development depended to some degree on outside capital, but it was still possible for one or two prospectors with few assets to strike it rich and come away wealthy men. This period ended in the late 1870s and early 1880s when oxidized surface ores, which could be readily mined and extracted, were exhausted. Further development depended upon deeper, lower-grade ores, which could be mined only with considerably greater investment. "The eyes of the mines," as one contemporary journalist put it, "were picked out."

During the last decade of the century Utah mining entered a more stable period, with the value of annual output ranging from $6.2 to $13.2 million and averaging $10.1 million. The value of gold and silver production continued at fairly stable high levels, but by 1900 copper output was increasing greatly and in 1907 copper for the first time exceeded gold and silver in value.

Lead was the only mineral other than sulfur of which Utah was a leading national producer in the nineteenth century. At no time did Utah produce more than six percent of the nation's gold; silver output reached as high as fifteen percent in 1882 and 1896, and it jumped to 22.5 percent in 1903; copper production never comprised more than three percent of United States output until open pit operations began in Bingham. Lead, however, amounted to 45.5 percent of national production in 1872 and comprised at least twenty percent most years through 1900. The aggregate value of all nonferrous metal output in the state was twenty-two million dollars in 1904.

Prior to the advent of the railroads, wagon-hauled coal and coke from mines at Coalville, Summit County, and Wales, Sanpete County, cost as much as forty dollars per ton in Salt Lake City. The Union Pacific made Wyoming coal available at lower prices but successfully resisted efforts to open up Utah's rich coal deposits to rail access until the 1880s. With the completion of the Denver and Rio Grande Western the coal that gave Carbon County its name was accessible, and the Utah Fuel Company, a D.& R.G.W. subsidiary, soon became Utah's largest producer. In 1890 there were four commercial mines in operation in the territory, producing about 235,000 tons of coal and employing 565 persons.

There was some development of other mineral resources before the turn of the century. Systematic large-scale harvest of salt from the Great Salt Lake began in the 1860s, leading in 1889 to organization with Mormon Church support of the Inland Salt Company. Production the first year amounted to nearly 50,000 tons. In 1890 Utah ranked fifth in the nation in the production of gypsum and first in sulfur production, though the uses of sulfur at the time were limited and the mineral was not in great demand.

There were persistent efforts throughout the nineteenth century to produce iron successfully on sites pioneered in southern Utah in the 1850s. A company was organized in 1869 for this purpose, selling its assets in 1873 to the Great Western Iron Mining and Manufacturing Company, which in turn sold out in 1883 to the Iron Manufacturing Company of Utah. The Mormon Church was influential in all these ventures. Though some iron was produced the companies were not economically successful, and development of these resources was not profitable until after the First World War.

The impact of the mining industry on the greater Utah population is difficult to assess. Church leaders did not support mining development as they had railroad building, with the result that nearly all capital and management came from outside the territory, much of it from English investors. Profits were taken elsewhere or spent in ostentatious living by the few wealthy, as the stately Victorian homes on Salt Lake City's South Temple Street attest. Mormon leaders did, however, conclude that it would be better for their people to work in the mines than for a flood of non-Mormons to enter the area, and they welcomed the new markets for farm produce, especially since payment was often in scarce cash. Saints were asked to seek permission of their bishop before taking employment in the mines to insure that their labor could be spared from local farming activities. In addition they were to promise not to indulge in the vices available in the boom towns and to work for cash rather than mining stock.

Work as miners and teamsters—supplying commodities to mining towns and hauling ores to the railheads—was of considerable importance, especially to young Mormons trying to establish themselves. Mine employees were paid from $3.14 to $5.27 a day for above-ground work and from $2.80 to $4.21 for work in the pits, an attractive contrast to the $1.50 to $2.50 per day paid for farm work. The diaries of youths coming of age in Utah in the last third of the nineteenth century suggest that seasonal mine work was a common experience. The Mormons apparently regarded such work only as an adjunct to their primary agrarian enterprises, however; few took up residence in the mining towns unless distance mandated it. Mormon branches were formed in Frisco, Eureka, and Park City in the 1880s, but Bingham and Mercur did not have Mormon organizations until Utah became a state.

Because of the availability of local labor, mining did not produce the inundation of Mormon population that General Connor had hoped for. One scholar has estimated that the total population of mining towns in Utah might have reached 2,000 in 1870, 8,000 to 10,000 in 1880, and 10,000 or more in 1890. At the most this would have meant that the mining population might have reached ten percent of the adult population of the territory. These figures, however, only estimate the people resident in mining towns. Undoubtedly the activities of these communities were sustained and supported by a significant number of gentiles living in Mormon towns, particularly in Salt Lake City.

As the number of non-Mormons increased, the character of the territorial population began perceptibly to change. The miners of the 1860s and 1870s came largely from other mining regions of the West, but in the 1880s and 1890s immigrants from eastern Europe, Italy, and then Greece found their way to Utah. The social and religious customs and cuisine brought by these people enriched the variety of life-styles observable in Utah at the turn of the century. Most were employed in Carbon County coal mines, in Salt Lake Valley smelting plants, or in the Bingham Canyon mines.

The mining towns had no standard design, though they tended to be situated in twisting narrow canyons with houses lining a main street and in some instances climbing kaleidoscopically one or two streets above the canyon floor. Buildings, commonly unpainted wooden structures with vertical board siding and tin roofs, were quickly put up. There were usually a general store, a livery stable, a blacksmith shop, a boarding house, a dance hall, and several saloons (in 1874 Bingham and Alta each had fifteen). In the larger towns the more imposing buildings might include a church, a community hall, and a Masonic or Odd Fellows hall. Most towns were served by a telegraph office and a Wells Fargo station. Appropriately, the most striking and enduring structures were the large, ungainly mills where ores were crushed and concentrated before shipment.

Agriculture

Development of other natural resources, land, water, and timber was not characterized by the dramatic changes taking place in mineral development during the last decades of the century. There were few changes in irrigation practices and few major engineering projects undertaken to expand the acreage already under cultivation. Through the century, new settlement, rather than improvement of lands near existing settlements, tended to be the characteristic response to overcrowding, with colonies established in Canada and Mexico in the 1880s and in the Big Horn Basin of Wyoming at the turn of the century. The Bear River Valley project, opening 150,000 acres of new land, was completed in the 1890s, the sole major new irrigation project in Utah before the turn of the century.

Also of importance to agriculture in Utah was the gradual introduction of improved strains of vegetable, fruit, and livestock crops. The church-related Deseret Agriculture and Manufacturing Association, chartered by the territorial legislature in 1856, maintained from the mid-1860s an experimental farm where new varieties were tested and cultivated so that starts could be distributed throughout the commonwealth when proven. Utahns also took considerable pride in their fruit industry, with excellent peaches, cherries, apples, and apricots grown on bench lands, especially in Davis and Weber counties, and figs, pecans, almonds, and grapes grown in southern settlements.

Probably the most significant development in agriculture between 1869 and the turn of the century was the rise of the livestock industry to a position of major importance in the 1880s and 1890s. Since the earliest days of settlement cattle had been important, with beef being the staple meat and with dairy and cheese-making being common enterprises. Oxen (castrated male cattle) were also in common use as draft animals, with the number in use increasing each decade until 1890 and dropping thereafter. Though the number of sheep in the territory became greater than the number of cattle during the 1860-70 decade, their total value surpassed that of cattle only in one year—1890. In that year nearly four million sheep were being grazed in Utah, the maximum ever attained.

The rapid growth of the livestock industry in the 1870s and 1880s did not, however, indicate a general move away from the wheat, corn, oats, and barley that made up the bulk of field production. Livestock were grazed, for the most part, on lands that hitherto had been of marginal value as farmlands, with the only major shift on improved lands being a diversion of some irrigated acreage to forage crops, especially alfalfa hay, which had become a major field crop by the 1890s. Some local economies, such as that of Kanab in southern Utah, became almost entirely devoted to the

Following the driving of the golden spike at Promontory, Utah, on May 10, 1869, the two engines are christened with bottles of wine as the chief construction engineers, Grenville M. Dodge (Union Pacific) and Samuel S. Montague (Central Pacific), shake hands.

livestock industries, while many older farming towns remained relatively untouched. Overgrazing in the late territorial period greatly damaged the groundcover in mountainous areas, leading to severe floods in several localities during the first decades of the twentieth century. Some restrictions in grazing were imposed after 1897, when the first forest reserves were set aside in Utah, though general control of grazing on public lands did not take place until the passage of the Taylor Grazing Act in 1934. Utah's sheep population has declined significantly since 1890, ranging between one and two million head. The number of cattle has grown slowly to about 750,000 head in recent years.

The growth of the livestock industry in the Great Basin was in part the result of an effort to develop all resources that might contribute to agricultural productivity. Another important development in that effort, dry farming, had its beginning in Davis

227

County in the 1860s. Other farmers adopted the method in the 1870s and 1880s, the quantity of dry-farm wheat from Cache Valley and eastern Box Elder, Tooele, and Juab counties becoming of considerable economic significance by the turn of the century. Shortly thereafter dry farming began to be widely established in the West, largely as a result of experiments conducted under the Utah Agricultural Experiment Station in Logan.

Utah has never produced sufficient timber for her own needs. William Chandless noted in the mid-1850s that firewood was "the severest item in household expenditure" and that "a family with two stoves burning will run very near to 300 dollars in the course of a winter." Though little data is available, it is clear that Utah's timber harvest in the territorial period was never enough to satisfy all the needs of the local citizenry.

Commerce and Banking

Economic changes after 1869 greatly stimulated the growth and proliferation of banking in Utah. Thirty-four banks were founded during the years 1864 to 1880, and another fifty were established between 1880 and the turn of the century. Those founded during the first period were located in metropolitan centers and seem to have primarily served the capital needs of mining and commercial enterprises. New banks opened between 1880 and 1900 were mostly in outlying areas. Though the bulk of their customers were also probably engaged in mining and commercial pursuits, the dispersion of these institutions suggests that the growing capital needs of farmers, particularly as the use of farm machinery became more common, were part of the demand for banking services.

Bank failures were common. The number of banks operating at any one time in Utah between 1864 and 1880 ranged from four to twelve; only two incorporated banks, Deseret National and Zion's Savings, survived the Panic of 1873, though several private banks, including Wells Fargo, McCornick and Company, and Walker Brothers Banking Company, survived as well. During the 1880s banking became the central concern of the Walker Brothers firm, which later acquired both the Wells Fargo and McCornick banking interests and assumed a major position among Utah's nineteenth-century banking establishments. Of all the early Utah banks only the Walker Bank, the Deseret National Bank, and Zion's Savings Bank survived into the twentieth century.

Commercial activity in the latter part of the nineteenth century is difficult to follow. The rise of the Mormon cooperative retail store system in 1869 has been discussed in the previous chapter.

Impressionistic evidence would lead one to conclude that the Z.C.M.I. system was probably the leading retailer throughout the region, despite the vigorous competition in Salt Lake City of many independent firms. In most towns other than Salt Lake City and Ogden, the local Z.C.M.I. enjoyed a near-monopoly position.

City directories published in 1869, 1874, 1884, and regularly from 1896 on give a rough indication of the directions taken in commercial activity in Salt Lake City. The 1869 population was estimated at 25,000. Among the businesses serving it were thirteen general stores, twenty dry goods stores, forty-one grocers, two breweries, three saloons, two banks, and seven "principal" hotels. Z.C.M.I. had, in all departments, thirty-four separate retail stores operating in the city. These were ward-operated cooperative stores; although not owned by Z.C.M.I., they were part of the Mormon Church-approved system. There were no businesses identified as relating directly to mining.

The 1874 directory estimated the population of Salt Lake City at 26,000, indicating either a surprisingly small growth rate for the five-year period or an unreliable census procedure on the part of the editors, probably the latter. Most dramatically, the mining industry had begun to make itself felt, with twenty-three different businesses engaged in various aspects of mining and smelting. Saloons had increased from three to thirty-eight and hotels from seven to eighteen. There were seven banks and forty-four retail grocers in the city. The 1884 directory, somewhat differently arranged and hence not readily comparable, indicates no major change, but the number of businesses increased greatly during the succeeding twelve years. The city had grown by 1896 to an estimated 72,684 persons. The mining industry had mushroomed, with 193 businesses either engaged in mining or offering assaying, engineering, stockbroking, smelting, and other directly related services and supplies. Outlets for liquor had kept pace with the capacity of the growing population, the number of saloons reaching sixty-nine. There were now twenty-nine hotels, sixteen banks, seventy general stores, and one hundred and seventy grocers in the city.

There was continuously even growth until 1900, when the city's population reached 84,606. Again the mining industries grew disproportionately, with over 400 establishments listed in related categories. Also evident in the directories is the gradual growth in city services, the introduction in the 1880s of electric services, and the growth of urban transportation and utility companies. There was a noticeable increase in the variety of businesses in operation by 1900, evidence of more finely articulated differentiation in goods and services offered to citizens of an increasingly cosmopolitan urban center. By the 1880s and 1890s new subdivisions were being opened regularly; real estate businesses, first appearing in 1874 with four firms, increased to sixty-eight in 1896.

Certainly a major contribution to this growth was made by the railroad, which increased the volume of goods brought overland sevenfold in the first year of its operation in the Salt Lake Valley. Serving as it did to support the mining industries, which in turn increased employment opportunities and the market for locally produced agricultural commodities, the railroad must be regarded as a major influence on the economic growth of Utah during the late nineteenth century. In 1873, for example, the Utah Central Railroad brought to Salt Lake City 117,000 tons of goods, the principal imports being general merchandise, coal, lumber and other forest products, iron ore, and coke. Exports over the same railroad amounted to 27,500 tons—principally crude bullion, lead, silver and copper ores, wool and hides, and general merchandise. The perennial problem of a provincial, developing area was expressed by the editors of the 1884 *Gazeteer,* who complained that "with the exception of mines, live stock and wool, nothing is done in the exportation of Utah products outside of mill stuffs, dried fruit, potatoes, dairy products and hides, pelts, and furs." Clearly the goal of self-sufficiency and regional autonomy was being replaced by an interest in how to assure a continuous supply of exports sufficient to balance the needed imports.

The United Orders

These developments stood in sharp contrast to the model of Utah's economic future that shaped the United Order of Enoch—Brigham Young's last-ditch effort to reverse the tide of economic events released by the railroad. The United Order was the most ambitious of the efforts by the church president to reshape Mormon economic and social institutions in directions Joseph Smith's revelations on consecration and stewardship had indicated. The two terms of the phrase "United Order," taken separately, expressed aptly the dominant temper of Mormon social philosophy since the founding of the faith. It had always been the aim of church leaders to counter the centrifugal forces in an individualistic, pluralistic society by building a people whose chief distinguishing traits would be unity and orderliness. Practiced briefly in Missouri between 1831 and 1833, there were no efforts by church leaders until 1854 to reinstate the system churchwide. In that year church members were asked to consecrate their properties to the church, with nearly half the heads of families responding. The movement did not alter existing economic patterns, however, because the church did not take possession of the consecrated properties.

Consecration was nonetheless an important expression of support for church economic plans and an indication that Brigham Young had by no means forgotten the communal ideals taught by Joseph Smith. Young himself was particularly enamored of the idea of rebuilding society into groups that, in the internal dynamics of their social and economic organizations, were like a "well-regulated family." The working models for the United Order were in Lorenzo Snow's Brigham City—a cooperative community which in its various shops and departments produced nearly all its own necessities, providing useful employment and comfortable security for its citizens—and in Brigham Young's own extensive household.

The church president's vision of the United Order was never clearly articulated or defined in the details of its workings, and local organizations were encouraged to improvise according to their circumstances and needs. Young's own preference was for a fully communal organization, with common dining facilities and collective ownership and management of all community resources. He was aware, however, that such an order would require an unusual degree of selflessness, and he accordingly asked bishops to improvise a form of organization acceptable to their own constituencies, even if it did not approach the more extreme communal ideal. He repeatedly emphasized that entry into the United Order was to be voluntary and that members should continue to love and fellowship those who did not join.

Again, as with the consecration and the cooperative movements, specific circumstances were important in precipitating the founding of the United Order. The discovery of silver in several southern Utah and Nevada localities had caused a number of Saints to enter into trading with the gentile mining settlements. The mining towns suffered severely from the effects of the Panic of 1873, causing serious repercussions in neighboring Mormon villages. Brigham City, by contrast, was hardly touched by the depression, confirming Young's longstanding bias in favor of local self-sufficiency. The United Order promised to reduce the need for trading and to keep it within church channels, permitting the central control and direction of economic development Young favored. There was also noticeable an increasing disparity between the incomes of the rich and the poor in Utah by the 1870s. Church leaders had long looked forward to a day "when there shall be no rich and no poor among the Latter-day Saints; when wealth will not be a temptation; when every man will love his neighbor as he does himself; when every man and woman will labor for the good of all as much as for self." The United Order promised to move the Saints towards the realization of these aims. With such considerations in mind the church president journeyed to his winter home at St. George in the fall of 1873, and there he launched the work of reform.

Organization spread quickly throughout the commonwealth, taking several forms, according to the preferences of local leaders. Most followed the St. George pattern, with those joining the Order pledging all their economic property and agreeing to receive wages and dividends according to the amount of labor and property contributed. Individual households were maintained. In communities that already had an operating system of consumer and producer cooperatives there was little change. Property was not consecrated, private households remained, and the most discernible effect of the new movement seems to have been to give added impulse to cooperative efforts already underway. In the wards of larger cities a single enterprise was taken up by each congregation, such as a soap factory, hat factory, or other such venture. They were financed by the ward membership and were apparently designed primarily to contribute to territorial self-sufficiency, creating jobs manufacturing goods that otherwise would need to be imported.

Communal orders, following Brigham Young's preferences, were established at Orderville, Price City (near St. George), Springdale, and Kingston, Utah, and at Bunkerville, Nevada, and several new settlements along the Little Colorado River in Arizona. Within these orders there was some variation, but most were distinguished by their devotion to communal dining, to community ownership of all productive property, and to community direction of labor. Orderville, the most famous of these communities, was founded for the express purpose of making a success of the more communal form of United Order. The Bunkerville and Arizona colonists used the communal order as a means of organizing their labors during the earliest stages of settlement.

There were not, of course, clear distinctions between the various forms of United Order, and some of the more than 200 wards and communities that established orders moved from one type to another in their effort to find a system that would serve them satisfactorily. Most variations fell somewhere within the loose cooperative system of Brigham City and the rigid communalism of Orderville. All sought self-sufficiency, a more harmonious community, and an evenly distributed prosperity for their members. All were touched with a strong moral fervor that enjoined the use of tobacco and alcohol; forbade rough language, immoral conduct, and ostentatious dress; and recommended regular prayers and church attendance.

All of the United Orders were discontinued or simply disappeared within a few years. A few, like Orderville, might have carried on past the mid 1880s except for the external pressures of the antipolygamy "crusade." Some did not move past the initial phases of evangelical commitment and the drafting of articles of organization. Many succumbed within a year or two to the same kinds of internal pressures and external attractions that have doomed utopian ventures in other times and among other peoples. And many persisted as cooperative enterprises which were "United Orders" only in name. The reluctance of a few men of greatest means no doubt inhibited some from entering the Order without reservation. Young himself acknowledged "laboring under a certain embarrassment, and so are many others, with regard to deeding property, and that is to find men who know what to do with property when it is in their hands. . . ." According to the most authoritative study of the United Orders, "such men apparently were never found." In one town, however, where a detailed study of the wealth of United Order members has been made, those favoring the most communal form of the Order were nearly twice as wealthy, on the average, as their fellow townsmen.

Brigham Young died in 1877 and was succeeded by men who seemed more willing to accommodate Mormon economic life to that prevailing in greater America. John Taylor, Young's successor as church president, sought to achieve coordinated marketing policies and to promote manufactures through the formation in 1878 of Zion's Central Board of Trade. Farmers in Cache Valley had initiated local boards of trade as early as 1872, cooperating to fix prices of farm produce sold to exporters. The later churchwide organization included these aims in a much broader effort to improve the general economic well-being of the Mormon people. The Central Board of Trade was to work with several stake boards of trade to promote general business activity, minimize competition among producers, encourage local manufacturing, disseminate "agricultural, manufacturing, commercial, and economic information," and to "secure to its members the benefits of cooperation in the furtherance of their legitimate pursuits."

Specific moves towards these ends were taken in the early 1880s as the Board of Trade organized the Utah Iron Manufacturing

Company to develop an iron industry in southern Utah, encouraged sugar manufacturing, and formed the Cooperative Wagon and Machine Company to import wagons, carriages, implements, and tools. The directors also took steps to increase production and sales of wool, silk, paper, leather, dairy products, soap, and salt. Functioning not unlike a chamber of commerce, the Board of Trade was flourishing in the mid-1880s when the antipolygamy crusade reached its peak. Then, for reasons not fully known, the organization ceased functioning without comment or explanation. Apparently its key members were forced underground to avoid prosecution and could not meet to sustain the organization. Zion's Board of Trade, unlike the United Order, was an organization in tune with the economic spirit of late nineteenth-century America. Accepting free enterprise and capitalism as the system within which Mormons would manage their economic activities, it proposed primarily to increase the chances, through cooperative action, that Mormons would get their fair share. There was little effort in the Boards of Trade to refashion an economic system more compatible with Mormon doctrines of equality and justice as had been done in the United Order, nor any vision of the self-sufficient precapitalist village communes proposed by Brigham Young.

Manufacturing

The development of Utah's economy has often been seen as a three-phase progression, beginning with agriculture, then supplemented with a mining sector in the 1870s, and finally supported by a manufacturing sector around the turn of the century. Actually, in terms of the total value of output and number of persons employed, manufacturing held its own against mining during all but two decades of the nineteenth century. The 1880 census showed mining products to total in value about one million dollars more than the products of manufacturing establishments, an edge that was increased to four million dollars in 1890 but lost by 1900 when the products of manufacturing establishments were reported to be worth a million dollars more than those of the mines. (See Table, pp. 714–15.) Complaints about the slow growth of manufactures in the territory were probably caused more by the narrowness of the range of local enterprises than their scale. A survey taken by the territorial legislature in 1875 outlined the problem clearly. Almost all manufacturing in the territory was involved in some way with the processing of products of mines and farms. Most of it, in addition, did not result in a finished product, such as clocks, nails, or shoes. Almost one-third of the $3.8 million manufacturing output was the product of ninety flour mills operating in the territory. The next most valuable product came from 128 sawmills, their lumber being valued at nearly $500,000. Planing mills were of major importance, as were brickyards—all relating to the home construction industry. Charcoal and coke production, which fueled the seventeen smelters then operating in the territory, was also important. The ten breweries and eight woolen mills then operating were the only enterprises producing finished products of major economic importance. The woolen mills, in fact, were the third most important manufacturing enterprise in the territory, producing $311,000 worth of cloth in 1875.

By 1890 the configuration of basic industries was little altered, though printing and publishing had become the third most important industry and the slaughtering of animals had become fourth; neither had been of major economic importance in 1875. Other changes included the rise in importance of metal founding and confectionary manufacturing. Through the century, then, most manufacturing in Utah involved converting locally produced raw commodities into forms suitable for household and domestic use by Utahns, including the construction of homes. There was, in addition, considerable intermediate processing of native products for shipment to manufacturers outside the territory. The perennial balance-of-payments problem was little helped by manufacturing before the turn of the century—mining and agriculture still provided the bulk of export items.

Attention was earlier given to several pioneer efforts, largely unsuccessful, to build the manufacturing industries, primarily to reduce dependency on imports but partly to produce exportable products. The Provo Cooperative Woolen Factory, a postrailroad undertaking, represented the most important and successful of these efforts. Built with a combination of private and church capital by the share-earning labor of local citizens, the mill began operations in 1872. Employing at times nearly 200 workers, it survived the various reorganizations until the Great Depression of the 1930s. Textile mills were established at about the same time in several other Utah towns, including Brigham City, Beaver, and Ogden. The cotton mill at Washington, near St. George, had been established earlier, but it was improved and enlarged during this period. Impetus to textile manufacturing was given by the railroad, which reduced the costs of importing equipment, with most Utah mills being founded soon after 1869. The mills produced about eight percent of total manufactures in 1874 and about four percent of manufactures in a considerably expanded and diversified economy in 1890. They exported some of their products—the Provo mill exporting about one-third of its output during its years of operation.

In 1870 a prolonged but futile effort to produce silk was begun, enjoying the support of Mormon women's organizations. As already mentioned, church efforts to manufacture iron and sugar continued. Some of the enterprises were costly failures, though such failure in most cases could be attributed to lack of capital and expertise more than to incorrect assessment of the region's manufacturing potential. The textile mills were reasonably successful from the beginning, and by the 1890s a sugar beet plant in Lehi, built with both church and private funds, was producing at least a palatable and competitive product. Private capital would develop the iron industry many years later, using the same ore and coal reserves Mormons had been attempting to develop since the 1850s.

Labor Organizations

The increasing influence and militancy of the labor union movement in the United States in the last third of the nineteenth century was only faintly reflected in Utah Territory. Guild-type unionism was represented in the 1850s and early 1860s by organizations of printers and theatrical workers, but by the time of the railroad both Mormon Church leaders and gentile businessmen, for not entirely dissimilar reasons, were moving toward an antiunion posture that would predominate in Utah for a century.

By the time the Deseret Typographical Union became the first nationally chartered trade union in 1868, the School of the Prophets was already committed to promoting local economic self-sufficiency through a variety of programs that included price and wage fixing. A proposal the next year to seek labor support for reducing wages by as much as one-third to one-half elicited little enthusiasm and does not appear to have affected wage levels significantly. Neither the cooperative movement nor the United Orders were hospitable to unionism, and the transient gentile mining population was not yet ready to consider collective bargaining. The Panic of 1873 weakened unionism everywhere for the balance of the decade.

In the 1880s skilled workers began to form local organizations, particularly in the building trades. As many as a thousand Utahns may have affiliated with the national Knights of Labor as it reached its peak around 1886, but overt Mormon Church opposition probably meant that most of the members of this semisecret mass labor movement were gentiles or somewhat disaffected Mormons. The resident miners and mill workers of the gold, silver, and coal towns were beginning to listen to labor "agitators," but the owners and managers would not face serious demands for collective bargaining rights until after the region recovered from the Panic of 1893.

By 1889 there were about twenty local unions in Salt Lake City, some of them with national affiliations. Trades represented included carpenters, painters, plumbers, railway firemen, brewery workers, cigar workers, machinists, iron molders, and retail clerks; they were generally conservative in tactics and strikes were rare and short-lived. Under the leadership of a Mormon typographer and printer, Robert G. Sleater, fourteen of these locals formed the Utah Federated Trades and Labor Council. Sleater represented the council at the American Federation of Labor convention in December 1889, and four years later the council was granted an AFL charter. Hard times and unemployment prevented any broadening of the trade union base during the balance of the territorial period.

The Panic of 1893

The economic development of Utah Territory had been characterized by an interesting and unusual interplay between central planning and free enterprise; between private and community capital; between individualistic and communal endeavor. In some sectors these approaches to development were sharply separated from one another; in other sectors they were combined. This mix of economic ideologies was evident as Utahns responded to their first major depression. Beginning with the Panic of 1893, the American economy went into a slump that lasted until the turn of the century, both nationally and in Utah. For Utah's Mormons the hard times were both an economic disaster and a bitter irony. Because of the previous independence of the Mormon economy, the Saints had been much less affected by the national panics of 1857 and 1873, although the gentile economy of Utah had suffered during the latter depression. By contrast, the total economy of Utah and the Mormon Church itself reeled under the impact of the depression of the 1890s. Production declined, businesses and mines failed, cash became scarce, and unemployment soared.

In an era unaccustomed to United States government intervention for the purpose of relieving economic distress, the economic ideologies of those who fostered the early Kingdom reasserted themselves in a vigorous program of relief by the Mormon Church.

Emigration to Utah was discouraged, colonizing efforts were renewed, and urban residents were advised to migrate to rural areas where the effects of the depression were less severe and the cost of living was less. The Mormon wards in Salt Lake City loaned unused lands to the poor for vegetable gardens. Church leaders urged their followers to support local industries and products in preference to purchasing imported goods.

In addition, the church took specific measures to stimulate the regional economy. To counter the scarcity of cash, the tithing office issued tithing scrip redeemable in foodstuffs, encouraging Utah's factories, businesses, and stores to do the same. The church established an employment service and provided many jobs by establishing the Inland Crystal Salt Company, the Intermountain Salt Works, the Saltair bathing resort, the Salt Lake and Los Angeles Railroad, the Pioneer Electric Power Company at Ogden (later Union Light and Power Company), and by expanding the operations of the Utah Sugar Company. Although undoubtedly mitigating the effects of the depression in Utah, the Mormon Church program of economic assistance required a calculated policy of deficit spending that resulted in enormous indebtedness. At his elevation to the Mormon presidency in 1898, Lorenzo Snow began to reverse this trend through emphasizing tithes and applying returns from church investments to debt reduction.

Under Snow's leadership the Mormon Church reduced its business involvement, either selling its interests outright or, in some intances such as Z.C.M.I., discontinuing its policy of exclusive control. As the twentieth century began, leaders redefined the objectives and characteristics of the Mormon Kingdom. President Snow indicated the new directions in his "Greeting to the World" on January 1, 1901, which he concluded with these words:

Let these sentiments, as the voice of the "Mormons" in the mountains of Utah, go forth to the whole world, and let all people know that our wish and our mission are for the blessing and salvation of the whole human race. May the twentieth century prove the happiest as it will be the grandest of all the ages of time.... Peace be unto you!

Conclusion

As the Utah economy regained momentum, it became possible for Mormon leaders to allocate more of their time to purely religious concerns. The lines demarking Mormon and gentile enterprise were becoming less clear, as the economy continued to grow and diversify, and as the autarchic aims of early leaders were abandoned in favor of integration into national patterns of business and trade. The accommodation was not without costs, however, for during most of the first half of the twentieth century the products produced most efficiently in the Great Basin—farm crops, metal ores, and livestock—were in great supply worldwide, putting Utah producers at a serious disadvantage in United States trade markets. Only after the Second World War did this condition begin to reverse itself, with Utahns finding their products in increasing demand at a time when a surfeit of skilled, industrious, human capital supported rapid growth in local manufacturing as well as in production of raw materials. The economic potential that Utah's early leaders recognized and labored to develop was supporting, under vastly altered circumstances, an affluence Brigham Young could hardly have imagined.

Chapter 12
Bibliographical Essay

Many of the studies recommended in the previous chapter overlap chronologically into the present chapter. *Great Basin Kingdom* should be the starting point for further reading. Several important articles on various aspects of the transcontinental railroad as they relate to Utah are found in the *Utah Historical Quarterly,* Winter 1969. Also helpful are Leonard J. Arrington's "Utah's Coal Road in the Age of Unregulated Competition," *UHQ,* January 1955; and "The Transcontinental Railroad and Mormon Economic Policy," *Pacific Historical Review,* May 1951. See also Merrill D. Beal, *Intermountain Railroads* (1962). A pictorial essay on other transportation facilities in Utah, "From Mules to Motorcars: Utah's Changing Transportation Scene," appeared in *UHQ,* Summer 1974.

Several important articles on mining in Utah are in *UHQ,* Summer 1963. These should be supplemented with data from Arrington, *The Changing Economic Structure of the Mountain West, 1850–1950* (1963); "Measures of Economic Changes in Utah, 1847–1947," *Utah Economic and Business Review,* December 1947; and from El Roy Nelson, *Utah's Economic Patterns* (1956). Additional information can also be found in each decennial report of the United States Bureau of the Census. Further information on the arrival in Utah of the various ethnic groups engaged in mine work is in Helen Z. Papanikolas, ed., *The Peoples of Utah* (1976). A vivid glimpse of Utah's mining towns in their heyday and today is in Stephen L. Carr, *The Historical Guide to Utah Ghost Towns* (1972).

Charles S. Peterson has provided an insightful view of changes in Utah agriculture at the turn of the century in "The 'Americanization' of Utah's Agriculture," *UHQ,* Spring 1974. A brief review of the history of dry farming is in John A. Widtsoe, *Dry Farming: A System of Agriculture for Countries under a Low Rainfall* (1911). The Summer 1964 *UHQ* was devoted entirely to studies of the cattle (though not the sheep) industry in Utah, possibly evidence of continuing grudges. Peterson has also reviewed the cattle industry in one Utah region, particularly as it relates to Forest Service range management, in *Look to the Mountains: Southeastern Utah and the La Sal National Forest* (1975).

There has been little work on Utah's commerce and banking in the last two decades of the nineteenth century. The Salt Lake City directories published in 1869, 1874, 1884, and then in continuous series starting in 1896 are a rich source of information on the subject, not yet subjected to systematic study. Also helpful, of course, are the Salt Lake City newspapers of the period. Leonard J. Arrington's "Banking Enterprises in Utah, 1847–1880," *Journal of Business History,* December 1955, is the source of most of what is known about banking in nineteenth-century Utah. See also Roland Stucki, *Commercial Banking in Utah, 1847–1966* (1967). *Building the City of God* (1976) by Arrington, Feramorz Y. Fox, and Dean L. May offers detailed material on the United Orders. Arrington's further study, "Zion's Board of Trade: A Third United Order," *Western Humanities Review,* Winter 1950–51, treats the Board of Trade movement.

There are few studies of manufacturing in nineteenth-century Utah. The principal ones deal with specific enterprises, such as Arrington's "The Provo Woolen Mills: Utah's First Large Manufacturing Establishment," *UHQ,* April 1953; and "Iron Manufacturing Company of Utah," *Bulletin of the Business Historical Society,* September 1951. The directories mentioned above and United States census reports provide additional information on various manufacturing establishments and occasional discussion of manufacturing problems in general.

Publications on the nineteenth-century labor movement in Utah are meager. Sheelwant B. Pawar, "An Environmental Study of the Development of the Utah Labor Movement" (Ph.D. dissertation, University of Utah, 1968), and Dee Scorup, "A History of Organized Labor in Utah" (master's thesis, University of Utah, 1935), are primary sources of information. Pawar's "The Structure and Nature of Labor Unions in Utah: An Historical Perspective, 1890–1920," *UHQ,* Summer 1967, deals mostly with the twentieth century. Two informative contributions by J. Kenneth Davies are "The Utah Labor Movement Before Statehood," *UHQ,* Summer

1966, and "The Secularization of the Utah Labor Movement," *UHQ*, Spring 1977. See also Davies, *Deseret's Son of Toil: A History of the Worker Movements of Territorial Utah, 1852–1896* (1977).

A summary of economic activities in the state at the close of the century is found in Leonard J. Arrington and Thomas G. Alexander, *A Dependent Commonwealth: Utah's Economy from Statehood to the Great Depression*, ed. by Dean L. May (Charles Redd Monographs in Western History, Brigham Young University Press, 1974).

Chapter 13
Government, Politics, and Conflict

Gustive O. Larson

T he demand of all the Western territories for a measure of home rule was intensified in Utah by the Mormon Kingdom of God concept, which contemplated the existence of a more or less autonomous theocracy within the American republic. While the United States military intervention of 1857–58 served as a reminder of federal sovereignty, it nevertheless left the Saints in control of the territorial legislative and judicial systems and of the local militia. The Mormon Church still dominated the political, social, and economic life of Utah communities, and plural marriage continued to be practiced in spite of national agitation for its suppression. On February 16, 1861, the territorial assembly, in defense of home rule, addressed a memorial to Congress that declared:

Your memorialists believe that the appointing of strangers as officers over the citizens of the United States in territories, though a time honored custom, is to say the least a relic of British Colonial Rule, and a direct infringement upon the right of self government, and opposed to the genius and policy of republican institutions.

This petition was given no more serious consideration than were the six unsuccessful bids for statehood made between 1849 and 1887. The two decades between the Utah War and the Supreme Court's 1879 decision upholding the first federal antipolygamy statute merely polarized politics in Utah and intensified national opposition to the aspirations of the territorial majority.

Beginning of Antipolygamy Legislation

After a decade of public pressure a predominantly Republican Congress passed the first federal anti-Mormon legislation in 1862. There was a little resistance since many believed that Congress should not interfere with established religion or its beliefs, but Vermont Representative Justin S. Morrill's antibigamy bill, which had first appeared in somewhat different form in 1856, passed both houses of Congress by overwhelming margins. In its brief on the bill, the House Judiciary Committee named the two major issues which for thirty years would block Utah's statehood—polygamy and the temporal power of the church that sponsored it. The new legislation struck at both polygamy and church power by prohibiting plural marriage in the territories, disincorporating the Mormon Church, and restricting the church's ownership of property to $50,000.

Abraham Lincoln signed the law but was content to overlook its enforcement while the Southern rebellion occupied his attention. Lincoln's policy toward the Latter-day Saints was aptly expressed when he told a church representative, "You tell Brigham Young if he will leave me alone, I'll leave him alone."

The Civil War Years in Utah

Although Young's first message over the transcontinental telegraph proclaimed Utah's loyalty to the Union, the territory residents played little part in the Civil War. The federal government asked Nauvoo Legion units to patrol part of the overland trail for several months in 1862 to curb Indian depredations, but their vigil ended when Union Army volunteers established Fort Douglas overlooking Salt Lake City. The war was interpreted by many prominent Mormons as divine retribution upon a nation that had allowed Mormons to be persecuted and driven beyond national borders without raising a hand to protect them. The carnage of battle was seen by church members as the beginning of the national dissolution that would precede the establishment of Christ's kingdom on earth.

While the Morrill Antibigamy Act was being debated in Congress, the Mormons drew up another constitution for the proposed State of Deseret, elected a full slate of officers, and applied a third time for admission to the Union. The application was rejected without serious congressional consideration, but the newly elected State of Deseret officers continued to function as a "ghost government" behind the territorial government from 1862 to 1870. Brigham Young, the governor of the phantom state, explained this unusual procedure to the Deseret legislature on January 19, 1863:

We are called the State Legislature, but when the time comes we shall be called the Kingdom of God. Our Government is going to pieces and it will be like water that is spilt upon the ground. . . . But I do not want you to lose any part of this Government which you have organized. For the time will come when we will give laws to the nations of the earth. . . . We should get all things ready, and when the time comes, we should let the water on the wheel and start the machine in motion.

Because of this feeling the management of federal business in Utah demanded wise, firm, and patient administration; reliance on the spoils system for federal appointees did not always produce governors, judges, and lesser officials with these traits. (See table, pp. 697–96.) Fortunately, Young's successor, Alfred Cumming, possessed these qualities and poured oil on Utah's troubled waters. The federal government generally supported him when there were disagreements with military and judicial officers, and his departure for his native Georgia at the outbreak of the Civil War was regretted by many Utahns. The concurrent closure of Camp Floyd and withdrawal of the army was little mourned.

Lincoln, as noted, sought to continue a conciliatory policy with Utah, but his first two gubernatorial appointments proved disappointing. John W. Dawson alienated the Mormons by insinuating their disloyalty, became involved in moral indiscretion, and fled the territory within a month. His successor, Stephen S. Harding, upon finding that his powers were more nominal than real, aroused Mormon indignation by petitioning Congress for changes in the territorial organic act that would restrict the local courts and place the selection of jurors and the appointment of militia officers in the hands of federal appointees. Two district judges also supported the petition. This threat to local control of judiciary and military powers was quickly reported to Young by William H. Hooper, Utah's delegate in Washington. A mass protest meeting was held; in response, Lincoln removed Harding as governor.

Lincoln finally found satisfaction when he appointed James Duane Doty, who had known the Mormons while he was Utah's superintendent of Indian affairs. Fully aware of the political aspirations of the Mormons, he chose to ignore them as long as they didn't interfere with federal business. In this spirit he explained to Secretary of State William Seward on January 28, 1865, that there were "three distinct governments" in Utah Territory—"the church, the military, and the civil." He continued:

But the leaders of "the Church" . . . have the appointment, and control in fact through its members, of all the civil and militia officers not appointed by the President of the United States. In addition, the same party, in 1861 formed an independent government in the "State of Deseret" whose boundaries include Utah and portions of Idaho and Arizona. This form of government is preserved by annual elections of all state officers; the legislature being composed of the same men who are elected to the Territorial Legislature, and who, in a Resolution, re-enact the same laws for the "State" which have been enacted for the Territory of Utah.

Restoration of peace between the North and South dimmed the prospects for the apocalyptic Political Kingdom of God. Union victory, which Utah's Mormons and gentiles celebrated together, pushed the millennial kingdom again into the indefinite future. The ghost government of Deseret faded out in 1870 while the territorial government remained; even so, Brigham Young, his colleagues in the Mormon hierarchy, the Council of Fifty, and other church instrumentalities continued to exercise considerable control. The Civil War had settled the states' rights issue in the South but not in Utah, where the fight to Americanize the Mormons was only beginning.

Governmental Activities

While war and political strife were the headlines of the 1860s, the territorial and local governments performed the prosaic tasks that a conservative populace was willing to assign to public agencies. Their jurisdiction was reduced when federal laws pruned Utah down to its present size between 1861 and 1868 (see map, p. 740). Since the federal appropriations for Utah Territory were never large and were often tardy, the chief revenue sources were property taxes and a percentage of the proceeds from toll roads, bridges, and other licensed monopolies. Levies in labor continued to be available, but it was more common to call on volunteer labor to construct public buildings and make other civic improvements. The Mormon Church often built facilities for public purposes—using local resources if the need was local but using churchwide resources if a general benefit was anticipated.

The Legislative Assembly continued to create and redefine counties, charter cities, organize business enterprises and special-purpose agencies, and appropriate funds for such entities as the Nauvoo Legion, the Deseret Agricultural and Manufacturing Society, the territorial penitentiary, and the University of Deseret. Appropriations for education were trivial until the 1870s, an aggregate ex-

246

penditure of $20,000 on the ill-fated Deseret Alphabet Experiment being an exception. Because localities were equally reluctant to tax themselves, the free school movement made little progress; the tuition-supported parochial-spirited community schools seemed adequate. County courts and city councils provided roads and ditches, animal pounds, minimal police protection, and even more minimal fire protection. The limited scope of governmental activity is suggested by the fact that in 1870 a territorial population of approximately 87,000 paid taxes, exclusive of federal levies, of $167,355. But Utah Territory was debt-free.

Mormons v. Gentiles

At the close of the Civil War the Utah populace was divided between those *of* the Kingdom and those *outside* the Kingdom. The "outsiders" had filtered into the Mormon commonwealth from among the forty-niners enroute to and from the California gold fields; from among those traveling the Oregon and California trails who were attracted to the commerce that centered in the Mormon capital; from among federal appointees and their dependents; from among Johnston's army, its camp followers, and the California volunteers who established Fort Douglas; from ministers who came to shepherd the gentile flocks and reclaim the "misguided" Mormons; and from miners and railroad workers.

This heterogeneous minority, composing ten to fifteen percent of the population in the 1860s and 1870s, understandably sought a place in Utah's political sun. They viewed with suspicion and resentment the Mormon domination of governmental, economic, and educational affairs, and they complained of taxation without representation. As their numbers increased, an ambitious and ardently anti-Mormon group launched a vigorous and unrelenting attack on the entrenched power of the Mormon majority. These anti-Mormon citizens were led by Fort Douglas commander Patrick Connor, who, after completing his military career in Wyoming and Montana, returned to Utah to carry on his mining interests and political activities until his death in 1891.

The strength of the minority position lay in Utah's territorial status. As long as the federal government exercised sovereignty through appointment of executive and judicial officers and retained final legislative control through the congressional power to override territorial laws, the gentiles could appeal to the nation's press, lobby for desired appointments and legislation, and exert pressure on appointees. During the 1860s the gentiles had insufficient numbers and cohesiveness for an effective united effort, but the completion of the transcontinental railroad in 1869 generated hopes of increasing numbers and, therefore, increasing effectiveness. The railroad town of Corinne, near the junction of the Union Pacific and Central Pacific railroads, flourished as Utah's "Gentile Capital" for several years; later when Ogden became the railroad center, the erstwhile all-Mormon city became an important base of gentile influence. By the end of 1869 there existed a nucleus of organized opposition to Mormon power. Headed by Connor, it found added strength in Robert N. Baskin, a young lawyer from Ohio who was sent to Washington to lobby for additional legislation.

Another factor in the gentiles' developing strength was apostasy in Mormon ranks. Particularly significant at the end of the decade were the so-called Godbeites, chiefly businessmen who objected to Brigham Young's "one-man power" and to certain economic policies of the church leaders. This "New Movement," which lost some of its influence when William Godbe and other leaders ventured into spiritualism, advocated abandonment of Mormon exclusiveness in economic affairs and urged development of the territory's rich mineral resources, two goals also sought by the gentiles.

Creation of Local Political Parties

The "reform" challenge was met with excommunications, and the leaders of the New Movement formed a temporary alliance with non-Mormon friends and organized the Liberal Party in February 1870. The following July, under Connor's leadership, the Liberals held their first convention at Corinne. George R. Maxwell, registrar of the federal land office in Utah, became the first of several Liberal candidates who tried unsuccessfully to unseat the Mormon delegates to Congress. William H. Hooper won reelection for a fourth term by a landslide. (A non-Mormon merchant, William McGrorty, had polled 105 votes in the previous election; his challenge to Hooper's right to the delegate seat was rejected by the House of Representatives.)

The *Mormon Tribune,* established by the Godbeites, became the Salt Lake *Tribune*—the voice of the Liberal Party. In response the Mormons created the People's Party, and the church-owned *Deseret News* became its journalistic voice. The newly established Salt Lake *Herald* also aggressively supported the People's Party. Liberal activities tended to find most of their national support among Republican politicians and press, while Southern Democrats, resentful of Reconstruction excesses, provided almost the only sympathetic ears outside the territory for the People's Party representatives.

Crowds wait outside the livery stable over which the case of Ann Eliza Webb Young v. Brigham Young *was being tried in 1875.*

However, the national political parties existed only in embryo in Utah Territory until the heat of the Mormon-gentile battle cooled in the early 1890s.

The Liberal leadership was quick to make plural marriage a political issue. The Antibigamy Act of 1862 had remained dead because the probate courts still claimed jurisdiction over most criminal offenses and Mormon grand juries could not be expected to indict persons arrested for polygamy. As a result there had been no convictions under the act, nor did it appear likely that there would be as long as the Mormons controlled the judicial machinery. Therefore, the polygamy issue became inextricably tied to the struggle for political control of the territory. The moral issue served as a convenient battle cry, not only for the political leaders in Washington bent on "Americanizing" the Mormon community, but for the politically ambitious local minority. The antipolygamy legislation that issued from Congress over the next two decades dealt largely with increasing federal controls over the executive, legislative, and judicial processes in the territory. Because they were seen as instruments of Mormon control, the laws also dealt with the territorial militia, public schools, naturalization of Mormon aliens, and the church economic monopoly.

As the Latter-day Saints continued to insist that the practice of plural marriage was protected under the First Amendment, the church-state issue received wide publicity. United States Vice-president Schuyler Colfax, speaking in Salt Lake City in October 1869, challenged the Mormon claim. "I do not concede," he said, "that the institution you have established here, and which is condemned by law, is a question of religion. . . . No assumed revelation justifies anyone in trampling on the law." In reply John Taylor said, "Allow me, sir, here to state that the assumed revelation referred to is one of the most vital parts of our religious faith; it emanated from God and cannot be legislated away." In a follow-up letter, Colfax set the issue in the context of post-Civil War politics:

> But the Nation resolved that wherever the territorial area of the Union extended, and wherever the flag of the Union has a right to float, there the laws of the Union should be respected. . . . It is time to understand whether the authority of the Nation or the authority of Brigham Young is the supreme power in Utah; whether the laws of the United States or the laws of the Mormon Church have precedence within its limits.

The Cullom Bill

Several bills were introduced in Congress during the late 1860s to strengthen the Morrill Act of 1862. None of them was enacted, though the bill sponsored by Illinois Representative Shelby M. Cullom came close in 1870. This extraordinary bill proposed to subject Utah to greater federal control by enlarging the governor's appointive power to include all local judges, notaries, and sheriffs. It also proposed to deny the probate courts all criminal jurisdiction and to place the selection of jury panels in the hands of federal appointees; to prescribe fines and imprisonment for both polygamy—the act of marrying again while a wife is still living—and cohabitation—the act of living together with two or more women concurrently—to exclude *believers* in plural marriage from jury service in polygamy and cohabitation trials; to exempt such offenses from the statute of limitations and permit wives to testify against husbands in such cases; to bar polygamists from naturalization, from voting, and from holding public office; and, finally, to authorize the president of the United States to employ military

250

force if and when necessary to enforce the provisions of the law.

An echo of recent measures to reconstruct the South, the Cullom Bill aroused nationwide interest. It also produced interesting results in Utah. Three thousand Mormon women gathered in the Salt Lake Tabernacle to formulate their protest to Congress. To the surprise of many who had assumed that Mormon wives were unwilling victims of "a priestly dominated polygamic system," the women denounced the proposed measures and threatened defiance. In the same month the territorial legislature formulated a bill that would grant Utah women the right to vote. The bill was signed into law by Acting Governor S. A. Mann on February 12, 1870, just two months after a similar enactment made the women of Wyoming Territory the first in the United States to receive the franchise.

The Cullom Bill passed the House of Representatives on March 23, 1870, but lobbying by the transcontinental railroad's financial interests succeeded in keeping it off the Senate floor. The prevailing sentiment, supported by many Utah Liberals, was that the railroad would in time introduce "civilizing elements" that would take care of the "Mormon problem." All of the provisions of the Cullom Bill reappeared under different sponsorship when the climate was again right for a crusade against the Mormons.

President Grant and the Mormon Question

President Ulysses S. Grant, fresh from crushing the Southern rebellion, adopted a get-tough policy toward the Mormons and appointed General J. Wilson Schaffer as governor and James B. McKean as chief justice for Utah. Schaffer is said to have boasted that "never after me will it be said that Brigham Young is governor of Utah." His health failed, however, and after appealing for passage of the Cullom Bill and briefly challenging Mormon control of the territorial militia, he died in October 1870. He was succeeded early in 1871 by George L. Woods.

Judge McKean, a New York lawyer who had been identified with Republican opposition to the "twin relics," was equally determined to break Mormon control of Utah's judicial system. Ignoring statutory limitations, he proceeded to adjudicate as if the Cullom Bill had become law. By allowing the United States marshal to impanel juries he made possible numerous convictions and he indicted Brigham Young for lascivious cohabitation. He announced that while the case listed Young as defendant, it was actually a case of "federal authority versus polygamic theocracy." He continued, "A system is on trial in the person of Brigham Young."

Before the trial could be held, a United States Supreme Court decision in *Clinton v. Englebrecht* (an appeal of an earlier Utah trial) declared on April 15, 1872, that all of McKean's juries had been improperly chosen. The decision resulted in the cancellation of 130 indictments, including Young's, and in the release of several imprisoned persons.

While McKean's judicial crusade was in process in January 1872, the Utah Legislative Assembly called for election of delegates to a constitutional convention to prepare a fourth bid for statehood. Governor Woods vetoed the measure on technical grounds, but the convention met anyway. The delegates who drew up the constitution and petition for admission in early March included nine gentiles from Salt Lake City. Of these, Thomas Fitch (who had ambitions to represent Utah in Congress) and former Acting Governor Frank Fuller were elected to accompany George Q. Cannon to Washington to join Delegate Hooper in presenting the petition. While the constitution did not include Fitch's proposal to outlaw polygamy, it said that if Congress offered a condition on which Utah would be admitted, the condition would be included in the state constitution if approved by a majority vote of the people. The application fared no better than those that had preceded it.

The Poland Act

The only congressional act passed concerning Utah in the 1870s was a measure introduced by Vermont Representative Luke P. Poland and signed by President Grant on June 23, 1874. The Poland Act restored Utah's judicial system to the original organic act pattern by giving the United States district courts exclusive civil and criminal jurisdiction and by limiting the probate courts to matters of estate settlement, guardianship, and divorce. It also abolished the offices of territorial marshal and attorney general, whose powers had overlapped the similar federal offices. It provided that jury lists should be drawn by the district court clerk and the judicial district probate judge, the assumption being that gentile and Mormon names would be drawn alternately. This procedure was followed with reasonable success during the next ten years.

Other Governmental Activities

Tension in Utah relaxed somewhat following the defeat of the Cullom Bill, the failure of President Grant's reform effort, and the adoption of the Poland Act. Whether Grant's visit to Utah in 1875 affected his perspective on the Mormon question is not clear; at least he saw the City of the Saints and shook hands with Brigham Young. A year later Utah's observance of the nation's centennial was limited to a parade and patriotic service in Ogden, a Ladies Centennial Exhibition in Salt Lake City, and patriotic exercises in some of the smaller towns. The territory held no official observance, and the Mormon hierarchy was not involved in the Ogden or Salt Lake City activities.

Governor Wood's stormy term of office was followed in the second half of the decade by two nonaggressive governors, Samuel B. Axtell and George W. Emery, whose congenial relations with the Mormons disappointed their opponents. The People's Party candidate for Congress, George Q. Cannon, swamped Liberal George R. Maxwell in August 1872 by a margin of 20,969 to 1,942; he won again in 1874 by 22,260 to 4,513. The frustrated minority presented no opposition in the next two elections, both won by Cannon.

As urban populations increased due to the railroad and as the non-Mormons began to press for services that the Mormons had been content to seek through church or other voluntary channels, the day-to-day business of government expanded in Utah. Following the Territorial School Act of 1874, both territorial and local governments increased contributions to schools. Land titles began being clarified and recorded in 1869 with the extension of the federal land system to Utah, but no federal lands were transferred to Utah for school or other revenue purposes during the territorial period. Salt Lake City and the other larger municipalities began to improve water and sanitation systems and security services, but private enterprise and Mormon Church initiatives brought the first fruits of late nineteenth-century power, communication, and transportation technology to the people. Refinements like surfaced streets and sidewalks were for the future.

In the 1870s government in mining and railroad towns with gentile populations resembled local government found elsewhere in the American West, and in Salt Lake City and Ogden contested elections pointed toward a day when Liberals would have a share of the offices and even control municipal government for a time.

The Death of Brigham Young

An epoch of Utah history ended on August 29, 1877, when Brigham Young died of cholera morbus at the age of 76. Intricate litigation to separate his personal property in the $1,626,000 estate from the Mormon Church assets, many of them associated with railroad and other business projects, was a posthumous reminder of the impact of his personality and leadership on Utah's first thirty years. A reorganized First Presidency, headed by John Taylor, found external pressure and internal sentiment for change mounting, but the course that it charted for the church did not depart significantly from that which Young had pursued.

The Reynolds Decision

The Supreme Court ruling that brought the new Mormon leadership to a crossroads was sought with the knowledge and consent of Brigham Young. In the mid-1870s the Mormons, elated over the defeat of radical antichurch measures, and the gentiles, pleased with the Poland Act, wished to test the Antibigamy Law of 1862 in the courts. George Reynolds, secretary to Young and the acknowledged husband of two wives, became the voluntary defendant in a test case. The first court proceeding in 1875 resulted in a mistrial; a second trial produced a conviction and a sentence of two years' imprisonment and a fine of $500. President Young died while the case was being appealed to the United States Supreme Court.

On January 6, 1879, the high tribunal upheld the decision of the territorial district and supreme courts. In *Reynolds v. the United States,* the court declared that the statute in question "is constitutional and valid as prescribing a rule of action for all those residing in the territories. Laws are made for the government of actions and while they cannot interfere with mere religious belief and opinions they can with practices. . . ."

Although the Supreme Court would later retreat from the position that religious belief cannot legitimize actions that would otherwise be subject to legal prohibition, its 1879 ruling left the Mormons without a constitutional defense for their practice of plural marriage. But they remained convinced that man's law conflicted with the law of God as revealed to them. Brigham Young's successor stated the dilemma in these terms:

We are placed—not by acts of our own—in a position where we cannot help ourselves. We are between the hands of God and the hands of the Government of the United States. God has laid upon us a command for us to keep; He has commanded us to enter into these covenants with each other pertaining to time and eternity, . . . I know they are true, . . . and all the edicts and laws of Congress and legislators and decisions of courts could not change my opinion. . . . The question resolves itself into this: having received a command from God to do a certain thing and a command from the State not to do it, the question is what shall we do?

254

With the law on the side of the federal officers and the Mormons appealing to a "higher law," the court decision brought little change in the legal impasse in Utah. So long as the church leadership could control the election of local officials and legislators and maintain the secrecy of plural marriage ceremonies, that impasse would remain. The Supreme Court ruled in 1881 (*Miles v. the United States*) that the testimony of a first wife was inadmissable as evidence, and the Legislative Assembly was not likely to make the changes in the law on evidence that the high court suggested. Another decade of conflict was destined to pass before the Mormon Church was willing to abandon the practice of polygamy and the effort to control Utah's secular development.

Chapter 13
Bibliographical Essay

For a general treatment of government, politics, and the church-state conflict from 1858 to 1879, see H. H. Bancroft, *History of Utah* (1890); B. H. Roberts, *A Comprehensive History of the Church*, vol. 5 (1930); and Orson F. Whitney, *Popular History of Utah* (1916). Edward W. Tullidge, in his *History of Salt Lake City* (1886), also gives some territorial coverage. T. B. H. Stenhouse, *Rocky Mountain Saints* (1873), reflects the view of one who was close to Mormon leadership before he apostatized with the Godbeites. Robert Joseph Dwyer, *The Gentile Comes to Utah* (1941; reissued 1971), emphasizes the political aspects of its subject. Howard R. Lamar points out unique features in his "Political Patterns in New Mexico and Utah Territories," *UHQ*, October 1960; see also Lamar's *The Far Southwest, 1846–1912: A Territorial History* (1966).

An explanation of the Mormon attitude toward the Civil War may be found in Gustive O. Larson, "Utah and the Civil War," *UHQ*, Winter 1965, and Ray C. Colton, *The Civil War in the Western Territories: Arizona, Colorado, New Mexico and Utah* (1959).

Controversial economic phases of the period are most broadly covered in Leonard J. Arrington, *Great Basin Kingdom* (1958). A critical phase of the Mormon-gentile conflict appears in Gustive O. Larson, "Land Contest in Early Utah," *UHQ*, October 1961, and Laurence R. Linfold, "Establishing and Maintaining Land Ownership in Utah Prior to 1869," *ibid.*, Spring 1974. With reference to early mining, see Arrington's "Abundance from the Earth: The Beginning of Commercial Mining in Utah," *UHQ*, Summer 1963, and Larson's "Bulwark of the Kingdom: Utah's Iron and Steel Industry," *ibid.*, Summer 1963.

Mormon colonization during the 1860s and 1870s is systematically covered by Milton R. Hunter in *Brigham Young the Colonizer* (1940). The Idaho phase appears in M. D. Beal, *A History of Southeast Idaho* (1942), and the advance into Arizona by Charles S. Peterson, *Take Up Your Mission* (1975). David E. Miller, *Hole in the Rock* (rev. ed., 1966), recounts the Mormon advance across the Colorado in an effort to control the San Juan area. Richard Sherlock gives a good summary of colonization in "Mormon Migration and Settlement after 1875," *Journal of Mormon History* (1975).

Utah's political struggle for statehood, including federal legislation and the local Mormon-gentile struggle for political control, is the subject of Gustive O. Larson, *The "Americanization" of Utah for Statehood* (1971). See also Klaus J. Hansen, *Quest for Empire* (1967), which treats Mormon ideological elements in the conflict. Richard D. Poll, "The Political Reconstruction of Utah Territory, 1866–1890," *Pacific Historical Review,* May 1958, concentrates on activities in Washington, D.C. Two important judicial figures are treated in Leonard J. Arrington, "Crusade against Theocracy: The Reminiscences of Judge Jacob Smith Boreman of Utah, 1872–1877," *Huntington Library Quarterly,* November 1960; and Thomas G. Alexander, "Federal Authority vs. Polygamic Theocracy: James McKean and the Mormons, 1870–75," *Dialogue,* Autumn 1966.

Other useful articles include Everett L. Cooley, "Carpetbag Rule: Territorial Government in Utah," *UHQ,* April 1958; G. Homer Durham, "A Political Interpretation of Mormon History," *Pacific Historical Review,* June 1944; and J. D. Williams, "Separation of Church and State in Mormon Theory and Practice," *Dialogue,* Summer 1966.

Chapter 14
The Crusade and
The Manifesto

Gustive O. Larson

With a population rapidly approaching 150,000 and a diversifying economy and society, Utah in 1879 possessed all of the requisites for statehood except one—a willingness of its Mormon majority to conform to late nineteenth-century norms of American political and social behavior. Not until federal authority imprisoned hundreds, disfranchised thousands, and threatened total destruction for the Mormon Church as an institution did the tenacious appeal to the church's "higher law" give way to a pragmatic acceptance of the nation's demands. The Woodruff Manifesto of 1890 opened the way for Utah Territory to enter the Union and for its dominant church to achieve eventual toleration among America's religious communities.

Renewal of the Anti-Mormon Campaign

A letter dated August 9, 1879, from United States Secretary of State William M. Evarts to the United States diplomatic representatives in each country from which the Mormon missionary system was drawing converts instructed diplomats to urge European governments to "prevent the departure of those purposing to come hither as violators of the law." Aside from indicating that the federal government intended to join the crusade and aside from placing the frustrated Mormon policy of the federal government in a somewhat ridiculous light, this effort to prevent the emigration of Mormon converts accomplished nothing.

President Rutherford B. Hayes, however, in his message to Congress in December 1879, made a statement prophetic of the course the government was soon to follow:

If necessary to secure obedience to the law, the enjoyment and exercise of the rights and privileges of citizenship in the Territories . . . may be withheld or withdrawn from those who violate or oppose the enforcement of the law. . . .

Governor Eli H. Murray, who arrived in Utah in February 1880, gave immediate support to the Liberal Party in its efforts to end Mormon political control of the territory. Because of support from the governor, the party reentered the competition for congressional delegate. Allen G. Campbell, a successful businessman, was chosen to challenge incumbent George Q. Cannon in November. When the election returns showed 18,568 votes for Cannon and only 1,357 for Campbell, the governor declared Cannon ineligible on the grounds that the native of England was not a citizen and that he was a polygamist; Murray gave the election certificate to Campbell. Cannon protested because the citizenship question had been cleared in a previous election and there was still no law against a polygamist holding public office. The question was finally referred to the House Committee on Elections. On April 19, 1882, the House accepted the committee's recommendation that the Utah seat be declared vacant. The decision was based on a provision of the Edmunds Act, passed a month before, which excluded polygamists from public office.

While Congress was determining Cannon's fate, the Utah Legislative Assembly adopted resolutions providing for a fifth statehood effort. As in the 1872 convention, a number of non-Mormons participated actively in formulating the proposed constitution. Significant also was the adoption of the name *Utah* instead of *Deseret*. While these factors suggested a trend toward accommodation in the Mormon struggle for statehood, the petition fared no better in Congress than did its predecessors. Locally a group of politically active gentiles opposed the move, and in Washington Congress said Utah would not be admitted without complete divorcement of church and state and abolition of plural marriage.

The Edmunds Act

President Hayes, whose visit to Utah in September 1880 was largely monopolized by Liberal Party Leaders, made some strong recommendations in his last State of the Union message in December. "Polygamy will not be abolished," he said, "if the enforcement of the law depends on those who practice and uphold the crime." As a minimum solution he urged "that the right to vote, hold office, and sit on juries in the Territory of Utah be confined to those who neither practice nor uphold polygamy." President James A. Garfield urged similar action prior to his assassination in 1881; at least one crusading journalist attributed the assassination to the Mormons. Chester A. Arthur emphasized that Mormon expansion beyond Utah's boundaries "imposes upon Congress and the executive the duty of arraying against the barbarous system all the power which under the Constitution and the law they can wield for its destruction."

The 1881-82 session of Congress was flooded with petitions on the Mormon question, and a score of bills and amendments were introduced. The Republicans responded generally with proposals to switch political power to Utah's non-Mormon minority; the Democrats sought to enforce existing antipolygamy statutes while keeping the good will of the voting masses of the territory.

The only proposal that became law was sponsored by Senator George F. Edmunds, a Vermont Republican who was active in the reconstruction of the South. The Edmunds Bill, in reality a series of amendments to the Morrill Antibigamy Act of 1862, not only declared polygamy a felony with a penalty of up to five years' imprisonment and/or a $500 fine, but also defined polygamous living, or unlawful cohabitation, as a misdemeanor punishable by six months' imprisonment and/or a $300 fine. The law disfranchised polygamists and declared them ineligible for public office. Those who practiced or believed in polygamy were disqualified from jury service in polygamy cases. All registration and election officers in Utah Territory were dismissed, and a board of five commissioners was to be appointed by the president to temporarily administer elections. The Utah Commission, as it became known, was to canvass Legislative Assembly election returns and issue certificates of election to those who were eligible and had been lawfully elected. The reconstituted legislative body was then expected to resume control of elections after passing laws consistent with the territory's organic act and United States laws.

Democrats opposed the bill because it deprived innocent citizens of their civil rights without trial. The Democrats also charged that federal commission control of the political machinery in Utah could effectively place the territory in the hands of the Republican Party. After heated debate the bill passed both houses and was signed by President Arthur on March 22, 1882.

The Utah Commission

The members of the Utah Commission, three Republicans and two Democrats, arrived in August 1882. The clash of interests between Mormons and gentiles immediately placed the commission-ers "between the devil and the deep blue sea," as expressed by member A. B. Carlton. The gentiles, realizing their inability to elect a Liberal Party delegate to Congress, urged unsuccessfully that the autumn election be cancelled. A request that woman's suffrage be abolished, though ignored at first, was recommended later by the commission. The Mormons, on the other hand, were outraged at the election officers appointed; from a population of 120,283 Mormons, 14,136 gentiles, and 6,888 ex-Mormons, the commission gave the Mormons eight, the gentiles seven, and the apostates nine positions. Mormons also protested the commission's ruling that forced polygamists who were registering to distinguish between those married before and after the passage of the Anti-bigamy Law of 1862. They also protested the introduction of a test oath that all prospective voters were required to sign, which in-cluded the clause: "I solemnly swear (affirm) that . . . I do not live or cohabit with more than one woman in the marriage relation." The Mormons found bitter satisfaction in the distinction made be-tween marriage—in which men acknowledged and lived openly with their wives—and the licentiousness alleged to be widespread among the non-Mormon populace.

On November 17, 1882, John T. Caine was elected as Utah's delegate. The vote was 23,030 for People's Party candidate Caine and 4,884 for Liberal Party candidate Phillip T. Van Zile, despite the disfranchisement of almost 12,000 Mormon men and women. (Three years later the commission's estimate of those excluded from the polls was 15,000.) The commission expressed confidence that "the steady and continuous enforcement of the law will place polygamy in a condition of gradual extinction, and that the dom-ination that is complained of by non-Mormons in Utah and else-where will, at no distant day be much ameliorated." The report also recommended public registration of all marriages. It added that should the next territorial legislature fail to pass appropriate registration and election laws, "Congress should have no hesitation in using extraordinary measures. . . ."

In contrast to the Utah Commission's initial deliberate approach in anticipation of early Mormon conformity with the law, the Lib-eral Party showed neither optimism nor patience. Liberal Party leaders sent a lengthy "statement of grievances" to Washington on November 28, 1882, claiming to represent "thirty thousand loyal American citizens of Utah who, it is estimated, pay more than a third of the taxes." Calling for the stripping of "all political power from the Mormon people," the memorial proposed "that the nation itself resume its authority over Utah," with the president appointing a legislative council to replace the locally elected legislature.

Notwithstanding some election commission success in reducing the Mormon franchise and certifying the elected members of the Legislative Assembly, the commission did not immediately respond to demands for legislative reforms. Still overwhelmingly Mormon, it sparred with Governor Murray while Caine continued to be elected to Congress and church members still filled most local offices. Despite its intended temporary status, therefore, the Utah Commission assumed permanency in Utah's political affairs. Its initial confidence that its objectives could be achieved "without resorting to measures destructive of local self-government, punishing the whole people . . . with political ostracism" gradually gave way. By 1887 the commission proposed direct federal control of the territory by an appointive governor and legislative commission and it supported passage of a federal law patterned after the 1885 Idaho Test Oath law, which practically disfranchised all Mormons in Idaho.

The Judicial Crusade

Mormon reaction to the Edmunds Law found clear and forceful expression through President John Taylor:

We have no fault to find with our government, we deem it the best in the world, but we have reason to deplore its maladministration. . . . We will contend inch by inch, legally and constitutionally, for our rights as American citizens and plant ourselves firmly on the sacred guarantees of the Constitution.

To test the constitutionality of the Edmunds Law in the courts, Mormons who had not been permitted to vote in 1882 filed a number of writs. On March 22, 1885, the United States Supreme Court upheld the disfranchisement provision of the law but declared the Utah Commission test oath "null and void" because it exceeded the commission's authority (*Murphy v. Ramsey*).

Meanwhile, with polygamous living defined as "unlawful cohabitation" and with all polygamists and their adherents excluded from jury service, the federal courts readied for action. The judicial system came to life with new appointees—Chief Justice Charles S. Zane and Associate Justices Jacob S. Borman and Orlando Powers presiding over the third (Salt Lake City), second (Beaver), and first (Ogden) districts, respectively. District Attorney William H. Dickson, his assistant Charles S. Varian, and United States

Marshal Edwin A. Ireland were other key men in the federal drive to finally stamp out polygamy. When the wheels of justice began to turn, sending hundreds of men and a few women to prison, it became a "judicial crusade," with attorneys and judges both lauded and denounced for their performance of duty.

The Mormons were not prepared to match this array of trained lawyers. During years of cooperative isolation when bishops' courts had served their needs, Mormons had developed a strong aversion to "going to law" against each other; attorneys were generally held in disrepute. However, with the non-Mormon influx, Brigham Young belatedly called attention to the need for Mormons trained in the law. One young man who heeded this advice was Franklin S. Richards, who, although largely self-taught, rose rapidly to meet the legal challenge of the time. With little more than a decade of experience, he became a leading figure in Mormon legal defense during the 1880s. As needs dictated, the church retained some of the recognized legal minds of the country to assist him.

The first polygamy case under the Edmunds Act was tried in Judge Zane's court in October 1884. It was that of Rudger Clawson, who had recently won high approval in Mormon circles for his courageous stand in Georgia when his missionary companion was murdered. Clawson was indicted on the double charge of polygamy and unlawful cohabitation. Among the witnesses called to establish that Lydia Spencer was Clawson's plural wife were President Taylor and his counselor George Q. Cannon. The case against the defendant could not be proved, and the hung jury was dismissed. The following morning Lydia, who had been in hiding, was discovered. When brought before the court in a second trial, she refused to be sworn as a witness and was committed to the penitentiary for contempt of court. The next day, at Clawson's request, she took the oath and admitted that she was married to Clawson. He was then found guilty and sentenced to three years and six months' imprisonment and a fine of $500 for the first count—polygamy—and six months' imprisonment and $300 for the second count—unlawful cohabitation. A plea for bail pending appeal was denied.

Certain developments in the Clawson case foreshadowed an uneasy future for the polygamists—the open venire in impaneling the grand jury, an all-gentile trial jury, imprisonment of a woman who refused to testify, severity of the sentence, and denial of bail. Bonds beyond reasonable measure were often required of those awaiting trial for a misdemeanor, and with a single exception the judicial interpretations challenged on appeal were upheld by the higher courts (*Clawson v. U.S., Cannon v. U.S., Snow v. U.S.*). The one extreme interpretation to which the Supreme Court took exception was the doctrine of "segregation," dividing the unlawful cohabitation into intervals so that several indictments could be handed down and the penalty for conviction could be extended. Apostle Lorenzo Snow, who later became president of the Mormon Church, was the appellant in this case (*ex parte* Snow).

By the end of 1884 the "wheels of justice" had ground out three convictions with prison sentences. The following year eighty-three polygamists were indicted, twenty-three were sent to the penitentiary, and forty-three awaited trial. Seventeen escaped imprisonment by promising to obey the law.

The antipolygamy campaign also reached into the territories of Idaho and Arizona. As a result of a vigorous effort headed by United States Marshal Fred T. Dubois (later a congressional delegate and senator), many polygamists were tried and imprisoned in Idaho and the already mentioned test oath law was adopted. While the crusade in Arizona resulted in several imprisonments, it was never as extreme as in Idaho. Late in 1884 John Taylor and his second counselor, Joseph F. Smith, visited the Mormon communities in the southern part of the territory and initiated a policy of "escape" colonization into Mexico. This program placed most Arizona polygamists out of United States jurisdiction.

Passive Resistance: The Underground

As the judicial activity intensified in Utah, Taylor was warned not to return to Salt Lake City. Despite the vigilance of the federal marshal, however, he quietly slipped into the city on March 31, 1885, to deliver in the Tabernacle what proved to be his last public sermon. After an emotional review of Mormon persecutions, of which he viewed the current happenings as a continuation, he described the United States as "no longer a land of liberty." "When such a condition of affairs exists," he said, "we must take care of ourselves as best we may, and avoid being caught in any of their snares."

Taylor then set the pattern of Mormon passive resistance by going on the "underground." He disappeared from public view to live among loyal friends, first in the vicinity of Salt Lake City, then northward where he spent the last eight months of his life in Kaysville. (He took another plural wife in Kaysville a few months prior to his death.) On occasion a select few church officials and political advisors were permitted covert contact with the president. During those two and a half years the leaders in hiding, with the

Among the polygamists confined in the Utah Territorial Penitentiary in the late 1880s were George Q. Cannon (wearing hat, standing in the doorway), first counselor in the LDS First Presidency, and Apostle Francis M. Lyman (wearing street clothes).

exception of Taylor himself, communicated under cover with Apostle Franklin D. Richards, whose office in the Church Historian's Building functioned as the "visible church."

Polygamous Mormons, taking the cue from their leaders, adopted various nonviolent measures to elude federal officers or to escape when overtaken. Going on the underground included taking refuge in ingenious hideouts in the home or on the premises, retreating into nearby canyons, escaping to the homes of friends in neighboring communities, or leaving territories where the crusade was in progress. For some leaders it meant accepting mission assignments overseas. The underground also developed highly successful communication systems, which included not only nocturnal trips between the hidden and the visible church but effective use of codes and warning signals. Marshal Ireland complained that most local telegraph, railroad, and police personnel were active collaborators with the underground. While he and his deputies were generally considerate and lawful in the conduct of their exasperating tasks, incidents of intimidation, harassment, and violence against individual Mormons, including women and children, did occur; one killing by a deputy marshal is recorded.

When Congress appropriated $45,000 in 1853 to construct a penitentiary in Utah Territory it could not have foreseen the structure's inadequacy in housing hundreds of Mormon polygamists during the last half of the 1880s. In 1884, when the prison population had reached an average of sixty, Ireland complained of inadequacies and unhealthy conditions. An 1885 congressional appropriation of $50,000 for necessary improvements was used instead for new construction, but long before this building was completed in 1888 it became evident that the enlargement would only mitigate the "miserable condition of the inmates." The accommodations were so crowded that the marshal asked district judges to delay prison sentences as long as possible. Congress finally appropriated $100,000 for additional construction; unfortunately, this was not completed until June 1891, when the crusade was over and prison sentences for polygamy were on the decline.

President Cleveland and the Mormons

The first Democratic victory since before the Civil War brought Grover Cleveland into the White House in March 1885, and a committee of church leaders addressed a petition to him that described the Mormon predicament in these terms:

> Contrary to good law, persons accused of crime are esteemed guilty until they prove themselves innocent. . . . Men fearful of not obtaining justice in the court, are avoiding arrest, believing no fair and impartial trial can be had under existing circumstances. . . . After the passage of the Edmunds Act and out of deference to its requirements, they have ceased to cohabit with their plural wives. Such men have violated no law and yet they are harassed and prosecuted.

In presenting the resolution to Cleveland, Delegate Caine stated, "All we ask is that the law be impartially administered." Cleveland promised, "You are entitled to that and so far as I am concerned, I shall see that it is done."

The first evidence of that impartial administration came when Cleveland changed Utah's governorship. Governor Murray's policy on civil service reform prevented any hasty response to Mormon complaints, but when his hostility towards the Legislative Assembly led him to veto the general appropriation bill, he was removed on March 16, 1886. As a gesture of good will the new governor, Kentucky Democrat Caleb B. West, made an early visit to the penitentiary to offer pardons to Lorenzo Snow and any others who would promise to obey the laws concerning plural marriage. Although West's intentions were appreciated, when the inmates declined to compromise he quickly discovered that Mormon polygamy involved deep-seated religious convictions and marital loyalties.

After this first unrewarding effort West turned to what he considered the supply line of polygamous marriages—immigration. In a letter to Secretary of the Interior L.Q.C. Lamar, somewhat reminiscent of Secretary Evart's circular letter of 1879, West noted that thousands of Mormons were still coming to America and suggested that "so long as these people maintain the attitude of defiance of the laws, every obstacle should be interjected to hinder, and, if possible, stop this immigration." In 1886 the governor warned prospective immigrants against entering the United States to participate in unlawful marriages. While the well-publicized proclamation proved that the fight against plural marriage was continuing, West's personal involvement in that fight lacked the rancor and vindictiveness that had characterized Governor Murray's administration.

The Edmunds-Tucker Act

The Edmunds Act of 1882, even with shifting interpretations, did not meet the expectations of those who wanted a comprehensive answer to the Mormon question. Democrats in Congress and on the Utah Commission were inclined to let existing measures prove themselves before they considered more extreme legislation, a viewpoint shared by President Cleveland. No such inhibitions restrained the Republicans, whose 1884 platform called for new laws and demanded "that the laws so enacted should be rigidly enforced by the civil authorities, if possible, and by the military if need be." In his last annual message President Arthur proposed "that Congress assume absolute political control of the territory of Utah. . . ."

Cleveland's State of the Union message in December 1885 asked for legislation to prevent Mormon immigration, and he indicated a willingness to approve "further discreet legislation" to rid the country of polygamy. But due to both humane and political considerations he slowed the judicial crusade, as already indicated, and he did not sign the next Congressional measure.

In 1882 Senator Edmunds introduced extensive amendments to the earlier Morrill and Edmunds acts, and in 1884 Congress debated at length a comprehensive measure aimed at plugging legal loopholes and at destroying the economic and political power of the

266

Mormon Church. Finally enacted in 1887, the hodge-podge Edmunds-Tucker Bill had potentially devastating implications.

To facilitate polygamy prosecutions, the bill required attendance of witnesses and permitted a lawful wife to testify against her husband; permitted initiation of adultery prosecutions by complaints other than a husband's or wife's; and required that all marriages be publicly recorded. Since county probate judges acted with the United States marshal in impaneling juries, they were to be appointed by the president. The bill also abolished women's suffrage in Utah and reinstituted a test oath for prospective voters, jurors, and office holders. The territory was redistricted and the Utah Commission was given the responsibility to conduct elections and administer the oath.

To destroy the church's secular power the Perpetual Emigrating Fund Company was dissolved and the Nauvoo Legion was abolished. The office of territorial superintendent of schools was replaced by a Utah Supreme Court-appointed commissioner in an effort to achieve free public education. On the basis of the Antibigamy Act of 1862, the church was again declared disincorporated, and the United States attorney general was directed to escheat to the United States all church property valued over $50,000. The forfeited property was to be used to benefit the territory's public schools.

Most provisions of the rejected Cullom Bill of 1870 were now revived with better prospects of enactment into law. While some Southern legislators objected to further federal invasion of state and territorial rights, the bill was pushed through both houses of Congress with predominantly Republican support. It became law on March 3, 1887, without Cleveland's endorsement.

The Utah Commission first applied the test oath four days later in an election in Brigham City. Some federal officers hoped the Saints would disqualify themselves by refusing to sign the oath, but nonpolygamist male Mormons signed the oath, registered to vote, and won another victory for the People's Party. The same pattern generally prevailed through the balance of the decade.

On July 30 (the day following President John Taylor's funeral) the government implemented the escheatment provisions of the Edmunds-Tucker Act by filing suits in Utah Supreme Court against The Church of Jesus Christ of Latter-day Saints and the Perpetual Emigrating Fund Company. Complex legal maneuvering followed; in November the court appointed United States Marshal Frank H. Dyer receiver of church properties in order to block the church from further dispersing assets to various church-related organizations and activities. When the marshal filed suits to recover some of this property, church leaders recognized that the mass of litigation might postpone appeal to the United States Supreme Court indefinitely and they agreed to pay $157,666 if the pending suits would be dismissed and no more claims would be presented. The total real and personal property in the hands of the receiver in June 1888 amounted to $807,000; most of it was still being used by the church on a rental basis. Scattered on the underground and limited to hasty, irregular council meetings, the church leaders compromised, believing that once their case was presented to the nation's highest court their legal position would be vindicated and their property restored.

Renewed Efforts for Statehood

In 1887 a sixth organized effort for Utah statehood was initiated. Visits and communications between the hidden and visible Mormon Church headquarters increased as People's Party leaders quietly invited the Liberals and the embryonic Republican and Democratic organizations to join the statehood movement. The non-Mormons declined, saying that the People's Party wanted to free Utah from federal control more than they wanted to force Mormon capitulation on polygamy and political domination. There is evidence that prominent church leaders saw the statehood project in these terms and that John Taylor's endorsement of the 1887 Constitution was predicated on this understanding.

John T. Caine presided at the June 30 constitutional convention, and the test oath prescribed by the Edmunds-Tucker Law was administered to the participants. Of major significance was the adoption of these provisions:

Article I, Section 3: There shall be no union of Church and State, nor shall any church dominate the State.

Article XV, Section 12: Bigamy and polygamy being considered incompatible with a republican form of government, each of them is hereby forbidden and declared a misdemeanor. . . .

Convention members, anticipating possible charges of duplicity, added a proviso saying the antipolygamy section could not be amended without consent of Congress and the president.

Discussions among church leaders, in which George Q. Cannon played a leading role, gave rise during the following days to the decision to let Mormons know "that the First Presidency and the Twelve see no reason why Latter-day Saints who are eligible to vote should not vote for this state constitution, and in doing so they would not offend God nor violate His laws. . . ." Mormon families were visited individually and asked to support the statehood movement. August 1, election day, brought an overwhelming vote for the constitution: 13,195 to 512. The support was in part a tribute to John Taylor, who had died July 27, and was a vote of confidence in those developing new policies.

The draft constitution was submitted to the Congress that convened in December 1887. House and Senate hearings continued intermittently for a year, but neither body acted favorably. The admission of Idaho, Wyoming, and four other Western states in 1889-90 accentuated the anomaly of Utah's predicament.

Utah's territorial Legislative Assembly, which now included five gentile members, considered several measures that supported the petition for statehood. Abandoning a previous policy of noncooperation with federal legislation, the lawmakers early in January 1888 enacted a law prohibiting the practice of polygamy, requiring all marriages to be of public record and restricting the authority to perform marriages to civil magistrates, ministers, and priests. Like the 1887 constitution, however, this measure was seen as a strategem by anti-Mormons for whom nothing less than a formal church capitulation, tested over time, would suffice.

Other significant enactments of the Legislative Assembly included the establishment of an industrial school in Ogden and the founding of the Utah State Agricultural College in Logan. For the first time the territory assumed a bonded indebtedness when $150,000 was appropriated for the improvement of various public institutions and properties. A committee headed by Governor West selected the site upon which Utah's present capitol is located. (No territorial capitol was built following the abandonment of Fillmore in the 1850s; governmental functions were scattered among a number of buildings in Salt Lake City and elsewhere during the long territorial period.)

President Cleveland also cooperated with the spirit of accommodation by appointing Elliot Sandford to replace Judge Zane, who consistently imposed heavy penalties on law-breaking polygamists. Taking office in August 1888, Judge Sandford purged the court of the crusading spirit that had bred such doctrines as segregation. Rendering judgment less severely, he encouraged many "cohabs," including George Q. Cannon and other church officials, to come out of hiding, plead guilty, and clear themselves of longstanding charges by serving moderate prison sentences. Before prosecutions were virtually abandoned in the early 1890s, over one thousand Utah Mormons were fined and/or imprisoned.

Political Movements within Mormon Ranks

Certain developments in the 1880s among the Mormons offered a more promising solution to Utah's church-state impasse than did the judicial crusade. Between 1884 and 1888 a group of young men of Mormon parentage challenged the traditional political alignment. As reported in the first issue of the Salt Lake *Democrat* on March 2, 1885, the group represented those who were "thoroughly dissatisfied with the deplorable condition of political affairs in this territory . . . and whose devotion to democratic principles would permit them to cooperate with neither the Liberal nor the People's Party." A program statement that they prepared earlier called openly for compliance with federal laws and for the end of ecclesiastical control in Utah. Such direct repudiation of both local parties and especially of the political position of their fathers sowed seeds of dissolution in their ranks and the *Democratic Club,* as it was called, soon expired.

Another effort was made in 1888 to challenge the established parties, but the short-lived "sagebrush Democracy" (so named by the Salt Lake *Tribune*) served primarily to remind old-timers that past undercurrents of dissatisfaction might sooner or later assert themselves more effectively. Democrats on the Utah Commission noted in a minority report on September 24, 1888: "From all the evidence before us, including personal observation, a radical reform in the near future is morally certain."

Included in the undercurrents of dissatisfaction were complaints made by prominent Mormon businessmen that a threat of heavy losses hung over them "as the gentiles are talking of confiscating their property in connection with the property of the church." They wrote to President Taylor in his retreat: the situation demanded yielding on the practice of plural marriage.

As pressures mounted and as political disabilities were suffered increasingly by nonpolygamists, restlessness increased and significant numbers of Mormons shifted their support from the People's Party to the Liberal Party. The Mormon political front cracked in August 1887 when the Liberals won the previously mentioned five seats in the Legislative Assembly. The following year the People's Party offered four places on its Salt Lake City ballot to the gentiles: the invitation was endorsed by non-Mormon conservatives headed by Governor West. The resulting Citizen's ticket candidates won the February 1889 election. In the same month the Liberals, aided by a group of strife-weary Mormons, captured Ogden City at the polls. In the August territorial election they increased the number of their legislature seats to eight. The Liberals next captured Salt Lake City in an exciting campaign in February 1890.

In the midst of the losing battle to retain control of their capital city, the Mormons suffered an additional blow when the United States Supreme Court upheld the Idaho Test Oath Law (*Davis v. Beason*). On the heels of their victories the Utah Liberals dispatched Robert Baskin to Washington with proposed legislation similar to the Idaho law. By April 1890 the legislation appeared in the Senate Committee on Territories as the Cullom-Struble Bill, coauthored by the same Illinois Republican who sponsored the drastic Cullom Bill of 1870. As the threat of total disfranchisement hung over the Mormons, the Supreme Court handed down a decision sustaining provisions of the Edmunds-Tucker Act by which the Mormon Church was dissolved and its property escheated (*The Church of Jesus Christ of Latter-day Saints v. U.S.*).

Equally conducive to social and political change in Utah were friendly warning voices from the outside. Supporting the increasingly tough federal legislation sponsored by the Republicans was an unpublicized but important program of personal contacts by high-ranking political leaders with the Mormons. General James S. Clarkson, editor of the *Iowa State Register* and twice chairman of the Republican National Committee, was one such contact. He claimed credit for inducing the Mormons to give up polygamy, and in another letter he said, "I have been made the one man in the Republican Party for over twenty years to look after the Republican interests in Utah and that region. . . ." This and similar labors by Isaac Trumbo, Leland Stanford, and others had a telling effect. Three months after George Q. Cannon was sustained as first counselor to Wilford Woodruff in July 1889, he stated:

I have been assured hundreds of times by men of wisdom and discernment that our overthrow was inevitable unless we conformed to the demands of public opinion and renounced all peculiarities of faith; . . . and that it was folly to suppose we could withstand these continued assaults upon us.

The Woodruff Manifesto

Although no official policy change was forthcoming at the time, authority for the performance of plural marriages was quietly withheld in 1889 and the Endowment House on Temple Square, where so many polygamous unions had been performed, was razed. Still pressure mounted, symbolized by the movement of some Mormon rank-and-file into the Liberal Party, by the adverse Supreme Court decisions, and finally by the Cullom-Struble Bill.

Church representatives desperately contacted the Washington sponsors of the Cullom-Struble Bill. With the help of Secretary of State Blaine, who gained Republican support from Utah, they delayed its passage conditioned on a promise that the church would stop practicing polygamy. According to Frank J. Cannon, when he brought this word from Washington to his father, George Q. Cannon replied, "President Woodruff has been praying . . . he thinks he sees some light. You are authorized to say that something will be done." In the meantime, the August 1890 report of the Utah Commission stated, in support of the Cullom-Struble Bill, "It is believed that forty-one persons have entered into polygamous relations in 1889." The press carried the report across the nation.

In response to the tidings from Washington, President Woodruff faced the inevitable. "I have arrived at a point in the history of my life as President of The Church of Jesus Christ of Latter-day Saints," he wrote in his journal on September 25, 1890, "where I am under the necessity of acting for the temporal salvation of the Church." The proclamation he issued to the press with the approval of his counselors and the Council of the Twelve was dated September 24; it became known as the Woodruff Manifesto. It stated that the Endowment House had been razed and it denied the Utah Commission's report that polygamous marriages had been performed in 1889. It concluded, "and now, I publicly declare that my advice to the Latter-day Saints is to refrain from conducting any marriage forbidden by the law of the land."

Upon notice from Delegate Caine that Secretary of the Interior John W. Noble would not accept the manifesto as authoritative "without its acceptance by the conference," it was submitted to the Mormons gathered in general conference on October 6, 1890, and unanimously approved.

The Woodruff Manifesto was received with caution in Washington since some thought it was a trick to secure statehood and that once statehood was gained, the practice of polygamy could be resumed without fear of vigorous prosecution. The Utah Commission Republican majority and President Benjamin Harrison warned against hasty steps towards Utah's admission. On the other hand, Governor Arthur L. Thomas, who as a former secretary of the territory and member of the commission had been zealous in the antipolygamy crusade, now urged acceptance of the Mormon action as the long-delayed fulfillment of the government's objectives. Charles S. Zane, once again Utah chief justice, showed confidence in the manifesto and ruled that membership in the Mormon Church should no longer constitute a bar against American citizenship. By such steps a road of mutual confidence was opened that led shortly to statehood.

Chapter 14
Bibliographical Essay

Historians have given generous coverage to the exciting Utah period from the Reynolds decision of 1879 to the Mormon capitulation on polygamy in 1890. Several of the works mentioned in chapter 13 also deal with this period. In *History of Utah,* Vol. 3 (1898) and *Popular History of Utah* (1916) Orson F. Whitney carries the Mormon point of view, as does B. H. Roberts in *A Comprehensive History of the Church,* Vols. 5-6 (1930). Gustive O. Larson, *The "Americanization" of Utah for Statehood* (1971), gives a detailed account of the crusade, the underground and the prison community, and developments leading to the Woodruff Manifesto. R. H. Baskin, in *Reminiscences of Early Utah* (1914), presents a typical gentile view of the Utah situation. Frank J. Cannon, who participated actively as Utah's delegate to Congress and later as senator, gives a version somewhat colored by his excommunication from the Mormon Church in Cannon and Harvey J. O'Higgins, *Under the Prophet in Utah* (1911).

Some light on the practice of polygamy and its relation to the political struggle appears in Juanita Brooks, "A Closeup of Polygamy," *Harpers Magazine,* February 1934; Orma Linford, "Mormons and the Law: The Polygamy Cases," *Utah Law Review,* Winter 1964 and Summer 1965; M. Hamblin Cannon, "The Prison Diary of a Mormon Apostle," *Pacific Historical Review,* November 1947; Gustive O. Larson, "An Industrial Home for Polygamous Wives," *UHQ,* Summer 1970; and Charles A. Cannon, "The Awesome Power of Sex: The Polemical Campaign against Mormon Polygamy," *Pacific Historical Review,* February 1974.

An unbiased evaluation of the crusading judge is found in Thomas G. Alexander, "Charles S. Zane, Apostle of the New Era," *UHQ,* Fall 1966. Three articles that throw interesting light on the Woodruff Manifesto are Kenneth Godfrey, "The Coming of the Manifesto," *Dialogue,* Fall 1970; Thomas G. Alexander, "Wilford Woodruff and the Changing Nature of Mormon Religious Experience," *Church History,* March 1976; and Henry J. Wolfinger, "A Reexamination of the Woodruff Manifesto in Light of Utah Constitutional History," *UHQ,* Fall 1971.

Matthias R. Cowley, *Wilford Woodruff* (1909), does not probe the political aspects of its subject. Samuel Taylor, *The Kingdom or Noth-*

ing: The Life of John Taylor, Militant Mormon (1976), combined extensive documentary research with some literary license.

Unpublished research that explores significant aspects of this period of Utah territorial politics and government includes Mark W. Cannon, "The Mormon Issue in Congress, 1872-82," (Ph.D. dissertation, Harvard University, 1960); Stewart L. Grow, "A Study of the Utah Commission, 1882-1896," (Ph.D. dissertation, University of Utah, 1954); and Judith Ann Roderick, "Historical Study of the Congressional Career of John T. Caine," (master's thesis, Brigham Young University, 1959). Richard D. Poll, "The Twin Relic: A Study of Mormon Polygamy and the Campaign by the Government of the United States for Its Abolition, 1852-1890," (master's thesis, Texas Christian University, 1939), contains a list of seventy-nine bills and resolutions that were introduced in Congress to deal with the "Mormon Question"; fifty-seven of them were introduced during the years covered by this chapter.

Chapter 15
Pioneer Society

Bruce L. Campbell and Eugene E. Campbell

In early February 1854 the starving, nearly frozen members of John C. Fremont's last expedition to the West straggled into Parowan, Utah. The inhabitants of the Mormon village received them warmly and nursed them back to health. Most of the group soon moved on to California, but Solomon Nunes Carvalho, the expedition's artist, was too weak to make the journey. He remained in Parowan to recuperate; later he traveled to Salt Lake City, where he became friends with Brigham Young. As Carvalho's health improved, he joined Young on a trip to southern Utah and so found himself again among his friends in Parowan. While there he was involved in a touching incident that he recorded in his journal:

> *The morning after my arrival . . . I arose early and, taking my sketchbook along, I sauntered around the city. In the course of my wanderings, I saw a man walking up and down before an adobe shanty, apparently much distressed. I approached him and inquired the cause of his trouble. He told me that his little daughter, age six, had died suddenly in the night. He pointed to the door and I entered the dwelling. Laid out upon a straw mattress, but very clean, was one of the most angelic children I ever saw. On its face was a peaceful smile, and it looked more like the gentle repose of healthful sleep than the everlasting slumber of death. . . . I entered very softly, and did not disturb the afflicted mother, who reclined on the bed, her face buried in the pillow, sobbing. . . . Without a second's reflection, I commenced making a sketch of the child, and in the course of half an hour, I had made a good likeness. . . . A slight movement in the room caused the mother to look around, and on seeing me, I apologized for my intrusion, telling her that I*

was a member of the Governor's party that had arrived the night before. I tore the leaf out of my notebook and presented it to her, and it is impossible to describe the delight and joy she expressed at its possession. She said I was an angel sent from heaven to comfort her. I bid her place her trust in Him "Who giveth and taketh away," and left her. . . . I continued my walk, contemplating the strange combination of events which gave this poor woman a single ray of peace for her sorrowing heart. When I was about starting the next day, I discovered in the wagon a basket filled with eggs, butter, and several loaves of bread, and a note containing these words: "From a grateful heart."

The next morning Carvalho left for California with a group of Mormon missionaries bound for the Sandwich Islands. From California Carvalho returned to his home in the East, where he wrote one of the more informative gentile memoirs of life in pioneer Utah.

In December 1886 Edward Meeks Dalton, a young Parowan polygamist who had been on the underground in Arizona, was betrayed by a disaffected Mormon neighbor and was killed by a United States marshal. The circumstances are disputed; the marshal was later acquitted on a grand jury indictment of manslaughter. Years later Delila, Dalton's second wife, died in California and was returned to Parowan for her funeral and burial. Emily, the first wife, was heartbroken at this event, which robbed her of the expected privilege of dying earlier and thus being the first to meet their mutual husband in heaven. Although Emily became reconciled enough to attend Delila's funeral, she would not allow Delila to be buried next to their husband—she saved that spot for her own final resting place.

Neither the experience of Carvalho nor of the Daltons is typical of pioneer life in Utah. Deaths of children were common but memorial sketches were not, and no other polygamist was killed in the prolonged struggle over "the Principle." However, many of the elements contained in each vignette are illustrative. Violence and untimely death were facts of life in frontier America, and Utah was no exception. Love, care, consideration, warmth, unity, cooperation, altruism, devotion, joy, and humor as well as conflict, division, fear, sorrow, indifference, prejudice, hate, dissension, and deceit are sentiments common to human experience—kingdom-builders and opportunity-seekers alike.

The social and cultural milieu of pioneer Utah was shaped by various forces. More important than environmental limitations and resources, which so powerfully influenced the development of adjoining territories, were the religious concepts and organizational patterns of the Mormon Church. Sponsorship of religious services, proselyting programs, plural marriage, education, newspapers, drama, dance, visual arts, music, and communal living demonstrate the pervasive influence of the church in the daily lives of the people. As gentiles arrived in increasing numbers, they challenged this Mormon domination of society, and the unique development of some social institutions can be understood only in the context of the bitter struggle that prolonged the territorial period. The ecclesiastical factor even affected the processes of urbanization and industrialization operating on the United States as a whole as they came to bear on nineteenth-century Utah.

Community Development

Two patterns of community development vied with each other in nineteenth-century Utah—the military, mining, and railroad towns which were typically American and the distinctive cities and villages of the Mormons, whose beginnings were discussed in chapter 6. The evolution of the relations of the communities from overt hostility through peaceful coexistence to a degree of integration would continue through the twentieth century.

The 1870 census, the first taken after Utah Territory had been trimmed to its present state boundaries, tallied 86,786 persons. Hardly reflecting the impact of railroads and mines, it reported 182 towns and precincts in the territory, with only three—Salt Lake City (12,584), Ogden (3,127), and Provo (2,384)—having more than 2,000 inhabitants. Eighteen towns had between 1,000 and 2,000 people, and twenty-eight had between 500 and 1,000. Thus, 133 of the 182 settlements reported in 1870 had fewer than 500 people; the territorial population per square mile averaged 1.1.

By 1900 Salt Lake City had a population of 53,531; Ogden and Provo had risen to 16,313 and 6,185 respectively; and Logan had 5,451 inhabitants. Thus, during the pioneer era most people lived in small towns; by the end of the century, however, urban centers were growing. The federal census described Utah as almost forty percent urban by 1900, and population density had risen to 3.4 per square mile. (It was almost thirteen per square mile in 1970.) Utah was also reaching her capacity to support a preponderantly agricultural society, and the outflow of population—for other than assigned colonizing purposes—was accelerating. In 1900 the number of Utah-born people residing in other American states and territories almost equaled the number born elsewhere in the United States who were residing in Utah.

Most of the gentile boom towns of the postrailroad generation became memories before World War I. Fairfield, whose population was built to 7,000 in the late 1850s by Johnston's Army and associated economic and social enterprises, became a farm and pasture area for the Mormons a few years after the troops departed. Corinne's boosters planned to convert the last "hell on wheels" construction camp of the transcontinental railroad into a gentile transportation and commercial center, but when Ogden instead was designated the main junction point of the Union Pacific, Central Pacific, and Utah Central railroad lines, Corinne became a ghost town within a few years. With less than a handful of exceptions, the gold and silver camps had similar fates. Alta, Frisco, Ophir, Silver Reef, Mercur, and Tintic followed the vicissitudes of the metals market and their own ore bodies; none achieved permanence. Stockton and Eureka survived as villages even though their ores played out, and Bingham disappeared in the mid-twentieth century because its copper ore did not. Park City lasted long enough to receive a stimulus from skiing and tourism. The smelting towns of the Salt Lake Valley and the coal towns of Carbon County received their largest gentile influx in the three decades before World War I. Their story is told in chapter 23.

Mormons were discouraged by their church leaders from working in the mines and smelters, and the non-Mormons who did work the mines were generally prejudiced against the Saints. In spite of these sentiments, however, some Mormons went to work in the gentile enterprises, often keeping their identity a secret. Many more Mormons sold agricultural and other produce in the mining towns and worked on construction projects. Such relationships tended in time to take the edge off the institutionalized Mormon-gentile hostility.

Estimates of the population breakdown between Mormons and non-Mormons vary, and their significance also varies because of the inactivity of some Mormons as the century waned. The 1890 United States census shows Mormons outranking all other religious denominations in Utah by 118,201 to 9,914, but it leaves over 82,000 persons unaccounted for. An 1883 estimate by Territorial Governor Eli H. Murray established Utah's population at about 150,000 inhabitants, nearly 40,000 of whom were non-Mormons or apostates. These elements of the population were not evenly distributed throughout the territory, but were concentrated in the mining towns and Wasatch Front urban centers, giving them more national visibility and political power than would otherwise have been the case. (See table, pp. 692–93.)

Social Divisions

While life in pioneer society was dominated by the division between Mormons and gentiles, there were other social dichotomies of importance.

Within the Mormon group there were persons of greater and lesser faith. Those who fell away from church practice and belief were called "Jack Mormons" or apostates. For many of these people, life in Utah became almost unbearable because they did not belong to either of the polarized groups. Mormons from President Brigham Young on down were not tolerant of those who left the faith. In an 1853 sermon Young said with characteristic hyperbole, "rather than that apostates should flourish here, I will unsheath my bowie knife and conquer or die." As a result many ex-Mormons left the territory, while some remained and tried to keep social communication open with both Mormons and non-Mormons. Other apostates sided with the gentiles. The Morrisite apostasy of 1861-62 and the Godbeite schism of 1870-71 were the most sizable defections, but attrition was continuous.

Within Mormon ranks there appears to have been some prejudice against different ethnic groups, most notably the Scandinavians. In 1900 sixteen percent of Utah's population was of Scandinavian stock; in some counties the proportion was higher. Many Scandinavian Mormons were from the lower classes and few spoke English at first, so they formed a convenient target for the frustrations some other Mormons felt. In some communities there was a Scandinavian section of town, and ward divisions reflected the community ethnic makeup. There were attempts by various Protestant churches to reconvert these Scandinavian Mormons, but they were not very successful. Both Scandinavian and German language newspapers were published intermittently in the later territorial years, when thousands of immigrant converts were learning English while still cherishing their mother tongues.

The impoverished conditions of the first years in most Utah settlements served to minimize class differences among the Mormons. Gradually some Saints prospered more than others, but church policy tended to distribute the wealth by requiring cash or produce tithing and contributions from the more affluent while asking the poor to contribute labor. In the construction of temples, tabernacles, and other public works, the unemployed were hired to work fulltime while the wealthy contributed of their means to help the projects along. Brigham Young was the only top Mormon official to amass substantial wealth in the first pioneer generation, and he was a major contributor to construction projects and other church-sponsored enterprises. The Perpetual Emigrating Fund redistributed wealth by encouraging the prosperous to help the poor gather to Zion. The United Orders of the 1870s, to the extent that they were implemented, also tended to decrease social class differences.

Holding a church position was one way to achieve high status in pioneer Utah. During much of this era, great secular influence was held by Mormon leaders; even local bishops and stake presidents were often very powerful men. D. Michael Quinn pointed out that a kinship network also developed in the church hierarchy with the passage of time, and it persisted well into the twentieth century. Doubtless abuse of ecclesiastical power and opportunity occurred— and was resented by less favorably situated Mormons as well as by gentile critics. President Young called attention to a temptation that some Mormon bishops succumbed to:

> When a good, handsome cow had been turned in on tithing, she has been smuggled, and an old three-titted cow—one that would kick the tobacco out of the mouth of a man who went to milk her—would be turned in to the general tithing office. . . . If one hundred dollars in cash are paid into the hands of a bishop, in many instances he will smuggle it, and turn into the general tithing office old, ring-bored, spavined horses instead of the money. I am inquiring after such conduct, and will continue until I cleanse the inside of the platter.

One important minority group with which the Mormons did not have very good relations was the army personnel stationed in Utah. The soldiers were not usually welcomed in Mormon communities and the gamblers, con men, prostitutes, and other camp followers were especially detested. While the relationships between the officers at Camp Floyd and the Mormon leaders was often cordially correct, the enlisted men generally did not like the Mormons. Of the Camp Floyd era, Thomas G. Alexander and Leonard J. Arrington conclude:

> Conflicts between the two ways of life were numerous, and defections from the faith occurred under the impact of these new temptations. If the diaries of the soldiers are any indication, the image which the Army took back of the people of Utah was extremely unfavorable and must have contributed to an already seething anti-Mormon sentiment in the country at large.

The founding of Camp Douglas in 1862 was not welcomed by Salt Lake City Mormons, and a generation of tension followed. On a smaller scale the same pattern prevailed during the military presence at Fort Cameron, near Beaver, from 1873 to 1883. On the other hand, many Mormons and soldiers appear to have developed friendly relations, and there were ties of employment and trade, but the United States Army was a source of social friction in territorial Utah.

Religious affiliation, as will be further noted in a later chapter, was a basis of social differentiation, both between Mormons and gentiles and among non-Mormons. Jews, Roman Catholics, and Protestants of all denominations entered the territory during the first generation, and Greek Orthodox communicants arrived in numbers before the end of the century. Generally the relationship between Jews and Mormons was good except when Mormon commercial policies bore down on Jewish and gentile firms alike. Catholics also generally had good interchurch relations with the majority group because they were not very evangelical in their approach; but many who came to work in the mines and smelters were ethnically "different" and so were viewed with suspicion by many Mormons. The official position of most of the Protestant groups was so emphatically anti-Mormon that social tension at the grass roots level was inevitable; the battle over schools was but one manifestation.

Thus of all the social divisions in Utah's society, the most important was between the followers of Joseph Smith and the rest. It presented some parallels to the last generation's racial division in America, including the range of relationships from acceptance and friendship to overt violence. The Mountain Meadows Massacre was one tragic manifestation. From 1866 to 1872 the hostility became so pronounced that Mormon hotheads attacked and may have killed some gentiles; the Brassfield and Robinson murders of 1866 were widely attributed to Mormons but were never solved. Gentile religious and secular meetings were disrupted and many non-Mormons carried weapons for self-defense. The Mormons were never pacifists, and in periods of stress some among them treated minorities in their midst like they themselves had been treated in Missouri and Illinois.

Health and Medical Care

The quality of life in pioneer Utah was, of course, affected by the available medical knowledge and care. That it was, in general, comparable to that available in many other parts of the United States and that it was primitive by present standards is clear. In the first generation almost one-third of the deaths were of infants under one year old, and another third were of children not yet five. Epidemics were not uncommon; diphtheria took 749 lives as late as 1880. Meager understanding of the causes of disease meant that preventive health care hardly went beyond the quarantining of known contagious diseases. Midwives and other medical practitioners were sometimes transmitters of infection.

Pioneer medicine relied primarily on Thompsonian herb doctors; local midwives; family remedies based on practical experience, tradition, and superstition; and "faith healing." Dr. John W. Bernhisel was a medical graduate of the University of Pennsylvania, but he devoted more attention to his assignment as Utah's delegate to Congress than he did to medical practice. Dr. Washington F. Anderson practiced in Utah for half a century and became a close friend of Brigham Young. Oberlin-trained George W. Hickman, on the other hand, was advised by Young not to practice medicine because the Mormons should be taught to rely on faith, and, according to his daughter's journal, he complied.

The advice to avoid the "poison doctors" was not too harsh when one considers the concepts that still dominated medicine in the mid-nineteenth century. According to Dr. Joseph R. Morrell:

The "humoral theory" of the ancients was still accepted. The humors were the body fluids: the blood, phelgm, yellow and black bile. When the humors were in balance, the body was in a state of health. When the balance was disturbed, disease appeared. Treatment was directed toward a restoration of the normal balance, and this was done by bleeding the patient, purging, inducing vomiting, and flushing the bowel with enemas. . . . The fear of bleeding, the standard method of treating most diseases, was intense. . . . No method of treatment used inspired confidence, and many felt that they were safer without the doctor. They were constantly warned from the pulpit to "let the doctors alone."

Early attitudes toward such physicians are reflected in this 1852 comment in the *Deseret News:*

Two physicians have moved to one of our most distant settlements, and gone to farming; three have gone to California to dig gold; three have taken to traveling and exploring the country; one has gone to distilling, and we are beginning to get some alcohol, which is desirable for gentlemen's shoe blacking, hatter's waterproofing, chemical analysis, washing bodies of the well to prevent sickness, and the sick that they may become well, when such there be. Those physicians who remain have very little practice, and will soon have less, we hope.

Some Thompsonian doctors, such as Brigham Young's second counselor, Willard Richards, had great influence because of their

Two decades after the death of Brigham Young this poster was still a popular tour-
ist item in Utah. The wives are, from left to right, top row: Emmeline Free Young,
Mary Ann Angell, Mary Van Cott Young, Augusta Adams Young, and Martha
Bowker Young; second row: Miriam Works Young, Eliza Burgess Young, Naamah
K. J. Carter Young, and Clara Chase Ross Young; third row: Lucy Decker Young,
Zina D. Huntington Young, Margaret Pierce Young, and Clara Decker Young; fourth
row: Harriet Cook C. Young, Lucy Bigelow Young, Harriet Barney Young, Emily
Dow Partridge Young, and Susan Snively Young; bottom row: Ann Eliza Webb
Young, Harriet Folsom Young (Amelia), and Eliza R. Snow Young.

positions in the Mormon Church. Their preference for such natural remedies as mild herbs, emetics, and "warming the blood with cayenne pepper" was not incompatible with the Mormon reliance on anointing and blessing the sick—a ritual then performed by both men and women. In the early 1850s the Thompsonian-led Council of Health contributed to the public bias against physicians.

Another factor that made it difficult for trained physicians to make a living in early Utah was the attitude concerning the morality of male doctors supervising the birth of children. The charge was made that a woman who sought such assistance was possessed of an "adulterous spirit." Young, who maintained that the most prevalent diseases in Utah were "fevers, which were not very common, and childbirths," encouraged midwives to superintend births, and until the end of the century they provided the only medical help available in most of the Mormon settlements. After the coming of the railroad the Mormon president encouraged Utah women to become trained physicians; about twenty of them, some financed by the Women's Relief Society, received medical training in eastern universities. These, in turn, trained midwives and nurses and helped to raise the level of medical practice and allay prejudice against trained doctors.

St. Mark's Hospital, sponsored by the Episcopal Church, began in 1872 in a converted residence in Salt Lake City and was used at first primarily for the care of miners suffering from lead poisoning and industrial accidents. Expanded four years later, it served as the Salt Lake County hospital until 1912. Holy Cross Hospital was built in 1875 not far from its present Salt Lake City location; like the short-lived hospital at Silver Reef, near St. George, it was operated by the Roman Catholic Sisters of the Holy Cross. Rather unique was Deseret Hospital, begun in 1882 and sponsored by the Relief Society. Most of the physicians at Deseret Hospital were women whose education had been assisted by the Relief Society. Though patient care services were suspended in 1890 because of financial problems, Deseret Hospital continued as a training school for nurses until 1905, when LDS Hospital was established.

The church strictures against physicians did not apply to dentists, and early Utah had the services of two trained practitioners, Alexander Neibaur and J. C. Kelley. Dr. Neibaur studied at the University of Berlin and practiced in England before converting to Mormonism and emigrating to Nauvoo. He practiced in Utah from 1848 until his death in 1883. His advertising mentioned "teeth cleaned, plugged, filled, scurva effectively cured, children's teeth regulated, natural or artificial teeth from a single tooth to a whole set inserted on the most approved principle." Dr. Kelley's ads listed many of the same skills and added extractions and filling by gold foil.

Little is known about the extent or treatment of mental illness in early Utah. Perhaps most mentally ill persons were cared for by their families, but there is some evidence that they were lumped together with the poor, infirm, and vagrant for such charitable care as might be available, as was the national pattern at the time. In 1869 Salt Lake City erected the first institution for the mentally ill in the territory at an isolated spot near the mouth of Emigration Canyon. Dr. Seymour B. Young took over operation and ownership in 1879, working under contract to the city; five years later he had twenty-nine patients, fifteen men and fourteen women.

In 1885 the Utah Territorial Insane Asylum was opened in Provo, where it remains today. Little is known of the type of care that was given there; it appears that most who entered the primarily custodial facility were not or were not expected to be cured. What is notable is that there was so little opposition to defining individuals as mentally ill, as opposed to being possessed of evil spirits or devils, given the general distrust of medicine and the emphasis upon the supernatural in everyday life.

Crime and Punishment

The measures taken to protect Utah communities from wrongdoers, like those protecting health, reflected nineteenth-century concepts and standards, with some variations in Mormon communities where disfellowshiping or excommunication might be employed against crimes as well as sins. Jails for temporary detention appeared early in many settlements, but serious offenders served their sentences in the territorial penitentiary or in federal institutions elsewhere.

The extent and type of crime in the territory have not been systematically studied. The full gamut of offenses, from juvenile deliquency, public drunkenness, and assault to counterfeiting, robbery, and murder, can be found in the records of both Mormon and non-Mormon communities.

Violations of laws defined by the stake high council during the first year in Salt Lake Valley were punishable by fines and whipping and, in some cases, seizure of property. Disturbers of the peace received a number of lashes on the bare back, not to exceed thirty-nine, or they were fined between $5 and $500, depending on the seriousness of the offense. Those found guilty of adultery or fornication were whipped and fined up to a maximum of $1,000. Convicted thieves were required to restore fourfold as well as receive lashes on the bare back. Actual whippings were apparently rare.

The same act of Congress that provided for organizing Utah Territory in 1850 also appropriated money for a territorial prison. The facility was completed in 1854 at a total cost of $34,000. It occupied three acres of ground southeast of Salt Lake City and was surrounded by a wall twenty feet high and four feet thick made of sandstone and adobe. Unfortunately fire, windstorm, and abuse by inmates brought the prison to a dilapidated condition by 1860. Prisoners were locked in their dormitories at night, but most were permitted to wander at will within the enclosure during the daytime. More dangerous convicts were kept in one of the sixteen cells made of iron bars placed in excavated holes covered with sheet iron. An iron cage called the *sweat box* was used to punish uncooperative inmates. Women prisoners were confined in the warden's quarters just outside the gate.

Prisoners escaped quite regularly. A memorial of the territorial legislature in 1869 asserted that the number of escapees plus those killed attempting to escape averaged about twenty-five percent of all the prisoners committed to the penitentiary between 1855 and 1868. The construction of the transcontinental railroad in 1869 was cited in the memorial as another reason for regarding the prison as inadequate for Utah's future needs.

By 1884 the prison population had reached sixty, and United States Marshal E. A. Ireland complained of the inadequate and unhealthful conditions. He was also aware of the pending influx of cohabs—Mormon polygamists being convicted of unlawful cohabitation under the Edmunds Act. Congress responded with a $50,000 appropriation and a new building was ready for occupancy by May 1888, but it was inadequate before it was completed when hundreds of cohabs were sentenced to serve prison terms. Ironically, a larger appropriation was made, but the additional construction was not completed until June 1891, when prison sentences for unlawful cohabitation were declining.

Imprisoned Mormon polygamists were segregated from other prisoners and were generally well-treated by the prison officials and guards. But there were complaints about the striped uniforms, shaved heads and beards, lack of time to eat, and ever-present bedbugs. (The dress and hairstyle codes were not consistently enforced.) Several prominent Mormon leaders were confined, including George Q. Cannon of the First Presidency and future President Lorenzo Snow. Even Brigham Young was forced to spend twenty-four hours in prison for contempt of court in connection with the 1875 suit for divorce filed by Ann Eliza Webb Young.

The penitentiary continued to serve as Utah's primary detention facility until a new state prison began being used at the Point of the Mountain in 1948. The walled prison at Sugarhouse was then demolished.

Family Life

While many other aspects of life in pioneer Utah were greatly influenced by the Mormon-sponsored community structure, family life—with the notable exception of plural marriage—was little different from family life elsewhere in America at the time. Gentile and Mormon families differed little except in ritual aspects like patterns of prayer and churchgoing. The nuclear family was the dominant type in the West as it was throughout America. The extended family—three generations in the same household—was never common in the United States and there is evidence to suggest that it was also uncommon in early Utah.

A man might marry a woman because she would be a good wife—cooking, sewing, bearing children, and so on—but romantic love was fast becoming the chief motivation for marriage. As a result, young adults were able to attend dances and other events together and build a personal relationship that would lead to marriage. People were expected to marry within their own race, religion, or ethnic group; marrying "outside the church" was a particularly serious taboo among the Mormons.

The husband was expected to hold a dominant position within the family in the nineteenth century, but visiting Europeans commented on the power and freedom of women and children in America. That some Mormon fathers acted in a despotic manner is clear from family records and from the frequency with which church leaders reminded that reasoning, love, and leading by example were the proper expressions of patriarchal authority. "I can pick out scores of men in this congregation who have driven their children from them by using the wooden rod," said Brigham Young on one occasion. Elder Orson Pratt advised parents in 1854:

Do not be so stern and rigid in your family government as to render yourselves an object of fear and dread. There are parents who only render themselves conspicuous in the attribute of justice while mercy and love should be

287

*the great moving principle interweaving itself in all your family adminis-
trations. . . . Govern children as parents and not 'as tyrants so they will be
parents in their generation and will be very likely to adopt that form of government in which they have been educated.*

Nineteenth-century Mormons, like their twentieth-century de-
scendents, were noted for having large families; fertility rates increased significantly in the areas where they settled. In response to
urbanization and industrialization, however, the birth rate decreased in Utah during the later pioneer period. Children were
economic assets in the rural villages, but in the cities, where fathers
were more likely to be wage-earners or shopkeepers than farmers,
children were liabilities. However, children were highly valued for
religious reasons and Mormon parents were instructed to rear their
children so children would "obey God and keep the commandments." Results varied. Levi Savage noted in his journal on a July
Sunday in 1873: "This afternoon has been *held sacred* by some
drunken boys, gambling and racing with horses." Later that same
month, while traveling through Nephi, he noticed a group of
young men drinking, loafing, and making comments about female
pedestrians—behavior not untypical of adolescence. Savage, however, felt that they, "being of the faith," should act better.

While paternal leadership was expected in the home, this was
more theory than fact for many Mormon families. Very often the
father was called to serve a proselyting, colonizing, or other mission for the church, and was sometimes absent for months or years.
For those not called on missions, the work of the church occupied
a great deal of time. Leonard Arrington notes the role played by
the Mormon wife:

*One is tempted to suggest that the process of settlement placed a heavier
burden on the women than on the men. Often away on missions . . . and other
assignments, the men left the women home to milk the cows, plant the crops,
and care for the children. A reading of the diaries kept by Utah's pioneer
women suggests that, in many instances, women provided most of the support
of their growing families by producing food and clothing, and, in some instances, even building the family dwelling places.*

While they were very similar to each other and to American
families in general, there were some differences between most gentile families and most Mormon families. The Mormons had more
children, and perhaps the Mormon fathers were somewhat less au-
thoritarian. In the Mormon system the women may have taken on
more responsibility than their non-Mormon contemporaries because of the church-related activities of the husband.

Plural Marriage

One unique aspect of social life in early Utah was the church-sponsored practice of plural marriage. Begun secretly by the Mormon leadership before the migration west, this form of marriage was publicly announced in 1852 and was thereafter defended as a religious principle. Although governmental pressure forced the church to discontinue official approval of such marriages in 1890, the institution continued to be a factor in Utah's social relations until well into the twentieth century.

It is still difficult to determine what percentage of the Mormon population practiced polygamy. Studies by Stanley Ivins, Kimball Young, and Nels Anderson indicate that at least ten percent of the eligible males entered into the practice; while two-thirds of them took only one additional wife, many had several wives, and a few of the leaders had more than twenty women "sealed" to them. Ivins' study indicates that the percentage of Mormons practicing polygamy fluctuated over the years, with the number of polygamous marriages increasing during the periods when federal opposition was particularly strong. He estimates that as many as fifteen or even twenty percent of the Mormon families may have been polygamous at times. During the Reformation years (1856-57) when religious conformity was particularly stressed, more plural marriages were contracted than during any other comparable period. The last upsurge of such marriages followed the passage of the Edmunds Act in 1882.

Plural marriage was supposed to be limited to those who were active and faithful church members. By reserving the right to authorize and perform such marriages, the leaders insured that only priesthood holders in good standing took additional wives. It is easier to document leadership action to encourage the reluctant than to discourage the unworthy. George Q. Cannon, then first counselor in the church's first presidency, is reported to have told a St. George congregation in 1884 while he and other leaders were eluding federal antipolygamy prosecution that he "did not feel like holding up his hand to sustain anyone as a presiding officer who had not entered into the patriarchal order of marriage." D. Michael Quinn has found that of the fifty-four Mormon general authorities appointed between 1844 and 1899, only nineteen were monogamous at the time of appointment; eleven of these took plural wives within four years of their appointment.

Some church members refused to practice polygamy because of personal feelings against it, lack of desire, or insufficient finances. Another limiting factor was the requirement that a man should secure the permission of the first wife. Some wives successfully blocked efforts by husbands or ecclesiastical superiors to secure entry into "the Principle," and a few may have actually sabotaged polygamous courtships. The fact that permission was sometimes given grudgingly and under considerable religious and social pressure did not make for harmonious relationships in such cases. However, there are numerous examples of women testifying of their conviction that polygamy was a divine system, and they not only permitted but encouraged their husbands to take another wife. A few wives assisted their husbands in selecting additional partners and even participated in the usually perfunctory courtship process.

Kimball Young's inaptly named study, *Isn't One Wife Enough?* (1954), suggests that over half of the polygamous marriages could be classified as highly successful or reasonably so. One-fourth are listed as moderately successful, and twenty-three percent are classified as having considerable conflict, with some ending in divorce. Recently discovered evidence of a large number of divorces among Mormon polygamists may indicate that Young's estimate of success is high. Certainly some polygamous unions were made and terminated for relatively casual reasons.

Although the primary rationale for plural marriage was theological, Mormon leaders defended the system as a means of solving many social problems. All women could have the opportunity of marriage and childbearing. A widow who wanted to marry again had little trouble in finding a man who would make her a part of his plural family. If the man were reluctant, he might receive a recommendation from Brigham Young that he "obey counsel." Girls immigrating from foreign lands, who might have been forced into domestic service or even prostitution in other societies, were able to marry and secure a respectable position in the community—and a mate for eternity. Defenders of polygamy frequently called attention to the fact that prostitution was found in Utah Territory only where the gentile population was concentrated.

Living arrangements in plural marriage varied with the economic circumstances and personal desires of the participants. Separate living quarters for each wife and her children were customary, and separate homes came to be regarded as preferable if feasible. Some of the polygamists with church assignments in more than one location had homes and families in more than one settlement. Emma, Rachel, and the thirteen children who accompanied John D. Lee to Lonely Dell on the Colorado River in 1871 represent a pathetic and heroic case. (The writings of Juanita Brooks have made Lee and his nineteen wives more accessible to modern readers than some of the other large polygamous families.) Husbands divided their time between families according to their assessment of the various considerations involved; with some of the wives there was apparently no sexual relationship at all. Since only a minority of the polygamists were affluent enough to support their partners in the life-style of upper middle class Victorian womanhood, wives and older children contributed substantially to the production of their own livelihood.

While some polygamous wives conducted virtually autonomous households, the more common pattern was for a degree of association among the wives and some division of labor. Cooking, baking, sewing, milking, teaching, and midwifing might be specialties; housecleaning and babysitting were usually shared activities. Children related freely with their half-brothers and half-sisters, as well as with their "aunt" or "aunts," thinking little of the distinctions until they grew older and possibly became aware of real or fancied differences in status among the wives and their offspring. Jealousy, varying in intensity, was common—especially when the first or earlier wives saw the husband's attention shifting to new partners, or when a plural wife perceived that she had not received an equal share in her husband's assets or affection. Overt competition between wives seems to have found expression in the household arts— sewing, cooking, cleanliness, appearance of the children, and budget management.

One of the most important aspects of plural marriage was its extra-legal nature. Because all polygamous unions except the tie with the first wife were not legal marriages and the customs and legal system in the United States were designed to regulate and support monogamy, plural marriage often resembled a ship without navigational instruments or maps. By the time experience with the institution might have been expected to develop appropriate norms, legal opposition began to drive it underground and made church regulation of participants' behavior increasingly difficult. As a result many of the polygamists—both male and female—who put up a happy face in public may have endured private dissatisfaction and suffering. Annie Clark Tanner's journal tells poignantly of her being taken back to her parents' home after her secret marriage in 1883 and of her disappointment when her husband failed to keep his first "appointment" with her two weeks later. On the other hand, Dr. (and State Senator) Martha Hughes Cannon, one of several plural wives who pursued active public careers in late nineteenth-century Utah, found that plurality had certain advantages for the wife: "If her husband has four wives, she has three weeks of freedom every single month."

If there had been no interference from the federal government, it is difficult to determine what would have become of plural marriage. It may have died out gradually because it was not economically feasible in an urbanizing society, or new ideas of romantic love and increasing stress on the family relationship may have caused younger Mormons to avoid the practice. However, it is clearly possible to maintain plural marriages in a modern industrial society, so the Mormons may very well have organized and regulated the system in such a way as to reduce the problems of the pioneer era.

Chapter 15
Bibliographical Essay

The best study on Utah community life is Lowry Nelson's *The Mormon Village* (1952). A brief survey of 1869 Utah towns by Eugene E. Campbell was published in *Proceedings of the Utah Academy of Sciences, Arts, and Letters*, Fall 1970.

Several studies of Mormon polygamy are helpful. Kimball Young, *Isn't One Wife Enough?* (1954), is probably the most detailed, but unfortunately the author failed to document his case studies. Stanley S. Irvins' "Notes on Mormon Polygamy," *Western Humanities Review*, Summer 1956, reprinted in *UHQ*, Fall 1967, is an important contribution, especially concerning actual numbers of people involved. Nels Anderson, *Desert Saints* (1942, repr. 1966), gives some interesting information on the southern Utah patterns. Gustive O. Larson, *The "Americanization" of Utah for Statehood* (1971), contains an excellent review of the practice in chapter two. For a helpful demographic study see Dean L. May, "People on the Mormon Frontier: Kanab's Families of 1874," *Journal of Family History*, December 1976. Two books with insights into the woman's view of polygamy are Annie Clark Tanner, *A Mormon Mother: An Autobiography* (1969, 1973), and S. George Ellsworth, ed., *Dear Ellen: Two Mormon Women and Their Letters* (1974).

Mormon Sisters (1976), edited by Claudia Bushman, contains articles about various facets of the lives and activities of pioneer women, including family life and plural marriage. *Sister Saints* (1978), edited and compiled by Vicky Burgess-Olson, contains detailed biographical sketches of twenty-six women who were prominent in Utah history, many of whom were partners in polygamous marriages. "The Mormon Family," by Bruce L. Campbell and Eugene E. Campbell, published in *America's Ethnic Families* (1976), Charles

Mindel and Robert Halberstein, eds., traces the historic development of the Mormon family and makes a current assessment of this important factor in Utah's growth.

S. N. Carvalho, *Incidents of Travel and Adventure in the Far West* (1857), captures some of the human interest of Utah pioneering. Richard F. Burton, *City of the Saints* (1861, repr. 1963, Fawn M. Brodie, ed.); Samuel Bowles, *Across the Continent* . . . (1865); Horace Greeley, *An Overland Journey from New York to San Francisco* . . . (1863); and Jules Remy and Julius Brenchley, *A Journey to Great Salt Lake City* (1861, repr. 1971), two vols., all present first-hand observations of early Utah through relatively unbiased, non-Mormon eyes. Elizabeth Wood Kane, *Twelve Mormon Homes* . . . (1874, repr. 1974, Everett L. Cooley, ed.), presents Mormon life in the early 1870s as perceived by Mrs. Thomas L. Kane.

John D. Lee (1961, rev. ed. 1972), by Juanita Brooks, is an important source of Mormon pioneer attitudes, which are further detailed in *A Mormon Chronicle* (1955), two volumes of Lee's journals coedited with Robert G. Cleland. Mrs. Brooks has also edited Hosea Stout's 1844-61 journals under the title *On the Mormon Frontier* (1964), two vols.

D. Michael Quinn's detailed study of the social, economic, and ecclesiastical relationships of the general authorities of the Mormon Church, "The Mormon Hierarchy, 1832-1932: An American Elite" (Ph.D. dissertation, Yale University, 1976), reveals a network of ties. Dale Beecher's monographs for the LDS Historical Department, *The Office of Bishop* (1975) and *The Bishop's Allowance* (1975), present a new look at the key men in Utah's pioneer settlements.

Chapter 16
Early Cultural and Intellectual Development

Bruce L. Campbell and Eugene E. Campbell

The cultural and intellectual history of pioneer Utah is primarily the story of the Mormon effort to build a self-contained society on the premise that God requires sacrifice and devotion but no more bleak austerity than earthly circumstances dictated. The non-Mormon and ex-Mormon minorities lacked the resources and cohesion required to develop an extensive counter-culture, though they produced enclaves of Western Americana, and their impact upon territorial education was next only to their political and economic influences.

As noted in earlier chapters, the cooperative, community-oriented Mormon colonization of Utah led to an urban development atypical of the American frontier. Mormon colonization was instrumental in creating an environment in which architecture, education, arts, and letters could find early expression. Even if only a few communities built separate churches, schools, theaters, dance halls, and civic centers, almost all communities combined the functions of these facilities in one or more buildings. (As civil government grew and in time conformed to the pattern of separation of church and state, litigation was required in some instances to determine ownership of these buildings.) The housing, of course, was less important than were the cultural strivings given outlet in tents and on hillsides, in log cabins and comfortable drawing rooms, in open air boweries, tabernacles, and that singular monument to the artistic aspirations of pioneer Utah—the Salt Lake Theater.

Architecture

During the first stages of community development structures reflected necessity rather than aesthetic or theological aspirations. Wagon boxes, tents, and hillside dugouts provided shelter while the community fort rose on—and usually out of—the omnipresent clay. Some of the first permanent homes were made of logs, but since conveniently accessible lumber was needed for fuel, fencing, roof timbers, and primitive furniture, adobe houses were more common. Properly constructed, adobe structures provided adequate shelter, though reports indicate that insects and even rattlesnakes found their way into these "dobie" homes, and the dirt floors were a frustrating challenge to tidy housekeepers. (A forty-day storm that began on Christmas Day, 1861, destroyed or damaged hundreds of mud-walled houses and shops in Utah's Dixie and collapsed Fort Harmony on the sleeping forms of two of John D. Lee's children moments before they could be evacuated.)

As economic progress permitted better living standards housing styles reflected individual means and tastes, memories of Nauvoo or Europe, changing American architectural fashions, and the special requirements of Mormon society. While plural marriage produced no special "polygamy" style, the chief functional requirement being that each wife have her own quarters, the Lion House that William Ward and Truman O. Angell designed for Brigham Young in 1853 is a unique monument to the multiple family. The Beehive House, with its combination of Federal and Greek Revival elements, and the no-longer-standing Gardo House, constructed in flamboyant Second Empire style, reflected both the substance and status of the man who presided over the Mormons for thirty-three years.

Rough-cut mountain stone and plastered adobe were the prevailing house materials until late in the nineteenth century, with varying architectural fashions reflected in floor plans, ornamental stonework, and increasingly intricate wood porches, pillars, stairways, widow's walks, gables, and trimmings. Mrs. Thomas L. Kane, who with her husband accompanied Brigham Young from Salt Lake City to St. George in 1873, found many of the dobie homes to her liking: "The walls of the best houses in Provo were white or light colored, and, with their carved wooden window-dressings and piazzas and corniced roofs, looked trim as if fresh from the builder's hand." Levi M. Savage, who traveled north along the same road from his home in southern Utah in the same year, was less enthusiastic about what he saw:

Dominating this 1870s view of First South Street in Salt Lake City is the Salt Lake Theater; St. Mark's School and Chapel are beyond the theater and the cupola of the City Hall is on the right.

There seems to be in some places a great lack of energetic enterprise in building and improvising. Miserable little huts "shingled with mud" are almost a universal sight in some places; fences, graineries, out-houses, yards, etc., all bear the same marks of confusion and bad taste.

The "fine homes" of territorial Utah were generally testaments to business success rather than to agrarian enterprise or ecclesiastical standing. Mormon merchant William Jennings remodeled the comfortable William C. Staines home, where Colonel Kane stayed during his 1858 visit to Salt Lake City, into the Second Empire-style Devereaux House. Mining and commerce produced most of Utah's late nineteenth-century fortunes, and the most elaborate renditions of European and American modes that appeared in Salt Lake City, Ogden, and Provo were as likely to be occupied by gentile as by Mormon families.

Public facilities, not private housing, most reflect the special architectural concerns of pioneer Utah. Leonard J. Arrington and Melvin A. Larkin assert that as one examines the early growth of Mormon communities "he gets the impression that the community was always in the process of building or creating some symbolic expression of its corporateness—its Zionic character—its communitarian single-mindedness."

The all-purpose meetinghouse appeared early in almost every pioneer settlement. None of the first generation of these log or adobe structures has survived, nor have the covered "boweries" that were built on Salt Lake City's Temple Square and elsewhere in the Mormon country where preaching services drew audiences of hundreds. Of the more permanent structures built after the Utah War, meetinghouses in Alpine, Grantsville, Parowan, and West Jordan, tithing offices in Fairview, Kanosh, and Paradise, and the Spring City Relief Society granary today display pioneer concepts of style and function. The lovely Pine Valley chapel witnesses that the Greek Revival found its way to the headwaters of the Santa Clara River.

It was in the same stage of community development that some of the most outstanding buildings were constructed—the stake tabernacles. Building a tabernacle was a major undertaking and only an organized, dedicated community could handle it successfully.

The Salt Lake Tabernacle, started in 1863 and used for several years before its dedication in 1875, was the achievement of three designers and the Church Public Works laborers. William H. Folsom conceptualized a self-supporting roof resting on pillars or buttresses that would support the great wooden arches that spanned the 150-foot width with a maximum height of eighty feet. Henry Grow superintended the construction, and Truman O. Angell designed the interior and trim. A gallery was added to the egg-shaped building in 1870, which lessened the effect of the vastness and improved the acoustics. Here Apostle Orson Pratt debated the biblical authority for polygamy with United States Senate Chaplain John P. Newman in 1870. And here, in 1884, Adelina Patti, world-renowned opera singer, performed for an audience that paid $1.00 for general admission and $1.50/$2.00 for reserved seats. Since that time many important religious and cultural events have taken place in the Tabernacle, and the organ and choir that have been associated with it for more than a century are probably the best-known symbols of Mormonism.

For sheer architectural brilliance, however, the Mormon tabernacles in Logan, Brigham City, St. George, Coalville, and Bountiful probably exceeded any other buildings of the pioneer era, including the four Utah temples. Like the Salt Lake Theater, the Coalville Tabernacle succumbed to "progress," but the others still stand. The pride evident in Juanita Brooks' description of the St. George Tabernacle is typical of feelings in all of these towns:

Completed, the St. George Tabernacle amply fulfilled the suggestions that it be an "ornament to your city and a credit to your energy and enterprise," for in its general lines it is perfectly proportioned with an upsweep of tower that satisfies the aesthetic sense. Simple in design, it is built of the red sandstone from the hills to the north, each block handcut for its special place, . . . the total effect is a building which some architects declare to be the most beautiful in the state.

The building of temples represented the most expensive pioneer accomplishment. Under direction of church leadership, the means necessary to construct buildings of this magnitude came from the cooperation of whole regions plus contributions of tithing and United Order labor and resources. Started in 1853, the Salt Lake Temple was forty years in progress. The St. George, Logan, and Manti temples were begun in the 1870s and completed in a decade or less. While perhaps not as architecturally significant as the tabernacles, the temples are the deepest expression of the Mormon faith. With their Gothic Revival styles, they are felt by some architects to be aesthetically heavy and formidable, but Arrington and Larkin suggest that they symbolize the mountains in which the Mormons found strength, shelter, and eternal perspective—"a spiritual fortress where they could not be cuffed about and mauled, where they would not quake in constant fear of their homes being burned and their leaders imprisoned and assassinated."

The two men largely responsible for the style and grace with which the religious spirit of Utah's pioneers was expressed in its tabernacles and temples were Truman O. Angell and William Folsom. Angell served as church architect for many years after having been sent to Europe by Brigham Young in 1856 to study the great examples of architecture to be found there. Folsom, a self-taught architect, served as chief church designer or as assistant to Angell during much of this era. Folsom also designed the Salt Lake Theater, the city hall now known as the Council House, and the iron front that still adorns Zion's Cooperative Mercantile Institution (Z.C.M.I.).

Early Schools

Education is another example of Mormon impact upon the growth of social institutions in pioneer Utah. The educational effort began early: within three weeks after her arrival in Utah in

1847, Mary Jane Dillworth was conducting school in a military tent in the old fort; a few weeks later Moses Julian was teaching older students. Clarilla Browning began teaching in a log house in Ogden in 1849. Six months after the founding of Manti, Jesse W. Fox had established a school for juveniles and was reading to the adults in the evenings by the light of a tallow dip and campfire. George A. Smith, leader of the Iron County colony, spent many of his evenings reading to the settlers by firelight.

In 1850 the *Deseret News* reported that common schools were beginning in all parts of Salt Lake City for the winter, and plans to construct schoolhouses in every ward were being made, with plans for a general citywide system of schoolhouses. Books for these schools were freighted from the states, and were partly paid for by one of the few appropriations Congress made for educational purposes during the territorial period. The first public school law, passed by the territorial legislature in 1851, created the office of territorial superintendent of schools and provided for the establishment of one or more schools in every town to be supported by local taxation. Ogden was probably the first city in Utah to levy such a tax; many communities failed to tax themselves until compelled to do so a generation later. Separate school buildings did not become commonplace until later, with church meetinghouses, community centers, and even homes housing much of the sporadic instruction that characterized the pioneer generation.

Unfortunately, most of the early schools were of inferior quality due to a lack of financial support or competent personnel. Tuition, often paid in kind, was required in almost all schools, and teachers were poorly and sometimes irregularly paid. Inadequate compensation led capable teachers such as Orson Pratt, Eli Kelsey, Orson Hyde, Mary Cook, and Karl G. Maeser to conduct private schools, which were more profitable. Family schools financed by such men as Brigham Young and Heber C. Kimball, each of whom had more than fifty children, formed a unique part of the educational scene. An expensive and finally unsuccessful fifteen-year effort to establish the Deseret Alphabet, a system of phonetic symbols designed to help non-English immigrants learn to read, was another novel feature.

The territory gradually assumed the burden of public education but was unable to obtain federal aid because of Congressional concern about Mormon control. Annual territorial appropriations for educational purposes were begun in 1874, and by 1876 each county had a board of examiners. Two years later a general school tax was inaugurated. Evidence of the shortfall between educational aspiration and accomplishment are these facts: the percentage of school-aged children actually enrolled in territorial schools fluctuated around sixty percent until 1890, and average daily attendance never reached fifty percent until 1893.

By the 1870s the schools had become a religious battleground. The pervasive Mormon influence in the school curriculum caused many gentiles to seek alternatives, resulting in a conflict over the support and control of territorial education. An 1874 letter from Philip H. Emerson, United States district court judge in Provo, expresses a common non-Mormon predicament:

I have three children whose ages range from six to fifteen years—they are at school in Michigan, my wife is with them. The inhabitants of this place are almost entirely Mormon; out of 3,000 inhabitants there are not to exceed six Gentile families. The schools are under the entire control of the Mormons, and I cannot think of keeping my children under such influences. . . .

Gentile church efforts to provide alternatives are discussed in chapter 17. By 1889 about 8,000 students were enrolled in 193 denominational schools in Utah. Many of these schools gave free tuition to Mormon children, and in some cases the studentbody was entirely Mormon. Westminster College in Salt Lake City and Wasatch Academy in Mount Pleasant are survivors of this Protestant effort, while Judge Memorial, also in Salt Lake City, is a remnant of the Roman Catholic system.

Non-Mormon educators and ministers joined with federal officials and other Liberal Party spokesmen to call for Congressional action; the government responded with the Edmunds-Tucker Act of 1887, which escheated Mormon Church property and proposed to apply the proceeds to a secularized public school system for Utah. It is hardly coincidental that the legislative assembly provided for the first territory-wide system of free tax-supported schools in 1890, the same year the Woodruff Manifesto was issued.

Alarmed by the influence of the non-Mormon schools and by what they saw as secular tendencies in education, the Mormon leaders began to develop a system of church schools. Brigham Young Academy was established in Provo in 1875 and Brigham Young College opened in Logan in 1877, the year of the Mormon leader's death. In 1888, in response to the Edmunds-Tucker Act, every Mormon stake was called upon to establish an academy in its area. Ultimately twenty-two institutions, most of them in Utah, were established as rivals of both the gentile and the territorial schools. Not until the turn of the century did the territorial-state schools finally emerge triumphant.

Higher Education

With the same aspirations that produced the framework of a university at Nauvoo, the first legislative body in the Great Basin chartered the University of Deseret on February 28, 1850, with an annual maintenance appropriation of $5,000. A chancellor (Orson Spencer) and a board of regents were commissioned to organize branch institutions elsewhere, prepare textbooks, and open a "free school institution for the benefit of orphans and other indigent worthy persons."

The free school for the worthy poor never materialized, and the early thrust of the University of Deseret was toward adult education and the training of teachers. The school first opened on November 11, 1850, in John Pack's home, and by February 1851 the forty male and female students in the "parent school" were meeting in the upper room of the Council House. Limited patronage and withdrawal of the territorial appropriation, however, led to the discontinuance of operations in 1852. Continuing efforts to secure federal land grant support were unavailing, and Deseret did not resume classes until 1867 when it opened as a commercial college.

The spirit of higher education was kept alive through individual lectures and by organized groups such as the Universal Scientific Society and the Polysophical Society. But it was not until 1869, under the leadership of John R. Park, that the University of Deseret began to offer a systematic collegiate curriculum. Park, who had practiced medicine in Ohio before turning to a career in education, had developed a small private school in South Willow Creek (Draper) before being called to head the University of Deseret. He proposed a two-course program, normal and collegiate—the late nineteenth-century concept of a normal course being enough high school and posthigh school work to qualify the graduate, usually a young woman, to teach in the public schools.

Dr. Park's program attracted 223 students, 103 of them women, during the first regular school year, and 152 in the summer term. At one point a faculty of ten were offering classes in the Council House. But the surge of interest again passed, and the regents decided in 1871 to suspend the higher education offerings because of lack of funds and a shortage of students with adequate college preparation. Park accepted an assignment to tour educational institutions in Europe, and he returned in 1872 to begin genuine university work on a less ambitious but more substantial basis, becoming president of the university, a position he held until June

1892. The move of the university from downtown Salt Lake City to the Fort Douglas military reservation and the name change from Deseret to Utah came in 1900 and 1902, respectively.

The University of Deseret-Utah represented the most substantial and sustained approach to higher education in pioneer Utah, but there were other efforts late in the period. By deed of trust prior to his death, Brigham Young set aside tracts of land in Provo, Logan, and Salt Lake City as sites for church-sponsored institutions. As noted, the academy and college that bore his name were launched before his death. However, the board of trustees for the proposed Salt Lake school contained five of his sons, and the land title was tied up for some time in the litigation of his estate. As a result, plans for Young University, intended to be the major church center for higher education, did not get underway until 1893. The financial panic then underscored the folly of having two fledgling universities competing for students in the capital city, so a compromise was worked out between the church and the University of Deseret. The church abandoned the Young University project and James E. Talmage, later a Mormon apostle, became president of the University of Deseret.

Both the territorial-state university and the church school in Provo, which changed its title to Brigham Young University in 1903, were in frequent financial straits until well into the twentieth century. Brigham Young College faced competition when the federal land-grant college was finally established in Logan in 1888; both schools offered high school as well as college curricula until well into the statehood period, when Utah Agricultural College became strictly a higher educational institution and BYC discontinued operations. A few other Mormon academies of the 1880s evolved into institutions of higher learning, with Weber, Dixie, and Snow eventually becoming state colleges. The LDS College in Salt Lake City went through an extended high school phase before becoming a business college.

Intellectual Endeavors

The foundation and growth of universities, while a good indication of intellectual striving, is not synonymous with intellectual development. Leonard J. Arrington has divided the intellectual tradition of the Mormons into four stages, two of which coincide with Utah's territorial period.

The *formative stage* of this tradition occurred while the Mormons were in New York, Ohio, Missouri, and Illinois. Some of the implications of the broad-ranging exploration of literary, philosophi-

Saltair, the largest of the lake resorts on the Great Salt Lake, endured through fires and changing entertainment fashions until World War II.

cal, and religious ideas by Joseph Smith and his companions have been discussed in chapter 6; these ideas came west in the intellectual baggage of the pioneers.

The *elaboration stage,* according to Arrington, lasted from the death of Joseph Smith to the revival of the School of the Prophets in 1867. Compared with the Nauvoo period, this was not a very creative era. Brigham Young was not an intellectual, nor did he perceive his mission to be one of adding new doctrines. Some of his elaborations were novel and pungently phrased; not all made their way permanently into the corpus of Mormon thought. The letters of Young's secretaries and advisers did, however, contribute to a deeper understanding of Smith's teachings and what his followers were trying to accomplish in Utah. Willard Richards, Orson Pratt, Orson Hyde, Franklin D. Richards, and John Taylor, men of intellectual substance, wrote important articles for the *Deseret News,* the British Mission's *Millennial Star,* and other church publications. *Peep O'Day,* an independent literature, science, and

304

art weekly edited by Edward W. Tullidge and E. L. T. Harrison, represents the variety of work produced outside formal ecclesiastical channels.

One expression of intellectual ferment in pioneer Utah was the Polysophical Society, founded in 1854 by Lorenzo Snow with the purpose of "impressing the mind with heavenly wisdom and with classic lore." Maureen Ursenbach Beecher describes a meeting:

The picture is delightful for its quaint ceremoniousness: ladies and gents in full finery—as far removed from frontier dress as they could manage, retrenchment not yet having been called for. Seated around a hall sparsely decorated with what few refinements the community offered, they listened to each other recite original poetry, perform on instruments, expound extemporaneously, and, on rare and special occasions, sing in tongues. A master of ceremonies apparently conducted the exercise, and "a small lad," wearing an appropriate badge indicative of his office, carried notes from the master of ceremonies to members of the group as their turn to perform approached.

The church-sponsored Deseret Theological Class, the Universal Scientific Society, and the Literary Musical Assembly were other intellectually oriented organizations that sprang up in the early days. Women were always a large part of the membership, assuming roles as leaders and performers as well as auditors.

In 1856–57 a religious reform movement swept Mormon Utah. This reformation emphasized the emotional-irrational side of human nature rather than the intellectual-rational side. Intellectual curiosity was seen by some community leaders as dangerous. Hannah Tapfield King's journal contains this wry observation:

Brother [Jedediah M.] Grant has done some strong preaching lately, and declared the Polysophical Society was "a stink in his nostrils." Brother [Heber C.] Kimball called out, "and in mine!" Said there was an adulterous spirit in it!! Well, there may be, for he says there is, and probably he understands it. To me it all seemed good and nice, with of course a little vanity and folly, and that one sees in the tabernacle and everywhere.

It would appear that there was more than a little intellectual rigidity and stress on doctrinal conformity in pioneer Utah.

The third stage of intellectual development Arrington calls the *purification stage*, which started in 1867 and ended with the achievement of statehood in 1896. Brigham Young appeared to be attempting to perfect the Saints so that they could resist the temptations the railroad would bring into the territory, and the effort continued beyond the event at Promontory Point and the death of Young eight years later. Publications such as the *Woman's Exponent,*

305

Contributor, Juvenile Instructor, and *Young Women's Journal* carried the principles and programs of purification into Mormon homes, and when the time for reconciliation with the world came, they were vehicles for that enterprise as well.

During this stage of development the church faced a challenge from a group of "liberal" Mormons who concluded that Young was beyond his religious authority when he endeavored to control the direction of economic growth in the territory. William S. Godbe, E. L. T. Harrison, Edward W. Tullidge, Henry W. Lawrence, and others publishing in the *Utah Magazine* opposed agrarian isolationism and advocated some accommodation with United States society. Many of the Godbeite leaders were excommunicated, but their ideas about Utah's future continued to have adherents in both Mormon and gentile ranks. Tullidge was a prolific writer, and his histories of that period are among the best sources of information. Another of the group, T. B. H. Stenhouse, was an editor and publicist for the church in the East before he and his wife defected.

What Arrington titles the *stage of creative adaptation* in Utah's intellectual evolution began with statehood and is considered later.

Literary Productivity

Nineteenth-century Utahns did not produce great literature, but there was a surprising amount of writing and publishing for a people colonizing a desert and coping with serious political, economic, and religious problems. Mormon pioneers were encouraged to keep journals and written records. Most of them contain only chronicles of daily events, but a few writers gave vent to their private feelings, recorded faith-promoting experiences, and indulged in religious speculations and creative writing.

Much of the published writing was polemical, with the Mormons on the defensive and some non-Mormons attacking Mormon beliefs and practices—especially plural marriage. Orson Pratt was the chief defender of the faith. Called to Washington, D.C., in 1852, he launched *The Seer,* a monthly publication that sought with limited success to change the popular image of Mormonism. John Taylor, Erastus Snow, and George Q. Cannon followed similar programs in New York, St. Louis, and San Francisco. Together they produced a sizable body of essays on Mormon and contemporary themes, but none of the publications survived the Utah War years.

Anti-Mormon literature varied from the broad humor of Mark Twain and Artemus Ward to the vitriolic writings of Kate Field and J. H. Beadle. Particularly significant among works produced by defectors from the Mormon Church is T. B. H. Stenhouse's *Rocky Mountain Saints* (1872), which reveals important insights about life in pioneer Utah despite its antagonism toward the Mormon hierarchy. Fanny Stenhouse's *Tell It All* (1879) is more personal and sensational, as is the semifictional narrative of Brigham Young's divorced wife, Ann Eliza Webb, called *Wife Number 19* (1875). Much more sympathetic is Elizabeth Kane's *Twelve Mormon Homes* (1874); the wife of Thomas L. Kane, Elizabeth accompanied her husband and Brigham Young on a tour through Utah in 1872.

Eliza R. Snow produced poems for all occasions and also wrote introspective and devotional poetry. Ultimately she published ten volumes of poetry, and she encouraged other women to write. Two of her friends were Hannah Tapfield King and Sarah Elizabeth Carmichael, each of whom published creditable verse. "Lizzie" Carmichael wrote on a wide variety of subjects, including the Civil War and the death of Lincoln. While Brigham Young expressed disapproval of some of her work, William Cullen Bryant placed one of her poems in a volume of "best American poetry."

Several competent historians emerged in Utah in the latter part of the nineteenth century. Two converts from England who became involved in the Godbeite protest wrote important volumes. Stenhouse has already been mentioned. Edward W. Tullidge's most lasting contribution is his *History of Salt Lake City* (1886), but he also published *Tullidge's Quarterly* and wrote histories of several other localities. Orson F. Whitney, who also wrote poetry, began producing his four-volume *History of Utah* (1892–1904), and Andrew Jenson began his important collection of Mormon documents, chronologies, and statistical information.

Perhaps the best history of Utah written during this period was by the California-based western historian, Hubert Howe Bancroft. A non-Mormon, Bancroft gained the cooperation of Mormon apostle and church historian Franklin D. Richards, who supplied him with important documents and guidance. Written so dispassionately that many accused the author of being pro-Mormon, Bancroft's *History of Utah* (1889) is still one of the best accounts of early Utah.

Newspapers

Newspapers played an important role in dispensing information to the Utah populace. The church-sponsored *Deseret News*, edited by Willard Richards and a succession of prominent and devoted Mormon journalists, first appeared in June 1850 and has continued to be the "voice of the Church" to the present. During much of the nineteenth century the *News* was involved in bitter rivalry with anti-Mormon newspapers. The *Valley Tan,* published at Camp Floyd by Kirk Anderson, was the first to challenge the Mormon journalistic spokesman. It survived only eighteen months and was shortly followed by the *Union Vedette,* established by Colonel Patrick Connor's troops at Fort Douglas in 1863. For two years prior to its expiration in 1867, the *Vedette* enjoyed the distinction of being Utah's first daily newspaper. The Godbeite leaders experimented with *Peep O'Day* and the *Utah Magazine* in the late 1860s before organizing the overtly anti-Brigham Young *Mormon Tribune* in 1870. The name was changed to the *Salt Lake Tribune* in 1871, and under new ownership the paper became a bitter critic of the Mormon Church and its policies. Not until 1910 did the *Tribune,* by then the property of silver magnate Thomas Kearns, begin to move away from this intransigeant editorial position.

Prominent among other Utah newspapers was the *Salt Lake Herald,* a pro-Mormon daily founded in 1870 as an unofficial counterweight to the *Tribune.* As national political parties began to emerge late in the century, it spoke for the Democrats and the *Tribune's* voice was Republican. Smaller communities produced an amazing number of newspapers, almost all short-lived. Newspaper life span depended upon advertising, politics, the editor's dedication, and the fickle nature of a cash-poor readership. County seats, no matter how small in population, generally had weeklies, and as partisan political divisions emerged, many of them had two. For example, five Cache Valley communities produced twenty-three different newspapers during the nineteenth century.

Hand-written newspapers appeared in many communities as individual enterprises and, after 1870, as Mutual Improvement Association projects. These papers, with names like "Knowledge Seeker," "Evening Star," and "Young Ladies' Thoughts," reflected the manners and morals of the people of the community. Usually short-lived, they were passed from home to home, serving as an outlet for sermons, stories, and news items.

Cultural and Recreational Activities

Despite the difficulties in establishing themselves in Utah, the Mormons found the time and means for relaxation and socializing. One of the favorite forms of relaxation was dancing. Richard Burton, the famous English explorer, observed in 1862 that "dancing seems to be an edifying exercise: the Prophet dances, the Apostles dance, the Bishops dance." A dance or grand ball was often listed as the climax of a holiday celebration. Missionary farewells and homecomings were similarly enlivened, and most towns had at least one community dance on the weekend. Frequently the entire family attended the affairs, leaving the infants on the benches or on the stage of the social hall. Often sandwiches were served at midnight, and dancing continued until two or three o'clock in the morning.

It was an era of square dancing. Quadrilles, the Varsovienne, the Virginia Reel, the Berlin Polka, the Schottishe, and the Polygamy Dance were all popular. Waltzing was considered somewhat risque, and the number of "round dances" permitted during an evening was often limited. In fact, one of the resolutions passed by the Cache Valley Young Women's Mutual Improvement Association was that the young ladies would not indulge in round dancing. (The effort to apply moral criteria to changing dance fashions persisted into the twentieth century.)

A second prominent feature of early Utah's recreational and cultural life was the drama. *The Triumph of Innocence* was presented in the first bowery in 1849, and a year later the Musical and Dramatic Company was organized in Salt Lake City. When completed in 1852, the Social Hall became the center of entertainment. During the 1855–56 season it was open three nights a week for such Deseret Dramatic Association productions as *Othello, Pizarro,* and *She Stoops to Conquer.*

Brigham Young was especially fond of theatrical productions, and on occasion he even took bit parts. He was quoted as saying, "if I were placed on a cannibal island and given the task of civilizing its people, I should straight-way build a theatre for the purpose." It took him a few years to build a theater in Salt Lake City, but the result of his efforts, the Salt Lake Theater, constructed in 1861–62, was magnificent. Realizing that the Social Hall was much too small, Young used surplus material cheaply purchased from Camp Floyd to make an improvement, and the new $100,000 edifice was dedicated on March 6, 1862. The Mormon leader expressed his philosophy of recreation in these words:

We shall endeavor to make our theatrical performances a source of good, and not of evil. . . . Our senses, if properly educated, are channels of endless felicity to us, but we can devote them to evil or good. Let us devote all to the glory of God and the building up of his kingdom, for in this there is lasting joy.

The theater became the social center of the entire territory and served as a valuable meeting place for both Mormons and gentiles.

Leading actors from the east were induced to perform there, it being one of the finest theaters between the Mississippi River and the Pacific Coast. Its design permitted covering the orchestra seats with a spring floor for dancing, and such galas as Utah's first Inaugural Ball, January 6, 1896, were held there.

Other communities in the territory followed the pattern of the mother colony. Cedar City and Parowan reported active dramatic associations in the 1850s. Several towns in Cache Valley were being entertained by their amateur actors not long after the towns were founded. The most outstanding dramatic efforts outside Salt Lake City appear to have been in Brigham City under the direction of Lorenzo Snow. The community supported the growth of theatre and eventually an opera house was built to accommodate patrons from miles around. Corinne, the short-lived "gentile capital of Utah," and the more enduring mining town of Park City both had opera houses, and most of the mining centers had facilities to accommodate itinerant players or local productions. Melodramas and morality plays were more common on the stages of territorial Utah than were the works of the dramatic and operatic masters, but the playbills of the Salt Lake Theater ran almost the full gamut.

Music also played an important role in early Utah. Captain William Pitt's brass band helped to raise the spirits of the pioneers as they crossed the plains, and it was a featured part of many Salt Lake Valley festivities. Within a few years almost every community had a band of some type. The Salt Lake Theater Orchestra, first directed by London-trained Charles J. Thomas, included many of Utah's leading musicians.

Ward choirs provided another musical outlet for the people. Their potential value to religious services and to public celebrations is attested by the offer of one pioneer bishop: "Ten acres of the best land in the settlement ... for a good bass, tenor, and soprano who are good members of society and good readers of music, and would settle in Mendon and attend meetings regularly." The Tabernacle Choir, of course, set a rising standard for musical organizations in the territory, and three of its conductors—George Careless (1869–80), Ebenezer Beesley (1880–90), and Evan Stephens (1890–1916)—produced some of Mormondom's favorite hymns and choral music. Joseph J. Daynes was the Tabernacle organist from the time Australian-born Joseph H. Ridges built the first organ until 1900.

The relative scarcity of women and the abundance of saloons produced a different cultural and recreational mix in the early railroad and mining towns. The aspirations of Corinne and Park City have been noted: mining centers that survived the boom phase—towns like Bingham, Park City, Helper, and Price—followed the cultural evolution of their counterparts elsewhere in the American West. Churches and ethnic organizations sponsored their musical and dramatic associations and many of their holiday activities. Masonic lodges and some other fraternal orders in early Utah excluded Mormons, and the first women's club in Provo was formed by gentile ladies whose social needs were not met by the multifaceted programs of the Mormon Church's Relief Society.

Holidays, of course, provided a change of pace for the Mormon majority as well. The traditional American events were observed with improvised rather than commercial diversions until a cash economy and transportation improvements made resorts at Utah's most accessible lakes and hot springs feasible. July 24—Pioneer Day—was the biggest event. The size of the Independence Day commemoration depended on the state of Mormon relations with the federal government; none of the top church authorities were official participants in the Centennial Fourth of July observance that brought Saints and gentiles together in a day-long program in Ogden in 1876, but Eliza R. Snow spearheaded the Ladies Centennial Exhibition held in the territorial capital. Most of the holiday observances were community affairs, consisting of parades and public meetings in the morning, sports in the afternoon, and a grand ball in the evening. The pioneer custom of beginning such diversions as theatricals, dances, and sporting events with prayer has persisted in Mormon Utah to the present.

The visual arts were less broadly supported but not unrepresented. One of the first artists to reach Utah was William A. Major, who accompanied Brigham Young to Salt Lake City in 1848. He was active in painting landscapes and portraits until his departure in 1853. Four years later Carl C. A. Christensen entered the territory "with the Danish flag flying from his cart and his trousers flapping in tatters around his legs." He gained local fame by painting scenes of Mormon history on a huge scroll and giving illustrated lectures throughout the settlements. Other Christensen paintings on a smaller scale, such as *Immigration of the Saints* and *Winter Quarters,* revealed considerable skill. Another Scandinavian convert, Daniel A. Weggeland of Norway, arrived in 1862 and was soon working with Christensen painting scenery for the Salt Lake Theater. He was also employed to paint scenes in the Mormon temples, and he became a teacher of many of the second generation of Utah painters.

The Salt Lake Theater was a center of Utah social life at the turn of the century.

The first art instructor at the University of Deseret, George M. Ottinger, arrived in 1861. He painted historical scenes such as *The Last Ride of the Pony Express of 1861,* as well as landscapes, seascapes, and mannequin-like portraits. The scenery in Utah inspired a number of artists, including Alfred Lambourne, John Tullidge, Harry L. A. Culmer, and John Hafen. Hafen, Lorus Pratt, and John Fairbanks were called on missions to France in 1890 for the purpose of developing their skills so that they could decorate the walls of the Salt Lake Temple. Pratt and Fairbanks had sufficient means to support their families during their extended absence, but the church assumed Hafen's debts, took care of his family, and supported the three artists during their study in Europe.

Of the photographers in Utah Territory, Marsena Cannon, Charles W. Carter, Charles R. Savage, and George C. Anderson left the richest legacy. Savage was perhaps the most skillful, but Carter's work may have the most historical significance.

Marsena Cannon was an unofficial Mormon Church photographer in the 1850s; his daguerrotypes include portraits of Brigham

Young and other prominent leaders as well as early views of Salt Lake City. Called to Dixie in 1861, he gradually declined in church activity and eventually participated in the Godbeite schism.

Charles Carter succeeded to the role of unofficial church photographer. His works include pictures of Mormon leaders, Indians, and important events such as the work on the Salt Lake Temple and the Salt Lake Tabernacle. Perhaps his most important contribution to history came from his habit of photocopying every interesting picture he came across; much of Cannon's work and some of the surviving photos of life in Nauvoo are Carter copies. Carter supported himself later in life by selling his photographs at Temple Square, and before he died in 1918 he sold his collection to the Mormon Church for $400.

Charles Savage arrived in Utah in 1860. His records of pioneer life and the scenic wonders of Utah are artistically noteworthy. His most famous pictures are a news photo of the driving of the golden spike at Promontory, which appeared on the cover of *Harper's Weekly,* and a portrait of Brigham Young at seventy-five years of age. The destruction of his negative collection in a Salt Lake City fire in 1883 was an artistic and historic tragedy. Savage was professionally active until 1906, and he initiated one of the late nineteenth- and early twentieth-century significant Utah social customs—Old Folks' Day.

George Anderson was trained by Savage and became an early user of the dry plate photography process. Based in Springville from 1881 to 1928, he not only photographed Utah and Utahns, but he photographed hundreds of scenes in the East and England for a pictorial history of Mormonism, which appeared in 1909.

The work of these frontier photographers is important not only because of the pictorial record they left but also because of what their presence signifies. Unlike many agriculturally based utopian movements, Mormonism did not imply that farming was the ultimate occupation. Life on the Great Basin frontier displayed a diversity of occupations and interests, including photography, that increased the richness of pioneer society and culture.

Chapter 16
Bibliographical Essay

General histories by Andrew L. Neff, Leland H. Creer, and Wain Sutton, cited previously, as well as the works by Orson F. Whitney and Edward W. Tullidge mentioned in this chapter, contain much information on Utah's early cultural and intellectual life. See also the accounts by non-Mormon visitors listed in chapter 15. A helpful introduction to anti-Mormon literature is Leonard J. Arrington and John Haupt, "Intolerable Zion: The Image of Mormonism in Nineteenth-Century American Literature," *Western Humanities Review,* Summer 1968. See also Arrington, *Kate Field and J. H. Beadle: Manipulators of the Mormon Past* (American West Lecture, University of Utah, 1971).

"Toward an Architectural Tradition" is the theme of the Summer 1975 issue of *UHQ,* which contains several excellent articles including Peter L. Goss, "The Architectural History of Utah," and Allen D. Roberts, 'Religious Architecture of the LDS Church: Influences and Changes since 1847." Leonard J. Arrington and Melvin A. Larkin, "The Logan Tabernacle and Temple," which adds interpretation to narrative, and Juanita Brooks, "Early Buildings," which includes the St. George Temple and St. George Tabernacle, appear in *UHQ,* July 1961. Stewart L. Grow's account of the Salt Lake Tabernacle, *A Tabernacle in the Desert* (1958), is well researched and very readable. David S. Andrew and Laurel B. Blank present important information on temple design and construction in "The Four Mormon Temples in Utah," *Journal of the Society of Architectural Historians,* March 1971.

The Fall 1975 issue of *UHQ* contains a number of important articles on Utah's educational beginnings, including non-Mormon schools. J. C. Moffitt's *The History of Public Education in Utah* (1946) and M. Lynn Bennion's *Mormonism and Education* (1939) give useful information on early educational developments. They should be supplemented with Stanley S. Ivins, "Free Schools Come to Utah," *UHQ,* October 1954, and C. Merrill Hough, "Two School Systems in Conflict, 1867–1890," *UHQ,* April 1960. The first volume of *Brigham Young University: The First One Hundred Years* (1976), four vols., edited by Ernest L. Wilkinson, presents a good account of nineteenth-century developments. *The University of Utah* (1960), authored by a long-time faculty member, Ralph V. Chamberlin, is a clear account of the University of Deseret growing into the University of Utah.

O. N. Malmquist's *The Salt Lake Tribune: The First 100 Years* (1971) and Wendell O. Ashton's *Voice of the West* (1950) give satisfactory accounts of the two leading newspapers of the territory; Monte B. McLaws, *Spokesman for the Kingdom* (1977), focuses on the nineteenth-century career of the *Deseret News.*

George D. Pyper's *Romance of An Old Playhouse* (1929) and Harold I. Hansen's "History and Influence of the Mormon Theatre, 1839–1869" (Ph.D. dissertation, University of Iowa, 1949) are excellent sources on early theatricals. *One Hundred Years of Utah Painting* (1965) by James L. Haseltine is an excellent survey with many illustrations. George W. James, *Land of the Blossoming Valleys* (1922), contains information on painters and sculptors. *The Valley of the Great Salt Lake* (1963), a revised version of *UHQ,* July 1959, features some excellent photographs of important early buildings. Nelson B. Wadsworth's "Zion's Cameramen: Early Photographers of Utah and the Mormons," *UHQ,* Winter 1972, contains a superb folio of nineteenth-century photographs, and his *Through Camera Eyes* (1975) presents more than a hundred pages of such pictures as well as an historical narrative.

Eugene E. Campbell's chapter on "Social, Cultural, and Recreational Life" in *History of a Valley, Cache Valley, Utah-Idaho* (1956), Joel E. Ricks, ed., summarizes these activities for a typical pioneer Mormon valley.

An invaluable aid in tapping pioneer writings both as literature and as social history is Davis Bitton, ed., *Guide to Mormon Diaries and Autobiographies* (1977), which describes almost 3,000 items.

Chapter 17
The Churches in
The Territory

T. Edgar Lyon and Glen M. Leonard

U tah has the distinction of being the only state in the Union
that was founded primarily as a religious colony and in
which the total population was almost all of one faith—perhaps as
high as ninety-eight percent—in its first decade. This condition created an unparalleled situation in which religious differences became inextricably entwined with the political, educational, and social life both of the territory and of the later state. No discussion
of denominational religious activities in Utah from its founding to
its statehood can be understood without recognizing this peculiar
phenomenon.

This synopsis of territorial period religious activities will treat a
number of divergent groups:

1. The Church of Jesus Christ of Latter-day Saints, whose secu-
lar policies and programs have been discussed in many chapters.
Here attention will be given only to certain aspects of Mormon
Church development.

2. The religious communities that primarily attended to the
needs of their own communicants. The Roman Catholics, Episcopalians, Jews, and Unitarians are the most prominent.

3. The evangelical Christian churches, much of whose effort
during the territorial period was directed toward converting individual Mormons and combatting Mormon Church influence.

This chapter will also consider the adjustments made by the several denominations when Utah became a state and when the long
Mormon-gentile conflict gradually came to an end. (For estimates
of denominational membership in the territorial period, see
Table H, pp. 692–93.)

Characteristics of the Mormon Church in Early Utah

Like many other Americans of their time, the Mormons believed that deeply held religious values should pervade all aspects of life. For them, Mormonism meant chopping wood for widows, answering the bishop's call to build roads into the canyons, and voting for church-approved candidates for public office as well as converting nonbelievers, healing the sick, and speaking in church. The Saints drew no lines between religious and other activities; this chapter will describe only activities considered to be religious from an institutional perspective.

When the Mormons established their new gathering place in the Great Basin they were just emerging from a period of transition in leadership. The succession crisis following Joseph Smith's death had created some splintering of allegiance. Nevertheless, the Council of the Twelve Apostles with Brigham Young as senior apostle retained the support of most church members. In December 1847 the Council of the Twelve nominated, and members assembled in special conferences sustained, Young as second president of the church. His influence dominated Mormon activities for the next thirty years, and the pattern of succession of the senior apostle to the presidency that was established with his appointment became a precedent since unbroken.

Under the hierarchical system of church government largely worked out under Joseph Smith's presidency, Brigham Young governed the Mormons, assisted by two counselors in the first presidency. Late in his life, the aging president appointed five additional counselors, but the basic decisions and the burden of executive and legislative leadership lay with the three-member presidency and the Council of the Twelve Apostles. Other general authorities included the hereditary office of Patriarch to the Church (retained in the Smith family), the missionary-oriented First Seven Presidents of the Seventy, and the Presiding Bishopric. During the nineteenth century the Presiding Bishopric shared with the church president responsibilities for finances—the collection and expenditure of tithing funds, the administration of the church public works and welfare programs, and the management of physical facilities.

Taken together, the twenty-six or more men who comprised the Mormon hierarchy represented a class of socially and economically prominent citizens in the community. One particularly noticeable characteristic of this ruling group was its domination by certain extended families. During the nineteenth century no less than

The Bowery and old Tabernacle, as they appeared in 1855, were the first meeting places of the Mormon pioneers on the temple block.

three-fourths of all general authorities were closely related, and about two-thirds of all new appointees already had either kinship or marriage ties with members of the hierarchy. The ties of blood and marriage (including plural marriage) strengthened a theological emphasis upon unity within presiding quorums. Outward appearances of bloodline favoritism caused some observers to view the benevolent dynasty in negative terms, but there were more important qualifications for leadership than kinship ties. Brigham Young identified those qualifications as personal righteousness, good natural judgment, and a humble reliance upon the Lord. When a "good man" was appointed to office in the church he was likely to remain in that office for decades; continuity in the leadership core was another significant characteristic of the Mormon Church.

Mormon Activities in the 1850s

For the Mormon in early Utah, life centered around the community and its ecclesiastical equivalent, the ward. Larger cities were divided into several wards, each with a bishopric to supervise temporal affairs and priesthood quorums to instruct in doctrine and foster fellowship. Each ward held a Sunday preaching meeting for adults and Sunday School for children. To a monthly Thursday afternoon fast and testimony meeting donors brought voluntary offerings (eggs, garden vegetables, wheat, etc.) for deposit in the bishop's granary or storehouse until needed by the poor. (The fast day was changed to Sunday in 1896, about the same time that most offerings, tithing, and other contributions went onto a cash basis.) A continuing activity was the monthly visit to each home by ordained and acting "teachers." As the bishop's messengers to the community the teachers were assistants for temporal concerns; in their visiting they often admonished members concerning their religious duties. They helped arrange for cooperative herds, surveyed the needs of widows and the poor, stoked the meetinghouse fire for gatherings, and helped manage road building, fencing, and irrigation ditching projects.

The development of a spirit of community in the ward led to a local unity that prepared the people to respond positively to calls for service. Loyalty to the direction of priesthood leaders among first-generation convert immigrants was strong; at the community, county, and territorial level the Mormon priesthood organization exerted its influence. To the few non-Mormons living in the territory it was clearly apparent that church and state were governed alike by churchmen.

The wishes of church leaders were communicated in the preaching meetings. Whether it was a local sacrament service or a stake or general conference, the regular meeting furnished opportunity for members to teach one another. In the Mormon system of a lay ministry, presiding officers regularly called upon the members to speak extemporaneously "by the spirit." Speak they did—about the coming millennium, or the mission of Jesus Christ, or the need for oxen to assist in the annual immigration, or men to work on the temple—about things temporal and spiritual, all part of Mormon religious concerns.

In the mid-1850s the frequent attention paid to internalizing religious values led to a movement known since as the Mormon Reformation. Brigham Young's counselor, Jedediah M. Grant, was among those most enthusiastic about touring the settlement to encourage members disheartened by drought and grasshoppers and lax in religious observances. His bold denunciations of sin and his vivid pleas for change brought direct responses. Members by the thousands recommitted themselves to a better Christian life and sealed that determination by being rebaptized in the nearest stream or millpond.

The Developing Church, 1860–80

The Mormon religion responded both to the need to care for the flock at home and to carry the saving gospel message to the world. Except when restricted by crises at home or abroad, missionaries actively proselyted among peoples around the world. In the 1850s short-lived missions were established in southern Europe, in eastern Asia, and in India. Greater proselyting success in these and later years was found among northern Europeans and among residents of the eastern United States and Canada. Not all of those who set out from their homelands to gather with the Saints in the promised land reached their destination. Untimely deaths, disaffection along the way, and poverty interfered with the religious impulse to join the community in the West. But census records clearly show the influence of Mormon missionary efforts in populating Utah during the early decades.

As the initial settlements moved out of the pioneering stages of the 1850s, greater interest was taken in enhancing cultural opportunities. In line with this the Mormons developed auxiliaries for young people, organizations that played an important role in community life. The movement began in the late 1860s when Brigham Young organized a Young Ladies' Retrenchment Society for his daughters. The idea quickly spread beyond his home, and soon young women in all Mormon towns were learning to retrench from worldly fashions. The development of the Young Women's Mutual Improvement Association, as it came to be known, fell under the supervision of Eliza R. Snow, who as general president of the adult women's Relief Society after 1866 oversaw all women's work in the church. Women of all ages received encouragement to raise their level of spiritual and cultural appreciation through their activities as homemakers and as involved citizens in the community. In 1875 a parallel organization, the Young Men's Mutual Improvement Association, was inaugurated churchwide, and three years later children were offered weekday religious training through the Primary Association. These auxiliary organizations, founded during a time of increased concern over the challenge to Mormon values from the outside world, played a significant role in Mormon history. Through succeeding generations, leisure time activities, organized sports, dancing, drama, speech, scouting, and other cultural and recreational activities became the province of the Mutual Improvement Association and Primary and dominated the after-school hours of young Mormons.

The 1860s and 1870s also saw a reaffirmation of the Mormon belief in temple building. Since the first groundbreaking for the Salt Lake Temple in 1852 work had proceeded slowly on that greatest of Mormon religious symbols. Brigham Young launched temple-building projects in St. George in 1871 and in Logan and Manti six years later. All of these smaller buildings were completed before the granite Salt Lake Temple was completed in 1893. Students of architecture have seen visual symbols of political sovereignty—castlelike towers and buttresses—in the Utah Mormon temples, but for the Saints these buildings represented the most sacred of sacred spaces, were reserved only for the most faithful of the Saints, and were established to administer ordinances of exaltation for the living and proxy ordinances of baptism, endowment, and marriage for deceased ancestors, many of whom had never heard of Mormonism.

One of the Mormon teachings that later became a minimum standard of behavior for those granted temple recommends was the Word of Wisdom. In the Great Basin, believers in Joseph Smith's 1833 revelation (warning against the use of tobacco, wine, "strong drinks," and "hot drinks") found the relative scarcity of these items (especially tobacco during the Civil War) an added, economic stricture against indulgence. Economic factors affected other religious activities as well, most notably temple building. Tithing collected locally and shared from general church funds employed stonemasons, sawyers, carpenters, and other skilled artisans in a direct economic boost to the communities where temples were being built. Construction of ward meetinghouses, stake tabernacles, and the Salt Lake Tabernacle likewise had economic significance.

Near the end of his life Brigham Young instituted administrative reforms within the church aimed at a more uniform organizational pattern in the stakes. Beginning at St. George in the spring of 1877 and continuing northward—as he had done in establishing the United Orders three years before—he and his associates reorganized stake presidencies and ward bishoprics, divided stakes and created new ones, and lessened the direct involvement of church general authorities in local affairs. The reform of 1877 eliminated many administrative variations, clarified the relationships between bishops and local priesthood quorums, and increased youth participation in the Aaronic Priesthood.

Schismatic movements caused concern in the 1860s and 1870s. The Godbeite movement had political and economic overtones, but William Godbe, E. L. T. Harrison, T. B. H. Stenhouse, Edward Tullidge, and others most active in the so-called *New Movement* were also expressing religious grievances. They trusted in seances and other manifestations of spiritualism, which Mormon leaders denounced, and they repudiated hierarchical authoritarianism and denied the uniqueness of the Mormon mission.

The New Movement was short-lived, as was Joseph Morris's earlier centrifugal thrust from 1860–62. Morris attracted followers to his Kingston Fort on the Weber River when he assumed a prophetic role and began issuing regular revelations. Failure of his specific prophecies of an immediate millennium to be fulfilled disheartened some followers, as did harassment by Mormon neighbors. Disagreements over the right to withdraw property from the communal pool heightened internal tensions and soon a *posse comitatus* made up of territorial militiamen faced Morris and his lieutenants in an armed confrontation. Morris, his chief assistant John Banks, and several others on both sides died in the exchange of fire. Soon afterward the Morrisite congregation scattered.

No study has been made of the less spectacular ongoing attrition from the Mormon ranks—an attrition born of all of the factors that can weaken human enthusiasm and commitment. That attrition was significant may be inferred not only from the testimony of some gentile and apostate observers, but also from the ambivalent attitudes of some church members during the hectic "crusade" years.

Conflict and Accommodation, 1880–1910

Church presidents in the remaining decades of the century faced the challenges of the crusade against polygamy and Mormon political domination of the territory. During these years President John Taylor and his successor, Wilford Woodruff, spent much time hiding on the underground. As a result, the Church Historian's Office became a *de facto* control center for religious operations.

Early in this period one complication in church financial affairs was resolved by the eventual settlement of Brigham Young's estate. After that, a clear separation of church and private property made it less confusing to account for church holdings. Another challenge was brought on by economic sanctions imposed by federal law upon the church, which, when combined with the depression of the 1890s, produced a decrease in voluntary contributions and brought the church into dire financial straits.

During the political crisis of the 1880s, authorities decentralized church financial holdings in anticipation of federally forced dis-

Independence Hall, completed in 1865, was not only the setting for Congregational, Methodist, Episcopalian, and Jewish services, but was the site of the establishment of Salt Lake City's first Masonic Lodge, the nomination of the first Gentile candidate for delegate to Congress, and the founding of the Women's National Antipolygamy Society.

incorporation. Placed in part under the care of stake presidents, these assets were utilized to further educational programs and to help build handsome stake tabernacles. Numerous stake academies were constructed and operated as high schools. Then, when the elementary grades were secularized in the 1890s, Mormons organized their own religion class program and taught children religion after school. Although directed toward grades one through nine, this was a forerunner of the high school-level seminaries and college-level institutes of religion founded early in the 1900s.

The polygamy manifesto of 1890 opened two decades in which the Mormon Church readjusted and reoriented its religious teachings and practices in many areas. Perhaps the church's greatest adjustment was in accommodating to the prohibition of new plural marriages. Opposition arose and the seeds of the later "fundamentalism" began to appear as those who were unwilling to accept the new interpretation continued to advocate and practice plural marriage regardless of the publicly announced church policy.

Economically the church entered an era of financial retrenchment and conservative capitalistic policies which, with the renewal of emphasis on tithing under President Lorenzo Snow, lifted a massive burden of debt. At the April 1907 conference, President Joseph F. Smith announced that the church was out of debt and operating on a cash basis. A new era, characterized by the building of hospitals, schools, and chapels—few of which had been constructed since the escheatment of church property in 1887—was inaugurated.

Politically, the church effected a great change in abolishing the one-party system that had existed in the territory. The membership divided fairly evenly on national party lines so that Jews, Catholics, Mormons, and evangelical Protestants began to associate together in political activities.

Other Mormon programs also underwent significant reexamination around the turn of the century. Curriculums were studied; teaching methods in church auxiliaries were professionalized; parents were given a larger voice in the auxiliaries; and the role of lay priesthood members was reassessed. The result was a revitalization of programs. In this way the adjustments of the 1890s and early 1900s contributed to a rethinking of how Mormonism, with its penchant for practical religion, should be translated into the lives of its members on a day-to-day basis in a world in which they were no longer gathered, isolated, and on the defensive.

The Roman Catholic Church

Roman Catholicism came into Utah with the Domínguez-Escalante expedition, and fifty years later fur trappers noted Ute Indians with crucifixes—evidence of continuing native contact with the missions in New Mexico. The rites of the church were performed at Camp Floyd for a few months in 1859, and were performed occasionally at Fort Douglas in the mid-1860s. Father Edward Kelly celebrated mass in Independence Hall and in the old tabernacle on Temple Square in the summer of 1866, and with some technical assistance from Brigham Young he purchased land for a church. The first resident pastor came two years later and his successor, Father Patrick Walsh, completed construction in 1871 on the first Catholic church in Utah, St. Mary Magdalene.

For the forty-two years from 1873 to 1915 Father Lawrence Scanlan, first as priest and then as bishop, directed Catholic activities in Utah. His policy was one of serving the members of that faith who resided in the territory, primarily in the mining and railroad towns and in the cities of Salt Lake and Ogden. By 1880 there were churches in Ogden and Silver Reef and mission stations at Alta, Beaver (for Fort Cameron), Corinne, Stockton, Ophir, and Park City. By the end of the territorial period the Roman Catholics had established seven chapels, three parochial schools, and two hospitals. The largest non-Mormon religious group in Utah at that time, the Roman Catholics constituted less than four percent of the population.

Toward the Mormons Father Scanlan maintained a policy of peaceful coexistence, carrying on no organized missionary program for the purpose of converting the Saints or their children. A remarkable example of interdenominational amity occurred in the St. George Tabernacle in May 1879 when the Catholic leader conducted services before a predominantly Mormon congregation of about 3,000 and the local tabernacle choir sang the mass in Latin.

The Protestant Episcopal Church

In 1867 Bishop Daniel S. Tuttle came to Utah to begin organized Episcopal Church activities and to begin an eighteen-year ministry in the territory. His congregation included only three confirmed Episcopalians, all women, and a mission committee that included a Roman Catholic, a Methodist, and an apostate Mormon. A thriving Sunday School was inherited from the chaplain at Fort Douglas, and a grammar school was just beginning.

The first non-Mormon chapel in Utah (excluding the multipurpose Independence Hall) was built by leaders of the Episcopal Church in Corinne. It was subsequently abandoned, but St. Mark's Cathedral, completed in 1871, continues to be a Salt Lake City landmark. Ogden's Church of the Good Shepherd was consecrated four years later. Bishop Abiel Leonard, who succeeded Tuttle, opened churches at Provo, Springville, Layton, Eureka, Park City, and Vernal. He also built a church and mission house on the Uintah-Ouray Reservation in 1895, and the next year when Congress allotted the reservations to various churches for religious and educational purposes, the Utes selected the Episcopalians. Facilities at Randlett and Whiterocks included church and school buildings and a small infirmary.

Bishop Tuttle, like Father Scanlan, pursued a policy of "constructive Christian fellowship with the Mormons and other people of Utah." The Episcopal Church built schools and St. Mark's Hospital, and Tuttle founded Mount Olivet, the first perpetual care cemetery in Utah, on land granted by Congress in 1877 from the Fort Douglas reservation; he later claimed credit for shaming "the Mormons into taking better care of their own ground." By 1895 the Protestant Episcopal Church had seven parishes, two schools, and one hospital in operation. The membership in the territory numbered less than a thousand.

The Jews

The first Jewish services were held in Salt Lake City in October 1864, at which time there were hardly more than fifty adult Jews in Utah Territory. They were a nonproselyting group, engaged primarily in business. Except when the Mormon campaign against non-Mormon businesses was being strongly pushed, Brigham Young showed a particular friendliness toward the Jews, donating land for their cemetery and permitting use of Mormon Church buildings for their services. Good relations were also maintained between the Jewish and Protestant communities; Jewish contributions helped to build Independence Hall, and one Utah Jew served for a time as one of its trustees.

The growth of Utah's Jewish population was slow, and problems of observing dietary and other ritual laws were severe. Major religious holidays were observed with some regularity in Jewish homes and were noted in the press. By 1895 there were a few more than 1,200 Jews in Utah; about 150 lived in Ogden, and almost all the rest lived in Salt Lake City. About evenly divided between the Reformed and Orthodox traditions, they collaborated to organize B'nai Israel of Salt Lake City in 1881 and to construct the first synagogue in 1883. Tension became pronounced before B'nai Israel Temple, a larger synagogue modeled after a famous Berlin temple, was dedicated in 1891. Congregation Montefiore had been organized two years earlier by several Orthodox and Conservative families, and its own synagogue was completed early in the new century.

The Unitarian Society

In 1891 the first Unitarian Society was organized in Salt Lake City. Its informal manner of extending membership, its disconcern about records, and its rapid turnover of members make it impossible to now list its membership or activities. At the beginning of Utah's existence as a state, its total membership was less than one hundred, and all of them lived in Salt Lake City. The Unitarians provided an intellectual prod to those who tended to become complacent about religion, politics, education, or social problems.

The Evangelical Christian Churches

The Presbyterians, Methodists, Congregationalists, Baptists, Lutherans, and members of the Church of Christ were the chief evangelical Christian bodies that operated in Utah during its territorial period. Following the Civil War these churches turned their zeal for service, which during the war years had been channeled into relief work, into new areas—renewed missionary work among the heathen nations abroad, among the recently freed Negroes of the South, and among "deluded Mormons, semipagan Mexicans, sunworshipping Puebloes, [and] demon-worshipping Alaskans."

The evangelical groups entered Utah to organize missions directed toward converting the "deluded" Mormons from what they sincerely believed to be a non-Christian religion. They soon discovered, however, that conversion of adult Mormons was almost impossible, for most of the Mormons had previously been converted from the evangelical Christian denominations. (Missionaries from the Reorganized Church of Jesus Christ of Latter Day Saints, who appeared first in Utah in 1863, had a comparable experience, though they won a few families to their version of Joseph Smith's teachings and built a chapel in Salt Lake City.)

It was obvious to the evangelical churches that the "Mormon Problem" must be attacked in another manner. Given the character of Utah's common schools, the children might be saved by providing a true Christian education for the Mormon youth, fewer than one-half of whom were enrolled in and were irregularly attending schools which might be operating for as few as three months a year. If free schools were established with a nine-month course of study and with certified denominational teachers from outside Utah, the evangelical church members thought that the more intelligent Mormon youth would flock to their classes. Along with the standard curriculum biblical, moral, and Christian education would be provided. Extracurricular activities in the Loyal Leagues, Liberty Brigades, sewing circles, and similar youth clubs would, it was hoped, bind them to Protestantism.

With this conviction, the evangelical churches turned to schools as their primary mission tool. By the time most of the mission schools closed near the end of the century, the sponsors claimed a cumulative total of more than 50,000 Mormon enrollments.

The Presbyterians began their first missionary work in Utah in 1869 at Corinne, a non-Mormon town on the Central Pacific Railroad near the north end of the Great Salt Lake. Two years later a church was established in Salt Lake City. By the close of the territorial period, twenty-five years later, twelve churches and forty-nine schools had been in operation in Utah, although not all of them had functioned at the same time. As many as sixty-five imported teachers and nineteen missionary-ministers had worked in the Presbyterian missions among the Mormons at one time. More than a million dollars had been invested in their educational-missionary effort.

Methodists also started their work in 1869 in Corinne, and they used Corinne as a base from which they invaded the Mormon centers. A quarter of a century later they had operated twenty-six schools with twenty-nine teachers at the height of their expansion, and they had forty-one churches or preaching stations staffed by twenty-two missionary ministers or pastors in the Mormon communities. Their total membership was 1,440 in 1895. Methodist expenditures exceeded $600,000.

The polemic dimension of Congregational missionary work was introduced in Utah when the Reverend Norman McLeod served for a year at the close of the Civil War as chaplain at Fort Douglas. He spearheaded the effort to build Independence Hall, which served as a gentile gathering place from 1865 to 1889, and together with Colonel Patrick E. Connor he called upon the nation to support a religious campaign against Mormonism.

Sustained Congregational activity began in Salt Lake City in the spring of 1874 when the regular missionary board of the Congregational Church, the American Home Missionary Society, entered the field. In 1880 an independent group, The New West Education Commission, which functioned within the framework of the Congregational Church, took over most of the schools already established and proceeded to establish more of its own. At its height twenty-eight schools and forty-eight teachers were serving the missionary effort. About fifteen congregations had been established, presided over by ten pastors in 1893. Expenditures were in excess of $625,000.

It was not until 1881 that the Baptist Church commenced permanent missionary work in Utah, although some efforts had been made as early as 1871. At the close of the territorial period the Baptists reported four schools and nine churches in Utah, with ten teachers and eight pastors serving during their greatest period of expansion. Their investment was about $230,000 and their membership numbered 478 persons.

Lutherans were late arriving in Utah. Their first church was established in Salt Lake City in 1882, and the second church was organized in Ogden in 1888. An Icelandic Lutheran Church was organized and a chapel was built in Spanish Fork in 1892. Only one school was operated, located in Salt Lake, for a few years. The total membership of the two Lutheran synods functioning in Utah in 1896 was less than two hundred. The Lutherans invested approximately $60,000.

The last of the evangelical groups to establish itself in Utah was the Christian Church (also having groups known as the Church of Christ and the Church of the Disciples of Christ.) A founder of this movement was Alexander Campbell, among whose followers had been Sidney Rigdon and many early Mormon converts. The Salt Lake church was organized in 1890. The following year a congregation was organized in Ogden, but it soon disintegrated because it was unable to sustain a minister. The territorial period closed with only one active Campbellite congregation, numbering fewer than one hundred. Its Utah investment was approximately $35,000.

As the years passed, the evangelical churches intensified their efforts to arouse American public opinion and thus block any attempt of Utah to acquire statehood until the territory adopted a tax-supported, free public school system, which would be removed from ecclesiastical control; until the Mormon Church agreed to abolish plural marriage; until the territory abolished the marked ballot, which they claimed gave the Mormon Church the means to coerce Mormon votes; and until the Mormons guaranteed the separation of church and state in Utah politics.

The story of the anti-Mormon political crusade is told in detail elsewhere; briefly, in cooperation with others, the evangelical churches generated a great amount of propaganda throughout the country. Their members sent petitions containing millions of names to Congress, demanding legislation to correct conditions they felt were incompatible with American democracy. Their efforts influenced passage of the Edmunds Law in 1882 and the more drastic Edmunds-Tucker Law of 1887.

By the 1890s all of the goals of the crusade had been at least nominally attained. With Utah admitted to the sisterhood of states in 1896, a new era dawned for the evangelical and other non-Mormon churches as well as for the Mormons.

Denominational Adjustments, 1890–1910

During these years the Jewish community, the Unitarian Society, the Roman Catholics, and the Episcopalians followed much the same course that had characterized their activities in the territorial period. Each enjoyed a steady, although small, growth drawn primarily from members of their denominations migrating to Utah. Many of these immigrants joined the local congregations and took an active part in promoting their respective faiths.

This was especially true of the Jewish groups in Salt Lake City, where two synagogues offered alternative rituals to divergent elements of that ancient faith. Ogden was able to establish a congregation and employ a rabbi during this period. The progress of the Unitarian Society was marked by the 1903 construction of Unity Hall, its first chapel. Two years later a congregation of the Greek Orthodox Church was established in Salt Lake City—the first fruits of the "new immigration" to Utah.

Increased mining and smelting activities brought many Roman Catholics into the state. The vigorous Bishop Scanlan founded parish chapels at Price and Tooele and established additional missionary stations for serving the sacraments. In 1899 he undertook construction of the present magnificent Cathedral of the Madeleine as the bishop's church for the Salt Lake City Diocese. It was dedicated in 1909 for what was then the most extensive diocese in the United States. St. Ann's Orphanage and the Judge Memorial Home for aged and ailing miners represented the continuing social thrust of the Roman Catholic Church.

The Protestant Episcopal Church established Emery House, a men's dormitory adjacent to the University of Utah campus. Constructed to care for both the physical and spiritual needs of out-of-town students, it was in 1910 the only religiously sponsored institution near the university. This facility and the Indian schools were big undertakings for an Episcopal membership that at the time probably numbered less than 1,500.

For the evangelical Protestant churches the years from 1890 to 1910 were, in contrast, a period of contracting activity. Their expansive school programs depended almost entirely on contributions from mission boards and private individuals; funds raised locally were negligible. In 1893 the economic panic produced a nationwide crisis in church finances, and the various church administrative units were forced to reduce expenditures. Utah's evangelical schools were subjected to careful scrutiny, and the few converts made from among the Mormons could not justify the continued outlay. A Methodist committee reported: "If 200 real Mormons have been changed into real evangelical Christians . . . we have been unable to discover them."

Retrenchment started immediately. The smaller schools were abandoned, and with them the small churches and preaching stations were closed. The Methodist, Presbyterian, and Congregational boards had operated academies (later known as high schools) in Salt Lake City, Mt. Pleasant, Springville, Logan, Ogden, Provo, Beaver, Nephi, Park City, and Lehi. Only one of three such institutions in the capital survived, and neither of the Ogden schools lasted. The Hungerford Academy at Springville and the New Jersey Academy at Logan continued until 1912 and 1934, respectively, but then they were combined with Wasatch Academy at Mt. Pleasant, the only school south of Salt Lake City that survived the mission board economy moves.

The Presbyterians had operated an academy, Salt Lake Collegiate Institute, since 1875. In 1895 and 1896 Dr. Sheldon Jackson, former superintendent of Presbyterian missions in the intermountain area, agreed to turn over a financial legacy he had received to establish a college in Salt Lake City; the new institution was designated as Sheldon Jackson College. A nationwide effort to provide financial support "to fight polygamy and save Mormon girls from polygamous slavery and debauchery" failed, but out of the movement Westminster College emerged early in the new century.

The evangelical churches manifested a continuing determination to fight the Mormon Church in the period following statehood. Their Utah leadership was instrumental in the successful fight against seating B. H. Roberts in the United States House of Representatives and in the unsuccessful effort to keep Reed Smoot out of the United States Senate.

In terms of service to their own membership, these Protestant churches were going through a transition period from denominational rivalry to a shared solution. Earlier attempts had been made to produce cooperation among them, but as the century opened they were still trying to maintain three and four competitive congregations in small Mormon towns where the combined gentile population wasn't enough to effectively support even one Protestant church. Not until 1915 did these Utah churches form the Home Missions Council to sponsor the community church concept. This technique has enabled the evangelical churches to maintain congregations in many of the small Utah towns that they could not have served by competing for members.

At the close of the period under discussion some noticeable changes had taken place in the religious climate of Utah. Tax-supported free public schools had become a reality; plural marriage had been officially abolished; the marked ballot had been replaced by the secret ballot; and the separation of church and state had been written into the state constitution. In contrast to the situation a half century earlier, when non-Mormons first commenced their missionary efforts, the Jews, Roman Catholics, Episcopalians, Unitarians, and Evangelical Protestants had sunk their roots deep in the soil of Utah. Although their parishes and congregations were neither widely scattered nor large in numbers, they were firmly grounded, some having become self-supporting and no longer mere missions of their respective national organizations. Their members were actively participating in the social, economic, political, and religious life of their communities. They were to be found cooperating with the Mormons in civic endeavors, moral problems, and community projects.

Chapter 17
Bibliographical Essay

General histories of Mormonism tend to follow political or settlement themes, but much about religious life can be found in the comprehensive survey by James B. Allen and Glen M. Leonard, *The Story of the Latter-day Saints* (1976). Illustrative documents are sampled in William Mulder and A. Russell Mortensen (eds.), *Among the Mormons: Historical Accounts by Contemporary Observers* (1958, 1973). Fuller visitors' accounts are in the detailed 1861 report of a British traveler, Richard F. Burton, *The City of the Saints and Across the Rocky Mountains to California*, Fawn M. Brodie, ed. (1963), and in the 1872 record of Mrs. Thomas L. Kane, Elizabeth Dennistoun (Wood) Kane, *Twelve Mormon Homes Visited in Succession on a Journey through Utah to Arizona*, Everett L. Cooley, ed. (1975).

Helpful for understanding administrative aspects of the Mormon Church are P. A. M. Taylor, "Early Mormon Loyalty and the Leadership of Brigham Young," *UHQ*, Spring 1962, and James B. Allen, "Ecclesiastical Influence on Local Government in the Territory of Utah," *Arizona and the West*, Spring 1966. Changes in the hierarchy can be followed in Reed C. Durham, Jr., and Steven H. Heath, *Succession in the Church* (1970). An unpublished analysis of special interest is D. Michael Quinn, "The Mormon Hierarchy, 1832–1932: An American Elite" (Ph.D. dissertation, Yale University, 1976).

Internal administrative developments are discussed in William G. Hartley, "Ordained and Acting Teachers in the Lesser Priesthood, 1851–1883," *BYU Studies*, Spring 1976, and in Leonard J. Arrington, "The Settlement of the Brigham Young Estate, 1877–1879," *Pacific Historical Review*, February 1952; see also D. Michael Quinn, "Utah's Educational Innovation: LDS Religion Classes, 1890–1929," *UHQ*, Fall 1975.

Articles of interest on specialized topics in nineteenth-century Mormon history in Utah include Gustive O. Larson, "The Mormon Reformation," *UHQ,* January 1958; Neal Lambert, "Saints, Sinners, and Scribes: A Look at the Mormons in Fiction," *UHQ,* Winter 1968; and Leonard J. Arrington, "Centrifugal Tendencies in Mormon History," in Truman G. Madsen and Charles D. Tate, Jr. (eds.), *To the Glory of God: Mormon Essays on Great Issues. . . .* (1972). See also the bibliographies for chapter 15.

On schisms of the 1860s and 1870s see G. M. Howard, "Men, Motives, and Misunderstandings: A New Look at the Morrisite War of 1862," *UHQ,* Spring 1976, and two fresh interpretations of the Godbeites: Davis Bitton, "Mormonism's Encounter with Spiritualism," *Journal of Mormon History,* 1974; and Ronald W. Walker, "The Commencement of the Godbeite Protest: Another View," *UHQ,* Summer 1974.

Much of the material on the non-Mormon religious groups of the territorial period is drawn from T. Edgar Lyon, "Religious Activities and Development in Utah, 1847–1910," *UHQ,* Fall 1967. The subjects are more extensively treated in the author's doctoral dissertation, "Evangelical Protestant Missionary Activities in Mormon Dominated Areas, 1865–1900" (University of Utah, 1962). Another useful unpublished monograph is R. Maude Ditmars, "A History of Baptist Missions in Utah, 1871–1931" (master's thesis, University of Colorado, 1931).

World's Fair Ecclesiastical History of Utah (1893) was a joint venture by Roman Catholics, Mormons, Jews, and seven Protestant denominations to present a summary of the status of organized religion in the Utah Territory shortly before statehood. Herbert W. Reherd, "An Outline History of the Protestant Churches in Utah," in Wain Sutton (ed.), *Utah: A Centennial History* (1949), vol. 2, is the most comprehensive summary in print of the Protestant efforts to establish themselves in the Mormon-dominated West. The Sutton volume also has sections on Roman Catholic, Christian Scientist, and Mormon activities. Robert J. Dwyer, *The Gentile Comes to Utah* (1941, 1971), has a heavy emphasis on political activities.

The more accessible books and pamphlets that deal with various Protestant denominational groups include: Ruth Walton, *A Century of Service in Utah, 1869–1969* (1969), which identifies eighty-nine localities where Presbyterian churches and schools were established; Henry Martin Merkel, *History of Methodism in Utah* (1938), which also tabulates schools, chapels, and ministers; *The First Century of the Methodist Church in Utah, 1870–1970* (n.d.), which has illustrations of all functioning Methodist buildings; *History of the First Con-*

gregational Church, 1865–1965 (1965); and Colin Brumitt Goody-kuntz, *Home Missions on the American Frontier* (1939). See also D. H. Christiansen, "Mission Schools in Utah," *Utah Education Review,* March 1915, and James W. Beless, Jr., "The Episcopal Church in Utah . . . ," *UHQ,* Winter 1968.

The Catholic story has not received definitive treatment. Useful are W. D. Harris, *The Catholic Church in Utah, 1776–1909* (1909), and Louis J. Fries, *One Hundred and Fifty Years of Catholicism in Utah* (1926). See also Robert J. Dwyer, "Pioneer Bishop: Lawrence Scanlan, 1843–1915," *UHQ,* April 1952, and Jerome Stoffel, "The Hesitant Beginnings of the Catholic Church in Utah," *UHQ,* Winter 1968.

Secular and religious threads of Jewish life in Utah are inter-twined in Leon L. Watters, *The Pioneer Jews of Utah* (1952) and Juanita Brooks, *The History of the Jews in Utah and Idaho* (1973). The story is summarized in Jack Goodman, "Jews in Zion," in Helen Z. Papanikolas (ed.), *The Peoples of Utah* (1976).

Chapter 18
Women in Early Utah

Ann Vest Lobb and Jill Mulvay Derr

A history of Utah women could well begin with Harriet Page Wheeler Decker Young, the pregnant plural wife of Lorenzo Dow Young, persuading her husband and her son-in-law, Brigham Young, to let her and three of her children accompany the original pioneer band of 1847. Eventually three plural wives—Harriet, her daughter Clarissa Decker Young, and Ellen Sanders Kimball— came in the company, as did Harriet's two small sons. During the next half century thousands of women followed these pioneer foremothers to Utah. A few came without kinship ties as schoolteachers, seamstresses, domestics, camp followers, and crusaders, but most, like these first three, were wives, mothers, daughters, and sisters who accompanied their families to the Great Basin.

Women as Colonizers and Homebuilders

By the end of July 1847 there were almost as many women as men in the Salt Lake Valley. Sixty women who had marched with the Mormon Battalion from Fort Leavenworth and who had wintered with the "sick detachment" in Pueblo, Colorado, came into the valley along with several Mormon families from Mississippi. As Utah population increased with the influx of Mormon emigrants from the eastern United States and Europe, males never substantially outnumbered females, a fact that distinguished Utah from much of the American West in the midnineteenth century. Utah, like New England, was originally settled by families committed to building a commonwealth. Through the 1850s and 1860s Brigham Young called upon those families to forward Mormon colonization beyond the Salt Lake, Weber, and Utah valleys settled in 1847–49. Families completed journeys of several thousand miles to the Mormon capital only to learn that they had one, two, or three hundred more miles to go to reach their particular haven in the intermountain Zion. Hundreds of women left whatever homes and gardens they had helped establish in burgeoning population centers and moved with their families to isolated, unsettled land—to Parowan in 1852 or Cache Valley in 1856 or Utah's Dixie during the years after the Utah War.

The frontier life of these Utah women approximated what other American women had experienced as the nation moved westward: sex roles were merged to the extent that women took as much responsibility for farm and field as they did for domestic chores. The diary of Christinia Oleson Warnick indicates that she not only helped build the Warnick home in Deseret, Utah, taking primary responsibility for the fireplace and chimney, but she plowed, planted, and fertilized the land and dug the irrigation ditches. She cut and stacked the wild hay from the river bottoms for the cows and she sheared the sheep. She grubbed brush, spun and wove cloth, and walked from one village to the next selling butter and eggs.

Upon the Mormon women often fell greater responsibilities than those typical for other pioneer women. Husbands and fathers were frequently away from home on missions or other church assignments, or were attending to plural families located elsewhere. For long periods and sometimes permanently a woman alone or with older children assumed management of the homestead and farm. If her household required more foodstuffs or provisions than her own land and handwork could provide, she pursued income from the various avenues of employment open to women: midwifery, schoolteaching, spinning and weaving, or the making of clothes, shoes, or hats. Some women picked and dried fruit to sell; others took in laundry or tore and wove rags into carpets.

Responsibilities were often shared among plural wives living in the same household, many of whom had to supplement the family income even when their husbands were present. Martha Cragun Cox described her own frontier household in St. George as "so systematized and so well ordered that we could with ease do a great deal." One wife was the family buyer and dressmaker. Another did the darning and repairing, while Martha herself did the ironing and brought in much-needed cash through teaching. The wives washed clothes together and nursed one another in ill health. "We enjoyed many privileges that single wifery never knew," Martha commented, adding, "We did not often all go out together. One always stayed at home and took care of the children and the

The cultivation and home manufacturing of silk is commemorated by this late nine-teenth-century group of Mormon women.

house. In that way we generally came home with a correct idea of
. . . the sermon."

Since Utahns were pioneering new settlements into the 1880s,
women's domestic activities varied from place to place at any giv-
en time. While women in Parowan were still sleeping in wagons,
their Salt Lake City sisters were putting carpets on floors. As
homes were built and fields and towns laid out, women turned
from making adobes and plastering walls to more traditional
home-centered activities. Child care, washing, cooking, and mend-
ing remained constants for women, but home maintenance and
beautification gained new importance. Some women began cultivating the fineries they had left behind them in the East, edging
their bed valances with hand-wrought lace, or purchasing furnish-
ings imported from the States, or reading *Godey's Lady's Book* and
other women's magazines for the latest hints on fashion and homemaking. For many women without the time or means for such lux-
uries, home maintenance meant supplementing the family income
with sewing, laundering, or other home-based employment.

Early Community and Cultural Involvements

In their weekly tabernacle sermons, Brigham Young and other Mormon leaders prescribed proper attitudes and activities for Mormon women. They admonished wives to obey their husbands in righteousness and named home as woman's "peculiar sphere." This was a prevalent theme about the time Horace Greeley visited Utah in 1859. "I have not observed a sign in the streets, an advertisement in the journals, of this Mormon metropolis, whereby a woman proposes to do anything whatever," Greeley noted with disdain. The journalist's overall impression was probably accurate, since most Utah women were anonymously occupied in their homes. But there were some notable exceptions.

Some women were active entrepreneurs. Fanny Brooks, an early Jewish immigrant to Utah, opened her own millinery shop and bakery on Salt Lake City's Main Street in 1853. A few years later advertisements in the city's *Deseret News* solicited young scholars for Mrs. Pratt's school and customers for Mrs. Read's fine dressmaking and cleaning. Women were more visible in the lecture and dramatic societies and musical assemblies that dominated Salt Lake City's cultural life in the 1850s. At least one such group, the Polysophical Society, involved men and women in a weekly program of poetry recitations, musical selections, and extemporaneous addresses on a variety of topics, some quite esoteric. Eliza R. Snow, sister of the society's founder Lorenzo Snow, described the gathering as "a magnificent moral, intellectual, and spiritual picnic," and she regularly presented her own poetry during the two years the group met.

In 1856 Eliza R. Snow published the first of her two volumes of *Poems, Religious, Historical and Political.* Increasingly through the 1860s the *Deseret News* carried the works of other female poets, including Sarah Elizabeth Carmichael, Hannah Tapfield King, and Emily Hill Woodmansee. The most celebrated of these was "Lizzie" Carmichael, whose work was praised locally by both Mormon and anti-Mormon presses and was occasionally reprinted in national newspapers and anthologies.

Emily Woodmansee, in addition to being a poet, gained some recognition as a player in the Salt Lake Theater. Previous to the opening of the theater in 1862, local women had participated in performances at Camp Floyd and the Social Hall, but the new theater substantially increased women's opportunities in drama. Several Utah actresses who began their careers with the Salt Lake Theater later became well known on the New York stage, including Julia Dean Hayne, Ada Dwyer Russell, and, most notably, Maude Adams.

As the sixties came to a close, Mormon leaders paid increasing attention to women's roles outside the home. In December 1867 Brigham Young asked bishops to help women organize Female Relief Societies within their wards. Originally organized for charitable purposes, these societies also served to mobilize women as a force in Utah economics and politics. As early as 1868 the Mormon Church president advocated education and training "without distinction of sex," and when the University of Deseret opened in 1869 eighty-eight women registered along with ninety-nine men. Affirming that "women are useful not only to sweep houses, wash dishes, make beds, and raise babies," Young declared that "they should stand behind the counter, study laws of physics, or become good book-keepers and be able to do the business in any counting house, and all this to enlarge their sphere of usefulness for the benefit of society at large."

Brigham Young's remarks signaled the commencement of a new era of individual and collective achievement for Mormon women, an era that had its parallel among the non-Mormon women of Utah. During the 1870s and 1880s both groups effectively organized and moved into the "society at large" to make their impact felt. These decades also marked the emergence of Utah's professional women—particularly in the fields of law, medicine, journalism, and education. Finally, it was during this era that the involvement of Mormon women in the practice of plural marriage brought Utah and its "poor, degraded women" national notoriety.

Gentile Women

A gazetteer for 1874 reflects the increasingly collective nature of the activities of Utah's non-Mormon women. It lists a Ladies' Library Association as the sponsor of one of Salt Lake City's three major libraries. Notices for lodges of the Independent Order of Good Templars indicate that women were espousing the temperance cause in Salt Lake City and Ogden and a number of Utah mining towns as well, including Corinne and Bingham. In 1877 the Ladies' Literary Club was founded by a group of thirty women interested in "literary pursuits and the development of mental culture." Meeting weekly on Fridays, this rapidly growing cluster of Utah women studied history, literature, and art. There were at the same time various sectarian organizations, including the Ladies' Benevolent Association of the Congregational Church and the Ladies' Hebrew Benevolent Association. As early as 1872 the

341

Jewish women sponsored fund-raising balls and parties that not only enhanced the social life of Utah Jews and Christians alike but that provided money to meet Jewish congregational needs and the needs of the poor.

Catholic women also began to make their presence felt during the 1870s. Father Lawrence Scanlan reported from Salt Lake City in 1875 that "a handsome colony of Sisters" had arrived from Indiana in June of that year, and that within two months these Sisters of the Holy Cross had secured land and laid the cornerstone for St. Mary's Academy of Utah. They had opened their school in September to over one hundred students, most of whom were non-Catholics. During the same autumn Sister M. Holy Cross and Sister Bartholomew leased a small building in the city for use as a hospital for sick and injured miners. Two additional sisters arrived the following year, but soon all four women were sleeping on the floor to make room for the overload of patients. In 1882 a full ten-acre block was purchased and work on a 125-bed hospital was undertaken. The "handsome colony" of Sisters of the Holy Cross expanded, and their efforts extended north to Ogden, where they established the Sacred Heart Academy, and south to the mining town of Silver Reef, where they established a school and a hospital. In 1901 Sister M. Cordelia began a training school for nurses in connection with the Holy Cross Hospital.

The Relief Society

The Relief Society "is the principle charitable institution in Utah," its "presidentess" Eliza R. Snow affirmed in 1876. Her report to the Ladies' Committee of the Philadelphia Centennial Exhibition indicated that more than 110 branches of the society were then functioning in various wards in Salt Lake City and other Mormon communities and that over an eight-year period they had collectively raised some $82,000. The Female Relief Society, first organized in Nauvoo by Joseph Smith, did not function from 1844 until the early 1850s, when it was briefly revived in a few wards mainly to provide relief for Indians. But when Brigham Young urged its reorganization in 1867 and commissioned Eliza R. Snow to help bishops establish Relief Societies throughout the territory, the movement took lasting hold.

The first and most constant obligation of a Relief Society was to help the ward bishop in his temporal care of the poor. Women not only donated money, food, and materials, but they met together to card, spin, and knit wool and to sew clothing, quilts, and carpets. Like their Jewish counterparts, Mormon sisters contributed extra

342

funds to build up their church—frequently providing curtains, carpets, and organs for ward meetinghouses and donating to temple, mission, and emigration funds.

In addition, Relief Societies secured their own properties. The president of one ward Relief Society indicated in 1868 that after the needy had been cared for the sisters found "an increasing treasury fund which it became our duty to put to usury." A lot was purchased and Utah's first Relief Society hall was dedicated in 1869. Built at the height of the Mormon cooperative thrust, these early halls often served as local cooperatives where the homemade goods of brothers and sisters from Mormon wards were sold, if not more cheaply than the Eastern finery on Main Street, then at least with the advantage that Mormon money did not exchange its way into gentile pockets. In fact, Mormon women stood to gain financially from such ventures. Their home manufactures— "clothing of all descriptions, shoes, bonnets, straw hats, artificial flowers, laces"—were sold on a commission basis. In 1876 the Relief Society sponsored the establishment of the Women's Cooperative Mercantile and Manufacturing Institution or Woman's Commission Store, where the homemade goods of women from throughout the territory were sold. At one point when the venture had just begun, Brigham Young offered male help to manage the financial transactions, but the ladies ignored his offer and proved themselves able to manage. Some Relief Society cooperatives were still operating at the turn of the century.

Relief Societies became involved in other business operations, including silk-raising and grain storage—two special commissions they had received from Brigham Young. As early as 1868 Young encouraged women to plant mulberry trees and undertake the cultivation of silk. One of his plural wives, Zina D. H. Young, became president of the Deseret Silk Association when it was established in 1875 to promote the manufacture of silk. The association disseminated information on sericulture, distributed eggs, and imported facilities for reeling the silk. Utah women filled bedrooms and parlors with mulberry leaves as they and their children tried to feed voracious silkworms. Relief Societies raised cocoons and reeled and wove silk, and in 1893 they put together a prizewinning exhibit of dresses, scarves, shawls, and hosiery of Utah silk for the Chicago World's Fair. By the century's close, however, due to lack of capital and support, the sericulture experiment was abandoned.

The program of grain storage undertaken by the Relief Society in 1876 continued into the twentieth century and had considerably greater impact than did the silk mission. Relief Society women, dedicated to preserving grain for times of scarcity, solicited donations of wheat or purchased it, gleaned fields, raised their own wheat, and built granaries in which to store it all. For nearly fifty years Emmeline B. Wells administered the Relief Society's widespread operation, which included buying, selling, and loaning of storage grain. The women drew some 2,000 bushels from their own stores to provide relief to southern Utah when that area was hit by a severe drought from 1898–1901. Carloads of Relief Society flour were sent to San Francisco following the 1906 earthquake, and to China the following year when that area suffered a famine. The Relief Society sold the remainder of the wheat, over 200,000 bushels, to the United States government during World War I.

Mormon Women and Medicine

Mormon women, like the Catholic Sisters, were concerned about medical care in Utah, but their efforts were centered on the primary occupational hazard of nineteenth-century women: childbearing. Dean May's study of eighty-one women living in Kanab in 1874 indicates that each mother bore an average of nine children during her lifetime. Four of the eighty-one women studied died in childbirth, and ten percent of the total 701 children born died before age one. Maternity and child health care obviously demanded attention.

As early as the 1850s Mormon women gathered under the direction of the Council of Health to hear lectures on midwifery and the health care of new mothers and infants. Later, Relief Societies sponsored lecture-study courses in women's physiology, and women from local societies were assigned to take obstetrics classes to provide their wards or communities with sufficient numbers of trained midwives. By 1879 some Relief Society sisters were advocating that the Mormons build a hospital for women and children that would also serve as a center for women's instruction in midwifery. The Deseret Hospital opened in 1882 in facilities rented from the Sisters of the Holy Cross. The hospital was managed by a female board of directors and was staffed by female Mormon doctors trained in Eastern medical schools. Some male board members and physicians were involved, but this first Mormon hospital in Utah was primarily a female enterprise. Funded through the contributions of Mormon Relief Societies, Young Ladies Mutual Improvement Associations, and Primary Associations (children's organizations), the Deseret Hospital treated sick and injured persons and handled difficult obstetrical cases. With its classes in nursing and midwifery it became the first nurses' training school in Utah.

Even after the 1890 closing of the hospital due to insufficient finances, the Relief Society maintained a sizable school of nursing.

The establishment of the women's hospital was an indication of the extent to which Mormon women had become involved in professional medicine. In response to the need for medical care a number of self-trained women had acted as midwives and doctors during Utah's first twenty years. These untrained "doctors," male and female, relied heavily upon botanic medicine or herbal cures. Midwives commonly administered saffron tea to infants directly after birth to clear their skin. They recommended that mothers administer ginger tea to ease the pain of teething, or that they use a half-teaspoonful of gunpowder as a remedy for children's diarrhea. One of Utah's early midwives, Patty Sessions, is said to have assisted in the birth of 3,977 babies. She also served at times, as did most other midwives, as a druggist, dentist, and surgeon of sorts.

During the 1850s there were ten trained medical doctors in Utah, three of whom were women who had received medical degrees outside of the United States before they emigrated to Utah and set up medical practices. Professional medicine surged ahead in Utah during the 1870s when Brigham Young, concerned that the coming of the railroad would lead to Mormon dependence on Utah's gentile population, encouraged men and women to obtain medical degrees in the East. By 1880 Romania Bunnell Pratt, Ellis Reynolds Shipp, and Martha Hughes Paul had all procured medical degrees from Eastern colleges and had returned to Utah to practice in their areas of expertise—eye and ear, obstetrics and pediatrics, and public health. Romania Pratt and Ellis Shipp both left children in the care of family members while attending the Women's Medical College in Philadelphia. All of these women were valuable assets to the Deseret Hospital and the Relief Society's program of medical training for women. By 1895 at least ten more women from Utah, both Mormon and non-Mormon, had traveled east for medical training and had returned to Utah to practice medicine.

Other Vocations

The advancement of Utah women in various trades and professions was celebrated by Utahns and other interested onlookers. Local newspapers proudly noted the admission of two women—Phoebe W. Couzins and Georgie Snow—to the Utah Bar in September 1872, and even some national papers picked up the story. Elizabeth Wood Kane, traveling through Utah the same year, observed with pleasure that female telegraph operators were employed at several of the settlements she visited. A series of *Woman's Exponent* articles followed the careers of Mary and Ida Cook, schoolteaching sisters whose journey to Utah to investigate Mormon tenets subsequently benefitted Utah schools. The Cooks, drawing upon their New York normal training, graded the schools and trained teachers in Logan, Salt Lake County, and St. George. During the 1870s each ran for election as a county superintendent of schools—Mary in Salt Lake County and Ida in Cache County—but, due to statutes prohibiting women from holding public office, neither was allowed to serve.

In spite of the political disability that hampered the development of the Cooks' careers, the development of women as professionals in Utah schools paralleled the development of the schools themselves. Through the 1850s and 1860s women opened schools in their homes or subscribed enough students to open schools in various wards. A few of the men and women who taught were trained teachers, but most were interested or needy persons simply volunteering to teach as much as they knew. As Utah's first academies and colleges developed—they were the equivalent of today's high schools—educated women became involved as teachers and administrators. Boards of the Presbyterian Salt Lake Collegiate Institute (later Westminster College), Morgan's Commercial College, and the Brigham Young Academies in Provo and Logan all appointed women as trustees, principals, or department heads early in the development of the schools. At the elementary and secondary levels teaching positions were fairly equally divided among males and females from the 1870s until the turn of the century, but most men's salaries were fifty to one hundred percent higher than women's salaries were.

As Utah developed full-fledged universities women were less involved in teaching and administration than they had been at the academies and colleges. Although women comprised one-quarter to one-third of the teaching staffs at the University of Utah and at Brigham Young Academy through the 1890s they advanced in rank more slowly than did faculty men. Not until 1904 did Maud May Babcock become the first female professor at the University of Utah. Even though Utahns encouraged the participation of women in medicine and education, the small number of women who actually became doctors and professors indicates that in the nineteenth century women generally did not expect to have a fulltime career away from the home.

On the eve of Utah's 1895 constitutional convention, Susan B. Anthony (seated in the center, wearing spectacles) and the Reverend Anna Howard Shaw (standing at the left with her hand on a chair) met with a group of Utah woman suffrage leaders, including Dr. Martha Hughes Cannon (standing farthest left), who would shortly be elected to the Utah Senate.

Publications By and For Women

News of Relief Society economic ventures, charitable activities, and educational efforts was carried in the *Woman's Exponent,* a semimonthly tabloid established by Mormon women in 1872 to discuss "every subject interesting and valuable to women." Owned, edited, and published by women, the *Exponent* reported the work of the three Mormon Church auxiliaries that women managed—the Relief Society, the Young Ladies' MIA, and the Primary Association. *Exponent* was an attempt by Mormon women to provide the world an accurate view of themselves as intelligent individuals and responsible wives and mothers, a view they hoped would substantially temper the popular image of Mormon women as "stupid, degraded, heart-broken" victims of polygamy.

At the same time the *Exponent* defended polygamy it advocated woman's rights. Utah's territorial legislature had granted suffrage to Utah women on February 12, 1870, but because the legislation did not enable women to hold public office the *Exponent* encouraged women to lobby for more extensive rights. News of national woman suffrage leaders and associations was a regular *Exponent* feature. By the 1880s the paper's masthead included the slogan: "The Rights of the Women of Zion and the Rights of the Women of all Nations," and feminist articles and speeches were frequently quoted.

The *Exponent* provided an opportunity for Mormon women to enter journalism as writers, editors, and even as typesetters. Louisa Lula Greene (later Richards), the paper's first editor, began work on the *Exponent* in 1872, a year before her marriage. By 1877 the demands of her family prompted her resignation, and Emmeline B. Wells, a notable Relief Society member, assumed editorship, a position she maintained until the last number of the *Exponent* was issued in 1914. The *Exponent,* along with the *Young Woman's Journal* (founded and edited by Susa Young Gates in 1889), did much to stimulate a local interest in poetry, autobiography, history, and fiction. Wells, Richards, and Gates established the Woman's Press Club in 1891 to further encourage women's literary efforts. By the turn of the century Mormon women had published more than three dozen books of poetry, autobiography, and history.

Advocates and Foes of Polygamy

Though Utah women distinguished themselves collectively and individually through the decade of the seventies, it was not their schools, their granaries, nor their practice of medicine that set them apart in the public mind from other women in the United States. Utah women gained national notoriety because they were at the center of the controversy over plural marriage. Many Mormon women lived polygamy and ardently defended it, and a tightly knit group of vociferous non-Mormon women opposed both the practice and the practitioners.

As Utah women became increasingly active in public life, they embroiled themselves in a conflict that had been gaining momentum since the 1862 passage of a federal law declaring polygamy a crime. Over two decades proposed legislation attempted to strengthen the 1862 law; at the same time anti-Mormon fiction, exposés, and tracts titillated the public with tales of Mormonism's depraved men and subjugated women.

When the Cullom Bill was before Congress in January 1870 some five or six thousand Mormon women convened in Salt Lake City to express their indignation at legislation that proposed to take away their husbands' civil liberties. They objected to the popular image of Mormon women that was presented nationwide over the pulpit and in the press, and they maintained that they could and would speak for themselves. They declared that they were women with high and glorious privileges and liberty "to leave at any time," and they defended plural marriage as a God-given institution, "the only reliable safeguard of female virtue and innocence; and the only sure protection against the fearful sin of prostitution and its attendant evils." While these Salt Lake City women were sending their resolutions to the nation's Congress, Mormon women held similar indignation meetings in every Utah settlement from Milton to Manti. Mass meetings and memorials served as the standard around which Mormon women rallied for twenty years in defense of their polygamous homes.

Not all Mormon women, of course, found happiness in the marital system prescribed for Latter-day Saints. Estimates seem to indicate that as many as seventy-five percent of them never lived in polygamy, though they strongly defended it as a religious tenet. The experience of those who did live "the principle" varied substantially, though plural wives commonly commented on the independence and individuality that polygamy encouraged. "The plural wife, in time, becomes conscious of her own power to make decisions," wrote Annie Clark Tanner, a plural wife who lived almost all of her married life apart from her husband.

Some women had ambivalent feelings. "I have taken pleasure in practicing this pure principle although I have been tried in it," one woman told her Relief Society sisters in 1870. Because husbands by necessity divided their time or through insensitivity neglected their wives, some women were plagued with loneliness. Jealousy was not uncommon. One plural wife commented, after leaving the Mormon Church, that she had watched her husband and his new bride trip off together "happy as children, while I remained rooted to the spot, tearing my pocket handkerchief to pieces, and wishing I could do the same with them." Some women, on the other hand, developed deep friendships with their sister-wives. One described "those two dear women with whom I served through hard work and poverty through so many years" as "more beloved of me than is any of my natural sisters." Women's responses to the practice of plural marriage were as many and varied as the responses of women to monogamous marriage. Some sought divorce since it was easily obtainable to women, though not to men; others ran away. More often the plural wife, like the monogamous wife, had a commitment to her marriage that made the difficulties bearable.

The vociferance of Mormon women in publicly acclaiming the virtues of polygamy also made the difficulties more bearable. In articulating their own defense Mormon women affirmed their positive perceptions of themselves in a system of mutual support that provided them a group identity to counter the devastating popular stereotype of Mormon women. But all told, their mass meetings and petitions and the *Exponent* did not measurably change the poor national image of Mormon women.

By contrast, the attempts of Utah's vocal antipolygamists did fan the fires of the nationwide crusade that resulted in the stringent legislation against polygamy in 1882 and 1887. Fanny Stenhouse, a Utahn who left the Mormon Church in 1870, published her famous exposé of polygamy, *"Tell It All,"* in 1874. She was followed by Ann Eliza Young, a recently divorced wife of Brigham Young, who in 1876 published her account of "life in bondage," a book that pleaded with the women of Utah to realize "how rich in love and happiness were the lives of women everywhere in the United States except in the fair territory of Utah." Unlike many other novels and confessions that had dealt with polygamy, both of these books were based on real experiences, though neither author resisted the temptation to fabricate.

The real crusade of Utah women against polygamy began in 1878 when two hundred women assembled in Salt Lake City to form the Anti-Polygamy Society and issued an invitation to the Christian women of the United States to join with them. Such notables as Harriet Beecher Stowe, Frances Willard, and Lucy Hayes (the nation's first lady) supported the Utah-based movement. In 1880 the society published its own exponent, the *Anti-Polygamy Standard,* a monthly by and for women that waged open war on polygamists. Two years later the *Standard's* editor, Jennie Anderson Froiseth, drew upon Stenhouse and Young and some of the paper's most heart-rending stories to compile *The Women of Mormonism or the Story of Polygamy as Told by the Victims Themselves.* The book, however, did not sell as well as the one that had preceded it in 1881, Cornelia Paddack's *The Fate of Madame La Tour, a Tale of the Great Salt Lake.* This alleged history of a Utah family, written by another member of the Anti-Polygamy Society, ran to 100,000 copies in the second edition.

In 1886 the Anti-Polygamy Society joined with Mrs. Angie F. Newman, a reform-minded evangelistic Methodist from Nebraska, in incorporating the Industrial Christian Home Association of Utah. Formed in the heat of the judicial crusade against polygamists, the association hoped to provide refuge for dissatisfied plural wives or for those who were left without support when their husbands were imprisoned in the raids. Mormon women objected en masse, saying that if these well-intentioned women were really sympathetic they would use their influence to stop the prosecution of polygamists. Mormon voices went unheeded, however, and Congress gave the association $40,000 to rent a home for plural wives. Additional federal moneys allowed for construction of the Industrial Christian Home in Salt Lake City in 1888–89, at which time the home fell under the jurisdiction of the Utah Commission. Proponents of the Industrial Christian Home were disappointed that only small numbers of women took advantage of their charitable invitation. Female occupants ranged from five to nine annually, with children and men bringing the annual total as high as twenty-seven. The project was abandoned as a failure in 1893; Utah's federal and local officials inherited use of the building.

Suffrage and Statehood

The Anti-Polygamy Society also worked for the disfranchisement of Utah women, declaring along with Utah's Liberal Party that Mormon women were merely puppets of their much-married husbands and were not free to vote as they opined; thus, they said, polygamists still governed in Utah's legislature. As the crusaders gathered petitions nationwide, memorializing Congress to divest Utah women of the vote, they incurred the wrath of such ardent suffragists as Susan B. Anthony, who supported Mormon women in the unsuccessful fight against the disfranchisement provisions of the Edmunds-Tucker Act.

The 1890 Woodruff Manifesto, which advised Mormons to refrain from new plural marriages, did not end tension between local Mormon and non-Mormon women. As Utah's 1895 constitutional convention prepared the territory for statehood, the question of female suffrage again divided Utah women along denominational lines. Mormon women had identified themselves with the suffrage movement since 1870 when Utah's legislature first granted women the franchise. They had enjoyed the support and attention of the National Woman Suffrage Association since that time and had attended some suffrage conventions in the eastern United States with the support of the Mormon first presidency. Following their disfranchisement in 1887 Mormon women attempted to align themselves with non-Mormon women in establishing a branch of the national suffrage association in Utah. Locally prominent non-Mormon women refused to become involved, not because they opposed woman suffrage in principle but because they feared that its restoration in Utah would assure the political domination of the Mormon Church. Thus it was primarily Mormon women who carried the standard for female suffrage through the early 1890s. Relief Societies spawned local suffrage associations throughout the territory; these associations carefully generated grassroots, bipartisan support for giving women the vote.

Widespread popular support ultimately decided the outcome of the battle that dominated Utah's 1895 constitutional convention—a heated debate over the political rights of women in the new state. Even Mormons lined up on both sides of the question. Prominent Mormon orator and Davis County Democrat B. H. Roberts was conspicuous in speaking out against the suffrage article as being injurious to Utah's chances for attaining statehood. Some non-Mormon delegates worked against equal rights by appealing to the familiar fear that through their women Mormons would dominate Utah politics. Also opposing the suffrage article were leading non-Mormon women, who assembled to draw up resolutions and circulate petitions arguing against inclusion of the article in the new state constitution, maintaining that the matter could be handled later by the state legislature. In rebuttal to these antisuffragists Mormon author and historian Orson F. Whitney pleaded with the convention to consider the capabilities of women and insure them equal rights through the constitution. He was backed by well-organized Mormon suffragists who were circulating their own petitions and reaping the benefits of their preconvention politicking. The suffrage article passed.

Once statehood had been achieved women not only voted, but women were elected: one to the Utah State Senate, two to the Utah State House of Representatives, and eleven as county recorders in 1896. At that time Martha Hughes Cannon became the first woman state senator in the United States when she won one of five district seats in the same contest lost by her husband, Angus M. Cannon, and her close friend, Emmeline B. Wells. Dr. Cannon, ardent Democrat and active woman suffragist, sponsored three significant welfare laws: one proposing to protect the health of female employees, another for compulsory education of deaf, dumb, and blind children, and the third creating a state board of health. Cannon worked for a number of other public health measures during her four-year term, then retired to practice medicine and work with the Utah State Board of Health.

Alice Merrill Horne, who was elected as a state representative in 1898 and 1912, authored a bill calling for the organization of the Utah Art Institute to advance the interest of the fine arts. The 1899 law provided for annual art exhibits in which the state would pay prize money and in turn would acquire the prize-winning paintings. Through exhibits held in Salt Lake City, Ogden, Logan, and Provo, Utah became the first state to establish its own fine arts collection.

Broadening the Utah Culture

During the last decade of the nineteenth century Utah women began to distinguish themselves in new fields, many of them seeking training elsewhere and then returning to give their home state the benefit of their exposure to new life-styles and ideas, as well as the benefit of their talents. In 1892, Alice Louise Reynolds enrolled at the University of Michigan at Ann Arbor; her graduate training there prepared her to teach the first classes in Shakespeare and Chaucer at Brigham Young Academy. Emma Lucy Gates left Salt Lake City for Europe in 1897; for several years she studied music and concertized there, returning at the outbreak of World War I to launch the Lucy Gates Opera Company. Utah-born Mary Teasdale traveled to Paris in 1899 and studied painting under the tutelage of Jules Simon and James McNeil Whistler. After her return to Utah she taught art and worked with the Utah Art Institute.

These educated travelers were substantially fewer in number than were the immigrants who were flocking to Utah mines and railroads at about the same time. Italian, Japanese, and South Slav women came first with their husbands and fathers; they were followed after the turn of the century by Greek and Mexican wives and daughters. Raising large families, running boarding houses, and participating in strikes along with their men, these immigrant women were as much pioneers as their well-established Utah sisters had been half a century earlier. Their roles are considered more fully in another chapter.

Women's Status in 1900

During Utah's first fifty years women's lives changed somewhat as cities expanded and modern conveniences became available, though at the turn of the century most Utah women were primarily occupied with homemaking, just as their predecessors had been. Census records indicate that in 1900 only eight percent of Utah's total female population over ten years of age were considered gainfully employed. Of these, thirty-seven percent were in domestic and personal services, over twenty-two percent were involved in manufacturing, and less than eighteen percent participated in professional employment areas. Generally, however, it seems that as the century progressed women gained enough freedom from home responsibilities to engage in activities outside the home. Most important for Utah women were activities sponsored by women's organizations. The proliferation of women's auxiliaries and clubs from the 1870s to 1900 reflected women's interest in pursuing avocations if not paid vocations. Lecture societies and women's newspapers provided women the opportunity to develop their skills as students and writers, while women's work in charity, suffrage, and antipolygamy campaigns provided them a way to participate in effecting community change. By 1892 Utah women's clubs had formed a federation, one of the first such groups in the nation.

The history of nineteenth-century Utah women cannot really be separated from the history of the territory itself. Along with men, women hewed homes and settlements out of desert and mountain frontiers. They delivered, raised, and often single-handedly supported the new generation who expanded settlements into towns and cities. Beyond their homes women's activities registered the development of Utah. They operated new telegraph stations, helped establish secondary schools, managed business cooperatives and hospitals, and assumed a prominent place among Utah's first trained educators, doctors, and artists. Far from separating themselves from the Mormon/non-Mormon tensions that plagued Utah in the nineteenth century, women entered into the thick of the conflict, both sides making certain their support of or opposition to polygamy was known nationally as well as locally. Women who had nurtured the developing Utah Territory witnessed the emergence of the newborn state and stood ready to help with Utah's twentieth-century upbringing.

Chapter 18
Bibliographical Essay

Those interested in pursuing the study of nineteenth-century Utah women will find an abundance of specialized interpretive and biographical studies, focusing primarily on Mormon women. Editor Vicky Burgess-Olson's *Sister Saints* (1978) and *Mormon Sisters: Women in Early Utah*, Claudia L. Bushman, ed. (1976), are both collections of essays including some biographical studies and assessments of Mormon women as feminists, educators, midwives, politicians, and as the subject of fiction. Also dealing with the lives of Utah's early Mormon women are four works published in the nineteenth century and recently reprinted or published in new editions. Edward W. Tullidge's *The Women of Mormondom* (1877, 1973) is the story of Mormon women told through autobiographical sketches. Elizabeth Wood Kane's *Twelve Mormon Homes Visited in Succession on a Journey through Utah to Arizona* (1874, 1974, ed. Everett L. Cooley) presents Mormon life as seen by the wife of Colonel Thomas L. Kane. Mrs. T. B. H. (Fanny) Stenhouse's *Tell It All . . . or An Englishwoman in Utah* (1874, 1971) and Ann Eliza Young's *Wife No. 19, or the Story of Life in Bondage* (1875, 1975) are views of life within the Mormon system written by disillusioned Mormon Church members.

Nineteenth-century Mormon women were dedicated record keepers who left behind a plethora of journals, reminiscences, and correspondence. Some of this material has been published in limited editions by families, and several notable works are widely available. *Not by Bread Alone: The Journal of Martha Spence Heywood, 1850–56*, Juanita Brooks, ed. (1977) and Mary Ann Hafen, *Recollections of a Handcart Pioneer of 1860 with Some Account of Frontier Life in Utah and Nevada* (1938) describe women's experiences in emigrating to Utah and settling in outlying settlements. *Dear Ellen: Two Mormon Women and Their Letters*, S. George Ellsworth, ed. (1974) presents 1850s correspondence between two young wives, one living in polygamy and the other in monogamy. *The Early Autobiography and Diary of Ellis Reynolds Shipp*, comp. Ellis Shipp Musser (1962), is Shipp's account of her personal life and medical training in the 1870s. Annie Clark Tanner's *A Mormon Mother* (1973) is the autobiography of a plural wife who married in the 1880s at the height of antipolygamy persecution. Also readily available are various women's documents that have been reproduced in the publications of the Daughters of Utah Pioneers: *Heart Throbs of the West* (1939–1951), *Treasures of Pioneer History* (1952–1957), and *Our Pioneer Heritage* (1958), all compiled by Kate B. Carter.

Other book-length studies focus on particular groups of women or women's organizations, including: Claire Noall, *Guardians of the Hearth: Utah's Pioneer Midwives and Women Doctors* (1974); Susa Young Gates, *History of the Young Ladies Mutual Improvement Association, 1869 to 1910* (1911); Katherine Barrett Parsons, *History of Fifty Years, Ladies' Literary Club . . . 1877–1927* (1927); and Relief Society of The Church of Jesus Christ of Latter-day Saints, *History of Relief Society, 1842–1966* (1966).

There has been a recent surge of periodical literature dealing with Utah women. Two articles containing a number of brief biographical sketches are Leonard J. Arrington, "Blessed Damozels: Women in Mormon History," *Dialogue: A Journal of Mormon Thought,* Summer 1971, and Raye Price, "Utah's Leading Ladies of the Arts," *UHQ,* Winter 1970. Other biographical essays include: Leonard J. Arrington, "Louisa Lula Greene Richards: Woman Journalist of the Early West,' *Improvement Era,* May 1969; Ronald W. Walker, "The Stenhouses and the Making of a Mormon Image," *Journal of Mormon History* (1974); Maureen Ursenbach Beecher, "The Eliza Enigma: The Life and Legend of Eliza R. Snow," *Essays on the American West, 1974–1975,* Thomas G. Alexander, ed. (1976); Chris Rigby, "Ada Dwyer: Bright Lights and Lilacs," *UHQ,* Winter 1975; Miriam B. Murphy, "Sarah Elizabeth Carmichael: Poetic Genius of Pioneer Utah," *UHQ,* Winter 1975; and Jill C. Mulvay, "The Two Miss Cooks: Pioneer Professionals for Utah Schools," *UHQ,* Fall 1975, and "The Liberal Shall Be Blessed: Sarah M. Kimball," *UHQ,* Summer 1976.

Much insight into women's roles in pioneer Utah may be drawn from Dean May's demographic study, "People on the Mormon Frontier: Kanab's Families of 1874," *Journal of Family History,* Fall 1976. Assessments of the thought and activities of Mormon women are found in Leonard J. Arrington, "The Economic Role of Pioneer Mormon Women," *Western Humanities Review,* Spring 1955; Jill C. Mulvay, "Eliza R. Snow and the Woman Question," *BYU Studies,* Winter 1976; Sherilyn Cox Bennion, "The *Woman's Exponent:* Forty-two Years of Speaking for Women," *UHQ,* Summer 1976; and Maureen Ursenbach Beecher, "Under the Sunbonnets: Mormon Women with Faces," *BYU Studies,* Summer 1976.

Information on the activities of the Catholic Sisters is found in Francis J. Weber, "Father Scanlan's Report of Catholicism in Utah, 1880," *UHQ,* Fall 1966, and "Catholicism among the Mormons, 1875–79," *UHQ,* Spring 1976, as well as Robert J. Dwyer, "Catholic Education in Utah, 1875–1975," *UHQ,* Fall 1975.

Suffrage and political activities of Utah women are examined by Thomas G. Alexander, "An Experiment in Progressive Legislation: The Granting of Woman Suffrage in Utah in 1870," and Jean Bickmore White, "Gentle Persuaders: Utah's First Women Legislators," *UHQ,* Winter 1970; and Jean Bickmore White, "Woman's Place is in the Constitution: The Struggle for Equal Rights in Utah in 1895," *UHQ,* Fall 1974. Finally, the antipolygamy campaign waged by Utah women is discussed in Gustive O. Larson, "An Industrial Home for Polygamous Wives," *UHQ,* Summer 1970; see also Robert J. Dwyer, *The Gentile Comes to Utah* (1971).

Chapter 19
The Indians in
Utah Territory

S. Lyman Tyler

For the Indians of the Great Basin and the Colorado Plateau, the first half of the nineteenth century was the beginning of the end for the isolation and cultural autonomy they had possessed for centuries. The expanding trade with Spanish California and New Mexico in slaves, horses, and other commodities took many Utes, Paiutes, and Navajo beyond their homelands. The fur trade brought hundreds of white invaders from Mexico, Canada, and the United States into the "land of the Yutas." Although none of these contacts displaced the native peoples, they began to establish patterns of interdependency that could—and did—evolve into dependent relationships in the last half of the century.

When members of The Church of Jesus Christ of Latter-day Saints moved into the Great Basin in 1847, they presented the first direct challenge to the territorial imperative of Utah's Indians. Traders, mountain men, and emigrants had preceded them, but hardly any had come to stay. The "Rocky Mountain rendezvous" had ceased after sixteen summers, and efforts to operate trading posts in the Uinta Basin had been abandoned. Only Jim Bridger's trading post on Black's Fork of the Green River and Miles Goodyear's year-old outpost on the Weber River were operational when Brigham Young declared that "this is the right place."

Utah was part of Mexico when the first Mormons arrived, but, with the exception of Goodyear, the only inhabitants of the land that became the state were different groups of Shoshonean-speaking Indians—the Ute, Shoshone, Gosiute (Western Shoshone), and Southern Paiute—and a few Athapascan-speaking Navajo. They numbered perhaps twenty thousand. Within the vast expanse Brigham Young proposed for the State of Deseret the only significant pockets of European culture were near the Great Salt Lake and in southern California. When Congress rejected Deseret in 1850 and organized the Territory of Utah, the Mormon settlements along the Wasatch were islands in Indian country that included present-day Colorado from the crest of the Rocky Mountains, the southwestern corner of Wyoming, and all of Nevada except the southern tip. The Territory of Utah encompassed most of the homeland of both the eastern and western Ute bands, the northwestern fringe of Navajoland, a great deal of Northern Shoshone territory, much of the land of the Western Shoshone, and the homelands of the Paiutes and Washoe all the way to the California border.

Mormon Indian Policy

The declarations, and in most cases the intentions, of the Mormon pioneers were friendly and constructive, but they were nevertheless carriers of cultural conflict and social disorganization insofar as the Indians were concerned. Mormon impact, complicated by ever-changing governmental policies, did not differ substantially from the outcomes elsewhere in the United States where white and red peoples encountered one another.

The Mormons were typical Englishmen-become-Americans in their drive to acquire land. Their Great Basin kingdom was basically a farming society; its two essential resource requirements were land capable of producing crops and water available for irrigation. Unfortunately, the best crop lands for the Mormons were also the best grazing lands for the livestock hunted by the Indians—for deer, elk, antelope, and so on—and the streams Mormons needed for irrigation also furnished water for the natural plant foods that Indian groups depended on for their sustenance.

The Indians soon realized that the Mormons had come to stay, and that they were not going to stay in one place. It was the good fortune of the first settlers that the Great Salt Lake Valley was a neutral zone betwen Ute, Gosiute, and Shoshone territory; a salt source for everyone, it was not hotly contested. This was not true of the area around Utah Lake, which had been an Indian gathering place "since time immemorial," as the legal documents say. As the Mormons moved south, the early friendship with the Utes ruptured.

In the meantime, representatives of the United States were approaching Ute territory from another direction, having acquired the land from Mexico by the Treaty of Guadalupe Hidalgo in February 1848. The first United States treaty with the Utes was negotiated by New Mexico Superintendent of Indian Affairs James S. Calhoun on December 30, 1849, and was ratified by Congress on September 9, 1850. On that same day the Utah Territorial Act was approved; under that act Brigham Young received his appointment as territorial governor and as superintendent of Indian affairs. Thereafter, relationships between Young and the Indians reflected his perceptions of the laws of the United States as well as the ideas and needs of the Mormon settlers. The possibilities for conflicts of interest were tremendous.

Because the Book of Mormon identified the Indians of the Americas as a branch of the house of Israel, "a chosen people," the Indians held a special significance for members of the Mormon Church. Missionaries had been sent to the Indians west of Missouri shortly after the church was organized in 1830. In the Great Basin setting the church and its members had an unusual opportunity to relate to the Indians both as a religious and as a social and political organization.

Brigham Young knew how important it was to maintain good relations with the Indians as a practical as well as a religious matter. In one of his messages to the territorial legislature he stated:

I have uniformly pursued a friendly course towards them [the Indians], feeling convinced that independent of the question of exercising humanity toward so degraded and ignorant a race of people, it was manifestly more economical and less expensive to feed and clothe than to fight them.

In a letter to Jacob Hamblin, one of the most effective missionaries to the Indians, Young sounded the same keynote as president of the church: "Continue the conciliatory policy toward the Indians which I have ever commended and seek by works of righteousness to obtain their love and confidence. Omit promises where you are not sure you can fill them. . . ."

With all credit for good intentions, what had occurred elsewhere in Anglo-America was soon repeated in the relationships between the Mormons and the Indians. Young's goal to convert Indians into communities of self-supporting Mormons met with failure. As early as November 20, 1850, he instructed John M. Bernhisel to work in Washington, D.C., for the complete removal of the Indians from the areas of projected Mormon settlement. (The policy of moving all of the eastern Indians westward to lands beyond the so-called Permanent Indian Frontier was still being implemented at the time, as the Mormons knew from their experiences in Missouri, Iowa, and on the plains.) Nothing came of Young's proposal, but the Mormons supported the reservation policy when it was proposed for Utah a decade later. Segregation, rather than accommodation and assimilation, would be most characteristic of white-Indian relations in Utah even to the present day.

The first hostility, a clash that took place at Battle Creek (Pleasant Grove) early in 1849, stemmed from cultural differences that always imperiled peaceful coexistence. A maverick band of Indians took some livestock from settlers in Tooele and southern Salt Lake valleys; the Indians were pursued to Utah Valley, where four of them were killed. Just a year later, as a result of Ute depredations against the new settlement of Fort Utah (Provo), about forty Indians were killed by the Mormon militia in battles observed by Captain Howard Stansbury, the United States Army surveyor. Such difficulties as these made it apparent that the Indians would like to have the material advantages available through the settlers without sacrificing their independence. Given Mormon policy and interests, they could not have both.

In November 1851 another clash occurred between Mormons, Utes, and Hispanic traders from New Mexico in connection with the well-established Indian slave trade. In this case Pedro Leon and other traders appeared in Utah bearing a license from the governor of New Mexico Territory that authorized them to engage in slave trading. Governor Young refused to recognize the license and ordered the license bearers out of the territory. Having come to depend on this trade to secure horses, guns, and ammunition, the Utes now resorted to a method that had been used with Spaniards for over 200 years: they threatened to kill the captive Indian children unless the Mormons bought them.

As a result, Young recommended legislation to legalize such purchases, and it was enacted in 1852. A number of Indian children were then brought into Mormon settlements where they were purchased and later adopted by Mormon families. Local church officials were given authority to oversee the treatment of these children, and family heads were made responsible for the adopted children's personal welfare.

In the 1850s Young and his ecclesiastical associates also advised missionaries to take young Indian women as wives because historically no more certain way had been found to cement relationships between peoples. Although the advice was not ignored, neither the Indian women nor the Mormon men seemed overly anxious to arrange such marriages. Like the child adoptions, most of the interracial marriages involved the Paiutes of southwestern Utah.

Various southern Utah and northern Arizona Indian tribes meet with United States commissioners on the Virgin River in 1874; Major John Wesley Powell is standing on the left.

The Walker War and Other Conflicts

The expansion of Mormon settlements in Utah and Sanpete valleys plus dissatisfaction with Mormon handling of the slave trade were important factors in the outbreak of the Walker War in 1853. The Indians under *Wahkara* (anglicized *Walker*) found through this conflict an outlet for antagonisms that had been developing for six years. (The baptism of Walker and more than a hundred other Utes in 1850 was no more effective in producing a cultural conversion than were most of the hard-won Indian baptisms performed by pioneer proselyters.)

The series of clashes, which lasted about a year, was hardly a war. Brigham Young instructed the settlers to "fort up" and to cut down the trade of weapons to the Indians. Less than twenty white men and an unknown number of Utes were killed. Of the whites, two died while on guard duty and the others were killed largely because they failed to take proper precautions. By October 1853 the war was over except for a few minor depredations against the southern settlements, and a formal peace was signed at Chicken Creek (Nephi) in May 1854. Chief Walker and Superintendent of Indian Affairs Young were the principal negotiators.

Walker died January 29, 1855. In less than a decade conditions in the region he had once ranged over freely had changed drastically. Forces from the United States now occupied posts in New Mexico and California. The Mormon colonies were persistently pushing outward in all directions from Salt Lake City. Walker's burial rites were, in this context, symbolic. Two slave women were killed and buried near the chief, three Indian children were buried alive, and a number of horses were slaughtered nearby.

The Mormon leaders hoped to avoid future disruptions by expanding the missionary effort among the Indians. Cultivating friendships and effecting conversions had been among the objectives in the founding of Provo, Manti, Fort Harmony (near Cedar City), and Fort Supply (near Fort Bridger). After a special missionary call at the April 1855 LDS conference, additional outposts were established in southeastern and southwestern Utah, northern Arizona, southern Nevada, eastern Idaho, and the Shoshone area of Wyoming. Some of these missions enjoyed limited successes, but the building of forts, the occupation of coveted Indian lands, and persistent attempts to get the Indians to change their life-styles led to friction and the early abandonment of the Elk Mountain (Moab, Utah), Las Vegas, and Fort Lemhi (Salmon River Valley) ventures.

Garland Hurt, an Indian agent stationed in Utah just prior to the Utah War, established three Indian farms with white supervisors in 1855–56. Though neither Indian Superintendent Young nor the commissioner of Indian Affairs in Washington, D.C., had previously authorized the ventures, both approved the actions and Congress grudgingly provided meager funds. These Indian farms were located at Corn Creek in Millard County, at Twelve Mile Creek in Sanpete County, and on the Spanish Fork River in Utah County. Hurt hoped that the farm areas would be permanently reserved for Indian use and that this would be one way of relieving their hunger.

When Brigham Young was replaced as governor and superintendent of Indian affairs in 1857, his successor viewed these farms as worthy projects and encouraged their continuance. A fourth farm was added to serve the Gosiutes at Deep Creek, south of present Wendover, in 1859. But the arrival of Johnston's Army in

1858 and Lincoln's proclamation concerning the establishment of an Indian reservation were both disruptive. For these and other reasons, including the pressure put on the Indians to change their life-style, federal sponsorship of the farms was discontinued by 1861. The Utes at Spanish Fork eventually went to the Uintah Reservation, but the Paiutes and Gosiutes stayed where they were, farming a little and depending on their white neighbors for part of their support.

The United States military forces were largely engaged in the East during the Civil War, but the vulnerability of transcontinental communications to Indian forays after the closing of Camp Floyd was a primary factor in the establishment of a permanent United States Army post in Utah late in 1862. Overland stage, mail, Pony Express, and telegraph stations were all targets of opportunity for the Ute, Shoshone, and Bannock Indians between Salt Lake City and Fort Laramie and for the Gosiutes west of the Mormon capital. In 1862 volunteer units of the Nauvoo Legion patrolled the routes east of Fort Bridger for several months. Then Colonel Patrick Connor and the California volunteers arrived to establish Fort Douglas and take over the Indian policing function. In January 1863 Connor's forces killed an estimated 200 to 400 Shoshone at the battle of Bear River, discouraging further disruptions of the overland mail service from that source.

But the predicament of the Indians was not changed. That situation was poignantly described by Jacob Hamblin in a letter written a few years later with specific reference to the Paiutes: "The watering places are all occupide by the white man. The grass that product mutch seed is all et out ... in fact there is nothing for them to depend upon but beg or starve." Since a third Indian option—to steal—was even less agreeable to the Mormon settlers than the two Hamblin mentioned, there was strong sentiment among Utah's white population to support a new federal policy that began to take shape during the Civil War years.

Treaties and Reservations

With the accelerating movement of easterners to Oregon, California, Texas, and New Mexico during the 1840s and 1850s, the Indian removal policy that began in the 1830s with the idea of holding the Great Plains as Indian territory ceased to be effective. As a result, the idea of reserving islands of land (reservations, usually a part of the Indian tribe's former, much larger territory) for Indian use, for "as long as the grass grows, the water runs, the sun shines," became the new Indian policy of the United States. The

Uintah Basin was referred to in the late 1850s as a likely place for a Utah Indian reservation. In 1860 Brigham Young sent a survey party to the Uintah Basin to determine whether the area would attract white settlers; the survey party returned a negative report. In 1861 President Lincoln declared the "entire valley of the Uintah River within Utah Territory" an Indian reservation.

A series of treaty gatherings was held in 1863 to work out agreements with these Indians. The first was signed at Fort Bridger in July; it included the eastern Shoshone (Chief Washakie was there) along with the other northern plains tribes. The second treaty was signed with the Western Shoshone at Box Elder in the same month. A third, involving other Western Shoshone, was signed at Ruby Valley, Nevada Territory, in October, and a fourth was accepted by the "Shoshone-Gosiute" in Tuilla (Tooele) Valley, also in October. Provisions worth thousands of dollars were distributed at the meetings. These were really gatherings of large numbers, not merely negotiating meetings between a few Indian representatives and a few United States agents. An Indian leader's power came from his people, and they were consulted before the leader committed them to any action.

In the treaties the United States asked for, and later required, safe passage for military forces; the right to establish military posts, wagon roads, and mail, telegraph, and railroad routes; and the right to build and maintain ferries on streams. In return, it was the custom for the government to guarantee the reservation lands to the Indians in perpetuity and to promise regular cash payments to the tribes for a specified number of years. (See map, p. 740, for Utah reservations today.) Ratification of the treaties by the United States Senate often took several years and was sometimes refused, although the terms were usually put into effect at once insofar as Indian obligations were concerned.

Congress did not implement Lincoln's 1861 proclamation creating the Uintah Reservation until 1864. In June 1865 Indian Superintendent O. H. Irish concluded a treaty with the Ute Indians at Spanish Fork to secure their removal to the new reservation. Knowing the prestige Brigham Young held in their eyes, Irish invited him to be present and to give the negotiations his support. Government officials agreed to pay the Utes $25,000 a year for ten years, $20,000 a year for the next twenty years, and $15,000 a year for the next thirty years; the amount was to be adjusted in proportion to population changes. The government also promised to sell the established Indian farms and to provide reservation schools at a cost not to exceed $10,000 a year.

As usual, the Indians were asked to give up their other lands and begin the move to the reservation immediately. In the meantime the treaty began its slow process through Washington channels, only to be rejected by the Senate almost four years later in March 1869. The Indians were thus left without their land and with no apparent legal claim against the United States, though Congress did appropriate funds for operating the reservation. (Eighty years later their heirs were awarded substantial financial compensation for these and many other broken promises.)

Dissatisfied with conditions, a minor Ute leader named Black Hawk invited members of other bands to a council in 1863 to plan some kind of retaliation against those who had invaded their territory. In 1865 a series of raids under Black Hawk's leadership began in the Sanpete area. To settlers in the West this was enough to constitute an Indian war. In the perspective of time, it may be seen that Indians who had been ravished by white men's diseases and displaced by white men were simply striking out at those who seemed responsible for their suffering and for the loss of the good life they had known. About fifty Mormon settlers were killed and several southern Utah villages were abandoned during the period of these intensified raids (1865–68). The pioneers learned that if they stayed inside during a raid and didn't try to pursue the Indians into the mountains few would be harmed. In addition to the hunger and privations Indians suffered during the hostilities, a much greater number of Indian lives were lost. Black Hawk died of tuberculosis in 1870. Sporadic raids continued until 1873, but the war that bears his name was the last forceful resistance to the white invasion of Utah that began in 1847.

In the late 1860s and early 1870s the Utah Utes gradually moved to the Uintah Reservation. There seemed to be no viable alternative. There were some bad agents and a few good ones, as was usual in the Indian Service of the period, and under the encouragement of better ones such as J. J. Critchlow some progress was made in agricultural pursuits, though most Utes did not find farming something that came naturally to them.

Turning to the Southern Paiute country in southwestern Utah, Irish negotiated a treaty in September 1865 that was actually an extension of the earlier Spanish Fork treaty. By its terms, these people also agreed to give up their lands in Utah Territory and move to the Uintah Reservation. The course seemed plausible, since the best lands that the Paiutes had once farmed were now agricultural settlements of white farmers. Transient miners and stockmen destroyed Indian crops, and miners in southern Utah and Nevada periodically killed members of the Indian bands. But when the time for removal came, the Paiutes realized that they did not want to share a distant reservation with the Utes, whom they remembered as the ones responsible for selling their women and children into slavery. The Paiutes refused to go.

At the time of the 1873 survey of Southern Paiute country by John Wesley Powell and G. W. Ingalls, the Utah bands were again encouraged to move to the Uintah Basin. They refused again for the same reasons. A second alternative was to go with Nevada's Southern Paiutes to the Moapa Reservation on the Muddy River in southern Nevada. The Utah groups agreed, provided the government supply the assistance necessary for the Indians to make the transfer and to reestablish themselves as farmers. The United States would neither provide the funds nor agree to move white settlers from the reservation on the Muddy. Gradually the Utah-based natives either withdrew into the surrounding unoccupied hills and desert areas or attached themselves in a dependent relationship to the white communities. Not until after the turn of the century were tracts assigned to the Kaibab, Shivwits, Cedar City, Indian Peaks, Kanosh, and Koosharem groups, some by local communities and some by the federal government.

Various recommendations were also made to move the Gosiutes to the Uintah Reservation or to the Fort Hall, Idaho, Reservation with other Shoshones. The Gosiutes did not like either idea so they stayed where they were, suffering continuing disturbances from the white people who had gradually surrounded them. For thirty years they were totally ignored by the federal Indian agencies, not even being counted in the late nineteenth-century censuses. Reservations were finally created for them by the Taft and Wilson administrations.

The sparse numbers of southeastern Utah Navajos were somewhat augmented by refugees from Monument Valley when Colonel "Kit" Carson and federal troops rounded up most of the Navajos and herded them off to internment at Fort Sumner, New Mexico. When this 1863–68 enforced confinement ended, some of the Navajos moved southward, but others were still there when Mormon and eastern farmers and stockmen moved into the San Juan region toward the end of the century to compete for resources. Although the land south of the San Juan River was incorporated in the Navajo reservation by presidential proclamation in 1884, federal Indian programs did not substantially affect the area until after 1900. Several modifications in the reservation boundary in Utah were made subsequent to that date.

Ute Removal from Colorado

After the 1859 discovery of gold in Colorado, the eastern Utes saw their territory invaded by a growing number of white men. Treaties in 1863 and 1868 reserved large tracts of land west of the Continental Divide for the White River, Uncompahgre, Moache, Capote, and Weeminuche bands. Prior to 1873 minerals were discovered in the San Juan Mountains of southwestern Colorado, and the number of miners increased until it seemed necessary, from the white point of view, to claim another piece of Ute territory. The San Juan Quadrangle was then removed from the reservation and opened up to miners who were already in the area. As a result, unrest among the Indians increased.

In 1879 Indian Agent Nathan Meeker's attempt to turn a White River Agency race track into farmland so upset the Indians that they killed Meeker and some of the agency employees. An encounter with federal troops ensued, and Colorado citizens cried that "the Utes must go." A responsive government then directed the Indians to Utah.

Colorado's White River Band, whose members bore responsibility for the Meeker massacre, was placed on the Uintah Reservation with the Utah Utes. Although the Uncompahgres had nothing to do with the incident at White River, they, too, were forced to leave Colorado and move to the Ouray Reservation in an undesirable area south of the Uintah Reservation. Eventually many Uncompahgres also moved to the Uintah Reservation because their assigned land would not accommodate farming. What little agricultural progress had been made by the Utah Utes was seriously upset by taunts of the White River Band, who had little respect for farmers and farming, and by the general confusion resulting from attempts to place new arrivals on a reservation that was already occupied and among people who had been told that the land belonged to them.

Changes in Federal Policy

The United States ended the practice of making treaties with the Indian tribes in 1871. No new treaties were negotiated; the treaties already in effect continued to be the legal basis for relationships between the government and particular tribes. Additional necessary legal arrangements were made by executive agreements and Congressional enactments.

In 1887 the General Allotment, or Dawes Severalty Act, allotted land to individual tribe members and then opened up the remaining reservation land for white settlement. The ostensible purpose of the law was to break up the reservations and stop governmental dealings with the Indians as tribal units. If the policy had been a success, Indians would have eventually been dealt with as individual landholders and ultimately would have received citizenship and clear titles to their land tracts.

One basic problem was that most western Indians, including the Utes, were not farmers, and the application of the new policy did not please them. Another problem was that much of the reservation land was not readily adaptable to freehold farming. The implementation of the new program among the Utah Indians began as Utah won statehood in 1896, and its traumatic impact upon the Uintah-Ouray Reservation inhabitants is still being felt.

Chapter 19
Bibliographical Essay

Two published bibliographies, Omer C. Stewart's *Ethnohistorical Bibliography of the Ute Indians of Colorado* (1971) and S. Lyman Tyler's *The Ute People: A Bibliographical Checklist* (1964), include articles, government documents, and monographic studies pertaining to the Utes, Paiutes, and Gosiutes both before and after contact by European-Americans.

Readers are referred to titles by Joseph G. Jorgensen that contain information about the Northern Ute; to the special issue of the *Utah Historical Quarterly,* Spring 1971, devoted to Utah Indians, with C. Gregory Crampton as guest editor; and to selections on the Indians in Helen Z. Papanikolas, ed., *The Peoples of Utah* (1976). See detailed citations following chapter 2.

Some of the earlier writers whose works contain significant material on the territorial period are Paul Bailey, whose *Jacob Hamblin: Buckskin Apostle* (1948) is still the basic biography for Hamblin; Leland H. Creer, "Federal Indian Policy, 1849–1865," *Utah and the Nation* (1929); Milton R. Hunter, *Brigham Young the Colonizer* (1940); Daniel W. Jones, whose personal experiences are recorded in *Forty Years Among the Indians* (1890); and William R. Palmer, whose many articles on the Southern Paiute appeared in *UHQ* from the first volume in 1928 until the 1940s.

Coulsen and Geneva Wright deal with the last years of the territorial period in "Indian-White Relations in the Uintah Basin," *Utah Humanities Review,* 1948. See also Dale L. Morgan, "The Administration of Indian Affairs in Utah, 1851–1858," *Pacific Historical Review,* 1948; Omer C. Stewart, "Ute Indians: Before and After White Contact," *UHQ,* 1966; and Gustive O. Larson, "Brigham

Young and the Indians," in Robert G. Ferris, ed., *The American West: An Appraisal* (1963). For essays on early White-Indian conflict, see Howard A. Christy, "Open Hand and Mailed Fist: Mormon-Indian Relations in Utah, 1847–52," *UHQ* 1978; and "The Walker War: Defense and Conciliation as Strategy," *UHQ* 1979.

Other important contributions to the literature on Utah Indians include Floyd A. O'Neil and John D. Sylvester, eds., *Ute People: An Historical Study* (1970); and Gregory C. Thompson, *Southern Ute Lands, 1848–1899: The Creation of a Reservation* (1972). For policy questions S. Lyman Tyler's *A History of Indian Policy* (1973) traces relations between European nations, the United States, and the Indian tribes from early contacts until 1972.

Recently the Indian tribes have themselves begun to sponsor histories, frequently under Indian authorship. Some titles available or in immediate prospect are James Jefferson, et al., *The Southern Utes; A Tribal History* (1972); Edward C. Johnson, *Walker River Paiutes: A Tribal History* (1974); and an official history of the Northern Utes now in final preparation for the press. The Intertribal Council of Nevada at Reno has published two titles pertinent to Utah history: *NUWUVI: A Southern Paiute History,* and *NUMA: A Northern Paiute History,* both in 1976; a third on the Western Shoshone is now in press.

Chapter 20
Opening the Colorado Plateau

Gustive O. Larson and Charles S. Peterson

The early colonization of Utah was largely confined to the Great Basin, its population centering in colonies along the foot of the Wasatch Mountains and spilling over the basin's south rim to the Virgin River Valley. The eastern half of the territory— the Colorado Plateau—long remained a hinterland disregarded by colonizers and more recently neglected by historians. Its potential was not always apparent to Utahns, and when that potential was conceded it was often in terms of exploitation or secondary uses. The result was the development of a Utah with a difference—a Utah to which Indians were removed, or from which water might be diverted, or into which livestock and mining frontiers extended from adjoining states. It was a Utah in which the Mormon question was muted and in which ethnic and racial minorities played a more important role.

These distinctions persisted beyond the pioneering years. The history of the Colorado Plateau to 1896 deals largely with exploration, surveys, Indian relations, and the gradual infiltration of settlers who established ranches and homes and identified the wealth of natural resources that would promote regional growth in the twentieth century.

Early Indian Inhabitants

White settlers were not the first occupants of the plateau and its canyonlands. As newcomers, they invaded the homelands of the prehistoric Anasazi cultures, whose crumbling ruins hang above the canyons or are tucked under the cliffs in places now labeled Mesa Verde, Hovenweep, Betatakin, and Inscription House. From primitive beginnings these people developed over the centuries an agricultural civilization whose sudden disappearance, sometime prior to A.D. 1300, continues to baffle archeologists.

Thereafter came a period in which a less brilliant and less extensive Pueblo culture persisted on the mesas of northern Arizona and New Mexico and along the Rio Grande River. On the Colorado Plateau and elsewhere in Utah the forefathers of the various Paiute, Ute, and Shoshonean stocks continued to follow primitive patterns until approximately 1750, when acquisition of the horse enabled some of them to broaden their operations and to develop more affluent cultures.

Spanish and Trapper Invasions

Spanish missionaries and traders were the first white men to become familiar with the Colorado Plateau as they pursued Ute trails westward and northward from Santa Fe. The Domínguez-Escalante expedition of 1776 took Europeans across the Green River and the Uinta Basin; the members carried information about the upper plateau region back to the New Mexican capital. Trading parties later shortened the route into Utah by crossing the Colorado River at present Moab and the Green River at Green River. (A variant from this approach to the Green River was by way of the Book Cliffs, farther north.) From here the route led across the San Rafael Swell to Castle Valley, through the pass by which Highway I-70 now crosses the Wasatch Plateau, and down Salina Canyon into Sevier Valley. It is likely that the Arze-Garcia trading party approximated this course on its way to Utah Valley in 1813. The route later became the Old Spanish Trail as it was extended from Sevier Valley to southwest Utah and on to southern California by the William Wolfskill Party in 1830.

For two decades the plateau was crossed by trading caravans bringing woolen goods from New Mexico to trade for horses and mules, which were then driven by the thousands back across the trail to Santa Fe. Lieutenant John W. Gunnison, whose 1853 survey followed the trail in its San Rafael sector, reported as many as twenty parallel trails the size of ordinary horse paths in a space barely fifty feet wide. An Indian slave trade also developed along the trail as children were purchased or stolen from the unfortunate Paiutes or bartered from the more aggressive Utes.

When Mexico won independence in 1821, trade restrictions were lifted and trappers and traders of many nationalities used Santa Fe and Taos as bases for operation in the Rockies and the Colorado Plateau. Trapping parties led by Etienne Provost and others reached Utah's Colorado and Green rivers as early as 1824. Missouri-based William H. Ashley came a year later; he is credited with the first boat trip made by white men on the Uinta section of Green River. Soon the canyon streams were widely explored for beaver. By the mid 1830s Antoine Robidoux and others had founded trading posts on the Gunnison and White rivers and in the Uinta Basin. For nearly two decades some of these trade centers continued to receive trappers' products in exchange for goods brought over the mountains in the first wagons known to penetrate the region.

Government Reconnaisance

Then came surveyors, often in United States Army uniforms, to explore the possibilities of transportation across land marked "unexplored" on existing maps. Growing geographic knowledge and national events in the 1840s shifted attention to the possibility of an American railway system to the Pacific Ocean. Under pressure to tie the Pacific slopes more closely to the Union, Congress appropriated funds in 1853 to support exploration of four possible routes by which this could be accomplished. One of the surveys sponsored by Senator Thomas Hart Benton and John C. Fremont was to roughly follow the fortieth parallel westward from St. Louis. When assignment of that route was given to John W. Gunnison, private interests backed Fremont for an independent survey. With Gunnison ahead, both men entered Utah near present Grand Junction and proceeded across the Colorado Plateau and on into the Great Basin. Upon reaching the Sevier River, Gunnison recorded satisfaction with having explored a passable wagon road but indicated that for a railroad it was far inferior to the central route via Medicine Bow and Fort Bridger, Wyoming. The records of both Gunnison and Fremont proved valuable in disclosing the mysteries of the plateau region, but only Fremont lived to see, thirty years later, the Denver and Rio Grande Western Railroad cross Utah's plateau by way of the Green River near the Old Spanish Trail.

Efforts made by United States topographical engineers to find additional routes into the territory during the Utah War resulted in two important explorations of the Colorado Plateau. Late in 1858 Lieutenant Joseph C. Ives steamed a shallow draft boat, the *U.S. Explorer,* up the Colorado River from the Gulf of California to Black Canyon, where Hoover Dam now stands, and then traveled overland into northern Arizona. Included in his party was geologist John S. Newberry, who the following year joined Captain

373

John N. Macomb to uncover many secrets of the almost unexplored Four Corners Region. Macomb was ordered to find the confluence of the San Juan and Colorado rivers and to determine the most direct route from the San Juan to the southern Utah Mormon settlements. In the discharge of that order he and Newberry recorded some of the earliest and finest descriptions of the breathtaking canyonlands scenery and called attention to such features as the juncture of the Green and Colorado rivers and Monument Valley. This report, which incidentally offered no route to the Mormon settlements, also described the course of San Juan River and the location of the La Sal and Abajo mountains.

Indian Relations in Southeastern Utah

Indians also figured strongly in the late nineteenth-century history of southeastern Utah. Slow in attracting white settlers because of its remoteness and harsh natural conditions, the Four Corners area was something of a last frontier for the native Americans—it was the traditional home for some, a recent refuge for others displaced by advancing whites, and a catchall for castoffs from more favored tribal lands.

The Utes dominated Utah when Anglo-Americans arrived, and they continued to dominate after the failure of the Mormon Elk Mountain Mission to the Utes in 1855. Moving restlessly to and from reservations in Uinta Basin and southwest Colorado, Ute bands grazed their stock and hunted in southeast Utah for the remaining decades of the century. Prompted by confused federal policy and noisy pressure from Indian removal interests, the entire population of the Southern Ute Reservation in Colorado appeared in San Juan County during the winter of 1894-95 and milled in disappointment and bitter cold while whites decided they had to return to Colorado.

Navajos, too, came and went from the earliest recorded times. After the mid 1860s their occupation south of the San Juan River took on permanent characteristics when Hoskaninni and others hid in the Monument Valley-Navajo Mountain country during Kit Carson's Navajo campaigns. In 1884, President Chester A. Arthur issued an order making all of Utah south of the San Juan River and its confluence with the Colorado part of the Navajo Reservation. Later Theodore Roosevelt added certain lands north of the San Juan, including the Aneth district. Finally, a small population of Paiutes and a handful of Weemuniche Utes found their way into the region. Both were reluctant to move from there to the Southern Ute Reservation.

While it was not one of the nation's great Indian battlefields, few areas have a history of more protracted trouble between Indians and whites or of such trouble extending into recent times. The Pinhook Battle of 1881, the Monument Valley killings in 1881 and 1884, the Blue Mountain and White Canyon skirmishes of 1884 and 1887, and the twentieth-century frictions—or, as Forbes Parkhill has called them, "the last of the Indian Wars"—marked four decades of nagging discord.

Racial friction had earlier brought conflict elsewhere on the lower Colorado Plateau when Mormon settlements (including Mt. Carmel, Glendale, Springdale, and Northrop) pushed up the East Fork of the Virgin River and a colony was tentatively established on Kanab Creek in the early 1860s. Almost immediately Indian disorders incident to Utah's Black Hawk War and Arizona's Navajo wars led to a general withdrawal from all these sites. Kanab was transformed into a fortified outpost that played an occasional defensive role. Otherwise the locality was abandoned until 1870, when peace brought the Mormons back to most of the old villages.

John Wesley Powell

In September of 1869 Jacob Hamblin, Indian scout and peacemaker, moved from Santa Clara on the lower Virgin River to Kanab, where he could better guard Utah's southern communities. The following fall Brigham Young visited the site in company with Major John W. Powell, who was to play an important role in the exploration and development of the entire Colorado Plateau. Powell needed a reliable Indian contact and an experienced guide; Brigham Young could offer the services of none better than Hamblin, who knew the Colorado crossings better than anyone else and who commanded the respect of Indians on both sides of the channel.

In 1870, Powell was already a nationally prominent figure because of his initial exploration of the Green and Colorado rivers the previous year. From his first launching of four boats with a party of ten men at Green River, Wyoming, he challenged the obstacles of Flaming Gorge, as William Henry Ashley had done in 1825, and the hazards of turbulent Ladore Canyon that had been faced by William Manly in 1849. As interest in the Far West soared, Powell came through the same series of roaring rapids, naming them Disaster Falls, Hell's Half Mile, and so on. After riding the rapids through the mountain gorges with the loss of one supply boat, he paused briefly in Uinta Valley to restock provisions at the White Rocks Indian Agency. That stop was his last

Major John Wesley Powell questions a Paiute Indian living on the Kaibab Plateau in northern Arizona.

contact with civilization for two months; when he left the valley on July 6, 1869, he headed into the unknown through a thousand cliff-bound miles. Before the party arrived at the Virgin River on August 30, they had passed the mouth of the Price, San Rafael, Dirty Devil, San Juan, Paria, and Kanab rivers and had named

Desolation, Cataract, Glen, and Marble canyons as well as various rapids through Grand Canyon. They started in Uinta Valley as a party of nine men with three boats; six men made it through to the Virgin with two badly battered crafts.

The fate of three men who parted company with Powell at Separation Falls within two days of final victory needed clarification; Powell sought out Jacob Hamblin for help. Conducting investigations among the Paiutes, Powell learned that the three explorers had been killed by Indians who mistook them for troublemaking prospectors. Powell also extended his contacts to the Hopis and Navajos, an experience that sharpened his interest in native cultures and later influenced him to direct the United States Bureau of Ethnology.

Looking forward to his second river expedition, scheduled for 1871, Powell also arranged for Hamblin to find a way to the mouth of the Dirty Devil and cache food supplies there for the exploring party. (Hamblin was unable to complete this assignment.) Then Powell was off to Washington, where he persuaded Congress to appropriate $25,000 for his exploration of the Colorado River.

In so doing Powell became serious competition for federally sponsored surveys headed by Clarence King, Ferdinand V. Hayden, and George M. Wheeler. Already well under way when Powell received his appropriation, the Hayden and Wheeler projects extended into the Colorado Plateau; the Wheeler surveys also overlapped Powell's work in the Dirty Devil and Paria river areas. East of the Colorado River, including and extending northward from the Four Corners Region, Hayden continued the surveys of Macomb and Newberry in the mid 1870s, mapping the topography with its geology and archeology. Important as the Utah work of Wheeler and Hayden was, it was peripheral in their overall programs and thus their surveys and reports were overshadowed, as far as Utah history is concerned, by those of Powell, whose activities centered on the Colorado Plateau.

Powell's second river expedition began at Green River, Wyoming, in May 1871 and arrived at Lee's Ferry by late October. There they met John D. Lee in his "Lonely Dell," and they left the river to set up survey headquarters in Kanab. In the months that followed Powell became well acquainted with the Mormons and their colonizing patterns. The opportunity of observing them helped him understand water value in arid lands and the worth of cooperative methods in its use.

Powell's survey of the Colorado Plateau was completed in 1879. A virtually unknown land had been made known, given boundaries, and labeled. Of all who gave names to the region—Indians, Spaniards, mountain men, government officials, explorers, and Mormons—none but the Mormons gave as many as did John Wesley Powell. Publications of the survey included Powell's own *Report on the Explorations of the Colorado River of the West* (1875, repr. 1961), Grove Karl Gilbert's *Geology of the Henry Mountains* (1890) and *Lake Bonneville* (1890), and Clarence E. Dutton's *Geology of the High Plateau of Utah* (1880). The last, with its vivid descriptive writings by Frederick Dallenbaugh, photography by Jack Hiller, and paintings by Thomas Moran and William Henry Holmes, was an impressive early witness to the region's unsurpassed natural beauty. Finally came Powell's *Report on the Lands of the Arid Regions of the United States With a More Detailed Account of the Land of Utah* (1878). It details his reactions to western lands, water supply, and climate as well as methods of utilizing economic resources he had learned from Indians, Spanish-Americans, and Mormons. The report emphasized differences between America's east and west, stressed aridity as the unifying feature of the West, and proposed reforms in federal land policy.

In addition to his role as director of the United States Bureau of Ethnology from 1879 until his death in 1902, Powell headed the United States Geological Survey from 1881 to 1894. He also directed the National Irrigation Survey, which by the end of 1889 had placed almost thirty million acres of possible irrigable land under study for withdrawal from public entry and which had selected 150 reservoir sites, many of them in Utah. Although Powell was forced from the Geological Survey by special interests, much of what he envisioned for Utah's water resources became a reality in the twentieth century.

Early Settlement in Southeastern Utah

With the close of the Black Hawk War, which had deterred expansion from the Great Basin but at the same time had acquainted settlers with the potential of the Colorado Plateau, Mormon settlements began to appear at the headwaters of the Green River and Colorado River tributaries. Price was established on the river bearing that name in 1877; Huntington, Orangeville, and Castle Dale were built on the affluents of the San Rafael at about the same time; Loa, Teasdale, and Bicknell were established on the sources of the Fremont River between 1876 and 1879; and Escalante was built on the Escalante River in 1875. In each of these settlements cattle and sheep became a mainstay of life. Livestock quickly exhausted ranges, contributing to serious flooding and erosion problems that were checked but not solved when forest reserves began to limit the number of stock grazed during the first decade of the twentieth century.

Meanwhile the Mormon fort built and abandoned in 1855 at present Moab was reoccupied in 1875 by George and Silas Green, who brought 400 head of cattle into the valley. Two years later, when George and Silas were both murdered by unknown killers, a black man locally called "Nigger Bill" and a companion vaguely referred to as a French Canadian arrived with more livestock, took possession of the fort, claimed the valley, and moved their cattle to the northwest slopes of the La Sal Mountains. Tom Ray located on the south slope in 1877 and was followed during the next three years by cattlemen who established ranches around the mountains or lived in Moab. The newly founded cowtown later became the seat of Grand County.

In 1879 a Coloradoan, Joshua B. Hudson, appeared with 2,000 head of cattle purchased at low prices in the Mormon settlements. Fattening the cattle on the Blue Mountains (Abajo) near present Monticello, he sold them at a good profit and returned with successively larger herds. He was soon joined by several other non-Mormon Colorado stockmen, who pastured on the Blues during the summer and on the sage and grass-covered plateaus of eastern Utah in the winter. Peter Shirts, whose cabin stood with a few others at the juncture of Montezuma Creek and the San Juan River, headed the only Mormon family in southeastern Utah in 1880 when the San Juan Mission established Bluff a few miles downstream.

The epic story of the hole-in-the-rock pioneers is a witness to the stubborn resoluteness of many Mormons who helped settle Utah. Fearful that outsiders would monopolize the San Juan country and anxious to cultivate good relations with the Indians, the Mormon Church leadership turned in 1879 to the time-proven device of the colonizing mission; settlers were called from Iron County and nearby parts of southern Utah. A scouting party crossed the Colorado River at Lee's Ferry and entered the San Juan Basin through Monument Valley, arriving at the mouth of Montezuma Creek in the spring of 1879. Satisfied with the country's prospects, the scouts returned by way of the Old Spanish Trail and the settlers prepared to make their move.

Ignoring the established but circuitous roads the scouts had traveled, the company of not less than 230 men, women, and children made its way east to the new village of Escalante, the jumping-off point into the trackless Colorado Plateau wilderness, with eighty-three wagons and a thousand head of cattle. At Forty-mile Spring, their first rendezvous, they learned of the almost impossible route ahead and of snow blocking their retreat; from November 1879 to April 1880 they challenged the impossible. Blasting a wagon-wide notch through a fifty-foot cliff, they built a road down to the Colorado River—an 1,800-foot drop in only three-quarters of a mile. At the end of January they crossed the river on a ferry they had built; then they pushed up perilous dugways onto land that had been described to them as impassable. Across slick rock and formidable ridges, through deep snow and dense juniper forests, they came at last to the sandy banks of the San Juan River a few miles below the mouth of Recapture Creek on April 5, 1880. Montezuma, where many of them had planned to settle, lay only eighteen miles ahead, but they had had enough. They made their camp overlooking the river and on the following days they established the town of Bluff.

The predicament of the settlers was difficult. For more than a year their contact with the Mormon settlements was through the Hole-in-the-Rock; finally an alternative route via Hall's Crossing was opened. Attempting to utilize the farm village pattern the Mormons had used to subdue desert oases elsewhere, Bluff's settlers struggled futilely to develop an irrigation system, watched as their limited land base washed down the San Juan River, and eked out an existence by grading railroad and freighting in the Four Corners area. The county seat was moved from Bluff to Monticello in 1895. By that time many of the pioneers had moved to Blanding.

Expansion of Livestock Interests

Attracted by grazing opportunities, outside livestock interests continued to invade southeastern Utah, and in the 1880s the small operators were pushed out by big companies. The L. C. Cattle Company, made up of herds from Texas, New Mexico, and Colorado, became a leading operation in San Juan County from its headquarters near Verdure. The Kansas and New Mexico Land and Cattle Company acquired Joshua Hudson's and other Blue Mountain holdings to become the largest cattle company in Utah and western Colorado. Owned by two English brothers, Edmond and Harold Carlisle, its extensive operations eventually centered around Monticello. The Pittsburg Cattle Company reached large proportions in the La Sal vicinity before selling out in 1895 to Cunningham and Carpenter, its local managers. Preston Nutter began to run a large outfit in the country north of Moab, while other operators, including the Indian Creek Company, pushed farther south and west toward the forbidding canyonlands. When the last of the big outfits arrived in 1888, most of the grazing lands were fully stocked and John Crosby drove his company's 2,000 Texas longhorns through Co Wash to Elk Ridge, a range first claimed by Mormons two years before.

With the great livestock companies threatening their existence in the country and with the San Juan River frustrating every attempt to establish a farming frontier at Bluff, the local Mormons shifted their emphasis to livestock in the mid 1880s. This move triggered a period of keen competition for grazing control. Utilizing the Bluff Pool (a livestock cooperative), Mormon stockmen vigorously pressed their claims. Scoring first in 1886, they bought a sheep operation that had pushed across the San Juan River to graze in pastures adjacent to Bluff. Two years later Mormons purchased the Elk Mountain Cattle Company longhorns. In 1887 settlers were sent from Bluff to establish Monticello and Verdure and to enter competing claims to water and pasture claimed several years earlier by the L. C. and Carlisle cattle companies. Monticello and Verdure both persisted, precipitating declining fortunes for the cattle companies; in 1911 a group of San Juan Mormons finally bought out the Carlisle successors. The La Sal Land and Livestock Company, a group of Mormon associates, bought out Cunningham and Carpenter in 1914; Scorup and Summerville bought the Indian Creek Company holdings four years later.

While the Mormon-gentile division had lost much of its meaning by the end of this period, a competition that had initially rested upon that distinction culminated with the southeastern Utah ranching magnates being Mormon and Utahn in background rather than belonging to the broader tradition of the American livestock frontier.

The expansion of settlements and the accumulation of livestock on the Colorado Plateau could not indefinitely escape the attention of the territorial Legislative Assembly. Utah's hinterland, so long ignored by both the colonizing church and its representatives in the territorial government, now presented problems that demanded attention. As already noted, white invasion of San Juan Indian lands did not proceed without friction. In addition, many livestock companies were exploiting grazing resources and escaping taxation in the absence of organized local government.

Recognition of these problems led the Mormon Church, as noted, to launch the San Juan Mission and to encourage settlers to move into Castle Valley and elsewhere in eastern Utah. It also led the legislature, in February 1880, to provide the areas in question with county government. Emery County, with its seat at Castle Dale, was carved from Sevier and Sanpete counties and included roughly what has since become Emery, Grand, and Carbon counties. San Juan included "all those portions of the counties of Kane, Iron, and Paiute laying east of the Colorado and Green rivers" and south of Emery County. Uintah County in northeastern Utah comprised part of the Green River portion of the Colorado Plateau. (See map, p. 732.)

Developments in Uinta Valley

The area composing Uintah County had undergone many vicissitudes in its progress toward political identity. In 1852 the territorial legislature created Green River County, covering a vast area of coincident boundaries with the northeast portion of Utah Territory as it was then defined. The county, along with the territory, suffered successive reductions with the enlargement of Colorado (1861), Nebraska (1861), and Wyoming (1868). Adjustment of county lines within Utah brought about the final extinction of Green River County in 1872. Thus the creation of Uintah County reflected a resurgence of interest in an area long ignored by local government.

Stretching 125 miles east and west between the Uinta Mountains on the north and the Colorado Plateau on the south, the Uinta Basin had seen many transients but few white residents since the days of Dominguez and Escalante. In 1852 Stephen B. Rose and George Washington Bean examined the region as a prospective area for Mormon colonization but returned an unfavorable report. A subsequent exploration in 1861 also reported negatively; according to the *Deseret News,* the country was "one vast contiguity of waste, and measurably valueless excepting for nomadic purposes, hunting grounds for Indians, and to hold the world together." With such a report it is less than surprising that President Lincoln, in response to a proposal originating in Utah, declared the Uinta Valley an Indian reservation. (See chapter 19.) Pending ratification of the Indian removal treaty of 1865, Pardon Dodds set up an Indian agency at White Rocks in 1868 where Antoine Robidoux had once maintained his trading post. Notwithstanding the United States Senate's 1869 rejection of the treaty, Ute bands from the Great Basin were pushed onto the reservation at the close of the Black Hawk War and were attached to the Uintah Agency.

As a result of the Meeker Massacre (1879) and the vigorous Indian removal movement that followed it in Colorado, the White

River and Uncompaghre Utes were moved to the Uintah Reservation during the early 1880s. Subjected to the general fortunes of Indian administration, including the application of the Dawes Act in 1895, the Utes saw their holdings steadily diminished. In 1897 the Uintah Forest Reserve was created, taking 1,010,000 reservation acres. Then in 1905 an additional 1,004,285 acres were opened to settlement by land-hungry white Americans. Demand for the available quarter sections exceeded supply by seven to one; soon the vastly reduced reservation was surrounded by white communities.

Beginning of Coal Production

The first production of coal in what was initially Emery County and later Carbon County was an extension of mining across the rim of the Great Basin from Sanpete County. By the mid 1870s digging was underway at Winter Quarters in Pleasant Valley—near where Scofield Reservoir was later impounded. With good markets existing in Utah's population centers, the Pleasant Valley Coal Company was organized in 1876, and within a few years it was the territory's largest producer. But it was not until the Denver and Rio Grande Western Railroad entered Utah in 1883 by way of the Green River that the Union Pacific coal monopoly was really broken. The Utah Fuel Company, a D & RGW subsidiary, pushed annual coal production in Emery County to 300,000 tons by the end of the decade, and by the century's close the Emery-Carbon area, with a million-ton production, had become the coal center of the West.

While cattle barons were invading the grasslands of San Juan County, Emery became a vital factor in the industrial development of the territory. As the city of Price grew, becoming the major population center in the region, its people sought to have the county seat transferred to Price from Castle Dale. Their effort cut across Mormon-gentile lines in addition to confronting the usual resistance to the loss of a county seat, so the more cosmopolitan populations around Price petitioned the territorial assembly for division of the county. The petition was granted and Carbon County was created in 1894.

Gold Seeking on the Colorado

Less significant but more exciting than coal mining were occasional metal mining booms. With gold and silver playing prominent roles in neighboring Colorado and in several parts of the Great Basin, booms frequently spilled over into southeast Utah

383

during the 1880s and 1890s. On the La Sal and the Blue mountains and along the San Juan River prospectors staked claims, talked big, and dreamed. A shifting community of will-o-the-wisp miners came and went and a few die-hards stayed to give such sites as La Sal Mountains Miner's Basin, the Blue Mountain Dream Mine, and Honaker's Trail along the San Juan River lasting impact on local folklore. But little came of strikes in the Four Corners region.

More widespread but scarcely more important were the Colorado River gold rushes. In the 1880s when river recluse and prospector Cass Hite leaked information that there was gold in the gravel banks of the Colorado River, newspapers grabbed the story and soon a minor rush brought hundreds of gold seekers, including aging Jack Summers, who had run the Colorado with Powell in 1869. They explored the length of Glen Canyon, the side canyons, and even the nearby mountains, but they found little gold. A second Hite-promoted boom in the economically-depressed 1890s had a similar outcome.

Before the dream of river gold faded entirely, the Pacific water-level railway scheme raised hopes of a revival. The Denver, Colorado Canyon, and Pacific Railroad did not materialize, but the engineer who headed the canyon survey, Robert Brewster Stanton, saw enough gold to inspire a plan to dredge the river's sand. Money was made available, and the Hoskinini Company was formed in 1898. An experimental dredge, 105 feet long, was hauled to Glen Canyon by wagons and was put into operation in 1901. But the Colorado River's gold was still elusive, and operation was suspended within a year because the extraordinary fineness of the dust made retrieval impossible. The dredge rested on the bottom of the river near Hall's Crossing for half a century, raising its superstructure in lonely witness to yet another unsuccessful effort to find golden treasure in the Colorado. Today the abandoned hulk lies beneath the waters of Lake Powell.

Oil, potash, uranium, gilsonite, and other industrial raw materials were in the Colorado Plateau all along, waiting for the takers, but only uranium and gilsonite were tentatively tapped before statehood.

Conclusion

The history of the Colorado Plateau is very much part of the story of Utah's development in the prestatehood years, but the region responded to the influences of time, nature, and neighboring societies in a way that gave it a character still recognizably its

384

own. Beyond the rim of the Great Basin, it was, except for the Virgin River area, slow to be settled and was in some ways exploited by the more heavily populated portions of Utah and adjoining states—as it has continued to be in more recent times. It was designated as an Indian territory, reflecting the importance of the Utes, Navajos, and Paiutes in its history. Many of the early settlers were not Mormons, and the related issues of church domination and polygamy did not figure as prominently in the political and social relations as in the Mormon country to the west. The exploitive industries of mining and ranching, rather than farming, dominated the early economy of the rugged and scenic Green and Colorado drainage areas, with transportation and tourism destined to play roles of increasing importance in the twentieth century.

Chapter 20
Bibliographical Essay

No single source covers the entire history of the Colorado Plateau, but scattered materials exist that, taken together, present a fair picture of the area's development. The Daughters of the Utah Pioneers county histories are useful for local information and may usually be used with confidence. For the approach of colonists to the area the several editions of Gustive O. Larson, *Outline History of Utah and the Mormons*, and Milton R. Hunter, *Brigham Young the Colonizer*, contain scattered material; with the exception of Utah's Dixie and the Virgin River region their treatment of the Colorado Plateau is incidental and general. A. K. Larson, *"I Was Called to Dixie," Virgin River Basin: Unique Experiences in Mormon Pioneering* (1961), and Angus M. Woodbury, "A History of Southern Utah and Its National Parks," *UHQ*, July-October 1944, provide much information that relates to the Colorado Plateau in the geographic sense, but in terms of timing and theme they are more closely related to Great Basin development.

Colorado Plateau prehistory is treated by Jesse D. Jennings in two articles, "Early Man in Utah" and "The Aboriginal People," *UHQ*, January and July 1960. For Indians of the historical period Floyd A. O'Neil and others, *Ute People: An Historical Study* (1970) is a beginning; O'Neil also provides some coverage for the process by which the Utes were put on the Uintah-Ouray Reservation in his dissertation, "History of the Ute Indians of Utah until 1890" (University of Utah, 1973). The entire issue of *Utah Historical Quarterly*, Spring 1971, is devoted to Indians, with many articles focusing on the Colorado Plateau.

The best general treatment of southeast Utah, C. Gregory Crampton's *Standing Up Country* (1965) is richly illustrated and thoroughly documented; it stresses nineteenth- and early twentieth-century history. Charles S. Peterson, *Southeast Utah and the La Sal National Forest* (1965), devotes considerable attention to settlement, Indian affairs, and livestock beginnings in San Juan and Grand counties but is also concerned with the influence of the La Sal Forest on twentieth-century developments. David E. Miller, *Hole-in-the-Rock: An Epic in the Colonization of the Great American West* (1959, 1966), is an outstanding study of one colonizing venture. Ranching on the Colorado Plateau occupies much of the Summer 1964 *Utah Historical Quarterly*, which is devoted to the state's cattle industry.

The official reports of government explorers, John C. Ives, John N. Macomb, E. G. Beckwith (who reported on the Gunnison explorations), F. V. Hayden, and G. M. Wheeler provide much early detail about Indians and the natural character of the country. Even more important are the Powell Survey publications listed in this chapter. Wallace Stegner, *Beyond the Hundredth Meridian: John Wesley Powell and the Second Opening of the West. . . .* (1954), is an interpretive treatment of Powell's role in Colorado Plateau history and his impact on resource management generally. Powell is also the subject of the Spring 1969 *Utah Historical Quarterly*, which commemorates his hundredth anniversary.

Essential for understanding regional political development is James B. Allen, "The Evolution of County Boundaries in Utah," *UHQ*, July 1955. Two other single-topic issues of *Utah Historical Quarterly* which contain much Colorado Plateau material are on mining, Summer 1963, and on the Colorado River, Summer 1960. See the chapter 24 bibliography for materials on the early settlement of the coal camps in Carbon County.

Chapter 21
The Forty-fifth State

Gustive O. Larson and Richard D. Poll

O nce the polygamy deadlock between Mormons and gentiles was broken by the Woodruff Manifesto of 1890, matters moved steadily toward Utah's admission to the Union. Following what Howard R. Lamar has called "the policy of superior virtue and patriotic conformity," Mormon Church leaders gradually disarmed most of the political opposition in Utah and Washington. Local political organizations disbanded and the Mormons, who still comprised almost ninety percent of the territorial population, found that gentile office-seekers were easier to vote for when they bore national party labels. Both Democrats and Republicans now courted the allegiance of Utah's voters and in the end the Republicans gained the most credit for statehood. When Utah's star was added to the national flag on January 4, 1896, the new state was moving rapidly away from her pioneer beginnings toward the social, economic, and political diversity that would characterize her history in the twentieth century.

Adoption of National Political Parties

As long as the People's Party functioned as the political arm of the Mormon Church, the church-state struggle was certain to continue, with the Liberal Party blocking every approach to membership in the Union. With the "twin relic" out of the way, it became increasingly clear to moderates in both parties that the road out of territorial subordination must be by way of national political affiliations.

In view of their failure to win statehood under Grover Cleveland's first administration, some of the Mormon hierarchy began to respond to Republican overtures even before the manifesto. But the Mormon Democratic tradition presented a problem. As a result of the prolonged Republican campaign to crush polygamy and the political power that protected it, the Mormons were naturally inclined towards the Democratic Party, with its emphasis on home rule and its resistance to extreme legislative measures. Although the Democratic movements in Utah in the 1880s proved abortive, the beginning of a permanent organization took place in 1890 with the campaign against the Cullom-Struble Bill. Although the Democratic Club movement was gentile in origin, it gathered its numerical strength from the Mormons as it evolved into the territorial Democratic Party in the ensuing months. Utah was considered as Democratic country by most observers in the early 1890s.

The Mormon First Presidency, fully cognizant of the Church's political bent, pondered how to move a Democratically oriented territory toward statehood through Republican channels. Both counselors in the presidency, George Q. Cannon and Joseph F. Smith, were ardently Republican; Cannon's political contacts dated back to the 1870s when he had been listed as a Republican delegate in Congress. After James G. Blaine's mid-1890 promise to halt congressional action on Mormon disfranchisement if the church "got into line," Cannon gave this significant report to his colleagues in the church hierarchy:

> Though rabid anti-Mormons are working against the people yet the Republican party are becoming more favorably impressed with the importance of securing Mormon votes and influence, and the leaders feel as though Utah should be admitted as a State in the Union. Even Secretary of State Blaine is desirous of Utah's admission; ... the Democrats might have won several states had they but possessed sufficient courage when Cleveland was President to admit Mormons to political power but they failed to do so and now realize their loss.

Cannon's extensive contacts included related business interests. Outside support for Utah's statehood was sometimes economically motivated, and the response of the debt-ridden church was not unrelated to economic necessity; tithes and other income had declined substantially as a result of the judicial crusade and the escheatment proceedings. James S. Clarkson of Iowa, who had been charged by the national Republican Party to work with the Mormons, effectively helped Mormon agents obtain loans substantial enough to meet current obligations and launch new industrial enterprises. A group of influential California Republicans—including Leland Stanford, Judge Morris M. Estee, and Colonel Isaac

Trumbo—foresaw Mormon aid in developing Utah's economic potential. To this end they hoped to elect Trumbo as one of Utah's first senators, and the hopeful candidate established residence in Salt Lake City's historic Gardo House and labored zealously for Utah's statehood admission.

In the nation's capital the Republicans narrowly controlled the Senate from 1889 to 1893. This advantage was lost with Cleveland's reelection, but was regained when hard times gave Republicans a 44-39 margin in the Fifty-fourth Congress (1895-1897). This struggle for control of the Senate explains the response of key Republicans to Mormon appeals for assistance in securing statehood. Such contacts brought a reminder that Utah, as a Democratic territory, could expect no help toward statehood from the Republicans. "We told them," Joseph F. Smith reported at a later date, "that we might show them more Republicans than they counted on. They replied that if we could make a good showing this way they would try to do something for us." Ironically, the politicians were now urging the church leadership to exercise political influence, the cessation of which had long been demanded as a requirement for statehood.

While the radicals continued the local People's-Liberal struggle, the conservatives of both camps sought political stability through the national party organizations. In response to the growth of the local Democratic clubs, and against bitter opposition from diehard Liberals and the Salt Lake *Tribune,* the Republican Party was launched at a meeting in the Salt Lake Theater on May 20, 1891. Opponents warned that it was a Mormon scheme to divide the non-Mormons for political advantage. Church members countered that the Liberal "ring" was trying to prevent division on national party lines in order to "continue the old antagonisms" and win control of the territory.

Although the Mormon leaders supported the shift from local to national parties, they approached the move fully aware that the Democratic strength among their membership might well work at cross purposes with what most of them perceived to be the best interests of church and territory. Apostle Abraham H. Cannon wrote in his journal on June 9: "The danger of our people all becoming Democrats . . . is feared, and the results of such a course would doubtless prove disastrous to us." He continued, "It is felt that efforts should be made to instruct our people in Republicanism and thus win them to that party."

A turning point in the affairs of Utah came with the dissolution of the People's Party on June 10, 1891. Ecclesiastical participation in the action and the political realignment that followed is reflected in Cannon's account of a meeting of some of the Mormon apostles and People's Party leaders:

Joseph F. Smith, Father, and Wilford Woodruff each spoke to the brethren and while they desired the Saints to join the different organizations, they did not want them to go en masse to either party. If we can divide about evenly between the parties, leaving an uncertain element to be converted to either side, it is thought best results will follow.

To counterbalance the anticipated Democratic strength, the meeting adopted a policy "that men in high authority who believed in Republican principles would go out among the people, but that those in high authority who could not endorse the principles of Republicanism should remain silent." Apostle John Henry Smith pursued the proselyting task with vigor. Apostle Moses Thatcher, who objected, identified actively with the Democratic cause, and the strained relationship with some of his colleagues contributed a few years later to his expulsion from the Quorum of the Twelve.

The folding of the People's Party did not escape attention in Washington, where both Democrats and Republicans followed developments aimed at strengthening their position in Congress. In fact, President Cleveland had already optimistically dispatched a telegram of "Congratulations to the Democracy of this Territory on their organization." In July both parties held nominating conventions for the territorial legislature; the Liberal Party, resisting pressures from both sides to dissolve, added a third list of candidates. In the August election the Democrats cast 14,147 votes; the Republicans cast 6,339; and the Liberals, who captured Salt Lake County, cast 7,404. Twenty-four Democrats and twelve Liberals were elected.

The adoption of the national two-party system in Utah resulted in considerable scrambling of Mormon and gentile forces. Religious differences yielded to new political alignment that often pitted church leaders against each other and found former opponents side by side on important issues. While the Mormon Church presidency, sustained by most of the Quorum of the Twelve, was covertly promoting Republicanism, the strength of the Democratic Party received the support of churchmen like Apostles Thatcher and Heber J. Grant, Bishop John R. Winder, Franklin S. Richards, William H. King, Brigham H. Roberts, Charles W. Penrose, and James Henry Moyle. In the first truly national political election in Utah, November 1892, the Democrats managed to carry the territory along with the Cleveland tide. Ex-Mormon Joseph L.

The same forty-five-star flag that decorated the Salt Lake Tabernacle for the state-hood celebration in January 1896 decorated the Salt Lake Temple when the pioneer semicentennial was observed a year later. (The incorrect location of the field of stars does not hint at lingering church-state tension; the ZCMI overall factory finished the flag on one side only, with the requirements of the Tabernacle display in mind.)

Rawlins, advisedly chosen to replace Mormon John T. Caine as candidate for delegate to Congress, defeated Republican Frank J. Cannon by 15,201 to 12,390 votes. Liberal Clarence E. Allen trailed with 6,986. With Cleveland's return to the White House came the appointment of Caleb W. West as governor.

Presidential Amnesty

Having formally quit the practice of polygamy and having disbanded the People's Party, the Mormons next sought pardon for all who were still liable to penalties under the federal anti-polygamy laws. On December 21, 1891, the church leaders submitted a petition for amnesty to President Benjamin Harrison; the appeal was endorsed by Governor Arthur L. Thomas and Chief Justice Zane. The president, unwilling to risk alienating voters in the states, procrastinated. But when Harrison failed to win reelection, Republican leaders pressed him to vindicate their party promises to the Mormons before his term expired. Mindful of the political significance of Utah's ultimate admission to the Union, Harrison granted amnesty and pardon on January 4, 1893, "to all persons liable . . . by reason of unlawful cohabitation . . . who since November 1, 1890, have abstained from unlawful cohabitation." The Utah Commission followed suit when it ruled in July that "amnestied polygamists be allowed to vote." Grover Cleveland continued the restoration process a year later by granting pardon and restoring civil rights to all persons who were disfranchised except those who had not complied with Harrison's earlier proclamation.

Moves Toward Statehood

After four decades of increasingly comprehensive control of the territorial government, it is not surprising that a proposal for home rule as a temporary substitute for delayed statehood gained support in Utah. The proposal to abolish the Utah Commission and replace the federally appointed governor and judges with elected officials failed in Congress, but the commission was stripped of its "carpetbags" feature on March 3, 1893, when a new law specified that its members must be residents of Utah.

Statehood now appearing to be merely a matter of time, Utah began to find more friends in Washington in both parties. Before his long service in Congress ended, John T. Caine introduced a bill on January 14, 1893, for a statehood enabling act. Although viewed favorably by many congressmen, it was lost in the closing rush of the Fifty-second Congress; but it became the pattern for a later bill introduced with better results by Caine's successor.

Delegate Rawlins introduced two bills in Congress in September 1893—one for statehood and the other for restoration of the church property seized by the government under provisions of the Edmunds-Tucker Law. Congress acted quickly on the latter, and personal securities in the amount of $400,000 were returned to the church's First Presidency the following January. The return of real property was delayed until statehood was granted; according to Leonard J. Arrington the returned assets comprised a "far different list from that originally possessed by the Receiver."

While action on the statehood bill was pending, Governor West urged its passage in his October 1893 annual report. Referring to "delicate and grave questions" and "radical differences" of the past that had now been peacefully resolved by the people, he expressed confidence that the "salutary lessons inculcated in the school of actual experience have admirably trained and fitted them for the duties and responsibilities of state government."

The election of territorial legislators in November 1893 revealed a significant trend in relative party strengths as the Republicans won fourteen seats, the Democrats won thirteen, and the Liberals won eight. Liberals who had resisted the shift away from local to national issues now realized the futility of continuing the anti-Mormon fight against statehood. On the advice of former Governor Thomas and *Tribune* editor and publisher C. C. Goodwin, the Liberals followed the People's Party into dissolution in December, leaving Utah for the first time politically organized solely on the American two-party system. Members of the disbanded party moved almost as a body into the Republican ranks. Here they discovered themselves beside increasing numbers of prominent Mormons who, representing the Saints' new economic directions, found the protective tariff to their liking.

The Rawlins Statehood Bill passed the House of Representatives on December 13, 1893, with only five opposing votes. With both Democrats and Republicans favorable and the local press now united in support of Utah's admission, its passage was assured. The bill emerged from Congress the following July as Utah's Enabling Act. Signed by President Cleveland on July 16, 1894, it provided for election of delegates to a constitutional convention to be held the following March.

Utah's Constitutional Convention

The economic depression of the 1890s weakened the national Democratic position, and in Utah the party suffered from a split Democratic-Populist vote on the silver issue in the November 1894 election. With added strength from former Liberals, from the Mormon business community, and from church influence filtering down through ecclesiastical channels, the Republicans won the territorial election. They elected not only Frank J. Cannon as delegate to Congress, but they also elected fifty-nine of the one hundred and seven delegates to the forthcoming constitutional convention.

The convention, which was presided over by Republican John Henry Smith and which included twenty-eight non-Mormons, met from March 4 to May 8, 1895. Its product was a constitution patterned generally after those of other American states, with the addition of certain special guarantees. As required by the Enabling

Act, an ordinance irrevocable without the consent of the United States government and the people of Utah declared:

That perfect toleration of religious sentiment shall be secured, and that no inhabitant of said state shall ever be molested in person or property on account of his or her mode of religious worship. Provided that polygamous or plural marriages are forever prohibited.

An important clause submitted by Charles S. Varian defined the antipolygamy proviso as covering only polygamous *marrying,* and this was the pattern of law enforcement after Utah became a state.

The hottest controversy in the convention involved woman suffrage. This was somewhat surprising in view of the prosuffrage pledges in both Democratic and Republican state party platforms and the record of female voting in the territory from 1870 to 1887. A mixed gentile-Mormon minority, for whom the oratorically gifted B. H. Roberts was the chief spokesman, fought the inclusion of a suffrage article on grounds of both moral principle and political expediency. The convention voted down a proposal to have this article voted on separately in the ratifying election, and when the constitution went into effect Utah joined Wyoming and Colorado in the slowly growing band of states who entrusted the ballot to women.

The completed document was presented to the people for ratification on November 5, 1895, when the voters also chose the first officials for the prospective new state. The most exciting feature of the campaign was the LDS First Presidency's conference criticism of two members of the hierarchy for campaigning for public office without clearance from the top ecclesiastical authority. Roberts carried the Democratic nomination for congressman and Moses Thatcher accepted the offer of a seat in the Senate if his party should win the state legislature. Despite this revival of the church-state issue, the Republicans disappointed Cleveland and a Democratic Congress by winning every statewide race and a commanding majority of seats in the new Utah State Senate and House of Representatives. Heber M. Wells, a Mormon, was elected governor and Clarence E. Allen, the non-Mormon who had carried the Liberal banner in territorial delegate contests, won the congressional seat. The legislature shortly elected retiring delegate Frank J. Cannon and a gentile attorney, Arthur Brown, as the state's first United States Senators.

The constitution was overwhelmingly approved by a vote of 31,305 to 7,687. Two members of the Utah Commission were delegated to deliver an engrossed copy to President Cleveland, and

Governor West and Senator Cannon joined them in Washington for the presentation on December 16. Unwilling to ascribe entire credit to the Republicans for the "Americanizing" of Utah, the president commented on his two-term effort "to bring about a change in the conditions that have existed in the Territory" and added, "in congratulating you all I have some excuse, I think, for self-congratulation." His disappointment at not being able to welcome a Democratic Utah may also have been responsible for his signing the statehood proclamation in his private office at 10 a.m. on January 4, 1896, while another Utah delegation waited in an adjoining room of the White House.

Inauguration Activities

If the depression- and winter-ridden nation was calm, the new state was not. It was Saturday, and impromptu parades, patriotic meetings, and general hilarity prevailed. "The Forty-fifth Star Shines Resplendent" headlined the Salt Lake *Tribune,* while the *Deseret News* simply affirmed, "Utah A State." Committees under the general direction of the three-state party chairmen put finishing touches on plans for Monday's formal inaugural activities. Henry Dixey's performance in *The Lottery of Love* drew only a fair crowd to the Salt Lake Theater, but after the performance a small fire on the roof of the venerable structure finished off the day with a touch of excitement.

Sunday's quiet in the capital city was punctuated by scores of sermons that rejoiced in the opportunities of a new year and a new era. State legislators and other prominent people from around the state gathered at the Cullen, Walker, Templeton, Knutsford, and Grand Pacific hotels. Five Seventh-Day Adventists were baptized in the sanitarium sulphur pool, and four Mormon ladies returning from a funeral were injured when their hack ran away on North Temple Street. During the evening a streetcar conductor named Brigham W. Young was waylaid, knocked unconscious, and robbed while walking to report that his car was stalled. According to the *Tribune,* "No arrests were made for violating the Sunday liquor law, and as the officers were on the outlook for offenders, it is presumed the saloon men were all good boys. . . ."

Inauguration Day, January 6, dawned cold and clear to the tooting of whistles, the tolling of bells, and the clanging of trolleys carrying participants and spectators to the first main event: the parade. Robert T. Burton, who thirty-eight years before had led cavalry of the Nauvoo Legion against Johnston's Army, was the parade marshal, and the Sixteenth United States Infantry troops and band from Fort Douglas marched amicably behind Burton in the long procession. Behind the state officials in their horse-drawn vehicles came, among others, Utah National Guard units, Held's Band, the veterans of the Grand Army of the Republic, firemen in black helmets and red shirts pulling an old-fashioned hand pumper, Knights of Pythias, Masons, Odd Fellows, the Ancient Order of United Workers, Scandinavian societies, members of the German *Turn Verein* performing on parallel bars on a float, and lastly "citizens on foot, horseback, and in carriages."

Estimates placed the throng in and around the Tabernacle at 15,000 when Acting Territorial Governor Charles C. Richards called the inaugural exercises to order shortly after noon. The vast Tabernacle ceiling was adorned with a 132-foot by 78-foot American flag made by the ZCMI overall factory. Through the cutout shape of the forty-fifth star, five "thirty-two candlepower" electric lights beamed down. Between the great pipes of the organ had been constructed an American eagle, and below it were the dates "1847-1896" and the word "Utah"—a spectacle that was termed "a magnificent electrical creation." A chorus of a thousand children, each with a small flag, was prepared to express patriotic sentiments in the national anthem, "America," and a number specially written for the occasion by choir director Evan Stephens, "Utah, We Love Thee."

Because of the ill health of eighty-nine-year-old Wilford Woodruff, his invocation was read by George Q. Cannon. Woodruff later confided to his journal: "I feel to thank God that I have lived to see Utah admitted into the family of states. It is an event that we have looked forward to for a generation." Joseph L. Rawlins read the statehood proclamation; then, as National Guard artillery boomed a forty-five round salute from the capitol site a mile to the north, retiring Chief Justice Zane administered the oath of office to the state officials. The inaugural address of handsome thirty-six-year-old Governor Wells combined the conventional felicitations with an extensive review of Utah's long struggle for statehood. A survey of economic resources and potential, appeals for silver legislation and for a railroad from Salt Lake City to Los Angeles, and a word of congratulation to the enfranchised ladies brought him to his peroration: "In the great firmament of nations, the United States is the constellation most beautiful, most sublime. Down the stream of time, through all ages and ages, may Utah be one of the brightest stars in that glorious constellation."

With the benediction offered by the Reverend T. C. Iliff, the crowd scattered to its holiday diversions while the members of the legislature made their way to the year-old City and County Building for a brief special session. While parties and programs were held in many communities, Salt Lake City, whose center was within a day's carriage drive for half of the state's population and within an hour's train ride for most of that half, was the social mecca. Theatricals at the Grand Opera House and the Lyceum drew capacity crowds. The dressing rooms at the Salt Lake Theater, however, were dark: the orchestra seats were covered with a spring floor and tickets were fifty and seventy-five cents to watch and one dollar to dance at the Inaugural Ball. Guests of honor were admitted free.

"Nothing ever attempted in Utah in the way of electric displays has approached this superb illuminative triumph," was the *Deseret News* judgment of the multicolored moving and flashing rendition of "Utah" that adorned the proscenium arch, beneath which a twenty-piece band performed a promenade concert while celebrities and ordinary citizens filled the theater's galleries and loges. At 9:30 p.m. Governor Wells escorted his mother to the gubernatorial box and then, his wife on his arm, led the gala assembly in the inaugural grand march. A varied program of lancers, waltzes, quadrilles, two-steps, a minuet, a schottische, a varsouvienne, a polka, and something called a Wentworth followed. But also on this same Monday evening a man was run over by a horse-drawn sleigh in Murray; the two occupants of the vehicle were arrested for drunken driving. As the *Deseret News* said: "Inaugural Day has been celebrated as no other in the history of Utah."

The State of the State

When she joined the Union Utah was already more populous than five of her sister states. Of her people, eight out of ten were American-born and nearly nine out of ten were Latter-day Saints. (See Tables F and G, pp. 690–691.) Apart from approximately 3,000 Indians, mostly located on reservations, the 571 Negroes and 768 Chinese counted in the 1895 territorial census were the largest racial minorities. Perhaps 2,000 polygamous families remained, but a considerable number of single men in the mining communities produced a small male preponderance in the total population of 247,324.

A minority of Utah's citizens lived in cities, although the inaugural festivities demonstrated that the capital's 50,000 residents enjoyed many of the amenities of urban life. Further evidence of progress were a maze of power and telephone lines in the downtown area, a university and eight academies, a limited distribution of natural and manufactured gas, sixty-eight miles of street railway, three daily newspapers, three theaters and two businessmen's clubs, a just-finished gravity sewage system with seven miles of mains, and a three-year-old fun spot, Saltair, perched on a foundation in the Great Salt Lake.

Twenty-seven years as a railroad center had brought Ogden 15,000 inhabitants, ten miles of street railway, two academies, one of the first hydroelectric projects in the United States (nearing completion), and some of the most eventful Saturday nights to be found outside the mining towns. Provo, with only 400 students in its Brigham Young Academy, was a quiet county seat with 6,000 people; its street railway was only six miles long, but it was steam powered. Logan, with 5,000 inhabitants, was beginning to orient its life around its eight-year-old land-grant college. As for the rest, the towns of Utah were either unpaved and unexciting farming centers or unpaved and uninhibited mining camps.

Agriculture and Mining

Farming and mining were the main businesses of the new state, and neither was prospering as 1896 began. The thirty-year decline in prices that brought populism to the farm belt had one more year to go, and the panic of 1893 had added mining distress to agricultural depression. Property values aggregated approximately one hundred million dollars in the state, but if absentee-owned railroads and mines were deducted, the accumulation of a half-century's effort averaged out at less than three hundred dollars per capita, and at least half of that was real estate.

Approximately one-third of Utah's employed population was engaged in agriculture. (See Table Q, p. 714.) All but 2,232 of the 19,916 farms were declared by Governor Wells to be free from encumbrances, but few mortgages were lifted during the winter of 1895-96 with wheat forty-six cents, corn fifty-eight cents, potatoes thirty-two cents, and apples forty cents per bushel; sugar beets and lucerne about four dollars per ton; wool seven-and-a-half cents per pound; and sheep one-and-a-half dollars per head. The New Year edition of the *Tribune* estimated that the value of all farm crops had declined by almost one-third between 1890 and 1894, and there had been little recovery since. These facts bear significantly on Utah's enthusiasm for William Jennings Bryan in the 1896 presidential election.

Reminiscent of the pioneer quest for self-sufficiency are 40,000 pounds of cotton and almost 3,000 gallons of wine produced in the Virgin River country in 1895 and 10,000 pounds of silk cocoons reported a year later. Recalling another dream that failed in the 1850s but that was now becoming a reality under Mormon Church sponsorship were the 40,000 tons of sugar beets processed by the Utah Sugar Company in the year prior to statehood. Although dry farming had begun in the 1870s, eighty-nine percent of the 467,162 cultivated acres (1894) was irrigated by methods largely developed in the founding generation. And although the Mormon Church was moving toward the abolition of tithing in kind, some produce still moved into the market through tithing offices and through script-using cooperatives like the cotton factory at Washington and the Provo Woolen Mills. Mormon Utah's bumper crop was children, and the declining support capability of agriculture was beginning to produce that export of young manpower that would characterize the first four decades of the twentieth century.

The condition of mining in Utah can be inferred from Governor Wells' appeal for silver legislation and the endorsement of bimetallism by both Republican and Democratic platforms in the pre-statehood election. At approximately sixty-five cents per ounce, Utah's mines had produced only $4,854,300 in silver in 1895, and that was produced largely from a few spectacular enterprises like the Centennial-Eureka and Bullion-Beck mines in the Tintic District and the Silver King Mine and almost-exhausted Ontario Mine at Park City. The total value of nonferrous metal production for the year was $8,464,500, down almost four million dollars from 1890. Gold discoveries in the Oquirrh Mountains Camp Floyd District and the resulting rush that led boomers to speak of a "New Johannesburg" when they incorporated Mercur two weeks before Inauguration Day did not disguise the fact that many mines were closed in 1895 and 1896 and that extensive unemployment was avoided largely because of the tendency for miners to move on when jobs disappeared.

The mining project with the greatest long-run potential was at Bingham. While the operating mines were still concentrating largely on the precious metals and the townspeople were rebuilding from a series of disastrous fires, Colonel Enos A. Wall and Samuel Newhouse were piecing together the claims that would become the foundation for Utah's greatest single productive enterprise, the Bingham copper mine. Except for coal, salt, and a very limited production of gilsonite, sulphur, and building materials, the other nonmetallic minerals that would eventually justify Lincoln's description of Utah as "the nation's treasure house" were either undiscovered or unappreciated.

Transportation and Manufacturing

The railroad network in January 1896 was substantially what it had become in 1880 with the completion of the Utah Southern Railroad extension to Milford, Frisco, and the Horn Silver Mine. The Union Pacific now owned 543, the Denver and Rio Grande Western owned 485, and the Central Pacific owned 157 of Utah's 1,225 miles of standard-gauge road; 150 miles of narrow-gauge track wound into the mines. Local stage lines still served parts of the state, and a gun battle between a sheriff's posse and two young horse thieves in City Creek Canyon in August 1895 was additional evidence that the frontier era had not yet fully passed. Telephone poles had started sprouting in 1879, and communities from Logan to Eureka were linked together by the Rocky Mountain Bell Telephone Company; there were still no rural phones. Western Union Telegraph Company, which joined Utah with the two coasts, purchased the Deseret Telegraph Company, the locally built enterprise that had spread the warning through southern Utah when the United States marshals were coming during the days of the underground. Salt Lake City had already enjoyed house-to-house mail delivery for a decade.

Hard times accelerated certain profoundly significant changes in the quality and direction of Utah's business activity. Like agriculture during the territorial period, industry, with the exception of mining and transcontinental transportation, had been largely in Mormon hands and had been devoted to regional self-sufficiency. The larger cooperative projects like iron, sugar, and cotton had fallen short of expectations, and most of the local manufacturing was in shops employing only a few hands. The 880 industrial concerns reported in 1894 had an average capital investment of about $6,000, a product value averaging approximately $8,000, and a total employment of 5,054 people; the Provo Woolen Mills, with 150 employees, was the largest remaining example of pioneer industry.

Unlike agriculture, industry reflected the revolution in economic policy taking place in the Mormon Church as it came to terms with late nineteenth-century American capitalism. The concern for the material development of the region remained, but the isolationist goals and communitarian methods largely disappeared. Numbers of existing Mormon Church concerns, like the Salt Lake Street Railroad Company, Salt Lake City Gas Company, and Provo Woolen Mills, were sold or secularized. The new church-supported projects recruited outside funds and functioned in conventional, even conservative, business fashion. The Utah Sugar and

400

Inland Crystal Salt companies, the hydroelectric development on the Weber River, the electric and gas utilities in northern Utah, and the Saltair Resort and the railroad serving it were all products of this expedient reinterpretation of the strictures against mingling Zion and Babylon.

Merchandising and the Consumer

At the counters and in the counting houses of Salt Lake and Ogden some of the earliest overtures toward Mormon-gentile peace had been made, and by 1896 the chambers of commerce and the forty Utah banks had replaced the Schools of the Prophets and Zion's Board of Trade as centers of business planning. Like the factories, most commercial establishments were small; the 1,974 stores reported in 1894 employed 5,023 people and had an average capital investment of over $7,000 and average sales of $17,000. Many Mormon-owned stores throughout the state still called themselves co-ops and did much of their purchasing through ZCMI wholesale, but the secularizing process already referred to in industry was also taking place in trade. The reincorporation of Zion's Cooperative Mercantile Institution as a million-dollar corporation on September 30, 1895, is a notable example. In 1891 it had discontinued tithing its earnings and had opened stock ownership to non-Mormons, and the new company functioned substantially as did its gentile competitors in the merchandise field.

How business functioned and how Utahns lived in the 1890s can be discovered from advertisements in the daily and weekly newspapers. They reveal a variety of goods and services now long forgotten and a level of prices almost beyond belief. *Vin Mariani, Cupidene,* and *Indapo, the Great Hindoo Remedy* were popular patent medicines. For those who preferred to see a medical practitioner, one doctor promised: "All classes of fits cured. Tapeworm removed with head or no pay." A dentist daily advertised: "Good set of teeth—$5.00. Better set—$8.00. Best set, no better made no matter what you pay—$10.00." Auerbach's was clearing ladies' tailormade suits at $3.85, footwarmers at fifty cents a pair, children's shoes at $1.00 a pair, and ostrich feather boas from $1.75 to $10.00. The corner grocers usually relied on handbills rather than on newspapers to call attention to their ten-cent beefsteak, fifteen-cent butter, and assorted penny candy. It should be remembered, however, that in 1896 two dollars was a good day's wages.

Educational and Social Services

Unlike their parents, Utah children could now go to school without tuition. Almost ninety percent of the 74,551 school-age children attended school at some time in 1895, and the pattern of available education was changing rapidly. The non-Mormon denominational elementary and secondary schools were now suspending operations, leaving only a handful of secondary schools and colleges to carry on in the twentieth century. The Mormon academies were, on the other hand, expanding in secondary education and in the normal course training of teachers, fields in which they matched public school enrollment until the first World War. The big growth, however, was in public elementary schools, where nearly 60,000 children were enrolled and almost 35,000 were in average daily attendance.

Most aspirants for university degrees and professional training still left Utah, but in Salt Lake City, Logan, and Provo institutions of higher education were taking shape. The University of Utah was still largely concerned with secondary and normal courses and adult education, and it had not yet begun to move to Fort Douglas. Five hundred students were in attendance, nine baccalaureate degrees had been awarded at the 1895 graduation exercises, and President James E. Talmage was trying to build a university on an annual appropriation of $35,000.

The faculty and 400 students of the Agricultural College of Utah at Logan might have complained at their $22,000 appropriation in 1896 if they had not also received a federal grant of $25,000. This raised their total budget from the level of Ogden's Reform School and Salt Lake's School for Deaf, Dumb, and Blind to a near-par with the Insane Asylum in Provo, whose $50,000 appropriation the first statehood year was the largest granted to any public institution. The asylum augmented its income by boarding "idiots and morons" at four dollars per week. Governor Wells' first message to the legislature, incidentally, raised the possibility of closing Ogden's Reform School since recent experience had shown that only one out of four of its inmates was rehabilitated. Instead the institution was relocated and named the State Industrial School a year later; the School for the Deaf, Dumb, and Blind was moved from Salt Lake City into the abandoned quarters in Ogden.

If the churches were abandoning some of their economic and political activities and transferring many of their educational functions to the state, they were by no means inactive. Most of the major Christian communions were represented in the church notices in the Salt Lake City papers, and St. Mark's and Holy Cross hospitals were already important examples of the testimony of the deed. Mormon-watching was still a mission of some of the gentile ministry; that fact had been apparent in the recent election and would become even more conspicuous when B. H. Roberts finally won a congressional election two years later. But the effort to rescue the Mormons from their religious delusions had lost its thrust, and the new policy of peaceful coexistence was symbolized by the prayers that opened and closed the inauguration ceremonies.

The Transformation of Mormonism

For the Mormon Church the traumatic consequences of the 1880s were more apparent than were the new interests and emphases that would prevail in the new century. Charges that the Mormon hierarchy still controlled politics and that plural marriage had not really been abandoned had to be denied frequently, and the effort to define and enforce policy in these matters produced some stresses within both the leadership and laiety. Efforts to carry on missionary, temple-building, educational, and business-promotion activities in the face of depression-shrunk tithes and rising debts contributed to an institutional cautiousness in financial matters that persisted through two generations. Twenty-five of the thirty-seven Mormon stakes were in Utah; the forty-eight wards in Salt Lake Valley were all in the Salt Lake Stake, which Angus M. Cannon had presided over for twenty years. Plans for observing the semicentennial of the pioneers' arrival included the construction of a monument to Brigham Young. The unveiling of the monument would be a highlight of the 1897 celebration and, in a symbolic way, an affirmation that the era of pioneer Mormonism— the dominant force in territorial Utah—was at an end.

Chapter 21
Bibliographical Essay

The general works by Whitney, Anderson, and Roberts listed in connection with chapters 9, 13, and 14 also deal with the closing phases of the statehood struggle. Gustive O. Larson's The "Americanization" of Utah for Statehood (1971) concentrates on the politics involved, and Leonard J. Arrington's Great Basin Kingdom (1958) interprets the economic and social changes that took place in the same period. Volumes by Dwyer, Baskin and Cannon, and O'Higgins are relevant.

Two thoughtful and provocative interpretations of the long political controversy are Howard R. Lamar, "Statehood for Utah: A Different Path," UHQ, Fall 1971, and S. George Ellsworth's 1963 Statehood Day Address, "Utah's Struggle for Statehood," UHQ,

Winter 1963. Particular facets of the accommodations of the 1890s are detailed in G. Homer Durham, "The Development of Political Parties in Utah," *Western Humanities Review,* April 1947; E. Leo Lyman, "Isaac Trumbo and the Politics of Utah Statehood," *UHQ,* Spring 1973; and Jean Bickmore White, "The Making of the Convention President: The Political Education of John Henry Smith," *UHQ,* Fall 1971.

Other articles that throw light on the 1895 convention include Stanley S. Ivins, "A Constitution for Utah," *UHQ,* April 1957, and Jean B. White, "Woman's Place Is in the Constitution: The Struggle for Equal Rights in Utah in 1895," *UHQ,* Fall 1974. See also Joan Ray Harlow, "Joseph L. Rawlins, Father of Utah Statehood," *UHQ,* Winter 1976.

The descriptive portion of this chapter draws heavily on the author's 1964 Statehood Day Address: Richard D. Poll, "A State is Born," *UHQ,* Winter 1964. If accessible, the contemporary files of the *Salt Lake Tribune* and *Deseret News* are invaluable for all facets of Utah life; the thirty-two-page issue of the *Tribune,* January 1, 1896, is rich in economic and social data. Much information about the social history of nineteenth-century Utah is found in the July 1959 issue of *UHQ,* which was revised and reissued as a paperback, *Valley of the Great Salt Lake* (1963). Noble Warrum, ed., *Utah Since Statehood, Historical and Biographical* (1919), four vols., is uneven in coverage but provides detail on many facets of Utah in 1896. The University of Utah Bureau of Economic and Business Research has produced two helpful data-based studies: *Statistical Review of Utah's Economy* (1960) and "Measures of Economic Changes in Utah, 1847-1947," *Utah Economic and Business Review,* December 1947.

Part III
Twentieth-century Utah
Introduction

Thomas G. Alexander

Perhaps the most important characteristic of twentieth-century Utah has been the decline of ecclesiastical domination of politics, society, and the economy and the rise of a secular life characterized by competition. Where nineteenth-century economic activity was divided between Mormon and gentile enterprises, twentieth-century businesses tend to be controlled by capital drawn from various sources. Three of Utah's governors—Simon Bamberger, George H. Dern, and J. Bracken Lee—have been non-Mormons, and a number of prominent Utah politicians and businessmen have been nominal rather than active Latter-day Saints. The Mormon Church continues to wield power in Utah's political decisions, but that power derives from moral suasion rather than from the threat of church excommunication or ostracism as it did in the nineteenth century. Beyond this, the church shares power with interest groups like the Kennecott Copper Corporation, the Utah Educational Association, the Associated General Contractors, and the American Federation of Labor-Congress of Industrial Organizations.

With the decline in ecclesiastical domination has come integration into the national economic, political, and social framework. A number of Utahns have made their mark nationally in the political, cultural, and economic arena. These include Reed Smoot, George Sutherland, James H. Moyle, George H. Dern, Ezra Taft Benson, and Esther Peterson in politics; Marriner Eccles, George Romney, and David Kennedy in economic life; and Cyrus Dallin, Mahonri M. Young, Avard Fairbanks, and Grant Johannesen in cultural activities.

This integration into the national economy and the willingness to share national concerns has not come without its costs. Cooperative enterprises like the Brigham City United Order were largely unscathed by the depression of the 1870s, but the depression of the 1890s, the distress in mining and agriculture in the 1920s, and above all the depression of the 1930s left Utah's economy and society terribly scarred. Utah's citizenry experienced unemployment nearing one-third in the 1930s and, despite popular mythology to the contrary, the Mormon Church was unable to care for its own under this extreme pressure.

Some advantages have accrued to the state, however, because of this integration. During and after World War II, the state was the beneficiary of inordinately high expenditures for defense installations and defense-related industries. In recent years the state has enjoyed a boom in service-related employment as tourism connected with the winter ski industry and the summer water and mountain resorts have attracted large numbers of people to the state. In addition, the recent energy crisis has made Utah's vast reserves of coal, uranium, and oil extremely valuable assets.

These changes have also brought about the secularization of Utah's culture. Though life centered around the Mormon Church continues to occupy the time of most of the people, secular cultural pursuits have added an increasingly diverse dimension to the state. Such familiar institutions as the Mormon Tabernacle Choir have been joined by the Utah Symphony Orchestra, Ballet West, and a large number of private and public theater companies to enrich the cultural life of the state. These have been supplemented by public and private sports events and activities sponsored by sport organizations, businesses, and educational institutions along the Wasatch Front.

Another aspect of twentieth-century life in Utah has been the increasing urbanization of Utah's population. The Wasatch Front (from Brigham City on the north to Payson on the south) serves as home for the majority of Utah's citizens. Contrary to the image of the state as basically agricultural, Utah is the tenth most urbanized state in the nation, with sentimental rather than actual ties to the agricultural sector and rural values. Problems of urban blight, crime, and pollution have plagued the state's largest cities in recent years, and those problems are far from solved. Beyond this, the burgeoning urban population is in need of additional water supplies that existing facilities seem unable to provide, and urban mass transit facilities are less than adequate.

Another major problem with which Utahns have had to cope in the twentieth century has been the increasing democratization of national society. Until the 1950s prominent hotels such as the Hotel Utah refused service to Blacks, and social and cultural discrimination included bans on swimming in public pools in Ogden. Hispanic-Americans have also been discriminated against—particularly if they came to the state as agricultural workers. Perhaps the most serious racial difficulty has been the relationship with the Native American population. Concentrated in the Uinta Basin and in San Juan County, these citizens have recently begun to assert their rights against the dominant Euro-American society. Indians have had the right to vote in Utah since World War II, and lawsuits currently under consideration are attempting to determine the jurisdiction of reservation authority.

Beyond this, the disadvantaged female majority has recently begun to assert itself in the state. Until recently discrimination in the form of lower pay for equal work and prejudice in hiring, securing loans, and control of property limited women to second-class citizenship. In spite of the rejection of the Equal Rights Amendment, in 1975 the legislature began to repeal male-dominated statutes on a case-by-case basis and began to curb discrimination in the private sector as well.

In practice, Utahns have proved surprisingly resilient in dealing with problems. State history in the twentieth century has displayed an extraordinary combination of the conservative and progressive. While electing conservatives like Reed Smoot, J. Bracken Lee, and Wallace Bennett, the state nevertheless became one of the national leaders in providing protection for women and children in industry and in promoting facilities for public health. These same conservative politicians, joined by moderates like Elbert D. Thomas and Frank E. Moss, have proved extremely resourceful in securing federal funds for the state by providing tariff protection for its businesses and grants for reclamation, resource management, and defense. Though state politics were tinged with McCarthyism, Senator Arthur Watkins served as chairman of the committee that recommended the censure of the opportunistic Wisconsin senator. It is perhaps this willingness to compromise with ideological orthodoxy that has allowed the state to function successfully in recent years and that may allow it to deal with the problems of enormous magnitude which face Utah in the future.

Chapter 22
Political Patterns of
Early Statehood, 1896-1919

Thomas G. Alexander

During the first twenty-three years of statehood Utahns faced many of the problems nationally associated with the Populist and Progressive periods and with the First World War. The process of politically and psychologically identifying with national issues and concerns was complicated, however, by far-reaching local changes. Urban and industrial expansion, the growth of commercial agriculture, and the rising influence of business corporations affected political decisions, and the relationship of the Mormon Church to state and local politics was questioned in a variety of ways. Not until the war years was it clear to all except the most jaundiced observers that Utah's political assimilation into the Union was complete.

Partly because the People's and Liberal parties broke up only a few years before Utah's first statehood election and partly because Mormon leaders continued to work for balance between the two major parties among church members, the elections of the late nineteenth century revealed considerable instability in party development. The injection of Populism and the silver issue compounded that instability by drawing voters into the Populist and Democratic camps who might otherwise have voted Republican. Nevertheless, the Republicans did well in the first election of state officers in 1895, and from 1900-1916 the Republican Party dominated Utah's political scene. Only during the war years did the Democrats gain control.

Launching the State Government

Apart from its provisions guaranteeing that there shall be "no union of Church and State" and that "polygamous or plural marriages are forever prohibited," Utah's first and only constitution contains little evidence of the long, unique, and stressful territorial experience. The provisions granting women suffrage, prohibiting the labor of women and children in underground mines, establishing the eight-hour day in public employment, and mandating industrial health and safety legislation reflect the progressive trend that would soon be strong nationwide. Utah's Declaration of Rights incorporates the federal Bill of Rights and other well-established principles of civil liberty.

The governmental structure provided in 1895 was conventional; it has not since been radically changed. Utah's bicameral legislature consists of a House of Representatives, whose members have two-year terms, and a Senate, whose members are elected for four years. Reapportionment is called for on the basis of a census every five years, and a tug-of-war between the rural counties and the Wasatch Front urban counties continues to be an ongoing phenomenon of Utah politics. Short annual sessions of the legislature are specified; since 1970 the pattern has been a sixty-day general session in odd-numbered years and a twenty-day budget session in even-numbered years.

The constitution originally designated six elective executive officers for the state—a governor, secretary of state, state auditor, state treasurer, attorney general, and superintendent of public instruction. In 1951 an amendment made the educational post appointive by a new elective state board of education. The executive officers serve four-year terms and are eligible for reelection. Pursuant to constitutional authority, over a hundred departments, commissions, and boards have been established to carry on state government business.

The constitution provides for a supreme court, district courts, and courts of specialized local jurisdiction. It also establishes the basic framework for county, city, and town government. Duchesne and Daggett have since been added to the twenty-seven initial counties. (See map, p. 732.) To amend the constitution requires a two-thirds vote of the legislature and a majority vote in a public election; more than fifty changes have been made since 1895. An amendment added during the Progressive era provides for popular initiative and referendum, but these instruments for voter participation in the legislative process have been rarely used in Utah.

The selection of the legislators and executive officers who would implement the new constitution in 1896 was complicated by the presence on the national scene of an important protest movement—the People's Party. Although its national strength was greatest in rural areas, the Populist Party was principally an urban movement in Utah. Its strength was in Salt Lake City and Ogden and in the mining districts of the Wasatch and Oquirrh mountains. Improvement of wages and working conditions, income tax, direct democracy, and especially the issue of the free coinage of silver at sixteen ounces to one with gold were important issues. Henry W. Lawrence, a well-known Salt Lake City businessman and former member of the Godbeite movement, was the Populist nominee for governor.

In spite of Lawrence's candidacy, Republican Heber M. Wells won the election. He polled 20,833 votes to 18,519 for Democrat John T. Caine, the former territorial delegate, and 2,051 for Lawrence. The breakup of the Liberal Party, the depression of the 1890s, and Republican support for the protective tariff appear to have outweighed other considerations. The Republicans captured all the major state offices and Clarence E. Allen, Bingham businessman and former Liberal Party activist, was elected congressman. The election of a Republican-controlled legislature meant that Arthur Brown, a lawyer and ex-Liberal, and territorial delegate and newspaperman Frank J. Cannon were named as Utah's first United States senators. The outcome suggested that during normal times Republicans could expect to emerge as the majority party in Utah.

As noted in chapter 20, considerable controversy developed during the 1895 election campaign because of ecclesiastical pressure put on Brigham H. Roberts and Moses Thatcher, Democratic candidates for the United States House of Representatives and Senate. The upshot was the formal adoption by the April 1896 Mormon Church general conference of a rule binding every leading church officer, before seeking or accepting a political or other secular position, to "apply to the proper authorities and learn from them whether he can, consistently with the obligations already entered into with the church . . . , take upon himself the added duties and labors and responsibilities of the new position." Another reflection of concern about church-state relations was the legislative practice of choosing one Mormon and one non-Mormon as United States senators, a custom that was followed until the Seventeenth Amendment placed the selection of senators in the hands of the voters in 1914.

Important Legislation

On January 6, 1896, following the inauguration ceremonies, the first state legislature addressed the task of turning the words of the

Utah constitution into laws. There being no capitol building, the representatives and senators met in the still-unfinished City and County Building on Washington Square in Salt Lake City. Governor Wells and most of the executives established offices in the former Christian Industrial Home (now the Ambassador Club), a facility built by the federal government in 1888–9 to house destitute polygamous wives and their children.

Even before statehood the pioneer custom of relying on Mormon Church programs and agencies to meet community needs was giving way to the conventional American practice of dealing with local problems through legislative enactment. In 1888 the territorial legislature established a reform school for delinquent children at Ogden and an agricultural college in Logan and had provided means to complete several buildings for the University of Utah. Two years later the basic legislation for a system of free public schools was enacted. To promote economic development, the 1890 legislature provided a bounty on sugar manufactured in the territory and provided a five-year tax exemption for new cement plants. In the early 1890s the legislature created a territorial board of medical examiners and boards to regulate pharmacies and dentistry. Agricultural regulations applied to fruit trees, beekeeping, livestock, and meat. Escape shafts and adequate timbering were made mandatory in coal mines, lien laws protected workmen and subcontractors, and eight hours became a statutory day's labor on public works.

The first session of the state legislature dealt with some similar problems as well as with the purely mechanical aspects of setting state government in operation. To assume the additional burden of territorial debts and salaries formerly paid by the federal government, Governor Wells recommended a combination of taxation and borrowing, which the legislature adopted. The state assumed control of the penitentiary in Sugar House, the mental hospital at Provo, and the Ogden reform school. The state also assumed operation of the Agricultural College of Utah at Logan and the University of Utah (then occupying buildings near the present site of West High School but later moving to a new campus on the Fort Douglas military reservation). Election laws were modified to replace the party ballot with the Australian ballot, and a commission was set up to codify territorial laws for the state.

Prior to the code commission activities the 1896 legislature passed a number of bills incorporating territorial legislation into state statutes. The bills included a number of regulatory measures, and attention was also given to implementing the economic and

412

Mercur celebrates Independence Day in 1901, shortly before a fire devastated much of the town.

social reforms that the convention had written into the constitution. Wells urged the lawmakers to consider railroad regulation, an eight-hour workday law, sanitary inspection of mines and company towns, a state board of arbitration, and the prohibition of blacklisting by employers. Business opposition defeated the railroad regulation bill. But despite opposition the legislature passed a bill limiting the hours of work to eight in mines and smelters and prohibiting the employment of boys under fourteen and girls and women of any age in such operations. On appeal after a Bingham businessman refused to obey the law, the United States Supreme Court upheld the Utah statute as a valid exercise of the state's police power over dangerous work; the decision, *Holden v. Hardy* (159 *U.S.* 366), became a landmark in the history of progressive legislation.

The legislature also created a state board for the voluntary arbitration of labor disputes, and it prohibited blacklisting. Though the arbitration provisions were strengthened in 1898 and 1901, the act was not effective in such bitter disputes as the 1903 Carbon

County coal strike and the 1912 Bingham Canyon strike. There is considerable evidence, however, that in minor disputes the board worked successfully.

Parties and Politics

National events and a shift in the public temper changed the complexion of Utah politics as the 1896 elections approached. Utah's delegation to the Republican National Convention was pledged to work for the free coinage of silver, and when that effort failed Senator Cannon and other westerners bolted the party and organized the Independent or Silver Republican Party, which supported the nomination of Democrat William Jennings Bryan. The Republican State Committee refused to go along with this, and it supported William McKinley. Further confusion resulted from the partial fusion of both the Populists and the Silver Republicans with the two major parties. Populists and Democrats offered a unified slate for the state legislature. The Silver Republicans and Regular Republicans also nominated a single slate, and they supported Lafayette Holbrook, the Silver Republican candidate for Congress. The Populists, unwilling to support Democratic congressional candidate William H. King, nominated newspaperman Warren Foster. The Silver Republicans, Populists, and Democrats offered a single list of three presidential electors, and Governor Wells supported Bryan. Bryan won a smashing victory in Utah, garnering more than eighty percent of the popular vote. King, a former federal judge and son-in-law of Mormon Apostle Francis M. Lyman, obtained sixty-three percent. The Democrats won control of both houses of the legislature.

In spite of their attacks on the trusts and their platform demands for progressive legislation, during the two terms in which the Democrats controlled the legislature (1897 and 1899) their record on the passage of regulatory legislation was quite modest. One bill passed was an important measure introduced by Utah's woman state senator, Martha Hughes Cannon, to establish a state board of health designed to improve sanitary conditions, regulate water supplies, and control disease. Other legislation included regulations for fishing, hunting, water rights, and mineral lands and a law to protect the spruce tree.

The Democratic victory in 1896, accomplished because of national Republican Party refusal to take the needs of the West into consideration, masked underlying weakness and disunity in the Utah party. Unable in caucus to agree on a senatorial candidate, the legislature required fifty-three ballots to elect former territorial

414

delegate Joseph L. Rawlins. The Democratic penchant for attracting trouble surfaced again in the 1898 election. Although Brigham H. Roberts defeated both Republican Alma Eldredge and Populist Foster, the House of Representatives refused to seat him after news of his polygamous marriages reached Washington.

After the legislature convened in 1899, party divisions were such that no senator could be elected. Support for Frank Cannon, William King, Salt Lake City businessman Alfred W. McCune, and former federal judge Orlando W. Powers produced a deadlock, and Utah was represented by only one senator for the next two years. A special election in 1900 chose King over Republican Secretary of State James T. Hammond to serve the remainder of Roberts's congressional term.

The 1900 special election was the last major election that the Democrats won until 1916. Prosperity had returned by 1900 and the Republican administrations in Washington and in Utah were able to claim responsibility; the Republicans renominated Heber Wells for governor and chose George Sutherland for Congress. The platform opposed monopolies, called for the coinage of both gold and silver, supported the protective tariff, and pointed to the return of good times. The Democrats chose James H. Moyle, a prominent attorney, as candidate for governor and renominated King for Congress. Wells and Sutherland won, McKinley beat Bryan, and the Republicans recaptured both branches of the state legislature. Thomas F. Kearns, a prominent mining magnate, was elected senator after twenty-two ballots.

Republican Ascendancy

From 1900 to 1916 the Republican Party controlled the politics of Utah, paralleling until 1910 its control of national elections. The return of prosperity, the popularity of Presidents Roosevelt and Taft, and the party's moderate-progressive stance on most local issues contributed to the Republican success in the state. In addition, the Democratic Party suffered from continuing internal problems. For a time it appeared that former Republican Senator Cannon might emerge as a leader of the Democrats, but in 1905 he committed political suicide by joining forces with Senator Kearns to denounce Joseph F. Smith, Apostle Reed Smoot, and the Mormon Church and began working for the anti-Mormon American Party. Former Apostle Moses Thatcher's fall from grace had earlier eliminated him from consideration, and Roberts, a charismatic leader, confined his politics to stump speaking for Democratic candidates after his rejection by the House of Repre-

415

sentatives. This left the field to such men as Rawlins, King, Powers, and Moyle. None of them had the ability to overcome the appeal of the Republican tariff to miners, sheepmen, cattlemen, and beet growers and the moderate-progressive Republican approach to other issues. Combined with prosperity and superior organization, the Republican Party presented a seemingly unbeatable combination.

Under these conditions a powerful political machine emerged that controlled the Republican Party until 1916. In 1903 the legislature elected Reed Smoot, a Provo businessman and Mormon apostle, as senator. Already a power in the Utah Republican Party, Smoot served in the senate for thirty years, becoming an influential figure in the postwar years when both he and his party were moving in a conservative direction. Utah's second and third governors, John C. Cutler, a Salt Lake City businessman elected in 1904, and William Spry, a Tooele politician and sometime businessman elected in 1908 and 1912, were members of Smoot's organization. The organization was often referred to as *the Federal Bunch* because many of its leaders were federal officeholders. Also closely associated with Smoot, though not machine members, were Mormon Church President Smith and Susa Young Gates, the leading Republican woman in Utah.

Smoot's rise to prominence and Thomas Kearns' lackluster record and independence led to a break between the senior senator and the Mormon president. Smith refused to support the mining millionaire for reelection; the 1905 legislature chose former Congressman George Sutherland as his successor. Sutherland's seat in Congress had been taken by Joseph Howell of Logan, who worked closely with the Federal Bunch.

While he was establishing his political base in Utah, Senator Smoot's membership in the Quorum of the Twelve caused serious problems in Washington. After his first election, a group of Salt Lake City ministers and laymen protested his seating on the ground that his allegiance to his church prevented his functioning as a free agent and obeying his oath to uphold the United States Constitution. One of the ministers also alleged that Smoot was a polygamist, but the Senate Committee on Privileges and Elections never seriously entertained the charge. Michigan Senator Julius Burrows headed the investigating subcommittee, whose inquiry about Smoot's church affiliation continued through 1906. Joseph F. Smith was the first to testify, and after him witnesses ranged from ardent supporters of the Mormon Church to dedicated opponents like Charles M. Owens, by whose efforts President Smith was fined for continued cohabitation with his polygamous wives. In 1907, though the Committee on Privileges and Elections recommended Smoot's exclusion, Theodore Roosevelt and the Senate's Republican leadership, impressed with Smoot's ability and loyalty, threw their support behind the Utahn, and he retained his seat.

The Smoot controversy and attendant allegations led the Mormon Church hierarchy to make the performing of plural marriages an excommunicable offense in 1904 and subsequently to drop John W. Taylor and Matthias Cowley from the Quorum of the Twelve for refusing to comply with this action. The charges of improper church influence in Utah politics led to the formation of the American Party in Salt Lake City. Although its candidates lost, the degree of its success in the 1904 election made members hopeful that it might capture Salt Lake City in the 1905 municipal election. Kearns had already purchased the pro-Republican and anti-Mormon Salt Lake *Tribune,* and after his reelection defeat he hired the embittered Frank Cannon as an editorial writer. The American Party now had its organ, and through effective campaigning and the divided efforts of Republicans and Democrats the party controlled city government in the state capital from 1905 to 1911. An irritant to the two major parties and to the Mormon Church, the American Party was never able to win statewide contests and it died out before the First World War.

Between 1896 and 1932 the average statewide voting pattern in Utah was sixty-six percent Republican. Although this was below the national preference of seventy percent, only Salt Lake and Carbon counties showed relative Democratic gains between 1900 and 1928. Members of the American Party, some Democrats, and a number of grateful Republicans believed that Mormon Church influence was principally responsible for Republican success. This seems unlikely. The Republican Party was unable to hold onto Utah in the 1930s in spite of opposition from a number of prominent Mormon leaders to the New Deal. In addition, as Smoot knew, the voice of the church on political questions was not unified. Democrat Charles Penrose, an apostle and editor of the church-owned *Deseret News,* was so independent that the Federal Bunch founded the *Intermountain Republican* (later the *Herald-Republican*) to plead their cause. Roberts and apostles Anthony W. Ivins and Heber J. Grant continued to be active Democrats. Even President Smith's efforts in 1908 and 1914 to stop opposition to Smoot from within the church came to naught.

In fact, the Republican Party appears to have succeeded because it delivered what the people of Utah wanted. It was only af-

Black soldiers returning from the Philippines campaign in 1899 parade through Salt Lake City on their way back to Fort Duchesne.

ter delivery stopped that the Democrats succeeded in gaining control of the state in 1916 and again during the Great Depression. What the party offered was a range of political choices from a moderate brand of progressivism to conservatism. On the national level Smoot set the example by his enthusiastic support of Roosevelt's conservation program; on the state level Governors Cutler and Spry established several commissions to regulate the use of natural resources. Smoot and Sutherland also advocated regulation of the railroads, whose rates were decidedly unfavorable to Utah, and increases in the tariff, which meant business and jobs to many Utahns. Sutherland spoke with pride of his support for Utah's eight-hour law, and he also helped draft national legislation for workmen's compensation in industrial accidents.

Progressive Economic and Social Legislation

After 1900 the efforts of the Republican-dominated state government to come to grips with problems caused by urbanism and industrialism increased, even as the two socioeconomic phenomena

418

became more characteristic of the state. During the first two decades of the twentieth century the state population grew from 276,749 to 449,396 (sixty-nine percent), but Salt Lake City and Ogden doubled in size, and by 1920 almost half the Utah populace was living in cities. Though legislative representation continued to be skewed in favor of the rural counties, the expanding demands of wage earners and urban consumers required attention.

In 1903 the legislature consolidated food regulation under the State Dairy and Food Commissioner and established standards of purity for certain foods. The scope and responsibilities of this office were gradually expanded thereafter. Laws to protect workers included an only partially effective prohibition against coercing employees into purchasing at company stores or living in company houses or towns. The tragic explosions at the Winter Quarters Mine at Scofield in 1900 and at the Daly-West Mine at Park City in 1902 forced the legislature to strengthen mine safety regulations. The offices of State Bank Examiner and State Insurance Commissioner were established, and the regulation of veterinarians, optometrists, doctors, and barbers was instituted or strengthened.

The rise of progressive reform in Utah began during Governor William Spry's two terms (1909-17). Despite the earlier prohibition of child labor in mines and smelters, it was estimated in 1910 that 3,231 children under sixteen were engaged in some form of gainful employment. In 1911, therefore, Utah became one of eight states to regulate the labor of children in street trades. In the same year, a general child employment act prohibited the hiring of children under fourteen in occupations that might be dangerous to their health or morals. Children were excluded from night work, and boys under fourteen and girls under sixteen were limited to fifty-four hours of work per week in all businesses except agriculture and domestic service.

The 1911 legislature also moved to correct abuses in the employment of women. The 1910 census showed that more than eighteen thousand women made up seventeen percent of the state's labor force. Most worked for long hours at low wages, and studies showed that many resorted to theft and prostitution to augment their meager incomes. The legislature established a nine-hour day and a fifty-four-hour week for women, exempting domestic service, canning, and farm labor. An expanded Bureau of Immigration, Labor, and Statistics was empowered to enforce all Utah's labor statutes except those concerning mine safety.

Utah also moved in the vanguard of states passing minimum wage and pension legislation. The 1913 law provided a minimum wage of $1.25 per day for experienced adult women, a rate so low that it affected only very poorly paid workers. Ironically, it was the United States Supreme Court decision written in 1923 by former Utahn George Sutherland in *Adkins v. Children's Hospital* (261 U.S. 525) that forced the repeal of this minimum wage law. The 1913 legislature also provided pensions for indigent mothers with dependent children.

Spry and the Republican legislators of his administration also attempted to deal with other problems. The Dairy and Food Commissioner's authority to deal with inferior and adulterated food was extended so Utah products would be more competitive in national markets. Mercantile houses were added to mines and smelters among those businesses in which eight hours was considered a day's work, but the Utah Supreme Court struck down this law as unconstitutional. A separate banking department was established in 1913 to regulate this burgeoning activity.

Utah also faced problems of inequity in its taxation system. Although the legislature had in 1901 adopted a five percent tax on inheritances over $10,000, the property tax was the primary source of state and local revenue. Large corporations, particularly railroads and mining companies, were able to escape part of their tax burden through underassessment and underreporting. Public demand for reform reached such a point that in 1911 the legislature directed Spry to create a commission on revenue and taxation to examine the subject. On the basis of its recommendations the 1913 legislature made some revisions in the tax system, but it was still unsatisfactory.

Regarded as a progressive measure at the time was the revival, under 1909 and 1911 statutes, of the occasional territorial practice of using convict labor on public roads. (The hiring out of prisoners for work on private projects was forbidden by the state constitution.) Seen by Spry as a way of reducing the costs of the state road system that the automobile was making necessary, the system was launched with fanfare in Box Elder County in 1911 and was continued on various state projects during the balance of the decade. Liberal criticism and changing ideas of prisoner rehabilitation led to the decline of the practice during the 1920s, though the 1911 statute was never repealed. Another territorial penal concept adopted by the state was the still-available option of receiving capital punishment by firing squad.

The movement for progressive reform and regeneration of society led the people of the United States and Utah to work for prohibition of the manufacture, sale, and use of alcoholic beverages. In spite of considerable statewide clamor, the governor vetoed a law providing for local option in 1909. Two years later, however, public support had reached such proportions that Spry signed a bill providing for mandatory local option elections. The required balloting on June 27, 1911, dried up most of Utah's towns and cities except for Salt Lake City, Ogden, and a number of mining camps.

The Progressive Party Challenge

The failure of the Republican Party to act on a number of proposals for economic and political reform led to an erosion of its support by 1912. The Democratic Party had stood for adoption of the initiative, referendum, and recall for some time, and both party platforms had called for the direct election of senators. The Republicans, however, equivocated on direct participation by the people in the governmental process and blocked Utah's ratification of the Seventeenth Amendment. Another issue of importance was workmen's compensation. Many citizens believed that the common law rule that virtually freed an employer from responsibility in industrial accidents should be overridden, and the Democrats had pressed for legislation for some time. Though Sutherland and other Republicans favored such action, the party had skirted the issue. In spite of recommendations by Governors Wells, Cutler, and Spry and platform pledges, the Republican legislature had also refused to create a commission to regulate railroads and other public utilities. (By 1915 Utah and Wyoming were the only states in the Union without public utilities regulation.)

It is probable that had the Utah Republicans bowed to their moderate and progressive factions to provide political reform, railroad regulation, and workmen's compensation by 1912, the Progressive Party never would have been organized in the state. In default of such actions, the group of Republicans principally from urban areas supported Theodore Roosevelt when he bolted the national Republican Party and nominated a Progressive ticket for state offices. Salt Lake City's Nephi L. Morris, a Mormon stake president and leader in the prohibition fight, was nominated for governor and Stephen H. Love, who had led the fight for railroad regulation, was ticketed for a congressional post. Roosevelt ran ahead of his party in Utah but carried only Weber and Uintah counties. Spry defeated both Morris, who carried only Uintah County, and the Democratic candidate, John F. Tolton. Utah and Vermont were the only states that preferred William Howard Taft over both Woodrow Wilson and Roosevelt.

The defection of the Progressives from the Republican Party caused Spry to be elected as a minority governor. In 1914 the Progressives formed an alliance with the Democrats who threatened Smoot's Senate seat. James Moyle, the coalition candidate in Utah's first direct senatorial election, barely lost. It has been argued that this was evidence of a decline in Smoot's power, but it seems probable that it was actually evidence of the staying power of the Republican Party and Utah's senior senator. After all, Smoot bucked the combined power of the Democrats and the dissident Republican-Progressives to win. The coalition managed only to elect Progressive James H. Mays as congressman from the first district; the Republicans still retained control of the legislature.

The Second Spry Term

After these challenges the 1913 and 1915 legislatures moved ahead to consider a number of progressive measures. In addition to the laws mentioned above, legislators also considered workmen's compensation, but in 1915 passed the hot issue to a commission charged with preparing recommendations for the next legislature. Several measures for regulating public utilities were introduced, but none was passed. The prohibition question again surfaced, this time in a demand for statewide prohibition that was spearheaded by Protestant clergymen and prominent Mormons. In response the legislature passed a bill in 1915 for complete statewide prohibition, but Spry, apparently unmindful of the possible consequences to his public career and to the Republican Party, pocket vetoed the bill.

The Spry administration was noteworthy for two other important events—the completion of the state capitol, formally opened on October 9, 1916, and the *Joe Hill* case. The latter episode, which became a national *cause célèbre*, began with the murder of Salt Lake grocer John G. Morrison and his son Arling during a robbery on January 10, 1914. Arling Morrison wounded one of the intruders. Later that evening a Swedish immigrant named Joel Häggelund, alias Joseph Hillstrom or Joe Hill, an itinerant laborer-poet and member of the Industrial Workers of the World, sought medical treatment for a rather severe gunshot wound. Subsequent investigation led to his arrest, trial, and conviction, and he was sentenced to execution by a firing squad. The IWW charged that the verdict was the result of a conspiracy against labor by the Utah Construction Company, the Utah Copper Company, and the Mormon Church. There is no credible evidence linking any of these organizations to Hill's prosecution. It seems probable that

Hill was rightfully convicted of the crime, but the state of public opinion in Utah makes the fairness of his trial questionable.

Hill's conviction on circumstantial evidence, his connection with the Industrial Workers of the World, and the question of the fairness of his trial led to a letter-writing campaign to induce Spry to commute the sentence to life imprisonment. Woodrow Wilson, Samuel Gompers, and the Swedish ambassador to the United States were among hundreds who urged commutation. After several delays and a reprieve, Hill was executed at the state prison on November 19, 1915. Evidence of the charged atmosphere in the state at the time are the firing of a University of Utah art teacher and the disbarring of Hill's lawyer for their outspoken public agitation in Hill's behalf. Since his execution, whether just or not, Hill has become a symbol of resistance to oppression for laborers, students, and others.

It seems unlikely, however, that the Hill case had much to do with the outcome of the 1916 election. The 1915 legislature's waffling on railroad regulation and direct democracy and the governor's prohibition veto spelled defeat for the Republican Party.

The Bamberger Administration and the First World War

An air of optimism pervaded the Democratic Party in 1916. President Wilson was increasingly popular in Utah and the people were dissatisfied with broken Republican promises. The Democrats nominated former Congressman King to run against Sutherland for the Senate, and Simon Bamberger, a German-born Jewish businessman and former state senator, to run for governor. Both the Federal Bunch and the Republican state organization were in disarray, even though most of the Progressives returned to the fold when Nephi Morris received the gubernatorial nomination. Bamberger and King swamped the Republican candidates, and the Democrats gained control of both houses of the legislature.

When Simon Bamberger took office in 1917, he led the state lawmakers to the passage of measures that completed the progressive program for the State of Utah. A public utilities commission was established to regulate the railroads and such other services as gas, lights, telephone, and water. The functions of the Bureau of Immigration, Labor, and Statistics, the Coal Mine Inspector, and the Board of Arbitration and Conciliation were turned over to a new Industrial Commission. Though Utah had lagged behind thirty other states in inaugurating workmen's compensation, the law that now came was one of the most stringent in the nation. But it still disappointed some reformers, excluding as it did domestic and farm workers and setting up a rather conservative compensation schedule.

The 1917 legislature also established provisions for the initiative and referendum; regulated the importation, sale, and use of narcotics; declared labor unions to be lawful organizations; and limited the use of injunctions in labor disputes. It set up new regulations governing water rights and irrigation districts and passed a corrupt political practices act. Perhaps the most popular piece of legislation was that providing for statewide prohibition after August 1, 1917. Utah was to remain legally dry until 1933.

International developments soon changed the focus of the Bamberger Administration, even as they attracted the attention and resources of the people of Utah and of the nation. The First World War brought the Progressive Era to an end and gave Utah the opportunity to demonstrate that any lingering doubts about the patriotism of her populace were unfounded.

The territorial Nauvoo Legion had been inactivated and then abolished during the antipolygamy crusade and the new Utah National Guard, organized in 1894 in the territory and carried over into the state, was representative of the new spirit of accommodation between Utah and the United States. When the Spanish-American War erupted in 1898, the response to Governor Wells' call for volunteers exceeded the War Department request; 663 Utahns served in the Philippines and in units that reached as far as Florida, California, and Hawaii before the short conflict ended. The only Utah battle casualties, nine dead and thirteen wounded, came during the suppression of the Filipino insurrection in 1899. Seventeen years later units of the National Guard served in the frustrating United States Army campaign against Pancho Villa in Mexico.

When war was declared against Germany in April 1917, civic and church leaders endorsed the calls from President Wilson and Governor Bamberger for money, materials, and men. Symbolic of the change in the posture of the Mormon Church since the days when the Civil War was interpreted as a judgment upon the nation was the service of Brigham H. Roberts and a son of President Joseph F. Smith, Calvin S. Smith, as chaplains of Utah units that went to Europe. Fort Douglas became an important training and supply center. Of the almost 25,000 Utahns who served in the army and navy, slightly more than half volunteered. Approximately 665 died in service, a third during combat and the balance from illness and other causes. President Heber J. Grant, who succeeded President Smith shortly after the armistice, and Smoot disagreed publicly over whether Wilson's League of Nations was an appropriate device for preserving the fruits of victory; to the extent that the 1920 election was a referendum on the League, a majority of Utahns followed Smoot and Harding.

Conclusion

The image of Utah that emerges from a study of these first years of statehood is at variance with the commonly held myths about the state's political history. Far from trailing other states, Utah generally stood in the first third of states of the Union in the passage of social legislation regulating conditions of work in dangerous occupations. Utahns moved quickly to deal with the conservation of natural resources, especially timber and water, and to adopt pure food legislation. The state also adopted progressive laws in the area of political reform. In the one area of utility regulation, however, Utah lagged far behind other states and the myth appears to have been based in part on this factor.

Beyond this, a reconsideration of the role of the Federal Bunch is also involved. The traditional judgment is probably derived from Senator Smoot's identification with the conservative wing of the Republican Party during the Harding-Coolidge-Hoover era. Smoot's organization was, of course, a political machine, but with the exception of its opposition to direct democracy there is little evidence that it formed a regressive force in the state in the prewar years. With the support of the Federal Bunch, the legislature enacted various measures of professional and business regulation; protected working men, women, and children; and launched an investigation that led to workmen's compensation. The Federal Bunch was among the forces that supported the creation of a public utilities commission, but other groups in the state were simply too powerful to allow its earlier passage.

This is not to say that the accomplishments of the Democrats during the Bamberger Administration were unimportant. Political reform was inaugurated and Utah had public utilities regulation, workmen's compensation, and metal mine inspection for the first time. Utah also had prohibition and the satisfaction of playing a patriotic role in the "war to end war."

Chapter 22
Bibliographical Essay

The only general study of Utah political development during the period is Noble Warrum, *Utah Since Statehood,* four volumes (1919-20), which is quite unsatisfactory because it tends to be uninterpretive. It should be supplemented with Frank H. Jonas, ed., *Politics in the American West* (1969); Jan Shipps, "Utah Comes of Age Politically: A Study of the State's Politics in the Early Years of the Twentieth Century," *UHQ,* Spring 1967; Jean B. White, "Utah State Elections, 1895-1899" (Ph.D. dissertation, University of Utah, 1968); and Brad E. Hainsworth, "Utah State Elections, 1916-1924" (Ph.D. dissertation, University of Utah, 1968).

A number of contemporary accounts ought to be consulted. They include: Frank J. Cannon and Harvey J. O'Higgins, *Under the Prophet in Utah: The National Menace of a Political Priestcraft* (1911), which must be used with care because Cannon had an axe to grind against the Mormons; and S. A. Kenner, *Utah As It Is: With a Comprehensive Statement of Utah As It Was* (1904), which goes to the opposite extreme. A chronological list of events thought important at the time will be found in Andrew Jenson's *Church Chronology* (1914). B. H. Roberts, *A Comprehensive History of the Church,* Vol. 6 (1930) is cursory on Mormon-related political events after the Smoot contest.

Two sources are useful for the state constitution: *Official Report of the Proceedings and Debates of the Convention . . . to Adopt a Constitution for the State of Utah,* two volumes (1898); and Stanley S. Ivins, "A Constitution for Utah," *UHQ,* April 1957.

The following master's theses relate to political movements during the period: Lauren H. Dimter, "Populism in Utah" (Brigham Young University, 1964); Reuben Joseph Snow, "The American Party in Utah: A Study of Political Party Struggles During the Early Years of Statehood" (University of Utah, 1964); C. Austin Wahlquist, "The 1912 Presidential Election in Utah" (Brigham Young University, 1962); and Bruce T. Dyer, "A Study of the Forces Leading to the Adoption of Prohibition in Utah in 1917" (Brigham Young University, 1958). See also Gibbs M. Smith, *Joe Hill* (1969).

Contemporary articles written about progressivism in Utah include: Peter Clark Macfarlane, "A Man of Utah," *Colliers,* January 17, 1914, which deals with Stephen H. Love, leader of the movement for railroad regulation and Progressive Party candidate for Congress; and Oswald Ryan, "Salt Lake City: A Municipal Democracy," *Harper's Weekly,* October 4, 1913. On the subject of Mormonism perhaps the most complimentary gentile article was Ray Stannard Baker's "The Vitality of Mormons: A Study of an Irrigated Valley in Utah and Idaho," *Century Magazine,* June 1904. Representative of attacks waged on the Mormon Church by a number of muckraking journals are "The Viper" series by Alfred

Henry Lewis in *Cosmopolitan*, March, April, and May 1911; and Burton J. Hendrick, "The Mormon Revival of Polygamy," *McClure's Magazine*, January and February 1911.

A number of biographical studies have been done of contemporary Republican leaders. Among the best are Milton R. Merrill, "Reed Smoot: Apostle in Politics" (Ph.D. dissertation, Columbia University, 1950), and a series of articles that grew from this study, including one in *Western Humanities Review*, Winter 1955. Joel Francis Paschal, *Mr. Justice Sutherland: A Man Against the State* (1951), slights Sutherland's political career in favor of his service on the Supreme Court. See also William L. Roper and Leonard J. Arrington, *William Spry: Man of Firmness, Governor of Utah* (1971). Two useful master's theses are Edward Leo Lyman, "Heber M. Wells and the Beginnings of Utah's Statehood" (University of Utah, 1967); and Kent Sheldon Larsen, "The Life of Thomas Kearns" (University of Utah, 1964). There are as yet no scholarly works on Joseph Howell, John C. Cutler, Nephi L. Morris, or Frank J. Cannon.

Among the best studies of Democratic leaders is Frank Thomas Morn, "Simon Bamberger: A Jew in a Mormon Commonwealth" (master's thesis, Brigham Young University, 1966). Quite disappointing is Robert H. Malan, *B. H. Roberts: A Biography* (1966), which simply fails to consider the issues of the progressive period. Work on Roberts should be supplemented with R. Davis Bitton's "The B. H. Roberts Case of 1898-1900," *UHQ*, January 1957. James H. Moyle, *A View of James Henry Moyle*, ed. Gene A. Sessions (1974), is a good introduction to Democratic Party politics. No satisfactory study of Moses Thatcher exists, but a starting point is Stanley S. Ivins, *The Moses Thatcher Case* (n.d.). There are no studies of James H. Mays or William H. King.

Anyone seriously interested in the career of Reed Smoot and the role of the Mormon Church during the period must consult the hearings of the Senate Committee on Privileges and Elections: *Proceedings . . . in the Matter of the Protests Against the Right of Hon. Reed Smoot, A Senator from the State of Utah to Hold His Seat*, four volumes (1904-1906). Also valuable for putting Smoot and his colleagues in the context of their times are: Jerome Martin Clubb, "Congressional Opponents of Reform, 1901-1913" (Ph.D. dissertation, University of Washington, 1963); two articles by Thomas G. Alexander, "Senator Reed Smoot and Western Land Policy, 1905-1920," *Arizona and the West*, Fall 1971, and "Reed Smoot, the LDS Church, and Progressive Legislation," *Dialogue: A Journal of Mormon Thought*, Spring 1972; and James B. Allen, "Personal Faith and

Public Policy: Some Timely Observations on the League of Nations Controversy in Utah," *BYU Studies,* Autumn 1973.

Biographies of the presidents of the Mormon Church during this period are available, but with the exception of the Aydelotte study they tell little about the political activities of these men. See Matthias F. Cowley, *Wilford Woodruff* (1909); Thomas C. Romney, *The Life of Lorenzo Snow* (1955); Joseph Fielding Smith, comp., *Life of Joseph F. Smith* (1938); and Loman Franklin Aydelotte, "The Political Thought and Activity of Heber J. Grant . . ." (master's thesis, Brigham Young University, 1965).

Chapter 23
Integration into the
National Economy, 1896–1920

Thomas G. Alexander

During the nineteenth century the Mountain West was the only section of the United States which, though it was significantly below the national average in industrial growth, exceeded the national level in per capita income. The income came principally from mining, and as soon as the relative proportion of those engaged in agriculture grew, per capita income fell below the national average. Utah did not share in this preliminary prosperity, however, because her economy was basically agricultural from 1847. Her per capita income lagged significantly behind not only the United States but all of the mountain states except New Mexico. (See Table P, p. 713.)

Though Utah exhibited rapid economic development during the first two decades of the twentieth century, by 1920 she was actually farther behind the United States than she was in 1890 in percentage of labor force employed in manufacturing. By contrast, the Pacific Coast states reached the national level of industrialization shortly before World War I. It was probably the inability of Utah's economic growth to keep up with the rest of the nation and the absolute and relative growth of her agriculture that contributed to the net population outflow from 1910 through World War II.

The period from 1890 to 1920, with which this chapter deals, marks the beginning of what might be considered the third phase of Utah's economic development. The first ended with the joining of the rails at Promontory Summit (1869), and the second ended with the achievement of statehood. The third phase—which continued until World War II—included the commercialization of agriculture, the emergence of a substantial business sector, and the development of corporate mining and manufacturing. By 1920 many of the development patterns that have persisted to the present were established. No longer was The Church of Jesus Christ of Latter-day Saints the principal force in Utah's economy. Absentee capitalists and engineers and managers born outside the state worked with homegrown businessmen and scientists to promote various undertakings. The separation of Mormon and gentile enterprises became outdated as Utah's arrangements for production and distribution were integrated internally and with the larger national economy.

These new patterns did not develop without dislocating consequences. The loss of the sense of community that had existed in the old ecclesiastical strongholds and the appearance of powerful and autonomous corporations led inevitably to bitter confrontations, especially in the mining districts of Carbon and Salt Lake counties. Farmers became increasingly tied to distant markets over which they had little control. National freight rate structures, which discriminated against the Mountain West in general and against finished products from that region in particular, became a constant disadvantage for both farmers and businessmen.

As pressures on arable lands increased, many Utahns migrated from the state. Census data show a net outflow of native-born white inhabitants between 1890 and 1920; they relocated in such diverse places as Oregon, Wyoming, Arizona, New Mexico, California, and even Mexico and Canada. By 1899 Mormon leaders concluded that it was no longer advisable to encourage converts to gather to Utah, and gathering was actively discouraged on occasion in the early twentieth century. The increase in population from 276,749 in 1890 to 448,396 in 1920 is attributable to two factors: a family size slightly larger than the national average and a substantial influx of southern and eastern European and other immigrants to work in the state's mines and smelters.

The Growth of Commercial Agriculture

By the 1890s Utah farmers had generally occupied the richest and most easily tillable land, and new lands were being opened in areas that proved marginal or submarginal. Farmers pushed into Pahvant Valley in Millard County, the Uinta Basin, and southeastern Utah's Grand Valley; as the prices of farm commodities rose during the second decade of the twentieth century the number of farms increased in every county except Grand, Juab, Morgan, and Wasatch. This development is attributable to the growth

The impact of sugar beets on Utah agriculture is witnessed by this George E. Ander-son photograph taken about 1900 at the Springville sugar factory.

of industrial and urban centers and to World War I. The total value of farm land and buildings increased from $39.5 million in 1890 to $311 million in 1920.

Although farmers expanded into outlying counties, the backbone of Utah agriculture remained near the Wasatch Front urban centers. About forty-eight percent of all farms were in the counties of Cache, Box Elder, Davis, Weber, Salt Lake, and Utah. The median size of Utah farms remained relatively stable at just over fifty acres. Since the absolute number of farms increased and the percentage of farms situated along the Wasatch Front remained approximately constant, it is clear that agriculture also moved onto marginal land in this part of the state.

During the years 1890-1920 the total acreage of Utah farms increased from 1.3 million to 5 million, or about 9.5 percent of the total land area. Most of the new acreage was taken up under the Homestead Law and other federal land laws during the speculative boom in land and commercial irrigation projects that accompanied other changes in Utah's economy in the 1890s. World War I gave an extra impetus to expansion. By 1920 improved land reached its virtual maximum of 1.7 million acres, 3.3 percent of the state's total land area; this was up from 0.5 million acres in 1890. The number of farms increased from 10,500 to 26,000 in the same three decades.

Almost all areas of the agricultural economy benefited from this expansion. Every category of farm commodity—truck, field, orchard, and livestock—registered increases in output between 1890 and 1920. Before 1914 superior grades of wheat seed were introduced and the Utah product became more easily marketable. The number of sheep rose from 1 million to 3.8 million in the 1890s, then declined to 1.7 million in 1910 and 1920 because of overgrazing. By contrast, the number of cattle and calves increased from 0.3 million in 1900 to 0.5 million in 1920. Owing probably to adverse freight rates, increasing numbers of cattle were shipped to the Midwest for fattening, but Utah's cattle industry remained strong.

Beyond the natural expansion of the market, promotional activities of state and private agencies helped to develop Utah's agricultural industry. The Utah State Fair Association, other state bureaus, and the Utah State Agricultural College Experiment Station promoted better quality products and more efficient practices. The bounties offered by the state legislature and the subsidies of the McKinley and Dingley tariffs helped sugar beet producers.

Also important, considering Utah's arid climate, were developments such as dry farming and reclamation. By introducing techniques that conserved the limited moisture, Utahns promoted successful experiments in farming without irrigation. After the passage of the Newlands Act in 1902, federal funds were made available to supplement reclamation projects that had been undertaken locally. The only federal project constructed in Utah before World War I was in Strawberry Valley, where water from the Colorado Drainage Basin was introduced into the Great Basin through a storage reservoir and tunnel. The prosperity of Utah County was enhanced by electricity from the Strawberry project in 1914 and by water a year later. (See map, p. 737.)

Easily the most significant factor in Utah's agricultural growth during these years was the opening of the sugar beet industry. While early attempts were unsuccessful in the 1850s, improved technology and financial subsidies provided the impetus for a second effort in the 1890s. Farmers generally reserved about ten acres of their best land for sugar beets, which produced a relatively high cash return and an assured income.

Utah's farmers shared with other industries, however, the problem of high shipping costs. This resulted not only from the relatively long distances to major markets but also from railroad rates that discriminated against the region. As a result, the prices of exported crops such as hay, wheat, barley, sugar, and potatoes were below the national average in Utah, whereas prices for imported crops such as corn, oats, and rye were higher. Most fruit crops had to be consumed locally because Utah fruit could not compete with that grown in the Midwest and on the Pacific Coast.

In spite of the problems, the life of the average Utah farmer improved tremendously in the first two decades of the twentieth century. Diversified farming was typical; according to one study, the average farmer received his principal income from sugar beets, with milk and dairy products second and potatoes and truck crops third. The typical farmer in 1914 had about $450 invested in farm machinery. Some farmers grazed cattle on public lands, but grazing permits were limited and stock raising was generally not sufficiently profitable to justify the irrigating farmer giving up field crops for pasture.

Much of Utah's livestock production was concentrated in a few big outfits. Beginning in the 1880s large cattle operations such as the Carlisle Cattle Company and Cunningham and Carpenter, financed by eastern and British funds, began pushing into southeastern Utah. Mormons who had established themselves at Bluff after the Hole-in-the-Rock expedition of 1879-80 began to challenge the larger ranchers in the late 1880s through the organization of a cattle pool under the leadership of Francis A. Hammond, who had been sent there as Mormon stake president. Their efforts succeeded; the outside ranchers sold out, culminating in the sale of Cunningham and Carpenter in November 1914. Charles Redd became manager of the newly organized La Sal Livestock Company. Together with other successful ranchers such as Al Scorup and Preston Nutter, Redd carried on large-scale livestock production in eastern and southeastern Utah for many years.

Per worker farm income, measured in constant dollars (1964 = $1), rose from $1,208 in 1900 to $2,260 in 1919-21. Farm tenancy was very low, reaching only ten percent in 1920. An aspect of the agricultural expansion that would not have pleased the pioneer generation farmers was the increase in farm mortgages. In 1890 about five percent of Utah farms were encumbered; by 1920 the figure was forty-eight percent.

Expansion of Mining and Smelting

If the largest single occupation of Utahns between 1890 and 1920 was agriculture, the leading export industry was mining. (See map, p. 736.) Metal mines were concentrated near the large urban centers and the principal farming region in the Wasatch and Oquirrh mountains and in the Tintic District of central Utah. From 1875 to 1890 the value of the major nonferrous metals produced in Utah averaged $7.4 million per year. From 1890 through 1900 the only year in which that average was not met or exceeded was the depression year of 1894. Annual production then spurted to almost seventeen million dollars and began a spectacular climb that reached ninety-nine million dollars in 1917. After 1890 Utah never produced less than twelve percent of the nation's silver and thirteen percent of its lead.

Undoubtedly the most significant factor in Utah mining expansion in these years was the development of the copper industry. Centered in Bingham Canyon, copper production surpassed silver in value in 1905 to become the state's leading mineral product. Though the precious metals at Bingham had been among the first developed in Utah Territory, it was not until 1896 that Samuel Newhouse and Thomas Weir formed the Highland Boy Gold Mining Company to make use of the newly perfected cyanide process and British investors formed the Utah Consolidated Gold Mines, Ltd., to provide capital for the venture. Exploratory work revealed extensive copper deposits that they decided to exploit. A smelter began operation in 1899 and Newhouse and Weir sold a controlling interest in Highland Boy to Standard Oil Company officials William Rockefeller and Henry H. Rogers. Newhouse and Weir had meanwhile purchased adjacent copper claims and with British investors formed the Boston Consolidated Copper and Gold Mining Company, Ltd.; they headed the operation until it was absorbed by the Utah Copper Company in 1910.

The Utah Copper Company was organized in 1903 by Daniel C. Jackling, Charles M. MacNeill, and Spencer Penrose following copper mining efforts by Enos A. Wall and others. Jackling's group secured financial support from Guggenheim banking interests, and they constructed the largest copper reduction facilities in the world. In 1906 they initiated open cut operations in the low grade porphyry ores of Bingham Canyon. By 1916 Utah stood fourth among the copper-producing states of the Union.

While Jackling achieved fame and fortune at Bingham, his first participation in Utah mining was at Mercur, the gold camp that is also associated with careers of two other prominent men. George H. Dern, later Utah's governor and United States Secretary of War, was general manager of the Consolidated Mercur Gold Mines Company; Lucien L. Nunn, already well-known for his pioneer work in generating alternating current, developed the long distance transmission of high voltage electricity from a plant near the mouth of Provo Canyon to Mercur, thirty-two miles away. By 1912, however, operations at Mercur had been submarginal, and a year later production ceased and the boom town of the 1890s quickly joined the list of Utah's ghost towns.

The Park City District, then Utah's principal lead producer, added its contribution to the gallery of industrial and political leaders by providing the source for Senator Thomas F. Kearns' fortune. Lead mining, closely associated with the simultaneous recovery of silver, rose to new heights under World War I demands. In 1916 Utah stood third in the United States in lead production and second in silver production.

By the summer of 1904 Salt Lake Valley was the home of three large copper smelters and a lead smelter. Those farming near these facilities suffered extensive crop damage from the sulphur dioxide emissions and filed suit in the United States district court. Eventually a verdict against the smelters forced the closing of all but one plant; it remained open only by reducing emissions and paying damages to the farmers. By 1910, however, the industry had rebounded and six smelters were in operation. As the price of metals rose, new methods made the smelting of old slag and tailings profitable. The Utah Copper Company reduced the cost for mining and smelting, which had been $89 per ton in 1872, to $1.25 per ton in 1913. Utah smelters handled ore from local mines and from such diverse areas as Nevada, Montana, Arizona, and the Coeur d'Alene District in Idaho. After a slump from 1912 to 1915, the war stimulated the smelting industry to such an extent that in 1919 Salt Lake Valley was the greatest smelting district in North America, producing 4.45 million tons of metal per year. Utah Copper Company also began converting the noxious sulphur into sulfuric acid, and a new chemical industry was added to Utah's economy.

Coal mining also became an increasingly important industry during the first decades of the twentieth century. Before the 1880s the principal supplier of coal for Utah had been the Union Pacific Railroad Company. As the Denver and Rio Grande Western Railroad pushed into Carbon County in 1882, however, the vast deposits of eastern Utah coal were opened and the Union Pacific hege-

Shoemaking was largely a handicraft in the ZCMI factory in Salt Lake City around the turn of the century.

mony was undermined by a D & RG subsidiary, Utah Fuel Company. Utah coal production first topped one million tons in 1900, and Utah Fuel mined ninety percent of it. After 1906 a number of independent companies cut into the monopoly in spite of Utah Fuel's efforts to stop them by the use of armed guards on public lands, and by 1916 the big company's share of the market declined to forty percent. Under the stimulus of an expanding local industrial market and the demands of World War I, Utah coal production increased to six million tons in 1920.

Although automatic machinery was introduced, expanding production increased the number of employees in this hazardous vocation. The safety record of the coal mines, in spite of legislative reforms during the Progressive Era, was not good. The Scofield disaster of 1900, which killed 200, was almost matched by the 172 deaths at Castle Gate in 1924. For the years 1914 to 1929 the fatality rate in Utah's coal mines was almost double the national average.

Considerable interest was shown in the development of other nonmetallic minerals. Oil and gas wells were drilled in various parts of the state, particularly from 1906 to 1910, and road construction increased the demand for asphalt. The discovery of radium by the Curies and the identification of carnotite on the Colorado Plateau opened a minor industry in the mining of carnotite and pitchblende. Salt production, based at the Great Salt Lake, was also important; the largest salt enterprise after 1897 belonged to the Mormon Church. Closing the shipping lanes to Germany during World War I pushed up the price of potash, a mineral used in explosives and as fertilizer, and a number of potash deposits were opened in Utah.

Industrialization and Manufacturing

As one might expect, Utah's manufacturing was based largely on the processing of agricultural and mineral products and was concentrated along the Wasatch Front. Fully half of the state's factories in 1911 were in Salt Lake City. The smelting and refining of nonferrous metals and the manufacture of beet sugar predominated. Utah stood second to Colorado both in percentage and absolute number of those employed in manufacturing in the mountain states. As a percentage of those employed, however, Utah slipped behind the United States as a whole between 1900 and 1920. What this meant is that although industrialization increased in Utah, it increased more rapidly in the nation as a whole. Strangely enough, Utah's rate of industrialization, as measured by the percentage of the population so employed, increased more rapidly between 1900 and 1920 than at any other time down to 1950. Utah was actually more industrialized after the first than after the second World War.

The prosperity of beet sugar manufacturers is indicated by developments during the years from 1890 to 1920. Organized in 1891 at Lehi, the Utah Sugar Company was soon employing more than one hundred people and processing 36,000 tons of sugar beets per year. To secure capital for expansion, the founders sold a controlling interest to the monopolistic American Sugar Refining Company in 1902. With the active participation of Mormon President Joseph F. Smith, Governor John C. Cutler, and others a number of plants were opened in northern and central Utah and in southern Idaho; they were united in 1907 as the Utah-Idaho Sugar Company, a thirteen million-dollar corporation. By 1915 the sugar manufacturing industry was second only to metal processing in value added by manufacture, and the next year Utah moved into third place among the sugar-producing states.

During this period of expansion the sugar companies, especially U&I, received considerable adverse comment. Critics pointed out that Utah sugar sold in Texas in 1913 for $4.15 per hundred pounds, while Utah citizens had to pay $5.25. During the war a growers organization charged that collusion between the United States Food Administrator, state officials, and the companies resulted in low prices to the farmers in order to enhance corporate profits. The culmination of war reduced both prices and profits for the sugar business.

A number of other industries, such as meat packing, were based on the primary processing of Utah and intermountain agricultural products. Until well after 1900 Denver was the only important livestock market between the Midwest and the Pacific states. In 1906, however, the Ogden Packing and Provision Company built a small plant that expanded in eleven years to become the largest packing operation west of Omaha. Several smaller firms also appeared, and by 1918 the estimated output of the meat packing industry was worth $8.3 million. New stockyards in both Ogden and Salt Lake City replaced less adequate facilities. But packers and stockmen were still dissatisfied; one observer pointed out that it was not uncommon to see a trainload of cattle followed by a trainload of grain followed by a trainload of hay all going from Utah to the same destination. Bankers were reluctant to loan money to livestock feeders, and freight rates favored live animals over dressed meats. Utah spokesmen petitioned the Federal Trade Commission to use its antimonopoly power to force rate changes, but by the end of the war they had achieved no success.

World War I also stimulated the milling industry, which was already supplying Utah's mining regions, the urban centers of the intermountain states, and part of the Los Angeles market. The increased emphasis on better strains of wheat and low hydroelectric power costs helped the industry. By December 1919 Ogden was one of the ten leading milling centers of America. A net exporter of flour, Utah was still a net importer of such processed grain products as breakfast food, probably because of adverse freight rates and a limited market.

Ogden became the center of the state's canning industry. The first two canneries were established there and in Woods Cross about 1890. Twenty years later there were fifty factories producing about 750,000 cases of canned goods a year. Competition and consolidation reduced the number of plants, but by 1914 Utah ranked fifth among the states in canning. In 1917 twenty-two Ogden canneries had government contracts; a year later the value of the industry's output was $3.4 million, of which sixty-four percent was sold outside the state.

Preeminent in wool manufacturing since territorial days, the Provo Woolen Mills, Utah's first large-scale manufacturing establishment, weathered the hard times of the 1890s and by 1900, ably led by Reed Smoot, was employing two hundred hands and producing between $250,000 and $300,000 in goods per year. Distance from consumer centers and obsolete machinery caused the company to suspend operations in 1904, and it remained idle until purchased by "Uncle Jesse" Knight in 1910. Thereafter the woolen goods market was good in the mining camps of New Mexico and Arizona and the lumber camps of the Pacific coast, where "Black Mormon Underwear" became synonymous with warmth and utility. Possibly owing to unfavorable freight rates, Utah had no scouring plants, so wool sheared in Utah was shipped to the east, scoured, dyed black, then shipped back. Two other large concerns, John Scowcroft and Sons of Ogden and Zion's Cooperative Mercantile Institution of Salt Lake City, produced work clothing, primarily for miners and construction workers.

Illustrative of the new directions in the Utah economy during this period was the construction of Utah's first evaporated milk plant at Richmond in 1904 for the Sego Milk Company. Sugar production also gave rise to commercial candy manufacturing; in 1920 Utah candymakers sold four million dollars' worth of sweets to consumers worldwide. Another economic indicator was that a number of Utahns became interested in the infant motion picture industry. While none of the prewar production ventures was a financial or critical success, a ninety-minute film, *One Hundred Years of Mormonism*, was made in 1913 with the active cooperation of the Mormon Church.

Prohibition, which began in Utah in August 1917, had a varying effect on Utah food processing industries. Soda water bottlers noted an increase in sales, but local cigar makers and distillers of legal liquor suffered. Saloons, which had handled Utah-made cigars, went out of business, and tobacco chain stores entered the state and pushed eastern goods in the major markets at Ogden and Salt Lake City. The major protection for the Utah cigar industry, which had been based partly on locally grown tobacco, had been the high shipping cost of the finished product.

Transportation, Utilities, and Banking

The Union Pacific Railroad had a virtual monopoly on most Utah rail traffic during the territorial period, since even the coal-hauling Denver and Rio Grande Western Railroad provided no access to the West Coast. Completion of the Salt Lake and Los

The coal mine disaster at Scofield, which took two hundred lives in 1900, filled the nearby communities with coffins (above) and mourning families (below).

Angeles Railway from central Utah to southern California in 1905 was resisted by the Union Pacific, but within a few years the transportation giant acquired the new line. A further challenge to the Union Pacific monopoly came from the Oregon Short Line, which consolidated several of the local companies founded in the intermountain region and which early in the twentieth century operated about 1,500 miles of track in Idaho, Montana, Wyoming, Oregon, and Utah. Headquartered in Salt Lake City, the Short Line allowed D & RGW traffic to invade Union Pacific territory in 1897, and the Union Pacific promptly cancelled its services to the Short Line. The conflict was not resolved until the regional railroad became a part of the Union Pacific system in 1899.

With the link to Los Angeles, Salt Lake City moved into a position to challenge Ogden as Utah's principal railway center. In November 1909 the Western Pacific completed construction between Salt Lake City and San Francisco, and the capital had routes in virtually all directions. Nevertheless, the railroad continued to be important to the Junction City. Union Pacific shops were housed in Ogden and the other E. H. Harriman-owned railroad, the Southern Pacific, was Ogden's leading employer, boasting an annual payroll of approximately one million dollars and employment of about 1,000. The completion of the $8.5 million Lucin Cutoff across the Great Salt Lake in 1903 shortened the Southern Pacific route west of Ogden by forty-three miles and strengthened the company's competitive position.

The automobile age meant opportunity for new road and bridge construction enterprises, though only modest improvements were made in the wagon tracks between cities until the enactment of the Federal Highways Act in 1916. Prior to 1918 Utah could boast only about thirty-four miles of paved roads, most of them urban, and some outlying areas were served by stagecoaches well into the twentieth century.

Perhaps nothing is more indicative of Utah's urban-industrial economic maturation than the expansion of urban utilities. The interurban Salt Lake and Ogden Railway, electrified in 1910, was called the Bamberger Line long before its president became Utah's first non-Mormon governor. The Salt Lake and Utah Railroad, nicknamed the *Orem* after its founder, Walter C. Orem, inaugurated service from the capital to Payson in 1916. The Utah-Idaho Central Railroad, owned by the Eccles family, carried local service from Ogden north to Logan and Preston, Idaho.

The Rocky Mountain Bell Company, which served Utah, Idaho, Montana, and Wyoming, became part of the Mountain States

Telephone and Telegraph Company in 1911. Service was expanded throughout the state and on July 28, 1914, crews set the last pole and spliced wires at Wendover to connect the first transcontinental telephone line. Electric service was extended to new urban areas, some of it by firms that pioneered hydroelectric power generation. Incorporated on January 1, 1913, from a number of small independent companies established in the 1890s, the Utah Power and Light Company supplied service within a decade to 205 communities between Ashton, Idaho, and Huntington (located in central Utah).

Utah's expanding economy demanded additional banking facilities. Between 1896 and 1919 the number of banks increased from 46 to 125, and total assets stood at $161.8 million. Efforts of Utah and southern Idaho bankers, led by the Salt Lake Clearing House Association, brought a branch of the Federal Reserve Bank of San Francisco to Salt Lake City. The Utah Bankers Association was formed in 1909 for educational and lobbying purposes.

The Utah Labor Movement

The strength of the economy during most of the period from 1890 to 1920 helped sustain a vigorous labor movement. Because of its anti-Mormon leadership the Knights of Labor had been unable to organize many Utah workers in the 1880s, but the American Federation of Labor, represented by conservative craftsmen like Robert G. Sleater, successfully organized the Salt Lake City Federation of Labor. This association of trade unions disbanded during the depression of the early 1890s but was reestablished in 1896. A similar organization was formed in Ogden in 1902 and the two city centrals worked together to form the Utah State Federation of Labor, which received an AFL charter in 1905.

The most serious setback to the labor movement and to Utah workers in general came with the depression of 1893. It is estimated that within a year forty-eight percent of Salt Lake City's labor force was unemployed. A workingmen's association led a movement to encourage employers and government agencies to provide jobs, and some groups tried rather unsuccessfully to form cooperative factories. The Mormon Church Relief Society organized an Industrial Employment Bureau to help employ people and provide aid for those without jobs. In addition, the Mormon Church promoted a number of public works projects to stimulate economic recovery.

Employers organizations were soon formed to oppose unionism. The first appears to have been the Salt Lake Contractors and

Builders Association, established in 1890 to resist pressure for union recognition, shorter hours, and higher pay. A Citizen's Alliance of Salt Lake City Employers formed in 1903 to fight collective bargaining, and the Utah Manufacturers Association, established in 1905, included antiunionism in its promotional program.

These antilabor efforts received little overt encouragement from Mormon Church officials, although many of the businessmen and publicists involved were Mormons. Though its position was somewhat equivocal, the church did not *oppose* union organization. At the time of the violent 1892 strike at Homestead, Pennsylvania, the *Deseret News* denounced the use of strikebreakers and Pinkerton detectives by the Carnegie Steel Company, but it advocated the use of state militia to maintain peace. The *News* editorially supported the eight-hour day movement and opposed the use of antitrust laws against labor, but it opposed legal restrictions on hours of work. Though the church paper was adamantly against the closed shop, it commented during some strikes on the just demands of the strikers; it also condemned the "yellow dog contracts" by which employers tried to keep workers from joining unions. In an apparent attempt to check the growth of divisions between workers and employers, Apostle Abraham O. Woodruff proposed in 1902 that the church organize its own labor unions, but President Smith preferred to allow individual Mormons the freedom to join national labor unions or not. When efforts were made, with some success, to recruit Mormons as strikebreakers during the bitter Carbon County coal strike of 1903-1904, the Mormon Church First Presidency published a categorical denial that the church was a party to the undertaking.

This rather neutral attitude probably gave moral support not only to union organizers in their fight against conservative pro-management forces but also to those resisting radical threats from within the labor movement itself. In the 1890s both the Western Federation of Miners and the Western Labor Union enjoyed some success at the expense of the AFL. After 1900 the WFM organized workers in many mines, mills, and smelters, and a few years later the Industrial Workers of the World launched a campaign among unskilled labor as part of a national free speech movement and in an effort to extend its influence beyond the mining areas, the IWW in 1913 increased its activity in Salt Lake City, in Ogden, and among railroad workers in various parts of the state. Indicative of the public reaction was the August 1913 riot in which a mob assaulted IWW speaker James F. Morgan and in which subsequent gunfire injured six men. The Joe Hill case a few months later showed radical unionism still to be anathema to most Utahns.

The prevailing attitude of the courts and of most elected officials made it virtually impossible for workers to bargain collectively unless their employers permitted them to do so. Vigorous attempts to unionize often led to violence as property rights clashed with personal liberty. Coal miners staged a bitter and unsuccessful strike against the Utah Fuel Company. During a strike against the Harriman railroad system in 1911, violence resulted from the attempt to bring in strikebreakers, and one striker was killed; the railroad broke the strike without public intervention in the case. In 1912 strikes occurred at the Murray smelter of the American Smelting and Refining Company and at the Utah Copper Company operations at Bingham. Battles between strikebreakers and strikers at Murray brought out the Utah militia; at Bingham the Salt Lake County Sheriff sent 400 special deputies who, together with 500 strikebreakers, succeeded in killing two strikers and in ending the strike within a year.

In contrast to the abject failure of labor to unionize such large corporations as Utah Copper, American Smelting and Refining, and Utah Fuel, employees of many smaller businesses in Salt Lake City were able to organize quite successfully. Especially between 1912 and 1914, when Congress and the state legislature were adopting various progressive labor reforms, such tradesmen as typographers, plumbers, electrical workers, and laundry workers succeeded in securing union shop agreements. In general relationships between employees and management in most small and middle-sized businesses appear to have been amicable. By 1916 reported violations of the minimum wage and maximum hour laws for women were infrequent and some firms were venturing toward welfare capitalism. Notable was the J. G. McDonald Chocolate Company of Salt Lake City, which provided dining and reading rooms, recreation facilities, a roof garden, and a small zoo for the benefit of its employees.

Conclusion

The growth of the union movement was only one result of the vigorous economy that developed in Utah between the time she won statehood and the end of World War I. Though the combination of agriculture, mining, manufacturing, and transportation produced a dependent relationship with the national economy, it also produced unprecedented prosperity for Utah's people. Per capita personal income in constant dollars (1964 = $1) increased

444

from $776 in 1900 to $1,023 in 1919-21. Though Utah per capita income lagged behind the national average and behind that of all of the Mountain States except New Mexico, it nevertheless enjoyed a thirty percent growth.

For most Utahns the period was one of improving material well-being and prospects. Few contemporaries would have quarrelled with Governor Simon Bamberger's assessment in January 1917 that:

while a portion of the stimulus may have been provided by the European war, the continuance of that war is in no wise essential to the continued prosperity of the state. Competent authorities hold that the present high price of metals will be maintained irrespective of the course of the warring powers. While food products may decrease slightly in price, the Utah farmer will not lose much, for he is learning by scientific intensive farming to produce a larger crop per acre each year and with an established market his future is assured.

That Bamberger's optimism was ill-founded became evident only after the end of the war.

Chapter 23
Bibliographical Essay

A general study of Utah's economic development during the period is Leonard J. Arrington and Thomas G. Alexander, *A Dependent Commonwealth: Utah's Economy from Statehood to the Great Depression*, ed. by Dean L. May (Charles Redd Monographs in Western History, Brigham Young University, 1974). Basic statistics will be found in "Measures of Economic Changes in Utah, 1847-1947," *Utah Economic and Business Review*, December 1947; Arrington, *The Changing Economic Structure of the Mountain West, 1850-1950* (1963); and Simon Kuznets *et al.*, *Population Redistribution and Economic Growth: United States, 1870-1950*, three volumes (1957-64).

Additional information will be found in El Roy Nelson, *Utah's Economic Patterns* (1956); Wain Sutton, ed., *Utah: A Centennial History*, three volumes (1949); and Noble Warrum, *Utah Since Statehood: Historical and Biographical*, three volumes (1919). Useful for specific data are the annual reports of the Utah Bureau of Immigration, Labor, and Statistics and its successor, the Industrial Commission. Articles in the *New West Magazine* give examples of local conditions.

Particularly helpful for labor problems during the period are Lynda Broadbent Gibbs, "The History of the United Mine Workers of America in Carbon County, Utah, up to 1933" (master's thesis, Brigham Young University, 1968); Dee Scorup, "A History of Organized Labor in Utah" (master's thesis, University of Utah, 1935), which is weakened by a number of unsubstantiated assertions; and three articles by Helen Z. Papanikolas in the *Utah Historical Quarterly:* "The Greeks of Carbon County," April 1954; "Life and Labor Among the Immigrants of Bingham Canyon," Fall 1965; and "Toil and Rage in a New Land: The Greek Immigrants in Utah," Spring 1970. Although predominantly a social history, Papanikolas, ed., *The Peoples of Utah* (1976), contains economic information and anecdotes. The best general study of Utah labor is Sheelwant Bapurao Pawar, "An Environmental Study of the Development of the Utah Labor Movement, 1860-1935" (Ph.D. dissertation, University of Utah, 1968), which makes use of union records and examines the movement in terms of current labor theory. A recent unpublished study is Glenn V. Bird, "The Industrial Workers of the World in Utah . . ." (master's thesis, Brigham Young University, 1976).

The Summer 1963 issue of *UHQ* is devoted to "A Century of Mining, 1863-1963." See also James B. Allen, "The Changing Impact of Mining on the Economy of Twentieth-Century Utah," *UHQ,* Summer 1970; and Arrington and Gary Hansen, *The Richest Hole on Earth: A History of the Bingham Copper Mine* (1963). The sugar beet industry is studied in Arrington's *Beet Sugar in the West: A History of the Utah-Idaho Sugar Company, 1891-1966* (1966).

For articles on several aspects of reclamation and conservation during the early twentieth century, see the Summer 1971 issue of *UHQ.* Electrical industry development is chronicled in Arrington, "Utah and the Depression of the 1890s," *UHQ,* January 1961.

Chapter 24
The New Immigrants

Helen Z. Papanikolas

As is true concerning the United States, Utah is a commonwealth born of immigration. The newcomers may be thought of as coming to the Great Basin and Colorado Plateau in four sequences. In the first cycle, the forebears of the Indians came so long ago that they are now thought of as Utah's indigenous population, and yet in complete refutation of the melting pot process neither the Mormon pioneer missionary efforts nor the federal government's vacillating policies were effective in accomplishing assimilation. Utah's Indians are still to a large extent separated from the mainstream of state development. Part of their story has been told in earlier chapters; their vicissitudes in the twentieth century are treated later.

The immigration of the Mormons—chiefly from the British Isles, Scandinavia, and Germany—was woven into the tapestry of Utah's territorial history as a second cycle. Diminishing numbers of immigrant converts have continued to come from northern and western Europe since the Mormon Church ceased to promote the concept of gathering to Zion, but most of the contemporary influx of Mormons is a homecoming for those who earlier went out into the world to seek their fortunes.

The third cycle of immigration began with the mines and railroads of the later territorial years and peaked during the first three decades of statehood. Southern and eastern Europeans, plus a smattering of other nationalities who comprised what is described in American history as the "new immigration," found their way to Utah's Carbon County and to the mining and smelting centers in and around Salt Lake Valley. Immigration restrictions and changing economic conditions drastically curtailed this influx by the 1930s, and the assimilation process has by now eliminated the pejorative references to *Bohunks* and *Wops*. The story of that gentile immigration follows.

In the final cycle the second World War launched the latest wave of newcomers—men, women, and children with Oriental or Spanish-American names or black skins to distinguish them from old-stock Utahns. Their story is also told in another chapter.

The New Immigrants

Granting of statehood and the rapid industrialization of the state are parallel themes in Utah's turn-of-the-century history. Although the Mormon preoccupation with building the political and economic kingdom of God on earth had been abandoned, the transitional years were not entirely smooth. There were still controversies without and within the church, and added to these was the unsettling inward rush of the new immigrants from the Balkans, the Mediterranean, and the Middle East in response to the labor needs for industrializing Utah.

Large labor gangs of these immigrants moved from mines to mills to smelters and from railroad section gangs to railyards. Among the agrarian Mormons, the throng of single men laying rails through sparsely inhabited terrain and filling up narrow canyons of mining towns with tents and shacks brought ancient fears for the safety of their women and of their Zion. Even before the immigrants had reached the state, its inhabitants had become conditioned to what was called their undesirability. Pronouncements on their biological and mental inferiority were regularly printed in newspapers and intoned in state legislatures and in Congress. The new immigrants relived the immigrant experience of the Irish and other immigrants of a half century earlier.

How many Greeks, Italians, South Slavs (Yugoslavs), and Middle-easterners came to Utah cannot be known. Census records are at variance with lodge, church, and employment figures, and the many ethnic neighborhoods with complete services for their inhabitants—boardinghouses, meat and vegetable peddlers, bakeries, cheesemakers, and ice, coal, and feed stores—give evidence that only a portion of the new immigrants were counted.

According to census figures, there were 1,062 Italians in the state in 1900 and 3,116 in 1910, and there were three Greeks in 1900 and 4,062 in 1910, making these two groups 11.3 percent of the state's foreign-born population. By 1920 the Italians had increased in number and the Greeks had decreased, but the percentage figure remained almost the same. The peak years of Italian, Greek, and South Slav population were reached between the 1910 and 1920 censuses just prior to the United States' entrance into the First World War, when mine, mill, smelter, and railroad activity was at its height. Yet immigrants of these national groups known to have been in the Salt Lake area at that time are not found in Polk's Directory. Census-taking was loosely carried on, and immigrant men were always moving in search of work.

South Slav census tabulations are particularly subject to criticism. Croats and Slovenes were listed as Austrians, as were Germans and Italians who were under Austrian jurisdiction. The 1910 census listed 275 Serbs and 2,628 Austrians in the state, yet records of seven Slovenian lodges throughout Utah indicate that more than 4,500 Slovenes had been enrolled prior to World War I. The 1920 census counted only 987 Serbs and Austrians, an obvious inaccuracy. In *The Croatian Immigrants in America* (1971), Croatian scholar George Prpic states that approximately 7,000 Croats were in Utah at that period—probably an inflated figure. The only definite statement that can be made about the Yugoslav population in Utah is that the Croats were greatest in number, the Slovenes were second, and lastly were the Serbs. Others, such as the Montenegrins and Bosnians, were too few to be numerically significant.

The Middle-eastern immigrants also have an inaccurate census record. There were far fewer Middle-easterners than other new immigrants, and they were relegated to the "all others" category in the census tabulations; they could also have been occasionally counted as Turks because they came from Turkish-held land. The 1920 census did report the presence of eighty Armenians.

Conditions of Living

If statistics on the new immigrants are unclear, their social history is fresh and vivid. Housing and wage discrimination was glaring. Railroad gang workers were separated into "white men's camps" where one railroad car was used for cooking, another for eating, and a third for bunkbed sleeping, and "foreigners' camps" in which one car was used for cooking and eating, with platforms constructed at either end for sleeping. In mining, smelter, and mill towns each group of immigrants clustered together for protection and mutual help. Many lived in shacks they had built out of blasting-powder boxes on company land; outside the shacks were separate streams for drinking water and sewage. Management took little responsibility for providing adequate housing.

449

Companies built boardinghouses over the years, but they proved to be insufficient. The lack of housing was a crushing burden to the first picture brides who came to Utah; almost all of them either ran boardinghouses or had brothers and cousins living in the house with them while they raised large families, cooked myriad meals, filled an endless number of lunch buckets, washed clothes by hand with homemade soap, baked bread (the Greeks used outdoor earth ovens), grew vegetables, and canned fruit. The *zagruda* family system of the South Slavs, in which families of parents and sons lived under the same roof, continued in Utah for many years. In their native countries the young mothers would have had older women in the extended families to help with housework and the raising of children; but in the new country they were struggling alone with the patriarchal society of their cultures. A few women saw the boardinghouse system as a means of acquiring security for their families, and they welcomed the opportunity regardless of the toil that accompanied it.

Poor housing, dangerous working conditions, and low wages were harsh aspects of immigrant life, but the extortionist practices of *padrones,* equally matched by management from straw bosses to superintendents, were most galling to workers. American laborers were free of the *padrone* system and were not subject to paying bribes. Bosses emulated labor agents to enrich themselves. The reminiscence of James Galanis of Helper (Carbon County) is typical of the immigrant experience:

I got a job at the Armour's packing house in Omaha for 2 or 3 hours a day at 23¢ an hour. Out of this sum five of us had to live. Fortunately, I thought, a labor agent offered us a job on a railroad 800 miles away, paying him $8 a piece for commission, which we borrowed, and on a freight train we reached our destination but there was NO JOB, neither were we allowed to return unless we paid the transportation charges back to Omaha.

We worked at some farm for 50¢ a day for 19 days and paid our way back to Omaha. From Omaha I went to Castle Gate, Utah, where I was offered a job at the coke ovens, provided I paid a $20 commission for the boss and his gang. When I reported to work, as agreed, the agent told me that someone else had bid the job with $10 more and since I had no more money I lost the job plus the $20 commission. . . . Then . . . I got me a job in the recently started coal mine at Kenilworth. The first month's check was $32.50. I got fired from there because not having any money to spare I refused to contribute towards buying a diamond ring for the superintendent's wife. (We had to please and pay everybody to hold our job.)

Because they were victims of labor agents and management with neither unions nor workmen's compensation to protect them and because maimings and deaths were a constant specter, immigrants were ever aware of the precariousness of life in America. The yearly State Immigrant Inspector's reports and those of mine inspectors that followed are filled with names of immigrants who were maimed and blinded by blasting powder, who died in explosions, and who were killed in collapses of coal and ore roofs. The largest coal mine explosions took place in Scofield's Winter Quarters Mine in 1900 where 200 men died, and in Castle Gate in 1924, an explosion that killed 172 men.

The Padrone System

Immigrants to Utah found themselves in despairing circumstances as a result of the connivance of mine and railroad officials with alien labor agents. Utah Copper Company records show several Serbian agents on their rolls; George (Gibran) Katter was an important Lebanese *padrone;* Mose Paggi, editor of the Salt Lake City Italian newspaper *Il Minatore* and a consular official, was in partnership with Leonidas G. Skliris, a Greek labor agent of formidable power. Only Edward "Daigoro Sama" ("Great Man") Hashimoto, an influential Japanese merchant, was considered as prestigious as was Skliris.

The Greeks had by far the greatest number of workers in the state; unlike other ethnic groups, their *padrone* system can be documented. When the opening of mines required extending the railroad through the West, Skliris and other daring Greeks left thriving Greek towns in New York and Chicago, drawn by the opportunity of providing labor for the allied industries of railroads, mines, mills, and smelters. The most important of these agents was Skliris, called by Americans the *Czar of the Greeks.* His authority radiated from Utah to all parts of the West.

As labor agent for the Oregon Short Line, the Denver and Rio Grande Western, and the Union Pacific railroads with their coal company subsidiaries and for the Utah Copper Company interests in Utah and Nevada, Skliris advertised in Greek newspapers in the United States, mainland Greece, and the island of Crete. Thousands of Greeks responded, some coming directly from their provinces wearing *foustanellas* (white pleated kilts) or Cretan breeches. Other Greeks worked their way westward when they were unable to find work in the factories, restaurants, and shoeshine parlors of eastern cities. Other Eastern Orthodox—Serbs, Albanians, and Lebanese (as distinguished from the Maronites)—also came to

451

Skliris for work. Each immigrant paid his lieutenants an initial fee of about twenty dollars and signed a contract allowing mine and railroad management to deduct one dollar a month from his wages for Skliris. With his control of a large portion of the state's labor supply, his agency for Greek, Italian, and Austrian steamship lines, and his partnerships in company stores where laborers had to trade or lose their jobs, Skliris became immensely wealthy.

Labor agents kept immigrants at their mercy. A common practice of *padrones* was to hire a man, take his fee, and then replace him within two or three months with a new arrival. The celebrated June 16, 1908, killing of a Skliris agent, George Demetrakopoulos, was the result of such a firing. Countrymen aided the killer to escape, eventually to Crete. Legend has two versions of his successful flight: one version was that he boarded a train disguised as a doctor wearing his black Sunday suit and carrying a physician's satchel; the other version was that he got on the train and was not recognized because his hair was freshly dyed red and he was sporting a false mustache.

Besides providing cheap labor for industry, *padrones* could quickly bring in large numbers of strikebreakers, readily recruited among wandering young immigrants who were desperate for work. Pitting one national group against another and setting opposing factions within each ethnic people initiated a bitter feuding that pervaded immigrant life for decades. Skliris's enlisting of mainland Greeks to break the Cretan-led Bingham copper strike of 1912 added to their old-country political differences and produced a schism, vestiges of which still exist.

Such schisms and the general welfare of their fellow countrymen were of no concern to *padrones*. They were contemptuous of those who worked with their hands. The American labor movement was giving dignity to manual labor, but this concept was so radical to immigrants that it would take more than a generation for them to become convinced that manual labor was not degrading. *Padrones* absolved themselves of insuring workers of proper housing, food, and other services—except for the Japanese labor agents, who assumed some responsibility for their countrymen.

The Movement Toward Unionization

The immigrants were not deterred by deaths, maimings, or discrimination; they continued to come to Utah, driven to America by the poverty of their countries. The rumors of work at higher wages in the West supplied an abundance of cheap labor to mines and railroads for the first quarter of the century. The labor scene was a paradox. Thousands of workers were needed for the major industries that were opening rapidly with the aid of eastern capital and to build branch rail lines, to change narrow-gauge rails to standard gauge, to maintain the rail lines, and to mine metal and coal. But Mormons, still following the dictates of their church leaders to stay on the land, were not able to fill the industrial demands and were not willing to see immigrant invaders among them.

If the immigrants had proved to be a docile people, they would have lived isolated from the state's rural population and would have been merely objects of curiosity; but, as unskilled workers, they became part of labor's chaotic push for unionization. Each group made its first appearance during labor strife, which was in itself disruptive and which presaged an unwelcome moving away from the agrarian life. The Americans and English-speaking immigrants who went on strike in the 1890s were replaced by Finns, Italians, and Yugoslavs. In the 1903 Carbon County strike the Italians and Yugoslavs led in unionization attempts and the Greeks were brought in as strikebreakers. In the 1912 Bingham copper strike and the 1922 Carbon County coal strike, Greeks led the strikers and Mexicans took their places in the mines.

The leap of aliens from strikebreakers to strikers was as disturbing to Mormons as it was to Americans elsewhere. The Mormons' early social experiments, the United Orders, and the union membership among the vanguard of British converts were being forgotten; any challenge to established authority was viewed as anarchy, and church leaders sided with industrialists during strikes.

Immigrants were suspected to be radical because of their quick initiation into the unionization struggle. Italians and Yugoslavs were especially responsive to striking for workers' rights; many had had the experience of traveling north for seasonal labor in their homelands and had learned of labor reform that was considered radical for the period. Others had come to Utah from the Northwest, where they had become involved in woodcutters' union activity, and from the coal mines of Red Lodge, Montana, one of the few socialist towns in the nation. The leading Utah labor figure in the United Mine Workers of America unionization fight, Frank Bonacci, came to Carbon County from British Columbia already a union member.

Greeks, however, had not had the experience in their country of going north for farm and industrial labor. Although they became leaders of two of Utah's biggest strikes, their reasons for joining

A Serbian fraternal lodge musters with uniforms and banners at Highland Boy, Bingham Canyon, in 1907.

unions were not for ideological principles but to rid themselves of their powerful labor agent and to protest such oppressive practices as being short-weighed on the scales. To Greeks, more than to Italians and Yugoslavs, labor in mines, mills, and smelters was temporary, a means of acquiring sufficient savings to become shopkeepers and property owners in their native land. Middle-eastern immigrants also had short-range plans for remaining in industrial work; they early accumulated the few hundred dollars that enabled them to become saloon proprietors, storekeepers, or merchants who traveled through mining camps with supplies of notions, laces, florid bedspreads, and embroidered tablecloths.

Labor Disputes

Charismatic leaders and immigrant conception of honor that required retaliation when cheated on the weighing machines and when forced to bribe weighers for cars were important aspects of strike activity. The lack of unity among Italian strikers in the Carbon County 1901 coal strike was altered in the 1903-1904 strike led by Charles DeMolli, an Italian organizer associated with the *Il La-*

voratore Italiano, a Trinidad, Colorado, newspaper that disseminated United Mine Workers' views to Italians. Young Italian women paraded down muddy streets in support of their striking men and one of them, Caterina Bottino, hid the famed labor organizer Mother Jones from authorities.

In the 1912 Bingham Canyon strike, Cretans, determined to free themselves from their *padrone,* Leonidas Skliris, conducted warfare from the foothills surrounding the mining town. The Western Federation of Miners was unable to convince them to descend to the town theater to hear Governor William Spry appeal for peace. In respect to their priest, who climbed the slopes wearing dusty black robes, a tall black priest's hat, and a glinting pectoral cross, they marched down to the theater but took their orders only from their leader, John Leventis. The strike did not result in unionization, yet the Cretans were jubilant because it forced Skliris to leave the state.

In the 1922 Carbon County coal strike Cretans joined to protest their being shortweighed on the scales. The strike was precipitated by Frank Bonacci, the Italian organizer for the United Mine Workers, who remonstrated with Kenilworth Mine officials at a decrease in wages while coal prices remained stable. Cretans became militant leaders of the tent towns that were established by the union after strikers and their families were forced out of company houses and led ambushes on trains rumored to be bringing in strikebreakers. The killing of a Cretan in an orchard inflamed them; seven hundred carrying small blue and white Greek flags followed the casket to the church and on to the graveyard.

In the 1933 Carbon County coal strike Yugoslavs led the Communist National Miners Union against Bonacci's United Mine Workers, each attempting to unionize the mines under the new legal sanctions of the National Recovery Administration (NRA). Yugoslav women led marches, assaulted guards, and humiliated sheriffs and managers alike with their tactics. One of them, however, rescued a sheriff from a mob gathered at the Helper Park. When Communist control of the National Miners Union was exposed, the United Mine Workers emerged victorious.

Nationalism and Ethnocentrism

For all Americans the strike proclivity of the new immigrants added to their foreignness, and the expression "Like oil and water, they don't mix" was common. There was no mistaking these later immigrant groups among the lighter-skinned Utah populace. Each group spoke its own language at work and on the street, had lodges, read foreign-language newspapers, belonged either to the Eastern Orthodox or the Roman Catholic churches, lived in "Greek Towns, Lebanese Towns, Bohunk Towns, Wop Towns, and Little Italies." The exotic customs, extreme nationalism, and rigid family systems that endowed enormous responsibilities to a large circle of kin were mystifying to the Mormons, among whom convert customs and languages had faded faster than the three generations usually taken for assimilation. The commonality of church participation brought intermarriage of convert groups within the first generation, and converts renounced native countries and old faiths for a new land and a young religion. (Armenians are an exception to the new-immigrant phenomenon in Utah. Most came as converts to Mormonism and were scattered across the state. They began to marry outside their ethnic group during the first generation.)

As soon as they arrived in Utah the immigrants demonstrated they were not interested in Americanizing themselves. On paydays they sent thousands of dollars in postal orders and bank drafts to relatives in their homelands. The money was for fulfillment of family obligations: to provide sisters with dowries and to help parents who had mortgaged their plots of land to pay for their sons' passage to America. These remittances were regarded by Utahns as sending the country's wealth abroad for the enrichment of other nations; during labor strife and the increased anti-alien attacks of World War I, immigrants were symbols of un-Americanism.

What was viewed as un-Americanism was a manifestation of the nationalism the immigrants brought with them. Centuries of invasions, wars, and foreign rule had coalesced each people's religion with a fiery nationalism. For the Italians ethnocentrism was centered in one's village, then in his province, and finally in either the fertile, literate, industrial north or the infertile, illiterate, agrarian south. This passion for religion and nation that was one and the same for the immigrants was fanatical; the oath "I swear by my country" was heard as often as "I swear by my God."

Of all the immigrants the Greeks were the most nationalistic. The first Greek church in Utah was built in 1905 when only one Greek woman had arrived. The first of several Greek language newspapers began publication in 1907, and Greek schools were established before 1920. During the Balkan Wars of 1912 and 1913, over two hundred Utah Greeks returned to Greece to fight the Turks and Bulgarians. Greeks had an additional element added to their distinctiveness: except for Serbs and Lebanese, who seldom attended liturgies because of the language barrier, their church was composed wholly of Greeks. In the Catholic churches various immigrant groups and Americans worshipped together.

Hostility that Americans displayed toward the immigrants because of their nationalism, cultural differences, and strike involvement and the instability of their life under labor agents and management were more than matched by ancient disputes and diversities between the nationalities and within each of them. Only when they were threatened by the outsiders—as in the attempted lynching of a Greek in Price for taking a "white" girl for a ride in his new automobile, and in the attempted lynching of another Greek in Salt Lake City accused of killing Jack Dempsey's brother, and during the Ku Klux Klan attacks of 1924—did the immigrants unite strongly and successfully.

Italians were listed on company rolls as either South Italians or North Italians. The principle of *campanilisimo*—everything alien beyond the sound of the village bell—was abandoned after the first few years in Utah; suspiciousness against other Italians was decided by one's birth in either northern or southern provinces, and early Italian lodges were so segregated. Italians from the north were the first to arrive in Utah; by the time those from the south came, they were well established, and many of them were businessmen. They were the fearful recipients of Black Hand threats nailed to their doors by compatriots from southern Italy.

The internal dissensions of the people classified as *Austrians* were even more complex than those of Italians. Serbs, Croatians, Slovenes, Dalmatians, Montenegrins, Herzegovinians, and Bosnians (united into the Kingdom of Yugoslavia in 1929) were instilled with ancient hostilities toward each other, especially the Eastern or Greek Orthodox Serbs and the Roman Catholic Croats. The July 1908 killing of a Serbian Orthodox, incorrectly reported in newspapers as a Greek Catholic or "of the Greek faction of Austrians," reflected centuries of religious and political divisions. The Austria-Hungarian Croats were Catholic and followed the New (Gregorian) Calendar; the Serbs were Orthodox and used the Old (Julian) Calendar. On holy days, particularly on Christmas and Easter when elaborate celebrations included old-country customs such as the roasting of suckling pigs, the danger of feuding between Orthodox and Catholics was always present.

The First World War brought Serbo-Croatian aggression to a peak. Croats and Slovenes were exempt from induction into the United States Army because they would be facing their own people, who were aligned with the Central Powers. Young Serbs, however, were being taken into the army—some of them were even returning to fight with the Serbian Army—and were angered at the uninvolvement of other South Slavs. In Bingham Canyon, the Serbs fought draft-exempt Croats and Slovenes. A tentative calm followed only after the belligerent Serb leaders were inducted into the army.

Greeks were listed on company rolls as either Greeks (mainlanders) or Cretans. Both were fervidly attached to the Greek Orthodox Church that had survived over four hundred years of Turkish oppression. The longer guerrilla life of Cretans made them alert to insurrection. They were liberals; most mainlanders were royalists. During political uprisings in the fatherland, Cretans and mainlanders in Utah avoided each other's coffeehouses. While fifteen Greeks and one Italian were on trial for the killing of a deputy sheriff in the 1922 Carbon County strike, feuding over old-country politics left one Greek dead. In labor wars Cretans were more prone to strike; in the 1911 Kenilworth coal strike (the "Greek War") mainland Greeks refused to follow Cretan strikers who were supplied with ammunition by other Cretans who infiltrated the mining camp at night.

The reactions of Utahns to the importation of old-country politics and cultural attitudes ranged from curiosity about vendettas, coffeehouses, marriage customs, and religious celebrations to active denunciations of immigrant "un-American" activities in joining the unions to extreme antiforeign demonstrations during the World War I years.

Opposition and Accommodation

The critical years in immigrant life were those of the early 1920s. The antiforeign sentiment of the war was kept alive by the American Legion, which insisted on instant Americanization, compulsory English education, and repressing of foreign languages and newspapers. During these years immigrants deserted manual labor to become store and property owners. Greeks graduated from supplying boardinghouses with lamb to becoming fullfledged sheepmen, driving their flocks to mountain ranges around Scofield, Park City, and Vernal in the summer and on the sagebrush plains of eastern Utah in the winter. The new prosperity of the immigrants, most of them American citizens by then, was resented by Utah's older residents. Together with their supposed unassimilability and the rising incidence of intermarriages with American women, that prosperity contributed to the 1924 Ku Klux Klan uprisings.

The Klan burned crosses on Salt Lake City's Ensign Peak, marched down Main Street, and threatened immigrants who were seen with American women. In Magna crosses were burned on the Oquirrh foothills and in front of a Greek's store: he had eloped with an American woman. Klansmen paraded down Magna's main street and were followed to the park by a gang of young Greeks, who pulled off the white Klan masks and exposed a number of leading townspeople. In Helper men rampaged through Greek stores, forced women employees to go home, and warned the women against working for immigrants. The Klan burned crosses in the railyards and on a mountain slope; Catholics answered with a burning circle on an opposite slope. The show of strength weakened the Klan although the explosive milieu it produced led to the 1925 lynching of Robert Marshall, a Black, south of Price.

The nationwide hysteria against aliens resulted in laws that drastically limited the number of new immigrants entering the country. The effect on immigrant life was instantaneous. The seemingly unending supply of industry labor was cut off, and workers who had been in the country for one or more decades were able to extricate themselves from the *padrones*. Labor agents had to turn to other means of making a living and proved to be profoundly unsuccessful. Lieutenants who had combined working for a *padrone* with running a business were the earliest prosperous immigrants; how they had accumulated their capital was almost forgotten with time, and they achieved a respectability among Mormons and other Americans. The passing of the restrictive immigration laws of 1921 and 1924 also brought the demise of the boardinghouse system, a cause for rejoicing by the women who ran them.

The restriction of immigration and the Ku Klux Klan attacks, symbols of fear and hostility, coincided strangely with the most economically productive years for the immigrants. Life was gregarious and exuberant. Lodges were in their prime; local, state, and national conventions were fertile ground for old-country matchmaking that continued for second-generation children born in the United States. Picnics, saints day celebrations, and the most important religious observance of the year, Easter, were ethnic community affairs. On June 15 the Serbs commemorated the battle on the Kosovo Plain (1389) that completely destroyed Serbian independence. On March 25 Greeks celebrated the revolt against the Turks with plays staged by Greek schools and members of the Star Theatrical Company—the theme of the plays concerned the heroic lives of the guerrillas. Italians succeeded in having Columbus Day declared a state holiday, and on this and other holidays the many Italian marching bands performed. Lebanese gathered from throughout the state for weddings and baptisms. At gatherings men played native instruments while people in national dress danced and sang their folk heritage. Among the celebrants were matriarchs, patriarchs, midwives, folkhealers, and evil-eye dispellers.

Although customs were continued and native languages were taught to the American-born generation, immigrant institutions— lodges, newspapers, the Catholic Church, and mutual aid societies that provided sickness and death benefits—were means of accommodation to life in the new country. Lodges imitated American civic organizations; they brought people out of their ethnic towns and into American life through participation in community affairs such as the Fourth of July and Pioneer Day parades. Lodges also became early spokesmen for ethnic groups in political life. Unions, at first hostile toward immigrants for working for lower wages than did the Americans, were an important aid in Americanization. All ethnic institutions, even the maligned Greek coffeehouses, brought immigrants together—the educated few, the many illiterate—and helped them learn about American life and its expectations.

Depression, War, and Assimilation

Following the prosperity of the 1920s, when immigrants began leaving the ethnic towns and moving into more desirable areas, the depression years of the 1930s brought the realization that they had settled for life in the United States. Not only did they fear the effects of the worldwide economic collapse on their historically poor homelands, but they had children who considered America home. American life had become increasingly more immediate and the life-style of their native countries had become increasingly more distant. Although still vitally interested in old-country politics, they had long been aware that America's educational opportunities for their children were unattainable in the lands of their birth.

World War II marked the end of the immigrant phase of life. Except for those associated with religious services, few Old World customs were followed. With children in the armed forces the immigrants fully recognized America as their country. When grandchildren began marrying outside the ethnic group, mainly with Mormons, immigrants faced the inevitability of assimilation.

After the war more immigrants arrived with the same zeal to accomplish as had the first aliens in the early years of the century. They have lived the immigrant experience with greater ease: they have come with better educations, and some have come with skills;

the war and increased communications had already taught them much about America. Their absorption has been easier and their economic rise faster.

These newest of the new immigrants have added vitality and diversity to Utah. However, the important role of having provided the brawn that changed Utah from an agricultural to an industrial state and of having led the long, rugged, and finally successful fight for unionization of mines, mills, and smelters was played by the first of the new immigrants—the disparate ones.

Chapter 24
Bibliographical Essay

The paucity of material on the new immigrants requires a detailed examination of past newspapers published in areas where immigrants congregated. Oral histories and court documents add other dimensions. Oral histories are at present filed in the American West Center, University of Utah; biographies and documents can be found in the Ethnic Archives, Western Americana Division, Marriott Library, University of Utah, Salt Lake City.

Investigators in the new immigrant field are few. All are represented in Helen Z. Papanikolas (ed.), *The Peoples of Utah* (1976): Philip F. Notarianni, "Italianita in Utah: The Immigrant Experience"; Joseph Stipanovich, "Falcons in Flight: The Yugoslavs"; Robert F. Zeidner, "From Babylon to Babylon: Immigration from the Middle East"; and Papanikolas, "The Exiled Greeks."

Fullrounded accounts of the immigrant roles in the coal mining industry are available in Allen Kent Powell's works: the definitive "A History of Labor Union Activity in the Eastern Utah Coal Fields, 1900-1934" (Ph.D. dissertation, University of Utah, 1976) and "Labor at the Beginning of the Twentieth Century: The Carbon County, Utah, Coal Fields, 1900-1905" (master's thesis, University of Utah, 1972); and two *UHQ* articles: "Tragedy at Scofield," Spring 1973, and "The 'Foreign Element' and the 1903-1904 Carbon County Coal Miners' Strike," Spring 1975.

Featuring "Immigrants and Mines," the Spring 1975 *UHQ* also includes: Joseph Stipanovich, "South Slav Settlements in Utah, 1890-1935"; Philip Notarianni, "Italian Fraternal Organizations in Utah, 1897-1934"; and Helen Z. Papanikolas, "Utah's Coal Lands: A Vital Example of How America Became a Great Nation." Two useful master's theses written at the University of Utah are Stipanovich's, published in 1975 as *The South Slavs in Utah: A Social History,* and Notarianni's "The Italian Immigrant in Utah: Nativism (1900-1925)" (1972).

461

Other Papanikolas publications in *UHQ* include: "The Greeks of Carbon County," Spring 1954; "Life and Labor Among the Immigrants of Bingham Canyon," Fall 1965; "Magerou: The Greek Midwife," Winter 1970; *Toil and Rage in a New Land: The Greek Immigrants in Utah,* second ed. rev., reprinted from *UHQ,* Spring 1970; and "Unionism, Communism, and the Great Depression: The Carbon County Coal Strike of 1933," Summer 1973. Two of her articles on cultural behavior are "Greek Folklore of Carbon County" in Thomas E. Cheney (ed.), *Lore of Faith and Folly* (1971), and "Ethnicity in Mormondom: A Comparison of Immigrant and Mormon Cultures," in Thomas G. Alexander (ed.), *Essays on the American West, 1975-1976* (Charles Redd Monographs in Western History, Brigham Young University, 1977).

Chapter 25
From War to Depression

Thomas G. Alexander

The tide of Progressivism that crested in Utah's 1917 legislature was followed by a change of mood and direction when the United States plunged into a war she had assiduously avoided for nearly three years. Already the European conflict had combined with rapid American economic growth to stimulate Utah's economic growth to new heights, and the 1917-19 wartime boom prolonged the trend. Then the national economy went through a quick depression-recovery cycle; Utah participated more fully in the deflationary phase than in the revival. A mixed performance in the economic sector throughout the 1920s was matched by mixed election outcomes, moderate to conservative political programs, and impressive performances by a few of the state's governmental leaders.

The Depression of the Early 1920s

Though less industrialized than the average American state during the prewar and war years, Utah was the most industrialized state in the Mountain West. Capital invested in manufacturing increased 175 percent from $47.3 million to $130.6 million between 1909 and 1919. Aggregate capital invested in the state's two basic economic activities increased almost as impressively in the same period—mining increased from $98 million to $187 million (81 percent) and agriculture increased from $150.8 million to $311 million (106 percent). Assets of Utah banks increased from $65.8 million in 1910 to $172.9 million in 1920.

Shortly after the end of the war, however, Utah's economy entered a depression that continued into 1922 and that affected agriculture, mining, and manufacturing significantly throughout the rest of the decade. Unlike most of the remainder of the country where the postwar contraction was severe but short, Utah and the Mountain West suffered a substantial setback and only a partial recovery.

When the war ended, the federal government moved away from financing sales of American farm products to Europe, and the overseas market shrank further as European production revived. The abrupt cancellation of war contracts impacted manufacturing and the mining and transportation upon which war production had depended. The release of shipping that had supplied the war zone also adversely affected Utah.

An important factor in the economic reversal was the shattering of marketing and production patterns that had developed during wartime. With ship traffic from the Atlantic to the Pacific curtailed, railroad freight rates enabled Utah business to penetrate coastal markets that could not be maintained upon the reopening of normal water routes. Freight rates gave Utah products an advantage in the Denver market, but Utah products were at a competitive disadvantage east of there. Efforts to secure more equitable rates through the Interstate Commerce Commission were no more successful in the postwar period than they had been before. (Even a 1924 ruling by the Federal Trade Commission stating that the steel industry should discontinue using the basing point system, which gave a price advantage to steel products originating in the eastern states, was ignored by the industry until after World War II.)

Also contributing to the economic distress were the fiscal and monetary policies pursued by the federal government as the war effort ended. In May 1919 the termination of most wartime business controls gave a new stimulus to inflation. Then in January 1920 the Federal Reserve Board shifted abruptly from an expansionary low-interest policy to a stringent high-interest policy. Coupled with a drastic cutback in federal spending, this threw cold water on the warborn economic boom, and Utah experienced more than a proportionate share of the hard times that affected the country during the next two or three years.

Distress in Mining

The depression had its earliest impact in the mining industry. After peaking in 1917, mineral prices generally lagged behind those of consumer goods. In 1919 Utah's total output of gold, silver, copper, lead, and zinc dropped fifty-four percent below the

464

1918 level. In 1919 and 1920 only eleven companies—about half the 1918 number—paid dividends. Even the industrial giants suffered from declining markets. Utah Copper Company's earnings dropped from $11.60 per share in 1918 to $3.03 per share in 1920. The company shut down its Magna flotation plant in February 1919 and the Arthur concentrator and Garfield smelter were closed in April 1921. Employment at the Bingham Mine dropped from 6,000 to a few hundred in three years, and all the copper-related towns similarly lost population. Utah Copper Company operations did not reopen until April 1922.

Distress in other sectors of the mining industry was not quite as severe or long lasting as it was in copper. Price supports under the Pitman Silver Act of 1918 assisted the silver, lead, and zinc industries. Even with that subsidy the price of silver began to decline in the spring of 1920. The Salt Lake *Tribune* reported early in 1921 that the past year had been the most "trying that the mines of this Tintic District have weathered through a great many years." But 1921 was even worse. Tintic Standard declared no dividend in the third quarter; most of the mines closed; and by the end of the year all major lead and copper companies were either idle or doing only maintenance work.

The depression was slower to affect coal mining, oil drilling, and the nonmetallics. As late as May 1921 the Federal Reserve Board announced that the price of bituminous coal, unlike many other prices, remained one hundred percent above prewar levels. Nevertheless, declining demand forced Utah mines to curtail production during the first half of 1921, and the mines ended the year with a production quota of about seventy-seven percent of the 1920 figure. The economic decline and other sources of instability also damaged several minor extractive industries. By the end of 1921 reports indicated that Utah's oil industry was adversely affected. In addition, the reopening of shipping lanes from Europe and the reorganization of the international potash cartel wiped out all but twelve of 128 potash companies by 1922, and five more closed down by 1926.

Agricultural Depression

Though mining suffered the initial shock, agriculture experienced the greatest long-term distress from the depression. Throughout the years from 1896 to 1914 wheat at a dollar a bushel had been a major agricultural goal. By 1922, however, the Bureau of Labor Statistics wholesale price index had risen forty-nine percent above the 1913 level. As the *Salt Lake Tribune* put it,

In 1920 the Utah Copper Company mine was still confined to Bingham Canyon; a generation later it would swallow up the mining towns in the foreground.

dollar-a-bushel wheat was no longer a goal but a dreaded disaster. Where in 1919 wheat had sold for between $3.35 and $3.50 per bushel, by November 1921 it had dropped to $.98.

Until October 1920 the price level for most agricultural commodities stood above prices that farmers paid for most other goods. During the winter of 1920, agricultural prices declined precipitately, and farmers began to hold onto storable crops. By May 1921 the price of wool, lambs, barley, and wheat had declined to about the 1913-14 level, and the price of cattle had dropped even lower. Wheat and corn were kept in silos and elevators and supplies of cheese, meat, fish, eggs, and fruits remained in cold storage. Sugar beets dropped from $12.03 per ton in 1920 to $5.47 in 1921, which was the lowest price they would be sold for between 1916 and 1932.

By mid-1922 agricultural prices seemed to be stabilizing, but as harvests began in the late summer, profits declined even more. Wheat prices equalled the lows of 1921, and corn, oats, barley, eggs, chickens, and peaches were actually below 1921 levels. Some apples and potatoes were not even harvested because prices were too low to pay for transportation to markets. Fortunately for stockmen, sheep and lamb prices were considered satisfactory and cattle prices improved slightly. It was the only bright spot for Utah farmers.

Manufacturing, Trade, and Banking

The effect of the depression on manufacturing seems to have more nearly paralleled that of mining than of agriculture. By 1919 Utah had developed more than 1,000 manufacturing establishments employing nearly 19,000 people. By 1921 the number of businesses declined to 645 and employment dropped to 13,300. Many primary metals manufacturing plants, sugar plants, and canning factories closed only temporarily, but Midvale's Utah Steel Company plant, founded in 1917 (Utah's only steel plant), closed and was never reopened.

Retail trade did not begin to suffer until 1921. Zion's Cooperative Mercantile Institution reported during 1920 transaction of the largest volume of business of any year in its history. Not until January 1921 did Salt Lake City retail stores experience any month during the depression when the volume of sales was less than the corresponding month of the previous year. Prices declined, and the cost of sirloin steak in Salt Lake City in July 1921 stood at 30.8 cents per pound, lower than prices in any other American city except Portland, Oregon. The cost of steak was twelve cents a pound lower than it had been in July 1913.

Utah's banking community shared the problem of a great many small units in small American towns that were unable to weather the financial stress. The number of banks in the state reached an all-time high of 134 in 1920 and declined every year of the decade except 1924, when the number of new banks equalled the number of failures. While the number of institutions decreased, however, assets of the largest banks climbed. Thus, in spite of failures, assets of Utah banks increased from $172.9 million in 1920 to $193.8 million in 1930.

Government Problems

As the economy experienced reversal, Utah's state and local governments also suffered. Assessed valuation of Utah property reached a peak of $716.9 million in 1921 and then began to decline. Much of the reduction in value came about as value fell on marginal agricultural property that had been purchased during and immediately after World War I. State revenues declined and the state government cut expenditures and fired employees.

To deal with the problem, state and local governments and school districts tried often contradictory measures. Though the state ran a deficit, made loans to farmers, and promoted a program of highway construction, Governor Charles R. Mabey asked the legislature and local governments to practice economy. At the same time, he urged local governments and the federal government to respond to the needs of the people by providing relief and employment. Total public school expenditures increased, but the number of employees and the salaries of existing employees were cut.

Despite opposition from the Chamber of Commerce and the Utah Manufacturers Association, Ogden and Salt Lake City inaugurated special public works projects to ease unemployment. Salt Lake City also opened a free employment service that doubled as a relief agency by distributing fish and potatoes to the needy.

Unemployment and Unrest

Even these efforts did not relieve the distress. As early as February 1919 the Twelfth Federal Reserve District reported increasing unemployment in Utah, and by March joblessness affected about 5,000 workers, mostly miners and the unskilled. Unemployment continued at abnormally high levels through 1920 and in June 1921 the United States Employment Service reported the improbability of any "improvement until the mining depression is relieved."

Groups of unemployed citizens pressed local and state officials to do more. Private relief agencies and charities came to the assistance of many, and public officials exhorted housewives to hire the unemployed to do their spring cleaning. Salt Lake City banks voted to subscribe $60,000 for stock in a foreign trade financing corporation in the hope of stimulating further employment, and many companies went on short shifts to try to spread the work around.

Distressing economic conditions and the example of revolution abroad led Utah laboring men to seek radical alternatives to their disappointing conditions. In February 1919 workers in Salt Lake County organized a Workers', Soldiers', and Sailors' Council on the Soviet model, and the Salt Lake Federation of Labor endorsed the Russian Revolution and the overthrow of all exploiting classes by a vote of sixty-seven to five. At the State Federation of Labor convention in September radicals won further endorsement of their aims; M. P. Bales, shortly to become a member of the Communist Party, was chosen president. During the depression Bales led the

Council of Unemployed, an organization that worked in favor of public works and better conditions for the unemployed.

In some ways the adverse immediate impact of the 1920s depression on Utah's economy was worse than that of the crash of the early 1930s, although the optimistic "boosterism" of business and governmental spokesmen camouflaged the earlier hard times to a degree. The aggregate current liability of Utah businesses that failed during the four years from 1921 to 1924 was actually greater than the liability of failures from 1931 to 1934. Retail sales during 1921 and 1922 were actually below the 1935-39 average. Annual cash farm income declined by about one-half in the early 1920s, and Utah's farmers did not reach the 1920 level of cash income again until another World War expanded their markets.

The Economy After the Depression

Though recovery from the depression was uneven, conditions began to improve early in 1922. The mining response was mixed. From a low of $40.6 million in 1921, the value of minerals produced in Utah rose to $115.1 million in 1929—only $2 million above the wartime production peak in 1917. After a spurt in 1923, silver production fell off again as the price of the metal declined steadily and then collapsed when hard times returned. Copper production, prices, and profits improved sharply and the other nonferrous metals experienced some recovery, but coal prices and employment in the coal industry both declined.

In mining, manufacturing, and agriculture, the massive capital formation of the previous decade did not continue. In fact, both mining and agriculture experienced a decline in total invested capital from 1919 to 1929. Value added by manufacture increased somewhat after 1921, but employment in manufacturing stood below the 1919 figure until the Second World War. Though some stability was achieved by tariff increases and federal loans, agricultural distress continued throughout the decade and the number of jobs declined.

Some sectors of the economy were not seriously affected by the depression. The dawning automobile age produced both business stimuli and social changes during the 1920s. Utah's motor vehicle registrations passed 100,000 for the first time in 1928, and the number of commercial vehicles was growing even faster than was the number of passenger cars. Taxicabs began to appear in Utah cities. An interstate trucking industry also developed in Utah, based on such firms as Pacific Intermountain Express and Interstate Motor Lines. Though the railroads had to reduce freight rates and though employment and revenues declined during 1921, traffic and employment grew during the balance of the decade.

Aviation and radio industries also began to affect the state. Geographic considerations made Salt Lake City an airmail center by 1925, and the first commercial air passenger traffic began two years later. Utah's first two radio stations, KZN (KSL) and KDYL, went on the air in 1922 and provided the printed media with new competition for the advertising dollar.

Electric energy consumption increased from 471 to 858 million kilowatt-hours from 1920 to 1929 (only to fall back to the 1920 level four years later). At the close of the war less than one farm in ten had electrical service; by 1930 fifty-five and a half percent, chiefly located along the Wasatch Front, were so provided. Much of the new hydroelectric power came into the state from Idaho, but new generating plants were built on some of Utah's canyon streams.

In spite of the relatively high price of building materials and high interest rates, the volume of new construction was hardly affected by the postwar depression. Apparently the demand for buildings had become so acute during the wartime curtailment of nonmilitary construction that demand was now great in spite of cost. In 1920 the value of building construction in Salt Lake City was only slightly lower than it was in 1919, and the next year construction recovered rapidly and moved to new heights. A high volume continued through the decade as projects such as the Ogden Arsenal, the Scofield Reservoir, the Salt Lake Federal Reserve Branch Bank, and the Bamberger and Orem Interurban Railway Station in Salt Lake City supplemented the demand for private housing and commercial structures.

Another bright spot in the economic picture was the revival—or reestablishment—of an iron industry. Columbia Steel Company developed a pig iron plant at Ironton, located between Provo and Springville. The company constructed short railroads to bring Carbon County coal to the Denver and Rio Grande Western Railroad line, and the Union Pacific Railroad built a branch line that carried both Iron County ore and tourists to Cedar City. Production at the Ironton plant began in October 1923; between May 1924, when the first iron flowed, and December 1931 the company produced 1.8 million tons of coke and a million tons of iron. Most of the iron went to California for further processing, but some businesses using iron for pipe and other products established themselves near the plant. The company also used coke to produce such byproducts as coal tar, ammonium sulphate, and benzol.

Access to southern Utah made tourism a service enterprise whose economic potential railroads and chambers of commerce began to exploit. The Utah Parks Company, a Union Pacific subsidiary, provided tours and tourist services at Zion, Bryce, Cedar Breaks, and the Grand Canyon. The motion picture potential of southern Utah scenery also began to be tapped, but the new developments were not sufficient to offset the economic consequences of agricultural decline in most communities in the southern half of the state. The net out-migration of Utah population from 1910 to 1940 came in part from those pioneer-founded villages that did not develop alternative economic support systems in the between-wars period. (See Table F, p. 690.)

Labor and the Decline of Unionism

The approximately forty-five percent of the Utah population over ten years of age that was gainfully employed was five percent lower than the national average both in 1920 and in 1930—possibly a reflection on the strengthening local commitment to education beyond the elementary grades. The composition of the labor market changed perceptibly; employment in agriculture, mining, and construction declined, and employment in manufacturing barely increased. New jobs for a population that grew from 449,396 to 507,847 were available in transportation, communications, public utilities, merchandising, services, and government. Per capita annual income stood at $537 in 1929, almost $150 lower than the national average in that peak year of American prosperity.

The trade union radicalism of the war years was short lived as businessmen and conservative workers staged a counterrevolution that broke the back of Utah's labor movement. A group of businessmen and civic leaders had in 1918 organized the Utah Associated Industries with the avowed purpose of ending labor disputes and establishing the open shop throughout the state. In early 1920 the Associated Industries moved to break the union movement in the construction trades, and by mid 1921 they achieved a partial open shop and wage reductions. Possibly the most vigorous battle developed between the employers' organization and the typographical union. Though the conflict raged for three and one-half years the union capitulated by September 1924. By the late 1920s the Utah Federation of Labor became little more than a name; its newspaper folded in 1924, and at the annual convention in 1929 only fifteen delegates representing seven unions—most of them from Ogden—even bothered to attend. In the meantime the legislature prohibited peaceful picketing and repealed the minimum wage for women.

An Economic Plateau

The Utah economy had reached what might be called a plateau by the mid 1920s. Agriculture, particularly staple crop production, remained in a depressed condition. Mineral prices, though higher than they were during the postwar collapse, remained unsatisfactory; manufacturing merely stabilized. Railroading, construction, and retail trade moved to new heights, and new developments in transportation and communication contributed to economic growth. But the combination of factors that gave the title "Prosperity Decade" to the national economy did not allocate to Utah a proportionate share of the boom.

Postwar Elections and Legislation

Contrary to the national trend that brought a hostile Congress to power in opposition to President Woodrow Wilson, Utah's 1918 elections resulted in continued Democratic control of the state. Congressmen Milton R. Welling and James H. Mays were renominated on a platform supporting the war, the graduated income tax, and the League of Nations. The Democratic advantage was heightened by an influenza epidemic that forced the closing of public meetings and incapacitated Mays's Republican opponent, ex-governor William Spry, during the campaign. In addition to winning both congressional posts, the Democrats retained control of both houses of the legislature by substantial margins.

Subjected to pressures for continuing the progressive trend of previous legislatures and for promoting the conformity demand by postwar sentiment, the 1919 legislature moved in both directions. To meet the needs of returning veterans it passed a soldier's settlement act, and it succumbed to antiradical sentiment by passing a criminal syndicalist act and a law that prohibited peaceful picketing. The legislature also strengthened the power of the state banking commissioner, improved workmen's compensation, passed an inheritance tax, increased fees for motor vehicles (now numbering 35,000), and enacted regulations against the sale of fraudulent or misrepresented securities in the state.

Coming as it did during both worsening economic times and a rather heated controversy over the League of Nations, the 1920 election brought a setback to the Democrats. The Republicans nominated Charles R. Mabey, a Bountiful businessman and former state legislator, as their candidate for governor. The Democrats chose Thomas N. Taylor, a Provo businessman and Mormon stake president, who was also Governor Bamberger's choice. Republicans Don B. Colton of Vernal and Elmer O. Leatherwood, a former district attorney, opposed James W. Funk and Mathonihah Thomas for the United States House of Representatives. Reed Smoot, running for the Senate for the fourth time, opposed Congressman Welling.

The election was unusual principally in that Parley P. Christensen, former secretary of the state constitutional convention and Salt Lake County Attorney, was the presidential candidate of the Farmer-Labor Party. The Republicans carried the state in a stunning reversal of their 1916 and 1918 performances. The worsening economy seems to have been the principal issue, and the mood of the state followed that of the country. Warren G. Harding's presidential electors carried every county in the state; the Republican Party elected a majority to both houses in the legislature; Smoot, Mabey, Colton, and Leatherwood won overwhelmingly; and the Republicans controlled every county in the state except Carbon. Christensen ran fourth behind Harding, James M. Cox, and Eugene V. Debs.

In spite of their success, the Republicans were deeply divided in the 1921 legislature. Rural sentiment in the party favored the passage of a state income tax law, but business opposition made that impossible. Basic consensus came about principally in reorganization of the executive department, continuation of the progressive crusade for moral reform, and continuation of nativist sentiment. Orientals were restricted in land acquisition, the sale of cigarettes was prohibited in the state until 1923, and a commission was created to propose the reorganization of the tax system. Besides blocking the passage of income tax legislation, the urban-rural split stopped reapportionment of the legislature.

Governor Mabey was unable to redeem his campaign pledge to institute economy in state government, and his efforts to achieve that end served further to divide the party. With the Federal Bunch's decline in power following Spry's unsuccessful renomination attempt in 1916 there developed in the Republican Party a new organization that tried to make itself the principal political power in the state. Built around Salt Lake City machine politician George Wilson, this *Order of Sevens* attempted to move in where Smoot had failed.[1] Shortly after Mabey's inauguration, Wilson is

---

[1] The Order of Sevens was a semisecret political organization within the Republican Party, the origin of which is somewhat in doubt. Made up of semiautonomous groups of seven

reported to have presented the governor with a list of names as a guide for appointments. Mabey refused the list because the proposal conflicted with his sense of propriety and with his desire for economy.

The result of this division was the inability of either Mabey or the Sevens to work their will in the party during the 1920s. The 1922 senatorial election pitted Ernest Bamberger, a prominent mining magnate and nephew of Governor Simon Bamberger, against Democratic Senator William H. King. The campaign was characterized by defections from the Republican ranks by such prominent Republicans as J. Reuben Clark, Jr., and Susa Young Gates, who preferred having King to having boss rule. Bamberger carried eighteen of the twenty-nine Utah counties, but King won a slim plurality by carrying Utah, Weber, and Salt Lake counties. In the same election Colton and Leatherwood successfully defended their house seats, and the Republicans again elected an overwhelming majority in both houses of the legislature.

The Emergence of George H. Dern

Republican Party conflict revealed itself even more sharply in the 1924 election when the Democrats nominated George H. Dern, mine operator and former progressive legislator, as their gubernatorial candidate. By this time Mabey had increased in unpopularity. His efforts at reducing state expenditures had largely failed, and his abrasive personality and tendency to self-righteousness alienated many in his own party who were not addicted to boss rule. His attempts at reorganizing the state government had been quite successful, but his successes were not enough to offset his lack of political acumen.

As the campaign developed, it became clear that even though he secured renomination Mabey was in deep political trouble. Dern played on two important themes by emphasizing his business experience and his progressive background; he received the endorsement of Progressive Party presidential candidate Robert M. LaFollette. In November he ran far ahead of the field, outdistancing the combined vote of LaFollette and Democrat John W. Davis and eclipsing Calvin Coolidge.

---

people, it seems actually to have been formed by Republican leaders James H. Anderson and Edward H. Callister during the antiprohibition fight. By the 1920s, however, the organization had fallen under the leadership of George Wilson, Ernest Bamberger, Clarence Bamberger, and George Odell and had become a means of organizing Republican Party machine politics. During the 1928 campaign many of the Mormons who had joined the organization left because of attacks by Mormon Church leaders and by former Governor Mabey on such secret organizations.

Dissatisfaction with national Republican policy was evident in the vote totals. Though Coolidge carried the state, the combined total of LaFollette and Davis votes surpassed those of the president. Nevertheless, the Republican sweep of state offices other than the governorship was only slightly less complete than in 1920 and 1922. All of the other executive and judicial offices went to the Republican Party, and only ten Democrats won seats in the state legislature. Congressmen Colton and Leatherwood handily won reelection, as they did again two years later.

The 1928 election further revealed the Republican split between the Order of Sevens and the remainder of the party. Charles R. Mabey opened an attack on the Sevens and Mormon members continued to withdraw from the secret organization, but Ernest Bamberger defeated J. Reuben Clark, Jr., for the senatorial nomination. Utah-Idaho Sugar Company executive William H. Wattis ran for governor, and Colton and Leatherwood ran again for Congress. The Republican platform called for continuation of the protective tariff, prohibition, and the institution of relief for farmers.

The Democratic Party renominated popular George H. Dern to head the ticket, but Senator King found opposition to his candidacy within the party because of his opposition to the protective tariff, to the child labor amendment, and to legislation passed to assist mothers with small children. Nevertheless, he was renominated. The party platform stood in favor of protection for sugar, wool, and lead, endorsed Dern's leadership in the Colorado River controversy, and called for a more equitable tax system.

Democrats Dern, King, and Milton Welling, the party's nominee for secretary of state, won, but the Republicans repeated their other victories. Republicans controlled both houses of the legislature, though by smaller margins than in 1926, and Herbert Hoover carried the state. Both Colton and Leatherwood successfully defended their House seats. The 1930 election was essentially a replay of the 1926 election as the Republicans posted substantial gains in the legislature and as Colton and Frederick Loofburrow, who replaced the deceased Leatherwood, won in Congress.

The efforts of the legislature during Dern's administration were aimed primarily at modifying and extending existing legislation rather than at breaking new ground. The 1925 session enacted compulsory certification for all school teachers, extended the jurisdiction of the Public Utilities Commission, revived the State Park Board, and expanded automobile regulation.

A notable feature of Dern's second administration was the promotion of tax revision. The 1929 legislature created a tax revision commission and proposed constitutional amendments that would require taxes on business profits, uniform rates for all tangible property, graduated rates on personal income, and centralized administration of the state's revenue system by a State Tax Commission. Partisan positions generally followed perceptions of interest: the Utah Manufacturers Association and the Salt Lake *Tribune* opposed the changes; the Utah Education Association, the Utah Farm Bureau Federation, the State Federation of Labor, and the *Deseret News* favored them. The amendments were approved by the voters in November 1929 and the 1930 special session of the legislature enacted implementing measures. (Even though the state constitution authorized an income tax, it required a mandatory amendment to institute the tax because of the business-agriculture standoff.)

Public Lands and the Colorado River Controversy

Perhaps the principal national concern of Utahns during the 1920s had to do with public lands. Since seventy percent of the land in Utah was owned by the federal government it was not subject to state taxation or control, and citizens wanted its use to conform to their needs. Senator Smoot's 1928 campaign emphasized his part in working with the Forest Service and the National Park Service to meet Utah needs and detailed his support of the appropriation of funds for the Strawberry, Scofield, and Echo reclamation projects. Governor Dern was particularly concerned about federal matching programs such as the highway program, by which the federal government gave the states seventy-four percent of the funds for construction of federal highways in return for twenty-six percent participation by the states. Dern pointed out that it was often difficult for states with such a large percentage of untaxable land to raise the money, and when President Hoover threatened to request congressional approval of a cut in the federal proportion, Dern protested.

Control of lands granted to the state by the enabling act also concerned Dern. Governor Mabey had already complained that the federal government was tardy in its survey of public lands so that the state had difficulty obtaining its share and, in addition, Washington had excluded all mineral lands from possible state ownership, even where they fell in school land sections. Mabey had attempted unsuccessfully to recover these mineral rights through a lawsuit. Dern considered the use of this land imperative because virtually all good agricultural land in Utah had already been occupied and the best grazing and timber land lay within the national forests. His activities and those of his supporters led to the passage of the 1927 Jones Act, which declared the transfer of these rights to the states a matter of public policy. Quite consistently, Dern adamantly opposed a 1930 proposal made by President Hoover to turn all public lands over to the states if mineral rights could be retained by the federal government. Dern called the proposal akin to "sucking the orange dry and handing the states the skin."

A particularly thorny problem that the Dern Administration faced was that of ownership and distribution of Colorado River waters. In November 1922 the representatives of the seven Colorado River states—Wyoming, Colorado, New Mexico, Utah, Arizona, Nevada, and California—completed an agreement for the control and division of river water. The 1923 Utah legislature ratified the interstate compact, and by 1925 when Dern took office all states had ratified the compact except Arizona, which demanded what the other states considered an excessively high share of water and power revenues.

In an attempt to circumvent Arizona's recalcitrance, California Congressman Phil D. Swing and California Senator Hiram Johnson introduced legislation providing for federal apportionment of the water and for construction of dams and reclamation projects. Dern immediately opposed the legislation, fearing that the doctrine of prior appropriation of water would grant water ownership to the lower basin states because, in the absence of a legally ratified agreement, the water would have been first impounded and used there. He also feared that federal ownership and control of the Colorado River might have the effect of denying the states through which it ran any rights to its regulation. He was not against federal construction of dams, but he wanted to be certain that the upper basin states got their share of the water. One-half of Utah is in the Colorado River drainage, but much of the land through which the water flows is virtually immune to either agriculture or urban development. (See maps, pp. 717, 720.) Dern pointed out that the construction of irrigation projects to impound Colorado River water and move it to the Great Basin would be expensive and time-consuming.

A complex sequence of interstate and congressional maneuvers followed. In collaboration with Utah's congressional delegation, Governor Dern insisted that before the Swing-Johnson Bill was voted on Congress should require ratification of the seven-state compact and recognize the Colorado River as a navigable stream. In taking this action, Congress would accept the principle that the banks, bed, and water of the river were the property of the states and not the nation and that the states were entitled to receive compensation if they used the river for power generation or other federal purposes. Eventually Congress passed the Swing-Johnson Bill with amendments designed to protect all state rights; on June 25, 1929, Hoover proclaimed the bill operative. Then, in order to further protect Utah's interests, Senator Smoot introduced a bill for the construction of a dam at Flaming Gorge similar to that authorized at Boulder Canyon.

After Utah entered suit against the United States, the Supreme Court declared in 1931 that the Colorado River is a navigable stream and that its banks and bed are the property of the states through which it runs.

Prohibition

A rather difficult problem for Utah citizens was the prohibition of the manufacture, sale, and distribution of alcoholic beverages. Inaugurated statewide in 1917 before the Eighteenth Amendment and the Volstead Act were passed, it apparently caused little dislocation to Utah business. A Prohibition Bureau was established, and volumes of more than five gallons of alcohol for medicinal or industrial purposes had to be purchased from a state warehouse.

Although public sentiment initially seemed to favor prohibition, sufficient opposition soon developed that rendered it impossible to strengthen the control legislation. In addition, many conservative people who favored prohibition in principle were unwilling to support the vigorous police action and reeducation necessary for its enforcement. As early as 1923 Attorney General Harvey Cluff reported that conditions in the larger cities were just as bad as they had been before prohibition. Huge profits made the illegal liquor trade impossible to stop, and the federal director at Milford alleged that the chief bootlegger there was the sister of the city marshal. Offduty policemen were at times caught in raids on speakeasies. By 1929 "booze" was being flown into the state.

The state kept no adequate figures, but federal statistics partially reveal the problems. From July 31, 1925, to June 30, 1932, federal agents in Utah seized more than 448 distilleries, 25,000 gallons of spirits, 8,000 gallons of malt liquors, 13,000 gallons of wine, and 332,000 gallons of mash. The Mount Olympus area of Salt Lake County and the Burch Creek area of Weber County earned reputations as locations of water supplies necessary for good quality moonshine. Prohibition in Utah appears to have been a fine example of a law that most people favored but whose enforcement most were unwilling to pay for. In 1933 Utahns would play an important role in the repeal of the "noble experiment."

A Political Plateau

On balance, the 1920s in Utah were a plateau between the rapid development and vigorous reform of the Progressive Era and the stagnation and antibusiness sentiment of the 1930s. It was a period of consolidation in which the executive branch of the state government was reorganized and in which the legislature tinkered with existing laws rather than moving out in new directions. Evidence of the relative impact of the several levels of government is the pattern of taxation during the decade. After the wartime levies were cut back in 1920-21, federal taxes claimed fewer dollars from Utahns than did state taxes, and the two combined did not equal local taxes until 1934.

The decade ought to be characterized as a time of moderation rather than reaction, even though it had its reactionary features—particularly in the Ku Klux Klan activity and the treatment the Utah labor movement received. It was also a time in which Utah citizens figured quite prominently in national affairs as Reed Smoot became a power in the United States Senate and George Dern gained national recognition for his championing of western needs in the public lands and Colorado River controversies.

Chapter 25
Bibliographical Essay

As one moves further into the twentieth century, secondary literature becomes more scarce. Those who intend to study the 1920s should also consult the bibliographies for the chapters on politics and the economy in the progressive era. The only general study of the period is found in Wayne Stout, *History of Utah, Vol. II* (1968) and *Vol. III* (1971), both of which are highly opinionated; they are principally valuable for the chronological material they contain. This study should be supplemented by Brad E. Hainsworth, "Utah State Elections, 1916-1924" (Ph.D. dissertation, University of Utah, 1968), and Dan E. Jones, "Utah Politics, 1926-1932" (Ph.D dissertation, University of Utah, 1968).

Politics during the period have been investigated in a number of studies. For the career of Governor Charles R. Mabey see Stanford John Layton, "Governor Charles R. Mabey and the Utah Election of 1924" (master's thesis, University of Utah, 1969), and Charles Rendell Mabey, *Our Father's House: Joseph Thomas Mabey Family History* (1947). The reader should also consult Thomas Sterling Taylor and Theron H. Luke, *The Life and Times of T. N. T.: The Story of Thomas Nicholls Taylor* (1959); J. Gordon Pasley, "Utah's George Sutherland as a Congressman and Senator" (master's thesis, Utah State University, 1970); and Joe Williams, "Political Parties of Utah" (master's thesis, University of Utah, 1933). On George Dern see Robert W. Wells, Jr., "A Political Biography of George Henry Dern" (master's thesis, Brigham Young University, 1971).

Basic economic information for Utah during the 1920s is found in the Bureau of Economic and Business Research of the University of Utah's *Measures of Economic Changes in Utah, 1847-1947* (1947), and ElRoy Nelson, *Utah's Economic Patterns* (1956). For information on specific industries see Leonard J. Arrington, *Beet Sugar in the West* (1966); K. A. Moser, "The Beet Sugar Industry and the Tariff with Special Reference to the Great Basin" (master's thesis, Utah State University, 1933); Roland Stucki, *Commercial Banking in Utah, 1847-1966* (Salt Lake City, 1967); Donald Quayle Cannon, "The History of the Trucking Industry in the State of Utah" (master's thesis, University of Utah, 1962); Lester T. Hansen, "An Economic Analysis of the Possible Implications of the Abolition of the Basing Point System of Pricing on the Steel Industry of Utah" (master's thesis, Utah State University, 1950); and Alexander J. Gardner, "The Regional Competition of the Iron Industry" (master's thesis, University of Utah, 1932).

The studies of labor history cited in chapters 23 and 24 are relevant here. See also Joseph C. Clark, Jr., "A History of Strikes in Utah" (master's thesis, University of Utah, 1953) and John Reese Evans, "A History of Labor Legislation in Utah" (master's thesis, University of Utah, 1959). More work needs to be done on the condition of women in Utah labor, but see Juanita Merrill Larsen, "Women in Industry with Special Reference to Utah" (master's thesis, University of Utah, 1933).

Larry Earl Nelson, "Problems of Prohibition Enforcement in Utah, 1917-1933" (master's thesis, University of Utah, 1970), illuminates a troublesome aspect of social and political history. Helpful in preparing this chapter were 1968 seminar papers by Brigham Young University students John R. Patrick and Charla Woodbury written on the National Guard role in labor disputes and on nativism in Utah institutions.

Chapter 26
The Great Depression

John F. Bluth and Wayne K. Hinton

Some perspective is needed to understand what happened to Utah during the 1930s. The initial development of the state's economy was a result of Mormon activities in the nineteenth century. By the end of the territorial period this structure was becoming unstable and the basic absentee-owned extractive and mineral processing operations were increasing in importance. These industries, Utah's main export enterprises, depended on national markets and prices. To an extent so did agriculture, which in 1930 employed nearly a quarter of Utah's 170,000 workers and, along with the rest of the state's economy, was none too healthy. Full recovery from the 1920-21 depression had not been achieved. Although the value added by manufacture had increased during the 1920s, the number of workers employed in manufacturing had declined. At the same time Utah moved strongly toward an urban-oriented economy. The 1930 census classified half the state population of 507,847 as urban nonfarm dwellers and found that 39.2 percent of Utah's workers were engaged in service activities.

In all, Utah's economic growth between 1900 and 1929 had not kept pace with that of the nation. (See Table P, p. 713.) In annual per capita income, Utah had moved from thirty-second to thirtieth position among the forty-eight states, and from seventh to sixth among the eight mountain states, but the $559 per capita figure was only 79.5 percent (down from 90.1 percent in 1900) of the national average. Jobs had not opened up fast enough to absorb those who wanted to work. From 1910 until World War II there was a net yearly migration out of Utah, a pattern that was the reverse of each of the other western states.

The era of the Great Depression and the New Deal constituted a significant phase in Utah's economic, political, and social development. These were years of human distress and unrest, of rejuvenation of the labor movement, and of startling political upsets—manifestations that Utah had indeed been Americanized and was becoming quite typical of the United States in general and urban states in particular. Indeed, Utah became part of the urban coalition that provided the political strength for the New Deal and that looked to Washington for clues and assistance. Because of this increased reliance on innovative federal programs, conservatives of both political parties found themselves, at least for the time, at an electioneering disadvantage in Utah.

Impact of the Depression

The Great Depression of the 1930s was unprecedented in American history both in scope and severity. Its causes are still disputed, but maldistribution of income, imbalances in international trade and payments, overextension of credit, and irresponsible speculation were among them. Since the causes involved human decisions Utahns were only incidentally involved, but their governmental and business leaders generally concurred in the national policies being pursued in the 1920s and regretted only that the state was not enjoying a fair share of the prosperity that was expected to last indefinitely.

When the 1929 stock market crash sent shock waves through the economy, Utah was quickly and seriously affected. Per capita income fell to 71.5 per cent of the national average by 1931, and when the state and the nation both hit bottom two years later, Utah's annual $300 per capita was still only 80 percent of the national average. Reasons for the magnitude of this impact range from dependence on such vulnerable export industries as mining and agriculture to excessive freight rates, weak labor organizations, a high birthrate, and a severe drought in 1931. At the depth of the depression, 61,500 persons—35.8 percent of Utah's work force—were unemployed, while comparable thousands on farms and ranches faced foreclosures and market prices that did not recover production costs.

All indicators of Utah's economic situation—prices, employment, marriage rate, postal receipts, electric power consumption, business failures, and others—showed the same pattern. Gross farm income declined from $69 million to $29 million by 1932. The value of total production of minerals plummeted from $115 million to $23 million, a drop of eighty percent. Utah's percentage of total national production declined from 1.96 percent in 1929 to 0.92 percent in 1933. The annual rate of corporate business failures, 127 in the 1920s, rose to 151 for the first four years after the crash. Of the 105 banks in Utah in 1929, 32 failed during the same period. Salt Lake City department store sales were off forty-one percent in 1933 compared to those in 1929. While the retail food price index in the Salt Lake market declined thirty-seven percent in the same period, this did not keep pace with the forty-five percent drop in per capita income. That only moderate improvement was achieved by World War II is evidenced by the fact that in 1939 the food price index was still seventy-five percent of 1929 levels, while per capita income had risen only to eighty-two percent of the pre-depression high. Utah's relative standing among all of the states and among her regional neighbors did not change significantly.

Welfare statistics showed another side of the same picture. In May 1934, 206 persons per 1,000 were on relief. Only South Dakota, Arizona, and Florida were higher. When Social Security was established two years later, 504 per 1,000 of the eligible elderly qualified to receive old-age assistance, a figure that was the second highest rate nationally. In March 1933, when regular public relief programs began, 36,151 families received assistance. Yearly increases averaged about 1,500 new families except in 1936, when a state-controlled direct relief program replaced federally administered direct aid. Some 48,000 families received direct relief, work relief, or Social Security aid in March 1940. About seven dollars were spent by the federal government in Utah for each dollar that was sent to Washington in taxes.

Responses to Hard Times

Utahns initially faced the Great Depression stoically. Governor George H. Dern responded to President Hoover's first inquiries about the state of the economy with optimistic assurances that the future looked good and the legislature could deal with any specific problems. Both men were influenced by three factors that hindered concerted, effective action before 1932. Most immediate was the perception that the depression would last only a short time; recovery was believed to be just around the corner. Second was the conservative leadership's reliance on private and voluntary charitable activity to bring relief. Third, and most significant, was the lack of funds. Budgets had to be kept in balance as revenue fell. These tradition-based convictions had broad bipartisan support until the sheer magnitude of the economic disaster produced new approaches.

In late 1929 hundreds of mine workers walked the streets of Salt Lake City looking for work. The governor talked tentatively about taking up the employment slack with a $3.25 million accelerated road construction program, but no substantive action was taken. Nor was the legislature that was elected in November 1930 prepared to break new ground, despite the march of 1,500 people, organized by the Communist Party, to demand unemployment insurance. This demonstration on January 31, 1931, provoked the legislators to issue a statement against any form of dole. No substitute actions were proposed except the belt-tightening measures of dismissal of working wives, no overtime work, and the saving of leftover food. Most of the lawmakers expected private charity to deal adequately with the problem.

Recognizing that falling assessed valuations were undermining the property taxes that provided eighty-one percent of state and local revenue in 1930, the legislature approved a graduated personal and corporate income tax. But with the continued economic decline even this new source of revenue failed to produce the expected funds. Utah's bonded indebtedness increased from $10 million in 1931 to $40 million in 1932, and the state was forced to cut back on its spending.

Due to the circumstances, the burden of meeting human needs fell primarily on private charities and county governments. The forms of voluntarism were varied and imaginative, but ultimately were unequal to the task. By the end of January 1930 the Utah Copper Company was using rotational employment to keep all its men doing some work. The Logan Chamber of Commerce requested business and municipal employees to donate two percent of their wages in order to employ 220 men on city improvement projects. At one point the Family Service Society was supporting over 2,700 people, giving fifteen dollars a month to a family of five for food while Salt Lake County's charity department could give less than eight dollars per family. During the winter of 1930-31 the Salt Lake Mayor's Advisory Council conducted a work relief program that provided temporary jobs to more than 10,000 unemployed. The most significant private charitable organizations were the churches and the Red Cross. Donations in kind and exchanges of services for food and clothing augmented the cash resources these agencies supplied. Surplus food purchased by the federal government to bolster farm prices was distributed by the Red Cross to about 70,000 Utah families beginning in the 1931-32 winter.

The depression reduced the income of churches and other charitable organizations. The Mormon Church, which had annually devoted more than $600,000 to charitable spending in the late 1920s and early 1930s, could afford only $413,000 in 1933. Pioneer Stake President Harold B. Lee, with 2,500 church members in need in his stake, experimented with production and sharing techniques that would later be incorporated in the Mormon Welfare Program. Financial stringency led the church to turn Dixie, Weber, and Snow colleges over to the state of Utah in February 1933. (Efforts to secure their return in the postwar period were unsuccessful.)

Although unemployment first impacted the mining towns and the cities of the Wasatch Front, it was soon statewide. By 1931 every county was giving some form of aid to the jobless. As local and private resources dwindled and the depression intensified, federal funds entered Utah in the fall of 1932 through the Reconstruction Finance Corporation. During 1932-33 these loans provided sixty-eight percent of the funds spent on relief in Utah, while private charities contributed twelve percent and state and local sources produced the remaining twenty percent. Handled by a five-man Governor's Committee on Emergency Relief, public money for shelter, food, and clothing reached 29,000 families during December 1932 at an average of twelve dollars per family. By March 1933 almost one-third of Utah's population was receiving some form of government aid from this source.

Symptomatic of growing unrest was the frequent disruption of sheriff's sales in urbanized Wasatch Front areas. In February 1933 a large crowd of protestors held up such a sale in Salt Lake County for several hours before being dispersed by tear gas and fire hoses. Many saw these disturbances as evidence that reforms were necessary. Others, perhaps disturbed by the 4,000 votes cast in 1932 for Socialist presidential candidate Norman Thomas and the 1,000 votes cast for a Communist candidate for governor, condemned the outbreaks as Communist-inspired.

Utah voting in the 1932 election followed national patterns. Democrat Franklin D. Roosevelt received almost fifty-seven percent of the popular vote; Democrat Henry H. Blood, Dern's choice as his successor, won the governorship by a similar margin; and Elbert D. Thomas unseated five-term Republican Senator Reed Smoot. With Democrats controlling both houses of the state legislature, the stage was set for a new approach to the problems of a depression-racked state.

Impact of the New Deal

Governor Blood indicated in his first inaugural address that Utah would now look to Washington for assistance and direction.

The statement was prophetic, but the legislature that met from January to March 1933 was still in a pre-New Deal environment and its approach was traditional: balance the budget, conform to Roosevelt's 1932 campaign and early presidential policy, cut appropriations and state payrolls, and "keep the faith." The legislators thought more in terms of mollification than correction. For example, they considered the sixty-day extension of the 1932 expiration date of automobile license plates a relief measure. When several hundred marchers appeared at the state capitol on March 2 to place their pleas before a joint session, legislators denounced the protestors for their aggressiveness and ignored their appeals.

As the Roosevelt Administration launched a multifaceted attack on the depression, Utah's governmental climate changed. Following the nationwide pattern, Blood declared a bank holiday for March 3-13, 1933. When the "Hundred Days" Congress established the Federal Emergency Relief Administration, the governor appointed a State Advisory Committee on Public Welfare and Emergency Relief, which administered relief programs in Utah for two years. On July 10, the opening day of a special session called to deal with school funding, protestors again paid a visit to the capitol. This time they demanded legislative action to facilitate cooperation with the recently enacted National Industrial Recovery Act. They also requested unemployment compensation. The protestors sang and shouted so loudly that the legislature was forced to adjourn and the governor had peace officers clear the halls. A joint committee heard the grievances of the demonstrators, but considered their demands for unemployment payments extravagant. Before adjourning, however, the special session did pass a Utah Industrial Recovery Act. It also enacted a two percent sales tax to match funds from the FERA for an expanded public welfare program.

While welfare expenditures were less than one percent of state spending in the fiscal year ending June 30, 1933, they jumped the next year to twenty percent under the impetus of FERA grants. Until December 1934 private charity organizations also helped the State Advisory Committee distribute federal money, demonstrating the attitude that relief was a private, not a public, responsibility. Since the depression had struck more people in Salt Lake County, they received the most aid. During 1933 about half of all state relief went to county residents for food that included salt pork, smoked pork, corned beef, canned beef, butter, cheese, eggs, flour, and beans. Per capita relief expenditures from all public and private fund sources were highest in Tooele County ($16.38) and lowest in Box Elder County ($2.31), with Salt Lake and Weber counties ($11.28 and $8.83) above the state average of $8.27.

In Utah, as well as in the nation's capital, sentiment increasingly favored programs of work relief that might meet the immediate needs of the unemployed while restoring confidence and completing useful community improvements. In Utah such an approach had been tried on a small scale in the depression of 1920-21. City governments in Ogden and Salt Lake City organized make-work projects late in 1930, and in Tooele in 1931, where two banks failed along with the crops. City and county governments established the Unemployment Relief Association to carry on work projects; wages were paid as relief allotments to 900 families. Until early 1934, however, over ninety percent of direct relief was in kind, an indication of its emergency nature. Only as statewide work programs replaced direct relief programs were cash payments more prevalent than relief in goods.

The first of the federal work relief programs was the Civil Works Administration. Underway by December 1933, it moved about half of the previous month's relief load to the ranks of the employed and reduced unemployment from more than 25 percent to 12.4 percent. Although the CWA only functioned during the winter of 1933-34, temporarily providing 20,000 jobs, other federally sponsored programs such as the Civilian Conservation Corps and the National Youth Administration provided work relief during all of the New Deal years. The CCC spent over $52 million in Utah before being terminated in 1941 and brought thousands of young men from all over the United States to work on conservation and recreation projects in the forest areas of the state. The NYA aided an average of more than 2,200 Utah young people per year to work their way through school; it continued operation until 1943.

These new programs did not start up closed smelters; instead they created new jobs. They emphasized relief, not permanent remedies. As the new Utah Emergency Relief Administration extended its coverage during 1934 to include needy teachers, students, and transients and to provide medical and nursing care and drought relief, per capita relief expenditures more than doubled the 1933 levels. Federal money supported over eighty percent of this burden, and now it was no longer in the form of loans. As 1935 began and a second federal winter work relief program ended, more than 46,000 workers were still without jobs, and a 1934 drought had aggravated the impact of hard times on the rural counties. Beaver, Duchesne, Emery, and Garfield counties had more than a quarter of their people on relief each month during 1934; Emery averaged thirty-six percent and Duchesne reached seventy-one percent in June. In March 1935 one-fourth of the state population received public assistance, a percentage exceeded only during 1933. Welfare jumped to forty-eight percent of all state spending.

Signs of recovery were by now appearing. However, for years it was unknown whether they were responsive to the codes and propaganda of the National Recovery Administration, the dollar devaluation and monetary experimentation, the production controls of the Agricultural Adjustment Administration, the expanded construction program of the Public Works Administration, the encouragement of the Roosevelt fireside chats, or simply the natural recuperative powers of the American economy. By 1935 a change in relief policy seemed appropriate. The national government moved away from providing funds to be disbursed by the states to the *unemployed* and the *unemployable*. Congress enacted a two-fold program: (1) provide federal work relief (the Works Progress Administration) for the employable jobless, and (2) extend partial financial support to state welfare plans (Social Security) for dependent children, the aged, and the blind. Utah followed the federal lead by creating a Department of Public Welfare, which replaced the UERA in May 1935. The WPA began activity in September and, with the inception of the Social Security program in February 1936, the emergency stage of the depression ended.

While Mormon leaders stated in 1933 that the church would try to provide relief for its members and urged them to refuse government relief, neither plans nor counsel could be immediately followed. As the New Deal unfolded, some church leaders argued against direct relief but encouraged the acceptance of work relief, the latter tending to maintain personal dignity. Following several steps behind the changing federal programs, the Mormon Church First Presidency announced a Church Security Plan in April 1936. Relief expenditures increased over threefold from 1935 to 1936 as projects to produce and rehabilitate useful commodities were established in many stakes. Primarily a direct relief program providing commodities and supplies along with work in their distribution, the Church Welfare Plan (as it was redesignated in 1938) had an accountable value in the late 1930s above $1.5 million yearly. While the effect of the program in meeting human needs and promoting an optimistic outlook among Mormons and non-Mormons was substantial, the undertaking only supplemented government action. Federal nonrepayable expenditures in Utah for the same years were ten times as great as the accountable value of churchwide Welfare Plan transactions.

As was indicated earlier, complete recovery did not come until World War II brought the American economy back to full employment. Consequently, the alphabetical agencies of the New Deal were prominent in Utah life for another half-dozen years. The WPA employed an average of almost 11,000 Utahns annually until 1942, the peak figure being over 17,000 on the eve of the 1936 election. More than $55 million of federal and state-local funds went into projects from building roads, schools, and airports to painting murals on public buildings and collecting and cataloging historical documents. Federal reclamation programs added Deer Creek and Pine View dams and five other projects to Utah's water storage and management resources at a cost of approximately $22 million. Utah's farmers, some of whom had flirted with radical measures to keep products off the market in 1933, turned increasingly thereafter to federal assistance. Through lobbying efforts by the governor, Utah's congressional delegation, and the State Farm Bureau, livestock farmers were given considerable federal aid in the form of a purchase and slaughter program during the severe 1934 drought. Utah farmers also benefited from the AAA, the Rural Electrification Administration, and from credit and mortgage protection programs. On occasion, groups of Utah farmers who took part in the participatory democracy that characterized the AAA accepted New Deal farm proposals unanimously.

Collective Bargaining and Labor Legislation

Section 7(a) of the National Industrial Recovery Act dealt with labor and provided for minimum wages, maximum hours, and a guaranteed right of collective bargaining. It was this provision that led to a renewed effort by Utah labor leaders to organize the state's mining industry. Competition between the United Mine Workers and the Communist-controlled National Miners' Union complicated the effort and divided the workers. In August 1933 Carbon County miners affiliated with the NMU went on strike seeking a shorter working week and recognition of their union. The mine operators refused to negotiate with them, and officials shut down the struck mines. County Sheriff S. Marion Bliss, Price Mayor Rolla West, and other local leaders initially sided with the operators in asking for National Guard assistance to break the strike. Governor Blood delayed response, hoping that he would be spared a decision by the publication of the NRA code for the bituminous coal industry. In the meantime incidents of violence occurred; mine officials accused the strikers of being Communists and insisted that the troubles were caused by outsiders living on relief. Finally granted arms and gas bombs by the National Guard, Bliss deputized 200 volunteers, some of them mine officials and some UMW miners, and soon approximately 300 strikers were in Carbon County jails.

Labor Day 1933 brought many messages of protest and sympathy from liberal leaders and spokesmen for the radical labor movement throughout the nation. Feelings ran high in the polarized communities, and on September 11 approximately 400 NMU sympathizers from Helper marched through the streets of Price toward the county jail. Deputies and the National Guard riot squad broke up the demonstration, and the city councils of both Helper and Price banned public gatherings. Gradually the tension relaxed; riot and criminal syndicate charges against NMU leaders were eventually dropped, but the union's influence in Utah was broken. Subsequent investigations criticized Sheriff Bliss for making arrests without warrants, denying hearings, and abolishing *habeas corpus.* With the publication of the applicable NRA codes, the mine operators capitulated and recognized the UMW as a bargaining agent. This victory, the first by miners in Utah's coal industry, was followed by the unionization of other mines in 1934, and it stimulated a spread of the organization movement to other sectors of the state economy.

The 1935 and 1937 legislatures, following additional clues from Washington, were more friendly toward labor than their predecessors had been since 1920. New laws legalized the withholding of union dues from wages, prohibited the deputizing of employers in lockouts and strikes, required registration of persons accepting work during a strike (an act later ruled unconstitutional by the Utah Supreme Court), established regular paydays, legalized peaceful picketing, and established an eight-hour day for state employees. When the NRA was invalidated by the United States Supreme Court in 1935, the Wagner Act sustained the national drive for collective bargaining. Coupled with the more favorable attitude toward labor in the state legislature, this finally killed the *American Plan* for labor that had crippled unionism in Utah in the years after World War I. Union membership in the state increased sixfold from November 1933 to February 1935 and reached its peak in 1937. Mechanics, factory workers, taxi drivers, and even salespeople were ultimately organized.

Repeal of Prohibition

President Roosevelt and the Democratic Congress moved quickly to redeem a campaign pledge by repealing the Prohibition Amendment to the United States Constitution. The proposed Twenty-first Amendment was supposed to be ratified by conventions elected specifically for that purpose in the various states rather than by state legislatures. The object was to give the voters a chance to express their sentiments solely on the liquor issue. In providing for an election, the Utah legislature also gave voters an opportunity to express opinions on the state's current liquor control laws.

In their April 1933 general conference as the Mormon Church observed the centennial of its Word of Wisdom, which teaches total abstinence from alcoholic beverages, an important emphasis was placed on dry-law preservation. As the election approached, President Heber J. Grant made frequent appeals for church members to vote for retention of prohibition. The dry advocates adopted the name *Defenders,* and the *Deseret News* became their chief voice. The state's other major daily, the Salt Lake *Tribune,* championed repeal of the Volstead Law and the Eighteenth Amendment. Aiding the repeal campaign were the Salt Lake Chamber of Commerce, the Utah Democratic congressional delegation, and the Democratic State Central Committee.

The vote on November 7, 1933, was three to two for repeal of the Eighteenth Amendment and two to one for repeal of the state's prohibition law. Since about sixty-five percent of the population was Mormon at the time, the outcome has often been interpreted as symbolic of the decline in church political influence. Actually that influence has waxed and waned since the 1890s, and the 1930s simply proved to be a period of decline. The election results more clearly indicate that the vote pitted the urban areas of the state against the rural. Except for Davis County, the Wasatch Front counties from Weber to Juab voted for repeal, as did counties with gentile railroad and mining centers. Seventeen rural counties voted against repeal. The urban coalition that has dominated Utah politics since the Great Depression had already emerged by 1933. Utah's was the thirty-sixth ratification of the Twenty-first Amendment—the decisive blow to prohibition.

Politics in the New Deal Years

In the 1932 election the Utah electorate voted against the status quo. Candidates associated with the Hoover Administration did not fare well. Although he had the open support of President Grant, conservative Senator Reed Smoot lost decisively to University of Utah political scientist Elbert Thomas, Republican gubernatorial nominee William W. Seegmiller ran far behind Henry Blood, and the Republican presidential ticket carried only seven counties, all of them rural. The New Deal quickly won the allegiance of Utah labor; agriculture, which had been a traditional Republican stronghold, was at least neutralized for a time by Democratic farm programs. In 1936 among the twenty-nine counties in the state only Kane County voted Republican. By 1940 the rural vote was returning to its Republican allegiance as six rural counties voted Republican, while the urban and labor areas remained strongly Democratic.

By 1934 spirited leadership and innovative federal and state programs of action were apparently winning approval. Candidates tainted with the past or apparently desirous of reversing the current trend began to experience difficulty at the polls. Coincident with this, a liberal-conservative division developed within the Democratic Party that at times threatened party control in Utah. This split led to acrimonious infighting for patronage and leadership posts in the state legislature. Disharmony was also evident in periodic battles to control county organizations and most notably in the races for nomination. The experiences of Senator William H. King, Governor Blood, and Herbert B. Maw illustrate the party factionalism and the growing popular preference for liberal candidates.

Senator King was not generally regarded as a New Dealer. He had opposed the Utah Education Association's request for federal aid for Utah schools because of avowed concern about the cost and the possible loss of state's rights. He was absent on crucial Senate votes on the Tennessee Valley Authority and on waterway development projects, and he was an early and outspoken critic of NIRA and public works expenditures. By early 1934 Democratic liberals were organizing support for State Senator Maw, a University of Utah professor of speech, to oppose King's renomination. In the state convention where the "Old Guard" predominated, King won over Maw and over New Deal Democrat Hugh B. Brown, who resigned as state party chairman and general counsel for the federal Home Owners Loan Corporation to make a late bid for the nomination. Maw supporters maintained that Maw would have beaten King in a direct primary.

King's Republican opponent, Don B. Colton, attempted to capitalize on the situation by campaigning as the more liberal candidate. He advocated fair minimum wages and maximum hours, vowed to fight for collective bargaining, advocated pensions for the aged and unemployment insurance, and announced general approval of the New Deal while condemning only President Roosevelt's alleged usurpation of power. King defeated Colton but ran well behind the Democratic ticket in the state.

The 1935 legislature looked increasingly to Washington for cues, and it produced significant reform legislation. The Senate contained nineteen Democrats and four Republicans; the House of Representatives had fifty-six Democrats and only four Republicans. A farmer-labor bloc dominated the session in spite of internal differences, and Herbert Maw gave liberal leadership as Senate president. Legislation permitted local governments to participate more actively in federal assistance programs, provided for a budget increase to meet relief needs at the risk of an estimated deficit of $350,000, and established a more progressive state income tax, a corporation tax, and a higher inheritance tax.

An attempt at the 1936 state convention to elect Senator King as a delegate at large to the Democratic National Convention was shouted down because of King's failure to support the New Deal. The same convention also settled a hotly contested race between Governor Blood and Maw, who was strongly supported by Townsend clubs. Blood narrowly won renomination, despite liberal threats to run a third party candidate. While Ogden Mayor Harman W. Peery's independent bid for the governorship failed to win the endorsement of the Progressive Democratic League, the league only agreed to support the state Democratic ticket after prolonged and bitter negotiations and a purge of conservative legislature candidates in Salt Lake County. The liberal purge, however, made it possible for the 1937 legislature to finally pass a direct primary law.

Despite a preelection *Deseret News* editorial strongly supporting Alfred M. Landon for president, the Democrats won the election by a two to one majority in most counties. Roosevelt received 69.3 percent of the vote. Blood ran generally behind the ticket but defeated his two opponents, Peery and Republican Ray E. Dillman. The legislature elected was one of the most one-sided in the state's history, with just one Republican in the Senate and only four in the House of Representatives.

The 1937 legislature proved to be the most liberal in Utah history. The legislative emphasis was on relief and assistance for the aged, underprivileged, and unemployed and on support for collective bargaining and other labor interests. More progressive taxation sought to cut the tax burden on the less affluent, and welfare spending was increased by $1,500,000. The legislature also passed the direct primary law that in 1940 tended to help the more liberal candidates in Democratic races for gubernatorial and senatorial nominations.

In 1938 Senator Thomas was reelected in spite of an anonymous letter sent to Mormon bishops expressing opposition to the New Deal and creating the impression that the Republican candidate, Brigham Young University President Franklin S. Harris, was the choice of the Mormon hierarchy. Two years later Herbert Maw secured the Democratic nomination for governor over Henry D. Moyle, who was also believed to have the support of the Mormon Church leadership. The direct primary proved to be the downfall of Senator King. By 1940 he was calling himself a "Constitutional Democrat" and waging war against the New Deal and Roosevelt on a broad front. It was almost inevitable that he would be opposed by a liberal, and Congressman Abe Murdock took up the challenge. In an extremely heavy primary election he decisively defeated King and went on to win in November. Maw defeated Republican Don B. Colton in a close race, and Roosevelt again carried the state.

Conclusion

Even with welfare programs and other new public expenditures, the financial condition of Utah was better in 1940 than it was in 1929. Until 1934 about seventy percent of Utah's yearly expenditures went toward education and highways. In 1935 public welfare temporarily displaced these two priorities, requiring approximately half of all state spending. From 1936 to World War II a more even balance was struck with schools, roads, and welfare dividing eighty percent of the total. State revenue dropped in 1933 to about $8.5 million, but new taxes carried it to $12.5 million in 1934, a total higher than in any previous year. Tax collections continued to grow each year thereafter, not showing any signs of the 1937 recession. Total local taxes hovered around $13.6 million per year for 1931-40, not varying more than $1 million. Federal revenue collections in Utah, however, changed sharply, falling from $3.7 in 1929 to $1.4 million in 1933, then climbing to $6.3 million in 1935 and $10.8 million in 1940. The financial situation of the state government by 1938 was rosy; debt was at a twenty-year low. Other states met the depression emergency with deficit spending. After reluctantly and tentatively venturing in that direction, Utah let federal money pay the way.

Assessment of the impact of the depression on Utah depends on what states are used for comparison, what data and data-guesses are used, and whose memories are consulted. Suffice it here to say that the depression struck a blow to the Utah economy and social order that they might not have survived without federal aid. Federal spending between 1933 and 1939 equaled about twenty percent of total personal income for the period. Utah received $289 million from New Deal spending and loan programs, a per capita amount of $569.49—which placed her ninth among forty-eight states. Full recovery was not attained, but the results of looking to Washington for solutions included a number of enduring public improvements, renewed vigor in the labor movement, plenteous social and reform legislation, a liberalization of Utah politics, and Democratic political control that lasted for almost twenty years.

Chapter 26
Bibliographical Essay

A great amount of research and interpretation awaits the historian before an adequate bibliography can be offered for the New Deal years. Besides Leonard Arrington's works little interpretation exists for economic aspects. By way of introduction two works stand out. James T. Patterson's *The New Deal and the States: Federalism in Transition* (1969) offers a national background. The first portion of Wayne Stout's *History of Utah*, Vol. III:1930-1970 (1971) is a compilation of data presented chronologically; no processing or refining has occurred.

While an even greater lack of refining is found in J. R. Mahoney, "Measures of Economic Change in Utah, 1847-1947," *Utah Economic and Business Review,* January 1947, it remains the single source offering in numbers a whole but disassociated skeleton of Utah's changing economy. Two other works add key data for evaluating the extent of depression: Simon S. Kuznets et al., *Population Redistribution and Economic Growth: United States, 1870-1950,* three volumes (1957-1964), and C. F. Schwartz and R. E. Graham, Jr., "Personal Income by States, 1929-54," *Survey of Current Business,* September 1955.

Leonard Arrington's interpretive works include *From Wilderness to Empire: The Role of Utah in Western Economic History* (1961) and *The Changing Economic Structure of the Mountain West, 1850-1950* (1963). While these two works are broad in treatment, a detailed analysis of federal expenditures during the years 1933-39 is reported in two articles: "The New Deal in the West: A Preliminary Statistical Inquiry," *Pacific Historical Review,* August 1969, and "Western Agriculture and the New Deal," *Agricultural History,* October 1970. Arrington's interest has also extended into a study coauthored with Wayne K. Hinton, "Origin of the Welfare Plan of The Church of Jesus Christ of Latter-day Saints," *BYU Studies,* Winter 1964.

Other works providing insight to the 1930s include F. E. Hall's "Poor Little Rich State," *Commonwealth,* February 9, 1940; Helen Z. Papanikolas, "Unionism, Communism, and the Great Depression: The Carbon County Coal Strike of 1933," *UHQ,* Summer 1973; J. R. Mahoney, "The Development of Manufacturing in Utah, 1860-1939," *Utah Economic and Business Review,* December 1941; and sections of Lowry Nelson, *The Mormon Village: A Pattern and Technique of Land Settlement* (1952).

Published studies on the political aspects of the New Deal years are even rarer than on the economic side. The best of several limited studies is probably Frank H. Jonas' contribution, "Utah: Sagebrush Democracy" to be found in Thomas C. Donnelly, ed., *Rocky Mountain Politics* (1940), which contains some good background information on personalities and issues of the New Deal era. Jonas has also edited and provided the section on Utah politics in *Western Politics* (1961.) Its emphasis is on the period from 1940 to 1960, with an historical perspective that touches on the 1930s.

Jonas and Garth N. Jones, "Utah Presidential Elections 1896-1952," *UHQ,* October 1956, read in conjunction with Edgar Eugene Robinson, *"They Voted for Roosevelt"* (1947), gives some understanding and perspective to Utah's voting behavior during the New Deal years.

For those interested in the types of research and questions yet unanswered regarding the New Deal years, James T. Patterson's "The New Deal in the West," *Pacific Historical Review,* August 1969, is suggested.

Chapter 27
The Impact of World War II

John E. Christensen

The outbreak of war in Europe, the feverish buildup in national defense, the Japanese attack on Pearl Harbor, and the full-scale American participation in World War II produced significant repercussions in Utah. Wartime spending lifted the state's economy from the depths of depression to the peaks of prosperity. Rapid population shifts subjected her citizens to stresses not found in the stability of peacetime. Political leaders had to deal with very different issues, though the years of hard times had conditioned them for more active roles than had traditionally been assigned to government in Utah.

As noted in an earlier chapter, the impact of the Great Depression was more severe for Utah than for most other states. Utah's expenditures for public assistance in relation to her income were among the highest in the nation. As late as 1938, compared to national averages, Utah had thirty-two percent more workers on WPA projects, forty-five percent more in the CCC, fifty percent more enrolled in the NYA, and sixty percent more on PWA payrolls. Not until the arrival of the defense industry during World War II was the state's economy revitalized. Comprised of both military and civilian operations, this activity transformed unemployment into worker shortages. Personal incomes climbed. Shifts in the relative importance of agriculture, mining, and manufacturing fashioned a new economic portrait for Utah.

Defense Industry

The state legislature that met in January 1941 responded to Governor Herbert B. Maw's suggestion to establish a Department of Publicity and Industrial Development to seek new war-related enterprises. Utah's location, natural resources, and transportation connections were assets for those who had lobbied in her behalf. As the Departments of War and Navy directed the mobilization and deployment of military forces, an expanding and frequently reorganized federal bureaucracy coordinated defense-related industrial production and plant expansion. In sequence the War Resources Board, the National Defense Advisory Commission, the Office of Production Management, and the War Production Board made procurement and production decisions that materially affected Utah's wartime roles.

National expenditures for defense purposes were of two categories. The first type of outlay was for hiring military and civilian personnel in the operation of government-owned and -operated facilities. During World War II Utah became the site of ten major military bases and an army hospital. The second category of defense expenditure was for procuring privately produced commodities and services, including steel, munitions, and other defense goods. Scores of existing or warborn enterprises, not all in the Utah metropolitan areas, became contractors and subcontractors. Since the defense industry was also an export industry, it brought income and employment into Utah from outside. It is estimated that the war brought 49,500 new jobs to the state.

Military Installations

Northern Utah was chosen as the site for three military training bases because of its security from possible attack, its equidistance from the ports of Seattle, San Francisco, and San Diego, and its accessibility by rail, highway, and air. Fort Douglas, established in 1862 to help protect the overland mail route, became the military nerve center of all states west of the Rockies when the Army's Ninth Service Command transferred to Salt Lake City shortly after the Pearl Harbor attack. The fort also served as a reception center for inductees and as a separation center for those being discharged from military service.

Between August 1942 and October 1943 over 90,000 airmen received basic training at the rapidly constructed Kearns Army Air Base. Following the war this readymade townsite became one of Utah's fastest growing communities.

Wendover Air Force Base was established to fill an acute need for heavy bombing and gunnery ranges and, covering three and a half million acres, it became the nation's largest military reserve. Twenty-one heavy bombardment groups, including the 509th

The crew of the Enola Gay trained at Wendover Army Air Force Base before drop-ping the first atomic bomb on Hiroshima, Japan.

Composite that dropped the atomic bombs on Hiroshima and Nagasaki, trained at Wendover.

In addition to location and transportation advantages, the arid climate and abundance of space made Utah an excellent choice for six military maintenance and supply depots, four in Weber and Davis counties. The Ogden Arsenal, a master depot responsible for distributing all items of ordnance supply and equipment to the western states after December 1943, had been opened as a small installation in 1920 when the War Department sought to disperse munitions away from the Atlantic Coast. Just prior to America's entrance into World War II, the federal government spent $9.6 million in reconstructing the facility, which was then also used for storage and ammunition, bomb loading, and artillery shell manufacture. At peak operations more than 6,000 people were employed there.

The Utah General Depot, also near Ogden, became the largest quartermaster depot in the United States after its construction in 1941; it prepared assorted supplies for distribution in the West and shipment overseas. Four thousand civilians and 5,000 prisoners of war helped to handle a larger volume of material than the combined volumes of the other depots in the Ogden area.

Repair and maintenance of aircraft were the major wartime activities at Ogden Air Depot (Hill Field). Later named the Ogden Air Materiel Area, Hill Field began as a WPA project late in the 1930s. By May 1943 it had become the state's largest employer, with more than 15,000 civilians and 6,000 military personnel working on base.

The Clearfield Naval Supply Depot, which began receiving materiel in December 1942, became overrun with supplies in 1945, as did other Utah depots when the war shifted to the Pacific.

Western Utah provided the other two military sites. The Tooele Army Depot, completed in January 1943 as an expansion of the Ogden Arsenal, received and shipped ammunition and material and overhauled vehicles, tanks, and artillery. The Deseret Chemical Depot, constructed in 1942, engaged in the top-secret storage and shipment of all types of chemical warfare materiel.

The Dugway Proving Ground, also located in Tooele County, was involved in large-scale testing and evaluation of chemical munitions, including incendiary and flame-throwing weapons and chemical mortars. The Dugway site was selected because of its climate, altitude, and space for expansion and isolation. Construction, which began in April 1942, encountered dust storms and high winds that also plagued completion of other defense facilities in and near the Great Salt Lake Desert.

Bushnell Military Hospital, located near Brigham City, had a patient capacity of 3,000 following its completion in 1942. The nine million-dollar, sixty-building facility was equipped to treat and rehabilitate amputees and soldiers who suffered neurosurgical and neuropsychiatric disorders; approximately 13,000 army personnel were treated. Following the war jurisdiction over the buildings was transferred to the Bureau of Indian Affairs for transformation into the Intermountain Indian School.

Manufacturing for War

Perhaps the best measure of the war's influence on Utah's industrial development is the "value added by the manufacturer." (This measure is computed by subtracting the cost of materials, supplies, power, and contract work from the total value of finished goods.) Between 1939 and 1947 the state's value added by the manufacturer increased 196 percent or by approximately $85 million. In the same period the number of manufacturing establishments rose from 549 to 772, an increase slightly larger than the state average for the nation as a whole. Utah received authorizations for $311 million in federal funds for facilities—thirty-eight percent of the total authorized for the mountain states. The national per capita expenditure for new industrial plants was $188; the Utah figure was $534. About ninety-one percent of Utah's wartime industrial expansion was financed by public funds. Generally the government financed construction of new plants while private investors supported enlargement of existing facilities.

The Remington Small Arms Plant was one of the major defense facilities to be built in Utah after the start of World War II. In June 1941, partly as a result of Governor Maw's urging during a visit to Washington in April, the War Department announced it would construct a $30 million installation in Salt Lake County to manufacture thirty- and fifty-caliber small arms ammunition. Six months later operations began at the plant, which took 7,000 workers to construct. The Remington Arms Company of Bridgeport, Connecticut, was awarded the $86 million contract to operate the facility. Employment reached 10,000 and remained steady until November 1943, when operations ceased. Besides being the second most expensive facility constructed in the state during the war years, the small arms plant accounted for eighty-five percent of the increase in Utah's manufacturing employment between October 1941 and November 1943. The buildings became the basis for a warehousing and light industries complex in the postwar period.

Undoubtedly the most important industrial development in the state during World War II was the construction and operation of the United States Steel Geneva Works in Utah County. Of the $310 million authorized by the Defense Plant Corporation (DPC) for new facilities in Utah, $190 million was spent constructing the Geneva plant. The details of its origin are illustrative of the genesis of Utah's federally financed industrial plants. In mid 1940 leaders of the nation's steel industry boasted that they could meet any increased demand for steel. But in March 1941 Congress passed the Lend-Lease Act, a law that committed seven billion dollars to the Allied nations. Thereafter an acceleration of the national defense program and an increase in consumer demand for steel made a steel deficit probable if existing facilities were not expanded more than had been planned. In April 1941 President Roosevelt mentioned in a meeting with Governor Maw and Utah's congressional delegation that the state was being considered as a site for a pig iron plant and steel mill. After months of deliberations, the Office of Production Management announced the location of a proposed integrated steel plant west of Orem.

Eight factors were significant in the decision. The proximity of large coal deposits in Carbon County, iron ore 252 miles southwest, and limestone and dolomite at nearby Payson were important. Adequate transportation facilities already existed with the Denver and Rio Grande Western and Union Pacific railroad lines converging at the plant site. Locating the plant in Utah was seen as a precaution against possible West Coast invasion or bombing or closure of the Panama Canal. Workers in Utah were considered productive, settled, and educated. The daily water needs of twenty-nine million gallons could be supplied by Deer Creek Reservoir and artesian wells that were located on plant property.

Approximately 10,000 men, many from surrounding towns and others from outside the county and state, were employed to construct the plant, which was designed by engineers of the United States Steel Corporation and built by Columbia Steel Company with the help of about a hundred subcontractors. Construction, which involved coke ovens, three blast furnaces, nine open hearth furnaces, a slabbing and blooming mill, a plate mill, a structural mill, and numerous complementary facilities, took place between 1942 and 1944.

In February 1944 steel production began with 1,500 workers. Peak employment reached 4,200 in January, 1945. During the period of governmental operation 634,010 tons of plate steel and 144,280 tons of structural shapes were produced. After the war the federal government sold the plant to United States Steel for $47.5 million with the stipulation that the company invest $18.6 million to convert the facility to peacetime operations. Thirty years after the war's end, the Geneva plant continues to be one of Utah's major industrial operations.

The Utah Oil Refinery in Salt Lake City was one of many refineries in the country that expanded to increase production of gasoline. Utah's alkylation plant, called the "number one war job in this area" during its construction, began operating in April 1944 in a facility that cost $15 million to expand. It set a world's production record of forty gallons of 100-octane gasoline from 100 gallons of crude oil in 1945. The following year the War Assets Administration sold the plant to the Utah Oil Refinery Company, a subsidiary of Standard of Indiana.

In addition to the small arms ammunition plant, the Geneva steel mill, and the Utah Oil Refinery, other plants were built for war purposes and some of them continued in postwar operation. One, the Lehi Refractory, supplied silica bricks for Utah's steel industry and was sold to a private firm at the end of the war. Another, the Eitel McCullough Radio Tube Plant, was built to fill the communications needs of the army and navy; it employed

1,500 people during peak operation and then closed with the cancellation of its War Department contracts. In Manti the Standard Parachute Company began manufacturing in June 1942 and a year later employed 450 workers. One of the few privately funded defense operations, this plant was converted to apparel manufacturing following cessation of its war-related operations in 1944.

Mining and Mineral Processing

Several mineral processing plants were added to the state's industrial facilities during the war. In 1940 the Army and Navy Munitions Board included aluminum, tungsten, and vanadium among the list of strategic and critical materials. Demand for aluminum airplanes spurred the Office of Production Management to authorize three million dollars for construction of a mill in Salt Lake City to process alunite, a low-grade aluminum ore. Completed in 1943 at a cost of $5.5 million, the plant was the first wartime facility to utilize Utah's alunite deposits near Marysvale. In 1945 what the Bureau of Mines called a disappointing operation was abandoned. Salt Lake City also hosted a tungsten retreatment plant between 1943 and 1946. Utilizing a chemical rather than flotation process, the mill produced more than 34,703 tons of concentrate. A vanadium processing unit was built at Monticello in 1942, the only federally financed plant built away from the Wasatch Front during the war years. By February 1944, when the government's vanadium purchasing program ended and the plant closed, nearly two million pounds of vanadium had been produced.

It was only with the stimulation of wartime need that the mining of coal, iron, dolomite, and limestone regained significance in Utah's economic picture. Peak production for coal before the war was six million tons, a record reached during the 1920s. That amount was not mined again until 1942. Two years later production exceeded seven million tons, and the production amount continued to increase.

Most of the privately financed industrial expansion during the war years was in connection with mining or mineral processing. Facility expansion by the American Smelting and Refining Company, International Smelting and Refining Company, Kennecott Copper Corporation, and Utah Copper Company totaled more than $15 million. The war stimulated production of some minerals and retarded the development of others. The copper mills at Magna and Arthur operated at 125 percent of their prewar capacity during the war years. With a decrease in mining in South Dakota, Utah ranked first in the nation in gold production. The natural gas industry, which had only 30,000 users in Utah in 1940, expanded all of its gas plants as rapidly as possible when the war broke out. Thereafter federal controls that prohibited manufacture of gas-burning appliances held consumption static. By the end of the war prices of other fuels had risen and this created an unusually heavy demand for gas service.

Construction

Construction of Utah's military and industrial installations affected the most extensive labor force changes in the economy. Prior to the war about 5,000 were employed in building trades. The number had jumped to 18,400 in October 1941 and 35,000 a year later. It still stood at 20,000 in 1943. Completion of the Geneva steel mill and the Utah Oil Refinery placed employment in the industry at about the prewar level. Many of the workers came from outside the state and left Utah after each project was finished. Civilian personal income in construction was $5 million in 1940, $70 million in 1943, and $14 million in 1945.

Agriculture

Graphic changes in other sectors of Utah's economy overshadowed developments in agriculture. Nevertheless, the war's impact was significant. On the whole demand for the products of agriculture increased. Cash farm income grew from $44 million in 1938 to $81 million in 1942. Government support and quotas helped push up prices and production. A newspaper poll in May 1942 revealed that the Utah farmers queried approved of federal marketing controls five to one. Gasoline rationing proved to be irritating because more machinery and equipment were being used to increase production. From 1940 to 1945 the size as well as the number of farms in the state increased. In 1940 25,411 farms averaged 287 acres in size. Five years later 26,332 farms had an average size of 392 acres each. Even though thousands of acres of rich farmland were withdrawn from use to make room for military and industrial installations, over three million acres were added to the state's farmland. Demands for reclamation and power projects, postponed during the war, increased immediately following the end of fighting.

Changing Economic Patterns

Utah's eleven military installations and numerous defense-related activities were largely responsible for alterations in her economic patterns during the war years. From 1940 to 1943 total em-

A group of children play at Topaz, the barracks-style relocation center near Delta, Millard County, in September 1942.

ployment jumped from 148,000 to 230,000. At the height of the war between 50,000 and 60,000 military personnel were stationed in Utah, and about the same number of civilians were engaged in defense-related work. Although there was a large decline in employment following the end of the conflict in 1945, a net increase of about 14,000 defense-related jobs remained after the postwar reconversion, and the unemployment rate held relatively stable.

Personal income was another economic factor that was drastically altered. Before 1940 Utah's total personal income was under $300 million. In 1943 it surged beyond the $700 million mark, then dropped back slightly for three years and continued upward thereafter. Per capita income was 81.8 percent of the national average in 1940 and 102.7 percent of the national average in 1943. Total assets of insured banks increased from $199 million in 1940 to $586 million at the war's close. In short, the tragedy of World War II led to the revitalization of Utah's economy.

Politics in the War Years

Nationally the war had the effect of turning the political focus from domestic to international issues. At the state and local levels politicians were required to deal with domestic problems that resulted from war mobilization.

In Utah the Democratic Party dominated the political scene from 1940 to 1945. The election of Herbert B. Maw in 1940 continued the pattern of Democratic governorship begun sixteen years earlier. Congressmen Walter K. Granger and J. Will Robinson and Senators Elbert D. Thomas and Abraham Murdock held posts that they or other Democrats had filled since 1933. In the elections through 1944 all major state offices were won by the party's candidates, and in the state legislature Democrats outnumbered Republicans in both houses by ratios of 2.5:1 and 3.7:1.

In choosing Murdock over anti-New Deal incumbent William H. King in the 1940 Democratic primary, Utahns demonstrated that their attachment to Franklin D. Roosevelt's programs and charisma was still strong. The state Republican organization brought presidential candidate Wendell Willkie to the Pioneer Day festivities, and the state Republican platform declared unqualified opposition to a third term for any president, charged New Deal administrators with using public payrolls to reward political favorites, demanded removal of quotas from domestic sugar beet production, and denounced the interventionist policies of the national administration. But in the November election Utah voters awarded Roosevelt and most Democrats running for state offices 60,000 vote pluralities. Willkie carried only six rural counties.

Except for the controversial chain store tax, Utah's 1942 election was barren of major issues. In an effort to protect small businesses in the state, the 1941 legislature passed an act that required all stores with two or more outlets to pay an additional tax for each new unit. Governor Maw signed the bill into law. Opponents of the measure acquired the necessary signatures from voters, and the proposition was placed on the 1942 ballot. The controversy drew national attention and became the campaign's liveliest issue. In the election, the first referendum ballot in Utah history, not one county approved the measure. Also defeated was a proposed amendment to the state constitution that would have increased compensation for state legislators.

In 1944 presidential tenure was the major political issue. Even though Roosevelt did not commit himself to seek reelection until just before the national convention, Utah Democrats instructed their delegates in May to nominate Roosevelt with Senator Elbert D. Thomas as his runningmate. (Senator Harry S. Truman received the nomination for vice-president.) During the ensuing campaign Democrats stressed the danger of "changing horses in mid-stream," and Republican Thomas E. Dewey was unable to devise a politically effective reply.

The influence of the war on Utah's politics in 1944 was reflected in the state platforms of both parties. The Democratic platform called for the establishment of a veterans advisory council, an end to war controls as soon as possible, support for private enterprise and small business, revision of discriminatory freight rates, and encouragement of price supports and soil conservation programs. The Republicans favored reemployment of veterans, pensions for their widows, rehabilitation of the disabled, and temporary unemployment benefits. They pledged support of state aid to education, import duties to combat foreign competition, protective tariffs on metals, and insurance supervision. Republicans opposed the direct primary and favored constitutional amendments that allowed nonpartisan selection of the judiciary and that established salary increases for state legislators.

Democrats won the 1944 election both nationally and in the major state races. As in 1940, the closest margin was in the gubernatorial contest, where Governor Maw defeated Price Mayor J. Bracken Lee by 1,056 votes. Senator Thomas defeated Adam S. Bennion, a Utah Power and Light Company executive, and Granger and Robinson returned to the House of Representatives. A constitutional amendment providing for nonpartisan judiciary selection was approved, as was an amendment to increase legislative salaries.

The Maw Administration

Insight into the problems imposed upon government leaders by the war may be gleaned from Governor Maw's messages to the state legislature. In 1941 he committed the support of Utah's people and her productive facilities to President Roosevelt's rearmament program. In 1943 he announced that the State Defense Council had enlisted tens of thousands of citizens in civilian defense units. He warned that federal contributions to relief and road building would be discontinued and that the drop in gasoline tax revenues would forbid new road construction. In 1945 he urged cooperation to provide for the security and prosperity of returning veterans, calling for the establishment of Veterans Service Centers. Throughout the period *economy* was the watchword.

Maw served two terms as Utah's chief executive and accomplished several important objectives in spite of wartime complications. First was an extensive reorganization of the state's executive branch. In 1941 he recommended that existing commissions, boards, and other governmental units be dissolved and be replaced by new departments, whose heads would be responsible directly to the governor. The new departments he suggested were finance, engineering, public welfare, lands and water, service and inspection, health, publicity, and industrial development. Recommendations for a board of higher education and for tax, industrial, and liquor commissions were also made. Most of his suggestions were implemented, but a special session of the state legislature was required to facilitate implementation.

Maw's second major accomplishment was initiated in August 1942 when, at the suggestion of the National Resources Planning Board, he authorized one of the nation's first postwar planning programs. He appointed Ora Bundy of the Department of Publicity and Industrial Development to direct a study of Utah's current economic conditions, problems, and possibilities and to recommend actions for postwar adjustment and development. Anticipating widescale unemployment following the end of the war, the governor urged that sales tax revenues be used only for direct relief purposes throughout the war years.

Another achievement of Maw's Administration came in 1943 when the governor personally delivered his budget message and announced that all of the state's services would be fully financed by June 30. Over two million dollars was used to retire the state's outstanding bonds, making the biennium ending in 1943 the first debt-free fiscal period in Utah's forty-seven-year history.

Apart from the major work of executive reorganization, activity of the Utah legislature during the war years could probably be categorized as maintenance rather than sweeping reform. In addition to measures already mentioned, appropriations for a crippled children's hospital, a general school financing program, and marriage and child adoption regulations were among the laws enacted. A 1944 special session provided the opportunity for citizens in the armed forces to vote.

Social Effects of the War

The military conflict that transformed the state's economy and politics also stimulated changes in social institutions, arrangements, and customs. Thousands of Utahns found themselves wearing military uniforms and fighting in foreign lands, and over 3,600 lost their lives. Thousands more at home altered their life-styles by working at the new defense installations. A large influx of construction workers and military personnel created acute housing shortages and strained the capacities of service establishments.

Food and other commodities were rationed. Naturally there was some resentment, but most Utahns accepted and adjusted to the wartime difficulties. Such demographic changes as a declining birth rate, a rising divorce rate, and an increase in ethnic diversity were probably direct outgrowths of the war.

Military Service

The war's direct impact on Utahns is disclosed by contrasting the number of residents in military service before the attack on Pearl Harbor and the number in military service four years later. In June 1941 the United States had total land and naval forces of 1.3 million. Nearly 7,000 of these were Utahns, including 2,000 men in National Guard units that had been activated nine months before the attack on Pearl Harbor. In June 1945 Utahns in uniforms numbered 62,107, including 60,764 men and 1,343 women. Of these 39,592 were on Army rosters, 8,306 were in the Navy, 4,638 were serving in the Marine Corps, and 1,740 were attached to Coast Guard units; 8,684 of them were commissioned officers. At the end of World War II 1,450 Utahns had been killed in action and a total of 3,660 were dead from all causes. Of course, the war's social and economic impact on families affected by death or disablement cannot be measured.

Worker Shortage

Whereas unemployment had been a critical problem prior to the war, a shortage of workers developed by the end of 1942. In December 1943 the War Manpower Commission placed building and construction trades on the critical shortage list, which meant construction workers could be hired only through arrangements with the United States Employment Service. The War Production Board halted work on a structural steel unit at the Geneva steel mill for three months so that workers could be used to complete the top-priority Utah Oil Refinery in Salt Lake City.

Employers used various tactics to obtain employees. Job requirements were lowered and intensive on-the-job training programs were sponsored. Men and women with physical disabilities were hired. At several installations women did metal work, repaired engines, loaded ammunition, and drove trucks, buses, and taxis. In Salt Lake City recruiting parades to obtain civilian defense workers were organized. Students and teachers from Cache Valley commuted to the Utah General Depot in Ogden to work weekends on an organized basis. German and Italian prisoners of war incarcerated at Utah General Depot were given work assignments, and Japanese-Americans from war relocation centers were allowed to work. To help compensate for employee shortages, work shifts and work weeks were extended.

Changing Population Patterns

The abrupt impact of the defense industry on Utah's population is illustrated by Tooele's growth from a city of 5,000 in 1940 to 14,000 in 1945. After three decades of net outward migration, Utah experienced a net inward migration of 18,400 persons between 1940 and 1946. The 25.2 percent population increase in the 1940's—from 555,310 to 688,862—occurred mainly in the seven Wasatch Front or neighboring counties (Salt Lake, Weber, Davis, Utah, Tooele, Box Elder, and Cache) where the major military and defense installations were located. Five other counties showed increases in population during the decade; seventeen counties registered declines. Decreases were probably due to increased mechanization on the farms and greater employment opportunities in the urban areas, where all but 11,000 of the population growth was registered. Utah's previously miniscule Black population grew rapidly during the war, and most of the newcomers left when defense jobs disappeared. The small Spanish-speaking population of the state increased substantially in size and diversity.

A memorable episode of World War II was the ill-advised relocation of Japanese-Americans from the Pacific Coast in 1942. The story of the Central Utah War Relocation Center, Topaz (located in Millard County), is told in another chapter. In spite of their unjust treatment, many of the almost 10,000 people who came to Utah under duress rendered valuable wartime service and remained in Utah when the conflict was over.

Housing and Community Problems

Utah's population shifts were similar to those in other defense-oriented regions of the nation, and the concomitant housing crisis was the same. In Weber and Davis counties the shortage was gravest, since 52,000 new jobs were created at Hill Field, Ogden Arsenal, Utah General Depot, and Clearfield Naval Supply Depot. In rural Tooele County a significant housing market did not exist before 1940, and the influx of war workers made difficult the location of even temporary quarters. Salt Lake City and the Provo-Orem area also experienced a deficit, particularly in family units. Utah's shortage of housing was resolved several years after the war as a result of cooperation between government and private concerns at all levels—federal, state, and local.

In August 1941 the Housing Committee of the State Defense Council was organized to coordinate construction of temporary and permanent facilities and to locate rental accommodations in already existing homes. Home registration bureaus known as hospitality centers were established locally. Homeowners and landlords registered vacant rooms or apartments and incoming workers were assisted in locating accommodations at no charge. During July 1942 the Salt Lake bureau processed between 150 and 200 applications daily. Through its local officials the Mormon Church also helped by locating available rooms in the homes of established families.

A variety of government-sponsored projects produced trailer villages, Quonset hut communities, on-base dormitories for civilians, multifamily frame buildings, prefabricated units, and conventional housing. The federal government built 6,000 units of permanent housing in Utah, and Federal Housing Administration loans financed most of the 8,000 units that were privately constructed. Following the war some units were annexed by neighboring cities and others, like Clearfield, Roy, and Washington Terrace, became incorporated bedroom suburbs for the megalopolis developing along the Wasatch Front.

The arrival of new defense plants, housing, and personnel upset some Utah residents. In 1940 farmers instituted lawsuits contesting condemnation of land for the Utah General Depot, and stockmen in Tooele County complained that the Wendover base would "wipe out a hundred outfits" and cost the state $1.5 million annually. Citizens living on or near the Clearfield depot site sent petitions to the Navy Department requesting an alternate location; state and Mormon Church leaders attempted to find one, but the navy rejected their suggestions. Local disputes developed over the dumping of sewage into canals and the routing of gravel trucks to the site of the Remington small arms facility. Wage scales were boosted in the Salt Lake area as a consequence of Remington's arrival, and local employers who were forced to compete with the higher wages objected. Some Provo residents resented the overcrowding of facilities during the construction of the Geneva plant.

Local residents were not the only ones to complain. Airmen at Kearns Army Base claimed that Salt Lakers were inhospitable, that there was little entertainment, and that USO (United Service Organization) facilities were inadequate. Many newcomers found Utah's Sunday closing ordinances archaic and its liquor laws oppressive. Wives of servicemen found rental housing scarce, particularly when they had children, and they found transportation facilities poor. Blacks and other minority groups experienced the same kinds of discrimination in housing and services as they did elsewhere in the United States.

War and the Lives of the People

World War II impacted the daily lives of Utahns in the form of rationing and price controls. Japanese conquests in the Pacific cut off sugar from the Philippines and rubber from Southeast Asia. Automobile tires and gasoline were among the first items to be rationed; sugar, coffee, meat, butter, canned fruits and vegetables, and other goods were later added to the list. Children collected aluminum, tin, and other scrap metal in neighborhood drives; women painted their legs to simulate hosiery because nylon had gone to war. An anti-inflation law passed by Congress in October 1942 gave the President authority to freeze wages, salaries, and prices at September 15 levels; the following July rents were also frozen. (Rationing controls on all food items but sugar were dropped in November 1945, and almost all other price controls were lifted in 1946.)

Following national patterns, Utah women took jobs in defense plants and military installations, performed volunteer services for hospitals, the Red Cross, and the USO, or cared for the children of mothers who were so engaged. Churches established activity and support programs for military personnel and their dependents. The LDS Servicemen's Committee tried to make religious services and supervision available worldwide to Mormons in uniform, most of whom came from Utah and adjoining states. Selective Service depleted the male population of Utah campuses; by 1945 enrollments in higher education had fallen as much as seventy percent below prewar levels.

Wartime conditions may have kindled other social developments. The Utah birth rate was approximately 25 per 1,000 population during the war, and it increased rapidly to 33.4 in 1947; the trend was nationwide, but the Utah figures were in all cases about one-fourth higher than the national average. The pattern of marriage went from 15 per 1,000 population in 1940 to an average of 10 in the war years; then the postwar reunions took the rate to 15.4 in 1946. A sharp increase in the divorce rate, a phenomenon also consistent with the national trend, took place in Utah toward the close of World War II. Through 1942 the rate was slightly above 2.5 per 1,000 population. This figure increased to a peak rate of 5.5 in 1946, and then it declined for more than a decade. While the marriage rate roughly equalled the national average, the Utah divorce rate was consistently higher; these were patterns that prevailed through the first eight decades of Utah statehood. (See Table D, p. 688.)

When Governor Maw set up the study of postwar problems and prospects and the legislature created a Centennial Commission to prepare for the hundredth anniversary of the Mormon pioneers' arrival in Salt Lake Valley, both actions affirmed that the World War II years were indeed a watershed in the history of Utah.

Chapter 27
Bibliographical Essay

Two important studies discuss the impact of World War II on Utah's economy. *Impact of Defense Spending on the Economy of Utah* (1967) by George Jensen and Leonard J. Arrington is, in the main, a theoretical treatment of defense industries and their impact on regional economies. *Federally-financed Industrial Plants Constructed in Utah During World War II* (1969) by Arrington and Anthony T. Cluff details the genesis and significance of the major industrial facilities built during the war years. Also of interest is the report of the state's Cooperative Planning Program, *After Victory: Plans for Utah and the Wasatch Front* (1943). Thomas G. Alexander and Arrington, "Utah's Small Arms Ammunition Plant During World War II," *Pacific Historical Review,* May 1965, deals specifically with the Remington plant's origins and impact. ElRoy Nelson, *Economic Patterns* (1956), mentions the effects of the war on particular industries in the state. Roland Stucki, *Commercial Banking in Utah, 1847-1966* (1967), briefly describes the war's influence on the economy by citing several banking indicators.

The origins, activities, and socioeconomic impact of individual military installations are described in a series of articles which appeared in *UHQ* between 1963 and 1966. Arrington and Alexander coauthored five articles: "They Kept 'Em Rolling: The Tooele Army Depot, 1942-1962," Winter 1963; "World's Largest Military Reserve: Wendover Air Force Base, 1941-1963," Fall 1963; "Sentinels on the Desert: The Dugway Proving Ground (1942-1963) and Deseret Chemical Depot (1942-1955)," Winter 1964; "Supply Hub of the West: Defense Depot Ogden, 1941-1964," Spring 1964; and "The U.S. Army Overlooks Salt Lake Valley: Fort Douglas, 1862-1965," Fall 1965. Arrington, Alexander, and Eugene A. Erb, Jr. wrote "Utah's Biggest Business: Ogden Air Materiel Area at Hill Air Force Base," Winter 1965; Arrington and Archer L. Durham collaborated on "Anchors Aweigh in Utah; The U.S. Naval Supply Depot at Clearfield, 1942-1962," Spring 1963. "Ogden's 'Arsenal of Democracy', 1920-1955," Summer 1965; and "Brief Histories of Three Federal Military Installations in Utah: Kearns Army Base, Hurricane Mesa, and Green River Test Complex," Spring 1966, were written by Alexander.

Information about World War II's impact on Utah's residents is dispersed throughout the articles just cited. In addition, James B. Allen's "Crisis on the Home Front: The Federal Government and Utah's Defense Housing in World War II," *Pacific Historical Review,* November 1969, describes the critical housing situation and outlines measures taken to relieve the shortage. Other articles dealing with the war's social impact are James L. Clayton's "An Unhallowed Gathering: The Impact of Defense Spending on Utah's Population Growth, 1940-64," *UHQ,* Summer 1966; and "Utah's First Line of Defense: The Utah National Guard and Camp W. G. Williams," *UHQ,* Spring 1965, by Alexander and Arrington. Statistics on Utahns in the military are contained in the reports of the Director of Selective Service, *Selective Service and Victory* (1948). Economic, social, and political statistics have been compiled by Merlin B. Brinkerhoff and Phillip R. Kunz in *Utah in Numbers: Comparisons, Trends, and Descriptions* (1969). The Mormon servicemen's program is treated in Eugene E. Campbell and Richard D. Poll, *Hugh B. Brown: His Life and Thought* (1975).

The only secondary source discussing Utah's politics during the years from 1940 to 1945 is Wayne Stout, *History of Utah* (3 vol., 1971). Despite editorial lapses and an interpretive bias, Volume III contains basic information on elections, summaries of legislative activity, and extracts of gubernatorial messages.

Chapter 28
Utah Politics Since 1945

F. Ross Peterson

V ery few states offer a student of geography and geology the
varied physical features that Utah does. The majestic Uintas
contrast with the salt flat deserts. The beautiful rock canyons are
preserved as national parks. The miracle of irrigation has greened
the flat agricultural lands. In the past thirty years these natural
beauties have been enhanced by protective laws and by a growing
appreciation of nature's gift to Utah. It has been a challenge to
Utah's post-World War II politicians to maintain Utah's splendid
physical and historical heritage.

In the three decades since the war ended, Utah has been served by
five governors who have guided the state through great population
and economic growth by advocating an alliance among state and
federal governments and business. Numerous Congressmen have
been elected to the House of Representatives; many of them
seemed to spend much of their time seeking advancement to the
Senate. Utah's seven United States Senators, although some served
multiple terms, have flirted with national prominence but have
rarely achieved it.

Rather than briefly discuss all sixteen postwar elections, this
chapter will discuss major trends in Utah politics and government
that have developed or continued during the postwar period. The
unusual voting behavior of Utah's electorate is illustrated by the
fact that Democrats held the governorship for sixteen of the thirty-
two years following the war and by the fact that the state's congressional delegation always included at least one Democrat, even
though Utah voted for Republican presidential candidates in six
out of the eight elections and the Republican Party controlled the

state legislature most of the time. (See Tables J-O, pp. 697–712.) Although basically conservative, Utah voters are difficult to classify and they repeatedly defy descriptions and pollsters' prognostications.

The Role of the Mormon Church

The Church of Jesus Christ of Latter-day Saints has continued to influence politics throughout the postwar decades. One dramatic and important change is that "the Church," as it is called in Utah, has evolved from direct participation in candidate selection toward attempts to influence voter response to specific issues. Perhaps the last major involvement in candidate selection was the 1950 senatorial campaign, in which many Mormon Church leaders supported Republican businessman Wallace F. Bennett in his attempt to capture the position of the New Deal Democratic incumbent, Elbert D. Thomas. Even though this participation was under the direction of lower echelon officials, it appeared that church spokesmen were desirous of a Bennett election. Although national political figures continually seek audiences with members of the church hierarchy, for the most part the presidents of the church have maintained outward and official neutrality.

That has not always been the case with some of the church's general authorities. In 1958 Ezra Taft Benson, Eisenhower's Secretary of Agriculture and a Mormon apostle, returned to Utah and campaigned for Senator Arthur V. Watkins. Watkins' seat was endangered because of the efforts of J. Bracken Lee, a former Republican governor running as an independent senatorial candidate after having lost to Watkins in the party primary. Frank E. (Ted) Moss, the Democratic challenger, persuaded Hugh B. Brown, another general authority of the church, to campaign on his behalf. Brown, a one-time Democratic state chairman, may have partially offset the Benson impact and helped Moss win the election. More than most other church leaders, Benson has played an active part in political campaigns. Generally loyal to the Republican Party, in 1974 he supported the American Independent Party, whose platform he called "God-ordained."

Mormon Church leaders have attempted to influence the outcome of numerous specific legislative proposals. In 1960 and again in 1967 the Mormon-dominated legislature passed church-desired Sunday closing laws, but both times the governors, Republican George D. Clyde and Democrat Calvin L. Rampton, vetoed the legislation. Nevertheless, the church position on Sabbath observance remains a strong political factor.

A similar desire to regulate personal behavior was more dramatically illustrated by a 1968 liquor-by-the-drink referendum. Many Salt Lake City businessmen, Utah resort operators, hotel managers, and tourism promoters have long contended that national conventions and many vacationers avoid Utah because of its stringent liquor laws. Also arguing that the current policy of a state liquor store and minibottles is corrupt, inconsistent, and potentially dangerous, the proponents of liquor-by-the-drink were able to get the controversial measure on the ballot as a referendum. Once the question was to be decided by popular referendum, many prominent Mormons openly fought against the proposal, which many came to understand as a religious issue. Since Utah's population is approximately seventy percent Mormon, the measure was soundly defeated.

Another issue that drew Mormon Church attention was the mid 1960s debate over a right-to-work bill. Since the nineteenth century the Mormon Church has been opposed to compulsory unionism, a view that has undoubtedly influenced the state legislature's actions on right-to-work measures and has undoubtedly dictated the stance of many congressional candidates. Finally, the federal Equal Rights Amendment has failed to gain ratification in Utah partly because of church opposition. In both the 1973 and 1975 legislative debates, official Mormon opposition was inferred and then was openly avowed. For instance, in 1975 the *Church News* editorialized its opposition and Barbara Smith, president of the Relief Society (an organization of Mormon women), also spoke against the ERA. A year later the church's First Presidency formally urged its defeat and the 1977 legislature again refused to ratify the constitutional amendment. Feminists in Utah were quick to blame church actions for the defeat of this reform, as well as for the conservative positions taken by the Utah International Women's Year Conference in June 1977.

Still, it should be pointed out that there is a real difference between church influence and individual party control. Very few informed sources would argue that the Mormon Church has controlled Utah's post-World War II politics. Mormon leaders can and do influence legislators and others, but they do not control candidate selection, platform construction, or elected officials, as was the pattern in the territorial years; the gubernatorial vetoes of the Sunday closing laws are significant illustrations of this point. During the 1950s the church sought to recover three Utah junior colleges turned over to the state for financial reasons during the 1930s, but the legislature rejected the church's offer.

A defeated 1976 Democratic gubernatorial candidate, John Preston Creer, described another trend in Utah politics as disturbing. Creer asserted that an active Mormon has difficulty rising to power within the state Democratic hierarchy. Consequently, he and others fear that the two major parties' leadership is determined by relationship to the Mormon Church—the active Mormons control the Republican Party and non-Mormons or inactive Mormons determine the fate of the Democrats. That the leadership of the Mormon Church has been predominantly and increasingly Republican in political orientation is apparent. When Apostle Hugh B. Brown keynoted the 1958 Democratic state convention, he wryly observed that he was present "with the approval of close associates, some of whom are mildly Republican." As a member of the church's First Presidency in the 1960s he repeatedly avowed the legitimacy of active Mormon participation in both political parties.

McCarthyism and Political Extremism

It is ironic that Utah has provided some fertile soil for the tactics of political extremists—ironic because those tactics clash with the principles of both political democracy and Christian ethics. In the generation since the Cold War gave rise to McCarthyism, political movements associated with ultraconservatism have had continuing impact on the local political scene.

Utah's 1950 senatorial election was a graphic example of McCarthyism in action. The incumbent, Elbert Thomas, was accused of presiding at Communist meetings and of sponsoring leftist organizations. He was cartooned as a puppet of the Communists and the radical unionists. It is not known who paid for the mass distribution of these fallacious charges, but the Republican candidate, Wallace Bennett, did nothing to deter the attacks.

Four years later another Utah Senator found himself entrenched in the last chapter of Senator Joseph McCarthy's crusading career. It was a credit to Utah that Arthur Watkins presided fairly and effectively over the special committee that recommended McCarthy's censure. However, Watkins' reputation in Utah apparently was not enhanced by this decision, and he was defeated for reelection in 1958. His loss can be attributed to many factors, including the J. Bracken Lee candidacy, but research has shown that many supporters of McCarthy considered Watkins a traitor.

The role of Ezra Taft Benson has been mentioned. In 1962 his son Reed ran for Congress in the Second District. Although Sherman P. Lloyd won the primary, the campaign was unique because

Utah Congresswoman Reva Beck Bosone introduces President Harry Truman during his campaign stop in Utah in 1952.

at the time the younger Benson was a paid recruiter for the John Birch Society. Throughout the 1960s John Birch Society representatives used Apostle Benson's endorsement of Birch founder Robert Welch—"the greatest living American patriot"—in their promotional work among Latter-day Saints in Utah and elsewhere.

In 1968 Utah rightists found a new leader in Alabama's George Wallace. During the hectic days of student and Black protests, Wallace developed a national following for his simplistic concept of law and order. Utah's American Independent Party was formed by Wallace supporters, but Wallace received less than ten percent of the Utah vote in the election as the state stood behind Nixon. The American Independent Party continued into the 1970s, but with the decline of Vietnam-related domestic turbulence and the fading of the Cold War its influence waned. Conservative resistance to big government, high taxes, and "welfare statism," on the other hand, contributed to the landslide proportions of the Utah majorities for Nixon in 1972 and Gerald Ford in 1976.

Political Personalities

Several young and potentially influential Utah Congressmen terminated their careers in the House of Representatives by unsuccessful, perhaps premature, bids to move on to the United States Senate. Two others were destroyed by more bizarre events outside the political arena.

After two narrow House triumphs, Second District Representative David S. King tried to unseat Senator Bennett in 1962 and lost. King, the son of four-term Senator William King, understandably aspired to his father's Senatorial seat, yet his lack of patience and his unwillingness to make a record in the House hurt him politically. His successor, Republican Sherman Lloyd, only waited one term before attempting political elevation, and he suffered the same fate at the hands of Senator Moss as King had from Bennett. Six years later a four-term Congressman from the First District, Laurence J. Burton, tried to defeat Moss. Despite—or perhaps because of—an expensive campaign and visits to Utah by President Nixon, Vice-president Spiro Agnew, Housing Secretary George Romney, Treasury Secretary David Kennedy, and the Nixon children, Burton failed. The most recent example of an unsatisfied House member is Wayne Owens, who after only one term made an attempt to win the Senate seat of retiring Wallace Bennett. In one of the biggest upsets of the postwar generation, Salt Lake City Mayor E. J. (Jake) Garn won the post. Owens' nationally televised appearance as a member of the Judiciary Committee that voted on the Nixon impeachment charges may have hurt him with some Utah Republicans; Republicans may have also looked unfavorably on his earlier service as an aid to both Robert and Edward Kennedy.

Undoubtedly the most dramatic occurrence in recent Utah politics was the strange case of Douglas R. Stringfellow. A handsome veteran who lost both legs in World War II, Stringfellow fabricated a fantastic tale of how he had slipped behind German lines during the war on a secret mission. He easily won election to Congress in 1952 as a Republican and seemed to do well in Washington. Finally, just before the 1954 election, Stringfellow, under heavy pressure, went before television cameras and confessed that his heroic adventures were inventions. Replaced by Utah State University President Henry Aldous Dixon, who easily won, Stringfellow slipped into obscurity and died a few years later.

520

Twenty-two years later a freshman Democratic Congressman lost his seat because of another unusual circumstance. Allen T. Howe, who had been an upset victor in 1974, was arrested for soliciting sex for hire on the streets of Salt Lake City following a political gathering. Although Howe claimed that he had been framed by political opponents and police decoys, he was convicted and subsequently lost his bid for reelection.

The national House of Representatives has been adequately served by Utah's delegation. However, the lack of interest in the House demonstrated by the collective behavior of the elected Congressmen indicates that the House has not been viewed as an end, but only as a means. If Democrat K. Gunn McKay builds on his longevity and party affiliation to become a power in the House of Representatives, he will be the first Utahn in the postwar period to do so.

During the postwar years Utah has produced one genuine political maverick—J. Bracken Lee. A non-Mormon from Price, Lee was elected governor in 1948 with the support of many prominent Mormons. He served eight years as Utah's governor and a similar period as Salt Lake City's mayor. Lee attempted a third gubernatorial term in 1956, but George D. Clyde defeated him in the Republican primary. Lee stayed on the ballot as an independent candidate but was defeated. Two years later, as already noted, he repeated the performance against Senator Watkins. By this time Lee was an embarrassment to some Utah Republicans, but in 1960 and again in 1964 he won as mayor in Salt Lake City. He fought the Internal Revenue Service over income taxes and as governor he refused to allow Utah to commemorate United Nations Day. At one time he allegedly said that he feared the government in Washington more than the one in Moscow. The Utah maverick was honored by right wing groups for his stand against big government.

As a public official Lee prided himself on cutting budgets and taxes and striving for economy. While many large corporations prospered, schools and other public agencies were underfunded. Unafraid of controversy, Lee was responsible for dismissing Utah State Agricultural College President Louis Madsen, and for firing Salt Lake Police Chief W. Cleon Skousen. Lee left the governor's office under a cloud of alleged corruption in the liquor commission and a charge that state employees were being used as Republican Party workers. It is ironic that when Lee campaigned in 1948 he accused the incumbent, Herbert B. Maw, of these same two malpractices.

Governor Calvin Rampton and Senator Frank Moss jointly led the Democratic Party in the 1960s and early 1970s. Moss, who served three terms in the Senate, was elected during the Watkins-Lee split. He attached himself to Lyndon Johnson's coattails in 1964 and soundly defeated Brigham Young University President Ernest L. Wilkinson in a bitter campaign. Six years later he bested Representative Burton. As Moss gained seniority, he had the opportunity to obtain prominence in areas other than sponsoring the ban on cigarette advertising on television. As a member of the Interior Committee, he performed valuable service to Utah in the areas of reclamation and conservation. He gained national attention for his investigations of doctors' abuses of the federal medicaid program. But in 1976 Orrin Hatch, a conservative lawyer with Ronald Reagan support, ousted Moss. Labor support for Moss and his basic liberal domestic record were used by Hatch to defeat the sixty-two-year-old veteran. Utah thus confronted a new Democratic president, Jimmy Carter, with a conservative, low-seniority Republican Senate delegation of Hatch and Garn—hardly the most politically advantageous circumstance for the state.

Calvin Rampton is a rare Utah political commodity. He was elected to three successive gubernatorial terms by overwhelming majorities. With an unimpressive platform appearance and a low-key verbal delivery, Rampton lacked charisma but he was politically astute and apparently so impressed the Republicans that they mounted only token opposition to him in 1968 and 1972. Rampton probably could have won an unprecedented fourth term in 1976. Instead he handpicked the Democratic candidate, Scott Matheson, to succeed him. As Utah voted overwhelmingly for Republicans Gerald Ford and Hatch, Matheson won easily, defeating Attorney General Vernon Romney.

Having guided both friendly and hostile legislatures in his desired directions, Rampton's administrations solved touchy problems such as legislative and congressional reapportionment and a restructuring of the state's tax system. Like his predecessors, Rampton's administration was beset by liquor commission troubles, and many state employees were found campaigning at Democratic headquarters in 1974. Rampton was more successful than his predecessors in bringing economic growth to the Beehive State.

Governmental Trends and Problems

Between 1950 and 1975 Utah state government expenditures from general revenues rose from $66 million to $680 million. Two years later it passed $900 million. (See Table B, p. 686.) Spending by various units of local government followed a comparable escalation, passing a half-billion dollars in 1975. Constitutional limitations and political decisions kept public indebtedness at a comparatively low level; still the increase in the state debt from less than $1 million in 1950 to $88 million in 1974 was impressive. The sheer increase in the scope and cost of public functions has presented the state government with a number of serious problems.

One of the state government's principal challenges has been to govern a state of more than a million people with a governmental system designed in 1895 for 250,000. Following recommendations of the state's 1965 Little Hoover Commission and a plan worked out by the 1967-69 state legislature, the executive branch was rationalized into a series of departments combined by function (such as social services, development services, and natural resources). The changes seem to have been generally satisfactory with a few exceptions, such as the inclusion of the Historical Society and Fine Arts in the Developmental Services Division and the inclusion of the State Archives under the Finance Division.

Problems of continuity and time pressures have always faced the legislators. Until 1947, the legislature met biennially for sixty days except for special sessions called by the governor. In 1947, however, the Legislative Council was created with a professional staff that was designed to make background studies and recommendations for legislation. A 1966 restructuring of the Legislative Council provided for interim committees dealing with budgets, legal services, and legislative operations. In 1970, this system was augmented by annual sessions when twenty calendar days in even-numbered years were devoted to budget matters. Other questions may be included on the budget session agenda by a two-thirds affirmative vote of both houses.

The Legislative Council and the annual sessions, together with a legislative auditor authorized in 1972, have been generally successful in dealing with continuity problems. The time problem generally remains unresolved. Perhaps the most unfortunate feature of the legislative structure is that both the compensation of legislative members and the length of sessions are fixed by the state constitution and can at present be revised only by constitutional amendment. The compensation is fixed at $25 per day and $15 for expenses, making service in the legislature a sacrifice for many. Legislators must have other sources of income; in addition, they must either resign their jobs, secure permission from their employer, or be self-employed in order to serve.

The structure of taxation established by the state constitution and the legislature is not greatly different from that of other states. Most tax-generated state revenue comes from sales taxes and corporate and individual income taxes. Though less than one percent of state revenue comes from property taxes, probably more controversy surrounds the property taxing system than any other taxation program because of the heavy reliance of counties, municipalities, and school districts upon income from this source.

The state constitution requires that property taxes be based on the market value of property, but studies made by the Utah Foundation in the early 1950s demonstrated considerable lack of uniformity between counties in making assessments. Legislation in 1953 mandated reevaluation of all taxable property every five years, but this was not accomplished until the legislature launched a program to improve property tax administration in 1969. By 1976 the new system, though more equitable than its predecessor, had proved far from perfect. Salt Lake and three other counties had not yet completed reevaluation, and a study by the Utah Foundation revealed that rates still ranged from a low of 6.31 percent in Sanpete County, which had not been reassessed, to a high of 20.28 percent in Juab County, which was reassessed in 1976. Some taxes on residential property in Davis, Utah, and Weber counties increased more than eighty percent in one year under the reevaluation program while business property, which was reevaluated annually in the same areas, received tax reductions.

The inequities in the assessment of real property also affected the financing of public education. The allocation of state equalization funds is based on the relative wealth of each local school district as measured by assessed valuation. Because of this system, schools in districts with a higher than average evaluation tend to receive proportionately less state support than those in districts with lower assessed valuations. A provision of state law requires that the state tax commission determine the ratio between the actual value of property and the value at which the property is currently assessed; the state contribution should be computed on that basis. This provision has never been enforced.

Utah's public schools face other problems as well. Though Utah contributes more per capita than do most other states for education, its high birth rate has maintained a large schoolage population so that its contribution per pupil tends to be low. In 1976 Utah had the highest student-teacher ratio in the nation, and the average per pupil expenditure for public education was $1,084, which placed it forty-second in the nation and last among states in the mountain west. In recent years money for improvement in teachers' salaries—which averaged $11,400 in 1976—has been taken out of funds that might have been used for other programs such as constructing new buildings and reducing the student-teacher ratio. The 1977 legislature mandated a reduction in the ratio in grades one through three, which may help to correct some of the problems.

Perhaps no other programs administered by the state generate as much controversy as do public welfare programs. In 1975, 3.7 percent of the state's citizens received some sort of welfare assistance, and 11 percent of the state budget went to welfare compared with 52.4 percent for education and 15 percent for highways. Public opinion to the contrary notwithstanding, the state administers no programs that give welfare assistance to able-bodied men who are unwilling to work. In 1975 seventy-nine percent of the welfare money went to assist families with dependent children—principally single-parent families with subteen children—and fourteen percent went for old age assistance and aid to the disabled. This left only seven percent for all other categories.

Though the greatest expansion since World War II has come in assistance to families with dependent children, undoubtedly the greatest change in recent years has come in the operation of mental health programs. Between 1962 and 1974 the number of persons treated at the Utah State Hospital in Provo declined by more than fifty percent. At the same time, an expansion took place in the role of community mental health centers that treat principally out-patients. The 1961 and 1963 state legislatures began the process of decentralization by making the Health Department responsible for developing an out-patient mental health program and assisting in the financing of community mental health services. These changes have not reduced overall expenditures for mental care, but they have allowed persons afflicted with treatable mental illnesses to live relatively normal lives within the community rather than suffering incarceration in an institution.

Utah's highway construction and maintenance program has faced some difficult problems in the past and will continue to face them in the future. Unlike many states, Utah chose to construct its interstate freeway system through the heavily populated urban areas first. This meant that the most expensive land acquisitions were completed first, but it also means that Utah remains behind other states in percentage of the projected interstate system completed. The recent energy crisis and the empoundment of Federal Highway Trust Funds have seriously depleted revenues needed not only for the interstate freeways but for other highway programs as well. This has left Utah woefully short of highway funds. At the same time considerable pressure has developed for further expansion of public transportation, particularly in urban areas.

In the years since World War II, and particularly since the 1960s, such state programs as education, welfare, mental health, highways, and law enforcement have benefited from—and have become increasingly dependent upon—federal funds. Local government units have also participated through revenue sharing and various categorical federal grants. While this assistance has significantly expanded revenues available for state and local programs, it has made these programs dependent upon the vagaries of federal income and budgetary policies and it has injected controls that many Utahns find capricious or oppressive. It also underscores the extent to which Utah is affected by decisions made in Washington, D.C.

The Impact of Federal Programs

Approximately one out of every ten Utahns is employed by the federal government. Another five percent are employed by defense-related industries or directly by the military. In fact, Ogden is almost a federal preserve. Gigantic Hill Air Force Base is on the outskirts of Ogden and regional offices of both the Internal Revenue Service and the United States Forest Service are located in the city. The Defense Supply Agency Depot is also a contributing factor of the Ogden economic picture.

Not only is the federal government the number one Utah employer, but it is also the state's greatest landowner, holding over seventy percent of Utah land. When the national forests, parks, monuments, and recreation areas are added to the Bureau of Land Management and the military holdings, it appears that the state is almost a colony of Washington, D.C.

Real political success for Utah's elected officials depends on whether they can obtain federal monies and influence federal agencies to aid the state. An example of this is the entire issue of reclamation. The congressional delegations and Utah's governors have combined forces in a bipartisan effort that has created two mammoth hydroelectric dams since World War II. The Flaming Gorge Dam on the Green River and the Glen Canyon Dam on the Colorado River were both completed in the early 1960s, providing power sources, water storage, and national recreation areas. (See map 20, p. 737.) The large Central Utah Project, designed to carry water to the heavily populated Wasatch Front and to irrigate portions of Central Utah, was far from completion when President Carter included it on his list of expendable governmental undertakings in 1977, but it narrowly survived. The political realities have made both conservative and liberal Utah officials advocates of federal spending for resource development in the state.

Federal presence is a constant political issue. Governors Lee and Clyde were concerned that along with federal expenditures come federal controls. Some of their fears were later realized under the aggressive policies of the Environmental Protection Agency, which seemed to threaten business, real estate, and tourism development in the mid 1970s. Senators Garn and Hatch campaigned almost exclusively on an antifederal platform. The 1976 ballot contained a proposition that the state should cut off all federal monies by 1980. Fortunately, this unrealistic measure was soundly defeated.

While Governors Lee and Clyde pursued probusiness tax and regulatory policies, Kennecott Copper, United States Steel, and other corporations prospered significantly. No genuine attempt was made by the state to control water or air pollution. Rampton, also intent on attracting outside businesses and jobs, was reluctant to push the mines and smelters toward emission regulation. It was left to the Environmental Protection Agency to try to reduce environmental abuses, while pollution along the Wasatch Front, especially in Salt Lake and Utah counties, remained a problem and while Utah Lake suffered greatly from refuse dumping. All Utah pollution, of course, is not the fault of the politicians or the mill and smelting operators; the number one violator is probably the automobile. None of the postwar governors or legislatures was willing to tackle the problems of providing a viable mass transit system for the Wasatch Front as it became a megalopolis.

The conflicting aspirations of the developer and the environmentalist will continue to hold the spotlight in Utah. Prosperity devotees argue that restrictive policies will hinder the growth and development of the state. Conservationists counter that Utah must be preserved for future generations to enjoy. It remains for state politicians, federal agencies, and the private sector to harmoniously develop plans that will lead Utah toward a necessary ecological balance.

Limiting Factors in Utah Politics

Very few politicians attain statesmanship stature during their careers. It takes time to develop programs and learn the methods of implementation. To expect political miracle workers is asking too much, yet it is probable that Utah politics may not attract the state's most able and qualified men and women. That is also true in other places, but there are some good reasons why Utah may be exceptional. For one thing, the nature of the Mormon Church discourages many capable people from seeking a time-consuming political office. While the church strongly advocates voter participation and attendance at party mass meetings, the fact that it operates with a lay clergy keeps some potential leaders out of politics. In the modern era most general authorities, stake presidencies, and bishoprics are reluctant to tilt their lances in politics for fear of dividing their ecclesiastical followers.

Finally, the increasingly conservative cast of political sentiment in Utah has tended to narrow the range of political debate. The state has lacked strong labor and minority movements to represent liberal political causes. Successful Democrats like Rampton and Moss have kept well to the middle of the road. Political emotions have tended to find expression in moralistic issues like liquor-by-the-drink and the ERA. Although Utah is one of the most urbanized states, its politics still hark back to the slogans and virtues of a less complex era. The voters rejected a land-use planning proposal in 1974 not because it was a poorly designed piece of legislation but because they feared anyone telling them what they could or could not do with private property. Those two great urban and rural planners to whom most Utahns pay homage—Joseph Smith and Brigham Young—would have been dismayed to see Utah's people trade quality for quantity.

The time has come for Utah's politicians to recognize the environmental as well as the political heritage that is theirs. Since its organization as a territory, Utah has produced many governmental leaders of courage and integrity. The contemporary politician who will do a great service to the state is the one who will convince the people that most of them are on a private island in a federal lake. A spirit of cooperation among all levels of government and the people is essential for Utah to achieve her human potential—citizens to match her mountains.

Chapter 28
Bibliographical Essay

When researchers begin working in post-World War II sources, they are amazed at the wealth of primary information and the few secondary publications on Utah politics and government that have so far been based on these primary collections. With time, good historical studies should come from the Elbert D. Thomas, J. Bracken Lee, and Frank E. Moss collections at the University of

Utah, the Arthur V. Watkins and Wallace F. Bennett papers at Brigham Young University, and the Edgar Brossard collection at Utah State University. The Utah State Archives maintains the official papers of all governors, and the University of Utah's Western Americana Collection has acquired the papers of many of Utah's postwar United States representatives.

As mayor of Salt Lake City and as governor of the state, Lee was in the limelight for nearly two decades. George B. Russell, *J. Bracken Lee: The Taxpayer's Champion* (1961), is narrow and ideological. Dennis Lythgoe has written several articles, the best of which is "Political Feud in Salt Lake City: J. Bracken Lee and the Firing of W. Cleon Skousen," *UHQ,* Fall 1974. Lythgoe's political biography of Lee should be forthcoming.

The author who has contributed most to an analysis of contemporary Utah politics is Frank H. Jonas, a political scientist at the University of Utah. Many articles have appeared in the *Western Political Quarterly, UHQ,* and *Proceedings of the Utah Academy of Sciences, Arts, and Letters.* His best works are two volumes that he edited, *Politics in the American West* (1969) and *Political Dynamiting* (1970). The former has an extended chapter on Utah, and the latter illustrates questionable political activities with material from recent Utah history, including the campaign against Senator Thomas. Jonas's *The Story of a Political Hoax* (1966) is the best and most objective discussion of the Douglas Stringfellow tragedy. His "Mormons and Politics," in Charles Press and Oliver Williams, eds., *Democracy in the Fifty States* (1966), briefly covers that essential topic.

There have not been many dissertations of note on Utah politics since 1945. Gerald E. Hansen, "The Conservative Movement in Utah after World War II" (University of Missouri, 1962), is excellent; Rulon Bradley, "The Use of Mass Media in the 1960 Election" (University of Utah, 1962), is also useful. Two master's theses that make genuine contributions are Roger D. Madsen, "The 1958 Senatorial Election in Utah" (Brigham Young University, 1972), and Brad E. Hainsworth, "Reapportionment in Utah, 1954-1965" (University of Utah, 1966).

A number of secondary works are also available. D. R. Haddock, et al., *Election Law Reform in Utah* (1967), is an excellent compilation of attempts to alter political participation. Oakley Gordon, Reed Richardson, and J. D. Williams, *Personnel Management in Utah State Government* (1962), is a good treatise on the growth of government but needs some revision. Senator Frank E. Moss wrote a book entitled *The Water Crisis* (1967) that foreshadowed contemporary difficulties. The Utah-United States military relationship is explored in Leonard J. Arrington and George Jensen, *The Defense Industry of Utah* (1965), and James L. Clayton, "An Unhallowed Gathering: The Impact of Defense Spending on Utah's Population Growth, 1940-1964," *UHQ,* Summer 1966.

Utah's post-World War II political history has an added dimension of significance—the findings of such excellent pollsters as Dan E. Jones, Bruce Mayfield, Ray Briscoe, and the Hinckley Institute of Government at the University of Utah. Important sources for examination of the fiscal activities of state government are the publications of the privately sponsored Utah Foundation, which include *Research Reports* on important matters of public policy and an annual *Statistical Review of Government in Utah.* The reports of the University of Utah's Bureau of Economic and Business Research are also helpful, as are the Bureau's two regular publications, *Utah Economic and Business Review* (monthly) and *Statistical Abstract of Utah* (annual).

Chapter 29
Contemporary Economic Development

James L. Clayton

U tah's postwar economy is perhaps best understood as an economy operating against serious physiographic odds in a relatively disadvantaged region while at the same time offering increasing and deeply felt satisfactions to those who lived there. Chief among the physiographic odds is the marked aridity of the entire state. Even those areas with the greatest rainfall (Davis, Weber, and Box Elder counties) do not receive enough precipitation to rise above the twenty-inch minimum annual rainfall barrier that separates arid from semiarid regions. Additional handicaps are a smaller than average manufacturing sector, remoteness from the larger economic centers, limited land usage potential (seventy-eight percent of the land in Utah is federal- or state-owned), a rising birth rate (since 1966) that tends to be causatively associated with a per capita income ten to twenty percent below the national average, and a long tradition of economic dependency on forces largely beyond the control of the state.

The economic benefits of living in Utah are evidenced by the small number of people who have left the state during the past thirty years and by the continuing return of those who once resided here. Among the economic benefits are a setting of relatively uncrowded and sometimes spectacular beauty; a healthful climate with four distinct seasons; a young, vigorous, and homogeneous population; an extraordinarily high number of males with four or more years of college education; a cost-of-living index that compares favorably with the nation as a whole; a low per capita tax rate (perhaps a mixed blessing); and a productive labor force. The Mormon life-style attracts some newcomers—both Mormon and non-Mormon—as well as returnees, even though the Mormon Church long ago stopped advocating the gathering. Finally, even if water resources are scarce, energy reserves are unusually plentiful.

Largely because of the limiting factors described above—and especially because of the state's rainfall distribution—the bulk of Utah's population and virtually her entire economic base are concentrated along a narrow one-hundred-mile-long line hugging the Wasatch Mountains from Brigham City in the north to Spanish Fork in the south. Located on what is commonly called the Wasatch Front, almost eighty percent of the state's residents live on less than five percent of the state's land. For this reason Utah is usually divided economically into two distinct areas: 1) the Wasatch Front (formerly Weber, Davis, Salt Lake, and Utah counties; more recently subtracting Utah County and adding Tooele and Morgan counties) and 2) the rest of the state. As in other desert regions, Utah's economy is an oasis economy, with the major oasis located in Salt Lake County, two smaller oases an hour by car to the north and to the south, and a series of much smaller watering places scattered out in every direction from that core.

Population Growth

Utah's economic development is closely tied to her population growth. During most of this century Utah has had one of the highest birth rates in the nation, but because of a very low in-migration rate her population growth has been lower than that for other mountain states. This pattern has also held true since 1950, though the regional configuration has changed markedly in the intervening years. Under the impact of America's latest westward movement Colorado, Nevada, and Arizona have grown rapidly, while the mountain states without substantial net in-migrations have lagged behind the regional average. Utah is in the latter group. The tide of transient workers has ebbed and flowed, and some natives have gone out into the world to seek their fortunes while others have returned for the same reason or to enjoy the fruits of retirement. Except for a moderate net in-migration in the 1950s and in recent years, almost all of Utah's net population growth since World War II has been from natural increase. The census totals have been:

1950 —   688,862
1960 —   890,627
1970 — 1,059,273
1980 — 1,461,037

There are both positive and negative aspects to Utah's birth rate profile during the past three decades. The population increase has been predictable, regular, and compatible with the existing population base. This allows an orderly economy with few demographic surprises or shocks. On the other hand, there are fewer productive workers in Utah's economy because of the higher percentage of children; and as a result, a higher percentage of the state's resources must go toward educating them. A striking economic tradeoff between high birth rates and low per capita income may also be evident, as will be noted later.

Utah's population growth patterns have varied widely since World War II. The Wasatch Front and its surrounding counties have been the fastest growing areas of the state for several decades. From 1950 to 1970, for example, the five Wasatch Front counties (using the current definition) grew sixty-five percent, the mountainlands (Summit, Utah, and Wasatch counties) grew fifty-two percent, the Bear River District (Box Elder, Cache, and Rich counties) increased twenty-nine percent, and central and southeastern Utah actually lost population. Within the Wasatch Front the most rapid increase in population occurred in Davis County, which grew 163 percent. Utah County, which moved to second place in the 1970 census primarily on the basis of Brigham Young University growth, has widened its population margin over Weber County in recent years because it has received a large share of the former Utahns (mostly Mormons) who have returned to the state.

Among other significant population features that have affected the state's economy in recent years is *Utah's birth rate.* Always at or near the top for the nation, Utah's birth rate nevertheless followed the national trend downward from the early 1950s until the mid 1960s, when it reached 22.4 per 1,000. At that point Utah's birth rate started up again, reaching 26.0 per 1,000 population in 1975, while the national rate continued to fall from 19.4 in 1965 to 14.8 a decade later. The result was that Utah's birth rate in 1975 was seventy-five percent higher than the national average, compared to twenty-nine percent in 1950. (See Table D, p. 688.)

Another factor in economic development is *Utah's youthful population.* Because of a high birth rate and a low out-migration pattern, Utah has a much larger percentage of people under twenty-five years of age than does the nation at large. That is one reason why public school expenditures have increased almost tenfold since 1950. The state unemployment rate has generally been higher than the national average since joblessness is largely concentrated among young people and women.

A third factor is *Utah's educational pattern*. Utahns typically stay in school longer than almost everyone else. In 1970, for example, fourteen percent of those twenty-five years and older had been to college four or more years; the national average was only 10.7 percent. This means that the state's work force is comparatively well educated, a situation that has prevailed for several decades and that affects the kinds of jobs people desire.

A final population factor that affects the economy is *Utah's minority population*. Utah has a relatively small minorities population, which has determined the scope and nature of ethnic conflict and the dimensions of the social welfare problems often associated with the disadvantaged.

Economic Growth

Utah's economic growth has closely paralleled her population growth over the years. During World War II there was a net in-migration of people as war industries were established here; following the war many employers decided to continue their operations in Utah partly because of Utah's high productivity and adaptability and partly because of low wages. The largest relative growth in employment since the war occurred in the manufacturing sector between 1945 and 1962. In 1945 manufacturing employees represented fourteen percent of Utah's work force; by 1962 they were nineteen percent. The second most significant growth sector during these years was in public services, which engaged ten percent of the work force in 1945 and thirteen percent in 1963. As manufacturing began to decline after 1963 with cutbacks in defense contracts going to Utah, services picked up the slack and rose to seventeen percent of the work force in 1974 (See Table Q, p. 714–15.)

Following the drastic 1944-45 cutback in war production, Utah's manufacturing industries were largely tied to agriculture and mining for a decade. Of the 35,000 manufacturing employees in 1955, almost one-fourth worked in food processing plants using agricultural products from Utah and surrounding states. Over one-third were employed in refining, smelting, processing, or fabricating Utah's metals or other mineral resources. Of the approximately 1,000 manufacturing companies, most were small, employing fewer than fifty persons. Within the food processing sector meat packing was most important, with four major plants (Cudahy, McFarland, Doctorman, and Jordan) located in the Salt Lake area. Within the minerals processing sector the Geneva Works of the United States Steel Corporation, established in Utah County during World War

II, is the key to understanding postwar developments. Since Utah is the only western state with major deposits of both iron ore and coking coal, her retention of a major steel plant made good sense. Later the Geneva plant influenced the establishment of many other steel fabrication firms; among the largest of these companies is Consolidated Western Steel, located adjacent to Geneva. Similar spinoffs also caused substantial growth in the construction and trade sectors during the first decade following the war.

Steel was the key growth factor in the first postwar decade; defense spending was even more important during the following decade. The most important economic development to occur in Utah since World War II was the creation of a major defense-oriented sector. During World War II when military bases were created or enlarged, approximately 100,000 persons found assignments or employment in the state. Following the war a sharp decline set in, only to be reversed by the Korean War when about 30,000 Utahns were employed by or were in the military. Only a slight decline during the years following the Korean War occurred. Beginning in 1956 in Utah, the United States Air Force started a major investment program in guided missiles. The first major defense industry was established in 1956 west of Salt Lake City by the Sperry Rand Corporation to begin producing Sergeant missiles. The largest defense contractor was Thiokol Chemical Corporation, whose facilities twenty-seven miles west of Brigham City manufactured solid-fuel propellants for Minuteman rockets. Hercules Powder Company, located twenty miles southwest of Salt Lake City, was also an important contractor of rocket engines.

When this development peaked in 1963, Utah had more than 17,000 employees in defense industries and defense was the state's single largest manufacturing sector. The significance of this buildup can be viewed another way: defense-generated employment, as a percentage of all public and private nonagricultural employment, made Utah the third most defense-oriented state in the nation in 1960 and the first in 1962. Since that time Utah has continued to rank near the top.

This new defense industry was added to an already substantial military establishment. During World War II Utah was the setting for ten major military bases, most of them supply and maintenance depots for the war in the Pacific. These operations were sharply cut back when peace came, but at the time of Utah's missile buildup Hill Air Force Base, located south of Ogden, was still one of the largest employers; in 1964 it had 15,000 workers. The Tooele Army Depot was the second largest defense installation with more than 3,000 employees in this period. Since the mid 1960s both military and defense production activities have declined in size and relative importance in Utah.

Concomitant with the Korean War defense expansion was the dramatic rise and decline of the uranium industry. For eight years following 1951 the federal government guaranteed the price of uranium ore and annual production skyrocketed from virtually nothing to $39 million per year. Much stock speculation accompanied the boom, giving Salt Lake City an unsavory reputation for questionable and even fraudulent stock manipulation. Uranium mining centered in San Juan County, and Charles Steen became Utah's first and only "Uranium King" when he struck it rich just as he was ready to give up prospecting. With the end of federal guarantees the boom collapsed, though some uranium production still continues.

Recent Industrial Trends

The years 1965-74 mirrored national economic trends, especially in the increasing need for energy and the shift to service enterprises. Since 1945 the value of Utah's mineral industries has tripled, amounting to nearly a billion dollars in 1974. More than one-third of the production that year was in copper, with another one-fourth in petroleum. From 1973 to 1974 the value of crude petroleum production climbed from $118 to $257 million, suggesting that Utah may have a bright future in oil. Several major oil companies have entered the Uinta Basin in recent years, with tankers and pipelines moving crude oil to Salt Lake City for refining. Aneth, located in San Juan County, is the center of another producing field. Oil shale and tar sands are also in the developmental process in the eastcentral part of the state. If the process of extracting oil from shale can be made less expensive or if the world price of oil climbs substantially, this oil field could make Utah one of the more significant producers in the country.

The largest increase in new jobs in Utah since 1965 has come in the trade, services, and government sectors—all of which reflect national trends. Most of these new jobs have been in professional and clerical occupations. Unfortunately for the overall health of the Utah economy, trade- and service-oriented jobs are not as well paying on the average as are jobs in mining, manufacturing, and construction; hence, the growth in services during the past ten years has not generally been as productive of income as was the defense industry growth of the previous decade.

Although not categorized separately, tourism is frequently claimed to be the second largest industry in Utah today and the largest single employer in Salt Lake Valley. It is estimated that the eight million or more tourists who visit Utah annually generate about $250 million for the economy. Most tourists come during the summer, and about half spend their time in Salt Lake County. Their major purpose is sightseeing. Utah contains some of this nation's most spectacular scenery and several of its most impressive national parks, monuments, and recreation areas. Poor accessibility and limited advertising have, however, kept most tourists away from all but the most famous spots in the past. Rising national incomes, more leisure, increased mobility, and intensified demand for solitude in virgin territory may be expected to spur this industry in the future—possibly even without great efforts by Utahns.

There are many signs of expansion, especially in the rising number of out-of-state skiers. Most come from California, but an increasing number are coming from the East—having learned that Utah's major resorts are about an hour from the Salt Lake City airport. The development of Utah's newest major ski resort, Snowbird, in Little Cottonwood Canyon was a major factor in placing the Wasatch ski slopes in the world limelight. Alta made Utah snow famous, but Snowbird is the only Utah ski area capable of competing with resorts like Sun Valley and Aspen for international competitions and the most affluent clientele. Since skiers spend more money, stay longer, and are much less dependent on gasoline shortages than are nonskiing tourists, Snowbird's recent development is expected to increase the state's recreational activity and income considerably—assuming the weather cooperates. But like defense spending, the major ski resorts are largely concentrated in the richest part of the state, and little financial help goes to those areas where it is most needed. The nearly snowless winter of 1976-77 demonstrated the vulnerability of this new component of the Utah economy.

Employment

Utah's work force has undergone several interesting changes since World War II. Of perhaps the greatest significance is the increase in the worker participation rate, especially by females and young people. In 1940 only forty-seven percent of the population over fourteen years of age was employed. By 1970 that figure had risen to fifty-six percent. The largest increase occurred among males from fourteen to seventeen years of age, who increased their participation rate from nine to thirty-one percent; the second largest was among females, whose rate jumped from eighteen to forty percent. (Both figures for 1940 may reflect residual unemployment from the Great Depression.) Over half of all women in Utah between the ages of eighteen and twenty-four are now working. The highest overall participation rate in recent years has been sixty-two percent in the relatively prosperous Wasatch Front; the lowest has been fifty-three percent in the southeastern section of the state.

The kinds of jobs Utahns hold have also been changing. The high-paying jobs in the mining sector have been steadily decreasing, dropping from ten percent of the work force in 1940 to three percent in 1974. A similar decline has occurred in the transportation and communication sectors. Since the manufacturing sector has not grown appreciably—and, in fact, has been gradually declining since 1963 as a share of the total economy—the only significant way for more Utahns to get work has been by expanding the number of jobs in government and in the service occupations. Like the defense jobs of the last generation, this employment is still highly concentrated. Of the state's 435,000 workers in May 1975, 113,000 were in government, 103,000 were in wholesale and retail trade, and 75,000 were in services. Almost all government employees earn their living in only three counties—Salt Lake, Davis, and Weber. Almost sixty percent of those employed in trade work in Salt Lake County, and two-thirds of the service employees work in Salt Lake and Utah counties.

Utah's unemployment rate has not followed national trends. From World War II until the defense industry boom of the mid 1950s the Utah rate was consistently higher than the national average. (See Table B, p. 686.) This was partly due to a heavy reliance on mining, two decades of relative economic stagnation prior to the war, an underdeveloped manufacturing sector, and a very high birth rate. Beginning in 1954 Utah's rate of unemployment fell below the national average for ten years until the missile industry was cut back. From 1964 until the national recession of 1974-75 Utah's jobless rate was again higher than that of the nation as a whole.

The indicators since 1975 have been more hopeful. Not only did Utah have a lower rate of unemployment during the recession, but the economic decline was also shorter—lasting only seven rather than seventeen months. One prime reason may have been because nationally the hardest hit sector was manufacturing, and Utah's relatively small manufacturing sector actually grew slightly during the recession. Another reason may have been because Utah lies in a region that is experiencing a boom in energy-related efforts and population growth. Other possible reasons were the stepped-up levels of tourism, a large increase in the number of malls and shopping centers constructed immediately prior to the recession, and an increase in industrial diversification. A final reason may have been Utah's good luck in suffering only a slight cutback in federal government employment, an area where the Beehive State is particularly vulnerable. From 1971 through 1975 increases in state and local government employment more than offset the loss in federal jobs. Recovery was comparatively rapid and pronounced. By June 1977 Utah's unemployment stood at 5.5 percent, approximately 1.5 percent below the national average.

The characteristics of Utah's unemployed are instructive. Those out of work tend to be males under twenty-five years of age who have been out of work for from five to fourteen weeks. They tend to be looking for jobs in trade, manufacturing, and construction. The unemployed also tend to be new entrants into the work force who have had little prior work experience and who lack extensive education. The majority of the unemployed have tended to be concentrated in the southeastern and central part of the state.

Data on the size, distribution, and growth of union membership in Utah prior to 1960 are sparse. In 1960 total union membership in Utah amounted to nineteen percent of the nonagricultural labor force. More than nineteen percent of those unionized were in manufacturing, mining, construction, and utilities and were concentrated along the Wasatch Front. Seventy percent of Carbon County employees were unionized, but several counties unionized less than five percent. By 1973 statewide union membership had declined to thirteen percent of the work force, with females comprising about one in ten of these members. Mining was the most heavily organized sector (seventy-three percent), and finance, insurance, and real estate were the least organized. Only a third of those in manufacturing and less than four percent in government were organized. The Right-to-Work Law passed by the state legislature in 1955 and the decline in union membership in both mining and manufacturing since 1960 are perhaps the key reasons for the declining fortunes of organized labor.

Income and Wealth

The most striking and in some ways the most alarming thing about Utah's income structure during the past three decades is that Utah has been gradually getting poorer compared with the rest of the nation. At the beginning and the end of the Great Depression Utah ranked twenty-ninth among the forty-eight states in per capita income. Following World War II the Beehive State had fallen to thirty-third place. The Korean War and the missile development of the late 1950s and early 1960s halted this downward trend, but with the cutback in missile production in Utah in 1963-64 Utah's rank began to fall again. In almost every year thereafter Utah's relative per capita income position fell until Utah stood in forty-second place in 1974; the average Utahn had an income only eighty-two percent of the national average. Because the national recession was more severe elsewhere, Utah's 1975 per capita income rose to thirty-ninth place; this may change as long-term trends begin to work again. (See Table P, p. 713.)

This relative decline in wealth has occurred despite a substantial increase in the percentage of the population that is working and the increased demand for Utah's defense-related production. Labor leaders blame the decline on the Right-to-Work Law; eighteen of the nineteen states with such legislation have lost ground in per capita income. A more objective reason is probably the already discussed population configuration. Because Utah's income per family has remained much closer to the national average—$9,320 compared to $9,586 in 1969, with a rank of twenty-fourth among the states—it seems clear that the nontypical Utah birth rate is the primary explanation for the downward slide in per capita income. The fact that some areas of the state have been falling faster than others seems corroborative. For example, of the 253 Standard Metropolitan Statistical Areas (SMSAs) in the United States in 1972, the Provo-Orem SMSA—with several thousand Brigham Young University student families—ranked 250th in per capita income. At the same time Utah County had the highest birth rate of any county in the state (32.7 per 1,000 population) and Utah had the highest birth rate of any state in the nation (23.5 v. 15.6 for the United States.)[1]

The economic cost of a rising birth rate when the rate in most other states is falling is, other things being equal, a falling rate of relative affluence. Such cost may, of course, be justified on social, religious, or other grounds. Still, if Utah's birth rate continues to go upward and the remainder of the nation's fertility continues to decline, it is quite likely that Utah's ranking in per capita income will continue to decline in the years ahead.

---

[1] In the 1970s Utah County experienced an accelerating in-migration of middle and upper income families, mostly middleaged or retired. A housing boom, only briefly slowed by the 1974-75 recession, was one indication that the level of affluence was probably rising as the student component of the county population became a declining proportion of the total. Between 1970 and 1977 the civilian work force in the county increased by fifty-six percent.

Even though Utah is relatively low in per capita income, Utah does not have a relatively high occurrence of poverty. A Census Bureau report based on 1969 data found thirty states had a greater percentage of poor families than did Utah. Among the mountain states only Nevada had a better record. If Utah has fewer people in poverty than the national average would indicate, it also has fewer who are wealthy. In 1969 twenty-one percent of the nation earned in excess of $15,000 annually. Only seventeen percent of all Utahns did. Overall, income distribution in the Beehive State seems to be not only lower on the average but also narrower in range than elsewhere.

When one looks at the different sections of the state strikingly different pictures emerge. The Wasatch Front is clearly the most prosperous section of the state and has been for several decades. In 1973 the only counties with a higher per capita income were Rich County, located east of Cache Valley with a population of less than 2,000, and Emery County, located south of Price with a population of less than 7,000, where income has been high only in the past few years. All but one of Utah's counties with an above average income in 1970 bordered on the Great Salt Lake. The exception was Daggett County in the Uintah Basin, which has less than 600 residents. All of the counties with more than the state average of families earning at least $15,000 in 1970 also front on Great Salt Lake.

As one would expect, Utah's wealthiest citizens also live in this area. Of the 1,421 families reporting incomes in excess of $50,000 in 1969, nearly 1,300 resided there. Within the Great Salt Lake area the most affluent people are to be found living in a crescent-shaped ring on the northern and eastern hills overlooking the capital city. The mean annual 1970 family income of residents of the Upper Avenues, for example, was $34,000—the highest in the state. The highest average home values are also to be found there.

In contrast to this affluence, much of the rest of the state, especially the central and southeastern sections, have had serious economic problems, particularly in recent decades. In 1959, the earliest year of record for family income by county, when Utah had a *higher* median family income than the national average, six Utah counties showed more than one-fifth of their families earning *less* than $2,000. All were located in central and southern Utah. In 1976 the counties with the lowest per capita income were located in the southeastern or westcentral part of the state. This extreme is probably related to aridity and to the large number of Indians living in southern Utah. Blacks living in Salt Lake City and Ogden are also poor; one-fourth to one-third have incomes below the poverty level. Spanish-speaking residents have a poverty level similar to that of the Blacks.

Conclusion

If one word had to be chosen to summarize the economic history of Utah for the past thirty years, a good choice would be *dependency*. More than any other factor the American government, and more particularly the Department of Defense, has been responsible for Utah's employment growth, overwhelmingly so in the largest economic sector (government) and to a commanding degree in the fourth largest sector (manufacturing). If Gross State Product data were available, as Gross National Product figures are, one could probably plot the course of Utah's economic development since 1945 largely on the basis of federal expenditures in the state for the storage, distribution, or production of military hardware and the maintenance of military bases. The rate of unemployment is a rough substitute. The only time since 1950 that Utah's unemployment rate fell below four percent was when defense spending in Utah was massive and accelerating (1951-53 and 1956-57). Nor should this dependency be surprising. As Leonard Arrington and Thomas Alexander have pointed out, dependency has been characteristic of Utah's economy at least since she achieved statehood.

A second theme has been *divergency*. Utah's per capita and family incomes are not only lower than the national averages, but the rankings among the states have been falling since 1945 largely because of a rising birth rate. A similar divergency has occurred within Utah. The growth rate of income (both per capita and total) in the Wasatch Front has generally been higher than the rest of the state and by 1974 the spread was substantial. In that year, for example, Salt Lake County's per capita income was ninety-three percent of the national average (the highest in the state), and it was eleven percent above the state average. Not only are incomes much lower outside the Wasatch Front, but for the most part they are growing less rapidly, thus further increasing the divergency within Utah between those who have and those who do not.

Despite continuing dependency and growing divergency, the economic future of Utah seems relatively bright to most observers. Defense employment seems destined to continue high, tourism is rising, Utah's popularity as a retirement area is growing, a new fertilizer industry is extracting potash and phosphate from the

Great Salt Lake, and new demands for energy—especially for Utah's shale oil and coal—are promising. Fiscally Utah is in excellent shape, partly because her constitution prohibits deficit financing for social welfare programs and partly because of occasional surpluses in state revenues. (See Table B, p. 686.) Whether these recent hopes will be realized in a new Utah—a Utah with rising relative income and diminished reliance on federal spending—or whether the longer-term historical trends of dependency and divergency will be more significant in the coming years is for future historians to answer.

Chapter 29
Bibliographical Essay

The most detailed studies of Utah's industry since World War II are Elroy Nelson, *Utah's Economic Patterns* (1956), and Elroy Nelson and Osmond L. Harline, *Utah's Changing Economic Patterns* (1964). A comparable work for the past decade does not exist, and for recent years one should consult the informative issues of the *Utah Economic and Business Review* and the research reports published by the Bureau of Economic and Business Research (BEBR) at the University of Utah. Particularly useful is the BEBR's *County Economic Facts— 1974*, published for the Utah Industrial Development Information System in 1974.

The 1976 *Statistical Abstract of Utah,* published by the BEBR, and the *Statistical Review of Government in Utah,* published annually by the Utah Foundation, are two excellent general statistical guides of Utah. The United States Census Bureau's *General Social and Economic Characteristics—Utah* (1972) is also indispensible for recent years, particularly for wealth and poverty topics. The United States Bureau of the Census *Statistical Abstract* and the Bureau of Mines *Minerals Yearbook* are also useful annals for comparative purposes.

Among government agency sources particularly useful are the Four Corners Regional Commission's *Utah State Preliminary Development Plan* (1969); the newspaper clipping files of the Western Americana section in the Marriott Library at the University of Utah; and the well-indexed reports of the Utah Department of Employment Security. The *Utah Historical Quarterly* has an excellent series of articles on defense spending written by Leonard J. Arrington, Thomas G. Alexander, and others in its 1963 and 1964 issues.

For more detailed information in understanding Utah's economy in recent years see: United States Bureau of the Census, *Census of Population and Housing: 1970, Census Tracts* (1972), for Utah's standard metropolitan statistical areas. This study is detailed on income, housing, and labor force characteristics. Also helpful are United States Bureau of the Census, Census of Agriculture: 1969, *Area Reports, Utah* (1972); United States Bureau of the Census, Census of Retail Trade: 1972, *Area Series, Utah* (1974); and *Utah Vital Statistics,* an annual publication of the Utah Department of Social Services.

For special topics see the following: Leonard Arrington and George Jensen, *The Defense Industry of Utah* (1965); Kenneth Bullock, *Minerals of Utah* (1967); Joe Peery and Reed Richardson, *Recreation in Utah: A Profile of the Demand for Outdoor Recreation by Out-of-State Travelers to Utah* (1966); Utah Mining Association, *Utah's Mining Industry* (1967); William B. Smart, ed., *Deseret, 1776-1976* (1976); Arrington, *The Changing Economic Structure of the Mountain West* (1963); and *The Future of the Human Environment in the Rocky Mountain States,* Tenth Annual Report of the Federation of Rocky Mountain States (1974).

Chapter 30
The Development of
An Urban Pattern

J. Michael Cleverley

The origins of Utah town and city patterns antedate the entry of the first settlers into Salt Lake Valley. Joseph Smith developed a master plan for the *City of Zion* to be built in Independence, Missouri, and it was this concept that the Mormon builders tried to follow when creating their communities in the West. Although modifications were common and each city seemed to display its own variations, all could easily be identified as Mormon towns by their square blocks, wide streets running north-south and east-west, central blocks for church-community buildings, and family farming activities on the large residential lots. The concept fit well with Utah's topography and limited water resources, and the spacing of buildings proved to be an excellent way of preventing urban fires from spreading.

Factors Influencing Urban Location

As the Mormons began implementing their city scheme throughout the Great Basin's eastern valleys, several factors influenced both where and how rapidly the cities grew. The supply of life-sustaining resources has always influenced urban patterns, but certain resources were especially important in the semiarid valleys that the pioneers claimed as their promised land. Water, timber, and irrigable land were to be found, but locations that provided all three in convenient proximity were scattered. This led to an isolation of settlements, and much of the development occurred along the Wasatch Range where water, land, and timber were most available.

Community development in these circumstances required a substantial degree of cooperation. In the spirit of early Mormon doctrine, work was ecclesiastically coordinated. Church members shared in bringing timber down from the canyons, constructing roads and bridges to the level of passability, and building meetinghouses and other public facilities. Water was utilized as a communal resource, and where private urban water companies were formed they were usually shortlived.

Cooperation was also necessary for the development of urban centers based on other factors such as mineral resources. Mining towns that developed in the late nineteenth century were established near rich ore deposits that brought an influx of capital, laborers, and service industries; corporations rather than religious organizations promoted a measure of cooperation for production purposes in the mining towns. Irregular terrain and private choices tended to give Utah's mining camps the same helter-skelter appearance as other boom towns until company towns began to appear.

Beyond these considerations, overland wagon routes and railroads promoted urban growth in various places. Salt Lake City quickly exceeded the optimum size contemplated for a City of Zion because of its functions as a supply source for the California gold rush and a receiving station for thousands of Mormon immigrants. A main wagon road from Fort Bridger to Camp Floyd, Carson Valley, and California went through Provo Canyon, and this no doubt stimulated the growth of Provo. The post-1869 decades saw Ogden become one of the major railway crossroads in the west, and rail connections also fed Salt Lake City's growth.

Other factors that influenced urban growth in the nineteenth century included Salt Lake City's religious, commercial, and civil influence. As headquarters for the Mormon Church, Salt Lake City was the spiritual and social center of Utah Mormon culture. In later years this religious influence was felt wherever Mormon settlers migrated, particularly in Idaho, Arizona, southern California, and parts of Mexico and Canada. In addition, as the largest city in the intermountain area Salt Lake came to play the role of regional commercial and business center. These factors as well as Salt Lake's political significance as the capital of Utah Territory provided a boon to the city as well as to its nearby Wasatch Front neighbors.

The existence of diverse and isolated resources has played a part in more recent urban development. The location of Provo at the junction of railroads from Carbon and Iron counties and available

The Broome Hotel, the Reed Hotel, the Opera House (with minaret), and the old City Hall were the center of Ogden activities in the 1890s.

land and water influenced the location of the pig iron plant at Ironton and the United States Steel Geneva Works. The availability of land and water together with railroads and a ready labor force influenced the construction of defense plants in Weber, Davis, and Tooele counties during World War II. More recently, scenic resources have caused the development of tourism and the growth of tourist services in urban centers. The uranium boom of the 1950s boosted Moab and other southeastern Utah cities, and Kanab has prospered both from tourism and from motion picture companies that have exploited the area's scenic resources.

Urban growth has from time to time been aided by community and civic promotion. The Ogden Chamber of Commerce, for example, helped secure federal defense installations during the 1940s by donating 383 acres of land for the construction of Hill Air Force Base, and, when the Senate appropriation turned out to be too small, by raising nearly $100,000 to help purchase the site for the Utah General Depot.

Urban Growth

These and other factors shaped the development of Utah towns and cities into complex and concentrated urban areas. In 1970, with 80.4 percent of its population living in urban space, Utah was the tenth most urbanized state in the United States. It is note-worthy that relatively few cities account for this extensive urban development. Salt Lake City, Ogden, and Provo make up nearly one-third of the state's population, while the Salt Lake, Ogden, and Provo-Orem Standard Metropolitan Statistical Areas account-ed for 77.6 percent of the population and 96.5 percent of the ur-ban population in 1970.[1] More than half of Utah's people lived in the Salt Lake SMSA alone. This suggests that the area called the Wasatch Front is not only the heart of Utah's urban population, but also the center of its entire population. From Brigham City on the north to Payson on the south, a near-megalopolis contains not only more than eighty percent of Utah's people but also eighty percent of the nonagricultural jobs, eighty-five percent of the man-ufacturing jobs, ninety percent of the jobs in wholesale sales, and seventy-six percent of the retail sales jobs.

In discussing the pattern of urbanization, two separate trends may be considered. The first is simply the number of people living in urban areas at various intervals as shown in Table C, p. 687, "Population in Utah Urban Areas, 1860-1970." But this does not give a complete picture. A second measure—the measure of *urban-ization*—shows how the urban population grew in comparison with the whole population. The chart on p. 683, "Percent of Population Living in Urban Areas, 1860-1970," presents this picture.

As can be seen, urban population rapidly increased between 1870 and 1890 when Utah cities felt their first growing pains. The depression of 1893 probably accounts for the drop in the urban-ization rate between 1890 and 1900. During World War II the large defense industries affected every Utah urban center, shown by the rapid growth between 1940 and 1950. Except for the period between 1910 and 1930, Utah's urban areas grew more rapidly than did the average urban areas across the United States.

These data also show that Utah was predominantly rural during its early history; not until the 1920s did a majority of the people live in urban areas. Before 1950 the state was slightly less urban-ized than was the nation, though the two trends closely paralleled. During the period between 1940 and 1970, however, urbanization in Utah outpaced urbanization in the rest of the United States, and in 1970 Utah was nearly eight percent more urbanized than the national average. Statistics confirm that the periods of most

---

[1]As defined by the 1970 census, a Standard Metropolitan Statistical Area (SMSA) for areas outside of New England is a county or group of counties with one city or twin cities of 50,000 or more inhabitants.

rapid urban growth occurred in the last part of the nineteenth century and during the past generation. By far the most noticeable period of urbanization has been since World War II began.

The process of urban growth can also be clarified by looking at Salt Lake City, Ogden, and Provo—the traditional and present urban centers of Utah.

Salt Lake City saw gradual growth throughout its history, and the trends characteristic of the territory and state explain urban patterns in its capital city. At first agricultural land was included in the city, and by 1860 its area of 57.2 square miles was exceeded by only four American cities. As electric trolleys replaced horse-drawn streetcars in the 1890s, providing easy access to the business district, the southern and eastern areas near Liberty Park became popular residential areas. The automobile made suburban living both practical and attractive and the commuter society was born. Although the population of the metropolitan area south of Salt Lake City increased steadily, the city itself actually decreased by over seven percent between the 1960 and 1970 censuses.

Ogden grew with the transcontinental railroad and the branch lines that followed its completion in 1869. When the decision was made to locate the permanent junction and principal railroad repair shops there, the city quickly eclipsed its only rival, Corinne, as the commercial center of northern Utah. Between 1870 and 1890 the population of Ogden doubled twice. The annual product of Ogden business establishments increased from $15,400 in 1860 to $370,110 in 1880. Growth was slower in the next half century, but as World War II approached, the same railroads that spawned the city's initial period of growth made it an ideal place for defense installations. The reconstruction of the Ogden Arsenal and the addition of the Utah General Depot, Hill Field, and the Clearfield Naval Supply Depot meant thousands of jobs, and after the postwar contraction in federal spending such defense industries as Marquardt, Boeing, and Thiokol provided new stimuli in the 1950s and 1960s. Suburbanization moved southward toward Salt Lake City, while Ogden itself peaked and then decreased in population.

Provo, as Table E illustrates, followed a somewhat different growth pattern. Provo grew rapidly during the 1850s, perhaps because of Camp Floyd and the road through Provo Canyon, and in 1860 it was Utah's second largest city. Growth was slower thereafter, and mines and railroads had relatively little local impact until the construction of the Ironton Works brought 500 jobs to the Provo area in the 1920s. This impact was modest compared to that experienced when Geneva Steel Company came to Utah County during World War II. The assessed valuation of property in the county increased from $57 million to $200 million between 1942 and 1944, and the population of Provo increased sixty percent during the decade. In the 1960s when Salt Lake City and Ogden were decreasing in population, Provo added nearly fifty percent, probably the result of the rapid expansion of Brigham Young University. Orem also developed into a substantial urban neighbor; more than merely a bedroom suburb, it became a business center for the Provo-Orem area.

In addition to Utah's three major urban areas, smaller towns and cities are scattered across the state. Although the great majority of these are agricultural communities originally settled by Mormon colonists (See Table A, pp. 684–85, and map, p. 730), distinctive communities developed to exploit mineral resources. Some of the boom towns became ghost towns, but others became urban centers. Many companies built and owned towns in the decades immediately after 1900, but few remained company towns by the mid 1970s since most were either abandoned or sold to their inhabitants. Though the company town is generally thought of as an oppressive and dull place, many Utah company towns were relatively attractive and modern during their time. Garfield, Spring Canyon, Castle Gate, Hiawatha, Copperton, and Dragertown are a few examples of communities that are, or have been, company towns.

The large influx of immigrants during the last half of the nineteenth century greatly encouraged the growth of cities. At first most immigrants came for religious reasons, but as the Mormon emphasis on gathering was abandoned after 1900, non-Mormons came from abroad to take advantage of new industrial jobs. In 1870 forty percent of the population of Salt Lake, thirty-five percent of Ogden's population, and twenty-seven percent of the population of Provo were foreign-born. The first immigrants were predominantly from Great Britain, but after 1870 the percentage of Scandinavians sharply increased, and after 1890 many southern Europeans—particularly Italian, Greek, and Slavic laborers—moved into the mines and smelters. Although the *number* of foreign-born whites continued to increase until 1910, the *proportion* of foreign-born city dwellers underwent a gradual decrease after 1870. In Salt Lake City, for example, immigrants constituted only twenty-five percent of the populace in 1900 and less than ten percent in 1940. Because most of the immigrants were from northern Europe and because the Black and Mongoloid races constituted very small minorities in Utah, the ethnic makeup of the urban population was—and for the most part continues to be—characterized by homogeniety.[2]

The Evolution of Urban Government

As urban areas grew in sophistication and complexity, changes in the forms of municipal organization occurred. City government in Utah began in 1851 when the General Assembly of the State of Deseret incorporated Great Salt Lake City—its official designation until 1868—and Provo, Ogden, Manti, and Parowan. The territorial legislature reaffirmed the charters, which provided for a mayor-council form of organization. Until 1888 Utah's three largest cities were each governed by a mayor, four aldermen, and nine councilmen, while smaller communities had fewer officials. The legislature then eliminated this complex structure and classified all cities and towns into three groups. Cities of 20,000 or more were to be considered first-class cities and were to have a fifteen-member council; cities of 5,000 to 20,000 were to be second-class with a ten-member council; and towns of under 5,000 were considered third-class with a seven-member council.

The city councils attempted to make each city function efficiently, despite generally low levels of pay and professionalism among municipal employees. In Provo council members were uncompensated until 1880 (though for a time they were fined two dollars for an unexcused absence from a meeting). City councils not only provided law and order and urban services, but they also passed ordinances like those in Provo that imposed fines for swearing and profaning and for Sunday horse racing.

Allegations that the Mormon Church unduly influenced municipal and state government continued beyond the territorial years and led to the formation of the American Party in 1904. It never gained control of county or state governments, but it did capture Salt Lake City government. While in power the American Party created a more partisan politico-religious conflict than before and caused a general letdown in municipal efficiency and civic spirit. An attempt at quasilegalized and controlled prostitution in the Stockade led to a dual clash between American Party adherents and a majority of the citizenry and between the city and county governments.

---

[2]As late as 1950, only 2,739 Blacks and 4,787 Chinese and Japanese resided in Utah. Of these 1,127 and 1,894 respectively lived in Salt Lake City, 928 and 638 in Ogden, and only 11 and 49 in Provo.

This 1904 photograph of South Temple and Main streets in Salt Lake City graphically portrays the maze of streetcar and trolley tracks that crisscrossed the downtown area.

In an effort to improve city government and divorce it from party politics, the state legislature in 1911 responded to public pressure by redefining the classes of cities and establishing a new form of government. A mayor and four commissioners were to govern first-class cities (over 30,000); a mayor and two commissioners were to govern second-class cities (5,000 to 30,000); and a mayor and five councilmen were to govern third-class cities (under 5,000). All larger cities thereby changed to a commission form in 1912; Utah was following a national trend.

The commission form of city government almost immediately brought more efficiency. It turned attention away from religious controversy, particularly in Ogden and Salt Lake City. The commissions instituted some governmental economies and upgraded the police and fire departments. In spite of these immediate reforms it is difficult to make an indepth comparison of the long-run performance of the mayor-council and city commission forms of government. The problems with which each was forced to deal were very different in size and in scope. The commissions found workable solutions for some problems that had beset the previous governments. Time would disclose that many urban problems are no more solvable in Utah than elsewhere, and some are barely manageable under any form of government.

The new system of city government did not satisfy the needs of many smaller communities. It was felt that the mayor and councilmen, none of whom gave full time to their city jobs, were unable to meet the technical demands of good government, and a number of third-class cities switched to a council-manager form. Brigham City and Tooele employed professional city managers in the 1920s, and several more small cities followed suit during the early 1940s. The city manager form of government was not available to first- and second-class cities until 1933, when a constitutional amendment providing for home rule was passed. Home rule was pursued in Salt Lake City, Ogden, and Provo during the postwar years. Ogden adopted a city manager form in 1951 and Provo adopted the same in 1955. However, Salt Lake City rejected such proposals in two elections, and Provo's city manager lasted only until 1961. Friction between the manager and elective council was too common, and it is not surprising that the form never became more popular than it did.

Development of Urban Services

The growth of urban areas brought a need for more complex and efficient public services. The earliest were provided by the ecclesiastical government—water in Salt Lake City was under the personal control of Brigham Young, and lesser church leaders performed or supervised court and police functions. But as cities expanded more comprehensive programs were needed. During the 1860s and 1870s the responsibility for urban services shifted to city governments, and population growth and new technologies expanded the scope of these tasks. It was during the early Progressive Era around the turn of the century that urban public services began to take modern form.

553

Water Supplies

Providing an adequate supply of water has historically been one of the large problems facing city administrations. For Utah's major cities it was a relatively simple problem in the 1850s and 1860s as local water resources, mostly distributed by gravity, were adequate. City Creek and private wells satisfied drinking water needs in Salt Lake City, while irrigation water flowed through ditches on each side of the streets. Irrigation water in Ogden was brought from the Weber River through canals built in the 1850s, and the residents of Provo obtained their domestic supplies from springs, shallow pump wells, artesian wells, and the same open ditches that watered their gardens and farms.

The postrailroad era saw a larger, more concentrated urban population demanding improved water services. In 1881 Ogden began laying pipes beneath its major streets to carry water from the Weber River. In the territorial capital, City Creek water was elevated to three major distributing points; by 1889 about 2,000 water users were connected with these supply centers by twenty-four miles of piping. Provo laid its first water mains at about the same time. Around the turn of the century the three cities embarked on new projects to quench their growing thirst. Salt Lake City had already gained rights to Utah Lake water, and between 1913 and 1916 a project in Big Cottonwood Canyon effectively doubled the amount of available water. While Provo laid more pipeline from the natural springs in Provo Canyon, Ogden invested about $150,000 in a seventy-five-acre plot of artesian wells in Ogden Valley in 1914.

The quest for additional resources began anew after a severe drought in 1934. The Metropolitan Water District of Salt Lake City, created the next year, looked toward the proposed Provo River Project for a solution, and when Franklin D. Roosevelt signed the authorization bill in 1935 the water districts of Salt Lake City, Provo, American Fork, Lehi, Orem, and Pleasant Grove-Lindon subscribed to almost seventy-five percent of the project's water. Upon completion in the 1950s and 1960s the Provo River scheme, which stored water from the Provo, Weber, and Duchesne rivers in Deer Creek Reservoir, brought a temporary solution to Salt Lake City's water problems. The dry winter of 1976-77 emphasized that the metropolitan Wasatch Front was once again vulnerable to the unpredictability of the Great Basin climate.

Schools

The early Mormons' attitudes toward education made schools in Utah a necessity. By 1849 there were elementary classes in Salt

Lake City, Provo, and Ogden. As noted in an earlier chapter, the first Utah schools were church-oriented and were financed primarily through tuition. Private parochial schools were founded in Ogden and Salt Lake City during the 1870s and 1880s as part of the gentile response to Mormon hegemony. The two-sided educational system changed in 1890 when the territorial legislature passed a free schooling law. The subsequent secularization, consolidation, and modernization of Utah's urban and rural schools is discussed elsewhere.

Police and Fire Protection

The three largest communities organized police forces during the early 1850s. The Salt Lake City force, composed of volunteers that were paid twenty-five cents an hour, at times numbered up to 200 men. Late in the century various technical improvements were made; the police department in Salt Lake City introduced uniforms, established a modern organization, added a patrol wagon, and situated alarm boxes throughout the city. By this time the police department was a small professional force, but law enforcement education was accomplished entirely on the job until well into the twentieth century.

In the statehood years Utah's urban police departments have been faced with demands for increased efficiency and professionalism while under the constraints of low pay and contradictory pressures. In Salt Lake City, for instance, churches and other groups such as the pre-World War I Civic Betterment League have wanted strict enforcement of moral reform legislation, including closing disorderly taverns, suppressing houses of prostitution, and conducting gambling raids. On the other hand, businessmen engaged in these occupations and some of the citizenry had urged the police to leave them alone. The American Party experiment with regulated prostitution was followed by a reform police chief, B. F. Grant, who cracked down on all violators. The subsequent pattern has been like a series of waves in which periods of public pressure have followed times of relative laxity.

Another force contradicting the development of police professionalism in Salt Lake City has been the tendency of incoming administrators to view the position of chief of police as a political plumb. B. F. Grant was removed after a new administration came to office, apparently because he was not liked by the new mayor. To some extent the same situation has continued until recent times—one example is the early 1960s feud between Mayor J. Bracken Lee and Chief of Police W. Cleon Skousen. Federal Law

Enforcement Administration programs and funding have been extensively used by Utah police forces for equipment and training in the 1970s.

Salt Lake City created its first volunteer fire department in 1856. The city purchased a fire engine and began work on an engine house that was not completed until 1870. Departments were not established in Provo and Ogden until devastating fires demonstrated the need. After a fire destroyed ten buildings in 1873, Ogden created its first fire brigade. The brigade expanded rapidly; fire hydrants were constructed in 1883, a fulltime department was established in 1890, and two stations were built the next year. Provo established a fire department in 1890, six years after Brigham Young Academy had burned to the ground. By then the Salt Lake City fire-fighting organization numbered fifty men who operated one Silsby steamer, two hand engines, five horse carts, one hook and ladder truck, and 5,400 feet of hose. Nine regular firemen were paid $60 per month; forty others were *call men* who received $50 a year.

Public Transportation

Farsighted planning gave Utah's early cities wide streets, but the users were reluctant to pay for surfacing, and so citizens wallowed alternately in mud and dust. As late as 1885 each railroad in Ogden donated twenty-five carloads of gravel to improve Twenty-Fifth Street from Wall Avenue to Washington. Asphalting began in 1893. About the same time Provo experimented with asphalt, but not until 1915 did systematic street paving begin. Salt Lake City was also slow in street improvement; by 1904 less than four miles of streets were paved. The projects undertaken between 1900 and 1907 concentrated on the city's core, and they were extended by 1920 to arterial routes such as State and Main streets, South Temple, Thirteenth East, Ninth South, and finally during the late 1920s to Twenty-First South. As pressure from automobile users became greater, the city was forced to pave more streets.

Horsedrawn streetcars made their first appearance in 1872 when the Salt Lake City Street Railroad Company was privately organized. The firm soon fell into financial difficulties following the Panic of 1873, and Brigham Young purchased most of the shares on behalf of the Mormon Church. The church's interest was probably related to transporting building materials to the Temple Block. The 1889 change to electricity greatly increased the efficiency of the system, and by 1890 a line had been extended as far south as Murray. The Mormon Church interest was sold during the transitional period associated with statehood attainment. By 1919 Salt Lake City boasted 146 miles of track, and the company had spent millions on double-tracking. Soon, however, automobiles cut into the trolley clientele. To overcome this difficulty, the world's first electric trolley busses were put into use in 1928, and finally during the 1930s the city shifted to motor busses. The last streetcar retired in 1941.

Muledrawn streetcars appeared in Ogden in the 1880s, to be supplanted by steam cars in 1889 and electric trolleys in 1891. A trolley system was attempted in Provo in 1890 but it folded two years later. Both Ogden and Provo had streetcars in the early twentieth century; in the 1930s and 1940s streetcars were displaced by busses which became losing propositions after World War II. Not until the development of the Utah Transit Authority in the 1970s did public transportation begin to make a comeback in Utah cities, principally in Salt Lake, Davis, and Weber counties. As late as 1977 the only public transportation in Utah County was a merchant's bus system connecting the Brigham Young University campus with the Provo and Orem business districts.

Other Urban Services

The Salt Lake City Gas Company was incorporated in 1872, and it soon came under Mormon Church control in much the same way as did the streetcar system. Electric lighting came to Ogden and Salt Lake City in the 1880s, and in 1890 an electric company headed by Reed Smoot was organized in Provo. The early twentieth century saw both gas and electric services concentrated in regulated private utility companies. Electric services were originally provided on a monthly rental basis; in Provo at the turn of the century each incandescent lamp burned until nine p.m. cost $1.25 per month. Hoping to lower the price of electricity, several cities in the 1920s and 1930s created municipal power departments to produce electricity or to buy it wholesale for distribution to city residents. By 1945 no less than thirty-seven cities and towns provided municipal power services; they included Provo, Logan, and several other of the state's larger communities. Utah's two largest urban centers—Salt Lake City and Ogden—were major exceptions.

Ogden planned and surveyed its first sewer in 1879 along Main and Fourth streets. It was intended primarily to drain water from the foundations of houses and to safeguard against sanitary problems caused by the high water table. A more comprehensive system was constructed for the entire city about ten years later. Meanwhile Salt Lake City planned a sewer system, and construc-

A steam-powered street railway briefly provided transportation in downtown Provo around the turn of the century.

tion began in 1893. The badly needed project served a dual function by providing employment following the business panic. By 1900 the city had twenty-two miles of sewers. Provo did not begin sewer construction until 1909. Utah's Wasatch Front cities dumped raw or partially treated sewage into the Great Salt Lake and Utah Lake until federal standards and subsidies helped to upgrade waste disposal systems beginning in the 1960s.

Several other urban services appeared in response to needs. City park development rapidly expanded after 1900. By 1940 Salt Lake City owned more park area per person than did any other large American city except Denver; the city boasted two parks in the canyons, sixteen within city limits, and three golf courses. Public welfare and social service programs received attention during the late nineteenth century, but they did not become permanent features of urban government until the depression of the 1930s. Their scope has expanded since that time.

Recent Urban Problems

During recent years urban services have been refined and broadened to the extent that larger urban areas are facing the problem of overlapping. This has occurred in the metropolitan counties composed of a large incorporated city and several smaller suburban and unincorporated communities. The metropolitan county has the responsibility for providing the same urban services that the large city provides for itself. Salt Lake County, for example, provides library, health, and fire and police services for much of the county, while Salt Lake City does the same for its residents. The obvious problem is that the city dweller pays taxes not only for those city services from which he accrues direct benefit, but also for those of the county which usually benefit only those living in unincorporated areas. To deal with this problem some urban areas have begun consolidating county and city services. Salt Lake County and Salt Lake City cooperate in providing jail and recreation facilities, while other county-city cooperation has been manifested in urban planning and zoning.

Perhaps the greatest challenges to urban development in Utah have come since World War II, although the problems began to appear much earlier. Air pollution, for instance, was an extremely severe problem in Salt Lake Valley at the turn of the century. Shifting from coal to natural gas for heating produced appreciable improvements in air quality, but the solution to pollution was generally avoided until the recent federal pressure from the Environmental Protection Agency. Salt Lake City inaugurated urban planning in 1920, but it was not taken very seriously. Despite master plans, economic pressures on and by developers and homeowners have conditioned patterns of urban development throughout the state. The result has been urban sprawl with the concommitant expense of providing services such as gas, water, electricity, streets, and waste disposal drastically increased because of the large distances involved.

During the same period the central city areas of Provo, Ogden, and Salt Lake City have tended to deteriorate. Each of the three cities in the 1970s began projects to try to rejuvenate the core area through urban renewal programs, tax increment funding, or special improvement districts. In addition the core of the cities, particularly in Salt Lake City and Ogden, tended to have the highest concentration of problems associated with urban blight. Welfare roles tended to expand in the early 1970s and the cities began to try to cope with them through local funding and federal poverty programs. A recent development of significance in the attempt to save central cities has been in the interest of urban heritage and has taken the form of reconditioning old homes for use as residences or office buildings. In many cases developers have found it more economical to refurbish the existing structure than to tear it down and construct a new one.

Conclusion

Utah's urban development may be seen as developing on a pioneer foundation of sparse resources and cooperation. The dependence on water, land, and timber caused towns and cities to be built near the mountains, and the discovery and development of mineral resources further favored the Wasatch Front. Both religious institutions and corporate enterprises found cooperation necessary for developing the dry desert and the ore-rich mountains. Other factors influencing urban patterns include the significance of Salt Lake City as headquarters of the Mormon Church, as state capital, and as economic center for the intermountain area and for the transportation routes that have crisscrossed Utah. Taken together these factors have worked to make Utah—despite its agrarian beginnings—an urban state, with its non-urban population comprising less than one-fifth of the total in 1970.

In looking back it appears that the cities began to take their modern form in the Progressive Era. It is true that throughout the period there was a lull in urban growth when compared to the growth of the 1870s and 1880s or of the modern period. But it was then that city government developed into its current form, secular authorities took over urban leadership, and those services characteristic of the modern city were created and developed. Once equipped with more modern tools and headed in a progressive direction, the cities were better prepared to meet newer and larger problems that the accelerated urbanization of later periods presented.

Along with the increasing proportion of Utahns living in urban areas, in recent years city dwellers have dispersed as Salt Lake City and Ogden have lost population to their suburbs. Some suburbs, such as Orem, may even pose threats to the economic life of their older city neighbors. Meanwhile the urban centers have become interlocked into a Wasatch Front megalopolis. Freeways have facilitated movement within this urbanized area, and it is not at all uncommon for a resident of Utah or Weber County to be employed in Salt Lake, or vice versa. The migration to the suburbs also dramatizes a growth pattern that disregards city and county boundaries. The future offers challenges that the cities and metropolitan counties will have to solve, and very possibly cooperation will again serve as the key to development.

Chapter 30
Bibliographical Essay

A theoretical framework for urban development in Utah is presented in Thomas G. Alexander, "Toward a Synthetic Interpretation of the Mountain West: Diversity, Isolation, and Cooperation," *UHQ*, Summer 1971. The reader should also consult Gunther Barth's *Instant Cities* (1975). The extent of urbanization along the Wasatch Front today is discussed in Leonard J. Arrington and George Jensen, *Utah's Emerging Metropolis: the Wasatch Front* (1962).

Edward W. Tullidge presents the best general history of early Salt Lake City in *The History of Salt Lake City and Its Founders* (1886). A very thorough inquiry into Salt Lake City's position in Utah and the intermountain west is Chauncy Dennison Harris, "Salt Lake City: A Regional Capital" (Ph.D. dissertation, University of Chicago, 1940). Useful also is Charles Brooks Anderson, "The Growth Pattern of Salt Lake City" (Ph.D. dissertation, New York University, 1945). The downtown development of the capital city is discussed in Dale L. Morgan, "The Changing Face of Salt Lake City," *UHQ*, July 1959; see also William Mulder, "Salt Lake City in 1880: A Census Profile," *UHQ*, July 1956. Unfortunately there are no histories available that cover Salt Lake City in recent decades.

For the history of Provo, refer to Edward W. Tullidge, "History of Provo," *Tullidge's Quarterly Magazine*, July 1884; J. Marinus Jensen, *History of Provo, Utah* (1924); or WPA Writers' Program, *Provo: Pioneer Mormon City* (1942). A more recent chronicle is J. Clifton Moffitt and Marilyn M. Miller, *Provo: A Story of People in Motion* (1974), which is notable for its pictures. See also Odell F. Scott, "Economic History of Provo, 1849-1900" (master's thesis, Brigham Young University, 1951).

Tullidge also wrote of early Ogden in *Tullidge's Histories* (1889), Vol. II. More comprehensive narratives are found in two volumes: Utah State Historical Society, *A History of Ogden* (1940), and its sequel by Elizabeth Tillotson, *A History of Ogden, 1940-60* (1961). Milton R. Hunter's *Beneath Ben Lomond's Peak* (1966) is another interesting history of Ogden. A useful specialized work is Alma W. Hansen, "A Historical Study of the Influence of the Railroad upon Ogden, Utah, 1869-1875" (master's thesis, Brigham Young University, 1953).

For insight into the company and mining towns of Utah see James B. Allen, *The Company Town in the American West* (1966), and

Duane A. Smith, *Rocky Mountain Mining Camps: The Urban Frontier* (1967). Helen Z. Papanikolas discusses the Greek immigration and associated ethnic problems in "Toil and Rage in a New Land," *UHQ,* Spring 1970. For ethnic groups that have figured into Utah's urban growth see also Papanikolas, ed., *The Peoples of Utah* (1976). O. H. Malmquist gives a fascinating account of early religious and journalistic controversies in Salt Lake City in his *The First 100 Years: A History of the Salt Lake Tribune* (1971). Insight into religious and political problems at the turn of the century is provided in Joseph Reuben Snow, "The American Party in Utah: A Study of Political Party Struggles During the Early Years of Statehood" (master's thesis, University of Utah, 1964).

Several studies of local and city government are available. See James B. Allen, "Ecclesiastical Influence on Local Government in the Territory of Utah," *Arizona and the West,* Spring 1966; Byron Muntz Oberg, "Personnel Management and the Forms of Municipal Government: A Case Study of Ogden's Commission and Council-Manager Forms" (master's thesis, University of Utah, 1948); Isaac B. Humphrey, "Commission Government in Salt Lake City, Utah" (master's thesis, University of Utah, 1936); J. D. Williams, *The Defeat of Home Rule in Salt Lake City* (1960); and Neil K. Coleman, "A Study of the Campaign for the Repeal of the Provo City Charter in 1961" (master's thesis, Brigham Young University, 1962). Early Mormon cities are discussed in John W. Reps, *Town Planning in Frontier America* (1969), while later city planning is studied in Kathryn J. Rigby, "Planning in Utah Local Government" (master's thesis, University of Utah, 1950). The problems of metropolitan counties are treated in Lynn Robert Webb, "A Case Study of the Need for Metropolitan Government in Utah County" (master's thesis, Brigham Young University, 1965).

The development of urban services is described in the general histories already cited, but particular references are Herbert Lester Gleason, "The Salt Lake City Police Department, 1851-1949: A Social History" (master's thesis, University of Utah, 1950); Alexander and Arrington, *The Provo River Project* (1966); and Arrington, *Great Basin Kingdom* (1958).

Chapter 31
Women in
Twentieth-century Utah

Maureen Ursenbach Beecher and Kathryn L. MacKay

I n the years since statehood Utah women have been more in the
mainstream of American life than would appear from the
uniqueness of their historical context. Even in their seemingly isolated Great Basin retreat, Mormon women from the beginning had
responded to impulses from their sisters in the more sophisticated
eastern United States, and with the incursions of the mails, the
telegraph, the railroad, and the increasing numbers of non-Mormon
women, they found themselves increasingly part of the national sisterhood. By 1900 the national women's movement focused almost
exclusively on the gaining of suffrage, and Utah women found
themselves begrudgingly honored for having already achieved the
vote, not only once in 1870, but again in the state constitution of
1895. In the battle for equal political status, Utah women had but
to cheer on their struggling contemporaries in an effort that would
not end nationally until 1920.

Religious Tensions

Polygamy, the practice that had separated Mormon women from
their gentile sisters, had diminished in importance with the Woodruff Manifesto. By the turn of the century the only polygamous
families left in Utah were the ones that were formed prior to the
1890 official injunction and those few unions that were contracted
secretly thereafter. For Mormon women the manifesto meant that
they no longer needed to defend the principle of plural marriage.
With the passing of the institution that had most pervasively influenced their lives, the last obvious barrier between the Mormon

women and their gentile sisters was officially eliminated even though vestiges of the problem remained.

One incident that occurred in 1909 illustrates that a gap still existed. Arrangements had been made to entertain delegates from the National Council of Women and the related International Council who were returning through Salt Lake City from a conference in Seattle. Emmeline B. Wells, who had long been active with both councils, chaired the affair, assisted by several Mormon and several gentile women. Plans were moving smoothly when non-Mormon Corinne M. Allen, the chairman of the welcoming committee, informed Wells that the welcoming committee objected to the presence of a "polygamist and a violator of the laws of this country" on the stand at the official banquet. The man in question was Mormon Church President Joseph F. Smith, who had been invited as the husband of Julina L. Smith, a committee member entitled to bring her spouse. Allen explained that she was objecting as a means "of publishing to those women who come here that the Christian women of Salt Lake City do not condone nor approve of the social ulcer which exists here."

The visit was a fiasco, and the result gave the impression that the Mormon and gentile women were consciously working against each other's participation. Accusations flew; an antipolygamist referred to the "craft and stealthy duplicity" of the Mormons, and the *Deseret News* answered that Allen had had no objection to sharing the platform with polygamists when it came to getting her husband, Clarence E. Allen, elected to Congress. More rational voices, however, expressed regret at the setback the incident had caused local club women, "who have labored for years to reconcile matters of religion in Utah."

Such an incident, while it reveals the barely hidden antipathies with which Utah women have long had to cope, is not indicative of the evident accomplishments of women on both sides of the religious fence, working singly and in cooperative ventures. In fact, the combined influence of women's clubs in Utah has a laudable history of its own.

Women's Organizations

That women's clubs in Utah should have developed along religious lines was inevitable, considering the state's history. Before they ever entered the Great Basin, Mormon women had been active participants in a church-sanctioned Female Relief Society of Nauvoo. Although that organization had disbanded before the Mormons began their move west, its advantages remained in the minds of the women such that in the early 1850s Relief Societies began springing up in several wards of Salt Lake City, and in 1867 Mormon Church president Brigham Young officially reestablished the society as the official organization for women in the church. (See Chapter 17.) Through its auspices were handled most secular and religious matters that pertained to women and their work, and its powerful and dynamic leader, Eliza Roxcy Snow, led the women through a wide variety of personal and community betterment projects. However, since the Relief Society also supported plural marriage, gentile women living in the communities where it existed were reluctant to join.

As the century turned, the Relief Society was still deeply committed to its original purposes: health, welfare, and other social services. Although its Deseret Hospital had been abandoned due to financial difficulty, the Relief Society's encouragement of nurses' training continued for a quarter of a century, setting a standard ahead of its time for training nurses' aids. Mothers' Classes within the organization set precedents for the educational programs with which the society would become increasingly involved, including classes in theology, literature, and social welfare. In 1919 the society opened a social services department in Salt Lake City. Directed by Amy Brown Lyman, the center served as an employment bureau for Mormon women and provided help for transients. Because the department functioned as the only licensed social work agency of the Mormon Church, its responsibilities continued to expand until 1970, when it was incorporated into a newly established general church agency for social services. During its half-century operation the department supervised adoption services and foster home care, the placement of Latter-day Saint Indian children in urban Mormon homes, and a youth service program. It also provided fieldwork training for the University of Utah Graduate School of Social Work.

In the 1920s funds from the wheat storage project the women had nurtured from its inception in 1876 were redirected into social services. Earlier in the century the wheat itself had been used liberally for disaster relief, and the balance was sold to the United States government in 1918 for war relief. In 1921 the Relief Society invested the wheat interest in such stake-sponsored programs as maternity homes and health clinics for babies and preschoolers. The Relief Society strengthened its social service programs by involving its leaders in national professional social work organizations and seminars. Since the 1870s Relief Society leaders had enjoyed fellowship in national women's organizations, including the

Woman's Suffrage Association and later the National and International Council of Women. Mormon delegates held offices in these organizations, with Relief Society President Belle Smith Spafford serving as president of the National Council of Women from 1968 to 1970.

In the meantime, other organizations had sprung up among the women of Utah. For the most part they began in the late nineteenth and early twentieth century as continuing education groups, with their main concerns the literary and artistic pursuits of their members. From their inception in the 1870s the Ladies' Literary Club and its parent group, the Blue Tea, held soirees devoted to the fine arts. By 1892, however, it was apparent that these clubs could better serve the public than the individual members. In 1892 Corinne M. Allen (the same woman who several years later would be protesting association with Mormon polygamists) chaired the first meeting of the Utah Federation of Women's Clubs, a mixed group of Mormons and non-Mormons that would be responsible for significant advances for Utah women. Charter members of the federation were members of the Salt Lake Woman's Club, Cleofan of Salt Lake, the Utah Women's Press Club (founded by Emmeline B. Wells, whom Allen would later so bitterly oppose), La Coterie of Ogden, and the Nineteenth Century Club of Provo. Added to its numbers would be members of such later organizations as the Women's League, a group organized in 1907 by Elizabeth Cohen aimed at bettering moral and civic conditions in Salt Lake City. Gathering momentum as it gathered member organizations, the Utah Federation of Women's Clubs became a powerful lobby in the state legislature; in 1912–13 its Legislative and Industrial Committee was organized as a specific lobbying group, Elizabeth Cohen serving as chairman.

The first World War brought the women's organizations in the state together in purpose as well as in body. Religious groups such as the Relief Society, Hadassah, the Catholic Women's League, Episcopal Women, and others became Red Cross auxiliaries, and, along with the other civic and social groups, they sent delegates to citywide governing bodies of the Red Cross. Organizing women in the war effort was a committee of leaders drawn from various religious and social groups, indicating that whatever enmities might exist between Utah women's groups could quickly vanish in the face of significant demands and dire needs.

The years after World War I and the years that marked the winning of suffrage for women have often been characterized as years of national retreat and frivolity. However, the numbers of organizations created and the continued participation by women in social, civic, and welfare efforts in both Utah and the nation would belie that characterization. For example, in 1923 Jeannette Acord Hyde formed what later became the Women's State Legislative Council of Utah, a powerful force in "bringing to fruition beneficial legislation for the state of Utah." In the same year Elizabeth Coray and Elizabeth Fitzgerald helped organize what became the Utah Federation of Business and Professional Women's Clubs. Joanna Sprague was its first president. Since its inception the Federation has waged a long and continuing campaign to secure equal rights for women in employment, in wages, and under the law.

The Great Depression of the 1930s and World War II again brought women's organizations throughout the state together in efforts to provide welfare and war-related services. In the years since, women's groups have continued to be formed and have continued to serve women's professional, labor, recreational, artistic, social, civic, political, welfare, and health needs. In the 1960s and 1970s a resurgence of the women's movement has served to galvanize and, in some cases, antagonize women's groups. With these latest incentives to participate in community affairs, the number of separate women's organizations in Utah has passed 160.

Women in the Family

The tradition that woman's primary responsibilities were dutiful wifehood and diligent motherhood—firmly established in Utah's pioneer culture—was still firm as the twentieth century began. A 1920 United States Census report noted with some amazement the results of this emphasis on family as a unit, and children as a value, in its statement that Salt Lake City ranked highest among American cities of over 100,000 population in ratio of children to native white women, and that smaller communities in the state generally upheld the same record. Only the Southern states came close to Utah in their ratios. "That Mormonism is the chief influence keeping the birth rate of Utah communities above that of the surrounding States cannot be questioned," the report commented. "And Utah is the best example in the United States of a community in which religion does exercise a decided influence on the birth rate."

Throughout the first three-quarters of this century a birth rate higher than the national average has been maintained in Utah. It has followed the national trends—dropping in the 1930s when times were hard and peaking in 1947 with the postwar baby boom—but has still kept above the national average. By 1970 it was one-third higher than the national average (25.5 births per 1,000 population compared to 18.4), and the disparity has continued to increase as the national birth rate has fallen markedly. (See Table D, p. 688.) At the same time death rates in Utah have been consistently lower than the national average, giving the state a relatively large increase in native population. In 1970 the national death rate was more than one-third higher than Utah's (9.5 deaths per 1,000 population against Utah's 6.7). The fact that out-migration has almost consistently exceeded in-migration suggests that the economy of the state was, at least until after World War II, unable to support the growing population. Even so, a recent turn of the migration pattern, with indications that the migrants are returning natives, suggests that the family standard, "to have and to hold," is still a force in Utah value systems. Parents are continuing to have large families, and family ties are remaining as strong bonding forces in the culture.

Utah has paralleled the national averages of marriage and divorce rates, generally being slightly lower than the average in marriage rate per 1,000 population and slightly higher, as are most Western states, in the divorce rate. While the marriage rate in the state has maintained a sustained level—it was 11.5 per 1,000 in 1906 and 11.2 in 1970—the divorce rate has more than trebled in the same interval—from 1.2 to 3.7 divorces per 1,000 population per year.

Beyond the statistics are the effects of family values on the individual women of Utah. In a thoughtful comparison of native Mormon and recently immigrant cultures, Helen Z. Papanikolas cites the effects of both continuity and clash on the members of both, especially in the areas of family traditions and assigned male-female roles. Commenting on the non-English-speaking immigrants, she tells of strong national traditions that held families in extended groups, that assigned to brothers responsibilities towards sisters, and that kept sisters submissive and catering to brothers, all for reasons that were no longer valid in the new environment. When immigrant boys courted Mormon girls (girls deemed immoral by the immigrant parents because of their freedom from supervision during dating), old country mores clashed with prevailing Utah values, causing problems with role identification. The immigrant family ideal of woman as the *de facto* ruler of the household contrasted with the Mormon priesthood ideal of shared responsibility; woman's traditional restriction to home and "woman's work" yielded under economic hardship to wives entering the marketplace; arranged, unromantic marriage contracts gave way to American-style unions based on emotional more than traditional familial ties.

Differences have since lessened, but women both of the dominant culture and of the now third-generation immigrant groups are coping with changing roles as they are brought about by automation, inflation and recession, education, intermarriage, vacillating standards of morality, widening opportunity, and changing family structures. In that sense Utah women are one with their sisters nationally.

Women in Education

By 1900 education on both elementary and secondary levels was available to both boys and girls. Utah was no exception in allowing and even encouraging women to attend school. An 1898 state law required *every* child to attend school until he or she had finished the work of the eighth grade or had reached the age of sixteen years. Utah also followed the national trend of more girls than boys regularly graduating from the eighth and twelfth grades. Boys left school in greater numbers to seek jobs, especially in times of war or economic depression. But in the 1950s the trend reversed itself both nationally and in Utah; to the present time, more boys than girls graduate from Utah high schools.

Beyond the public schools, university education was available for women when Utah's first university, now the University of Utah, opened its doors in 1869. However, many more men than women have received university degrees in Utah. A higher percentage of women now attend colleges and universities than ever attended in the past, a rise dramatically evidenced over the past quarter of a century; however, women continue to cluster in what might still be considered the "womanly pursuits": education, homemaking, nursing, and the liberal arts. For example, in the years 1967–72 the University of Utah granted to women 3,932 bachelor's degrees, of which 3,333, or eighty-five percent, were in the colleges of education, letters and science (later humanities), fine arts, and nursing. In April 1975 Brigham Young University graduated 1,510 women, of whom 1,180 were in two colleges: family living and education. This does not suggest that other fields were closed to women; the same graduating classes found women in all colleges, albeit in only token numbers in business, engineering, and mining. About half as many women as men received the bachelor's degree in those years, and about a third as many women as men were awarded graduate degrees.

Considering the numbers of women who have entered the educational professions it would be expected that they would dominate the field at all levels. Such has not been the case. The feminization of schoolroom teaching that swept nationwide in the nineteenth century moved schoolmasters out of the elementary classroom but into the advanced classes and supervisory posts, leaving women to handle the instruction of young children. That pattern still prevails with the exceptions of a small increase in numbers of women in supervisory posts and the entrance, since the 1950s, of some men into the elementary school classrooms.

There have always been women serving on city, county, and state boards of education, and on the boards of Utah universities and colleges, but never in proportion to female teachers or students. Only one, Emma J. McVicker, has ever held the office of State Superintendent of Education—and that was by a fluke. In its 1895 convention, the Republican Party nominated her for that office, offering John R. Park as an alternate in case the courts decreed that women were ineligible to stand for office in this pre-statehood election. The decision did go against the women; Park was nominated and elected superintendent. He died in office, however, and McVicker was appointed to finish out the last three months of his term.

About that time universities, whose women students had been almost exclusively in teacher training programs, began offering courses in the new field of domestic science. Susa Young Gates opened the department at Brigham Young University in 1894, James E. Talmage established the department at the University of Utah in 1896, and in 1903 Utah State Agricultural College (now Utah State University) founded a school of domestic science and arts in the belief that "the state owes as much to the housekeeper in educational opportunities as it owes to the farmer, the mechanic, and the engineer." As advanced as the efforts might have seemed at the time, they were in fact still furthering the attitude that education for women was essentially a means of extending their traditional roles: a way of making them better mothers and more able homemakers. Education for women was not oriented towards careers.

Despite such slow beginnings, many women have influenced education in Utah in this century. Amelia Brotherhood and Maud May Babcock were the first women appointed to the faculty of the University of Utah; Rebecca Little and Antoinette B. Kinney served on the Board of Regents of that institution. Kinney later became a state senator, continuing a very active life as a civic leader. A moving force at the University of Utah was Lucy May Van Cott, whose little housekeeping tasks seem to belie the real power she wielded in behalf of her women charges during her tenure as first Dean of Women. A woman with Victorian ideas about women and women's roles, she pressed hard for scholarships for women and for home economics studies, the successor to the domestic science department of the 1900s.

At Brigham Young University Alice Louise Reynolds, who in the 1890s had attended graduate school at the University of Michigan, served long as *grande dame* of the Department of Literature, which she founded at Brigham Young University upon her return. Active in public library projects, she was the first woman to address Founders Day assemblies at that institution. Ida Smoot Dusenberry was one of the leaders in the kindergarten movement in Utah, and she was elected president of the State Kindergarten Association for three separate terms beginning in 1901. A widow, she taught at Brigham Young University, where she headed the Kindergarten Normal Training School and later held a post as professor of psychology.

Women now are no longer the exception on university faculties, and since the passage of federal bills requiring greater equality of employment opportunities, they are becoming increasingly visible in the higher ranks of educational pursuits.

Women in Arts and Letters

Utah has a strong tradition in arts and letters, and women have been and continue to be a part of that tradition both in promotion and in participation. In 1899 legislator Alice Merrill Horne wrote the law that established the first state association in the United States to foster the fine arts with an annual art exhibit and a state art collection at the state's expense—the Utah Institute of Fine Arts. Alice Horne had studied art for many years, but she sacrificed being an artist for the chance of being a teacher and promoter. She helped organize the Utah Art Colony, collected works by Utah artists, and launched numerous exhibits. Her *Devotees and Shrines: a Handbook of Utah Art* (1914) was the only book published on the subject for fifty years. Many women joined her and followed her in encouraging arts in Utah—they established the Salt Lake Art Center and built collections in the Utah Museum of Fine Arts, the Bertha Eccles Art Center, and the Springville Art Museum.

Among the many other women artists were also several respected educators: Mary Teasdel, who studied under James Whistler and exhibited in the French Salon; and Florence Ware and Irene Fletcher, who were part of the Works Progress Administration Artists' Project during the 1930 depression. Others included Rose Hartwell, Mabel Frazer, Mary Ruth Ballard Snow, Rose Salisbury, and Elaine S. Michelsen. Alice Morrey Bailey, who represented sculptors in the Utah Fine Arts Institute, is also a well-known poet. In the early 1900s Mary Meigs Atwater, a prominent American handweaver, started a weavers' guild that has since lifted weaving to the level of art.

Emma Lucy Gates Bowen, who studied voice in Germany and who recorded for Columbia Records, organized the Lucy Gates Opera Company, which toured the Rocky Mountain West in the 1920s. Other noted singers are Virginia F. Barker, Annette Richardson Dinwoodey, Blanche Christensen, and Naomi Farr. Pianists Cybella Clayton Bassett, Becky Almond, Mabel Borg Jenkins, and Gladys Gladstone are some of the many fine Utah performers and teachers. Since its beginnings as the Utah Works Progress Administration Orchestra women have been a part of the Utah Symphony, and they have likewise been a part of the world-renowned Tabernacle Choir.

Utah has become a major American center for dance due in large measure to the successes of Ballet West, Repertory Dance Theatre, the [Shirley] Ririe-[Joan] Woodbury Dance Company, and the efforts of such theorists and innovators as Children's Dance Theater founder Virginia Tanner and Dr. Elizabeth R. Hayes, whose long teaching career at the University of Utah began in 1941.

One of America's greatest stage actresses was Maude Adams, a diminutive woman from Salt Lake City. From her first appearance in 1906 as Peter Pan she became identified with that and other Sir James Barrie roles. Although she lived most of her life outside of Utah, her appearances on hometown stages were enthusiastically supported. Other Utah actresses were Viola Pratt Gillette, who became famous for playing roles of boys in musical comedy, and Hazel Dawn, who starred in musical comedies, farces, and Zeigfield Follies. Her sister Margaret Romaine sang with the Metropolitan Opera. Leora Thatcher and Ethel Baker Callis both toured with the Moroni Olsen Players during the 1920s. Thatcher later garnered accolades for her starring role in the Broadway production of *Tobacco Road*.

Dr. Maud May Babcock, while on the faculty of the University of Utah, organized the first college dramatic club in the United States and turned the University's theater department into the major Utah drama center, particularly after the Salt Lake Theater was torn down in 1929. Lila Eccles Brimhall, one of Babcock's students, carried on her efforts and became the first lady of Utah theater.

The Woman's Exponent, continuing until 1914, was one of the few publications that afforded women writers the opportunity to see their works in print. The Mormon Church sponsored the *Relief Society Magazine, The Children's Friend,* and the *Improvement Era,* which were filled with poetry, stories, and articles written by women such as Ruth May Fox and Vesta P. Crawford. Some Utah women writers have risen from amateur and local status to gain national reputations: Claire S. Boyer, Christie Lund Coles, Maryhale Woolsey, Alberta H. Christensen, Eva W. Wangsgaard, Caroline E. Miner, Judith Rosenfeld, and May Swenson are nationally recognized poets; Kathryn Kay was a freelance writer in Hollywood; Olive Wooley Burt is a prolific writer of mysteries and children's stories; Virginia Sorensen won the Newberry Medal for *Miracles on Maple Hill* (1956); and Maurine Whipple's book, *The Giant Joshua* (1941), remains a powerful and poignant description of women in Mormon polygamy.

Utah seems to have a sense of history. It is, therefore, not surprising that history is of particular interest to Utah women writers. Kate B. Carter, Daughters of Utah Pioneers president from 1941 to 1976, collected and compiled a lot of historical material. From her sponsorship of the Works Progress Administration historical records survey, discussed later, Juanita Brooks moved into a distinguished career as a historian; her studies of *John D. Lee* (1962) and *The Mountain Meadows Massacre* (1950) brought light and understanding to a tragic and controversial aspect of Utah history. Ann W. Hafen is recognized for her individual writings and for coauthoring with her husband several histories of the Far West and the Rockies. Fawn M. Brodie has written provocative biographies of Joseph Smith, Thaddeus Stevens, and Thomas Jefferson that have earned her a national reputation.

Women Under the Law

The constitution of the State of Utah guarantees that "both male and female citizens of this state shall enjoy equally all civil, political, and religious rights and privileges," a sentiment decisively supported by the people of the territory who approved it in 1895. The sense of that statement is very close to that of the federal Equal Rights Amendment, which the 1973, 1975, and 1977 Utah legislatures declined to ratify. Between the sentiment in the state constitution and the feelings of opposition to the Equal Rights Amendment lies an ideological struggle that may be extremely difficult to resolve. Basically the question is one of the position of women in the society: are they creatures to be cared for and protected, or are they agents with the same responsibilities as men? The complexity of the issue lies in the overlap between the two positions, in questions such as whether protection in some areas does not produce unfair discrimination, or whether equal rights do not remove guarantees necessary to women in their reproductive function.

Thirty years before the turn of the century Utah women had received the right to vote, and their franchise, lost along with the right to hold public office in 1887 through federal legislation, was restored with the coming of statehood. By the 1890s Utah, like most states in the Union, had modified the English common law doctrine of *femme couverte,* under which women were considered chattels of their husbands, so that the state constitution specified the equality of parties in a marriage by guaranteeing the wife's right to her own property.

These early laws establishing equal rights for women were joined by laws securing protection for women. The Mines and Smelter Act of 1896 prohibited the employment of women in Utah's mines and smelters. The next year a seating law required managers of stores, hotels, and restaurants that employed women to provide them with chairs for resting when they were not working. The concept that women needed these protective restrictions or facilities was based on the traditional definitions of their roles in society; similar laws protecting men would have been seen as a violation of their freedom of contract, a freedom from which women were exempted by virtue of their special status.

Succeeding legislatures, paralleling actions of other states in the country, enacted laws in 1911 restricting women to a nine-hour day and fifty-four-hour week and later to an eight-hour day and forty-eight-hour week, with exceptions granted for emergency situations. In 1913 a compromise measure set a minimum wage for women, responding to a strong lobby from the Utah Federation of Women's Clubs that had demanded, but lost, the establishment of a wage and working condition supervisory commission. The aim of that early bill was finally achieved with the 1933 Minimum Wage Law, which granted to the Industrial Commission power to fix minimum wages, maximum hours, and conditions of work.

By then the Federation of Women's Clubs had been supplemented as a lobby for women's interests by another body, founded in 1923 as the Women's Legislative Committee. This group, later called the Women's Legislative Council, represented most of the women's groups in the state and concerned itself not only with employment conditions for women but with child welfare and such issues as racing, prohibition, and gambling. In its promotion of protective laws, this group went on record in 1945 against the passage of a women's rights amendment.

The counter action to protective legislation—the move for equal rights—began a new groundswell in the national capital in 1923, and an equal rights measure was proposed to every session of Congress until a constitutional amendment was finally submitted to the states in 1972. A strong voice in its behalf had been heard in Utah as early as 1938, when the Utah Federation of Business and Professional Clubs took its stand against gender-based legislation with the statement that all legislation intended for women only should be stamped out. The effort gained new momentum in the 1960s and 1970s. In 1973 the Utah State Legislature heard Representative Rita Urie, with support from the Governor's Commission on the Status of Women, present the Congressional proposal for ratification. Supporters were surprised, however, when the bill went down to defeat; they had not anticipated, nor could they match, the powerful backing of the opponents of the amendment. Following the first defeat, Utah women promoters organized what became the Equal Rights Coalition, an umbrella organization to promote passage of the bill in subsequent sessions of the legislature. The bill, however, was defeated again in the following two legislatures, the Mormon Church taking at first an indirect and then an official position against it.

Despite this action, Utah's legislature is actively correcting its own statutes to fulfill the intent of the state constitution. It has found that most of the alterations needed to equalize the legal status of women and men are minor word changes rather than major repeals. Utah has not witnessed the repressive legislation against women that some states have, and her women have occupied an enviable position vis-a-vis the law.

Women in Politics

Utah women have been effective in local, state, and federal offices. Democrat Martha Hughes Cannon set the standard in 1896 when she won a seat in the Utah State Senate, the first woman in the United States to do so. It is one of the delights of Utah political history that she outpolled her Republican husband, who failed to gain a seat in the same body. Cannon, a physician, secured some of the first public health legislation in Utah, and her example in promoting social welfare measures was followed by many of the women who succeeded her in the legislature. Ten women sat in the Utah State Senate and more than 130 were elected to the House of Representatives during Utah's first eighty years.

Most of the women who have run for office in Utah have been Democrats. During the 1930s hundreds of women became involved in New Deal programs and in Democratic Party affairs. Even after the Republican Party regained control of the state at the end of World War II, overwhelmingly more Democratic than Republican women sought and won seats in the state legislature. One example was Nellie Jack, who was credited with running Salt Lake City's west side politics for thirty years. First elected to the House in 1936, she served in the Senate in 1956 and as county recorder in 1958. In all she won seats in the Utah House in fourteen separate elections.

In local politics as well as in the state legislature a Utah woman pioneered a place for her sex by being elected as one of the first woman mayors in America. In 1912 Mary W. Howard and her all-woman town council in southern Utah's Kanab did not limit themselves to the social welfare types of legislation usually promoted by women, but addressed such problems as building a dike above the town, taxing peddlers whose competition threatened town businesses, building bridges over the town's irrigation ditches, and controlling stray dogs. They also tackled issues of morality, banning gambling and enforcing liquor control laws.

Utah women have frequently been appointed to state and national positions: Jeanette Acord Hyde was appointed collector of customs in Hawaii; Florence E. Allen was judge of the Sixth Circuit's court of appeals; Ivy Baker Priest was appointed Treasurer of the United States; and Esther E. Peterson served as Assistant Secretary of Labor and as a consumer advocate in a variety of appointments. But only one Utah woman has thus far been elected to Congress: in 1948 Reva Beck Bosone went to the House of Representatives and there became the first woman to serve on the Interior Committee. She won a second term in 1950, but during the McCarthy era she was attacked as a Communist sympathizer and lost elections in 1952 and 1954. In retrospect, her career, first as state representative and then as floor leader of the Democratic majority, as city judge, and as national representative, qualifies her for a significant place among Utah politicians. In an interview after her retirement, Bosone expressed regret that so few Utah women entered the field of politics: "I can't help but feel that maybe it is the women. . . . I think we have just as many fine women as we do fine men. I think they need to step out and raise a little Cain about it!"

Women Earning

In 1970 the United States Census reported that nearly half of the women in Utah sixteen years old and over were gainfully employed. The forty-one percent figure, which reflected a sharp increase in the 1960s, contrasts with the eleven percent of the female population gainfully employed in 1900. As the century opened, the majority of earning women were single girls under twenty-five years of age, and the low wages paid to them were justified in the public mind by the thought that they supposedly were merely supplementing a family income and required only pin money. The drive for acceptance of the equal pay for equal work doctrine has accelerated since women moved into traditional male work during the Second World War, and the nature of the female working force has altered so markedly that many women are not merely supplementing an existing income but are the sole support of a family.

In the first decades of the century there was strong feeling in the public mind about the appropriateness of certain jobs for women. Brigham Young expressed it earlier when he spoke proudly of courses at the University of Deseret that would train women to be "bookkeepers, accountants, clerks, cashiers, tellers, payers, telegraphic operators, reporters, and fill other branches of employment suited to their sex." His list bears strong resemblance to the jobs women were filling in 1900-20: teachers, stenographers, office clerks, laundry operatives, telephone operators, and candy factory operatives were most numerous.

What Young had not foreseen was the hardship that their working conditions would place upon women: the long hours, the low wages, the split shifts, and the inability to rise in seniority above men to more responsible, less dreary jobs in the factory or office. It is not surprising that in January 1910, just two months after the famous "Uprising of the Twenty Thousand" garment workers, the first significant strike of women workers in the East, a group of female employees in a large candy factory in Salt Lake City went on strike. Their action was ineffective—the management brought in replacements to take their jobs—but the benefit ball given in their aid and the support of other labor groups in boycotting the factory's products were indications of pressures that would eventually improve conditions for women workers.

In 1913 the Utah legislature narrowly passed a minimum wage law without the surveillance body that had been requested by lobbying women. The set wage, 90 cents a day for unskilled women and $1.25 a day for skilled women, was totally inadequate in meeting the prevailing cost of living. With the onset of the First World War, women who were hired in small numbers to replace men called to military duty were in many cases paid the wages of the men they replaced. The *Deseret News* editorially supported the equal pay doctrine, noting that "the women who are coming into the employment of equal rights in other fields of human activity should not be denied them in the labor market."

The war, however, did not make a lasting change in the opportunities for women in the labor market; they were hired as temporary replacements, often with fanfare as they filled unaccustomed jobs; they were expected to return to home and hearth after the war. Some small shifts of women workers remained. A 1917 story in the Salt Lake *Telegram* dealt in an offhand way with one of these changes. Female elevator operators had been hired to replace men in Salt Lake City's Newhouse Hotel. The uniforms provided by the management offended the fashion-conscious women, and they went on strike. The deadlock was broken only when management agreed to let the girls wear their own civilian clothes.

With the end of the war there was a small decrease in the percentage of women earning an income, the figure standing at 13.7 percent in 1920. The next decade saw a gradual rise, possibly influenced by the tight national immigration policies. As before the war, most of the employed women were single; the prejudice in Utah against married women working outside the home remained so strong that some businesses expressed the feeling as policy. At the same time the labor unions, including those comprising women workers, declined in both effective power and grassroots support. The radical elements earlier prominent in the labor movement in Utah had weakened public acceptance, and courts were deciding more frequently in favor of management. By 1929 only seven unions were represented at the annual convention of the Utah State Federation of Labor. Garment Workers Local 107, active in Ogden since 1912, was the only women's group there.

The Great Depression was particularly severe in Utah because important sectors of the economy were already lagging behind the national level of activity in the 1920s. Women earners fared better than did men during the hardest times; they were more often employed in service occupations that were not so quickly hit. Those women, however, who worked in woolen factories, electrical sup-

Eager that their votes be counted, women at the June 1977 International Women's Year Conference crowd into the room where issues are being debated. Abortion on demand, the proposed Equal Rights Amendment, and related issues were soundly defeated both in workshops such as this and in plenary sessions.

ply, food processing, and other industries closely tied to the overall economy suffered badly.

What it meant to women to be caught in the depression might be seen in the experiences of one Cedar City woman. Annie Chamberlain Esplin's family had left rural Orderville some time earlier, but were still being supported by the father's sheep flocks when the 1931 drought brought the livestock operation to an end. Men out of work in a small city were hard pressed; Annie's husband Frant (Francis) bartered money owing for services he could render or bargained with local merchants for short-term hauling. Annie Esplin reminisced:

One bill he traded around and four fellows paid their bills and there wasn't a penny cash exchanged. Frant would haul coal and I'd scout around and find a place to sell it, and trade it for things that we needed. The boys needed overcoats, and so I went down to Clint Beesley, he was a friend of ours and the manager of the J. C. Penney store. I asked him if he couldn't use a load of coal and we talked about it. I told him we surely needed some clothes. He said, "You tell your husband to bring me the coal. I can use it." So we did and he paid us but we turned right around and bought them clothes. So when we had to go over to Orderville to bury Carolyn [an infant daughter] why the kids looked quite respectable.

In other depression-hit towns women found ingenious ways of bringing extra income—or any income at all—into their families. In St. George, for example, Mormon Stake Relief Society President Juanita Brooks won federal support for a Works Progress Administration project of collecting documents on southern Utah history. Converting the spare room of her home into an office, she hired women—widows, daughters, anyone who could type—to transcribe the handwritten manuscripts. The monthly wage was thirty dollars, raised later to thirty-six dollars—"a literal godsend," Brooks later recounted.

The organization of female workers into unions proceeded slowly or not at all during the depression. The previously active Garment Workers Local 107 became an early casualty, disbanding quietly when the major employer discontinued its effort to run a union shop. A labor leader characterized the potential female union members of Utah as "in the main a bunch of very weak sisters." An exception was the Culinary Alliance, a union of restaurant help, two members of which focused public attention on unfair legislation by picketing a cafe to protest the management's refusal to run a union shop. The two peaceful picketers were arrested—the law against such demonstrations was still on the Utah statute books—and although the union forces could not raise enough money to defend them until a higher court could declare the law unconstitutional, their action led to the eventual clarification of the rights of organized labor in the state.

A major involvement of women in the labor movement, however, was in the organization of women's adjuncts to the unions. A Central Council of Women's Auxiliaries was organized in 1931 under Anna P. Kelsey, wife of a union man. In her attempts to broaden the power base of the male-dominated unions she urged the wives of the workers to join the struggle, using such rhetoric as that she used in a 1934 speech to a convention of the Utah State Federation of Labor:

Believe it or not, but it is the women who practically control the destiny of organized labor. That may sound rather foolish to some of the men here who think that a woman's place is in the home tending the children and doing the housework, but it is the wife who spends the bulk of the wage-earner's money, and it depends largely upon how and where she spends that money whether or not organized labor will prosper . . . or whether it will stay in the half-baked state it is in at the present time.

As the state pulled itself out of the economic deprivation of the depression, fears of the return of such a condition prompted some discriminatory legislative proposals, including a bill that would have prevented the husband of an earning wife, or the wife of an earning husband, from holding a job. The bill did not pass, but its introduction reflects the failure of some Utahns to take into consideration that most earning women had left their homes because of the poverty of their families and that most women were employed in jobs that men would not or could not have filled at that time.

In 1940 one out of six Utah women was earning an income, about the same ratio as prevailed early in the depression, ranking Utah second to the lowest in the nation in the percentage of women gainfully employed. The big increase in female employment took place in the following decade, the major prod being the Second World War. An estimated 24,000 Utah women, many of them married with children in school, left their homes for the first time to fill jobs vacated by men, this time on a much larger scale than during the previous war. They worked in transportation, in wholesale and retail trade, as unskilled laborers, and as skilled mechanics in defense plants. One study estimated that nearly thirty percent of the earning women were in war industries during that time. Unlike the women who filled men's jobs in the first war, these women hired on as permanent employees and many expected to remain at their jobs when the men returned; statistically they did. By 1950 there had been an increase in female employment to the extent that one-fourth of Utah's women now held remunerative jobs. And despite a new emphasis on domesticity that swept the country during the 1950s, more married women worked, changing patterns of life making it increasingly possible for them to do so. In 1900 the average woman married at twenty-two years of age, had her last child at thirty-two, and died at fifty-one. By 1950, however, the average woman married at twenty, bore her last child at twenty-six, and died at sixty-five. Work was an alternative to staying at home after the children started school or were grown.

The trend continued. In 1960 the majority of earning women in Utah were married and between thirty-five and fifty-five years of age. They made real contributions to the family income. In Utah more than one-half of the families with middle class annual incomes of $7,000 to $15,000 had both an earning husband and an earning wife. The issues of equal pay for equal work and employment opportunities continues to be vital. In 1960 the median income of fulltime women earners in Utah was fifty-five percent of the median income of men, a proportion lower than the national average. The main occupations filled by women continued to be clerical and service occupations rather than professional and operative. Women and women's organizations pushed hard for the amended Utah Anti-Discrimination Act of 1965, which prohibits discrimination in employment matters based solely on grounds of race, color, national origin, sex, religion, or age.

The proportion of women in Utah's labor force increased considerably during the 1960s. While the population of women fourteen and over rose by twenty-nine percent, the number of women earners increased by fifty-seven percent. In 1970 more than three-fifths (sixty-two percent) of the women earners in Utah were married and were living with their husbands. In 1970 about 20,000 families (eight percent of all Utah households) were headed by women. The majority of these women were wage earners.

Conclusion

As Utah women approach the last quarter of the present century they find themselves increasingly cosmopolitan, increasingly drawn into the mainstream of American culture, and, albeit with a conservative lag typical of contemporary Utah, into the women's movement at large. As the latest available report of the Governor's

Committee on the Status of Women suggested, Utah women in the various facets of their lives must deal with the same problems of employment opportunity, threats to the family, housing, and gender and minority discrimination as do women across the nation.

As that same report stated, the women of Utah, whether Mormon or gentile, are influenced by the doctrines and practices of the predominant church: "Any analysis of social, economic, welfare, recreational, or educational problems within the state of Utah must be developed in relationship to the role of the LDS Church," the report observed. It noted in some detail how Mormon welfare systems affect community services, how Mormon emphasis on education results in Utah's high percentages of school and university attendance, and how Mormon regional meetings bring about a high level of communication and a sharing of cultural and recreational advantages among members. But this condition also creates pockets of isolation and conflict for those who do not belong to the Mormon Church, both as individual families in rural areas that are predominantly Mormon and as groups in the urban areas where the population may be only half Latter-day Saint. Women, the report pointed out, have been particularly affected by this cultural segregation because many of the basic conflicts deal with the realms of family life, sex roles, and sex values.

That circumstances had not changed radically since the 1909 confrontation between Corinne Allen and Emmeline Wells was demonstrated in the discussions and voting at the June 1977 state conference of the International Women's Year in Salt Lake City's Salt Palace. Nearly 14,000 women attended the meetings, which were planned by Utah women as part of a federally sponsored national observance. Mormon Church leaders encouraged women to attend, a fact that ultraconservative political activists utilized by calling preconference meetings where women, many erroneously assuming the meetings to be church-sponsored, were instructed on issues and warned against conspiratorial tactics attributed to International Women's Year organizers.

As a result, the meetings were characterized by an almost immediate polarization of participants. Voting became the prime purpose of the conference, and discussion was mostly about tactics rather than issues. In one session on the Equal Rights Amendment, for example, the first motion from the floor called for the voting to precede both the panel presentation of the issue and the discussion of the task committee recommendations. Voting split about 6,000 to 400 against ratification of the Equal Rights Amendment; this ratio was paralleled in the voting against elective abortions, public funding of birth control centers, sex education in the schools, child care centers, and other issues.

More significant than the issues and the voting, however, was the effect of the conference on Mormon-gentile relations in the state. Feminist factions blamed Mormon Church leaders for the worsening of relations. "This has set us back fifty years!" commented one participant, referring to the antipathies that the conference had reinforced.

Apart from the record-breaking attendance, what happened at the Salt Lake conference was not unique. The Right to Life organization and other groups, liberal as well as conservative, dominated International Women's Year conferences in several other states, and factional polarization also occurred elsewhere, all of which suggests that Utah women, for all their peculiarities, are very similar to other American women. The majority of Utah women are probably more conservative in their attitudes toward their careers, morality, fashions, families, education, and politics, but they are still certainly mainstream, and certainly American.

Chapter 31
Bibliographical Essay

The history of Utah women is part of the general history of women in the United States. Books helpful in describing the general history include Eleanor Flexner, *Century of Struggle: The Women's Rights Movements in the United States* (1973); William Henry Chafe, *The American Woman: Her Changing Social, Economic, and Political Roles, 1920-1970* (1972); Jean E. Friedman and William G. Shade, ed., *Our American Sisters: Women in American Life and Thought* (1973); William O'Neill, *Everyone Was Brave: The Rise and Fall of Feminism in America* (1969).

Very little has been published specifically pertaining to Utah women and especially to women of the twentieth century. Readers wishing to investigate further need to use many primary documents, unpublished theses, archival collections, oral interviews, local newspapers, and ephemeral materials.

Some of the few articles, pamphlets, and books that are available include Susa Young Gates, *Utah Women in Politics* (pamphlet, c. 1913); Katherine Barrette Parson, *History of 50 Year Ladies Literary Club, 1877-1927,* (1927); Mrs. Gould B. Blakely, "History, Utah Federation of Women's Clubs," in *Official Year Book 1918-1920* (at Utah State Historical Society); Max Binheim, ed., *Women of the*

West; a Series of Biographical Sketches of Living Eminent Women in the Eleven Western States of the United States of America (1928); Helen Z. Papanikolas, "Toil and Rage in a New Land, The Greek Immigrants in Utah," *UHQ*, Spring 1970; Papanikolas, "Ethnicity in Mormondom: A Comparison of Immigrant and Mormon Cultures," in Thomas G. Alexander, ed., *Essays on the American West, 1975-1976,* (Charles Redd Monographs in Western History, Brigham Young University, 1977); *Women in Utah,* Report of the Governor's Committee on the Status of Women in Utah (1966).

Statistical information—labor records, demography trends, census reports, and school reports—is available from federal and state government agencies, much of it in published form.

Scholars at the University of Utah have interpreted various segments of the history of twentieth-century Utah women in theses and dissertations. Some of these are Madeline Stauffer Lambert, "Women at Work in Salt Lake City: A Comparative Study of Select Problems of Women's Labor" (master's thesis, 1914); Edith Berghout, "The Effect of War upon the Employment of Women with Special Reference to Utah." (master's thesis, 1944); Juanita Merrill Larsen, "Women in Industry with Special Reference to Utah" (master's thesis, 1933); Eunice Louise Wheeler, "Female Labor Force Participation: Economic and Religious Trends in Utah, 1940-1970" (master's thesis, 1970); Shauna McLatchy Adix, "Differential Treatment of Women at the University of Utah from 1850 to 1915" (Ph.D. dissertation, 1976); Ronald Quayle Fredrickson, "Maud May Babcock and the Department of Education at the University of Utah" (master's thesis, 1965); Jean Bickmore White, "Utah State Elections, 1895-1899" (Ph.D. dissertation, 1968); Sheelwant Bapura Pawar, "An Environmental Study of the Development of the Utah Labor Movement: 1860-1935" (Ph.D. dissertation, 1968); Karl Alwin Elling, "The History of Organized Labor in Utah, 1910-1920" (master's thesis, 1962); Walter McGregor Douglas, "A History of the Utah State Federation of Labor, 1930-1940" (master's thesis, 1962). See also Mavis Gay Gashler, "Three Mormon Actresses" (master's thesis, Brigham Young University, 1970).

Scrapbooks and minute books of many women's organizations are located in various archives in the state, and personal accounts left by individual women can also be found in archives. Oral interviews with Ann Amelia Chamberlain Esplin (Mormon Church Archives), Reva Beck Bosone (University of Utah), and Nellie Jack (University of Utah) are examples. Autobiographies such as that of Eva B. Poelman (Mormon Church Archives) and papers of such outstanding Utah women as Reva Beck Bosone and Amy Brown Lyman (Brigham Young University) have been useful in the present study.

Chapter 32
Education and the Arts
In Twentieth-century Utah

James B. Allen

Reflecting a cultural penchant for proving Utah's excellence in almost everything, the author of a 1952 text on education reported with "deep humility and grateful appreciation" that his state ranked first in the nation in median years of school completed, first in general educational attainment, first in the production of "men and women with great ability," and among the top five states in preparation of teachers. Such a barrage of self-congratulatory statistics, whether right or wrong, suggest the appropriateness of considering at least some aspects of Utah education in the twentieth century. Achievements in the cultural arts—quantitatively more modest—also merit consideration.

The End of Denominational Schools

Three trends characterized elementary and secondary education in Utah in the first quarter of the century: the decline of denominational schools, the growth of public schools, and the consolidation of districts. The move away from denominational schools was particularly impressive. In 1890, when Utah's first compulsory attendance law was passed, there were some 8,000 students in private non-Mormon schools and 1,500 in private Mormon schools. The result of increasing public school taxes and facilities was a rapid decline of church schools, and by the mid 1920s there were only 525 students in five non-Mormon schools, and the Mormon academies (secondary schools) had all been turned over to the state.

As late as 1915, three years after the Mormon seminary program was launched in the Granite School District, Mormon President Joseph F. Smith still openly opposed the expansion of the public high school system, fearing that it would interfere with efforts to indoctrinate students with religious and moral teachings. Officials of the Mormon Church and of the schools worked in close cooperation to mitigate these concerns. The seminary experiment continued, and in January 1916 the state board of education granted limited high school credit for Bible history and literature that was taken on a released-time basis. This encouraged seminary enrollment, and in 1920 the Mormon Church finally decided to transfer all its secondary schools to the state and to focus its own attention on seminaries, colleges, and teacher education.

The released-time policy did not escape challenge. In 1930, for example, the state high school inspector raised questions about its constitutionality. The use of public school buses by pupils who also attended religious classes, and the sometime use of seminary teachers to conduct study periods, assist in registration, and even conduct some classes for the schools seemed to violate the principle of separation of church and state. Within a year the state board ordered everything related to the seminaries and their faculties totally dissociated from the high schools, but a resolution to deny credit for released-time Bible study was defeated. In succeeding years there were attempts to challenge the system in the courts, but a judicious separation of seminary and school activities helped ward off such actions.

Growth and Consolidation

Contemporaneous with the discontinuance of church schools was the rapid growth and consolidation of public schools. In 1888 there were 344 school districts in the territory, twenty of them in Salt Lake City. An 1890 territorial law required consolidation of districts in first- and second-class cities. As in other states, consolidation became an emotional issue, pitting champions of larger, more economical districts against the advocates of strictly local control. Despite the difficulties of the task, the five largest cities in the state soon complied with the law. After a bitter political battle combined Salt Lake County's thirty-six school districts into two, a bill for statewide consolidation was adopted by the legislature in 1905. Permissive in nature, it was followed ten years later by a statute that made consolidation mandatory; the combined districts were to supervise both elementary and high schools. Utah's multiple districts were thus reduced to forty.

Consolidation of schools within the districts came about more slowly because it was left to the discretion of local boards. Prejudice, disagreement over the values of consolidation, and the natural impulse to fight the elimination of small hometown schools all slowed down the process. Improved roads, school buses, and increasing costs of operating small facilities maintained the pressure for merging units, but local controversies continued as late as the 1970s.

All this was only part of a renaissance for education in Utah in the early years of the twentieth century. In 1916 it was reported that in just over ten years the number of high schools had grown from five to forty-five, and that only four counties had no public high schools. Moreover, a 1919 law made school attendance mandatory until age eighteen. The public mind seemed favorable to education, and the legislature even went so far as to provide year-round supervision of some educational activities, to create divisions of Health Education and Americanization in the Utah State Department of Education, to enact a county library law that would help rural areas, and to put new emphasis on vocational and industrial training.

At the same time Utah adopted another innovation that was becoming popular throughout the country—the junior high school. Beginning about 1914, many school districts adopted the six-three-three plan, whereby students would attend six years of elementary school and three years each of junior and senior high school. The result was greater interest in continued schooling on the part of teenage students and a decline in the dropout rate.

The Problem of Finances

The problem of financing public education was complicated by the fact that Utah was consistently among the lowest states in the nation in ability to pay the costs. At the same time Utahns tended to remain in school longer than did students elsewhere, the state had one of the highest ratios of children between the ages of five and eighteen, it frequently spent more per capita on education than did any other state, and it was always among the top states in the proportion of its per capita income devoted to schools.

In general, school finance in Utah followed national trends. For at least the first half of the century local property taxes provided the main revenue; after that funding the state assumed the major burden. Like most states, Utah began in the Progressive Era to consider statewide equalization. A 1905 law guaranteed state funds to any district whose other resources could not support a minimum annual salary of $300 per teacher. In 1911 a state property tax was established to be apportioned to high schools, and in 1920 a State District School Fund was created by constitutional amendment;

589

the proceeds of the fund were to be distributed according to school population. Inequities in local tax bases remained, however, and even the creation of a Uniform School Fund in 1937 left the depression-racked school districts far short of the resources needed to maintain desired minimum programs. Then, in 1946, two constitutional amendments created the Minimum School Program of 1947, which, with modifications, became the foundation program still in existence. All state revenue from income and franchise taxes was earmarked for education, and all state school funds were merged into a new Uniform School Fund. The Minimum School Program also developed a complicated but more equitable formula for determining classroom units (later defined as distribution units) and the amount of money to be distributed per unit, and it defined more precisely the minimal educational program acceptable. The most extensive overhaul of this program came in 1973 when the legislature provided even greater equalization and significantly increased the amount of state aid available.

But even though Utah seemed to keep pace with national trends in such matters as school law, teacher certification, and curriculum development, teacher salaries remained comparatively low. In 1926, for example, a federal survey revealed that Utah's elementary school teachers were paid much lower than those with similar qualifications outside the state. Utah, nevertheless, had an unusual ability to attract and hold teachers, even with its low salary schedule, and it ranked high in teacher preparation. By 1976 teacher compensation was still below the national average but it had reached the average of the eight mountain states.

In 1964 this combination of high educational aspirations, limited resources, and low pay made Utah the first state in which a statewide teacher recess was staged. It was also the first state against which the National Education Association declared national sanctions. On March 16, 1963, some 8,000 Utah Education Association members voted overwhelmingly to cut off contract negotiations in protest against the failure of the legislature to provide adequate funding. Throughout the summer the teachers refused to negotiate until Governor George D. Clyde agreed to appoint a school study committee. Most of the teachers were in their classrooms in the fall, but dissatisfaction continued; the following May the teachers staged their unprecedented two-day recess (condemned as a strike by critics), and the National Education Association soon declared its sanctions. Within a year the sanctions were lifted, although only moderate increases in funds were forthcoming in the ensuing years.

A men's club at Brigham Young College, Logan, demonstrates the current vogue in campus transportation in 1900.

Federal Funding

A controversial but increasingly important source of help to Utah education came in the form of federal aid. The beginning of dollar grants for secondary education came in 1917 with the Smith-Hughes Act, under which Utah accepted $35,000 for vocational education. The state was required to match these funds. Agricultural education profited first, but many schools soon began offering more training in the trades and industrial skills.

During the Great Depression of the 1930s federal aid became increasingly significant. Between 1932 and 1934, for example, the Civil Works Administration provided a half-million dollars in labor to renovate school buildings; the Federal Emergency Relief Administration approved some $535,000 for building projects; and the Public Works Administration gave $172,000 for remodeling or new construction. World War II enlarged Utah's tax base and brought federal funds to defense-impacted school districts, but it also generated some long-lasting educational problems. Much of

591

the Wasatch Front was suddenly inundated by defense workers. In many districts this resulted in overcrowded schools, and it was not unusual to find classes meeting in improvised facilities. The condition did not abate after the war, and the result was a surge of building activity that substantially increased the educational budget of the state.

Since the war federal agencies have provided direct aid to school districts where defense industries created especially heavy burdens. They have helped with school lunch and milk programs, have expanded vocational training, and have subsidized scientific education. By 1969 nearly eight percent of all school revenue came from the federal government, though a report a year later showed that Utah ranked only thirty-seventh among the states in percentage of total public school funds obtained from Washington.

Recent Trends

The number of Utah public schools increased by about thirty percent between 1945 and 1971, while the number of teachers grew from 4,000 to 10,000 and the number of pupils grew from 122,000 to 312,000. Since Utah's birth rate in the 1970s remained well above the national average, the nationwide contraction in public school enrollments was not matched statewide, although some central city and rural schools experienced declines.

In spite of its financial problems, Utah tried to keep pace with the nation in program innovations; federal dollars assisted in this effort. By 1970 these programs included special training for some 22,000 educationally disadvantaged children and for 1,000 handicapped children; provided educational opportunities for migrant workers; established a program of driver education; initiated environmental education; provided for advanced placement programs to help students obtain a head start on their college education; established special bilingual programs; provided for the expanded use of instructional media, including educational television; initiated career counseling; and augmented adult education programs and other special services. In addition, the State Board of Education supervised the state's two technical colleges in Salt Lake City and Provo, schools for the deaf and blind in Ogden, plus ten area centers for the improvement of vocational and technical instruction.

Utah's Colleges and Universities

In the field of higher education, the twentieth century opened with a contest over teacher education between the University of

Utah and Brigham Young Academy. Though both institutions were still largely secondary schools, the University of Utah was leading the way in moving into higher education. At the same time Brigham Young Academy had begun to compete by offering a teacher education program. Because of church financial difficulties, some Mormon leaders were almost persuaded to abandon the field, but in the end the church decided that it must maintain the teacher education program. Both universities grew during the century to attain distinction for Utah.

The state of Utah currently supports two universities, two four-year colleges, three junior colleges, and two technical colleges. The major institution is the University of Utah, originally founded in 1850 as the University of Deseret and now the oldest university in the far west. It was only after the turn of the century that collegiate-level work became the primary activity of the university, though as early as 1906 President J. T. Kingsbury happily reported that ". . . students of college grade now outnumber those of high school grade." That year there were over 500 college students enrolled.

As the century began, the university was attempting to become a diversified institution of higher learning, and a number of professional schools were added. A school of mines, a medical course, a law school, and a school of graduate studies were established before World War I. Eventually the University Medical School became a leading research institution and was especially noted for training heart surgeons. In 1974 the university was named by the National Academy for Educational Development as among the thirty-six leading research universities in the nation.

The Utah State University of Agriculture and Applied Sciences was originally founded in 1888 as a land grant college; it attained university status in 1957. Because of its special emphasis on agricultural and mechanical training, it initially attracted students from a broader area outside the state than did the other Utah institutions, and by 1904 over 600 students were registered. By 1970 it was offering degrees, including graduate degrees, in agriculture; business; social sciences; education; engineering; family life; forest, range, and wildlife management; humanities; and the sciences. In addition, it was the home of certain professional publications including the prestigious *Western Historical Quarterly*.

The state's four-year institutions are Southern Utah State College and Weber State College. The former began in Cedar City in 1897 as a branch of the State University, although the work then offered was secondary in nature and school was held in a Mormon meetinghouse. By 1913 the desirability of expanding to collegiate work was clear, and the legislature transferred the school to the Agricultural College at Logan. At first the Branch Agricultural College offered only a two-year course, but it gradually expanded until it offered a four-year degree in 1962. It was renamed the College of Southern Utah in 1962, and in 1965 it became administratively independent. Its present name was adopted in 1969.

Three of Utah's public colleges were Mormon academies in 1900: Weber State College in Ogden, Dixie College in St. George, and Snow College in Ephraim. The same considerations that led to Mormon Church withdrawal from the high school field led to extended discussion in the 1920s and the 1930 decision to turn the three junior colleges over to the state. The transfer was completed in three years. A plan for the Mormon Church to reabsorb the schools was enacted by the cost-conscious legislature and was endorsed by conservative Governor J. Bracken Lee in 1953, but a citizen-initiated referendum decisively rejected the proposal.

Weber State College expanded rapidly after World War II, moving to a new campus in suburban Ogden in 1954 and becoming a four-year college in 1959. Dixie continued to be affiliated with the local high school until 1963, when it moved to a new campus. Dixie College functioned under the State Board of Education until 1969, when jurisdiction over all state colleges was given to the newly created Utah State Board of Higher Education. Snow College became a branch of Utah State University in 1951, and until 1969 it was administered by a resident director.

The College of Eastern Utah, formerly known as Carbon College, was founded in Price in 1938. Until 1959 it also offered high school work, but then separate campus facilities were provided and the high school connection was broken. The legislature also placed the college under the University of Utah Board of Regents, where it remained until its reorganization in 1969.

The state of Utah also operates Utah Technical College at Provo, founded in 1941, and Utah Technical College at Salt Lake City, dating from 1947. Enrollment in these schools followed the national trend; between 1966 and 1974 the headcount at both more than doubled. Governing responsibility was divided in 1969 between the State Board for Vocational Education and the Board of Higher Education; the presidents of the schools met with both boards. Several area technical schools also offer some posthigh school vocational courses.

As Utah's colleges and universities grew in size and scope, it became clear that better statewide planning was necessary to assure the most effective system compatible with the best economy. The first legislative step was taken in 1959 with the creation of the advisory Coordinating Council of Higher Education. Ten years later the Utah Higher Education Act created the Utah State Board of Higher Education, later renamed the Board of Regents, and eliminated all separate governing boards. G. Homer Durham, former vice-president of the University of Utah and president of Arizona State University, became the first Commissioner of Higher Education.

The new board began vigorously pursuing its responsibilities after first weathering an attempt by the State Board of Education to have it declared unconstitutional. By the mid 1970s the nine institutions with which the board was concerned were becoming more closely coordinated, and the transferability of credit among them was an accomplished fact. In addition, the board was beginning to make institutional role assignments, some of them on an exclusive basis. In 1976 Durham was succeeded by T. H. Bell, who had served as State Superintendent of Public Instruction and United States Commissioner of Education.

Two privately sponsored institutions have also figured prominently in Utah higher education in the twentieth century. Westminster College in Salt Lake City, initially a Presbyterian academy, adopted its present name and mission in 1911 and has maintained its place as an independent liberal arts college in the face of rising competition from the state's public education system.

During the first half of the century Mormon Church commitment to the support of Brigham Young University was periodically reviewed, and the Provo school's future was uncertain until the 1940s. Its name was changed from Brigham Young Academy to Brigham Young University in 1903, and its first master's degrees were awarded during World War I. Primary emphasis at the university remained on teacher education until the culmination of World War II brought a flood of veterans and a diversification of curricular emphases to the campus. Mormon leadership then reaffirmed church support and assumed direct governance of the school. Under the presidency of Ernest L. Wilkinson, 1951-70, Brigham Young University began granting doctoral degrees and became the largest university in Utah and the largest church-related university in America. Most of its former students are now living out-of-state, but Brigham Young University ranks only behind the state university as an educator of Utahns.

The Arts in Utah

Along with their efforts to support education, Utahns have professed interest in the arts, although in 1926 the young Bernard De-Voto looked at his native state from afar and wrote: "Who ever heard of a Utah painter, or Utah sculptor, or Utah novelist, or poet or critic, or educator or publicist—who ever heard of a Utahn?" Despite significant works by Cyrus Dallin and Mahonri Young, the early years of the twentieth century were relatively lean ones for the arts in Utah. During the Great Depression of the 1930s new hope and opportunity for the arts came through a variety of federal projects; after World War II there was a significant flowering of both the visual and the performing arts.

The Utah Art Institute, established by the legislature in 1899, struggled with meager resources to promote literature, music, and other fine arts; in 1937 the institute was renamed the Utah State Institute of Fine Arts. In honor of Alice Merrill Horne, the legislator who was instrumental in founding the institute, a state-owned art collection was begun. For years the institute board met only irregularly, but it was able to purchase some works of art and hold exhibits at the state capitol. In 1967 it became the Division of Fine Arts within the newly created State Department of Development Services. At last it had a staff, a home in the renovated carriage house on the Utah State Historical Society grounds in Salt Lake City, an order from the governor to care for state-owned art, and funds to carry out its responsibilities, which included promotion of all the arts in the Beehive State.

The Choir and the Symphony: Utah's Showpieces

Nothing represented Utah's cultural achievements to the world better than its two major performing groups, the Mormon Tabernacle Choir and the Utah Symphony Orchestra. Founded in the 1860s and consisting of nearly 400 voices, the Tabernacle Choir was the official choir of the Mormon Church. In 1929 it began a series of weekly broadcasts over the Columbia Broadcasting System; the program became the oldest continuous coast-to-coast broadcast in America. In the 1940s the choir began recording, both with the Tabernacle organ and with the Philadelphia Symphony Orchestra; "Battle Hymn of the Republic," recorded with the symphony, was a best-seller in 1959 and won the recording industry's Grammy Award. In addition, the choir made a number of national and international tours and performed at the presidential inauguration in Washington in 1969. One Utah music critic wrote

Utah's two most famous cultural organizations in the period since World War II have been the Mormon Tabernacle Choir and the Utah Symphony, shown here during an early joint appearance.

about the choir in 1968: "Theirs is a distinguished history, a promising future." But he chided, "Largely a 'prophet without honor,' they receive greater acclaim outside the Church, state, and community than within."

It remained for the Utah Symphony Orchestra to achieve international fame and at the same time regularly perform for audiences throughout the state. In the early years efforts to bring symphonic music to Utah were frustrating, and various orchestras maintained only sporadic existences. In 1936, however, the Works Progress Administration inaugurated the Utah Music Project. Beginning with only five musicians, the project rapidly expanded, and in 1940 the new Utah Symphony Orchestra gave its first performance in the University of Utah's Kingsbury Hall.

In 1947 Maurice Abravanel was engaged as music director. Told that Utahns were not sophisticated enough to take the full orchestral repertoire, the young but experienced conductor set about to build a superior orchestra and to introduce the people of the state to the best in symphonic music. He succeeded. In 1966 the symphony was honored by Abravanel's native country when the Greek government invited the orchestra to perform at the Athens Festival. En route the orchestra performed in Carnegie Hall in New York and in five European countries. Since 1968 it has toured regularly and its recordings have established a worldwide reputation.

The most important contribution of the Utah Symphony for Utahns was bringing them musical experiences hardly thought possible in earlier years. It has traveled throughout the state more than any other performing group, and it still gives about seventy-five school concerts annually as well as ten or fifteen concerts outside the state. In addition it performs regularly with the University of Utah opera and Broadway musical productions, and it is an integral part of the school's ballet program. One publication on the arts in Utah declared that Abravanel was "the most significant artistic figure of the state's second century," and "almost single-handedly changed the cultural face of Salt Lake City and Utah."

Expansion of Music, Dance, and Theater

Other musical interests also became important. In 1947 musical theater saw a modest revival as traveling groups went throughout the state in connection with the pioneer centennial celebration. The next year the University of Utah inaugurated a summer festival of operas and musicals that continued for eighteen years. In addition, the University of Utah and Brigham Young University regularly sponsored operatic productions, and the Utah Valley Operatic Association, organized in Provo in 1959, presented three productions each season for many years.

First performed in Salt Lake City as part of the 1947 celebration, the musical pageant *Promised Valley* has been frequently repeated. *All Faces West,* a similar production based on the Mormon pioneer experience, played annually in Ogden for about two decades. Other performing groups have become prominent in the state: the Salt Lake Oratorio Society presents Handel's *Messiah* each Christmas and Mendelssohn's *Elijah* each Easter in the Salt Lake Tabernacle; Provo is the home of the Utah Valley Symphony and the Ralph Woodward Chorale. Other various amateur and semiprofessional groups carry on the singing tradition that goes back to pioneer times.

In addition to its performing groups, Utah produced a few outstanding individual performers and composers in the twentieth century, many of whom left the state to find greater opportunities. Perhaps most famous was pianist Grant Johannesen, a graduate of the former McCune School of Music in Salt Lake City and winner of various international recognitions and awards. Emma Lucy Gates Bowen was the first Utah operatic singer to achieve an international reputation. Alexander Schreiner, Mormon Tabernacle organist, received wide acclaim for his performances in Europe in 1967-68. Pianist Reed Nibley enjoyed notable concert success before choosing the academic life as a Brigham Young University professor. Other important Utah performers have included Glade Peterson (tenor), Robert Cundick (organist), and Roy Samuelson (baritone).

Among prominent Mormon composers are Arthur Shepard, who helped establish a professional symphony early in the century and who later became assistant conductor of the Cleveland Symphony; Leroy Robertson, chairman of the music departments at both Brigham Young University and the University of Utah, whose *Trilogy* won the Reichhold Award in 1917 and whose *Book of Mormon Oratorio* is one of the most important Mormon-related compositions; and Crawford Gates, composer of *Promised Valley,* who in 1966 became musical director and conductor of the Beloit (Wisconsin) Symphony Orchestra.

Critics suggest that Utah still has weak spots in its musical life. The Utah Symphony has a limited budget, which makes its salaries the lowest among the nation's thirty major symphony orchestras. There are few programs for assisting Utah musicians to develop their potential, but taken as a whole Utah music has seen significant development in this century.

Dance and Drama

Dance, and particularly ballet, became one of Utah's leading performing arts in the years after World War II. In 1951 William Christensen, founder of the San Francisco Ballet, established the first school of ballet in an American university at the University of Utah. A performing group was soon formed, and in 1963 the Utah Civic Ballet became a professional company. The University of Utah remained its official home, and the Ford Foundation provided $175,000 to enable the company to commence professional operations. In 1968 its name was changed to Ballet West.

Like the Utah Symphony, the Utah Civic Ballet and Ballet West gained fame outside the state but also provided local cultural opportunities. In 1955 Christensen joined forces with Abravanel and the Utah Symphony to produce the first of its annual Christmastime performances of Tschaikovsky's *Nutcracker.* Ballet West had a successful tour of six European countries in 1971, in addition to visiting many parts of Utah and giving sixty-nine school and community concerts.

At the same time ballet was gaining prominence, other forms of dance became increasingly popular in Utah. The University of Utah pioneered in modern dance under the leadership of Elizabeth Hayes. The Ririe-Woodbury Dance Company and Virginia Tanner's Children's Dance Theatre have achieved wide recognition. Utah's dancing children made the covers of *Life* and *Newsweek* magazines in 1953, and this program is now federally funded. In addition, the University of Utah received a $370,000 Ford Foundation Grant to establish a professional company, the first associated with an American university. The Repertory Dance Theatre began its work in 1967. At Brigham Young University, the International Folk Dancers were organized in 1956 by Mary Bee Jensen; in 1964 this group became America's first official representative at European dance festivals and it has toured worldwide ever since.

In the field of drama, the century began with commercial theater still in vogue as the Salt Lake Theater continued to attract nationally known performers. By the 1920s, however, a decline was apparent, possibly because of the competition of the movies, and in 1928 the Salt Lake Theater was sold by the Mormon Church to make way for an office building. Critics decried not only the passing of the theater but also the destruction of an historic landmark. In later years various groups, including the Mormon Church, joined forces to construct a partial replica of the building on the campus of the University of Utah.

With the decline of commercial theater the colleges and universities in the state took over the legitimate stage. By midcentury each major institution had wide-ranging theater programs. In addition, both the University of Utah and Brigham Young University made special efforts to promote and give awards for new plays, especially those written by students. Also noteworthy is the Utah Shakespearean Festival, produced annually since 1961 by Southern Utah State College in Cedar City. The college now has an Elizabethan-style outdoor theater and a national audience and reputation.

Various community groups had formed throughout Utah by the 1970s. In tourist-oriented Park City two competing groups presented old-fashioned melodramas to the summer crowds. In Salt Lake City the Promised Valley Playhouse, owned by the Mormon Church, presented a variety of productions often staged by student performers from the University of Utah and Brigham Young University. In Ogden a Summer Festival of Theater and Arts was produced annually with the cooperation of Weber State College, the Bertha Eccles Community Art Center, and the Chamber of Commerce. And in Logan the old Lyric Theatre was restored by community action in the 1960s to become the home of summer drama activities. There were also such summer enterprises as the Sundance Theater in Provo Canyon and the Sherwood Hills Theater near Logan. In addition, the ambitious amateur drama activity fostered by the Mormon Church kept young Utahns involved in productions of widely varying quality in every community throughout the state.

The Visual Arts

Almost all art critics agree that in the twentieth century Utah has demonstrated a certain degree of backwardness in the visual arts. Some place part of the responsibility on the dominant Mormon Church which, they say, fosters art that is didactic, illustrative, and commemorative in nature as opposed to the imaginative, expressionistic, and impressionist trends in modern art. While many Mormon artists share this view, some still find ways to express their religious feelings through artistic innovation. The Festival of Mormon Arts, sponsored annually by Brigham Young University since 1968, gives many of them an opportunity to show what artistic innovation may say and do for the life of the spirit.

Other factors contributing to Utah's lag in the visual arts reflected the general problems of artists. Patronage was one problem; Utah citizens, already heavily taxed as well as donating their means for religious purposes, did not always respond with enthusiasm to appeals for public support of artists and museums. At least for the first half of the century it seemed that the most talented artists left the state if they did not want to sink into oblivion. Many, such as Mahonri Young and Cyrus Dallin, did just that, and became successful as a result.

Another problem was the lack of adequate exhibition space. By the 1970s there were still only a few centers devoted exclusively to the display of visual arts, including the Salt Lake Art Center, founded in 1933; the Springville Museum of Art, built with the help of the Works Progress Administration in the 1930s; and the Bertha Eccles Community Art Center in Ogden. In addition, the Harris Fine Arts Center on the campus of Brigham Young University and the University of Utah Museum of Fine Arts became two of the finest galleries in the West in the 1960s.

Despite difficulties, twentieth-century Utah has produced some significant artistic talent. Among pioneer painters who continued to contribute in the early statehood years were Dan Weggeland, sometimes called the father of Utah art, and George M. Ottinger. As the nineteenth century ended, Weggeland and Ottinger were urging their students to study in the art centers of Europe. Many followed their advice; the first to go was James T. Harwood, who went to Europe in 1888 and who became head of the Art Department at the University of Utah in 1923. Harwood was especially well known for landscapes, figures, portraits, and etchings. Close behind him was John Hafen, one of several Utahns who was sent to Paris by the Mormon Church to study painting and who was commissioned to paint the murals in the Salt Lake Temple. A third important artist of this generation was Edwin Evans, who also studied in Paris and who became especially famous for his watercolors. Evans was a stimulating teacher who believed that a student could develop his own best form of expression if mechanical and stultifying methods were not imposed upon him. For three years he fought to have such inhibiting teaching methods eliminated from the Utah public schools; he finally succeeded. Other important painters of this generation included John W. Clawson, Lee Green Richards, and Donald Beauregard. A number of women artists, such as Mary Teasdel, Rose Hartwell, and Myra Sawyer, also left Utah to study in Europe.

Perhaps the best-known Utah artists who were active during the first decades of the century were Cyrus E. Dallin and Mahonri M. Young, both of whom were among the Utah artist colony in Paris. Even before he went abroad, Dallin established a reputation as a sculptor; by 1888 he had received the Gold Medal of the American Art Association and a commission to execute the statue of Paul Revere that now stands in Boston's Paul Revere Mall. His best-known works in Utah include the Angel Moroni atop the Salt Lake Temple, Brigham Young Monument on Main Street in Salt Lake City, and *Massasoit,* an Indian statue now in Massachusetts, with a replica at the Utah State Capitol Building. Dallin is especially well known nationally for his Indian statues; in 1975 his heroic-sized bronze, *The Last Arrow* or *Passing of the Buffalo,* sold at auction for $150,000—a record price for an American sculpture.

Mahonri Young, like Dallin, will be best remembered for his sculptures. Outside Utah he is known for such works as *The Man with the Pick* (1912) in the Metropolitan Museum and for *Joe Ganz* (1929), a life-sized figure of the black prize fighter that is in New York's Madison Square Garden. Utahns know him best for the statues of Joseph and Hyrum Smith (1908) on the Salt Lake Temple grounds, the Temple Square Seagull Monument (1913), the This Is the Place Monument (1947), and the Brigham Young statue in the Capitol Rotunda in Washington, D.C. (1949). In addition, Young created life-sized groups of Hopi, Apache, and Navajo Indians. A major collection of his paintings, etchings, and sculptures is housed at Brigham Young University.

In recent years a number of Utah artists have received some recognition outside the state, although it is the general assumption among art critics that there is as yet no major art renaissance in the state. Among the central figures in Utah painting are V. Douglas Snow of the University of Utah, one of the few contemporary artists who has exhibited outside the state and the first major Utah abstractionist; Harrison Groutage of Utah State University, who is nationally recognized for his oils and watercolors; Farrell Collette of Weber State College, who is a prominent illustrator, particularly of wildlife; George Dibble of the University of Utah, whose textbook on watercolors is widely circulated; Gary Smith, formerly of Brigham Young University, whose impressionistic religious paintings promise to add something to the dimensions of Mormon art, as do the works of sculptor Dennis Smith and painter Trevor Southey; Edith Roperson of Salt Lake City, whose works have been described as possessing a "magic realism" in their almost photographic detail; and Alvin Gittins, another University of Utah painter, whose portraits have received considerable attention. Avard Fairbanks has also produced several monumental sculptures.

Literary Arts

In the field of literature Utah lagged behind its achievements in the performing arts, at least as far as the number of writers and poets it produced. One of Utah's most famous and controversial sons was Bernard DeVoto. DeVoto left his native state while he was still a young man; in the 1930s, 1940s, and 1950s he wrote widely in such journals as *Saturday Review* and *Harper's*. In 1948 he won a Pulitzer Prize for his historical narrative, *Across the Wide Missouri*, and in 1953 he won the National Book Award for *The Course of Empire*.

In 1974 *The Uneasy Chair*, a biography of DeVoto, appeared; the book was written by another Utahn, Wallace Stegner, himself a prize-winning author. Although not born in the state, Stegner was schooled here and taught for a time at the University of Utah. His book, *The Gathering of Zion* (1964), is a sympathetic and colorful account of the people who traversed the Mormon Trail. In 1971 he published *Angle of Repose,* the novel that won Stegner the Pulitzer Prize. Most Utah writers of national reputation have used Utah or Mormon themes. Maurine Whipple's *The Giant Joshua* (1941) depicts life in southern Utah in the nineteenth century. Virginia Sorenson's *A Little Lower Than the Angels* (1942) traces the problems of a Mormon woman converted in Nauvoo as she adjusts to the new faith and to the practice of plural marriage. Samuel W. Taylor's *Family Kingdom* (1951) was an historic novel about his own father, excommunicated apostle John W. Taylor, and his plural wives. In his more recent *Nightfall at Nauvoo* (1971), Taylor exercises some latitude in his interpretation of the facts. In spite of the skill and sensitivity of such Utah writers, most critics suggest that the great Mormon novel or the great Utah novel remains to be written.

In the twentieth century Utah also produced a handful of professional historians whose research and writings had a significant impact upon their discipline. Perhaps most widely published of all, LeRoy R. Hafen's specialty is Western American history, especially history of the Rocky Mountains and the mountain men. Leonard J. Arrington's *Great Basin Kingdom* (1957) deals with the economic history of the Mormons in the nineteenth century. Juanita Brooks is widely respected among historians of Western America for her edited works and interpretive writings on John D. Lee, Hosea Stout, and the Mountain Meadows Massacre, while Dale Morgan contributed to the field not only with his biography of Jedediah Smith but also with the editing of many texts pertaining to the mountain men. Fawn M. Brodie won the Knopf Biography Award for her 1945 biography of Joseph Smith, *No Man Knows My History,* but in later years her interests broadened beyond her Mormon-Utah background and her biographies of Thaddeus Stevens, Richard Burton, and Thomas Jefferson showed her to be unusually talented in biographical writing. Equally sensitive and well recognized for their literary style were two biographies by the team of Jack Adamson and Harold Folland; they wrote biographies of Sir Walter Raleigh and Sir Harry Vane the Younger.

Utah poetry was just beginning to come into its own by the 1970s. It was promoted mainly at the universities and through the League of Utah Writers and the Utah State Poetry Society. Generally recognized as among the major Utah poets are May Swenson, who moved to New York; Radcliff Squires, who accepted a teaching position in Michigan; Brewster Ghiselin of the University of Utah; Clinton Larson of Brigham Young University; and Robert Pack Browning. Carol Lynn Pearson and Emma Lou Thayne have captured much of the Mormon spirit in their writing. Clarice Short has also achieved distinction for her poetry.

The Mass Media

In tapping the cultural, recreational, educational, and other potential of the mass media, Utah in the twentieth century has followed national patterns. The Salt Lake *Tribune* surpassed the Mormon Church-owned *Deseret News* in statewide circulation early in the century, and both owed their economic viability in the post-World War II generation in part to combining their printing, advertising, and circulation operations in 1952 into the Newspaper Agency Corporation. The Ogden *Standard-Examiner,* Provo *Daily Herald,* and Logan *Herald Journal* were the only other Utah daily papers to survive the impact of television and rising costs.

Television, the brainchild of Utah-born Philo T. Farnsworth, came to the state in 1948 when KTVT went on the air in Salt Lake City. Other stations followed, including educational channels at the University of Utah and at Brigham Young University. Stereophonic and FM broadcasting added cultural dimensions to radio's outreach. Thanks to the technology of the space age, no mountain hut or desert hogan in Utah is now inaccessible to the messages of the electronic media.

Conclusion

The contribution of Utah to the arts, as well as its support and enthusiasm for various artistic forms, was somewhat spotty in the twentieth century. Support for the arts was difficult to come by, especially in the early years, but after World War II various factors combined to increase the understanding of the arts among the people of the state: legislative appropriations for state-supported activities increased; Maurice Abravanel and the Utah Symphony brought symphonic music to every community; dance groups widened their performances and gave lessons in the high schools; and Utah's institutions of higher learning, especially its three universities, became important centers for fostering all the arts. It took time and considerable effort, but by the 1970s the people of Utah enjoyed cultural opportunities unusual among the thinly populated states of the mountain west.

The twentieth-century record is more solid in education. The federal government's *Digest of Educational Statistics for 1971* reported that there were only three states in the nation with lower illiteracy rates, and Utah had the lowest portion of adult population with less than five years of school. It was number eight in the nation in terms of median school years completed, number one in percent completing high school, and number three in percent of college graduates. On the other hand, a survey by the State Board of

Education found that on advanced placement examinations Utah's high school students ranked below national norms, although the gap narrowed significantly between 1966 and 1970. Utah scores on the American College Tests were below the national mean in 1965-66 but above it in every category by 1970.

Chapter 32
Bibliographical Essay

The standard general history of education is John C. Moffitt, *The History of Public Education in Utah* (1946), but it is now outdated; most of Moffitt's historical insights relate to the nineteenth century. See also Moffitt, *A History of Public Education in Provo, Utah* (1944). Reuben D. Law, *The Utah School System: Its Organization and Administration* (1952) provides a general historical summary, but it is filled with apologia that is almost religious in tone. Moffit, *A Century of Service 1860-1960* (1960), is a history of the Utah Education Association. E. T. Demars, ed., *Utah School Organization and Administration* (1964), is light on history but provides a much better discussion of the philosophy and administration of education than do either Moffitt or Law. A very important work for the first part of the century is the United States Department of the Interior *Survey of Education in Utah* (1926), a thorough 510-page study conducted by the United States Commissioner of Education. There is no adequate book on the history of Mormon education, but M. Lynn Bennion, *Mormonism and Education* (1939), provides a beginning.

The history of Utah State University to 1938 may be found in Joel E. Ricks, *The Utah State Agricultural College: A History of Fifty Years, 1888-1938* (1938), but a new history of the institution is needed. More interpretive in nature is Ralph V. Chamberlin, *The University of Utah: A History of Its First Hundred Years, 1850-1950* (1960). See also LeRoy E. Cowles, *The University of Utah and World War II* (1959). *Brigham Young University: The First One Hundred Years* (1975-1976), four volumes, is by a former president of the institution, Ernest L. Wilkinson.

A number of theses and dissertations provide further historical insight into Utah education. These include James R. Clark, "Church and State Relationships in Education in Utah" (Ed.D. dissertation, Utah State University, 1958), which is a particularly important study on this topic, although chronologically it extends only into the first few decades of the twentieth century; Jeffrey N. Eastmond, "A Study of the Trends in Public School Finance in the United States with Particular Reference to the State of Utah" (master's thesis, Brigham Young University, 1948); Ray L. DeBoer, "A Historical Study of Mormon Education and the Influence of its Philosophy on Public Education in Utah" (Ph.D. dissertation, University of Denver, 1951); John W. Fitzgerald, "One Hundred Years of Education in a Utah Community" (Ed.D. dissertation, Stanford University, 1958); Joseph J. Jeppson, "The Secularization of the University of Utah to 1920" (Ph.D. dissertation, University of California at Berkeley, 1973).

Among other useful reports, articles, and surveys are the biennial reports of the State Superintendent of Public Instruction (more recently titled *Utah School Report*), which summarize yearly activities and occasionally provide valuable historic insights. The annual reports of the Utah State Board of Higher Education (since 1969) also provide periodic reviews of policy and problems. The *Utah Educational Review* seldom publishes historical material, but its pages throw light on the problems and activities of its sponsor, the Utah Education Association. See also Utah State Board of Education, *Historical Perspectives of Major Educational Changes in Utah, 1847-1966* (1966); John C. Evans, Jr., *Utah School Crisis, 1963* (1963), a diary-style account of the 1963 teacher crisis; Utah State Board of Education, *How Good Are Utah Public Schools?* (1971); Utah Educational Survey Committee, *Public Education in Utah: The Report of the Fact-Finding Body Appointed in 1939 by the Governor of the State of Utah* (1939).

There is no general historical survey of Utah arts and artists. Material for this chapter came from consultation with Utah art teachers, as well as from printed sources. *Report on the Fine Arts in Utah 1968* (study made under a grant from the National Endowment for the Arts, directed by the Utah State Institute of Fine Arts, conducted by the Bureau of Economic and Business Research, University of Utah, 1968), briefly discusses the history and status of all the arts in Utah. James L. Haseltine, *100 Years of Utah Painting* (1965), is a well written and illustrated survey of major Utah painters and the best single source available. Other sources on the visual arts include Monte B. DeGraw, "A Study of Representative Examples of Art Works Fostered by the Mormon Church with an Analysis of the Aesthetic Value of These Works" (master's thesis, Brigham Young University, 1959); Dale T. Fletcher, "Art and Belief: A Group Exhibition," *Dialogue: A Journal of Mormon Thought,* Spring 1967; James L. Haseltine, "Mormons and the Visual Arts," *Dialogue,* Summer 1966; Wayne K. Hinton, "A Biographical History of Mahonri M. Young, A Western American Artist" (Ph.D. dissertation, Brigham Young University, 1974);

Kaysville Art Club, *Pioneers of Utah Art* (1968); Thomas A. Leek, "A Circumspection of Ten Formulators of Early Utah Art History" (master's thesis, Brigham Young University, 1961); Utah Centennial Commission, Arts Division, *Final Report of Arts Division, Utah Centennial Commission, September 15, 1947,* which contains brief biographical sketches of artists whose works were exhibited in the centennial touring art shows; Lorin F. Wheelwright and Lael J. Woodbury, eds., *Mormon Arts* (1972), Vol. I, which was published in connection with the first annual Festival of Mormon Arts on the Brigham Young University campus; Maida Rust Winters, "Art and the Church," *Dialogue,* Autumn 1968; Peter and Marie Myer, "New Directions in Mormon Art," *Sunstone,* Spring 1977; Rell G. Francis, *Cyrus E. Dallin: Let Justice Be Done* (1976).

Additional insights into some aspects of music may be found in Maurice Abravanel, "The Utah Symphony Orchestra: An Orchestra in the Deep Interior," in Henry Swoboda, ed., *The American Symphony Orchestra* (n.d.); Lowell M. Durham, "On Mormon Music and Musicians," *Dialogue,* Summer 1968; Herald Gregory, "Next Time They Should Stay Longer," *Music Journal,* April 1967; Hope Stoddard, "Music in Utah," *International Musician,* April 1955; and Donald George Schaefer, "Contributions of the McCune School of Music and Art to Music Education in Utah, 1917-1957" (master's thesis, Brigham Young University, 1962). Some interesting articles on miscellaneous aspects of Utah culture are Jack Anderson, "There's More Than Sand and Sagebrush Here," *Dance Magazine,* August 1967; Leonard J. Arrington, "The Intellectual Tradition of Mormon Utah," *Proceedings of the Utah Academy of Sciences, Arts, and Letters* (1968); and Samuel W. Taylor, "Peculiar People, Positive Thinkers, and the Prospect of Mormon Literature," *Dialogue,* Summer 1967.

Chapter 33
Religion in
Twentieth-century Utah

James B. Allen

The history of organized religion in twentieth-century Utah reflects many of the patterns established in earlier years, as well
as certain new elements. It was only natural that The Church of
Jesus Christ of Latter-day Saints (Mormon) should remain the
dominant faith and that some of the stresses between Mormons
and other missionary-minded Christians should continue, at least
for a time. By midcentury, however, most of the old antagonisms
seemed to have disappeared. Missionary zeal remained, but it was
generally tempered with a spirit of amity and good will.

A few statistics reveal the unique pattern of religious activity in
Utah. Since early in the century about three-fourths of Utah's
population have professed church membership, and nine out of ten
of these have been members of the Mormon Church. (See Table
H, pp. 692–93. Estimates of denominational strength vary widely;
numbers used in this chapter are based on this table.) This suggests that a high birth rate and local proselyting have maintained
the Mormon preponderance, despite the heavy influx of non-Mormons into Utah mining and industrial centers, especially in connection with two world wars and the defense buildup of the 1950s.

The state's second most prominent denomination has been the
Roman Catholic Church, which claimed approximately 2.5 percent of the total population in 1914 and 4.4 percent in 1975. Catholics constitute the major non-Mormon group in the Salt Lake,
Ogden, Oquirrh, Provo, and Price regions. The third largest religious body in the early years was the Greek Orthodox Church,
which was 1.3 percent of the total population on the eve of World
War I. Most of these were Greek and Southern Slav immigrants

associated with the mines and smelters of Salt Lake Valley and Carbon County. By 1975 the Greek Orthodox community constituted less than .6 percent of all Utahns, and several congregations made the Baptist Church the third largest denomination, with about .7 percent. The major Protestant faiths have been Baptist, Methodist, Presbyterian, Congregational, Episcopal, and Lutheran, but none has ever embraced one percent of the state population. Other religious groups that have maintained congregations include Jews, Seventh-day Adventists, Church of Christ, Disciples of Christ, Jehovah's Witnesses, Reorganized Latter Day Saints, Unitarians, and Protestant fundamentalists. Buddhist congregations have been formed among Utah's Japanese.

Anti-Mormon Evangelism

In spite of their relatively small numbers, the major non-Mormon groups have made significant contributions to the state. Some of their energy, particularly in the early part of the century, went into efforts to combat the dominant influence of the Mormon Church. This evangelistic zeal led to the establishment of denominational academies in the nineteenth century and was one of the factors in the founding of Westminster College in Salt Lake City. In the 1920s James E. Clark, a Westminster faculty member, expressed the spirit of those who felt themselves still battling against religious odds in Utah when he published *An Appealing Missionary Opportunity.* In a state with 500,000 population, the pamphlet declared, there were only 10,000 Christians; it urged Presbyterians, especially, "to supply the pressing need of one of the most difficult mission fields in the United States." Other denominations also felt a continuing urge to change the religious balance, and as late as the 1940s appeals by Catholics for financial aid in Utah took on a similar tone. A nationally distributed pamphlet entitled *A Foreign Mission Close to Home* declared, "Perhaps in no other place in the United States is the need for expanded Catholic activity so pressing as in Utah." Such undertakings revealed the natural frustrations faced by minority religious groups in a region so overwhelmingly dominated by one church.

Evangelistic efforts met with only limited success, even though many Protestant churches continued to demonstrate a certain missionary zeal. In 1951 a survey of Protestant evangelism in Utah reported that the Baptists were converting some forty to sixty Mormons each year, but the executive secretary of the American Baptist Home Mission Society wrote, "The results are not spectacular and I am sure that we are not going to wipe out the Mormon empire within the foreseeable future." Other churches reported similar discouragement with respect to missionary work, but they were optimists with regard to their own denominational activities. Both the Methodist Church and the Board of American Missions of the United Lutheran Church of America, for example, said that they no longer conducted missions in Utah. The most positive comment came from the field representative of the Presbyterian Church of the United States, Dr. A. Walton Roth, who declared that even though its numbers were small his church was receiving about four times as many members from the Mormon Church as it was losing to them.

In addition to this denominational evangelism, at least two independent missions began intensive efforts to convert the Mormons in the twentieth century. The first was the Utah Gospel Mission, founded in 1900 by the Reverend John D. Nutting, with headquarters in Cleveland, Ohio. This society conducted door-to-door visits, distributed literature, and held evangelistic meetings. The other group was the Utah Christian Mission, Inc., of Phoenix, Arizona. Founded about midcentury by the Reverend Harry A. McGinney, this mission distributed evangelistic Christian literature; its representatives could be seen in Salt Lake City each April and October passing out tracts to the Mormons attending their semiannual conferences.

Protestant Activities

Among Protestant churches, the early years of the century saw at least two major shifts in emphasis. One was the decline in number of church schools. Begun as an effort to compete with Mormon hegemony as well as to provide adequate elementary and secondary training in pioneer Utah, these schools were unable to compete with the growing public schools by 1900, and most of them were closed soon after that.

A second change was a decline in the number of individual congregations, together with a shift in the distribution pattern of Protestants. This was largely due to comity agreements that reflected a general trend among Protestant churches in early twentieth-century America. Comity agreements sought to build one church in a community with enough members to support it adequately rather than to establish several smaller competing congregations. Such agreements were voluntary, but Utah's major Protestant groups generally respected the recommendations of the interdenominational comity committees. By 1915 they were actively cooperating with each other, and the result was fewer local churches but larger membership and better facilities in each congregation. Such agreements did not affect the areas of population concentration around Salt Lake City and Ogden.

Comity agreements led to some realignment in membership. The Congregational Church in Park City, for example, was closed early in the century. By the 1930s the Presbyterians dominated the Protestant group in the central Utah valleys after the Methodists voluntarily moved out. In 1937 a conference in Salt Lake City was attended by representatives from the Methodist, Presbyterian, Baptist, Disciples of Christ, Episcopal, and Congregational churches, and it resulted in the strengthening of comity agreements throughout the state. In later years these patterns began to change again as the major denominations all grew in numbers.

The story of the Baptists in Utah is one illustration of the influence of the comity movement. At the beginning of the century most Baptists were located in Salt Lake City and Ogden, although there were a number of small churches and missions in various rural areas. The quest for membership, however, met with practically no success, and in the midthirties the last circuit mission was closed. In the meantime comity agreements resulted in the removal of all Baptist churches from much of the state by 1940, leaving only Ogden, Salt Lake City, and southeastern Utah near Moab as centers of Baptist activity; in southeastern Utah the Baptists claimed 100 percent of the non-Mormon population. In that same year, however, an Episcopal Indian Mission was established at Bluff; the Indian Mission soon did away with the Baptist hegemony. In addition, Baptists soon began to appear again in other parts of the state, particularly in Carbon County. In 1926 the Baptist Church was only the sixth largest Protestant denomination, but it climbed to first place by 1960, partly as a result of the movement of Southern workers into the mining, missile, and other defense industries. In 1975 there were some 8,400 Baptists in Utah.

Like the Baptists, the Methodists also continued their early attempt to convert Mormons, and in the first years of the twentieth century they occasionally established schools and a number of rural churches. By 1930, however, comity arrangements led the Methodists to move out of Provo and central Utah and to increase their numbers in Park City and in other railroad and mining communities. Methodist membership was estimated in 1975 at 3,700.

The Presbyterian Church claimed over 6,000 members in 1969, the centennial year of Presbyterianism in Utah; the Lyon survey (Table H) lists its membership as 4,928 in 1975. Most of its members have been located in Salt Lake City and Ogden, and one of its major contributions to the state has been the continuing operation of two institutions of learning, Wasatch Academy in Mt. Pleasant and Westminster College in Salt Lake City.

Wasatch Academy had its beginning in 1875 as a mission school. Despite initial Mormon opposition, it soon became an important secondary school in Sanpete County. Today it is a boarding school serving not only Presbyterians, but also other students.

In 1911 Westminster College was founded, offering students two years of college training. The following year it also began to offer high school work when the old Collegiate Institute was closed and its functions were taken over by the new college. In 1944, after weathering serious financial problems in connection with World War II, it became a senior college, and in subsequent years enrollment steadily increased. Symbolic of the new feeling of good will between the Presbyterians and the Mormons was the fact that for a time, until the mid 1950s, the Mormon Church gave modest annual grants to Westminster College in recognition of the fact that a number of Mormon students were enrolled.

The work of the Episcopal Church in the early twentieth century was also in part a continuation of early efforts in mission and educational activity. Outside Salt Lake City its most significant growth was in the Uinta Basin. In the late nineteenth century the Federal Government had allocated Indian reservations to various churches for religious activity, and in 1896 the Episcopalians opened a school near Roosevelt. When the Uinta Basin was opened for white settlement in 1905, Episcopal missions were established in Duchesne, Myton, and Roosevelt. Like other denominations, however, the Episcopal Church gave up most of its schools early in the century as the public school system grew.

A particularly noteworthy contribution of the Episcopalians to Utah was the founding and operation of St. Mark's Hospital in Salt Lake City. When established in 1872 it was the first hospital between Denver and San Francisco. Until 1912 it also served as the Salt Lake County hospital. Its activities were substantially expanded in 1925 when the Intermountain Unit of the Shriner's Hospital for Crippled Children was located within its walls; this facility moved to its own location in 1951. From 1894 until 1970 St. Mark's Hospital operated a School of Nursing, which then was succeeded by the St. Mark's Hospital School of Baccalaureate Nursing of Westminster College, a cooperative venture between St. Mark's Hospital and the college. In 1973 the hospital moved into a new fifteen-million-dollar facility in southeastern Salt Lake City. Episcopal membership in Utah in 1975 was estimated at 4,100.

The Roman Catholic Church

The Catholic Church remained the largest non-Mormon faith through the twentieth century with over 53,000 members in Utah in 1975. By then six different bishops had headed the Salt Lake diocese, and in each case they were able to create and maintain a spirit of good will with the rest of the community and to make important progress for the church.

At the turn of the century Bishop Lawrence Scanlan was a well-known Utahn. He had come to Salt Lake City in 1873 and was particularly active in acquiring property, promoting Catholic education and mission work, and directing a building program. A young Irish priest when he first arrived, his early activities led him into mining camps as well as into other parts of Utah. He cultivated and maintained friendly relations with the heads of other churches. Under his direction the magnificent Cathedral of St. Mary Magdalen was completed, and on Easter Sunday in April 1908 he conducted the first Solemn Pontifical Mass in the basement of the new structure. The building was dedicated in 1909.

Scanlan was succeeded in 1915 by Bishop Joseph M. Glass. Under his direction the cathedral received a major renovation and was rechristened as the Cathedral of the Madeleine. Glass devoted time and energy to the establishment and improvement of Catholic schools in Utah, and he sent a number of Utah students to seminaries to study for the priesthood. He was instrumental in enlarging the Kearns St. Anne's Orphanage and in establishing a center in Salt Lake City for self-supporting Catholic girls. Six new parishes were created in the diocese (which included Utah and Nevada), and the number of priests was increased from seventeen to forty; the growth of the church in southern Utah was especially pronounced.

After the death of Glass in 1926, the Right Reverend John J. Mitty became the third bishop of the Salt Lake Diocese. His contributions included the establishment of a mission among the Mexican people and the broadening of educational opportunities. Religious vacation schools were established, and weekly radio broadcasts of Catholic sermons and services were instituted.

Mitty was succeeded in 1932 by Bishop James E. Kearny, who had the difficult task of guiding the Utah church through some of the worst years of the Great Depression. He succeeded in dedicating several new chapels and in increasing Catholic membership in Salt Lake City and in some of Utah's mining communities. The highlight of his Utah service was the retirement of the debt on the

Cathedral of the Madeleine; the edifice was consecrated on November 28, 1936.

On August 6, 1937, the Most Reverend Duane G. Hunt was appointed Bishop of Salt Lake—only the eleventh convert in America to be elevated to the Episcopacy. His first assignment as a new priest in 1920 was in Utah, and he spent his entire career in this state. From their inception in 1927 he had been giving the Catholic radio addresses over KSL radio in Salt Lake City, and he continued to do so on a regular basis until 1952. One of Hunt's most important achievements was his part in the establishment in 1947 of the Trappist monastery near Huntsville. That year thirty-four monks took up their residence in Quonset huts, and within ten years the monastery accommodated sixteen priests and forty-four lay brothers who were preparing either for the priesthood or for the Trappist brotherhood.

Hunt's policy of expanding the diocese through missionary effort began in earnest in 1938 when the Paulist Fathers, an order of missionary priests, accepted the responsibility for the Uinta Basin parish with headquarters at Vernal. Over the years new parishes were opened in other areas, and regular priests often traveled long distances to offer Mass to scattered Catholics. In the 1940s, for example, Father Blase Schumaker used his skills as a pilot to offer Mass in the missions of the Uinta Basin and of northwestern Colorado. A number of orders of nuns came to Utah for missionary and education work, including the Missionary Sisters, with convents in Salt Lake City, Ogden, and Bingham; the Sisters of St. Francis of Perpetual Adoration, with a convent in Provo; the Sisters of the Atonement, with convents at Bingham, Draggerton, and Roosevelt; the Carmelite Sisters in Salt Lake County; and the Sisters of the Holy Family, who worked in Tooele and Helper.

Hunt died in 1960 and was succeeded by Bishop Joseph Lennox Federal, who had come to Utah in 1951 as auxiliary bishop of Salt Lake. Under Federal's guidance the Utah Catholic Church shifted its emphasis toward internal growth and organizational solidarity. Stimulated by the Second Vatican Council (1962-65), Federal's main contributions were to implement the decrees of that council in Utah and to cope with the rapidly changing patterns and problems of American life in the 1960s and 1970s. Greater participation in church affairs by laity was achieved, and the church also began to involve itself more in civic affairs. Of special significance to the broadening of lay participation was the ordination on December 27, 1976, of fourteen married men to the permanent diaconate, which empowered them to administer baptisms, perform marriages, preach, distribute communion, and teach the Catholic faith. The diaconate as a permanent office had been restored in the United States in 1968, but the new deacons were the first to be ordained in Utah.

One of the major concerns of the Catholic Church in twentieth-century Utah was the support of Catholic education, continuing a tradition established in the territorial years. In 1967 the church operated eleven parochial grade schools and five high schools, all locally financed. One such institution was the Cathedral of the Madeleine Grade School in Salt Lake City, established in 1921. The construction of a new building, undertaken in 1947, marked the first time in Salt Lake City history that the laity had been called upon to contribute directly to the building of a Catholic school. Other elementary schools founded since 1900 included four in Salt Lake City and one each in Price, Provo, Bountiful, Murray, and Kearns. Rising costs and changing educational patterns adversely affected parochial education in Utah as it did elsewhere in the nation, and by the end of the 1960s a number of Catholic schools in the state had been forced to close.

The Catholics also operated two colleges in Salt Lake City. All Hallows, opened in 1889, served as a college for young men until it was closed in 1918. Of longer duration was St. Mary-of-the-Wasatch, founded in 1875 by the Sisters of the Holy Cross as a secondary school. It was considered to be the "cradle of Catholic education in Utah," serving young women from local areas and out-of-town boarding students. The College and Academy of St. Mary-of-the-Wasatch was opened as a junior college in 1925 and soon became an accredited four-year institution. In 1959, however, the collegiate program was discontinued, and in 1970 the high school was closed.

In addition to the combined secular and religious programs offered in its own schools, the Catholic Church took advantage of Utah's released time law to provide weekday religious education for Catholic students who were enrolled in public high schools. There were similar concerns at the college level, and in 1920 the first Newman Club in Utah was established at the University of Utah. Later a building was purchased for the Newman Center, which provides social opportunities as well as religious services, instruction, and counseling. Newman Centers were dedicated at Utah State University in 1961 and at Weber State College in 1974.

Another important Catholic contribution was the continued support for the operation of two Utah hospitals, St. Benedict's in Ogden and Holy Cross in Salt Lake City. With partially local funding St. Benedict's was finished and dedicated in 1946; ground was broken for new facilities in 1974. Holy Cross Hospital, founded in 1875, grew in the twentieth century to become a 353-bed facility with both research and care facilities. Until 1973 it also conducted an accredited school of nursing. At the dedication of a new wing in 1960 a hospital consultant from New York complimented both Holy Cross Hospital and the Utah community:

Your recognition of the nonpartisan nature of disease has given mute evidence to the fact that there is no such thing as Catholic Cataracts, Mormon Malignancy, or Jewish Jaundice. You have typified so ably the American way, which affords us all the inalienable right to help our neighbor.

Jewish Activities

The major non-Christian religion in Utah has been Judaism. Relationships between Jewish leaders and the Mormon community were cordial from the early territorial days, so the Mormons supported construction of the first synagogue in the state. On August 13, 1903, Mormon President Joseph F. Smith spoke at the laying of the cornerstone of the synagogue of Congregation Montefiore; that same year the Mormon Church donated $650 toward the cost of the synagogue.

At the turn of the century there were actually two competing congregations among the Jews in Utah: the orthodox B'nai Israel Congregation and the more liberal Congregation Montefiore. By 1915 another split occurred within the liberal group when differences of opinion over the seating of women and over other procedural matters caused some fifty families to form their own group, the Congregation Sharey Tzedek. The new congregation required the men to sit in the main hall and the women to sit in the gallery during worship services, thus moving toward a more orthodox ritual. With little youth appeal, however, the new congregation did not last.

A spirit akin to Zionism linked prominent Utah and Eastern Jews in 1910 in sponsoring the agricultural colony of Clarion. Established near Gunnison as a place to resettle Jewish immigrants from urban ghettos in the eastern states, the colony numbered fifty-two families at its peak in 1913. Meager agricultural skills, underfunding, undependable water supplies, and uncooperative neighbors contributed to the project's failure. By 1915 most of the colonists had left. Benjamin Brown, a founder of the Utah Poultry Producers Cooperative Association, and Maurice Warshaw, founder of two retail market chains, were Clarion pioneers who later became substantial contributors to Utah's growth.

Utah's Jews were scattered throughout the state, but the major groups were in Salt Lake City and Ogden. Expressive of the concern that Jewish young people remain within the faith was the 1923 purchase of the Enos A. Wall home in Salt Lake City for a religious and cultural center to be known as the Covenant House. Under the direction of Rabbi E. M. Burnstein, who arrived to serve Congregation Montefiore in 1924, the Covenant House sponsored clubs, study groups, and an extensive social program. One social program was the Maimonides Club, which lasted until 1933. Later other groups were organized at the University of Utah and at other places where sufficient numbers of Jewish youth were located.

The years following World War II saw increased efforts at cooperation between the Salt Lake City B'nai Israel and Montefiore congregations. The Jewish Community Center, dedicated in 1959, was a joint venture between the two. By 1969 the congregations decided to combine their religious education for children, and the new United Jewish Religious School graduated its first class in 1971. All this was precursory to an even more important merger: the gradual unification of the two congregations. Under the direction of Rabbi Abner Bergman, the new Congregation Kol Ami was formed in the early 1970s.

The Mormon Church

The activities of The Church of Jesus Christ of Latter-day Saints naturally continued to dominate Utah religious life. Responding to the secular challenges of the modern world, the church augmented its programs for individuals and families while moving away from religious and economic practices that had brought it into collision with nineteenth-century America. The Mormon people became much more a part of the larger community, no longer culturally or economically isolated from the rest of the nation.

One of several fundamental adjustments that the church was making at the beginning of the twentieth century was the final abandonment of plural marriage. Even though the Woodruff Manifesto of 1890 had presumably brought the practice of polygamy to an end, evidence presented at the Reed Smoot hearings in the United States Senate and elsewhere showed that the performing of such marriages continued on a limited basis until 1904. In that year an official statement by President Joseph F. Smith declared that anyone who performed or entered into such a marriage would henceforth be excommunicated. The action served to calm the tide of criticism against the church, although it did not convince all church members; two apostles who refused to support the declaration were dropped from their positions, and one was subsequently excommunicated. Both publicly and privately the church vigorously pursued its new policy, although various splinter groups have continued the practice to the present.

The Mormon Church also made substantial economic adjustments. In 1898 it had a debt of some $1,125,000 due to the confiscation of church property during the antipolygamy campaign and due to other problems incident to the depression of the 1890s. In that year the income of the church was only $600,000, barely enough to cover administrative costs. Increased emphasis on the payment of tithing together with improvement in other financial resources resulted in the complete liquidation of the debt by 1907. At the same time the church was reevaluating its general economic policy. Instead of promoting such ventures as the united orders and the cooperative merchandising companies of the nineteenth century, it began to invest in business enterprises that were based more solidly on the philosophy of private enterprise and profit-making. Thus Mormon economic development reflected more fully the economic patterns of the rest of the nation.

The church encountered other problems and controversies, since it was inevitable that the dominant religion of the state should become involved in important political and social issues. Although ostensibly above partisan politics, the Mormon hierarchy could not effectively prevent members and leaders from expressing personal opinions on issues about which they felt deeply. Moreover, church leaders felt obliged to speak out on what were considered to be moral issues, such as prohibition and liquor-by-the-drink. The church supported prohibition, for example, and came out officially against its repeal in 1932. It opposed liquor-by-the-drink legislation in Utah, supported a Sunday closing law in the state, and came out against any legislation dealing with the legalization of abortion. Even when the church involved itself in such issues the action was not always decisive. National repeal of prohibition was approved by the Utah legislature against the publicly announced wishes of Mormon leaders. Church opposition, however, may have helped defeat the Equal Rights Amendment in the 1977 legislature.

Almost as if it were intentional, the activities of some Mormon leaders in the twentieth century demonstrated that they could hold opposite political views and still maintain their basic faith as well as their leadership positions. In 1919, for example, Apostle Reed Smoot, Presiding Bishop Charles W. Nibley, and at least two other general authorities were outspoken critics of the League of Nations; the president of the church, Heber J. Grant, and Apostle George F. Richards, just released as European Mission president, and other leaders were equally public in their support of it. In the 1930s Grant was an outspoken critic of the New Deal, as was his counselor J. Reuben Clark, Jr.; Brigham H. Roberts, a member of the First Council of the Seventy, was one of its most ardent defenders. In the 1950s Clark was an outspoken critic of the United Nations while David O. McKay, then president of the church, said that there was at least enough good in it to justify its existence. And in the 1960s Hugh B. Brown, a member of the church's First Presidency, was an active participant in the Democratic Party and praised the various federal welfare and antipoverty programs of the so-called Great Society while Republican Ezra Taft Benson, a Mormon apostle and Secretary of Agriculture under Dwight D. Eisenhower, pubicly condemned such programs. In each case some Utah Mormons saw the official endorsement of the church in statements of their favorite leaders, but these assumptions were mistaken for political pluralism.

Perhaps the most frustrating public dilemma faced by the church since World War II has been the issue of race relations. As the Black revolution in America unfolded, Mormon leaders joined with other groups in publicly upholding the principle that all races should have full constitutional rights and they urged church members to "do their part as citizens to see that these rights are held inviolate." But the church continued its own policy of withholding the priesthood from members of the Negro race, a practice that elicited widespread criticism. In the late 1960s protest rallies were held in Salt Lake City, delegates from civil rights groups (including many Blacks) sought audiences with church leaders, Brigham Young University athletic teams were picketed on road trips, and a few schools even severed athletic relations with Brigham Young University. Church leaders pointed to many opportunities for Blacks within the church, but they maintained that the priesthood policy could not be changed without direct revelation, and that people who did not accept the Mormon faith had no right to attempt to dictate policy to the church.[1] In 1974 an NAACP suit was

---

[1] A revelation announced by church President Spencer W. Kimball in 1978 extended priesthood eligibility to all races.

filed alleging only priesthood holders could become patrol leaders in Mormon Boy Scout troops. When the church clarified that these positions were open to all boys, the suit was dropped.

All these events, both political and social, were significant in the history of twentieth-century Utah, for they demonstrated how widely the policies and activities of the Mormon Church still influenced all aspects of society. In spite of such strains, its members maintained a high degree of religious solidarity in other matters and thus continued to promote the major programs of the church throughout the state.

One of those programs was education, and the twentieth century brought significant changes in this area. In the pioneer generations the church had established many academies or secondary schools. Like other groups, however, the Mormons became increasingly conscious of the expensive duplication of effort as public high schools increased in number. By the mid 1920s all Mormon academies in Utah had been discontinued or had been transferred to the state. In 1912 a weekday religious education program known as the seminary system was inaugurated to replace the academies, and within a few years the seminary program spread to nearly every high school in the state. For college students the church began in 1926 to establish institutes of religion adjacent to colleges and universities. Professionally trained teachers were employed in both seminaries and institutes in an effort to ensure that classes compared academically with those of the adjacent institutions; but the ultimate purpose was to build and maintain the faith of Mormon students in the face of secular challenges of the modern world.

Perhaps the most significant development in the religious activity of college-age Utah Mormons was the 1956 beginning of student wards and stakes. In that year students at Brigham Young University were organized into a stake with twelve wards designed to give them opportunity for religious development and training. By 1976 there were twelve stakes and 130 wards—now designated as branches—on the Brigham Young University campus alone, and similar organizations have been established at each of the other colleges in the state.

The needs of modern life brought further changes within the Mormon Church, one of the most dramatic being the Church Welfare Program. Organized in 1936 to provide emergency relief for families affected by the Great Depression, the welfare program soon became a permanent program of economic aid to needy church members. In Utah its activities were soon seen in scores of welfare farms, canning plants, and storage facilities that were operated by donated labor and in Deseret Industries, which provided work for needy people in the repair and sale of various used consumer goods.

It was inevitable that the vast operations of the welfare program should raise questions in Utah about the propriety of welfare farms being tax-free. Mormon leaders argued that, far from raising taxes, these farms and other welfare activities of the church kept so many people off public welfare rolls that they actually tended to keep public expenditures, and hence state taxes, down. Support for this position was given in September 1972, when the church released comprehensive figures on its welfare expenditures. These were total figures, but a major share of the expenditures were within Utah. Total assistance in cash or commodities amounted in 1971 to $17,722,800, in addition to 3,990,515 hours of donated labor for welfare purposes. The program also provided 1,480,000 hours of work for the handicapped.

As the twentieth century progressed, the church saw the need to expand its social services beyond the traditional bounds of charity and self-help. In 1905 it opened the LDS Hospital in Salt Lake City, and eventually this hospital established a fully accredited school of nursing. Beginning in the late 1940s, the church took over several local Utah hospitals that were financially floundering. With the advantage of a unified administrative system, it was able to maintain the hospitals and to improve the quality of professional services that they rendered. By the 1970s the church operated some fifteen hospitals in Utah, Idaho, and Wyoming; outstanding among them was the Primary Children's Hospital, which became the major pediatric center in Utah. In 1971 all Church hospitals, as well as a variety of other services, were combined under the new Health Services Corporation. In 1974, however, the expanding cost of operating a local hospital system led Mormon leaders to turn over all church hospitals to a private, nonprofit corporation. The Health Services Corporation continued to provide other health-related programs for Mormons in Utah and elsewhere.

Early in the twentieth century the church also began to institutionalize its response to other social needs and to have an impact on state programs. It was partly under the prodding of Amy Brown Lyman, general secretary of the Relief Society, that the state began its public welfare department and began to match federal welfare grants. Within the church the Relief Society began during World War I to conduct its welfare activities on a casework system. It was not until 1969, however, that the social welfare activities of the church were brought together under one administrative head. That year a Social Services Department was established to provide help to local church leaders in connection with psychiatric and psychological needs, youth guidance, vocational and marriage counseling, rehabilitating the handicapped, Indian placement programs, and the adoption of children of unwed mothers. In addition, the Social Services Department worked with drug abuse, alcoholism, divorce, and crime and continued a previously experimental program of assisting Mormons in prison.

Such responses to broad social needs were only extensions of the concerns for the quality of Mormon life that had already produced far-reaching augmentation of the religious programs of the church. Beginning in about 1908, for example, a general priesthood reform movement resulted in a more consistent, well-planned training program for teenage boys. In 1911 the Boy Scout program was officially adopted, and shortly thereafter a parallel program was developed for girls. The Mutual Improvement Association, founded in Brigham Young's day, was expanded to include sports, drama, dancing, homemaking for girls, and various other cultural activities. The Primary Association provided weekday religious instruction for children under the age of twelve, and the Deseret Sunday School Union prepared systematic courses of study for all ages. The Women's Relief Society provided special training in theology, homemaking, and various cultural pursuits. Publications which in the nineteenth century had borne the impress of their editors gave way to such organizational voices as the *Improvement Era* (MIA), the *Relief Society Magazine,* the *Children's Friend* (Primary), and the *Juvenile Instructor* (Sunday School).

As the church continued to place increasing emphasis on the strengthening of individuals, families, and congregations, *home teaching* to other families became a regular priesthood assignment; welfare, genealogy, temple, and missionary assignments absorbed much adult time. Administrative demands upon local leaders proliferated, and bishops and stake presidents with twenty-five-year tenure became rare and then nonexistent. In effect the local ward became, more than ever before, both the spiritual and cultural center of nearly every Utah community and for Mormons of every age.

These programmatic developments were accompanied by important administrative changes. As early as 1913 church leaders attempted to correlate the programs of the priesthood and auxiliary groups more effectively. Such efforts were continued sporadically until the 1960s, when a new and more permanent correlation program was instituted. All church programs, courses of study, manuals, and periodicals were thereafter to be cleared by a committee whose responsibilities were to eliminate overlap, approve doctrinal content, and hopefully improve general quality. In 1970 existing church magazines were supplanted by three official, advertising-free monthly publications—the *Ensign* for adults, the *New Era* for youth, and the *Friend* for children. In 1972 a newly organized Department of Internal Communications was assigned the worldwide correlation function.

The Mormon Church also responded to what it saw as certain special needs among the American Indians—Lamanite descendants of ancient Israel, according to the Book of Mormon. Beginning in 1947, members of the church in the vicinity of Richfield volunteered to take Mormon Indian children into their homes during the school year to help them gain better educational opportunities in the public schools. This effort was so successful that by 1954 the church officially inaugurated an Indian Student Placement Program. Soon white families in various Utah communities, mostly at their own expense, began to take Indian children into their homes during the school year. While there was some criticism of the program, there was also evidence that genuine benefits resulted.

In recent years special emphasis has been placed on the family as the basic unit of the church and society. *Family Home Evening* began to receive priority attention in the 1960s, and soon the church designated each Monday night for that purpose. As the scheduling of athletic events, school events, and other community activities was adjusted to accommodate Mormon family night, some Utahns expressed resentment at this church influence, but such were the realities of living in a culture dominated by a single religious tradition.

The Mormon State

The years since World War II have seen the Mormon Church transformed from a Utah-based American church to an international religious movement, an increasing fraction of whose members are outside the United States. But Utah remains the center, even though only about one-fourth of the church members now live there. An expanding administrative bureaucracy has made the church an important Utah employer and has brought Mormons with technical and management skills back to careers in the state. Of the presidents of the church since Joseph F. Smith—Heber J. Grant (1918-45), George Albert Smith (1945-51), David O. McKay (1951-70), Joseph Fielding Smith (1970-72), Harold B. Lee (1972-

73), and Spencer W. Kimball (1973-1985) — only Kimball came to the hierarchy from a career outside Utah. Most of the Mormon general authorities are Utahns, although increasing numbers are being called from other states, and non-Americans are beginning to appear in positions above the ward and stake levels. Not until the 1970s did more than half of the voluntary fulltime missionary force come from homes outside the Beehive State.

The unique role that The Church of Jesus Christ of Latter-day Saints continues to play in the unfolding story of Utah is evidenced by the worldwide tendency to associate the term *Mormon* with the name of the state. By the latter part of the twentieth century states like Massachusetts, Pennsylvania, Maryland, and Rhode Island have largely broken the ties with their churchly founders. Utah has not.

Chapter 33
Bibliographical Essay

The scholarly literature on religion in twentieth-century Utah is meager, but there is a rapidly growing body of literature on Mormonism in recent generations, and the generalizations there may usually be applied to Utah. With regard to non-Mormon religions, however, very little has been done. Sources consulted for this chapter include newspaper accounts, brochures, mimeographed flyers, and other miscellany. Very useful to students interested in doing primary research is Utah Historical Records Survey, *Inventory of Church Archives of Utah*. Vol. I, *History and Bibliography of Religion* (1940), contains valuable statistical data; Vol. II., *Baptist Church* (1940), has some brief historical material; Vol. III, *Smaller Denominations* (1941), has little historical data but is a valuable inventory of records. A brief summary of the status of Utah religions in about 1916 is contained in William Noble Warrum, *Utah Since Statehood* (1919). See also Paul A. Wright, "The Growth and Distribution of the Mormon and Non-Mormon Populations in Salt Lake City, 1970" (Ph.D. dissertation, University of Chicago, 1970).

A useful statistically oriented study is Milford R. Rathjen, "The Distribution of Major Non-Mormon Denominations in Utah" (master's thesis, University of Utah, 1966). A. Walton Roth, *A Century of Service in Utah, 1869-1969* (1969), is a sketchy summary of the Presbyterian Church activities. Some insight into Baptist objectives and activity may be found in "Utah Baptists in the Mormon Empire," *Crusader*, October 1951; Janice Singleton, "Winning the Mormons to the Right Way," *Royal Service*, February 1953; and R. Maud Ditmars, "A History of the Baptist Missions in Utah, 1871-

1931" (master's thesis, University of Colorado, 1931). An interesting general article on evangelism in Utah is Louis M. Ader, "Evangelical Missions Among the Mormons," *The Review and Expositor,* July 1952. See also Robert Keith Cox and James Joseph McCormick, "A History of St. Mark's Hospital" (master's thesis, University of Utah, 1971).

Information on the Catholic Church came from various materials supplied by the Office of Education, Diocese of Salt Lake City. Included are "Twenty Years of Progress," in *Intermountain Catholic Register* (1957), a special issue on the twentieth anniversary of the consecration of Bishop Duane G. Hunt, and 1971-72 accreditation data from Judge Memorial Catholic High School. See also Gordon R. LeBaron, "Study of the Religious Education Program of the Roman Catholic Church in Utah" (master's thesis, Brigham Young University, 1965). Information on Jewish congregations is contained in Juanita Brooks, *The History of the Jews in Utah and Idaho* (1973), and Greek Orthodox congregations are treated in Helen Z. Papanikolas, *Toil and Rage in a New Land, UHQ,* Spring 1970, and Papanikolas, ed., *Peoples of Utah* (1976).

The most complete discussion of twentieth-century Mormonism is in James B. Allen and Glen M. Leonard, *The Story of the Latter-day Saints* (1976). This one-volume history of the Mormon Church incorporates most of the research accomplished by scholars of the past two decades. The exhaustive bibliography includes almost all books and articles of consequence that appeared prior to early 1976. Other useful volumes include two documentary works, William E. Berrett and Alma P. Burton, *Readings in LDS Church History* (1958), Vol. 3, and Richard O. Cowan and Wilson K. Anderson, *The Living Church* (1974), which contains particularly informative material on administrative developments. James B. Allen and Richard O. Cowan, *Mormonism in the Twentieth Century* (1967), is a sketchy preliminary survey. Joseph Fielding Smith, *Essentials in Church History* (1973 ed.), has been periodically updated since its first appearance in 1922, but it is still unsatisfactory regarding information about the twentieth century. B. H. Roberts, *Comprehensive History of the Church* (1930), Vol. 6, contains extensive material on the period to 1930.

Thomas F. O'Dea, *The Mormons* (1957), is the best sociological study of the Mormons to date; it contains a particularly perceptive chapter on stresses and strains within the modern church. Marvin S. Hill and James B. Allen, eds., *Mormonism and American Culture* (1972), contains several interpretive articles. The only major books since O'Dea that have attempted to analyze modern Mormonism have been written by popular journalists rather than by historical scholars, and none is adequate as a history of the contemporary church. These include William J. Whalen, *The Latter-day Saints in the Modern-Day World* (1964); Wallace Turner, *The Mormon Establishment* (1966); and Robert Mullen, *The Latter-day Saints: The Mormons Yesterday and Today* (1966).

Chapter 34
Utah's Unassimilated Minorities

Richard O. Ulibarri

In 1909 a Jewish immigrant, Israel Zangwill, wrote *The Melting Pot,* a play about American immigrants. Its successful Broadway run created for the English language an expression of faith in American homogeneity, and for many years thereafter Americans pretended that the melting pot myth really worked. But in the 1960s Americans finally realized that the melting pot motif was actually restricted to those in the United States whose ancestry, heritage, and traditions are European.

It is estimated that approximately eighty-five percent of the United States population represent this European background. The other fifteen percent is composed of four groups of people who have generally not been successful in assimilating with the majority: Black Americans, various small Spanish-speaking groups, American Indians, and Asian Americans. These are the real ethnic minorities of this country. Because of racial or cultural differences they are treated as groups who are apart, or they regard themselves as aliens here, and they are held in low esteem and deterred from certain opportunities that are open to the dominant group.

Reasons for Nonassimilation

The primary reason these minority people have not been assimilated is not because they have not wanted it, but because the cultural majority has refused to accept them as equals. This refusal is based upon five factors.

First, the unassimilated minorities have physical characteristics that immediately set them apart—skin color, texture of hair, stature, and facial features.

Secondly, their non-European cultural patterns set them apart from the white Anglo-Saxon Protestant norms that predominate. Asian Americans came from the Orient; Blacks were brought from Africa against their will; Indians were, of course, already here; and the Spanish-speaking share a European background through their Spanish forefathers, but are the cultural progeny of intermarriage between Spaniards and the nonwhite peoples in the Americas.

Thirdly, these people do not fit the conventional category of immigrants. If one defines an American immigrant as someone who made a definite decision to leave the Old World and to establish a home and family in the New, this definition simply does not fit the unassimilated minorities. The Native Americans wished only to be left where they were. The Blacks came involuntarily as slaves. The Chicanos were a cultural creation of this hemisphere. The first Orientals—like some of the first Greek, Slav, and Italian immigrants—were most often interested in making a fortune and then returning home; they did not see themselves as typical immigrants.

Of critical importance in understanding the unassimilated minorities is the fourth trait, which is shared by only three of the four groups. The Indian, the Black, and the Chicano all share the experience of having been subject or slave peoples in this country and incurring the consequence of this status: deculturalization and cultural isolation.

Finally, the only way these minorities shared the American frontier experience was on the unprofitable side of the action. With specific reference to Utah, the Indians suffered the loss of their lands to the early white settlers at precisely the same time the land of the Mexican fathers of the present-day Chicanos was taken over by the United States government. Those Blacks who came during the settling of the Utah frontier were slaves or servants, and the Orientals came to stay only after the original settlements had been made, and they participated on the periphery as basic laborers. These experiences were not unique; they followed a pattern developed elsewhere during America's westward sweep.

In Utah the minorities are truly in the minority. While their number increased about sixty-three percent from 1960 to 1970, they still comprised only a little over six percent of the total population. The Spanish-speaking formed the largest segment, numbering more than 43,000, or 4.2 percent of the populace. The other groups were significantly smaller: Indians from various tribes numbered approximately 11,300; Asians numbered about 6,500, including increasing numbers from India, Korea, and elsewhere in southern Asia; and Blacks also numbered about 6,500.

With the exception of the Indian tribes, Utah's minorities are concentrated along the Wasatch Front, particularly in Salt Lake City and Ogden. Blacks and Chicanos live in communities close to the military installations where they most readily find employment. The very small number of Chinese reside in the densely populated areas where many are engaged in small businesses such as laundry, dry cleaning, and restaurants. Most of the Japanese Americans also live relatively close to the major population centers; many, however, are engaged in farming activities, particularly truck farms. Younger generation Orientals, now graduating from college, are entering the professions.

Most Indians still reside on the reservations; almost half of Utah's total Indian population lives in San Juan County alone. However, in the 1960s an important shift took many Indians from the reservations to the urban areas. During that decade the Indian population in metropolitan Utah more than doubled.

Blacks: Servitude and Service

Although always few in number, Blacks have figured prominently in the history of Utah since the early nineteenth century. James P. Beckwourth, a member of the Rocky Mountain Fur Company from 1823 to 1826, was one of the noted *Mountain Men*. Jacob Dodson, another Black, was with John C. Fremont's expeditions; Fremont recorded that he "performed his duty manfully."

Blacks were also among the Mormon pioneers. The Brigham Young Monument and the This Is the Place Monument contain the names of three Blacks who were in the vanguard of July 1847: Green Flake, Hark Lay, and Oscar Crosby. The first Black slaves in the area, they were soon joined by others, since a great number of the Mormons emigrated to the Great Basin from the Southern states and brought their slaves with them. The Mississippi Company in 1848 included fifty-seven white members and thirty-four Blacks.

Some Blacks immigrated to Utah as free men and others immigrated as slaves. Mormon pioneer John Brown consecrated property to the Mormon Church in the 1850s that included real estate valued at $775, livestock, farm equipment, tools, household articles, and one "African Servant Girl" valued at $1,000. According to the 1850 census there were twenty-four free Blacks and twenty-six slaves in Utah; ten years later the enumeration listed thirty free Blacks and twenty-nine slaves.

In 1851 the Utah territorial legislature passed an act protecting slavery. The obligations of master and servant were defined in

Isom Dart (left) was a cowboy in the Brown's Hole area of eastern Utah in the late nineteenth century and detective Paul Cephas Howell was Salt Lake City's first black policeman.

terms similar to the milder Southern slave codes. While the slave trade was never legal in the territory, dealing in human bondage did take place. The legal institution ended, of course, when the United States Congress abolished slavery in the territories in 1862. Many of the Black people at that time, both slave and free, were Mormons, and they chose to remain in the territory. Some Blacks in the state today trace their ancestry to these pioneers.

After the Civil War Blacks continued to be involved in western settlement. Two who worked the range in the Brown's Hole area where Utah, Wyoming, and Colorado meet were Albert Williams (called *Speck* because of his freckles), who operated a ferry on the Green River, and Isom Dart, a cattle driver and bronco buster. A third Black cowboy of interest to Utah was Nat Love. One of the few cowboys to leave an autobiography, he entitled his history *The Life and Adventures of Nat Love: Better Known in the Cattle Country as Deadwood Dick* (1907). When he retired from the range, Deadwood Dick worked as a pullman porter; during the 1890s he and his family lived in Salt Lake City.

Completion of the transcontinental railroad brought more Blacks into Utah, as did the expansion of federal military installations. The threat of a Ute Indian outbreak in 1884 led the Bureau of Indian Affairs to recommend the establishment of a fort near the Uintah Reservation. What followed is commemorated on a plaque at the site of Fort Duchesne:

August 21, 1886, two companies of colored infantry commanded by Major F. W. Benteen and four companies of infantry under Captain Duncan arrived at this site to control the activities of Indians. . . . The troops hauled logs from nearby canyons, built living quarters, a commissary, storehouses, and a hospital, thereby establishing Fort Duchesne. . . .

Much disliked by the Indians, Benteen's Ninth Cavalry troops received from them the name of *Buffalo Soldiers* because of their curly hair. Their task was to defend the tri-state frontier area. They served for nearly twelve years at the fort.

Another unit of Black soldiers, the Twenty-fourth Infantry Regiment, was stationed at Fort Douglas and participated with distinction in Cuba and the Philippines during the Spanish-American War. These were the men who swept up San Juan Hill and, along with other Black cavalry units, scored a victory for Colonel Theodore Roosevelt. Following the battle they served as nurses in the yellow fever hospital at Siboney.

The Black population of Utah grew very slowly. When Utah's entire population reached 277,000 at the turn of the century, there were only 678 Black residents, including approximately 200 soldiers at Fort Duchesne. The civilians were chiefly employed by the mines and railroads in Salt Lake, Weber, and Tooele counties. Despite the removal of the soldiers and their dependents from Uintah County, the number of Blacks in the state doubled during the years from 1900 to 1920. To the economic opportunities along the Wasatch Front were added jobs in the expanding coal mines of Carbon and Emery counties. However, the next two decades slowed the upward trend. Employment, especially during the Great Depression, was extremely scarce, and Black people left the state in search of jobs elsewhere. The decline in coal mining presented particularly difficult conditions, and by 1940 ninety percent of the remaining Blacks lived in Salt Lake and Weber counties. With World War II the Black population again increased, and most of the newcomers settled near the military installations and defense plants from Ogden to Salt Lake City and in Tooele County.

The influx of Black workers in the precivil rights years created a demand for business and service facilities that would provide accommodations and services refused by many white-owned firms. In both Salt Lake City and Ogden several hotels, restaurants, and clubs near the railroad centers, such as the Porters and Waiters Club, were operated by Blacks. In addition, Blacks created their own social and cultural organizations—churches, fraternal associations, literary clubs, press services, and community centers. The first Black church, the Trinity African Methodist-Episcopal Church, was founded in Salt Lake City in the 1890s. The Calvary Baptist Church was organized shortly thereafter, and the Wall Street Baptist Church in Ogden was established early in the new century. The earliest Black newspapers appeared during the 1890s. The *Broad Ax*, published by Julius Taylor, was discontinued in 1899, but William W. Taylor's *Utah Plain Dealer* continued until 1909.

When one examines the pattern of discrimination in Utah, it is apparent that it has been simply a microcosm of Black history in the United States. Until as recently as 1963 Utah had a miscegenation law prohibiting marriage with whites. Black entertainers were brought to Lagoon, Saltair, and Rainbow Gardens, but Black residents had to sit in balcony sections of theaters and stand outside ballrooms to hear their music. Concert singer Marian Anderson was allowed to stay at the Hotel Utah on the condition that she use the freight elevator. Harry Belafonte was refused rooms at the Hotel Utah but was accepted at the Hotel Newhouse, which had previously barred Blacks. Other Black celebrities experienced similar indignities.

Three lynchings of Blacks are recorded in Utah history. In 1869 an unidentified man was shot and hanged in Weber County. Sam J. Hairney was lynched in Salt Lake City in 1885; in 1925 Robert Marshall was hanged repeatedly in one day by a large mob in Price. During the 1920s and 1930s the Ku Klux Klan was active in Utah, and, as elsewhere, Blacks were the prime targets.

In 1939 Salt Lake City commissioners received a petition bearing 1,000 signatures asking that Blacks living in the city be restricted to one residential area. Initiated by a local realtor, the petition failed to accomplish its purpose. However, other forms of discrimination continued to limit Black opportunities in housing. Statistics now show that the core areas of Salt Lake City and Ogden, where at least eighty percent of Utah's total Black population resides, are in zones peripheral to the business districts.

As noted, employment opportunities have historically been very limited for Blacks in Utah. Affirmative Action and Equal Employment laws have not helped a great deal. Rarely have Blacks been employed in businesses and agriculture operations that are not directly federally sponsored. Most active in the field for equal rights have been two chapters of the National Association for the Advancement of Colored People in the state. The Salt Lake City chapter was organized in February 1919, only ten years after the founding of the national body. The Ogden chapter was not formed until 1943.

Perhaps of greatest concern to the Black population in Utah has been the Mormon Church denial of its priesthood to Black members. This issue was resolved in June 1978 when President Spencer W. Kimball announced that "all worthy male members. . .may be ordained without regard for race or color." Black and white religious and civic leaders greeted the announcement with enthusiasm.

The Spanish-speaking Peoples

Spanish-speaking people comprise Utah's largest minority. Most of them now call themselves *Chicano;* included in that group are the Spanish Americans or *Hispanos* from New Mexico and Colorado, the *Californios* from California, and the immigrants from Mexico. The term *Spanish-speaking* is often used as a noun to include Latin Americans from elsewhere in the hemisphere; however, the number of these residing in Utah is small. Consequently, the terms *Chicano* and *Spanish-speaking* may be used here interchangeably.

Utah's first Spanish-speaking people were transient explorers. While settlement did not follow the Rivera and Domínguez-Escalante expeditions, subsequent trade in furs, Indian slaves, horses, and firearms brought increasingly frequent visits by Chicanos from the Sante Fe region in the late eighteenth and early nineteenth centuries. It also left many Spanish names on the land.

The passing of the fur trade, the coming of the Mormons, and the Mexican-American War of 1846-48 disrupted the old patterns, but some trade—predominantly in Indian slaves—continued following the annexation of both Utah and New Mexico by the United

States. The Walker War of 1853-54 finally terminated this trade, and Mormon leaders also opposed New Mexican trader participation in enterprises in Utah Territory. Chicano contacts thereafter were largely limited to employment in the livestock operations in southeastern Utah.

Culturally, two groups built the Spanish-speaking population of twentieth-century Utah. The Chicanos in the livestock country, principally in San Juan County, were linked to the Spanish-American population of southern Colorado and northern New Mexico. In Utah they found work as sheepherders and ranch-hands, with a few owning their own homesteading ranches and farms. The Mexican immigrants who came later into the more industrial areas of Ogden and Salt Lake City formed the second group. To some extent the distinction remains significant in Chicano affairs today.

As late as 1900 the United States Census listed only forty individuals of Mexican nativity living in the state, and Catholic records reveal only eleven baptisms of Spanish-surnamed children in the first decade of the new century. Economic attractions drew increasing numbers of Mexicans in the period from 1910 to 1930, and the increasing numbers justified the designation of a Mexican consul in Salt Lake City in 1912. In 1920 Utah inhabitants of Mexican birth were numbered at 1,666; the 1930 census reported 4,000. But because of the clandestine immigration that has consistently taken place from Mexico to the United States, such figures are highly suspect.

Immigrant laborers were sometimes used as strikebreakers; Utah Copper Company used 4,000 Mexicans during their 1912 labor troubles. Others found work with the mills, smelters, and railroads. By the end of World War I a number of Mexicans were becoming part of Utah's agricultural picture, mostly as itinerant labor recruited to meet the war-born labor shortage; others immigrated voluntarily because of the revolutionary tumult in Mexico. A notable feature of the 1930 census tally was the substantial increase in the number of Mexican *families* reported in the state.

In 1920, under the initiative of Juan Ramón Martínez, who came to Salt Lake City from southern Utah, the Mormon Church established the Provisional Lamanite Branch, a fledgling missionary effort for the Spanish-speaking people. Four years later it was officially organized as the *Rama Mexicana*, or Mexican Branch. Personal contention handicapped operations, and from 1924 to 1965 no Spanish-surnamed individual headed the branch.

In 1927 the Catholic Church also established a mission for the benefit of Salt Lake City's Mexican community. In 1930 it was designated as the Mission of Nuestra Señora de Guadalupe, or Our Lady of Guadalupe, with Father James Earl Collins as administrator.

These years were particularly important in the development of Utah's Spanish-speaking population. Heavy Mexican and Spanish-American movement into the state encouraged organizational activity and the development of a sense of community. The Mexican Protective Association and the Mexican Blue Cross in Salt Lake City and the *Union y Patria* in Bingham were established as mutual aid societies. By 1930 almost half of the Spanish-speaking inhabitants of Utah were native-born.

With the onset of the Great Depression, a sharp decrease in the size of the Spanish-speaking community took place. The competition for the few available jobs saw Mexicans and Chicanos losing even the most basic and menial jobs to English-speaking workers—commonly lumped together as *Anglos.* One of the adopted solutions for unemployment was to deport large numbers of Mexicans who had come to the United States when labor was in short supply. Between 250,000 and 500,000 immigrants returned to Mexico either voluntarily or through forced deportation during the Great Depression decade. By 1940 the number of Mexican-born living in Utah had dropped to 1,069.

World War II pulled the state and the nation out of the depression and created a new labor shortage. In Utah the rapid growth of government facilities was the single most important factor that attracted Chicanos from surrounding states. The supply depots in Weber, Davis, and Tooele counties demanded laborers, and the copper mines in Bingham Canyon, coal mines in Carbon County, and railroads and farms throughout the state needed hands. Active recruitment programs were conducted, attracting hundreds of Chicanos from Colorado, New Mexico, and other states. Interestingly, the number of immigrants from Mexico who came and remained in the state was quite small. Census figures show an increase of only 327 between 1940 and 1950, although this tabulation did not record Mexicans who came for limited periods as migrant laborers.

In the postwar years Utah participated in the growing national trend of using migrant labor in the fields, orchards, sugar factories, and canneries. Recruitment of Spanish-speaking workers in Texas, Arizona, and elsewhere in the southwest, as well as Mexican *brazeros,* increased into the mid 1960s, when almost 8,000 itinerant workers were in Utah in a single year. Two interesting features of

Utah's migrant labor story are the number of Navajo Indians from Arizona who were involved and the number of farmers with Japanese surnames who employed migrant hands.

The United States Employment Service generally oversaw migrant labor under terms of federal laws and agreements with Mexico. State agencies were slow to become involved, and standards of housing, health care, and schooling available to the transients received only belated attention. Legislation upgrading wages and the terms of contract labor encountered both economic and social resistance on the part of Utah employers. In expressing a preference for Mexican rather than Indian labor, an Ogden sugar company official made a revealing observation: "They tend to mind their own business and do not try to mix with the white race."

During the years after World War II a number of organizations designed to protect the interests of Chicanos were formed. In 1946 Demetrio Trujillo formed the Mutual Protection Society of United Workers, a chapter of a fraternal society that had been established in Colorado in 1900. The Texas-based American G. I. Forum organized a Utah chapter in 1947. The forum mirrored a changing orientation of the Spanish-speaking community in Utah and elsewhere. It did not stress Mexican nationalism, but was instead aimed at solving Mexican-American problems in an Anglo-American society. The G. I. Forum lagged in the late 1950s but revived activities and membership during the activist 1960s.

Not until 1968 with the formation of SOCIO (Spanish-speaking Organization for Community, Integrity, and Opportunity) was there a broadly based statewide organization to represent the Chicano minority. By 1974 SOCIO had grown to 27,000 members, with nine chapters located throughout the state. It was successful in creating increasing awareness in state government of the concerns of Utah's Spanish-speaking populace.

Utah's Chinese

The discovery of gold in California was the initial attraction that brought the Chinese to the American West. Their history in Utah began with the construction of the transcontinental railroad, when more than 10,000 Chinese laborers were employed on the Central Pacific portion. Across Nevada and into Utah these crews laid up to ten miles of track a day. When the project was completed in 1869, Promontory became the gateway for the Chinese who remained in Utah Territory. Between 1870 and 1880 Box Elder County was the home and the railroad was the employer of most of them.

From the railroads the Chinese moved to employment as miners and independent small businessmen in mining and railroad towns. Soon, however, their industriousness and ethnic separateness became a concern throughout the West. California was the center of the agitation that produced Chinese exclusion laws beginning in 1882. That similar feelings existed in Utah is clear from an editorial that appeared in the Ogden *Junction* on January 29, 1879:

... But when every argument in favor of the Chinese is exhausted, the case of today is not covered; for times are hard, work in places is difficult if not impossible to get, and the wages of white men, as a consequence, have dwindled to such an extent that there is at least but a trifling difference between the prices paid for work performed by the white man and that done by the copper-colored incubus. ... To divide what little [work] there is with the inferior and alien race, is not good nor a just policy. ...

Under the immigration ban Utah's Chinese population remained small. By the turn of the century Salt Lake City, Ogden, and Provo all had Chinese laundries and restaurants, some of which have continued to the present time. Park City had a Chinatown in its early years, and places as remote as the Uinta Basin and Silver Reef accepted the services of Chinese entrepreneurs while manifesting the conventional prejudices. In spite of the continued harrassment, the decades between 1900 and 1930 were years of growing Chinese activity around Salt Lake City's Plum Alley and in Ogden's Chinatown. But the Great Depression caused mass unemployment, and by 1940 the number of Chinese in Ogden and Salt Lake City had declined to fewer than five hundred. Most of the eligible young men performed military service during World War II.

When the Chinese Exclusion Act was repealed in 1952, Chinese immigrants again began to settle in the United States. Many students came from Hong Kong and Taiwan to Utah universities, and some remained to become citizens of the state. The 1970 census counted 1,281 Chinese. Almost half were owners or employees of Chinese restaurants; others were operators of laundries, dry cleaning establishments, and other small business concerns.

The only Chinese organization in the state today is the *Bing Cong Tong* or *Bing Cong Benevolent Association.* Only a vestige of the organization that once provided a place for Chinese to meet and to speak their native tongue, its membership consists almost entirely of men of the older generation. Although the second- and third-generation Chinese are more Americanized than their parents, assimilation is by no means total.

Utah's Japanese

After Congress passed the Chinese Exclusion Act, American industrialists turned to Japan for cheap labor. The liberalization of Japan's emigration laws in 1885 facilitated this shift. The results were striking: in 1890 there were 107,448 Chinese and 2,039 Japanese in the United States; twenty years later there were 71,531 Chinese and 72,157 Japanese.

The first Japanese recorded in Utah were some fifty members of an official delegation touring America in 1872. Ten years later the first reported immigrants were female prostitutes who worked in the railroad camps. The first male workers came in the 1880s to fill railroad jobs abandoned by the Chinese. But riots in Wyoming and at the Carbon County mines drove most of them from the region. Consequently the 1890 census showed only four Japanese in Utah.

The beginning of the twentieth century saw 417 Japanese in the state, only eleven of them females. By 1910 there were 2,110 Japanese Americans, and by 1920 2,936 were residing primarily in the Salt Lake Valley and working as farm laborers, tenants, or sharecroppers. Many men came through the auspices of labor contractor Daigoro Hashimoto, and they sent money back to families in Japan through the same channel.

During the 1920s many of the Issei (first-generation Japanese Americans) worked in the state's mining industry—about 800 worked at Bingham and a thousand worked in the coal mines around Helper. Japanese also worked in the smelters of Salt Lake and Tooele counties. Issei also contributed to the growth of truck farming in Box Elder, Davis, Weber, and Salt Lake counties; the celery and tomato culture and the sugar beet industry particularly grew to depend upon them. By the late 1920s and early 1930s areas in Salt Lake City and Ogden began to be known as Japanese centers, with religious shrines, specialty stores, and a few hotels. Then the depression reduced the Japanese population; many moved to California or returned to Japan.

The largest influx of persons of Japanese ancestry took place during World War II. Even before Executive Order 9066 ordered the relocation of all Pacific Coast Japanese on March 27, 1942, Nisei (second-generation Japanese Americans educated in America) and Kibei (second-generation Japanese Americans educated in Japan) were instructed to move out of strategic areas on their own. About 1,500 moved to Utah, adding to the more than 2,000 Japanese already living here.

With the activation of the Central Utah War Relocation Center, *Topaz,* located near Delta in Millard County, over 8,000 Japanese Americans were brought into Utah. Between September 11, 1942, and October 31, 1945, the involuntary occupants of the tar-paper barracks of Topaz—one of the ten quasiconcentration camps established in the United States—comprised what was at its peak Utah's fifth most populous city.

Closely supervised, the Topaz residents were permitted at first to take only farm work and other nonsensitive jobs. Some of the restrictions were eventually relaxed, but the sentiments of many Utahns were reflected in several ways. After Governor Herbert Maw vetoed a bill prohibiting Japanese Americans from buying or leasing real estate, a ban applying only to land was enacted. Neither the University of Utah nor Utah State Agricultural College would admit applicants from Topaz.

Despite being forced to live under these trying circumstances, the people of Topaz proved not only their patriotism but their industry as well. As strange as it may seem, the headquarters of the Buddhist Church of America was at Topaz during World War II, having been transferred from San Francisco. The *Topaz Times* was published, art classes were held for adults, and 3,000 students were enrolled in the Topaz schools. The names of eighteen Japanese American war dead from Utah are inscribed on the Nisei War Monument in Salt Lake City.

Even before the war ended, the War Relocation Authority began to permit the internees to move from relocation centers to places where employment was available. In Utah the Tooele Ordnance Depot became one of the chief employers of Japanese; by the end of 1944 300 new families had been added to the existing Japanese community there, and many still live in the area. In all, some 5,000 Japanese Americans settled in Utah after World War II. Thereafter the number of Japanese Americans gradually declined, and by 1970 a Census Bureau sampling found that fewer than 3,500 Utahns were natives of Japan or had at least one parent born there.

Out of the war experiences came a strong Japanese community in Utah. The Japanese American Citizens League was influential in securing the repeal of the Alien Land Law in 1947, and one of its spokesmen, Mike Masaoka, was a key lobbyist for the Evacuation Indemnity Claims Act that was passed by Congress in 1948. *Utah Nippo,* founded in 1914 and now published twice weekly, has been effective in holding the Japanese Americans together. JACL chapters carry out social and athletic programs, sponsor scholarships, and conduct youth activities affecting nearly every Japanese family in the state. Religiously the Japanese are aligned with the Japanese Church of Christ, the Salt Lake Buddhist Church, and the Nichiren Buddhist Church. Several hundred are Mormons. The newest generation, the Sansei, is nearly a century removed from the first Japanese immigrants to Utah, but the traditions of their forefathers continue to provide them with the cultural attributes that have assisted them in periods of duress.

Indians: The Era of the Dawes Act

In 1871 the United States ended the practice of making treaties with Indian tribes. The treaties already in effect continued to be the legal basis for relationships between the federal government and the individual tribes, but the Native Americans became in most respects subject to the changing laws and policies administered by the Bureau of Indian Affairs.

In 1887 the General Allotment, or Dawes Severalty Act, set the pattern by which agreements were to be made alloting tribal lands to individual members and then opening up the remainder of the reservations for white settlement. The ostensible purpose of the allotment was to break up the reservations and to stop governmental dealing with the Indians through their tribal leaders. If the policy had been a success, all relationships would have eventually been with Indians as individuals, for they would have received citizenship and clear titles to their pieces of land. One basic problem was that most of the western Indians did not want to farm and so disliked the new policy from the outset.

The only Utah reservation seriously affected by the allotment policy was the Uintah-Ouray Reservation. In 1895 a commission was appointed to survey and allot lands. The fact that three mutually distrustful Ute bands were involved, that most of the good agricultural land was on the Uintah section of the reservation, and that the Utes wanted to retain their hunting and grazing lands and avoid farming turned the whole experience into a fiasco. By 1905 allotments were made to individual Utes, often against their will, and the Uintah-Ouray Reservation was opened for white settlement. That same year Theodore Roosevelt withdrew 1,100,000 acres from the reservation to create the Uintah National Forest Reserve. In 1909 another 56,000 acres were withdrawn for the Strawberry Valley reclamation project. Between the 1880s and 1909 the Ute lands in the Uinta Basin decreased from 4,000,000 to about 360,000 acres. The effect on the Northern Utes was demoralizing.

642

With the assignment of agents, later called superintendents, to work with the Indian groups and with the continuing infringement of the neighboring white communities, the real power of traditional Indian leaders was weakened. Cultural influences such as schools, churches, and the surrounding economy increasingly affected the attitudes and actions of the Native Americans. The first decades of the twentieth century were particularly difficult. Not only were the Indians very poor, but they had poor health, and the United States was slow to make health care available except to the children attending government boarding schools. Even there the death rate from tuberculosis and other diseases was high as young Indians were brought together in environments that were unnatural to them.

The Utes that married into white families, and particularly the children of these marriages, seemed to adjust better to the surrounding society, and soon the fullbloods saw these mixed bloods taking more and more active roles in the relationships between the two cultures. Differences continued to assert themselves until Congress, in 1954, under pressure from the fullbloods, designated the mixed bloods as Affiliated Ute Citizens entitled to a share of tribal claims and resources but removed from the jurisdiction of the Bureau of Indian Affairs. Since then tribal business has been under the control of fullbloods (having over fifty percent Ute ancestry).

The Paiutes and Gosiutes were too few to present a comparable problem, and the more numerous but isolated Navajos experienced relatively few interracial marriages until the latter part of the twentieth century.

Renewal of Tribal Governments

There was no relief from the allotment policy until independent studies in the 1920s made it clear that the Dawes Act had been a mistake. The policy had been successful in securing Indian lands for the white man, but it had not made farmers out of the Indians and it had not taught them to retain their individual holdings against the pressures and blandishments of white farmers, ranchers, and businessmen. The Indians had not learned to think like whites.

Along with other reforms that appeared during the Depression, the Indian Reorganization Act (Wheeler-Howard Act) was passed by Congress in 1934. This legislation encouraged Indian tribes to reconstitute their tribal governments and to elect leaders to represent their interests. Although what occurred was not usually a renewal of the traditional Indian leadership, the new organizations, encouraged by representatives of the Bureau of Indian Affairs, offered an alternative to almost complete control by appointed agents of the federal government.

Most Utah Indian groups accepted the new system, under which they elected a tribal council, or business committee, which in turn elected a tribal chairman. The actions of these governing groups were controlled by tribal constitutions and by relevant laws. Tribal charters established the tribe or group as an entity capable of doing business with other private or government agencies. These were mechanisms that largely grew out of the white man's experience, and sometimes they failed to satisfy demands made on them by their Indian constituents.

The 1930s brought difficulties for the Native Americans as well as for other citizens of Utah, but bad times were not new to them, and in their rural communities they were sometimes able to adjust more readily than were their urban neighbors.

During World War II Utah Indians enrolled in the armed services in proportionately greater numbers than was the case with the nation generally. Some Utah Indians received special recognition for distinguished service. As these men returned from the war their plans for the future varied; some had learned trades and wanted to continue in them, some wanted to use their G.I. educational benefits, and some were anxious to resume their former places in the community.

In 1948, largely to meet the needs of Navajos, the Bureau of Indian Affairs offered job placement services through offices in Salt Lake City, Denver, and Los Angeles. The relocation program was soon extended to other Indians, and Chicago was added to the group of field offices that were available to Utah Indians. Many Navajos obtained permanent employment and moved their families to these cities.

Revival of the Termination Policy

The postwar era also saw a movement back to the "old, bad days" of the Dawes Act when, between 1953 and 1958, it became congressional policy to terminate the special relationship between the United States and selected Indian tribes "as rapidly as possible." In a 1957 article, Utah Senator Arthur V. Watkins spoke of the period under the Indian Reorganization Act of 1934 as an aberration:

Unfortunately, the major and continuing congressional movement toward full freedom was delayed for a time by the Indian Reorganization Act. . . .

Amid the deep social concern of the depression years, Congress deviated from its accustomed policy under the concept of promoting the general Indian welfare. In the postdepression years Congress—realizing this change of policy—sought to return to the historic principles of much earlier decades.

Possibly because Watkins was chairman of the Senate Indian Affairs Subcommittee, the first termination hearings dealt with "Tribes of Utah (Shivwits, Kanosh, Koosharem, Indian Peaks Bands of Paiutes, Skull Valley Shoshone, and Washakie Shoshone)." The reason heard most frequently for terminating these small and scattered Indian groups was that they did not really receive any assistance from the federal government. While this was largely true, experience that followed the termination process proved that it brought little increase in attention from agencies in Utah that were supposed to assume the responsibilities formerly assigned to federal agencies. By the time termination was again abandoned in 1958, the Southern Paiutes, Gosiutes, and Affiliated Utes had all been affected. In a few years all the Southern Paiutes except the Shivwits had largely lost control of the small plots of land that had been assigned to them.

New Approaches to Self-Determination

A movement in the 1950s to involve Indians more in programs that served other citizens resulted in the Public Health Service taking over responsibilities for Indian health, the public schools becoming responsible for the education of most Utah Indian children, and state agencies undertaking to provide welfare services for Indians. In the late 1950s and 1960s it became the custom to include Indian reservations in congressional legislation; both the federally-impacted-area legislation of 1958 and the manpower development and training program of 1962 were made applicable to Utah reservations. Under the Economic Opportunity Act of 1964, the Office of Economic Opportunity (OEO) created an Indian Desk to simplify relationships between tribal representatives and that office. Soon other federal agencies followed this lead, and Utah tribes were benefited.

During the same period state legislation created an advisory State Board of Indian Affairs and a Division of Indian Affairs within the Department of Social Services to coordinate and improve state services to Utah's Native Americans.

A major factor in transforming Indian life in recent decades has been the successful prosecution of claims against the United States for violations of nineteenth-century treaties that guaranteed tribal land holdings. The Utes first brought such a claim in 1909, and they received an award of over $3,500,000. The post-World War II years saw more comprehensive lawsuits, and by 1962 Ute awards amounted to about $47,700,000, of which the Northern Ute (Uintah-Ouray) share was approximately $30,500,000. The Affiliated Ute Citizens participated in these awards; in the 1970s the Southern Paiutes and Gosiutes were each awarded settlements in excess of seven million dollars.

In addition to making use of claims money, the Northern Utes have been interested in developing the mineral resources on the reservation; attracting visitors to the Bottle Hollow motel, convention center, and recreation area; and utilizing their water rights. Industrial development to provide employment for tribal members and to insure continuing income from tribal investments has also been given high priority. Oil, coal, and other minerals on both Ute and Navajo lands promise additional income in the future.

The Indians of Utah Today

A comparison of federal census data for 1960 and 1970 shows representative recent trends. The Native American population increased sixty-two percent in the decade, increasing from 6,961 to 11,273; the distribution shows some net migration into the state as well as some significant internal relocation.

There was a substantial increase in the number of Navajos in San Juan County (2,668 to 4,740), associated in part with new employment opportunities in the Aneth oil field. The Ute population in the Uinta Basin increased only slightly (from 1,190 to 1,337). But there was a dramatic increase in the number of Indians in Salt Lake County and elsewhere in the urban areas along the Wasatch Front (from 1,182 to 3,129). As was the case elsewhere in America, the urban Indian movement reached significant proportions in the 1960s, and steps were taken to organize these groups. In Utah the United Council for Urban Indians, followed by the Utah Native American Consortium, enabled city dwellers to follow national developments and receive benefits on the same basis as did other citizens. (See map, p. 738, for the location of Indian reservations today.)

Utah's Indians continue to be caught between cultures. While they make continual efforts to maintain some of the old ways, the surrounding white environment, with all the impact of its institutions, forces change upon them. The paternalistic and exploitive pattern of federal administration undermined tribal authority in the late nineteenth and early twentieth centuries, and recent efforts to reassert Indian autonomy, funded by claims awards and mineral contracts, have found traditionalists at odds with advocates of comprehensive assimilation.

On Navajo land today adults and children wear both Indian and American dress. Horses and pickup trucks share the dusty roads to trading posts. Some Navajos attend the Episcopal mission church, and some attend Catholic, Mormon, and other Protestant services. Meanwhile much homage is still paid to ancient tribal religious practices. For medical services Navajos utilize both their medicine men, the undistinguished medical facilities near trading posts, and larger hospitals in centers such as Gallup, New Mexico. The children ride long hours on school buses for elementary education and look ahead to distant boarding schools as well as reservation schools for junior and senior high school opportunities.

The Utes on the Uintah-Ouray Reservation anticipate a brighter future with income derived from oil and natural gas leasing, an expanding cattle industry, a furniture factory, and the Bottle Hollow facilities. As among the Navajos, improved income has meant improved housing and changing life-styles for many. The Ute children are enrolled in the public schools of Uintah and Duchesne school districts, but so little attention is paid to the cultural differences between the Indians and whites that many families still prefer to send their children to Bureau of Indian Affairs boarding schools such as the Intermountain School at Brigham City, Utah, and institutions in other states.

Meanwhile the Paiutes, whose trustee relationships with the federal government have been terminated, struggle to maintain their identity and to survive. Federal and state programs have been largely unsuccessful in converting them to white patterns of behavior, but the native language is heard less often today, and claims awards may assist the few hundred remaining Paiutes to assimilate with their neighbors.

Southwest of the Great Salt Lake the Gosiutes experience much the same trauma as do the other Utah tribes. Today less than sixty-five Skull Valley Gosiutes remain, and most of these have migrated to Tooele and Grantsville for school and employment. At Deep Creek some eleven families remain. Whether federal claims awards will permit them to survive or will accelerate their disappearance as a Native American cultural entity remains to be seen.

In his special message on *The Forgotten American,* delivered March 6, 1968, Lyndon B. Johnson called for an end to the old debate about termination and stressed self-determination as a new goal for the Indians. President Nixon stressed the same theme in 1970. A typical reaction of Indians from Utah and elsewhere was expressed by one Indian leader: "We have often heard the thunder but have yet to feel the rain." In the words of James Jackson, speaking for his tribal council, self-determination will have become a reality when the tribe "has assumed active control of the land it now controls on paper.... When we are harvesting the economic benefits of the great resources we hold; when our governing body has an educated and competent leadership.... It will come when we are ready, and at our request."

Conclusion

In summary, Utah's Chicanos, Blacks, and Indians have not yet been able to succeed economically and have encountered serious social dislocations and discrimination. On the other hand, the Oriental races in Utah have discovered a means of maintaining their identity and cultural backgrounds while surviving in the highly competitive environment of the United States. With the civil rights reforms of the 1960s and the continuing pressure against bigotry and prejudice carried on by minorities and many sensitive whites, these groups may yet become equal citizens. Compared to many other states, Utah has had only a small percentage of ethnic minorities. Nevertheless, the task of assuring them full citizenship has not been significantly different from that in other states in the Union, and much still remains to be done.

Chapter 34
Bibliographical Essay

This chapter relies heavily on groundbreaking essays in Helen Z. Papanikolas, ed., *The Peoples of Utah* (1976). Particular use has been made of the contributions of Ronald G. Coleman, "Blacks in Utah History: An Unknown Legacy"; Don C. Conley, "The Pioneer Chinese of Utah"; Papanikolas and Alice Kasai, "Japanese Life in Utah"; and Vicente V. Mayer, "After Escalante: The Spanish-speaking People of Utah." The informative chapters on Indians by Clyde J. Benally and Floyd A. O'Neil concentrate primarily on the nineteenth century. An unpublished manuscript on federal Indian policies by S. Lyman Tyler, University of Utah, has been very helpful. An overview of the subject of this chapter is Richard O. Ulibarri, "Utah's Ethnic Minorities: A Survey," *UHQ,* Summer 1972.

A number of sources are available for the study of Utah's Blacks. See Dennis L. Lythgoe, "Negro Slavery in Utah," *UHQ,*

Winter 1971; Philip T. Drotning, *A Guide to Negro History in America* (1968); and United States Bureau of the Census, *Negro Population, 1790-1915* (1918). For the military experiences of Blacks in Utah, see Thomas G. Alexander and Leonard J. Arrington, "The Utah Military Frontier, 1872-1912: Forts Cameron, Thornburgh, and Duchesne," *UHQ,* Fall 1964. Extensive demographic information is to be found in George Ramjoue, "The Negro in Utah: A Geographical Study in Population" (master's thesis, University of Utah, 1968).

For an examination of the establishment of the Northern Ute reservation, see Floyd A. O'Neil, "The Reluctant Suzerainty: The Uintah and Ouray Reservation," *UHQ,* Spring 1971. On the Navajo see J. Lee Correll, "Navajo Frontiers in Utah and Troubled Times in Monument Valley," *UHQ,* Spring 1971. Two publications of the American West Center, University of Utah, provide some historical background in connection with Indians who have moved into Utah metropolitan areas: Mary Ellen Sloan, *Indians in an Urban Setting: Salt Lake County, Utah (1972)* (1973); and Stephen M. C. Hunt, *Native American Adjustment to the City: The Salt Lake County Case* (1976).

In addition to the Conley article on the Chinese mentioned above, see George Kraus, "Chinese Laborers and the Construction of the Central Pacific," *UHQ,* Winter 1969; and Kate B. Carter, comp., "The Early Chinese of Western United States," in *Our Pioneer Heritage* (1958), Vol. 10.

Sources on the Chicanos are somewhat more limited than they are for other ethnic groups. See the bibliographies for chapters 2, 3, and 4 for the early Spanish and Mexican contacts with Utah. *Toward a History of the Spanish-speaking People of Utah* (1973), a publication of the University of Utah's American West Center, includes Paul Morgan and Vincent Mayer, "The Spanish-speaking Population of Utah: From 1900 to 1935"; Ann Nelson, "Spanish-speaking Migrant Laborer in Utah, 1950 to 1965"; and Greg Coronado, "Spanish-speaking Organizations in Utah." Helen Z. Papanikolas, "Life and Labor Among the Immigrants of Bingham Canyon," *UHQ,* Fall 1965, describes the use of Chicanos as strikebreakers. An oral history project at Weber State College has explored Chicano experiences in Utah; an interview with Manuel Fernandez, November 18, 1971, has been used in this chapter.

Basic statistical information on Utah's minorities may be found in United States Bureau of the Census, *General Social and Economic Characteristics, Utah: 1970 Census of Population* (1972).

Chapter 35
Natural Resource Utilization

Charles S. Peterson

T he collective effort of Utahns and the United States government to develop and regulate natural resources has been a major theme of the twentieth century. It has involved the management of widely separated water and land resources in an effort to bring them together to permit utilization. This process has been vital to Utah's economic and social wellbeing. It has also been extremely costly; in early Utah history such costs were met by collective efforts at the local level, but since the turn of this century, costs have been met by a different sort of collective effort—one often financed and organized at the national level. Consequently, development of Utah's resources attracted both attention and controversy as the various local and national interests sought to work out their respective roles.

The history of resource development and regulation in Utah may be organized under three overlapping but distinct headings: *irrigation and reclamation, conservation,* and *preservation.* Reclamation has been concerned with development of water and waste areas; conservation has concentrated on perpetuating productive capacity through the wise use of resources; and preservation has been concerned with the protection of scenic, historical, and natural sites of extraordinary quality. These three functions have much in common, including many of the historical impulses from which they grew. In timing they were similar, with each program emerging in its modern form in the early years of the twentieth century and then following a course dictated by national and local politics, war, and economic conditions. Each theme was profoundly influenced by environmental considerations as Utahns became in-

651

creasingly aware of scarcity as a human problem in the third quarter of the century. And while it oversimplifies, each may be said to have fallen under the primary administration of great federal agencies: respectively, the Bureau of Reclamation, the Forest Service, the Bureau of Land Management, and the National Park Service.

Utah interests have paralleled and worked with the federal agencies. In some ways local participation has been private, but in Utah, as in the nation, the trend has been to place these functions under public control, and various state agencies have emerged and made important contributions to the overall effort.

Irrigation and Reclamation

Irrigation has been important to Utah in fact as it has been in tradition. Pioneer Mormons developed many of the technical and social patterns necessary for life in the arid region. Small land holding practices, cooperative economic activities, and ecclesiastical control were initiated; streams were diverted, diversion dams were constructed, and miles of canals were developed. The seasonal rhythm of ditch work and irrigation became a way of life. The legal instruments of irrigation, too, were developed. Progressive and effective early doctrines included public ownership and control of water; acquisition of private rights by priority of appropriation; the inalienability of water from the land upon which it was used; and cooperative local development by the water users. Of particular importance were the laws of 1852 and 1865 that respectively defined the role of the courts in controlling water for the public interest and established the irrigation district system of local administration.

Although it lacked the capital and the science to impound vast reservoirs or convey streams from one watershed to another, early Utah irrigation was successful. For several decades intensive cultivation and progressive utilization of primary waters met minimum needs for new farming opportunities. Crop productivity was above the national average, while farm debt and tenant farming were lower in Utah than almost anywhere else in America. Furthermore, Utah's small irrigated farms and neighboring villages did not involve people in the relentless isolation of farm life that existed elsewhere in the west. Authorities—notably John Wesley Powell—saw in Utah the rudiments of a workable national policy for the administration and distribution of the public domain in arid regions. While the inefficiency of overlapping and uncoordinated irrigation systems must be acknowledged, it has generally been conceded that Utah's irrigation performance compared favorably with other frontrunning irrigation states.

Private and State Projects

In 1880 a new territorial irrigation act heralded the waning of cooperative and local development and the dawn of a new era. The act's most important provisions reduced the public character of water, making it essentially private property that could be bought and sold independent of land. The two decades that followed saw private companies undertake great speculative reclamation projects that required heavy financing and advanced technology. By 1897 twenty-three companies existed. They were capitalized at a total of $17,000,000 (at least on paper) and proposed to open 846,000 acres to irrigation. Ingenious schemes and in some cases truly progressive agricultural systems were worked out in an effort to help farmers to quickly get into paying production. In addition, extensive advertising campaigns were conducted throughout America and even in Europe.

But big capital and advancing technology notwithstanding, private commercial enterprises were mostly unsuccessful. Many never got beyond the talking stage. Others encountered engineering problems too complex for the technology and scientific knowledge of the day.

Some companies, however, apparently had good prospects. One, the Bear River and Bear Lake Water Works and Irrigation Company in Box Elder County, actually succeeded in reclaiming almost 45,000 acres and delivering the water necessary for irrigation. The Bear River Company was capitalized at nearly $2,500,000, enjoyed the services of Samuel Fortier and Elwood Mead (two of the finest water engineers produced by America during those years), employed 7,000 men damming the Bear River and building a model system of canals, and carried on a successful promotional campaign that brought hundreds of hardworking farmers to Utah from Illinois and elsewhere in the midwest. (See map 20, p. 737.)

But, for all its good prospects, the Bear River Company went through a series of reorganizations and a welter of costly litigations before its collapsed interests were purchased by the Utah-Idaho Sugar Company in 1902 for $450,000. Among the problems contributing to its failure were distrust of its massive size and a lack of enthusiasm growing from its break with the older system that had been based on cooperation and local development. Homesteaders, speculators, and even farmers who bought company lands often found it in their interest not to buy company water. In short, while the company controlled the water it did not monopolize control of the land, and it lacked the necessary legal instruments and public support to make the project pay out.

Thus the Bear River Company and most other commercial enterprises failed to make lasting contributions. The 1890s were the high tide of capitalistic irrigation activity; some companies carried on into the new century.

Meanwhile, important related developments were underway in Utah and in the nation. Spread over a decade or more, these were part of a hard-fought movement by which the major initiative for reclamation of arid lands shifted from the local and the private to the public and ultimately to the national level.

Awakening federal interest in the matter was evident as early as 1888 when Congress established the Powell Irrigation Survey. Under its provisions Frederick H. Newell collected a mass of information concerning water supply, canals, and thirteen reservoir sites in Utah. Another evidence of mounting national interest was the Senate Special Committee on the Irrigation and Reclamation of Arid Lands, chaired by William M. Stewart of Nevada, which took testimony in Utah during 1889. The Stewart Committee found Utahns anxious to advance the cause of irrigation. It was also apparent that future development of Utah water would require a vastly greater capacity than had earlier systems, and that coordination was badly needed. Public opinion was divided on the proper role of the federal government, territorial government, and private capital in the development of water and land resources.

Utah's interest in irrigation also led the territory to play a leading role in the development of a national irrigation movement. The first National Irrigation Congress, which met in Salt Lake City in 1891, called for the federal government to grant public lands within the confines of arid states to those states. The Salt Lake resolution entered a national situation of growing complexity where the voices of private enterprise, states' rights, and the eastern states who saw little immediate gain in western reclamation contended with an initially weak but mounting cry for federal development of public lands and water.

In partial response to the Irrigation Congress resolution the Carey Act was passed by Congress in 1894. Sponsored by Senator Joseph M. Carey of Wyoming, this act permitted the government to grant up to 1,000,000 acres to individual states for development by those states. The Carey Act proved to be largely unworkable in Utah; its provision that the state be the agent of development was precluded by the state constitution. By 1913 some 830,494 acres had been approved under twenty-five Carey Act applications, but by 1920 no more than 23,000 acres had actually been reclaimed.

More successful were state projects growing out of the Utah Enabling Act of 1894. Section 12 permitted the state, as soon as the formalities of admission to the Union were completed, to select 500,000 acres of unappropriated public lands for the establishment of permanent reservoirs. In 1897 the legislature created a reservoir fund into which proceeds from the sale of 485,607 acres ($819,110) had been paid by 1920. Acting on this provision, the state made loans to seven irrigation companies between 1907 and 1913. It also undertook two major reclamation projects—the Hatchtown Project in Garfield County and the Piute Project in Piute County. Both promised success. But in 1914, after the Hatchtown Project was complete and some 6,000 acres had been sold to farmers, the dam washed out. The Piute Project reclaimed 35,000 acres at a cost of $790,000 to the state; in 1920 the water users purchased the entire project for $1,300,000.

In the meantime, cooperative irrigating companies, many of which had by this time assumed a secular organization by incorporating as mutual companies, continued to control most of the actual irrigating in Utah and to develop additional projects, a few that were of considerable size. Perhaps the most successful was the East Canyon Dam. Built in 1899 at a cost of $50,000, it impounded 3,834 acre-feet of water. During the first year of its use, added crop productivity more than paid for the dam. With this encouragement, the Davis and Weber Canal Company more than doubled the reservoir's capacity by adding twenty-five feet to the dam's height late in 1900. Other pioneer cooperatives that later became mutual companies made less spectacular gains.

Federal Projects

The 1902 passage of the National Reclamation Act—called the Newlands Act after its chief sponsor, Nevada Senator Francis G. Newlands—ushered in Utah's third and modern era of water development. More rightly characterized by the term *reclamation* than by *water development* or *irrigation,* the Newlands Act repudiated private enterprise and abolished local or state dominance. Arid states joined in a cry for immediate action, and by 1905 twenty projects—many of them of gigantic size—had been hastily authorized.

One of the soundest of the projects was the Strawberry Valley Project in central Utah. The first large-scale transmontane diversion from the Colorado River drainage to the Great Basin, it was also one of the earliest Bureau of Reclamation projects to develop hydroelectric power. In 1906 construction was initiated on supporting roads, a power plant, and a 19,500-foot tunnel. The storage unit consisted of a dam on Strawberry River and a diversion dam and collector canals on neighboring creeks. Construction continued until 1922. By the 1940s two additional power plants had been added and the delivery system had been improved. In the years after 1950 plans were laid to expand Strawberry Reservoir as part of the Central Utah Project, extending its capacity nearly four times and providing additional water for Utah Valley and new water for the enlarged Mona and Sevier Bridge reservoirs. (See map 20, p. 737.)

Not surprisingly, some friction was experienced between the Bureau of Reclamation and the Strawberry Valley Water Users. Disputes involved the claims of previous water users, the project costs, and the time allowed for repayment. As result of such problems combined with World War I and the agricultural depression of the 1920s, the project was not turned over to the local water users until 1926. Despite these problems, the Strawberry Valley Project may be judged a success. Some 16,000 new acres were opened to agriculture, and supplemental water was provided for an additional 26,000 acres. Several new agricultural industries were opened, hydroelectric plants contributed to the well-being of the community, the reservoir became a boon to recreation, and in general the southern part of Utah Valley showed a new economic vitality.

Although federal reclamation has continued to develop Utah's water potential, its story can be quickly concluded here. No new federal projects were undertaken until the 1920s. Following a 1924 independent study, the Bureau initiated a modest new program late in the decade. As the New Deal took shape in the 1930s with its philosophy of federal spending, a drive was launched that changed the face of Utah.

The 73,900 acre-foot Echo Reservoir near Coalville was commenced late in 1927 as the major feature of the Weber River Project, which was itself part of the vast Salt Lake Basin Project that had been briefly proposed in the 1924 report. Beginning with the Hyrum Dam in Cache County, seven New Deal reclamation projects were initiated. Including Moon Lake, Newton, Ogden River, Provo River, Sanpete, and Scofield, these projects were completed at a cost approximating $29,300,504 and impounded about 379,393 area feet of water. Along with irrigation, electrical power, and domestic water they opened new opportunities for recreation.

The depression projects were in turn dwarfed by projects that were authorized after World War II. The Colorado River Storage

Project harnessed the tumultuous waters of the Colorado drainage system with great reservoirs that fall largely within the State of Utah at Flaming Gorge on the Green River and Glen Canyon on the Colorado River. Reclaiming no land under their immediate dams, these mammoth projects focused upon the storage and distribution of the Upper Colorado Basin waters and upon recreation and hydroelectrical generation. As planned, the Central Utah Project will be even more important to Utah. Extending over the central and eastcentral part of the state, it provides Utah the opportunity to utilize most of the water allotted under the Colorado River Compact of 1922 and the Upper Basin Compact of 1948. By the terms of these two agreements, California, Arizona, Nevada, Utah, New Mexico, Colorado, and Wyoming—the Colorado River Basin states—have attempted to adjust their various interests in the river. The Central Utah Project will provide additional waters to the highly developed industrial and urban portions of Utah and will ultimately be used for municipal and industrial purposes, irrigation, hydroelectric power, recreation, and flood control and water quality control.

Importance of Reclamation

The reclamation movement was conceived in controversy and has continued to attract both ardent support and strong opposition. Politically and financially vulnerable because of its high costs and regional character, reclamation has also been attacked for what is said to be its wholesale and insensitive tampering with forces of nature, the longterm effects of which cannot be fully understood. Sentiment against reclamation was particularly strong after 1960, when the Sierra Club and other environmentalist forces came to the fore. But with much to gain in the immediate sense, Utahns have, in the main, favored reclamation. The state's people have found employment in its vast projects, opportunity in its new agricultural and hydroelectric potential, and pleasure in its recreational facilities. Not surprisingly, a number of Utah politicians have made it their stock-in-trade. Senator Reed Smoot (1903-33) often opposed federal control of waterways but worked for a coordinated program for conservation that adjusted the relative interests of private groups, of states, and of the nation. Democrat Elbert D. Thomas, who defeated Smoot, was instrumental in securing many of the Depression projects for the state. In the 1960s and 1970s Democratic Senator Frank E. Moss also emerged as a major voice in reclamation politics. But Utah's most ardent senatorial champion of reclamation was Arthur V. Watkins, who approached the matter during the 1940s and 1950s with a fervor opponents called evangelical. He was a major factor in many of the decisions leading to the Colorado River Storage Project and the Central Utah Project.

By merit of her irrigation tradition and the realities of her natural endowments, Utah has continued to be fully involved in water development, and her political and economic fortunes have been closely connected with it. Since 1880 Utah water development and reclamation have, in the main, followed the patterns that have been unfolding nationally. Like other arid states, Utah had a period (1880-1900) of capitalistic water development notable only for its limited success. The states' rights impulse with respect to reclamation has been strong in Utah as it has been elsewhere. And the overwhelming reality of federal reclamation projects has altered the state in many of its social and economic characteristics as it has in its natural profiles.

Conservation and Land Resource Management

Conservation in Utah has paralleled reclamation in a number of respects. Historically the two movements have grown from local and national concerns about natural resources, and they have been similar in timing. On the other hand, while reclamation's primary mission has been to salvage resources unusable or nearly unusable in their natural condition, conservation has focused on accessible resources and their wise use through management and regulation.

Nationally the conservation movement probably began in 1875 when the American Forestry Association was organized. The movement already boasted a number of achievements by 1905 when the Forest Service was created as part of the Agricultural Department. In 1891, Congress had provided for the designation of forest reserves that were closed to entry by private interests. During the next six years thirty-three million acres in thirty forest reserves were set aside by presidential order. In 1897 President Grover Cleveland withdrew vast additional tracts shortly before he left office. Thus, in its first three decades, the national conservationist movement had shown a special concern for forest resources and had developed strong connections with the Forest Service.

Conservation began early in Utah and continued in the twentieth century. Public control of water, timber, land, and grazing grounds for the good of the community had characterized the earliest settlement. As conservationist elements in Mormon stewardship yielded to speculative impulses in the 1890s a new conservation fortunately began to emerge. In 1894 the territorial legis-

Shafer #1 was drilled on the Colorado River near Moab shortly after World War I; it burned in 1925.

lature made it illegal to pollute streams, and concern for recreation led to the early establishment of a Fish and Game Commission. Support from Utah encouraged President Grover Cleveland to include the Uintah Reserve in the 21,379,400 acres that he withdrew for forest purposes. The next year the state legislature requested a grant of certain lands near Fish Lake in Sevier and Wayne counties; this led to the establishment of the Fish Lake Reserve in 1899. The Mormon Church voted to support federal withdrawal of public lands for protection of watersheds at its April Conference in 1902, and various communities petitioned the United States to withdraw their watersheds from grazing use by the end of that year.

But for all its support of conservation, Utah was not conservationist in the way national leaders of the movement were. What Thomas Alexander has called *advanced-progressive conservationists*, those favoring governmental development and suspecting the motives of state and business interests, stood at the head of the national movement. By contrast, most Utah leaders were what

Alexander has termed *business-minded conservationists.* The latter group favored some federal action but believed that private and state interests "ought to be included in conservation considerations." This stance was apparent in each of Utah's first three governors. Heber M. Wells favored positive action by the general government, but reacted with fear when over 4,000,000 acres of land were withdrawn in 1902 and 1903. His successors, John C. Cutler and William Spry, also had misgivings about the magnitude of Utah's national forests. Congressional leaders generally favored the reserve concept and gave cautious support to the creation of Utah's forests.

The Forest Service in Utah

In the year after 1902 a series of forests totalling nearly 4,000,000 acres were established extending from Cache Valley in the north to Pine Valley Mountain in the south. These forests, together with the Uintah and Fish Lake Reserves that had previously been established, comprised the natural base of Utah's national forests. (See map 21, p. 738.) By 1908 an administrative system had been developed that consisted of the Forest Service in Washington, D.C.; Forest Region IV, with headquarters in Ogden; the various forests, each of which was administered by a supervisor officed at some adjacent town; and the ranger districts, which were the local administrative units.

The Forest Service quickly began to exert a practical, if limited, control over a variety of economic activities which, taken together, accounted for much of the state's income. While timber, mining, transportation, and recreation were all important, the major concern of the Utah forests was with the related problems of overgrazing and watershed. With a much greater potential for winter grazing on its vast deserts than for summer grazing on its mountains, Utah stockmen had badly overgrazed the state's upland pastures by 1900. Together with extraordinarily heavy traffic in transient herds, this had depleted mountain grazing and cut away high elevation ground cover. Runoff from snow pack and from summer rains created unmanageable erosion that worsened progressively with time.

In controlling this, the first obligation of the Forest Service was to bring the number of livestock into line with the amount and condition of summer ranges. Numbers were immediately reduced. A million sheep were said to run in 1900 on the portion of the Wasatch Plateau that became the Manti Forest; permits for sheepherding were reduced to 191,000 by 1909. This process continued for both sheep and cattle, with each progressive cut in numbers being presented by the Forest Service as necessary because of over-grazing and watershed problems. The opposition of Utah stockmen and of their political allies slowed but did not frustrate the Forest Service in its determination to reduce livestock numbers.

To reduce friction and acquire insight into the local point of view, Utah forests employed many Utahns. This policy was largely successful in bridging the communications gap between the Forest Service and the community, though after a few years of work for the Forest Service even tradition-bound natives found that their basic commitments lay with the agency that employed them. On the other hand, the policy of employing locals provided an important source of employment for the sons of Utah's struggling small farms. A tradition exists that certain Utah ranching areas have virtually mothered the Forest Service by filling its ranks with their sons.

By the 1930s Utah's Forest Service had made much progress in controlling the grazing industry; some pressure on overgrazed mountains was relieved, but groundcover and eroded slopes were not restored. Indeed, the problem of watershed management proved to be almost beyond the capacity of the Forest Service—a fact that was apparent as devastating floods continued, notably at Farmington in Davis County and at Willard in Box Elder County. Also pointing to the magnitude of watershed control was a growing mass of technical data developed by such agencies as Utah State Agricultural College, the Great Basin Experiment Station, and the Intermountain Forest and Range Experiment Station.

Conservation in the Great Depression Years

During the depression the Soil Conservation Service and a number of relief programs provided funding and manpower necessary to arrest the progressive damage that forest drainage systems had suffered. Leaving much initiative in the hands of local residents, the Soil Conservation Service organized local districts throughout the state and provided technical staff members to be placed at the disposal of state and local governments as well as at the disposal of other federal agencies. District-wide plans were developed, some aspects of which extended to the public domain and to the national forests. Before 1936 ended numerous soil conservation projects were underway. In a typical report, the Manti National Forest called attention to 32.5 miles of contour furrows, 940 rods of log fence, 480 rods of barbed wire fence, and the transplanting of

5,000 Douglas firs, all carried on under Soil Conservation Service auspices. In the following decades the Soil Conservation Service directed and financed a wide variety of projects throughout the state.

The Federal Emergency Relief Administration and the Works Progress Administration also made substantial contributions to conservation in Utah during the 1930s. Their input was often in cooperation with that of the Civilian Conservation Corps, which established twenty-six camps in Utah before the end of 1933. Twenty were Forest Service camps, one was a National Park Service camp, and the remainder were state camps. During the eight remaining years of the Civil Conservation Corps' existence, many camps worked in conjunction with the Soil Conservation Service and the Grazing Service (later the Bureau of Land Management). An estimated $52,756,183 was spent by the Civil Conservation Corps in Utah, contributing to a much-improved situation by 1940.

Another development of the depression years was the Taylor Grazing Act, passed in 1934. By its terms some 173,000,000 acres of unreserved federal lands were withdrawn from public entry and placed under the administration of the Grazing Service in the Department of the Interior. During the decades that preceded this event, public and official opinion had divided on the desirability of placing the remaining public domain under federal regulation. Many Utahns, including livestock men, acknowledged that the open range system was outdated. Unlike most neighboring states, Utah did not favor cession of the public domain to the states, nor did it favor outright management by private interests. Congressman Don Colton led in the federal control movement prior to his defeat in 1932. Utah appears to have welcomed the advent of the Grazing Service, which involved local stockmen in the policy-making processes with characteristic New Deal concern for popular participation. Responding willingly if not eagerly, livestock men soon created grazing districts and associations to help govern them.

The Bureau of Land Management

In 1946 the Bureau of Land Management replaced the Grazing Service as chief proprietor of public lands. Although more than forty-seven percent of Utah's total land area, about twenty-four million acres, came under its jurisdiction, the Bureau of Land Management initially recognized only one constituency—Utah's livestock operators. Almost immediately, however, demands on the public domain began to broaden until the Bureau of Land Management's role extended to mineral leases, recreation, wildlife, water development, and various other functions under the multiple-use concept. Not surprisingly, the Bureau of Land Management dealt in substantial sums of money. From the inception of public lands management through 1975 some $234 million had been received in Utah—$20 million in 1975 alone. Of this sum mineral leases accounted for seventy-one percent. Under the terms of the Taylor Grazing Act and subsequent legislation, about one-third of the Bureau of Land Management receipts were passed on to the State of Utah.

Other federal agencies, including the Forest Service, the National Park Service, and the military, control additional land in Utah, bringing the total amount of land under federal jurisdiction to nearly thirty-five million acres (seventy-three percent). The State of Utah is also a great land proprietor: millions of acres of land allotted to the state for public schools, universities, and other institutions were sold at minimum prices during the early years of the century in keeping with policy that seemed more concerned with land exploiters than with the institutions to which land grants were made. Nevertheless, the state continues to administer more than three million acres.

The Rise of Environmentalism

A marked change in mood regarding the functions of land and of the entire environment took place after 1960. The growing national consciousness that scarcity, rather than abundance, was the norm brought new concern. Various forms of pollution were recognized to be of critical proportions. Industry was concentrated in the valley fold of the Wasatch Front. The number of automobiles multiplied. When temperature inversions turned valleys into giant exhaust tanks, residents gasped in some of the nation's filthiest air. Coal-burning power plants built in the late 1960s in Emery County and in neighboring Arizona provoked angry outbursts from environmentalists, and controversy peaked with the proposal to build a giant plant on Kane County's Kaiparowits Plateau in the mid 1970s. After a bitter confrontation the project was abandoned in 1976 with the environmentalists the apparent winners.

The Kaiparowits controversy was accentuated by the multiple problems of the energy crisis which, by the early 1970s, had penetrated the consciousness of all Utahns. Coal, a vast deposit of oil shale in eastern Utah, petroleum, and various potential sources of energy were all approached with new vigor that resulted from escalating prices and the need to establish domestic sources of energy. Exploration was greatly accelerated, and Price and other mining towns enjoyed a sharp upturn in economy. (See map 19, p. 736.)

In 1975 the Bureau of Land Management let two prototype oil shale leases on tracts southeast of Vernal amounting to about 10,000 acres for a total of $115 million. Geothermal steam energy leases were also issued on several tracts, the most notable of which was Roosevelt Hot Springs northeast of Milford. In addition, three proposed coal-fired generating plants are under consideration in southern Utah. At this writing all of these projects, and others like them, are still in the prestatement or public hearings stages. Whatever their prospects in terms of energy, it is apparent that many Utahns are concerned with the threat that the state will become an energy colony and a pollution dump to areas with the wealth and power to manage and control natural resources from afar.

Preservation and the National Parks

For Utah the growth of preservationist impulses has coincided closely with the development of reclamation and conservation. By 1900 Utahns and Americans generally recognized that in her canyons, deserts, and plateaus Utah possessed unique scenic and natural history attractions. Pioneers had viewed such inhospitable, but magnificent, areas with a pragmatic mix of antipathy and awe. John Wesley Powell and the scientists who followed him to Utah had found a motherlode of geological knowledge. And a small but influential fraternity of archaeologists, geologists, Indian traders, and river runners had sensed the romance and character of the southern and eastern half of the state—that portion coinciding with the Colorado Plateau. The region's champions dramatized successive areas in books, magazine articles, and scientific treatises. Some—like Theodore Roosevelt, who made the exhausting but richly rewarding trek to Rainbow Bridge in 1909—were widely publicized. Gradually the state and the nation awakened to the potential of Utah's natural wonders.

Beginning with the Natural Bridges National Monument in San Juan County, twelve national parks and monuments had been created by 1970. All but three of these were in southern Utah, and all but the Golden Spike National Historic Site at Promontory were designated for reasons of scenery, prehistory, geology, or a combination of the three. Acting under the terms of the National Antiquities Act of 1906, national monuments were created at the Natural Bridges in 1908, at Zion Canyon and the Rainbow Bridge in 1909, and at the Dinosaur Quarry in Uintah County in 1915.

No provisions were made for the administration of these first monuments, except for such care as neighboring national forests could provide. With Utah's Senator Reed Smoot taking a leading role in the movement, the National Park Service was established in 1916 and provision was made for the maintenance of Utah's four national monuments. In 1919 Zion National Monument (which had previously gone under the name *Mukuntuweap*) was accorded national park status and, fortunately, its name was changed. During the 1920s Hovenweep National Monument, Bryce Canyon National Monument, Timpanogos Cave National Monument, and Arches National Monument were all created, and in the 1930s Cedar Breaks and Capitol Reef national monuments were established. Bryce, Arches, and Capitol Reef were subsequently made national parks. In 1964 the Canyonlands National Park was created and in 1969 the Golden Spike National Historic Site was added. (See map 21, p. 738.)

Until midcentury the State of Utah limited its official interest in preservation and park programs to such support activities as highway development and the promotion of national parks by the State Travel Council. In 1957, however, mounting interest in parks of a historical, scenic, and recreational character led to the establishment of the Division of State Parks and Recreation, which has subsequently been administratively lodged in the Department of Natural Resources. Harold Fabian, a Salt Lake City lawyer with long-time interests in Virginia's Colonial Williamsburg, was instrumental in the Utah state park movement and was appointed the first chairman of the State Park and Recreation Commission. Serving in this capacity for many years, Fabian's interest in historical preservation was reflected in the early acquisition of several important historical properties, including the Territorial Statehouse at Fillmore, the stagecoach inn at Fairfield, and the Brigham Young and Jacob Hamblin homes which had for years been part of the Dixie State Park in Washington County.

Placing increasing emphasis upon its recreation function, the Division of Parks and Recreation also moved to acquire other sites until in 1973 its operations included eight state beaches, nine historical monuments, twelve recreation areas, seven state reserves, the Museum of Natural History at Vernal, and six state parks. Included in the latter category is the Great Salt Lake State Park, created in 1969 on the north end of Antelope Island to provide historical, recreational, and natural history activities. Likewise pointing to increasing sophistication are the division's important archaeological sites at Anasazi Indian Village in Garfield County,

Newspaper Rock and Edge of the Cedar Ruin in San Juan County, and Danger Cave northeast of Wendover. Originally known as Hands and Knees Cave, the latter was excavated from 1939 until 1955, and has yielded artifacts indicating that its first occupancy occurred prior to farming in the Euphrates and Nile valleys in the Old World. State Park and Recreation properties are located in twenty-four of the state's twenty-nine counties, with only Daggett, Iron, Sevier, Wayne, and Weber counties without state park facilities.

Water and winter sports, camping, fish and game opportunities, and scenic attractions join with historical and archaeological interest to draw an increasing number of visitors to Utah. With nearly 3,000,000 visits in 1972, State Park and Recreation facilities vie with the National Parks as popular sites for vacation activities. While somewhat less oriented than its federal counterpart to preservation for utilization by coming generations, the State Parks program nevertheless does much to regulate the use of natural facilities and to maintain them for extended use.

Conclusion

The continuing importance of the natural resources as contrasted to the cultural or industrial resources is highlighted in Utah's twentieth-century preoccupation with reclamation, conservation, and preservation. The national government assumed the primary burden for development and control in each field, and it progressively broadened its role by exerting increasing regulatory control, by spending more money, and by affecting the lives of a growing number of people. The State of Utah, too, enlarged its involvement in water development and in the regulation and preservation of resources during this era, with policies and expenditures growing to meet new needs.

Much was accomplished. The idea of public management of water and land resources and their development was widely accepted. The political and administrative machinery necessary to the task evolved. Progress was made toward full utilization of water, the key resource. Steps were taken to avert the worst excesses of resource exploitation. A number of scenic and natural history resources were preserved for the enjoyment of this and future generations. Economic opportunity was enhanced, lives were enriched, and the most exploitive methods were moderated and rationalized. Yet as 1976 came and went it was clear to all that resource management was a continuing problem that would have to be solved again and again in the face of changing times.

Chapter 35
Bibliographical Essay

The historical literature on the topics treated in this chapter is much more extensive at the national and regional levels than it is for Utah. Fortunately there is considerable overlap, and many broader works extend to Utah. In terms of reclamation Alfred R. Golz, *Reclamation in the United States* (1961), is among the better general works. More closely related to Utah is Norris Hundley's *Water and the West: The Colorado River Compact and the Politics of Water in the American West* (1975). The summer 1971 issue of *UHQ* was devoted to reclamation in Utah. Among the worthwhile articles appearing there are Thomas G. Alexander, "An Investment in Progress: Utah's First Federal Reclamation Project, The Strawberry Valley Project"; Leonard J. Arrington and Thomas C. Anderson, "The 'First' Irrigation Reservoir in the United States: The Newton, Utah, Project"; Stephen A. Merrill, "Reclamation and the Economic Development of Northern Utah: The Weber River Project"; and Kenneth W. Baldridge, "Reclamation Work of the Civilian Conservation Corps, 1933-42." Also useful is William Peterson, "History of Federal Reclamation in Utah by Projects," in Wain Sutton, *Utah: A Centennial History* (1949), Vol. I. Among the Bureau of Reclamation's most useful publications is *Reclamation Project Data* (1961).

Early irrigation in Utah has been widely treated in general histories of the territory and of the Mormons. More specialized works on water development include Charles H. Brough, *Irrigation in Utah* (1898); George Thomas, *The Development of Institutions Under Irrigation . . . (1920)*; and William E. Smyth, *The Conquest of Arid America* (1899), which has two chapters dealing with Mormon irrigation. Of these three, Thomas is the most complete and authoritative. Alexander, "John Wesley Powell, The Irrigation Survey . . . in Utah", *UHQ,* Spring 1969, points up Powell's role in the second phase of water development while George Dewey Clyde, "History of Irrigation in Utah," *UHQ,* January 1959, provides a helpful survey. Three illuminating government publications also merit mention: *Report of the Special Committee of the United States Senate on the Irrigation and Reclamation of Arid Lands* (1890); John Wesley Powell, *Report on the Lands of the Arid Region of the United States, With a More Detailed Account of the Lands of Utah* (1879); and Elwood Mead, *Report of Irrigation Investigations in Utah* (1903).

For the conservation movement three general works may be cited. Gifford Pinchot, *Breaking New Ground* (1947), portrays the developing conservation movement and the Forest Service as Pinchot conceived them. Elmo Richardson, *The Politics of Conservation: Crusades and Controversies, 1897-1913* (1962), deals with the movement's early politics and touches briefly on contributions of Utah's first three state governors. Paul H. Roberts, *Hoof Prints on Forest Ranges* (1963), portrays the grazing conditions out of which the Forest Service emerged in its regional context and treats a number of Utah situations in the process. Charles S. Peterson, "Albert F. Potter's Wasatch Survey, 1902 . . .", *UHQ,* Spring 1971, considers the survey from which nearly 4,000,000 acres of Utah highlands were designated as national forests, and his *Southeastern Utah and the La Sal National Forest* (1975) treats one national forest in its regional context. His "Small Holding Land Patterns in Utah, and . . . Forest Watershed Management," *Forest History,* July (1973) calls attention to practices leading to overgrazing and flooding. Walter P. Cottam, *Our Renewable Wild Lands—A Challenge* (1961), collects six bulletins and position papers by Cottam, including "Is Utah Sahara-Bound?"

For the National Park movement Donald C. Swain, *Federal Conservation Policy, 1921-1933* (1963) and *Wilderness Defender: Horace M. Albright and Conservation* (1970), provide good general information. For the Utah parks Angus M. Woodbury's "A History of Southern Utah and Its National Parks," *UHQ,* July-October 1944, is the most complete but is still sketchy. Andrew K. Larson, "Zion National Park With Some Reminiscences Fifty Years Later," *UHQ,* Fall 1969, provides an intimate glimpse of one park during its early period. Of the dozens of *National Geographic Magazine* articles that treat parks and national monuments in Utah, the following are especially useful: Lewis F. Clark, "Amid the Mighty Walls of Zion," January 1954; William Belnap, "Nature Carves Fantasies in Bryce Canyon," October 1958; Neil M. Judd, "Beyond the Clay Hills: An Account of the National Geographic Society's Reconnaissance of a Previously Unexplored Section of Utah," March 1924; and Byron Cummings, "Great Natural Bridges of Utah," February 1910. Another popular account of special merit is W. W. Dyar, "The Colossal Bridges of Utah . . .", *Century,* August 1904. Charlie R. Steen, ed., "The Natural Bridges of White Canyon: A Diary of H. L. A. Culmer," *UHQ,* Winter 1972, brings to the fore the magic of one great natural wonder and the unpenetrated rawness of the country in which it is found.

Chapter 36
An American Commonwealth

Richard D. Poll

U tah's experience has been in many respects unique, as these chapters have abundantly demonstrated. Not only have the ties—and tensions—between church and state been unprecedented in scope and duration in American history, but the Mormon thread has been the preoccupation of most of the historians who have worked with the records of the Beehive State. It may be appropriate, therefore, that *Utah's History* close with a reminder that for all its distinctiveness, the forty-fifth state has much in common with her sisters. For, as S. George Ellsworth emphasizes in *Utah's Heritage* (1972), "The history of Utah and the history of the United States have always run side by side. Utah history cannot properly be considered separately."

This judgment may be validated by going back to the recorded beginnings—noting in passing that the people of Utah's prehistory belong to the epic of the American southwest, which anthropologists are gradually piecing together.

As the bicentennial commemorations of the Domínguez-Escalante expedition noted, Utah's documented story is as old as the United States. But for accidental delays, the two Franciscan *padres* and their companions would have left Santa Fe on the very day that the founding fathers were adopting the Declaration of Independence. Washington was in retreat and the prospects for the new nation were bleak when the little band of missionary explorers bade farewell to the Indians of Utah Valley on September 25, 1776, promising to return within a year. Had they done so, Utah's history might be merged in the American chronicle with that of New Mexico or California.

The Utah Bicentennial Statehood Day observance on January 3, 1976, recalled the first statehood celebration on January 6, 1896, with a flag-draped Tabernacle, a chorus of children, a military band, and comments by Mormon Church President Spencer W. Kimball and Utah State Governor Calvin L. Rampton.

Following Spain's failure to plant mission and presidio here, the region knew only occasional, transient white men until the fur trappers arrived a half-century later. From the British Northwest, Mexican Santa Fe, and American Missouri came Peter Skene Ogden, Etienne Provost, Jim Bridger, and their companions, converging in the mid 1820s on what journalist Samuel Bowles would later describe as "a region whose uses are unimaginable, unless to hold the rest of the globe together, or to teach patience to travelers." For twenty years the mountain men harvested beaver and geographic lore, respecting no political boundaries and leaving few memorials. The people of Utah's first seven decades—from the

Spanish trailblazers to John C. Fremont and Lansford W. Hastings—were in many ways distinctive, but they clearly belong to the main lines of historical development of the United States.

What may be said of the people of the next half-century—the pioneer settlers and state builders? How American were they?

Not to be forgotten are the thousands who came to Utah in the territorial period to build railroads, man military posts, found business houses, dig mines, operate stage lines, explore rivers, and fill governmental appointive offices. They were as American as the melting pot, the gold rush, the business cycle, and the political machine. These gentile Utahns never numbered more than twenty percent of the territorial population, but they provided many of the closest connections between Utah and the Union.

Also important were the Utes, Paiutes, Gosiutes, Shoshones, and Navajos who were already here in 1847. Under the influence of the policy that it is better to feed the Indians than to fight them, they were exposed to such well-meant experiments as Indian farms, Indian missions, and the adoption of Indian women and children. But in the end they were pushed onto reservations under conditions hardly different from their tribal kinsman elsewhere in the West. They would be part of the nation's Native American problem in the twentieth century.

Most prominent, of course, were the Mormons—from 1847 to 1896 the most numerous and stubborn human facts in the Utah story. Had they been permitted to express their convictions and capabilities in isolation, they might have produced a unique and autonomous theocratic society. But this was not to be. Whatever may have been the hopes or expectations of the Mormon leaders when they picked the Great Basin for a haven, the American victory in the Mexican War subjected them to the vicissitudes of national and sectional politics and territorial government.

Any assessment of their Americanism in this context must dismiss the grotesque stereotypes of anti-Mormonism and the unworldly images of Mormon folklore. The Mormon founders of Utah were men and women who were seeking happiness for themselves and their children in spartan circumstances. Their religion profoundly influenced their lives, but it did not lift them out of their surroundings or their century. Whether gathered from Europe and the East or born in the mountain valleys, they reflected and related to the world outside Utah in many ways.

The Mormon migration was spectacular for its extent and planning. But the same kinds of conestoga wagons carried Oregonians and Californians along the same Platte River and across the same South Pass. The Donner Party served the Mormons by clearing the last part of the road into the Salt Lake Valley, and the Latter-day Saints provided ferries and roads for tens of thousands of gentile emigrants on the transcontinental trails. Human fallibility led many of the Donners to tragic death in the Sierras and many of the Mormon handcart pioneers to tragic death on the high plains of Wyoming.

The uniqueness of Utah colonization lay in the motivating religious zeal, the existence and widespread acceptance of strong leadership, the practice of plural marriage, and the pervasive cooperative elements of the Law of Consecration and the United Order. The individual exertions that built homes, farms, businesses, and sometimes fortunes had their parallels elsewhere, and the impressive achievement of the Mormon founders has undergone the same mythologizing process by which Americans have made folk heroes out of Washington, Lincoln, and other builders of the republic.

As for the details of pioneering, potatoes were planted in the Great Basin the same as they were planted elsewhere. Adobes were made, horses were shod, hams were smoked, candles were dipped, flour was milled, pottery was fired, wine was pressed, and cloth was woven according to the techniques of the time. Even irrigation was not original to Utah, though substantial additions to its technology were developed here.

Pneumonia, smallpox, childbed fever, and Indians were hazards to health in Utah as they were throughout the West. The settlers of Utah called in the Mormon elders when they were sick, but they also called in herb doctors such as Willard Richards and Philadelphia-educated physicians such as Romania Pratt and Ellis Shipp. Midwives performed many medical tasks according to nineteenth-century understanding; some appreciated the importance of sanitation and others did not. A diphtheria epidemic took 749 lives in Salt Lake City in 1880, Mormons and gentiles alike.

Women were as busy in Utah as they were in other parts of America, and they were doing mostly the same things. They produced impressive quantities of poetry, quilts, articles on woman suffrage, silk pillowcovers, corn puddings, burial clothes, and babies. They were frequently breadwinners as well as homemakers. Their interest in secular culture was sometimes criticized by conservative community leaders, but the minutes of the Polysophical Society and the files of the *Woman's Exponent* show the scope and quality of their strivings. How plural marriage affected the ten to twenty percent of Mormon women who entered the practice needs more study than it has received; spokeswomen like Emmeline B. Wells and Belinda Pratt contended vigorously that they were not oppressed. Dr. Martha Hughes Cannon, who served in Utah's first state senate, maintained that a plural wife was not as tied down as a single wife: "If her husband has four wives, she has three weeks of freedom every single month." It is not improbable that such imported ideas as romantic love and female emancipation contributed to the waning interest in polygamy late in the century.

In many ways the Mormons of Utah Territory were involved in the business of America. They manned the Pony Express stations and helped build the transcontinental railroad. Few of them fought in the battles of the Civil War, but a Mormon cavalry unit patrolled the overland telegraph line in 1862, and when Lincoln died the people of Utah mourned. To a degree their cities reflected Joseph Smith's plan for the City of Zion, but the buildings that replaced the first dugouts and cabins showed contemporary architectural styles. The Salt Lake Theater was Greek Revival in design and American eclectic in programming—a very important bridge to the world beyond the Wasatch.

The boys of Orderville preferred "store-bought" pants and the daughters of Brigham Young favored eastern fashions because they belonged to an era as well as to a church. Men of the priesthood read the Salt Lake *Tribune* and their wives shopped in stores owned by Jews and gentiles in response to the crosscurrents that were blowing in Utah. (Despite their editorial antagonism, eighty percent of the content of the *Deseret News* and the *Tribune* was interchangeable.) An eastern journalist watching Utahns celebrate the nation's centennial in Ogden in 1876 would have found it difficult to tell which of the participants were Mormons. If he were a knowledgeable journalist, of course, he would have noticed that no major Mormon leader was present, and it would have strengthened his awareness of one respect in which territorial Utah was definitely different.

From the Nauvoo days when Joseph Smith first taught the concept of the political Kingdom of God and created the secret Council of Fifty to assist in its planning, the Mormon attitude toward the government of the United States was ambivalent. On the one hand, America was declared to be a choice land, its Constitution divinely inspired. On the other hand, the government was expected to give way before the millennium to a theodemocracy manned by priesthood holders and like-minded non-Mormons. For a generation the Mormon leaders in Utah conducted their relations with the government in Washington on the premise that they were dealing with a transitory institution. Brigham Young and his successor, John Taylor, preserved the shadow structure of the State of Deseret and periodically restaffed the Council of Fifty because, as Young put it in a message to the ghost legislature in the midst of the American Civil War: "Our government is going to pieces and it will be like water that is spilt upon the ground. . . . The time will come when we will give laws to the nations of the earth."

Given this expectation, together with the frequently perverse behavior of federal officials, it is not surprising that expressions of patriotism in early Utah were frequently muted. Yet in both kingdom-building and statehood-seeking, Utah's early leaders were notably and increasingly pragmatic. And in following what Howard R. Lamar has called "a different but essentially American path," they found themselves in a by no means unique predicament. According to Lamar:

> . . . in trying to establish cultural and institutional pluralism in the United States in the nineteenth century the Mormons came up against deepset conformist beliefs, in defense of which anti-Mormon Americans proved to be willing to suspend civil rights, use force, and violate traditional constitutional limitations on the powers of government.

In espousing plural marriage and church control of the economy and polity of Utah Territory, the Mormons found themselves under increasing attack from a national government and public that branded these practices as immoral and unAmerican. Their responses were as expedient as circumstances and conscience required. They were neither the first nor last Americans to appeal to a higher law.

When Lot Smith, about to put the torch to a government supply train during the Utah War, met the plea, "For God's sake, don't burn the trains," he coolly replied, "It is for His sake that I am going to burn them." Comparable convictions sent John Brown to Harper's Ferry two years later. When John Taylor called for civil disobedience after the passage of the Edmunds Act, he was in the American lineage of Susan B. Anthony and Martin Luther King, Jr. The Deseret Telegraph girls who used their technological marvel to warn polygamists that United States marshals were advancing were in tune with the antislavery conductors of the underground railroad. As George Q. Cannon donned his prison stripes for a publicity photo at the Utah Territorial Penitentiary, he might have quoted Thoreau: "Under a government which imprisons any unjustly, the true place for a just man is also in prison."

The nature of Utah's participation in the 1876 centennial celebration reflects this context. Railroads, mines, and commerce were undercutting the socioeconomic order of the pioneers, and the battle to end church control of elective offices was already joined. That the biggest commemoration of America's centenary took place in Ogden—the Mormon city where the old and new orders were in most intimate contact—is symbolic.

The next twenty years changed matters radically. Federal legislation disfranchised at least 12,000 voters and stripped the Mormon Church of its property. The courts stamped more than 1,300 polygamists as criminals. When tacit indications of willingness to compromise on polygamy, plus energetic lobbying in Washington, did not reverse the national tide, Mormon Church President Wilford Woodruff took the decisive public step, announcing in September 1890 that the church would no longer perform plural marriages. The abandonment of the Kingdom of God policies of political solidarity and economic self-sufficiency quickly followed.

Though some clung to the old priorities, it was for most Utahns as if a great load had been lifted. Since the millennial fulfillment of what Thomas O'Dea called "the theocratic and separatist aspects" of Mormonism was apparently to be postponed, the burdensome conflicts of loyalty could now be resolved in favor of the "democratic and patriotic motives which were equally genuine and equally well grounded in Mormon doctrine."

Utahns overwhelmingly approved the 1895 constitution, with its female suffrage and its prohibitions on polygamy and the mingling of church and state. The governor-elect was Heber M. Wells, a son of Daniel H. Wells, who had commanded the Nauvoo Legion when the forces of the United States were forbidden to enter Utah Territory almost forty years earlier. In reviewing the long struggle for statehood, Governor Wells congratulated both the state and the nation:

The State, because of the great benefaction of Constitutional government bestowed by a wise and generous Congress; the Nation, because of the addition of a new commonwealth, pledged to the perpetuity of the Union, and possessed of infinite treasures which the State, upon her admission, lays at the feet of the Nation.

The years of Utah history that have followed statehood span one generation in which the distinctive elements of the territorial period were eliminated or papered over as rapidly as possible, and two more generations in which the state and the nation became so interlocked that one might ask what meaningful distinctiveness remains.

Of the transitional years between 1896 and the end of World War I, Charles S. Peterson has written:

Most Utahns, particularly its Mormon society, wanted statehood, and the symbol of belonging to the larger society of America that it implied, with a fervor that is difficult for us to grasp. . . . Once they had achieved this membership, they went about the business of proving that they merited it with enthusiastic and sometimes uncritical energy.

All thoughts of self-sufficiency were abandoned as Utah's land, water, and minerals became the basis of an economy whose prosperity depended on outside capital and markets. Strawberry Reservoir water began to flow to the orchards and sugar beet fields in Utah Valley. Hydroelectric power, in whose development Utahns pioneered, began to flow to the cities along the Wasatch Front and the mines and smelters of the Oquirrh Mountains. The new immigrants came in increasing numbers into the mines and mills of Carbon County and the Salt Lake Valley, exciting fears of trade unionism and other alien ideologies, and a Utah firing squad gave Joe Hill to the folklore of the labor movement. Seven billion dollars' worth of copper began to emerge from what Arrington and Gary Hansen have called "the richest hole on earth."

A level of prosperity was achieved in these first statehood years that Utah did not enjoy again until World War II. In the process, however, Utah took on much of the economic configuration of the other mountain states—dependence upon extractive industries and external funding and subjection to federal transportation, tariff, and public land policies that reflected the greater political clout of other parts of the country.

If statehood did not immediately erect a wall of separation between church and state, the political problems of B. H. Roberts and Reed Smoot reinforced the resolve of most Utahns that elections and government should be conducted within the conventional framework of American politics. The effort of Thomas Kearns and others to recreate Mormon-gentile political division through the American Party had less impact on Utah as a whole than did the national Progressive movement of the early twentieth century. The pendulum swings that still characterize Utah elections appeared early; from William Jennings Bryan to William Howard Taft and back to Woodrow Wilson was quite an oscillation in twenty years. Public differences of opinion between

Mormon leaders on such issues as prohibition and the League of Nations further emphasized that the day of obligatory Mormon positions on political questions was past. Fullfledged support of the national effort in the Spanish-American War, the Pershing expedition into Mexico, and the World War set the direction that Utah would follow in more recent conflicts.

There is, Ellsworth's text affirms, "little uniqueness to Utah's history after 1920." The era of the flapper and the speakeasy produced its rebellions and its reactions in Utah—the predominance of the reactions reflecting the conservatism that has prevailed in Utah during most of the twentieth century. Business and government policies blunted the drive to strengthen the labor movement. More insubstantial manifestations were a short-lived statute outlawing the sale of cigarettes and a legislative proposal that was never adopted specifying the maximum permissible clearance of ankle and Adam's apple in feminine fashions.

Like the other mountain states, Utah experienced the economic troubles of the between-wars era. The nation's depressions were felt somewhat more severely because of the dependent nature of the state economy. Utah's agriculture never recovered from the collapse of 1920-21 until another world conflict brought a new world market, and mining reached 1918 production levels only briefly in the late 1920s before being hit by the Great Depression. For the thirty-five percent of the working force who were unemployed in 1932, even potatoes at a half-cent per pound and hamburger at two pounds for nineteen cents were hard to get. In 1938 Utah had thirty-two percent more workers on Works Progress Administration projects and forty-five percent more young men in the Civilian Conservation Corps than the national average. The 1930s were the third consecutive decade in which more people moved out of Utah than moved in.

Economic conditions made Utah so solidly Democratic that she voted four times for Franklin D. Roosevelt, despite anti-New Deal pronouncements by Mormon Church President Heber J. Grant and his strong counselor, J. Reuben Clark, Jr. The governor's office was in Democratic hands for six consecutive terms, and the party controlled the legislature for almost twenty years. (It should be noted that the Democratic Party in Utah, even during the New Deal, was more moderate than liberal, and that during the statehood years its more successful leaders, from James H. Moyle and William H. King to Calvin L. Rampton and Frank E. Moss, have concentrated on issues of local concern and avoided the "liberal" label. Only Senator Elbert D. Thomas and Governor Herbert B.

Maw, both products of Depression politics, identified strongly with the reform elements in the Democratic Party.)

With World War II the integration of Utah and the United States became virtually complete. Most of the military and defense installations continued beyond the peacemaking and were supplemented by other federal agencies and programs that have been fundamental to Utah's recent economic growth and well-being. The benefits have not been without a price, as Utah has experienced the same federal constraints as have the other public land states of the West. The development—or exploitation—of the timber, water, minerals, and even the scenery of seventy percent of the state's area is subject to policies made outside Utah. The pronounced political swing to the right in the 1970s reflects an anti-Washington sentiment that is faintly reminiscent of the feelings many Utahns had a century ago.

Most national trends of the late twentieth century—urban sprawl, civil rights reform, rising divorce rates, the Vietnam malaise, environmental pollution, women's liberation, TV-addiction, rising affluence, high taxes, Indian "self-determination," chronic poverty, and energy shortages—have been manifest in Utah. Such phenomena as the high birth rate and the majority opinions on welfare statism, right-to-work, feminism, liquor-by-the-drink, right to life, anti-Communism, and detente reflect the prevailing political conservatism of the American West and the still powerful influence of the Mormon Church when the leadership obliquely or directly defines a Mormon position.

Utah's observance of the United States Bicentennial was in notable contrast to the restrained 1876 celebration. In exercises in the Salt Lake Tabernacle patterned after the statehood ceremonies eighty years earlier, Governor Rampton and Mormon Church President Spencer W. Kimball extolled Utah's patriotic heritage, and flag-waving children helped to envision the future in terms of the American dream rather than the millennial hope. As Utah moves with the nation into her third century, many of the signs are favorable, though the challenges are great. Such major problems as urban congestion, air pollution, remote and limited water resources, unassimilated ethnic minorities, and continuing political and social tension between some Mormons and some non-Mormons call for solution. Such valuable assets as educational development, community pride, a strong allegiance to the work ethic, and those "infinite treasures" of natural wealth extolled by Governor Wells in 1896 justify some optimism in assessing the future of the Beehive State.

Chapter 36
General Bibliographical Essay

Much of this chapter is based upon the author's "The Americanism of Utah," *UHQ*, Winter 1976, and language taken therefrom is used with the permission of the Utah State Historical Society. The chapter also reflects impressions and judgments formed while editing other chapters of *Utah's History*.

Among works more or less comprehensive in scope, the following titles have been particularly useful to the authors and editors of this volume.

General surveys of Utah history begin with Hubert Howe Bancroft, *History of Utah, 1540-1886* (1889), the pioneer work by a non-Mormon historian, with copious footnotes that are a resource which is still being mined. Orson F. Whitney, *History of Utah* (1892-1904), four volumes, has a heavy political emphasis and Mormon bias; its last volume is biographical. Whitney's one-volume *Popular History of Utah* (1916) and Levi Edgar Young's *The Founding of Utah* (1923) were staples in libraries and schools for more than a generation. Milton R. Hunter, *Utah, the Story of Her People* (1946), appeared in several formats and was the public school text for many years. Leland H. Creer's editing of the first part of Andrew Love Neff's unfinished in-depth study gave college classes a basic text, *History of Utah, 1847-1869* (1940), until it went out of print. Gustive O. Larson, *Outline History of Utah and the Mormons* (1958 and revisions) has since provided a synoptic text with a Mormon emphasis but with objective perspective. S. George Ellsworth, *Utah's Heritage* (1972), information-packed and profusely illustrated, is the current public school text.

Cooperatively produced works that are useful for reference include Noble Warrum, ed., *Utah Since Statehood: Historical and Biographical* (1919), three volumes; Frank Esshom, *Pioneers and Prominent Men of Utah* (1913); Utah Writers Project, *Utah, A Guide to the State* (1941); and Wain Sutton, ed., *Utah, A Centennial History* (1949), three volumes. Wayne Stout, ed., *History of Utah* (1967-1971), three volumes, is excessively argumentative.

Although focused on the Latter-day Saints, several works are invaluable concerning many facets of Utah history. B. H. Roberts, *A Comprehensive History of the Church of Jesus Christ of Latter-day Saints, Century I* (1930), six volumes, is political in emphasis and defensive in tone in dealing with the Utah period. Two useful reference works by Assistant Church Historian Andrew Jenson are *Latter-day Saints Biographical Encyclopedia* . . . (1901-1936), four volumes, and

Encyclopedic History of The Church ... (1941). Nels Anderson, *Desert Saints: The Mormon Frontier in Utah* (1942), has valuable insights into pioneer life. Leonard J. Arrington, *Great Basin Kingdom: An Economic History of the Latter-day Saints, 1830-1900* (1958), is undoubtedly the most frequently cited volume on Mormon and Utah history to appear since World War II. James B. Allen and Glen M. Leonard, *The Story of the Latter-day Saints* (1976), is a sympathetic but comprehensive survey based on current research; its bibliography lists hundreds of books and articles that relate to Utah history. The forthcoming sixteen-volume sesquicentennial history of the Mormon Church will contain much information for students of Utah history.

Two recent works of general interest, both illustrated, are Helen Zeese Papanikolas, ed., *The Peoples of Utah* (1976), and *Deseret, 1776-1976: A Bicentennial Illustrated History of Utah by the Deseret News* (1975). David E. Miller, *Utah History Atlas* (1977 ed.), is valuable for both maps and historical explanations.

The files of *Utah Historical Quarterly* (1928-   ) document the important work of the Utah State Historical Society in sponsoring research and publication; the reviews in the quarterly evaluate virtually every book that has appeared in the last half-century of even marginal relevance to the Beehive State. An index is available for volumes 1-33. Another collection of general reference value is that of the Daughters of Utah Pioneers, which has appeared under three titles, all compiled and edited by Kate B. Carter: *Heart Throbs of the West* (1939-1951), twelve volumes; *Treasures of Pioneer History* (1952-1957), six volumes; *Our Pioneer Heritage* (1959-1975), eighteen volumes.

Supplementary Bibliography

The most useful source for recent Utah history research is the *Utah Historical Quarterly,* which contains, both articles and reviews of relevant books. Some important findings have also appeared in *Western Historical Quarterly, Sunstone* (quarterly) *Dialogue: A Journal of Mormon Thought* (quarterly), and *Journal of Mormon History* (annual). The following list of books was selected by the editor from a much larger number of titles that have been published since *Utah's History* first went to press.

Alexander, Thomas G., and Jessie L. Embry, eds. *After 150 Years: The Latterday Saints in Sesquicentennial Perspective.* Charles Redd Monographs in Western History, No. 13. Midvale UT: Signature Books, 1983.

Alexander, Thomas G., and James B. Allen. *Mormons and Gentiles: A History of Salt Lake City.* Boulder CO: Pruett Publishing, 1984.

Arrington, Leonard J. *Brigham Young: American Moses.* New York: Alfred A. Knopf, 1985.

Beecher, Maurine Ursenbach, and Davis Bitton, eds. *New View of Mormon History: A Collection of Essays in Honor of Leonard J. Arrington.* Salt Lake City: University of Utah Press, 1987.

Bringhurst, Newell G. *Brigham Young and the Expanding Mormon Frontier.* Boston: Little, Brown & Company, 1986.

Bushman, Richard L. *Joseph Smith and the Beginnings of Mormonism.* Urbana: University of Illinois Press, 1984.

Campbell, Eugene E. *Establishing Zion: The Mormon Church in the American West, 1847-1869.* Salt Lake City: Signature Books, 1988.

Carter, Thomas, and Peter Goss. *Utah's Historic Architecture, 1847-1940.* Salt Lake City: University of Utah Press, 1987.

Crawley, Peter. *The Constitution of the State of Deseret.* Provo: Friends of the Harold B. Lee Library, 1982.

Embry, Jessie L. *Mormon Polygamous Families: Life in the Principle.* Salt Lake City: University of Utah Press, 1987.

Firmage, Edwin B., and R. Collin Mangrum. *Zion in the Courts: A Legal History of the Church of Jesus Christ of Latter-day Saints, 1830-1900.* Urbana: University of Illinois Press, 1988.

Geer, Deon C., Klaus D. Gurgel, Wayne L. Wahlquist, Howard A. Christy, and Gary B. Peterson, eds. *Atlas of Utah.* Ogden/Provo: Weber State College/Brigham Young University Press, 1981.

Gerlach, Larry R. *Blazing Crosses in Zion.* Logan: Utah State University Press, 1981.

Godfrey, Kenneth W., Audrey M. Godfrey, and Jill Mulvay Derr. *Women's Voices: An Untold History of the Latter-day Saints, 1830-1900.* Salt Lake City: Deseret Book, 1982.

Jackson, Richard, ed. *The Mormon Role in the Settlement of the West.* Charles Redd Monographs in Western History, No. 9. Provo: Brigham Young University Press, 1978.

Kimball, Stanley B. *Historic Sites and Markers Along the Mormon and Other Great Western Trails.* Urbana: University of Illinois Press, 1988.

Kimball, Stanley B. *Heber C. Kimball: Mormon Patriarch and Pioneer.* Urbana: University of Illinois Press, 1981.

Logue, Larry M. *A Sermon in the Desert: Belief and Behavior in Early St. George, Utah.* Urbana: University of Illinois Press, 1988.

Long, E. B. *The Saints and the Union: Utah Territory During the Civil War.* Urbana: University of Illinois Press, 1981.

Lyman, Edward Leo. *Political Deliverance: The Mormon Quest for Utah Statehood.* Urbana: University of Illinois Press, 1985.

Madsen, Brigham D. *Corinne: The Gentile Capital of Utah.* Salt Lake City: Utah Salt Lake City: University of Utah Press, 1983.

Madsen, Brigham D. *Corinne: The Gentile Capitol of Utah.* Salt Lake City: Utah State Historical Society, 1980.

May, Dean L. *Utah: A People's History.* Salt Lake City: University of Utah Press, 1987.

McCormick, John S. *Salt Lake City: The Gathering Place.* Woodland Hills, CA: Windsor Publications, 1980.

Newell, Linda King, and Valeen Tippetts Avery. *Mormon Enigma: The Biography of Emma Hale Smith.* New York: Doubleday, 1984.

Powell, Allan Kent. *San Juan County: People, Resources, and History.* Salt Lake City: University of Utah Press, 1983.

Roberts, Richard C., and Richard W. Sadler. *Ogden: Junction City.* Northridge CA: Windsor Publications, 1985.

Stott, Clifford L. *Search for Sanctuary: Brigham Young and the White Mountain Expedition.* Salt Lake City: University of Utah Press, 1984.

Van Wagoner, Richard S. *Mormon Polygamy: A History.* Salt Lake City: Signature Books, 1985.

Chart A
PERCENTAGE OF THE POPULATION LIVING IN URBAN
AREAS: UTAH AND THE UNITED STATES, 1860–1970

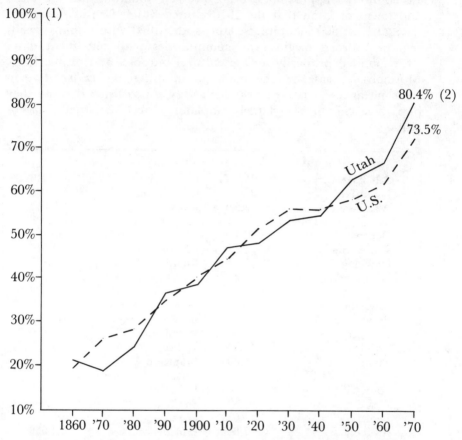

Notes:
1. The vertical axis uses a logarithmic scale in order to show the rate of change rather than absolute change. The slope of the line between two points on the chart indicates the rate of change from one point in time to another.
2. The percentages for 1970 are based on the new Bureau of the Census definition of *urban* (Standard Metropolitan Statistical Area). The change exaggerates the urban shift between 1960 and 1970 but does not affect the relative positions of Utah and the United States.

Source: United States Census for 1860-1970.

Table A
UTAH'S URBAN BEGINNINGS

Listed in the approximate order of their founding are the cities and towns of Utah that the 1970 United States Census showed to have at least 500 inhabitants. Unless identified with mining, smelting, or railroad origins, the communities with settlement dates were founded primarily for agricultural purposes and primarily by Mormons. A case can be made for a different *founding* date in some instances. The *expansion communities* are so listed because they owe their existence to largely unplanned overflow from adjacent cities.

1847		Fillmore		1,411
Salt Lake City	175,885	Cedar City		8,946
Bountiful	27,853	Grantsville		2,931
Farmington	2,526	Midvale		7,840
1848		Pleasant View		2,028
Ogden	69,478	**1852**		
Centerville	3,268	Mt. Pleasant		1,516
Holladay	25,000	Ephraim		2,127
West Jordan	4,221	**1853**		
1849		Perry		909
Kaysville	6,192	**1856**		
Provo	53,131	Beaver		1,453
Granger	13,800	Washington		750
Tooele	12,539	Wellsville		1,267
Manti	1,803	Mapleton		1,980
1850		**1859**		
Harrisville	603	Plain City		1,543
Pleasant Grove	5,327	South Jordan		2,942
Lehi	4,659	Logan		22,333
Alpine	1,047	Providence		1,608
American Fork	7,713	Heber City		3,254
Lindon	1,644	Midway		804
Payson	4,501	Coalville		864
Spanish Fork	7,284	Fairview		696
Springville	8,790	Richmond		1,000
Layton	13,603	Smithfield		3,342
North Ogden	5,257	Gunnison		1,073
1851		Moroni		894
Parowan	1,423	**1860**		
Brigham City	14,007	Kamas		806
Salem	1,081	Hyde Park		1,025
Willard	1,045	Hyrum		2,340
Santaquin	1,236	Morgan		1,586
Nephi	2,699	Huntsville		553

		1879	
1861		Riverton	2,820
Saint George	7,097	Wellington	922
1862		**1880**	
Hebron (Enterprise)	844	Moab	4,793
1863		Milford (railroad)	1,304
Monroe	918	**1884**	
Salina	1,494	Green River (railroad)	1,033
1864		Helper (railroad)	1,964
Richfield	4,471	**1887**	
Kanab	1,381	Monticello	1,431
Panguitch	1,318	**1890**	
Clinton	1,768	Garland	1,187
1866		Tremonton	2,794
Honeyville	640	**1896**	
1867		Hurricane	1,408
West Point	1,020	**1904**	
1869		Blanding	2,250
Eureka (mining)	753	**1905**	
1870		Duchesne	1,094
Randolph	500	Roosevelt	2,055
Lewiston	1,244	**1906**	
1871		Magna (smelting)	8,000
Sandy (railroad)	6,438	**1907**	
1872		Delta	1,610
Murray (smelting)	21,206	**1909**	
Park City (mining)	1,193	Wendover (railroad)	781
Riverdale	3,704		
1875		**Expansion Communities**	
Escalante	638	Clearfield	13,316
1876		East Carbon City	2,900
Sunset	6,268	Kearns	18,200
1877		North Logan	1,405
Castle Dale	541	Orem	25,729
Ferron	663	River Heights	1,008
Huntington	857	Roy	14,356
Orangeville	511	South Ogden	9,991
Price	6,218	South Salt Lake	7,810
Syracuse	1,843	Washington Terrace	7,241
1878		Woods Cross	3,124
Vernal	3,908		

Sources: Milton R. Hunter, *Brigham Young the Colonizer* (1940), pp. 361-367; Andrew Jenson, *Encyclopedic History of The Church of Jesus Christ of Latter-day Saints* (1941), *passim*; and "Cities and Towns: 1970 Census (Incorporated places and unincorporated places of 1,000 or more)," *Utah Highway Map 74/75* (1974).

Table B
MAJOR FISCAL INDICATORS, 1950-1975

Year	Total State Expenditures (1) (millions)	Government Taxes (2) (per capita)	Taxes as Percentage of Personal Income	Public Assistance Expenditures (3) (millions)	State Debt (millions)
1950	$66	$334	26.9	$11	$1
1955	96	462	29.8	14	5
1960	167	660	34.2	16	15
1965	305	778	34.2	21	30
1970	474	1091	36.8	44	103
1975	680 (4)	1544	34.7	66	88 (1974)

Notes: 1. Expenditures from general revenues for the fiscal year ending June 30, excluding state liquor store operations and funded pensions.
2. Includes federal, state, and local taxes.
3. Includes federal and state expenditures, mostly for aid to families with dependent children (sixty-four percent in 1975), aid to the disabled (seventeen percent), and old age assistance (fifteen percent).
4. Expenditures for fiscal year 1976 were $837 million, and authorizations for fiscal year 1977 were $971 million.

Sources: *1976 Statistical Abstract of Utah,* VII-1, VII-6, and VIII-6; State of Utah, *Annual Budget,* 1971-72, 1976-77, and 1977-78, 2; *1976 Statistical Review of Government in Utah,* vi, 44, and 56.

Table C
POPULATION IN UTAH URBAN AREAS, 1860-1970

	1860	1870	1880	1890	1900	1910
Salt Lake City	8,236	12,854	20,768	44,843	53,531	92,777
Ogden	1,464	3,127	6,069	14,889	16,313	25,580
Provo	2,030	2,384	3,432	5,159	6,185	8,925
No. of urban places (1)	1	2	4	6	12	16
No. living in urban places	8,236	15,981	33,665	75,155	105,427	172,934

	1920	1930	1940	1950	1960	1970
Salt Lake City	118,110	140,267	149,934	182,121	189,454	175,885
Ogden	32,804	40,272	43,688	57,112	70,197	69,478
Provo	10,303	14,766	18,071	28,937	36,047	53,131
No. of urban places	17	21	25	30		
No. living in urban places	215,584	266,584	305,493	412,518		

Note: 1. Until 1950 *urban places* were defined as towns or cities of 2,500 or more inhabitants. Thereafter the Standard Metropolitan Statistical Area (SMSA) became the Census unit for measuring urbanization.

Source: United States Census for 1860-1970.

Table D
UTAH VITAL STATISTICS, 1850-1970[1]

Date	Utah Population	Birth Rate (per 1,000) Utah	Birth Rate (per 1,000) U.S.	Death Rate (per 1,000) Utah	Death Rate (per 1,000) U.S.	Marriage Rate (per 1,000) Utah	Marriage Rate (per 1,000) U.S.	Divorce Rate (per 1,000) Utah	Divorce Rate (per 1,000) U.S.	% of Pop. Children under 10 yrs. Utah	% of Pop. Children under 10 yrs. U.S.	% of Pop. Males Utah	% of Pop. Males U.S.
1850	11,380		43.3[2]							45.4	29.1	53.1	50.4
1860	40,273		44.3[2]							50.0	28.7	50.3	51.2
1870	86,786		38.3[2]							48.3	26.8	50.8	50.6
1880	143,963	41.9	39.8							45.1	27.1	51.8	50.9
1890	210,779	26.9	32.9			11.0	9.0	0.7	0.5	40.3	24.3	53.1	51.2
1900	276,749	27.2	32.3		17.2	9.8	9.3	1.0	0.7	40.8	23.7	51.2	51.1
1910	373,351	30.7	30.1	10.8	14.7	11.5[3]	10.5[3]	1.2[3]	0.9[3]	40.5	22.2	52.7	51.1
1920	449,396	31.2	27.7	11.5	13.0	11.7[3]	12.0	1.6[3]	1.6	37.6	21.7	51.6	51.0
1930	507,847	25.4	21.3	9.9	11.3	11.1	9.2	2.0	1.6	35.6	19.6	51.2	50.6
1940	550,310	24.3	19.4	8.8	10.8	15.0	12.1	2.7	2.0	31.4	16.1	50.6	50.2
1950	699,962	30.9	24.1	7.3	9.6	10.2	11.1	3.0	2.6	33.5	19.5	50.5	49.8
1960	890,627	29.2	23.7	6.7	9.5	7.9	8.5	2.4	2.2	37.5	21.8	50.0	49.4
1970	1,059,273	25.5	18.4	6.7	9.5	11.2	10.6	3.7	3.5	33.3	18.3	49.4	48.9

Notes: 1. Spaces left blank indicate that reliable figures are not available.
2. White only.
3. Figures are for 1906 and 1916 respectively; figures for 1910 and 1920 are not available.

Sources: United States Bureau of the Census, Seventh through Nineteenth Censuses of the United States: Population. University of Utah, Bureau of Economic and Business Research, *Statistical Abstract of Utah, 1976* (1976), I-1, II-1, II-2.

Table E
POPULATION GROWTH, 1850-1970
UTAH, THE MOUNTAIN STATES, AND THE UNITED STATES

	UTAH		MOUNTAIN STATES (1)		UNITED STATES	
	Population	% Increase	Population	% Increase	Population	% Increase
1850	11,380 (2)		72,927		23,191,876	35.9
1860	40,273 (2)	253.9	174,923	746.1	31,443,321	35.6
1870	86,786	115.5	315,385	60.0	39,818,449	26.6
1880	143,963	65.9	653,119	78.5	50,155,783	26.0
1890	210,779	46.4	1,213,935	75.5	62,947,714	25.5
1900	276,749	31.3	1,674,657	31.9	75,994,575	20.7
1910	373,351	34.9	2,633,517	66.8	91,972,266	21.0
1920	449,396	20.4	3,336,101	30.4	105,710,620	14.9
1930	507,847	13.0	3,701,789	33.6	122,775,046	16.1
1940	550,310	8.4	4,150,003	16.7	131,669,275	7.2
1950	699,962	25.2	5,074,998	40.9	150,697,361	14.5
1960	890,627	29.3	6,855,060	39.0	179,323,175	19.0
1970	1,059,273	18.9	8,281,562	20.8	203,235,298	13.3

Notes: 1. Utah, Idaho, Wyoming, Colorado, Montana, New Mexico, Arizona, and Nevada.
2. Includes population of those parts of the Territory of Utah now included in Colorado, Nevada, and Wyoming.

Sources: United States Bureau of Census, *Historical Statistics of the United States: Colonial Times to 1970* (1975); Bureau of Economic and Business Research, *Statistical Abstract of Utah: 1976* (1976).

Table F
ORIGIN AND IN-OUT MIGRATION OF UTAH POPULATION 1870-1930 (1)

	A	B	C	D	E	Gain/Loss Due to Interstate Migration (C-E)	Net Change (Change in C + Change in D - Change in E)
Year	Population	Born in Utah	Born in Other States	Foreign-Born	Born in Utah Living in Other States		
1870	86,786	41,426	14,658	30,702	3,674	+ 10,954	
1880	143,963	92,130	18,253	43,994	10,414	+ 7,839	+ 10,147
1890	210,779	140,270	31,857	53,064	20,489	+ 11,368	+ 12,599
1900	276,749	181,886	40,245	53,777	38,534	+ 1,612	- 8,944
1910	373,351	243,054	60,655	63,393	61,442	- 1,259	+ 7,118
1920	449,396	314,006	73,999	59,200	94,832	- 20,833	- 24,239
1930	507,847	378,778	78,713	48,015	142,582	- 63,869	- 54,221

Note: 1. Reliable figures for other decades are not available.

Source: United States Bureau of Census, Ninth through Fifteenth Censuses of the United States: Population.

Table G
ETHNIC CHARACTERISTICS OF UTAH, 1850-1970

Census Date	Utah Population	White	Negro	Indian	Other	% of Population Foreign-Born Utah	U.S.
1850	11,380	11,330	50			18.0	9.7
1860	40,273	40,125	59	89[1]		31.7	13.2
1870	86,786	86,044	108	179[1]	445	35.4	14.4
1880	143,963	142,423	232	807[1]	501	30.6	13.3
1890	210,779	205,925	588	3,456	810	25.2	14.2
1900	276,749	272,465	672	2,623	989	23.9	13.6
1910	373,351	366,583	1,144	3,123	2,501	17.6	14.6
1920	449,396	441,901	1,446	2,711	3,338	13.2	13.1
1930	507,847	500,124	1,108	2,869	3,746	9.5	11.5
1940	550,310	542,920	1,235	3,611	2,544	6.0	8.8
1950	688,862	676,909	2,729	4,201	5,013	5.4	6.9
1960	890,627	873,828	4,148	6,961	5,690	3.6	5.4
1970	1,059,273	1,031,917	6,617	11,273	9,466	2.8	4.7

Note: 1. Until 1890 census data did not include Indians living on reservations.

Sources: United States Bureau of the Census, Seventh through Nineteenth Censuses of the United States: Population. University of Utah, Bureau of Economic and Business Research, *Statistical Abstract of Utah, 1976* (1976), I-1, I-5.

Table H
MEMBERSHIP OF RELIGIOUS DENOMINATIONS IN UTAH—1870-1975[1]

Denominations	1870	1884	1890	1914	1926	1939	1975
Adventist			37	205	290	500	NA
Baptist		50	327	1,170	1,121	1,612	8,403
Roman Catholic		1,700	5,958	10,000	13,595	14,000	53,794
Christian Science			100	500	601	700	NA
Congregational and United Church of Christ		400	460	1,522	1,594	1,600	1,852
Disciples of Christ			270	275	350	450	150
Episcopal	400	600	751	1,650	3,837	3,596	4,100
Eastern Orthodox (Greek)				5,000	6,000	7,000	6,400
Jehovah's Witnesses							908
Jewish			100	175	1,290	1,400	2,000
Latter-day Saint (Mormon)	85,000	106,000	118,201	269,980	337,200	400,000	851,050
Lutheran			84	392	1,200	1,500	2,675
Methodist	300	450	1,055	1,820	2,198	2,500	3,710
Presbyterian	30	350	688	1,863	2,218	2,500	4,928
Reorganized Latter Day Saint		386	250	740	216	200	400
Unitarian				75	150	150	350
Others			80	500	1,000	1,475	1,260
TOTAL MEMBERSHIP	85,730	109,936	128,361	295,867	372,860	439,183	941,980
Total Utah Population	86,786	168,600[2]	210,779	403,500[2]	485,000[2]	546,000[2]	1,219,000[2]
Membership as % of Population	98.8[3]	65.2[4]	60.9[4]	73.3	76.9	80.4	77.3
Total Non-Mormon Membership	730	3,936	10,160	25,887	35,660	39,183	90,930

Mormons as % of Total Membership	99.1	96.4	92.1	91.2	90.4	91.1	90.3
Mormons as % of Total Population	97.9	62.9	56.1	66.9	69.0	73.3	69.8

[1]The source for the denominational data for 1870-1939 is the Utah Historical Records Survey, *Inventory of the Church Archives of Utah*, Vol. I (1940), 49-55. A survey of Utah churches by T. Edgar Lyon generated the data for 1975. Many figures are estimates by denominational spokesmen, gazeteers, and historical researchers, and some are not consistent with the United States Bureau of the Census special reports on *Religious Bodies* for 1906 (1910), 1916 (1919), and 1926 (1930). It is believed that the table correctly illustrates relationships; individual numbers and percentages may in some cases be inaccurate.

[2]Except for the census years 1870 and 1890, the Utah population figures are estimates. The 1975 figure is a University of Utah Bureau of Economic and Business Research estimate; the others are based upon the assumption that the rate of growth from one census to the next was uniform.

[3]The United States Census figures for 1870 church membership are clearly estimates; they apparently count most unchurched gentiles as well as apostate Mormons as being Latter-day Saints.

[4]Two factors may possibly account for the low percentage of the population identified as church members in 1884 and 1890. Non-Mormons in the growing mining and railroad communities may have lacked the opportunity and/or inclination to identify themselves with church congregations, and some Mormons may not have been identified with the Mormon Church for reasons associated with the legislative and judicial campaign against the church in this period.

Table I
UTAH TERRITORIAL OFFICIALS, 1850-1896

GOVERNORS

Brigham Young (1850-1857)
Alfred Cumming (1857-1861)
Francis H. Wootton (1861)*
John W. Dawson (1861)
Frank Fuller (1861-1862)*
Stephen S. Harding (1862-1863)
James Duane Doty (1863-1865)
Charles Durkee (1865-1869)
Edwin P. Higgins (1869)*
S. A. Mann (1869-1870)*
J. Wilson Shaffer (1870)
Vernon H. Vaughan (1870-1871)*
George L. Woods (1871-1874)
Samuel B. Axtell (1874-1875)*
George B. Emery (1875-1880)
Eli H. Murray (1880-1886)
Caleb W. West (1886-1889)
Arthur L. Thomas (1889-1893)
Caleb W. West (1893-1896)
*Territorial secretary, serving as acting governor

TERRITORIAL DELEGATES*

John M. Bernhisel (1850-1859)
William H. Hooper (1859-1861)
John M. Bernhisel (1861-1863)
John F. Kinney (1863-1865)
William H. Hooper (1865-1873)
George Q. Cannon (1873-1882)**
John T. Caine (1883-1893)
Joseph L. Rawlins (1893-1895)
Frank J. Cannon (1895-1896)
*Elected
**Denied seat in House of Representatives, 1882

SECRETARIES

Broughton D. Harris (1850-1851)
Willard Richards (1851-1852)*
Benjamin G. Ferris (1852-1853)
Almon W. Babbitt (1853-1856)
William H. Hooper (1856-1857)*
John Hartnett (1857-1860)
Francis H. Wootton (1860-1861)
Frank Fuller (1861-1863)
Amos Reed (1863-1867)
Edwin P. Higgins (1867-1869)
S. A. Mann (1869-1870)
Charles C. Crowe (1870)
Vernon H. Vaughan (1870-1871)
George A. Black (1871-1876)
Moses M. Bane (1876-1877)
Levi P. Luckey (1877-1879)
Arthur L. Thomas (1879-1887)
William C. Hall (1887-1889)
Elijah Sells (1889-1893)
Charles C. Richards (1893-1896)
*Acting

CHIEF JUSTICES

Joseph Buffington (1850)*
Lemuel G. Brandebury (1851)
Lazarus H. Reed (1852-1853)
John F. Kinney (1853-1857)
Delena R. Eckles (1857-1860)
John F. Kinney (1860-1863)
John Titus (1863-1868)
Charles C. Wilson (1868-1870)
James B. McKean (1870-1875)
David P. Lowe (1875)
Alexander White (1875-1876)
Michael Schaeffer (1876-1879)
John A. Hunter (1879-1884)

Charles S. Zane (1884-1888)
Elliott Sandford (1888-1889)
Charles S. Zane (1889-1894)
Samuel A. Merritt (1894–1896)
*Did not take office

ASSOCIATE JUSTICES

Perry E. Brocchus (1850-1851)
Zerubbabel Snow (1850-1854)
Leonidas Shaver (1852-1854)
George P. Stiles (1854-1857)
William W. Drummond (1854-1857)
Emery D. Potter (1857)
Charles E. Sinclair (1857-1860)
John Cradlebaugh (1857-1860)
R. P. Flenniken (1860-1861)
Henry R. Crosbie (1860-1861)
Thomas J. Drake (1862-1869)
Charles B. Waite (1862-1864)
Solomon P. McCurdy (1864-1868)
Enos D. Hoge (1868-1869)
Obed F. Strickland (1869-1873)
Cyrus M. Hawley (1869-1873)
Philip H. Emerson (1873-1876)
Jacob S. Boreman (1873-1880)
John M. Coghlan (1876-1880)
Stephen P. Twiss (1880-1885)
Philip H. Emerson (1881-1885)
Jacob S. Boreman (1885-1889)
Orlando W. Powers (1885-1886)
Henry P. Henderson (1886-1889)
John W. Judd (1888-1889)
Thomas J. Anderson (1889-1893)
John W. Blackburn (1889-1893)
James A. Miner (1890-1893)
George W. Bartch (1893-1894)
Harvey W. Smith (1893-1895)
William H. King (1894-1896)
Henry H. Rolapp (1895-1896)

UNITED STATES DISTRICT ATTORNEYS

Seth M. Blair (1850-1854)
Joseph Hosmer (1854-1858)
Alexander Wilson (1858-1862)
Hosea Stout (1862-1866)
Charles H. Hempstead (1868-1871)
George C. Bates (1871-1873)
William Carey (1873-1876)
Sumner Howard (1876-1878)
Philip T. Van Zile (1878-1881)
William H. Dickson (1881-1887)
George S. Peters (1887-1889)
Charles S. Varian (1889-1893)
John W. Judd (1893-1896)

UNITED STATES MARSHALS

Joseph L. Heywood (1850-1855)
Peter K. Dotson (1855-1859)
(Incumbent not identified, 1859-1862)
Isaac L. Gibbs (1862-1866)
Josiah Hosmer (1866-1869)
Joseph M. Orr (1869-1870)
M. T. Patrick (1870-1873)
George R. Maxwell (1873-1876)
William Nelson (1876-1878)
M. Shaunessy (1878-1884)
Edwin A. Ireland (1884-1886)
Frank H. Dyer (1886-1889)
Elias H. Parsons (1889-1892)
Irving H. Benton (1892)
Nat M. Brigham (1893-1896)

MEMBERS OF THE UTAH COMMISSION

Alexander Ramsey (1882-1886)
A. B. Carlton (1882-1889)
A. S. Paddock (1882-1886)
G. L. Godfrey (1882-1894)

J. R. Pettigrew (1882-1886)
J. A. McClernand (1886-1894)
A. B. Williams (1886-1894)
Arthur L. Thomas (1886-1889)
R. S. Robertson (1889-1894)
Alvin Saunders (1889-1893)
H. C. Lett (1893-1894)*
Jerrold R. Letcher (1894-1896)*
Erasmus W. Tatlock (1894-1896)*
Albert G. Norrell (1894-1896)*
Hoyt Sherman, Jr. (1894-1896)*
George W. Thatcher (1894-1896)*
*Utahns at time of appointment

Lorenzo Snow (1872-1882)
Joseph F. Smith (1882-1884)
W. W. Cluff (1884-1886)
Elias A. Smith (1886-1890)
Franklin S. Richards (1890-1892)
William H. King (1892-1894)
M. A. Breeden (1894-1896)

*Presidents of the
House of Representatives*

William W. Phelps (1851-1852)
Jedediah M. Grant (1852-1856)
Hosea Stout (1856-1857)
John Taylor (1857-1862)
Orson Pratt (1862-1863)
John Taylor (1863-1869)
Orson Pratt (1869-1882)
Francis M. Lyman (1882-1884)
James Sharp (1884-1886)
William W. Riter (1886-1890)
James Sharp (1890-1892)
William H. Seegmiller (1892-1894)
Albion B. Emery (1894-1896)

PRESIDING OFFICERS OF
THE LEGISLATIVE
ASSEMBLY

Presidents of the Council

Willard Richards (1851-1854)
Heber C. Kimball (1854-1858)
Daniel H. Wells (1858-1864)
George A. Smith (1864-1872)

Sources: Compilations are based on information in the following works, among which there are some inconsistencies on dates and the rendering of names: C. E. Carter, ed., *The Territorial Papers of the United States* (1934), Vol. 1, 29-30; Earl S. Pomeroy, *The Territories and the United States, 1861-1890* (1947), appendices; Noble Warrum, ed., *Utah Since Statehood* (1919), Vol. 1, 786-788; Russell R. Rich, *Ensign to the Nations* (1972), 633-635; Everett L. Cooley, "Carpetbag Rule: Territorial Government in Utah," *UHQ*, April 1958, 119; B. H. Roberts, *A Comprehensive History of the Church* (1930), Vols. 3-6; Gordon Irving, *Roster of Members of the Legislative Assembly, Utah Territory, 1851/52 to 1894* (Task paper, L.D.S. Historical Department, 1975).

Table J
ELECTED STATE OFFICIALS OF UTAH, 1896-1977

GOVERNORS

Heber M. Wells (R) (1896-1905)
John C. Cutler (R) (1905-1909)
William Spry (R) (1909-1917)
Simon Bamberger (D) (1917-1921)
Charles R. Mabey (R) (1921-1925)
George H. Dern (D) (1925-1933)

Henry H. Blood (D) (1933-1941)
Herbert B. Maw (D) (1941-1949)
J. Bracken Lee (R) (1949-1957)
George D. Clyde (R) (1957-1965)
Calvin L. Rampton (D) (1965-1977)
Scott M. Matheson (D) (1977-

SECRETARIES OF STATE

James T. Hammond (R) (1896-1905)
Charles S. Tingey (R) (1905-1913)
David Mattson (R) (1913-1917)
Harden Bennion (D) (1917-1921)
H. E. Crockett (R) (1921-1929)
Milton H. Welling (D) (1929-1937)
E. E. Monson (D) (1937-1949)

Heber Bennion, Jr. (D) (1949-1953)
Lamont F. Toronto (R) (1953-1965)
Clyde L. Miller (D) (1965-1969)
Lamont F. Toronto (R) (1969-1973)
Clyde L. Miller (D) (1973-1977)
David S. Monson (R) (1977-*
*Position changed to Lieutenant-Governor.

AUDITORS

Morgan Richards, Jr. (R) (1896-1901)
Charles S. Tingey (R) (1901-1905)
J. A. Edwards (R) (1905-1909)
Jesse B. Jewkes (R) (1909-1913)
Lincoln G. Kelly (R) (1913-1917)
Joseph Ririe (D) (1917-1921)

Mark Tuttle (R) (1921-1925)
John E. Holden (R) (1925-1929)
Ivor Ajax (R) (1929-1933)
Julius C. Anderson (D) (1933-1937)
John W. Guy (D) (1937-1941)
Reese M. Reese (D) (1941-1945)

Ferrell H. Adams (D) (1945-1949)
Reese M. Reese (D) (1949-1953)
Sherman J. Preece (R) (1953-1957)
Sid Lambourne (R) (1957-1961)
Sherman J. Preece (R) (1961-1965)

Sharp M. Larson (D) (1965-1969)
Sherman J. Preece (R) (1969-1973)
David S. Monson (R) (1973-1977)
Richard Jensen (R) (1977-

TREASURERS

James Chipman (R) (1896-1901)
John D. Dixon (R) (1901-1905)
James Christiansen (R) (1905-1909)
David Mattson (R) (1909-1913)
Jesse B. Jewkes (R) (1913-1917)
Daniel O. Larson (D) (1917-1921)
W. D. Sutton (R) (1921-1925)
John Walker (R) (1925-1929)
A. E. Christensen (R) (1929-1933)
Charles A. Stain (D) (1933-1934)
Joseph Ririe (D) (1935-1937)

Reese M. Reese (D) (1937-1941)
Oliver G. Ellis (D) (1941-1945)
Reese M. Reese (D) (1945-1949)
Ferrell H. Adams (D) (1949-1953)
Sid Lambourne (R) (1953-1957)
Sherman J. Preece (R) (1957-1961)
Sharp M. Larson (D) (1961-1965)
Linn C. Baker (D) (1965-1969)
Golden L. Allen (R) (1969-1973)
David L. Duncan (D) (1973-1977)
Linn C. Baker (D) (1977-

ATTORNIES GENERAL

A. C. Bishop (R) (1896-1901)
M. A. Breeden (R) (1901-1909)
Albert R. Barnes (R) (1909-1917)
Daniel B. Shields (D) (1917-1921)
Harvey H. Cluff (R) (1921-1929)
George P. Parker (R) (1929-1933)
Joseph Chez (D) (1933-1941)
Grover A. Giles (D) (1941-1949)

Clinton D. Vernon (D) (1949-1953)
E. R. Callister (R) (1953-1961)
Walter A. Budge (R) (1961-1962)
A. Pratt Kesler (R) (1963-1965)
Phil D. Hansen (D) (1965-1969)
Vernon B. Romney (R) (1969-1977)
Robert B. Hansen (R) (1977-

SUPERINTENDENTS OF PUBLIC INSTRUCTION

John R. Park (R) (1896-1901)
A. C. Nelson (R) (1901-1914)
E. G. Gowans (D) (1915-1919)
George N. Child (D) (1919-1921)
George Thomas (R) (1921-1925)

C. N. Jensen (R) (1925-1933)
Charles H. Skidmore (D) (1933-1945)
E. Allen Bateman (D) (1945-1953)*
*Position became appointive 1953.

SUPREME COURT JUSTICES

George W. Bartch (R) (1896-1906)
James A. Miner (R) (1896-1903)
Charles S. Zane (R) (1896-1899)
Robert N. Baskin (D) (1899-1905)
William M. McCarty (R) (1903-1918)
Daniel N. Straup (R) (1905-1916)
Joseph E. Frick (R) (1906-1927)
Elmer E. Corfman (D) (1917-1923)
Samuel R. Thurman (D) (1917-1929)
Valentine Gideon (D) (1917-1927)
Albert J. Weber (D) (1919-1925)
James W. Cherry (R) (1923-1933)
Daniel N. Straup (R) (1925-1935)
Elias Hansen (R) (1927-1937)
William H. Folland (R) (1929-1939)
Ephraim Hanson (R) (1929-1938)
David W. Moffat (D) (1933-1944)

James H. Wolfe (D) (1935-1954)
Martin M. Larson (D) (1937-1946)
Roger I. McDonough (D) (1939-1966)
Eugene C. Pratt (R) (1941-1951)*
Lester M. Wade (D) (1943-1966)
Abe W. Turner (D) (1944-1946)
George W. Latimer (R) (1947-1951)
J. Allen Crockett (D) (1951-
F. Henri Henriod (R) (1951-1976)
George W. Worthen (R) (1954-1959)
E. R. Callister (R) (1959-1975)
A. H. Ellett (D) (1967-
R. L. Tuckett (D) (1966-1976)
Richard J. Maughan (D) (1975-
D. Frank Wilkins (D) (1976-
Gordon R. Hall (R) (1976-
*Military leave 1942-1946

Sources: Utah Secretary of State, *Biennial Reports,* 1896-1954; Utah Supreme Court, *Utah Reports,* 1896-1977; Noble Warrum, ed., *Utah Since Statehood* (1919), Vol. 1, 788-790; *Deseret News.*

Table K
PRESIDENTIAL ELECTIONS IN UTAH, 1896-1976
Only major candidates are listed; votes are recorded to the nearest thousand

Year	Republican Candidate *Winner	Utah Votes	Democratic Candidate *Winner	Utah Votes
1896	William McKinley*	13,000	William J. Bryan	78,000
1900	William McKinley*	47,000	William J. Bryan	45,000
1904	Theodore Roosevelt*	62,000	Alton B. Bunker	33,000
1908	Willam Howard Taft*	61,000	William J. Bryan	43,000
1912	William Howard Taft	42,000		
	Theodore Roosevelt (Prog.)	24,000	Woodrow Wilson*	37,000
1916	Charles E. Hughes	54,000	Woodrow Wilson*	84,000
1920	Warren G. Harding*	82,000	James M. Cox	57,000
1924	Calvin Coolidge*	77,000		
	Robert LaFollette (Prog.)	33,000	John W. Davis	47,000
1928	Herbert C. Hoover*	95,000	Alfred E. Smith	81,000
1932	Herbert C. Hoover	85,000	Franklin D. Roosevelt*	117,000
1936	Alfred N. Landon	65,000	Franklin D. Roosevelt*	150,000
1940	Wendell L. Wilkie	93,000	Franklin D. Roosevelt*	154,000
1944	Thomas E. Dewey	98,000	Franklin D. Roosevelt*	150,000

Year				
1948	Thomas E. Dewey	124,000	Harry S. Truman*	149,000
1952	Dwight D. Eisenhower*	194,000	Adlai E. Stevenson	135,000
1956	Dwight D. Eisenhower*	216,000	Adlai E. Stevenson	118,000
1960	Richard M. Nixon	205,000	John F. Kennedy*	169,000
1964	Barry M. Goldwater	182,000	Lyndon B. Johnson*	220,000
1968	Richard M. Nixon*	239,000	Hubert H. Humphrey	157,000
1972	Richard M. Nixon*	324,000	George McGovern	126,000
1976	Gerald Ford	338,000	Jimmy Carter*	182,000
1980	Ronald Reagan*	436,000	Jimmy Carter	124,000
			John Anderson (Ind.)	30,000
1984	Ronald Reagan*	467,000	Walter Mondale	155,000
1988	George Bush*	425,000	Michael Dukakis	209,000

Sources: United States Bureau of the Census, *Historical Statistics of the United States: Colonial Times to 1970* (1975); *Deseret News*.

Table L
GUBERNATORIAL ELECTIONS IN UTAH 1896-1976
Only major candidates are listed; votes are recorded to the nearest thousand

Year	Winning Candidates			Losing Candidates		
	Name	Party	Votes Cast	Name	Party	Votes Cast
1895	Heber M. Wells	R	21,000	John T. Caine	D	19,000
				Henry W. Lawrence	(Pop.)	2,000
1900	Heber M. Wells	R	48,000	James H. Moyle	D	44,000
1904	John C. Cutler	R	51,000	James H. Moyle	D	38,000
1908	William Spry	R	53,000	Jesse W. Knight	D	42,000
1912	William Spry	R	43,000	John F. Tolton	D	24,000
				Nephi L. Morris	(Prog.)	9,000
1916	Simon Bamberger	D	78,000	Nephi L. Morris	R	60,000
1920	Charles R. Mabey	R	84,000	Thomas N. Taylor	D	55,000
1924	George H. Dern	D	81,000	Charles R. Mabey	R	72,000
1928	George H. Dern	D	103,000	William H. Wattis	R	72,000
1932	Henry H. Blood	D	116,000	William W. Seegmiller	R	86,000
1936	Henry H. Blood	D	110,000	Ray E. Dillman	R	80,000
1940	Herbert B. Maw	D	129,000	Don B. Colton	R	118,000
1944	Herbert B. Maw	D	124,000	J. Bracken Lee	R	123,000

702

Year	Winner	Party	Votes	Opponent	Party	Votes
1948	J. Bracken Lee	R	151,000	Herbert B. Maw	D	124,000
1952	J. Bracken Lee	R	181,000	Earl J. Glade	D	147,000
1956	George Dewey Clyde	R	127,000	L. C. Romney	D	111,000
				J. Bracken Lee	(Ind.)	94,000
1960	George Dewey Clyde	R	196,000	William A. Barlocker	D	176,000
1964	Calvin L. Rampton	D	227,000	Mitchell Melich	R	171,000
1968	Calvin L. Rampton	D	289,000	Carl W. Buehner	R	132,000
1972	Calvin L. Rampton	D	332,000	Nicholas L. Strike	R	144,000
1976	Scott M. Matheson	D	281,000	Vernon B. Romney	R	248,000
1980	Scott M. Matheson	D	329,000	Bob Wright	R	265,000
1984	Norman H. Bangerter	R	351,000	Wayne Owens	D	276,000
1988	Norman H. Bangerter	R	259,000	Ted Wilson	D	248,000
				Merrill Cook	(Ind.)	136,000

Sources: Utah Public Documents, *Secretary of State Biennial Reports*, 1896-1954; *Deseret News*.

Table M
UNITED STATES SENATORIAL ELECTIONS IN UTAH 1896-1976
Only major candidates are listed; votes are recorded to the nearest thousand

	Winning Candidates			Losing Candidates		
Year	Name	Party	Votes Cast	Name	Party	Votes Cast
1896	Frank J. Cannon (2)	R	(1)			
	Arthur Brown (3)	R	(1)			
1897	Joseph L. Rawlins	D	(1)			
1901	Thomas Kearns (4)	R	(1)			
1903	Reed Smoot	R	(1)			
1905	George Sutherland	R	(1)			
1909	Reed Smoot	R	(1)			
1911	George Sutherland	R	(1)			
1914	Reed Smoot	R	56,000	James H. Moyle	D	53,000
1916	William H. King	D	81,000	George Sutherland	R	56,000
1920	Reed Smoot	R	83,000	Milton H. Welling	D	56,000
1922	William H. King	D	58,749	Ernest Bamberger	R	58,188
1926	Reed Smoot	R	88,000	Ashby Snow	D	59,000
1928	William H. King	D	97,000	Ernest Bamberger	R	77,000
1932	Elbert D. Thomas	D	117,000	Reed Smoot	R	86,000
1934	William H. King	D	98,000	Don B. Colton	R	84,000
1938	Elbert D. Thomas	D	102,000	Franklin S. Harris	R	81,000

Year	Candidate	Party	Votes	Candidate	Party	Votes
1940	Abe Murdock	D	155,000	Philo T. Farnsworth	R	92,000
1944	Elbert D. Thomas	D	149,000	Adam S. Bennion	R	100,000
1946	Arthur V. Watkins	R	101,000	Abe Murdock	D	96,000
1950	Wallace F. Bennett	R	142,000	Elbert D. Thomas	D	121,000
1952	Arthur V. Watkins	R	177,000	Walter K. Granger	D	149,000
1956	Wallace F. Bennett	R	178,000	Alonzo F. Hopkin	D	152,000
1958	Frank E. Moss	D	113,000	Arthur V. Watkins	R	101,000
				J. Bracken Lee	(Ind.)	77,000
1962	Wallace F. Bennett	R	167,000	David S. King	D	152,000
1964	Frank E. Moss	D	228,000	Ernest L. Wilkinson	R	170,000
1968	Wallace F. Bennett	R	225,000	Milton L. Weilenman	D	192,000
1970	Frank E. Moss	D	210,000	Laurence J. Burton	R	159,000
1974	E. J. (Jake) Garn	R	210,000	Wayne Owens	D	185,000
				Bruce Bangerter	(Am.Ind.)	25,000
1976	Orrin G. Hatch	R	290,000	Frank E. Moss	D	242,000

Notes:

1. Elected by the state legislature until the Seventeenth Amendment introduced popular election in 1914.
2. Elected for four years; legislative stalemate left seat unfilled, 1899-1901.
3. Elected for two years.
4. Elected for four years.

Sources: Utah Public Documents, *Secretary of State Biennial Reports*, 1896-1954; *Deseret News.*

Table N
UNITED STATES HOUSE OF REPRESENTATIVES ELECTIONS IN UTAH, 1896-1976
Only major candidates are listed; votes are recorded to the nearest thousand

Year	Winning Candidates			Losing Candidates		
	Name	Party	Votes Cast	Name	Party	Votes Cast
1895	Clarence E. Allen	R		Brigham H. Roberts	D	
1896	William H. King	D	47,000	Lafayette Holbrook	R	28,000
1898	Brigham H. Roberts (1)	D	35,000	Alma Eldredge	R	30,000
1900	William H. King	D	26,000	James T. Hammond	R	22,000
1900	George Sutherland	R	46,180	William H. King	D	45,939
1902	Joseph Howell	R	44,000	William H. King	D	38,000
1904	Joseph Howell	R	53,000	Orlando W. Powers	D	37,000
1906	Joseph Howell	R	43,000	Orlando W. Powers	D	27,000
1908	Joseph Howell	R	53,000	Lyman R. Martineau	D	33,000
1910	Joseph Howell	R	51,000	Ferdinand Erickson	D	33,000
1912	Joseph Howell (2)	R	43,000	Tillman D. Johnson	D	37,000
	Jacob Johnson	R	42,000	Mathonihah Thomas	D	37,000
1914	Joseph Howell	R	28,000	Lewis Larson	D	32,000
	James H. Mays	D	13,000 (3)	E. O. Leatherwood	R	13,000

706

Year	Candidate	Party	Vote	Candidate	Party	Vote
1916	Milton H. Welling	D	40,000	Timothy C. Hoyt	R	30,000
	James H. Mays	D	40,000	Charles R. Mabey	R	28,000
1918	Milton H. Welling	D	25,000	William H. Wattis	R	20,000
	James H. Mays	D	24,000	William Spry	R	16,000
1920	Don B. Colton	R	42,000	James W. Funk	D	28,000
	E. O. Leatherwood	R	39,000	Mathonihah Thomas	D	28,000
1922	Don B. Colton	R	33,000	Milton H. Welling	D	28,000
	E. O. Leatherwood	R	29,000	David C. Dunbar	D	26,000
1924	Don B. Colton	R	41,000	Frank Francis	D	34,000
	E. O. Leatherwood	R	42,000	James H. Waters	D	32,000
1926	Don B. Colton	R	44,000	Ephraim Bergeson	D	27,000
	E. O. Leatherwood	R	42,000	William R. Wallace, Jr.	D	27,000
1928	Don B. Colton	R	50,000	Knox Patterson	D	32,000
	E. O. Leatherwood	R	46,866	J. H. Paul	D	46,025
1930	Don B. Colton	R	46,000	Joseph Ririe	D	29,000
	Frederic C. Loofbourow	R	35,000	J. H. Paul	D	34,000
1932	Abe Murdock	D	48,000	Don B. Colton	R	45,000
	J. Will Robinson	D	62,000	Frederic C. Loofbourow	R	47,000

Year	Candidate	Party	Vote	Candidate	Party	Vote
1934	Abe Murdock	D	56,000 (4)	Arthur Woolley	R	30,000
	J. Will Robinson	D	63,000 (4)	Frederic C. Loofbourow	R	34,000
1936	Abe Murdock	D	69,000	Charles W. Dunn	R	30,000
	J. Will Robinson	D	81,000	Arthur V. Watkins	R	35,000
1938	Abe Murdock	D	53,000	LeRoy B. Young	R	36,000
	J. Will Robinson	D	58,000	Dean F. Brayton	R	35,000
1940	Walter K. Granger	D	63,000	LeRoy B. Young	R	47,000
	J. Will Robinson	D	87,000	A. Sherman Christensen	R	50,000
1942	Walter K. Granger	D	36,297	J. Bracken Lee	R	36,028
	J. Will Robinson	D	44,000	Reed E. Vetterli	R	35,000
1944	Walter K. Granger	D	60,000	B. H. Stringham	R	44,000
	J. Will Robinson	D	90,000	Quayle Cannon, Jr.	R	54,000
1946	Walter K. Granger	D	44,888	David J. Wilson	R	44,784
	William A. Dawson	R	56,000	J. Will Robinson	D	51,000
1948	Walter K. Granger	D	67,000	David J. Wilson	R	46,000
	Reva B. Bosone	D	93,000	William A. Dawson	R	69,000
1950	Walter K. Granger	D	54,000	Preston L. Jones	R	52,000
	Reva B. Bosone	D	84,000	Ivy B. Priest	R	74,000

Year	Candidate	Party	Votes	Candidate	Party	Votes
1952	Douglas R. Stringfellow	R	77,000	Ernest R. McKay	D	50,000
	William A. Dawson	R	105,000	Reva B. Bosone	D	95,000
1954	Henry A. Dixon	R	56,000	Walter K. Granger	D	49,000
	William A. Dawson	R	91,000	Reva B. Bosone	D	68,000
1956	Henry A. Dixon	R	74,000	Carlyle F. Gronning	D	48,000
	William A. Dawson	R	120,000	Oscar W. McConkie, Jr.	D	88,000
1958	Henry A. Dixon	R	58,000	M. Blaine Peterson	D	50,000
	David S. King	D	91,000	William A. Dawson	R	87,000
1960	N. Blaine Peterson	D	65,939	A. Walter Stevenson	R	65,871
	David S. King	D	121,000	Sherman P. Lloyd	R	117,000
1962	Laurence J. Burton	R	59,000	M. Blaine Peterson	D	57,000
	Sherman P. Lloyd	R	108,000	Bruce S. Jenkins	D	93,000
1964	Laurence J. Burton	R	76,000	William G. Bruhn	D	60,000
	David S. King	D	150,000	Thomas G. Judd	R	111,000
1966	Laurence J. Burton	R	101,000	J. Keith Melville	D	54,000
	Sherman P. Lloyd	R	96,000	David S. King	D	61,000
1968	Laurence J. Burton	R	139,000	Richard J. Maughan	D	65,000
	Sherman P. Lloyd	R	130,000	Galen Ross	D	81,000

Year	Candidate	Party	Votes	Candidate	Party	Votes
1970	K. Gunn McKay	D	95,000	Richard Richards	R	89,000
	Sherman P. Lloyd	R	98,000	A. H. Nance	D	87,000
1972	K. Gunn McKay	D	127,000	Robert Wolthius	R	96,000
	Wayne Owens	D	133,000	Sherman P. Lloyd	R	107,000
1974	K. Gunn McKay	D	125,000	Ron Inkley	R	63,000
				L. S. Brown	AmInd	12,000
	Allen T. Howe	D	106,000	Stephen M. Harmsen	R	100,000
1976	K. Gunn McKay	D	156,000	Joe Ferguson	R	107,000
	Dan Marriott	R	145,000	Allen T. Howe	D	111,000

Notes: 1. Rejected by the House of Representatives; King elected to replace Roberts in an interim election held April 2, 1900. See next entry.
2. Two districts were created in 1912. First District is listed first throughout.
3. Exact figures unavailable; Mays had a plurality of 158 votes.
4. Incomplete newspaper returns.

Sources: Utah Public Documents, *Secretary of State Biennial Reports, 1896-1954; Deseret News.*

710

Table O
POLITICAL COMPOSITION OF THE UTAH STATE LEGIS-LATURE, 1896-1977

Year	House of Representatives		Senate	
	Republicans	Democrats	Republicans	Democrats
1896	31	14	12	6
1897 (1)	2	40	0	17
1899 (2)	15	26	2	14
1901	28	17	8	10
1903	38	7	12	6
1905	41	4	15	3
1907	37	8	18	0
1909	43	2	18	0
1911	37	8	16	2
1913	30	15	17	1
1915 (3)	23	19	12	5
1917 (4)	1	44	4	14
1919	10	37	0	18
1921	46	1	11	7
1923	45	10	19	1
1925	46	9	19	1
1927	49	6	19	1
1929	29	26	11	9
1931	41	14	11	9
1933	9	51	10	13
1935	4	56	4	19
1937	4	56	1	22
1939	15	45	2	21
1941	16	44	4	19
1943	21	39	6	17
1945	15	45	5	18
1947	39	21	11	12
1949	19	41	11	12
1951	30	30	8	15
1953	39	21	15	8
1955	33	27	16	7
1957 (5)	40	23	15	10
1959	22	42	10	13
1961	28	36	11	14
1963	34	30	13	12
1965	30	39	12	15
1967	59	10	23	5

1969	48	21	20	8
1971	29	40	16	12
1973	44	31	16	13
1975	35	40	14	15
1977	40	35	12	17

Notes: 1. Three Populist members of the House; one Populist Party member in the Senate.
2. Four Independent Party members of the House; two Independents in the Senate.
3. Four other party members in the House; one in the Senate.
4. One Socialist Party member in the House.
5. One Independent Party member in the House.

Source: Utah Senate and House of Representatives, *Journals,* 1896-1977; *Deseret News.*

Table P

PER CAPITA PERSONAL INCOME OF UTAH, THE MOUNTAIN STATES, AND THE UNITED STATES, 1880-1975

Year	Utah Per Capita Income (dollars)	U.S. Per Capita Income (dollars)	Utah as Percent of U.S. Per Capita Income	Utah's Per Capita Rank Among the States	Utah's Rank Among the Eight Mtn. States[1]
1880	$ 134	$ 175	76.6	31	7
1900	183	203	90.1	32	7
1919-1921 av.	556	658	84.5	31	7
1929	559	703	79.5	30	6
1930	505	624	80.9	29	5
1933	300	375	80.0	26	5
1935	392	472	83.1	31	7
1940	487	595	81.9	30	6
1945	1,128	1,234	91.4	25	5
1950	1,309	1,496	87.5	29	6
1955	1,625	1,876	86.6	27	6
1960	1,977	2,216	89.2	30	6
1965	2,377	2,770	85.8	31	7
1970	3,227	3,966	81.4	39	7
1975	4,819	5,834	82.6	39	7

Note: 1. Utah, Idaho, Wyoming, Colorado, Montana, New Mexico, Arizona, and Nevada.

Sources: Data to 1921 is compiled and calculated from Simon S. Kuznets and Dorothy S. Thomas, eds., *Population Redistribution and Economic Growth: United States, 1870-1950*, Vol. 1, 753. Since 1921, *Statistical Abstract of the United States*, various years.

Table Q
DISTRIBUTION OF THE UTAH LABOR FORCE, 1850-1975[1]

	Agriculture	Government	Trade	Manufacturing	Services	Transportation, Communication, Utilities	Mining	Construction	Finance, Insurance, Real Estate	Labor (unspecified)[2]	Unemployment Utah	Unemployment U.S.
	Percentage of Total Labor Force in Each Occupational Group[2]											
1850	50.4	0.4	2.0	15.6	2.5	0.4	0.7	8.1	0.2	19.7		
1860	54.5	0.4	2.4	13.8	5.1	1.1	0.2	4.5	0.3	17.7		
1870	48.5	1.0	2.8	10.5	7.5	5.0	3.0	5.6	0.1	16.1		
1880	36.3	1.7	5.1	12.3	9.9	4.9	7.1	5.2	0.3	17.3		
1890	29.9	1.8	7.2	11.5	13.0	6.4	6.2	8.3	2.9	12.8		
1900	34.6	1.0	5.8	10.9	13.0	6.7	8.6	4.7	4.3	10.5		
1910	28.3	2.1	9.3	11.9	14.5	8.9	7.7	11.7	5.4	[3]		
1920	28.9	1.9	10.3	14.5	13.7	7.9	6.9	8.0	7.9	[3]		
1930	24.3	2.2	12.0	12.4	16.3	8.6	6.3	9.2	8.7	[3]		
1940	19.2	4.9	19.4	11.0	18.2	10.5	7.0	5.4	3.0	1.6		
1950	12.4	9.4	20.4	12.2	18.5	9.7	5.5	7.4	3.2	1.3		
1960	5.8	10.3	19.8	16.0	21.8	7.9	4.0	6.9	4.0	2.7		

Percentage of Non-Agricultural Employees in Each Occupational Group[4]

Year											
1945		30.9	19.0	14.1	10.1	13.7	6.7	3.1	2.4		
1950	(21.6)[5]	23.2	22.6	15.5	11.3	11.2	6.5	6.4	3.3	5.5	5.3
1955	(17.4)	23.8	22.3	15.6	11.2	10.2	6.4	6.4	4.1	4.1	4.4
1960	(14.4)	23.6	22.5	17.8	12.6	8.4	5.2	5.6	4.3	4.8	5.5
1965	(11.2)	26.4	22.5	16.4	14.2	7.1	3.9	5.3	4.2	6.1	4.5
1970	(7.8)	27.9	22.3	15.3	16.2	6.5	3.5	4.1	4.2	6.1	4.9
1975	(8.2)	25.0	23.7	15.3	16.7	6.1	3.0	5.5	4.5	7.2	8.5

Notes:

1. Because of differences in the studies used, the data for 1850-1960 and 1945-1975 are not entirely comparable. They both indicate directions of change in Utah's economic development.

2. This analysis is based on occupational data gathered by the United States Bureau of the Census. It does not reflect unemployment, and the occupational classifications did not remain entirely consistent through the eleven censuses.

3. The *Labor* classification was discontinued from 1910 to 1930.

4. This analysis is based upon United States Employment Service data. It does not include agricultural employment or self-employment, and the *Government* classification includes employment in defense industries as well as in governmental agencies.

5. This column gives the percentage of the total labor force that is engaged in work not classified as "nonagricultural employees." Agricultural employment and self-employment are the primary components, with agriculture a declining factor in Utah employment.

Sources: For the 1850-1960 analysis: Leonard J. Arrington, *The Changing Economic Structure of the Mountain West, 1850-1950* (Utah State University Monograph Series, June 1963), 39-49, and 1960 calculations by Wayne K. Hinton.

For the 1945-1975 analysis: *1976 Statistical Abstract of Utah* IV-2, IV-4, IX-9; *1976 Economic Report of the President*, 199; *1976 Statistical Review of Government in Utah*, 6; *Monthly Labor Review*, July 1976, 86; and Utah Department of Employment Security, R & A Section.

Physical Divisions of Utah

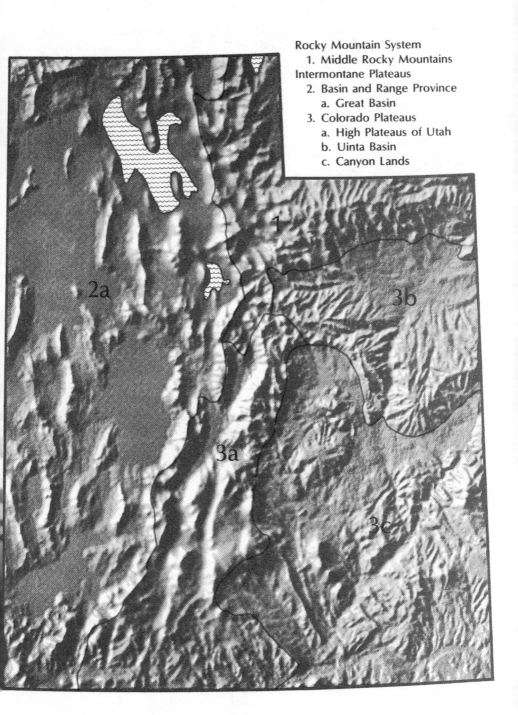

Rocky Mountain System
1. Middle Rocky Mountains
Intermontane Plateaus
2. Basin and Range Province
   a. Great Basin
3. Colorado Plateaus
   a. High Plateaus of Utah
   b. Uinta Basin
   c. Canyon Lands

CLASSES OF LAND-SURFACE FORM

Adapted from Edwin H. Hammond

Scale 1:2,914,560

0   50   100   150   200

SCHEME OF CLASSIFICATION

SLOPE (Capital letter)

A   More than 80% of area gently sloping

B   50–80% of area gently sloping

C   20–50% of area gently sloping

D   Less than 20% of area gently sloping

LOCAL RELIEF (Number)

1   0–100 feet

2   100–300 feet

3   300–500 feet

4   500–1000 feet

5   1000–3000 feet

6   Over 3000 feet

PROFILE TYPE (Lower-case letter)

a   More than 75% of gentle slope is in lowland

b   50–75% of gentle slope is in lowland

c   50–75% of gentle slope is in upland

d   More than 75% of gentle slope is in upland

CLASSES OF LAND-SURFACE FORM

PLAINS

| A2 | Smooth plains |

TABLELANDS

B4c	Considerable relief
B5c	High relief
B6c,d	Very high relief

PLAINS WITH HILLS OR MOUNTAINS

B4b	With high hills
B5a,b	With low mountains
B6a,b	With high mountains

OPEN HILLS AND MOUNTAINS

| C5 | Open low mountains |
| C6 | Open high mountains |

HILLS AND MOUNTAINS

| D6 | High mountains |

OTHER CLASSES

Sand

Standing water

Lakes

Irregular peaks
Regular cones

Crests

Escarpments and valley sides

In the last three symbols, width of line is directly proportional to height of feature above its base.

718

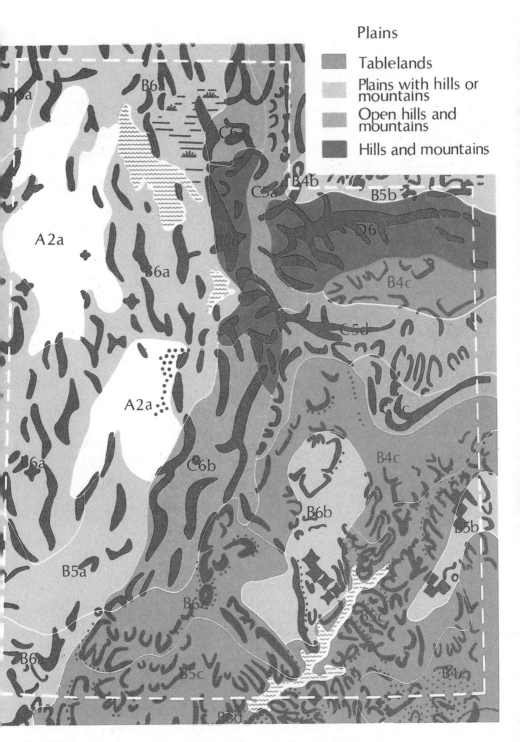

Plains

	Tablelands
	Plains with hills or mountains
	Open hills and mountains
	Hills and mountains

Climate of Utah
Variation Between Selected Locations

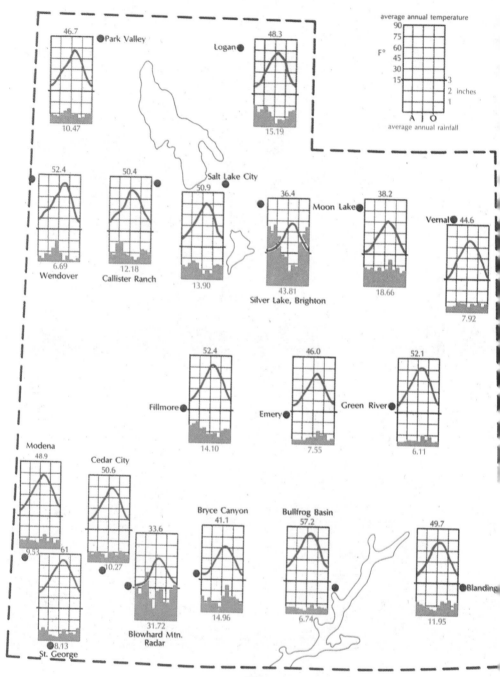

average annual temperature

F° 90 75 60 45 30 15

3 2 inches 1

A J O

average annual rainfall

Park Valley 46.7 10.47

Logan 48.3 15.19

Wendover 52.4 6.69

Callister Ranch 50.4 12.18

Salt Lake City 50.9 13.90

Silver Lake, Brighton 36.4 43.81

Moon Lake 38.2 18.66

Vernal 44.6 7.92

Fillmore 52.4 14.10

Emery 46.0 7.55

Green River 52.1 6.11

Modena 48.9 9.53

Cedar City 50.6 10.27

Blowhard Mtn. Radar 33.6 31.72

St. George 61 8.13

Bryce Canyon 41.1 14.96

Bullfrog Basin 57.2 6.74

Blanding 49.7 11.95

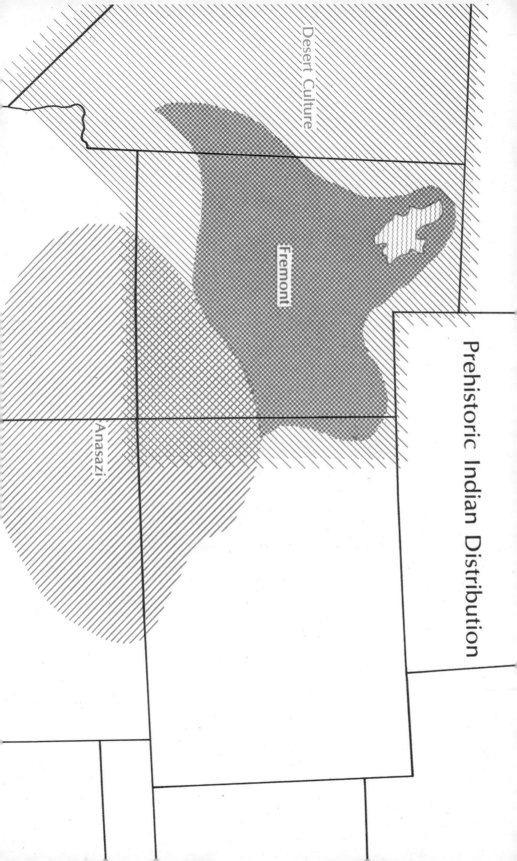

Prehistoric Indian Distribution

Desert Culture

Fremont

Anasazi

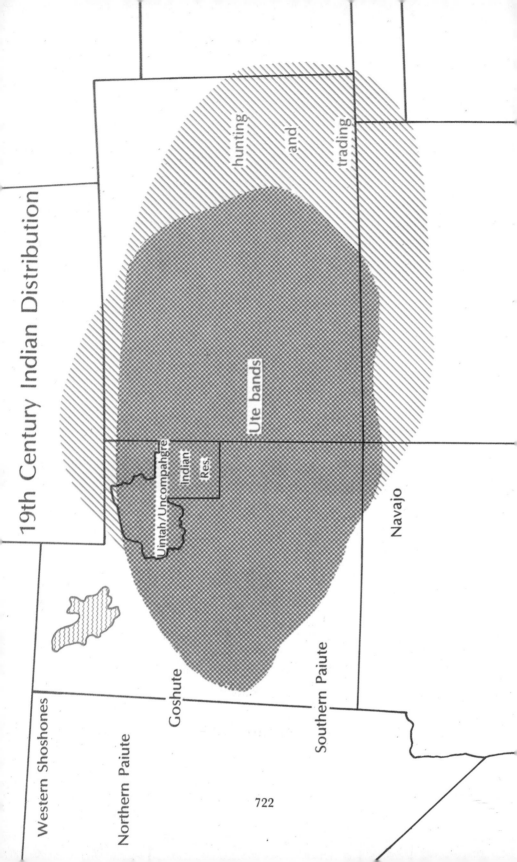

19th Century Indian Distribution

hunting and trading

Ute bands

Uintah/Uncompahgre Indian Res.

Navajo

Western Shoshones

Northern Paiute

Goshute

Southern Paiute

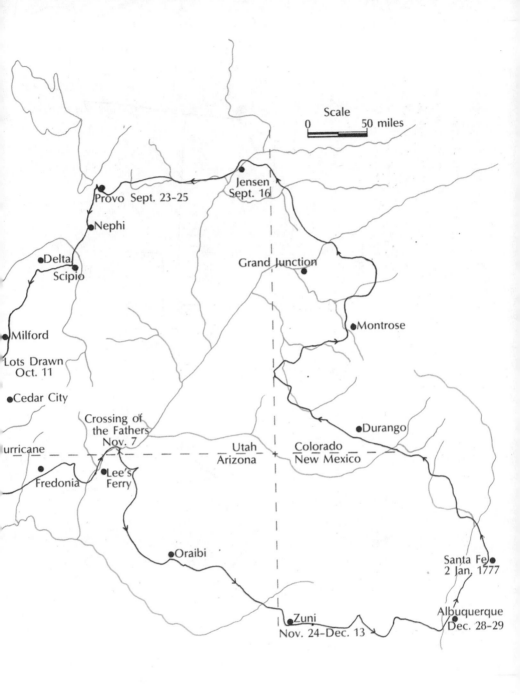

Dominguez-Escalante Route 1776

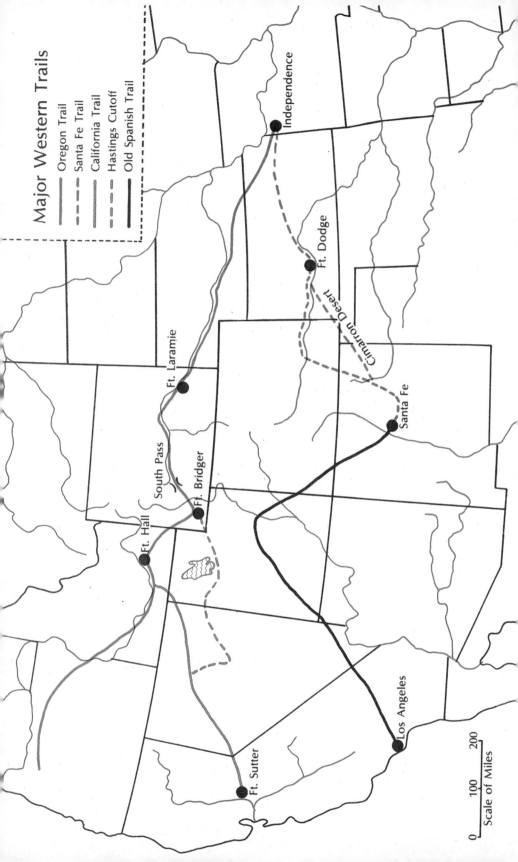

Major Western Trails

- Oregon Trail
- Santa Fe Trail
- California Trail
- Hastings Cutoff
- Old Spanish Trail

Independence

Ft. Dodge

Cimarron Desert

Ft. Laramie

South Pass

Santa Fe

Ft. Bridger

Ft. Hall

Los Angeles

Ft. Sutter

Scale of Miles

0   100   200

———— 1823–24
———— 1826–27
———— 1827–30

0   100   200
scale in miles

Great

Basin

Western Explorations of Jedediah S. Smith

Ogden's Route into Utah, 1825

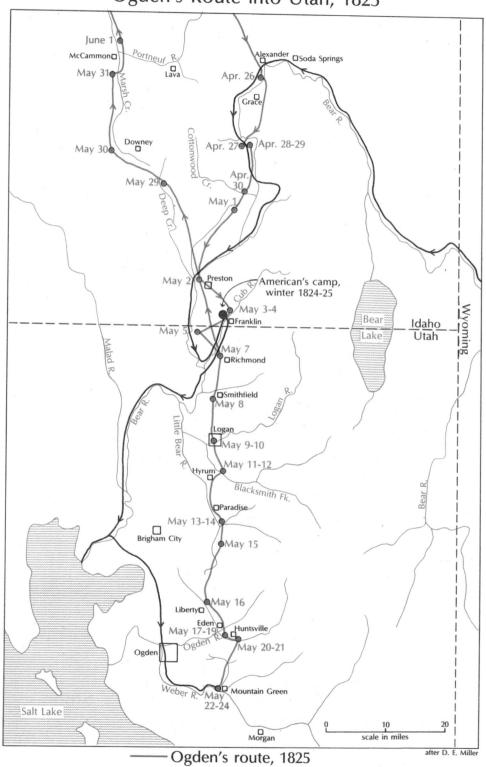

McCammon☐ June 1
Portneuf R.
Lava☐
May 31 Alexander☐ ☐Soda Springs
Apr. 26
Grace☐
Marsh Cr.
Bear R.
Downey
May 30 Cottonwood Cr.
Apr. 27 Apr. 28-29
May 29 Apr. 30
May 1
Deep Cr.

May 2☐ Preston☐ American's camp, winter 1824-25
Cub R.
May 3-4
Bear Lake Idaho / Utah
May 5 ☐Franklin
Malad R. May 7
☐Richmond
Bear R.
☐Smithfield
May 8
Logan R.
Logan☐ May 9-10
Little Bear R.
May 11-12
Hyrum☐
Blacksmith Fk.
Bear R.
☐Paradise
May 13-14
Brigham City☐ May 15

May 16
Liberty☐
Eden☐ ☐Huntsville
May 17-19
Ogden R. May 20-21
Ogden☐
Weber R. May 22-24 Mountain Green☐
Salt Lake
Morgan☐

Wyoming

0   10   20
scale in miles
after D. E. Miller

——— Ogden's route, 1825
——— American's route, 1824-25

726

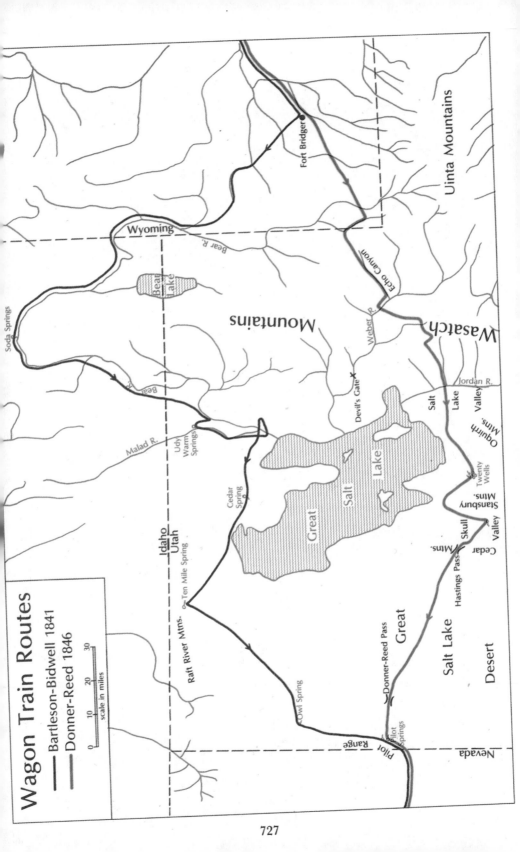

Wagon Train Routes

— Bartleson-Bidwell 1841
— Donner-Reed 1846

scale in miles

0   10   20   30

Uinta Mountains

Fort Bridger

Wyoming

Bear R.

Bear Lake

Soda Springs

Mountains

Wasatch

Echo Canyon

Weber R.

Devil's Gate

Jordan R.

Salt

Lake

Valley

Oquirrh Mtns.

Malad R.

Bear R.

Udy Warm Springs

Cedar Spring

Great Salt Lake

Twenty Wells

Stansbury Mtns.

Skull Valley

Cedar Mtns.

Hastings Pass

Idaho
Utah

Ten Mile Spring

Raft River Mtns.

Owl Spring

Donner-Reed Pass

Great

Salt Lake

Desert

Pilot Range

Pilot Springs

Nevada

----1842
——1843–44
——1845–46
----1848
——1853–54

Ancient

Lake

Bonneville

0   100   200
scale in miles

Western Explorations of John C. Fremont

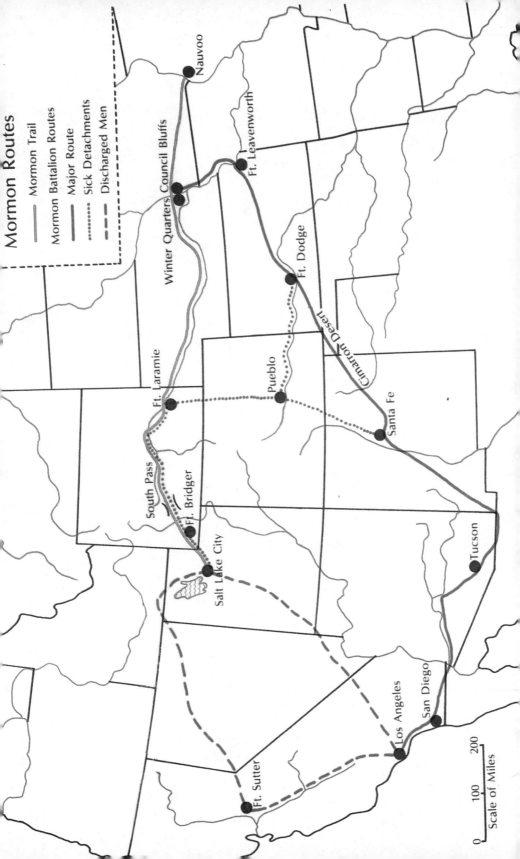

Mormon Routes

- —— Mormon Trail
- Mormon Battalion Routes
- —— Major Route
- ········· Sick Detachments
- – – – Discharged Men

Nauvoo

Ft. Leavenworth

Winter Quarters, Council Bluffs

Ft. Dodge

Ft. Laramie

Pueblo

Cimarron Desert

Santa Fe

South Pass

Ft. Bridger

Salt Lake City

Tucson

Ft. Sutter

Los Angeles

San Diego

Scale of Miles

0   100   200

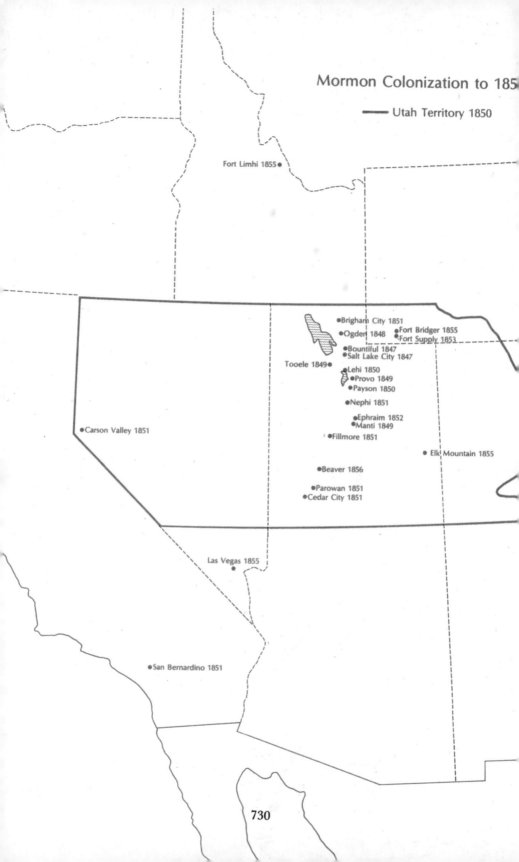

Mormon Colonization to 185[...]

—— Utah Territory 1850

Fort Limhi 1855 ●

●Brigham City 1851
●Ogden 1848   ●Fort Bridger 1855
             ●Fort Supply 1853
●Bountiful 1847
●Salt Lake City 1847
Tooele 1849 ●
●Lehi 1850
●Provo 1849
●Payson 1850

●Nephi 1851

●Ephraim 1852
●Manti 1849
●Fillmore 1851

●Carson Valley 1851

● Elk Mountain 1855

●Beaver 1856

●Parowan 1851
●Cedar City 1851

Las Vegas 1855
●

●San Bernardino 1851

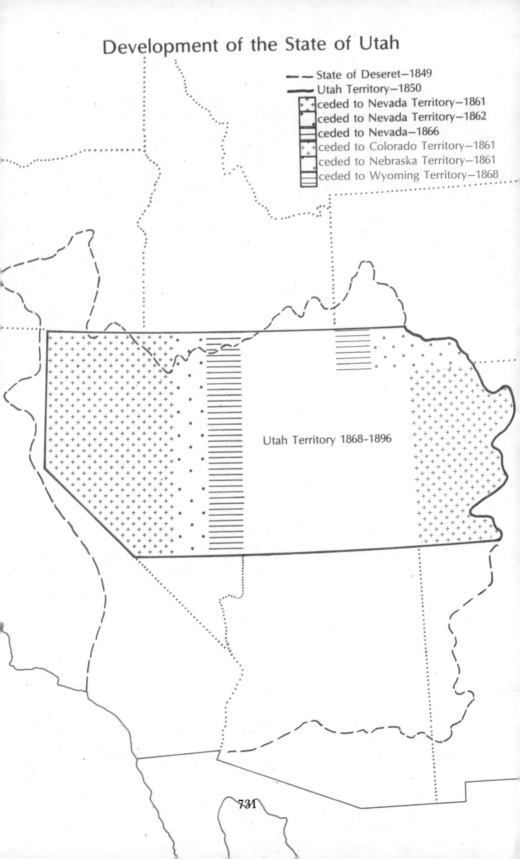

Development of the State of Utah

State of Deseret—1849
Utah Territory—1850
ceded to Nevada Territory—1861
ceded to Nevada Territory—1862
ceded to Nevada—1866
ceded to Colorado Territory—1861
ceded to Nebraska Territory—1861
ceded to Wyoming Territory—1868

Utah Territory 1868-1896

Development of Utah Counties

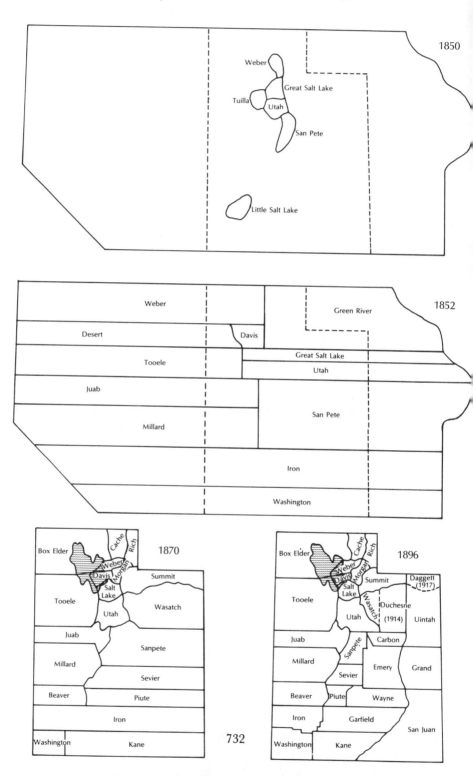

A Typical Mormon Townsite
of the 1870 s

733

Pony Express, Stage, Telegraphs

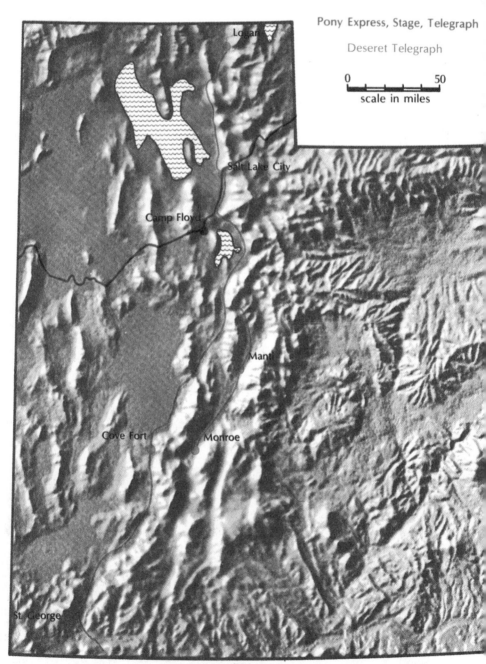

Pony Express, Stage, Telegraph

Deseret Telegraph

0   50

scale in miles

Logan

Salt Lake City

Camp Floyd

Manti

Cove Fort   Monroe

St. George

Major Utah Railroads to 1896

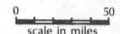

Railroads into Utah
- – – – Union Pacific
- ·········· Central Pacific
- —— Denver & Rio Grande

Mormon Railroads
- ·········· Utah Northern
- —— Utah Central
- – – – Utah Southern

Extension Lines
- – – – Utah Western
- —— Utah Southern
- ·········· Utah Eastern & Summit County

0   50
scale in miles

Logan

Promontory

Ogden

Coalville

Salt Lake City

Park City

Stockton

Provo

Spanish Fork

Nephi

Price

Delta

Frisco   Milford

Sites of Principal 19th Century Mining

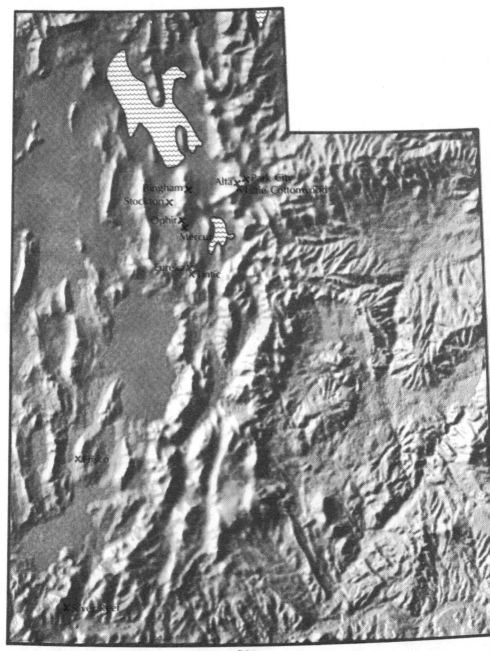

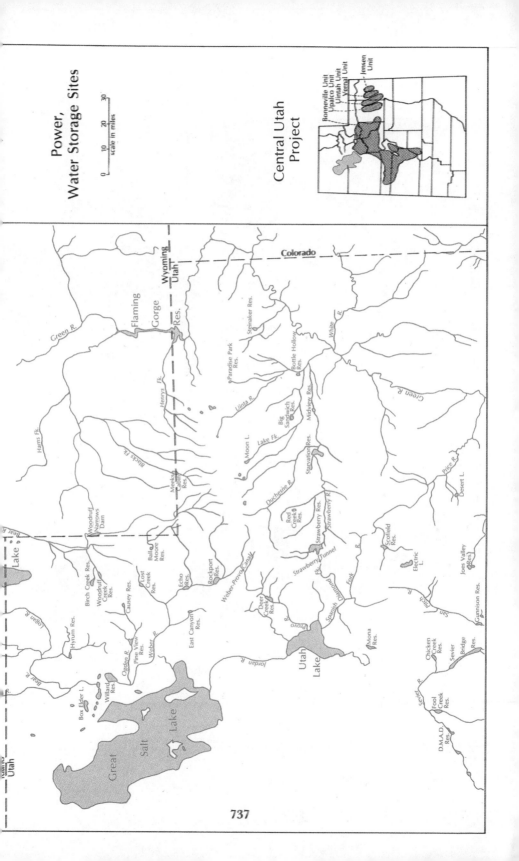

Power,
Water Storage Sites

scale in miles

0   10   20   30

Central Utah
Project

Bonneville Unit
Upalco Unit
Uintah Unit
Vernal Unit
Jensen Unit

Green R.

Flaming Gorge Res.

Wyoming
Utah

Colorado

Hams Fk.

Henrys Fk.

Blacks Fk.

Paradise Park Res.

Steinaker Res.

Bottle Hollow Res.

Uinta R.

Big Sandwich Res.

White R.

Lake Fk.

Moon L.

Midview Res.

Green R.

Meeks Cabin Res.

Starvation Res.

Duchesne R.

Price R.

Bear R.

Woodruff Narrows Dam

Red Creek Res.

Strawberry Res.

Strawberry R.

Desert L.

Lake

Logan R.

Birch Creek Res.

Woodruff Creek Res.

Causey Res.

Ball Moore Res.

Lost Creek Res.

Echo Res.

Rockport Res.

Weber-Provo Canal

Strawberry Tunnel

Scofield Res.

Electric L.

Diamond Fork

San Pitch R.

Joes Valley Res.

Hyrum Res.

Box Elder L.

Pine View Res.

Ogden R.

Weber R.

East Canyon Res.

Deer Creek Res.

Provo R.

Spanish Fork

Mona Res.

Gunnison Res.

Chicken Creek Res.

Willard Res.

Jordan R.

Utah Lake

Sevier

Bridge Res.

Bear R.

Great Salt Lake

Sevier R.

Fool Creek Res.

D.M.A.D. Res.

737

Utah Recreation Areas

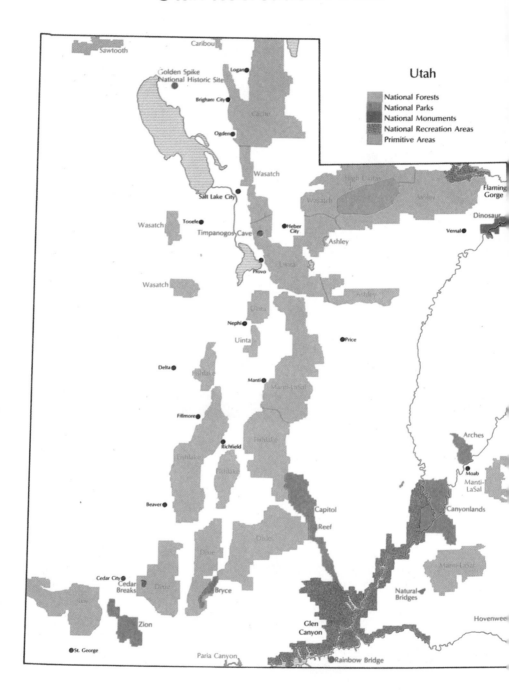

Industrial Minerals of the 20th Century

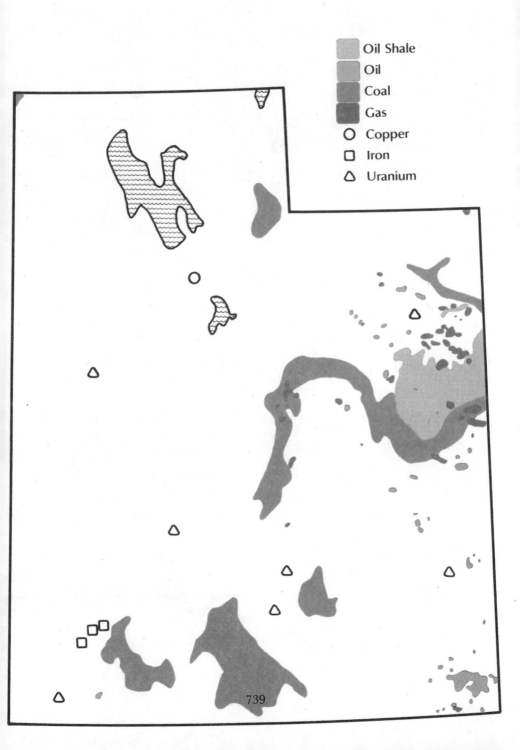

Oil Shale
Oil
Coal
Gas
O Copper
□ Iron
△ Uranium

739

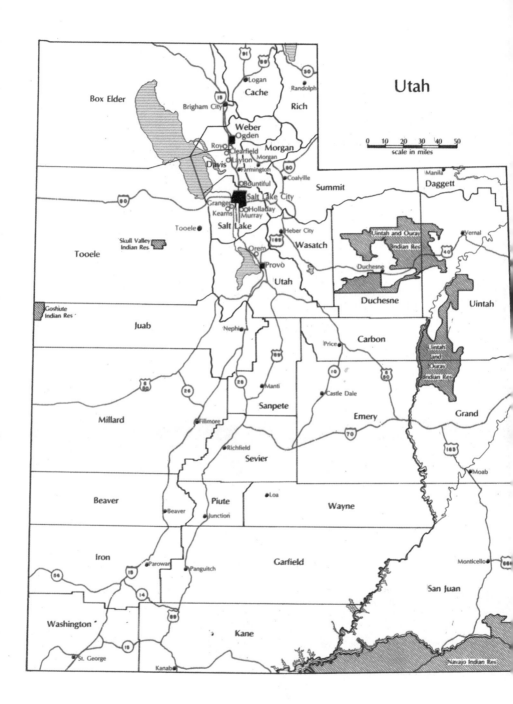

Utah

scale in miles

Index

751

United Mine Workers, 489
United Order (of Enoch), 201, 218, 230–233, 280
United States Forest Service, 526
United States Steel Geneva Works, 501–502, 504, 527, 547
Universal Scientific Society, 302, 305
University of Deseret, 246, 302, 303, 593
University of Utah, 412, 593
University of Utah Medical School, 593
University of Utah Museum of Fine Arts, 601
Upper Basin Compact of 1948, 657
Upper Sonoran Zone, 19
Utah, admitted to the Union, 395
Utah Agricultural College, 303, 406
Utah Anti-Discrimination Act of 1965, 582
Utah Art Colony, 571
Utah Art Institute, 596
Utah Associated Industries, 471
Utah Bankers Association, 442
Utah Central Line (Railroad), 220, 222, 230
Utah Christian Mission, Inc., 611
Utah Civic Ballet, 599
Utah Commission, 259, 261, 392
Utah Consolidated Gold Mines, 434
Utah Copper Company, 434–435, 444, 451, 465, 484, 503, 636
Utah Education Association, 476
Utah Emergency Relief Administration, 487
Utah's Enabling Act, 393–394, 655
Utah Farm Bureau Federation, 476
Utah Federation of Labor, 471, 476
Utah Federated Trades and Labor Council, 237
Utah Federation of Business and Professional Women's Clubs, 567
Utah Fuel Company, 223, 383, 436
Utah General Depot, 499, 509, 510, 511, 549
Utah Gospel Mission, 611
Utah-Idaho Sugar Company, 437
Utah Institute of Fine Arts, 571
Utah International Women's Year Conference, 517, 579, 583
Utah Iron Manufacturing Company, 233

Utah Lake, 9, 10
Utah Magazine, 306, 308
Utah Manufacturers Association, 443, 468, 476
Utah Museum of Fine Arts, 571
Utah Music Project, 597
Utah National Guard, 424
Utah Nippo, 641
Utah Oil Refinery Company, 502, 504, 509
Utah Parks Company, 471
Utah Power and Light Company, 442
Utah Shakespearean Festival, 600
Utah Southern Railroad, 220, 222, 404
Utah State Agricultural College, 269
Utah State Board of Health, 353
Utah State Board of Higher Education, 594
Utah State Fair Association, 432
Utah State Historical Society, 523
Utah State University of Agriculture and Applied Sciences, 593
Utah Steel Company Plant (Midvale), 467
Utah Sugar Company, 238, 403, 437
Utah Symphony Orchestra, 572, 596–598, 605
Utah Technical College, 594
Utah Territorial Insane Asylum, 285, 406, 412
Utah Territorial Prison, 286
Utah Territory, 160–164, 358
Utah Valley, 138
Utah Valley Symphony, 598
Utah War of 1857–1858, 143, 145, 188, 196, 243
Utah Women's Press Club, 566
Utah's Declaration of Rights, 410
Ute Indians, 23, 27, 38, 357, 358, 365, 367, 643
Valley Tan, the, 198, 308
Van Cott, Lucy May, 571
Van Vliet, Stewart, 166–167
Van Zile, Phillis T., 260
Varian, Charles S., 261
Vasquez, Louis, 144
Volstead Act, 478, 491
Wagner Act, 490
Wahkara (Chief), 361–363
Walker Brothers Banking Company, 206, 228
Walker, Joseph Reddeford, 43, 66, 77

Walker War of 1853, 139, 146,
361–363, 636
Wall, Colonel Enos A., 399
Wallace, George, 519
Walsh, Father Patrick, 325
Wangsgaard, Eva W., 573
War Production Board, 498
War Resources Board, 498
Ward, William, 296
Ware, Florence, 572
warm front, 15
Warnick, Christinia Oleson, 301, 332,
613
Wasatch Mountains, 10, 434
Watkins, Arthur V., 516, 518, 644–645
Wattis, William H., 475, 492–493
Weber State College, 303, 593, 594
Weber, John H., 56
Weber River, 8
Weeminuche Indians, 27, 28, 371
Weggeland, Daniel A., 311, 602
Weir, Thomas, 434
Welling, Milton R., 472, 475
Wells, Daniel H., 160, 168, 210
Wells, Emmeline B., 344, 348, 352,
565, 583
Wells, Fargo, and Company, 197, 208
Wells, Heber M., 394, 411, 660
Wendover Air Force Base, 498
West, Caleb B., 265
West, Caleb W., 391
West, Rolla, 489
Western Federation of Miners, 443,
455
Wheeler, George M., 377
Whipple, Maurine, 573, 604
White River Agency, 367
White River Indian band, 27, 28, 31,
383
White Rocks Indian Agency, 375
Whitney, Orson F., 307, 352
Wilkinson, Ernest L., 522, 595
William Wolfskill Party, 372
Willie Handcart Company, 182
Willkie, Wendell, 506
Wine Mission, 187
Winter Quarters, 118, 176, 182, 383
Women's Christian Industrial Home,
412
Woman's Commission Store, 343
Woman's Exponent, 305, 347, 573
Woman's Press Club, 348

Woman's Suffrage Association, 566
Women's Cooperative Mercantile and
Manufacturing Association, 343
Woodbury, Joan, 572
Woodmansee, Emily Hill, 340
Woodruff Manifesto of 1890, 271–272,
301, 351, 563, 618
Woodruff, Wilford, 177, 271, 323
Woods, George L., 251
Woolsey, Maryhale, 573
Word of Wisdom, 322, 491
Workers', Soldiers', and Sailors'
Council, 468
Works Progress Administration, 488,
497, 663
Workman, James, 33
Yamparka Indians, 27, 28
"yellow dog contracts," 443
Young, Ann Eliza Webb, 249, 283,
307, 350
Young, Augusta Adams, 283
Young, Brigham, 103, 109, 117,
138,143–144, 154, 160, 164–165,
176–178, 180, 182, 184–185, 193,
195, 201, 203, 208, 218, 231, 233,
246, 249, 253, 262, 283, 287, 300,
318
Young, Clara Chase Ross, 283
Young, Clara Decker, 283
Young, Clarissa Decker, 121, 337
Young, Eliza Burgess, 283
Young, Emily Dow Partridge, 283
Young, Emmeline Free, 283
Young, Harriet Barney, 283
Young, Harriet Cook C., 283
Young, Harriet Folsom (Amelia), 283
Young, Harriet Page Wheeler Decker,
121, 337
Young, Joseph W., 182
Young Ladies' Retrenchment Society,
321
Young, Lucy Bigelow, 283
Young, Lucy Decker, 283
Young, Mahonri, 596, 601
Young, Margaret Pierce, 283
Young, Martha Bowker, 283
Young, Mary Van Cott, 283
Young Men's Mutual Improvement
Association, 321
Young, Miriam Works, 283
Young, Naamah K. J. Carter, 283
Young, Samuel C., 83–85

756

Young, Seymour B., 285
Young, Susan Snively, 283
Young Women's Journal, 306
Young Women's Mutual Improvement
  Association, 321
Young, Zina Diantha Huntington, 283,
  343
Ytimpabichis (Timpeabits) Indians, 31
Yubuincariri (Uinkarits) Indians, 31
zagruda (family) system, 450
Zane, Charles S., 261, 272, 391

Zion (definition of), 101
Zion's Camp, 101
Zion's Central Board of Trade, 233,
  234, 401
Zion's Cooperative Mercantile
  Institution, 206–208, 218, 229, 238,
  299, 401, 439, 467
Zion's National Park, 471, 664
Zion's Savings Bank and Trust
  Company, 208, 228
Zuni, 38